INTERNATIONAL FINANCE

Ephraim Clark

Second Edition

INTERNATIONAL FINANCE

THOMSON

Australia • Canada • Mexico • Singapore • Spain • United Kingdom • United States

THOMSON

International Finance – Second Edition

Copyright © Ephraim Clark 2002
The Thomson logo is a registered trademark used herein under licence.

For more information, contact Thomson, High Holborn House, 50/51 Bedford Row, London, WC1R 4LR or visit us on the World Wide Web at: http://www.thomsonlearning.co.uk

British Library Cataloguing-in-Publication Data
A catalogue record for this book is available from the British Library

First edition published in 1993 by Chapman & Hall

ISBN 1–86152–971–6

Typeset by Saxon Graphics Ltd, Derby

Text design by Design Deluxe

Printed in Great Britain by TJ International, Padstow, Cornwall

Contents

List of exhibits, figures and tables

Tables

Preface

The financial environment has undergone a profound change over the past 30 years that has been nothing short of spectacular. The elimination of most controls on cross-border capital movements, the exceptional technological advances in the processing and dissemination of information, the general liberalization of financial markets and reduction of transaction costs: all these have been at the source of a veritable financial revolution. This revolution has led to the appearance of new financial markets for products such as futures, options and swaps, the renovation of the traditional domestic money and stock markets, and the development of powerful and efficient offshore capital markets that are largely immune from troublesome government meddling. It has also led to a transformation in the role of financial intermediation played by banks and other financial institutions, as well as to the increased importance of the finance departments in commercial and industrial enterprises.

Besides the ongoing financial revolution, the past 30 years have also been marked by the internationalization of commercial and industrial activity. World imports and exports have increased many-fold, thanks to reduced customs barriers, lower transport costs and increased reliance on comparative advantage for economic development. These exchanges of goods and services have generated their corresponding financial flows and it is now the rule rather than the exception that a firm must manage payments and receipts in currencies other than its own. As a result, multi-currency borrowing and lending is also commonplace. Furthermore, as international barriers to free capital movement have disappeared, firms have sought to exploit their comparative financial advantage and diversify their sources of funds by borrowing internationally rather than limiting themselves to their own domestic market. For reasons of market access and productivity, many firms have also embarked on programs of direct investment in foreign countries, with all the risks that this entails.

It is clear that modern day financial management and investment is international in scope and requires the corresponding knowledge and expertise in order to be successful. Consequently, financial training in general should include the international aspects of the field, and international financial training in particular should reflect the current revolutionized environment. This is the goal of this book.

Primary audience and pedagogical approach

This book is designed for MBA and masters level finance and banking students as well as for financial professionals working in corporations or on the markets. It can also be used by senior level undergraduates majoring in finance. Basic courses in corporate finance, descriptive statistics and international economics would be useful primers: for example, knowledge of international economics would make Chapters 1–3 easier to read. Familiarity with discounting techniques and a knowledge of basic statistics such as standard deviation, correlation and covariance would help with some of the other chapters.

However, this book is, for all practical purposes, self-contained. It is intended to be accessible to students and professionals without recent training in modern financial theory. The basic principles models and techniques of finance and investment are explained and illustrated with examples as they arise. The techniques particular to the international dimension are then developed, analyzed and illustrated with numerous examples. The more complicated mathematical tools necessary for the more advanced applications are presented in the end of chapter appendices. Solutions to end of chapter problems are provided on the web site, as are further questions, problems, exercises and suggested solutions (see www.thomsonlearning.co.uk/accountingandfinance). This web site also contains teaching aids for adopters of the book as well as open access resources for students.

Besides the technical aspects of international finance, I have also taken care to develop the institutional aspects. There is, however, no specific national perspective such as the "American" or "European" perspective taken in the book. The major international institutions, both public and private, as well as the major markets and market participants have been presented and analyzed. The book can thus be used effectively throughout the world. Because institutional, market and participant details are continuously evolving, I have also included their web addresses so that students can keep up with changes in real time.

Book structure

This book is divided into eight parts. Given the importance of exchange rates in all international financial transactions, we begin the book with a detailed analysis of what determines the exchange rate and how currencies are borrowed, lent, bought and sold. Part I deals with the economics of international transactions. Its three chapters are designed to provide a clear understanding of the relationship between a national economy, its balance of payments and the exchange rate. Part II shows how the international financial system is organized for handling cross-border financial flows and currency trading. These three chapters detail the international institutional framework and conventions that form the backbone of the international monetary system.

Part III deals with the international derivative markets. It describes the major derivative markets and shows how they are organized. It also describes the major instruments they trade, shows how these instruments can be used and how they can be priced. One whole chapter is devoted to the over-the-counter markets that trade some of the more complicated products used in international financial transactions such as swaps and exotic options.

In Part IV I look at assessing the risk that is specific to international transactions such as country risk and political risk. I also show how the standard financial models, such as the capital asset pricing model, arbitrage pricing theory, and value at risk, can be applied at the international level. Part V is devoted to managing foreign exchange risk. These four chapters are designed to provide a thorough grounding in currency risk management using straightforward techniques such as in-house hedging, netting and leads and lags, as well as the more complicated techniques that employ forwards, futures, options and swaps. Part VI deals with the institutional aspects of the major international debt markets and how interest rate risk can be managed, while in Part VII I look at two other markets: the international commodity markets and the world equity markets. Finally, in Part VIII I examine capital budgeting and foreign direct investment.

New to this edition

This edition represents a major revision in terms of both content and presentation. It reflects significant changes in the international financial system. The euro has replaced most of the venerable old currencies of the European Union. The emerging markets and transitional economies play a more prominent role in world economic and financial activity. The Mexican peso crisis of 1994, the South-East Asian economic meltdown of 1997 and the Russian default of 1998 have introduced the world to a possible systemic breakdown and made it more sensitive to country and political risk.

Four completely new chapters have been added to this edition and all chapters have been updated and extensively rewritten to reflect changes in the international financial environment. The most important changes are as follows:

- Chapter 4 has been rewritten to incorporate the introduction of the euro.

- Chapter 7 is a new chapter devoted to the organized futures exchanges. It has been added to provide a better understanding of how futures markets are organized and how they can be used to hedge the risk inherent in financial and commercial transactions.

- Chapter 8 (formerly Chapter 11) is devoted to options and has been extensively rewritten to improve its pedagogy. The presentation is clearer and more structured and addresses several issues that were missing in the last edition. The section on option pricing has been extended to include an underlying other than an exchange rate. From this the chapter shows how to price options on currencies, commodities with convenience yields, futures contracts, stocks with dividends and assets with no intermediate payouts at all. Some methodologies for pricing American style options are also presented.

- Chapter 9 is a new chapter devoted to exotic options and other over-the-counter products, such as swaps, swaptions, caps, collars and floors. Products such as these are popular but not easy to understand. The chapter shows how they can be used to manage risk and how they can be priced.

- Chapter 10 on country and political risk analysis is a new chapter that reflects the importance of these factors in the new international financial and economic organization. It covers the sources and effects of political risk, a comprehensive presentation of the methods and techniques for assessing this type of risk and several approaches for incorporating the analysis into the capital budgeting process.

- Chapter 11 (formerly Chapter 8) on portfolio investment has been extensively rewritten to improve its pedagogical content. It has also been expanded to include arbitrage pricing theory and the relatively new "value at risk" technique for risk management.

- Chapter 12 (formerly Chapter 7) on advanced techniques for country and political risk assessment has been rewritten and expanded to include the estimation of systematic country risk.

- Chapter 17 describes the major world debt markets, both primary and secondary, their instruments and their procedures. The markets include the United States, Japan, the United Kingdom, the international bond market and syndicated Eurocredits. Brady bonds are also examined in this chapter.

- Chapter 18 deals with interest rate risk management. It reviews the concepts and techniques of bond pricing and management, including yield calculation, duration and convexity. It goes on to analyze techniques for hedging long-term and short-term interest rate risk on the futures markets and concludes with applications of over-the-counter products such as swaps, caps, floors and collars.

- Chapter 19 is a new chapter on the international commodity markets. It describes the spot markets, data sources, major participants and trading conventions. It then describes the derivative markets and how they can be used to hedge commodity risk.

- Chapter 21 on capital budgeting for foreign direct investment has been rewritten and expanded to include the real option approach to investment under uncertainty and evaluation techniques outside the mean-variance paradigm.

- Chapter 22 on measuring and managing risk in foreign direct investment has been rewritten and improved in several ways. The section on estimating a project's required rate of return has been expanded to include systematic country economic and financial risk. In the appendix at the end of the chapter we show the relationship between the CAPM, which is used to measure systematic economic risk, and the Black-Scholes options pricing model, which is used to measure systematic financial risk. We also show the various approaches for including political risk in the analysis. Finally, we review the internal and external hedging techniques that can be used to manage exposure to political risk.

Acknowledgements

I hope that this book will fulfill the needs of students in advanced undergraduate, post-graduate and post-experience courses in international banking or finance. I also hope that corporate financial officers will find it interesting and helpful. The work itself owes much to the interest and comments of my students at ESC Lille, HEC Paris, Vrije Universiteit and Middlesex University, as well as to my colleagues at these institutions. It also owes much to my co-authors of the first edition, Patrick Rousseau and Michel Levasseur. The first edition benefited from many helpful comments and suggestions from Professor Bernsden of Erasmus University, Dr. Duffhues of Tilburg University, Dr. Prodham of the Oxford Centre for Management Studies, Professor Theobald of the University of Birmingham and Michael Turner of the University of Southampton.

For this edition I would especially like to thank my colleague at Middlesex, Dr. Radu Tunaru, for his insights, analysis and support. Special thanks are also due to Dr. Geeta Lakshmi (Plymouth University), Dr. Kostas Kassimatis (Middlesex University), Dr. Magid Gadad (Finance Institute of Tripoli), Dr. Amel Zenaidi (IHEC Tunisia), Professor Bernard Marois (HEC), Professor Theo van der Nat (Vrije University), Professor Octave Jokung (EDHEC), Dr. Vincent Dropsey (University of California at Fullerton), Professor Bertrand Groslambert (CERAM), Professor Michel Bouchet (CERAM), Dr. Gérard Mondello (Latapses), Dr. Edgar Ortiz (Universidad Autonoma de Mexico), Dr. Jean Batiste Lesourd (GREQAM), Professor René Thiéblemont (Université de Savoie) and Professor Dilip Ghosh (Rutgers).

The international in our lives

Commerce between different peoples and nations is as old as recorded history. We all know about Marco Polo, the Phoenicians and the ancient Egyptians. There are those who even suspect Neanderthal and Homo Erectus of some primitive commercial collaboration. As old as the origins of international trade may be, however, it did not really become an important factor in the general public's standard of living until the fairly recent past. Nowadays, thanks in large part to the development of communications and transport technologies, the international element in our daily lives is pervasive and virtually inescapable.

To appreciate how pervasive and inescapable the international element has become in your life, try a little test. Go into your clothes closet, your kitchen, your living and dining rooms.[1] Look at the "made in" labels on the clothes, appliances, food and furniture that you see. You will probably find exotic names like Taiwan, Hong Kong, USA, South Korea, France, Germany, Vietnam, Japan, Tunisia, etc. Then look at the trademarks on the products. Many of the goods produced in one country will have the trademark of a company owned in another country. In fact, if you take the trouble to find out, you will probably discover that many trademarks you thought native to your own country are actually owned by foreigners. The international influence on your life doesn't end there. Most of the goods produced in your own country by nationally owned firms contain parts or materials that have been produced in another country. Thus, your habits and standard of living depend to a large degree on what happens in many far-away lands.

Table I.1 gives an idea of what this means to residents of some of the world's major economies. It shows imports of foreign goods and services as a percent of GDP. In Germany, for example, roughly 30% of a resident's consumption in 1990 depended directly or indirectly on goods or services produced abroad. It is also interesting to note that the proportion of imports in total output grew considerably in most of these countries between 1960 and 1990.

Since a large percentage of the goods and services that we consume directly or indirectly come from abroad, it follows that our well-being or standard of living depends to a large extent on events in the countries that produce these goods. Oil importing countries, for example, benefit if oil prices fall as a result of a discovery of new reserves in Saudi

---

[1] Impoverished students with few worldly possessions can extend the test outside their own immediate lodgings to the cars they drive, the vacations they take outside their country of residence, their favorite restaurants, discotheques and bars or even their parents' homes.

Arabia or the development of a new technology for more efficient exploitation of existing reserves. On the other hand, they lose if oil prices rise due to war or social unrest in oil-producing regions. By the same token, the level of output in countries exporting manu-factured goods can rise or fall due to changes in demand in the countries that it counts as clients. Changes in demand can stem from normal economic conditions associated with the trade cycle, competition or economic performance as well as from natural catas-trophes, political change or social unrest. Many developing countries, for example, were obliged to cut back on imports in the 1980s when the debt crisis reduced their credit capacity at the same time that debt servicing was eating up an increasing share of their export earnings. Resulting lower standards of living caused political and social unrest that further reduced output, exports and imports. Foreign exporters that counted these countries as clients were hurt by falling sales and the inability to collect on what had already been sold.

Foreign events affect more than marginal flows of goods and services across national borders. Since each commercial transaction implies a corresponding financial transaction or currency exchange, cumulated trade deficits and surpluses translate into cross-border financial assets and liabilities with effects on the whole international financial and monetary system. Take, for instance, the debt crisis mentioned above. The inability of the crisis countries to service their foreign debt weakened the balance sheets of the banks that had lent to them. This in turn contributed to weakening the monetary systems in the banks' home countries. By the late 1980s many banks were facing bankruptcy, many were paying higher interest rates on borrowing than their commercial clients and others were forced to merge in order to remain solvent. Another one of the most revealing examples of world financial interdependence was the startling stock market crash of October 1987 that spread from the United States throughout the whole world in a matter of hours.

International economic and financial interdependence means that there can be no effective insulation of domestic markets from international markets. The risks and rewards

Table I.1 Imports as a percent of gross domestic product for selected countries

	1960	1970	1980	1990
Australia	16.8	14.7	17.8	17.7
Belgium	33.9	41.6	60.3	68.1
Canada	18.5	20.0	26.4	24.4
France	11.3	15.3	22.8	22.7
Germany	17.4	20.6	28.8	29.6
Ireland	37.2	44.9	63.0	53.9
Italy	13.9	16.6	24.0	19.5
Japan	11.1	10.2	15.8	10.1
Korea	12.8	23.6	41.5	32.2
Netherlands	48.6	46.6	53.0	52.0
New Zealand	25.6	25.0	31.6	27.9
South Africa	24.6	24.5	27.4	20.5
Switzerland	29.7	34.5	40.3	35.8
United Kingdom	21.6	21.7	25.0	27.3
United States	4.4	5.5	10.7	11.2

Source: IMF, *International Financial Statistics*, several issues.

associated with international trade and investment also play an important role in determining the risks and rewards associated with purely domestic trade and investment. For this reason, the study of finance should be considered in its international context.

Organization of the international economic and financial system

The first element determining the features of international trade and investment is the environment in which they occur. Today's economic and financial system is organized around the concept of the nation state and national sovereignty. Current international law recognizes the right of individual national governments to organize and administer the economic and financial framework within the geographic boundaries that they control. This means that they have the power to make and enforce the laws that determine how and where goods and services will be produced, who will own them, and how they will be exchanged. The degree of government involvement can vary considerably from country to country but it usually falls somewhere between the pure *laissez-faire* capitalism of the 19th century and the discredited comprehensive central planning of 20th century communism. Most of the world's rich industrial countries, for example, have established systems based on markets and individual choice. Within this basic philosophy, however, we find many different models ranging, among others, from American rugged individualism to French state capitalism, Japanese oligopoly and Swedish socialism.

The jurisdiction of the individual national systems effectively ends at each country's border. There is no real supranational authority with the power to impose its will on the rest of the world. This is especially true since the collapse of the Soviet empire and the dissolution of the Eastern bloc. Relations between countries have to be negotiated. Negotiations can be undertaken on a narrow country-to-country basis or they can be more comprehensive and include several countries. The tendency since World War II has been to multilateral agreements and many international organizations have been created to facilitate the multilateral format. The International Monetary Fund (IMF), for example, oversees international payments and exchange rates, the World Bank (International Bank for Reconstruction and Development) promotes economic development, and the General Agreement on Tariffs and Trade (GATT) is the format for negotiating international trade. The Bank for International Settlements (BIS), which was created after World War I to facilitate the transfer of funds among European countries whose currencies were not then convertible into one another, now serves as a kind of central bank to the industrial countries' central banks as well as a forum for monetary authorities from different countries to meet and exchange ideas. Other organizations, such as the Organization for Economic Cooperation and Development (OECD), which groups the world's 24 industrial economies, the European Community (EC) and the Organization of Petroleum Exporting Countries (OPEC) were founded to further the economic interests of particular groups of countries. Many other international organizations, too numerous to mention and covering a wide range of fields, also exist. Although all the foregoing organizations represent little or no explicit supranational enforcement power, many have acquired institutional strength that enables them to exert considerable influence over the behavior of individual countries.

Today's international economic and financial environment can thus be described as being comprised of a number of sovereign nation states with distinct internal organizational structures competing against one another according to a set of guidelines determined by multilateral negotiation and monitored by the moral authority of the international organizations created for that purpose. The competition, or cooperation for that matter, can involve governments as well as resident firms and individuals of the different countries. The outcome is reflected in each country's national accounts, balance of payments and exchange rate. As we will see, the balance of payments and the exchange rate determine the economic and financial limits of domestic policy. They are also particularly sensitive to monetary phenomena. Since most countries associate monetary policy with national sovereignty and, consequently, issue and manage their own separate currencies, the balance of payments and the exchange rate play a prominent role in how the system works. In fact, much of this book is concerned, directly or indirectly, with these two subjects.

Advantages of international trade and finance

International trade and comparative advantage

In the study of international finance, international financial transactions are often presented in a way that make them seem independent and unrelated to the transactions involving the exchange of goods and services. Although the development of international financial activity can be singled out as one of the major causes of the growth of international trade, it should not be forgotten that without international trade there would be no international finance. If goods and services could not be exchanged between residents of different countries there would be no reason for borrowing, lending or investing between countries since nothing could be bought with the product of the loan or investment. On the other hand, international trade can exist and has existed in the absence of any international financing arrangements. Direct exchange or barter and cash payments in gold at one time were the rule. They still exist today.

With this in mind, one question that we should answer before we go any further is why trade between nations exists in the first place. To answer this question it is obvious that on the most elementary level international trade makes it possible to procure goods and commodities that are not available in the home market. For example, certain raw materials such as oil and minerals are necessary inputs for many if not most consumption and investment goods. If they are not available domestically, they have to be purchased abroad. It is only a short step from here to Adam Smith's theory of absolute advantage, which holds that all nations benefit from international trade by specializing in the goods and commodities they are best suited to produce because of natural or acquired advantages.[2] In this case, if one country can produce wheat more efficiently than another country while the second country can produce cars more efficiently than the first, the first country will specialize in producing wheat and the second country will specialize in producing cars. Because they are specialized in the good they produce most efficiently, total output of the two goods is higher than it would be if they both allocated resources to the less efficiently produced goods. This theory assumes that every country has at least one product with an absolute cost advantage that can be exported in exchange for the other goods it needs to import.

What happens, however, if a country has no advantage in the production of any good? Ricardo's theory of comparative advantage answers the question.[3] The theory of comparative advantage holds that even in the absence of an absolute cost advantage, a country will export the good that it produces the least inefficiently and import the good that it produces the most inefficiently. Suppose that Japan produces both wheat and cars more cheaply than the European Community but the cost advantage is relatively greater for cars than for

[2] Adam Smith, *An Inquiry into the Nature and Causes of the Wealth of Nations* (New York: Random House, 1937).

[3] David Ricardo, *On the Principles of Political Economy and Taxation* (New York: Dutton, 1948).

wheat. According to the theory of comparative advantage, it will be advantageous for both Japan and the EC if Japan exports cars to the EC in exchange for the EC's wheat. An example will make it clear why this is so.

Table I.2 shows the situation of the two countries before any international trade takes place. We see in section (A) that Japan has a lower absolute cost for producing both wheat and cars. It takes 20 units of labor to produce one unit of wheat in the EC and only 15 units of labor to produce the same unit of wheat in Japan. For cars the difference is even more pronounced. It takes 10 units of labor to produce one unit of cars in the EC and only 2.5 units of labor for the same car in Japan. In section (B) we see that there is a total of 100 million workers employed in the EC, 60 million employed in wheat and 40 million in cars. In Japan 30 million are employed in wheat and 15 million in cars for a total of 45 million. In these conditions section (C) shows that the EC will produce 3 million units of wheat (60 million employed / 20 units of labor per unit of output) and 4 million units of cars (40 million employed / 10 units of labor per unit of output). Japan will produce 2 million units of wheat (30 million employed / 15 units of labor per unit of output) and 6 million units of cars (15 million employed / 2.5 units of labor per unit of output). Before international trade, the total output of wheat is 5 million units (3 million in the EC + 2 million in Japan) and the total output of cars is 10 million units (4 million in the EC + 6 million in Japan).

Figures I.1(a) and I.1(b) show the consumption – production possibilities curves for the EC and Japan respectively if there are constant opportunity costs.[4] Opportunity costs refer to the number of units of output of one good that must be sacrificed in order to increase output of the other good by one unit. Constant opportunity costs imply that the factors of production are perfect substitutes for one another when used in the same proportions and that there are constant returns to scale. Constant returns to scale mean that output increases in direct proportion to the increase in the factors of production.[5] Thus the opportunity cost of one extra car produced in the EC is $\frac{1}{2}$ units of wheat and the opportunity cost of one wheat unit is two car units. Consequently, the slope of the EC's consumption–production possibilities curve is $-\frac{1}{2}$. In

Table I.2 Situation before trade

	EC	Japan	Total
(A) Workers per unit of output			
Wheat	20	15	
Cars	10	2.5	
(B) Number of employed (mn)			
Wheat	60	30	
Cars	40	15	
Total	100	45	
(C) Consumption and output (mn units)			
Wheat	3	2	5
Cars	4	6	10

[4] Assuming constant opportunity costs facilitates the exposition but is not necessary for the demonstration to hold.

[5] The production function is homogeneous of degree one.

Figure I.1 Consumption–production possibilities curves assuming constant opportunity costs

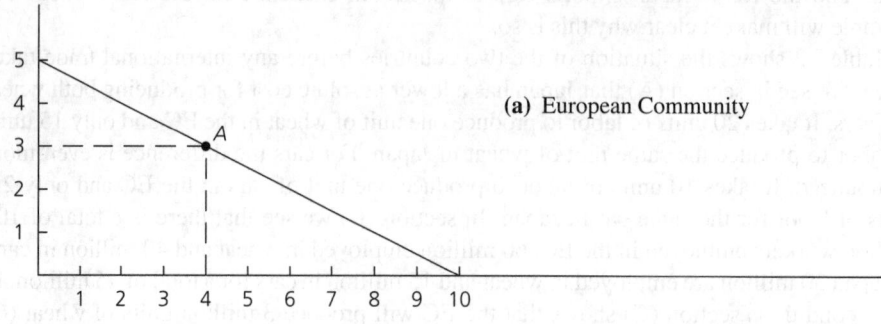

(a) European Community

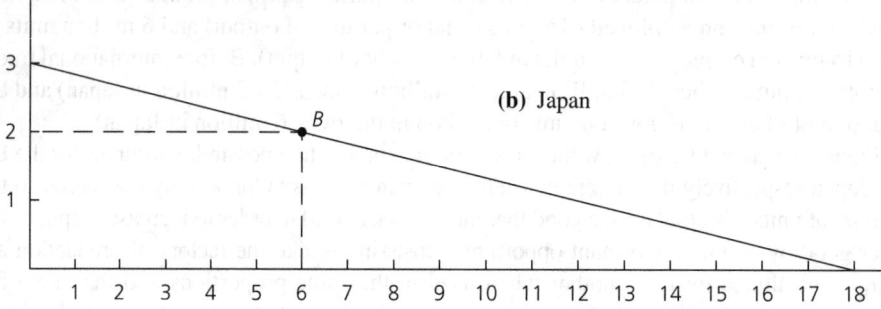

(b) Japan

Japan the opportunity cost of one wheat unit is six car units and the opportunity cost of one car unit is $\frac{1}{6}$ units of wheat. The slope of Japan's consumption–production possibilities curve is thus $-\frac{1}{6}$. If all the EC labor is devoted to the production of wheat, 5 million units will be produced; 10 million car units will be produced if all labor is devoted to the production of cars. In Japan if all labor is devoted to the production of one good, either 3 million wheat units or 18 million car units can be produced. Point A indicates the EC's actual output of wheat and cars and point B indicates Japan's.

Since the opportunity cost of one unit of wheat in the EC is only two cars whereas it is six cars in Japan, the EC is said to have a comparative advantage in the production of wheat. Since the opportunity cost of one car unit in the EC is $\frac{1}{2}$ wheat units while it is only $\frac{1}{6}$ wheat units in Japan, Japan is said to have a comparative advantage in the production of cars. Hence, according to the theory of comparative advantage, the EC will export wheat and import cars while Japan will import wheat and export cars.

Suppose that after trade begins, the EC shifts 20 million laborers to producing wheat and Japan shifts 10 million laborers to the car industry. Section (A) in Table I.3 shows that the EC will have 80 million employed in the wheat industry and 20 million in the car industry, while Japan will have 20 million employed in the wheat industry and 25 million in the car industry. In section (B) we can see that this employment distribution will lead to output of 4 million wheat units and 2 million car units in the EC and 1.33 million wheat units and 10 million car units in Japan. Total wheat output is 5.33 million units, 0.33 million units higher than the before-trade situation. Total car output is 12 million units, 2 million units higher than the before-trade situation.

How the increased output is distributed between the EC and Japan depends on the reciprocal demand for the two products in both countries. Nevertheless, trade will take place and benefit both countries as long as the opportunity cost of international trade, otherwise known as the international **terms of trade**, lies somewhere in between the opportunity costs

Table I.3 Situation after trade

	EC	Japan	Total
(A) Number of employed (mn)			
Wheat	80	20	
Cars	20	25	
Total	100	45	
(B) Output (mn units)			
Wheat	4	1.33	5.33
Cars	2	10.00	12.00
(C) Consumption (mn units)			
Wheat	3.20	2.13	
Cars	5.20	6.80	

in the two countries. Remember that the opportunity cost of an extra unit of wheat is two car units in the EC and six car units in Japan. Thus, the EC will trade wheat as long as trading will earn more than the two car units that it earns at home. Japan will buy wheat as long as each unit costs less than the six car units it costs in Japan.

Suppose, for arguments sake, that the international terms of trade are four car units for one wheat unit. Figures I.2(a) and I.2(b) compare the consumption–production possibilities curves of the EC and Japan before and after international trade takes place. The solid lines are the before-trade consumption–production possibilities curves. The dashed lines are the after-trade consumption–production possibilities curves and, since the international terms of trade are the same for both countries $\frac{1}{N}$ one to four $\frac{1}{N}$ they both have a slope of $-\frac{1}{4}$. P_{EC} and P_J represent the after-trade output combinations of the EC and Japan respectively as shown in Table I.3 section (B). Starting from point P_{EC} in Figure I.2(a) and following the dashed line, we can see the various combinations of the EC's output and consumption when wheat is transformed into cars by trading with Japan. All the points lie above the no-trade possibilities curve. The same goes for Japan. Starting from point P_J, the dashed line represents Japan's consumption–production combinations when cars are transformed into wheat through trade with the EC. All points on this curve are above the no-trade possibilities. Trading is clearly beneficial for both countries.

To take an example, suppose that the EC exports 0.8 million wheat units. In equilibrium it will thus import 3.2 million car units. Table I.3 section (c) shows the consumption in both countries that results. After trade the EC consumes 3.2 million wheat units and 5.2 million car units (point *C* in Figure I.2(a)) where before trade it only consumed 3 million wheat units and 4 million car units (point *A*). By the same token, Japan consumes 2.13 million wheat units and 6.8 million car units (point *D* in Figure I.2(b)) as opposed to the 2 million and 6 million units before trade (point *B*).

This is an important result. Both countries have become richer because of trade even though one country had an absolute advantage in the production of both goods. More complicated examples of comparative advantage involving demand curves, utility functions and variable returns to scale only serve to confirm this basic conclusion.[6] International finance

---

[6] For a complete exposition of comparative advantage and international trade see Franklin R. Root, *International Trade and Investments*, 6th edition (Cincinnati, Ohio: South-Western Publishing Co., 1990).

Figure I.2 Consumption–production possibilities curves before and after international trade

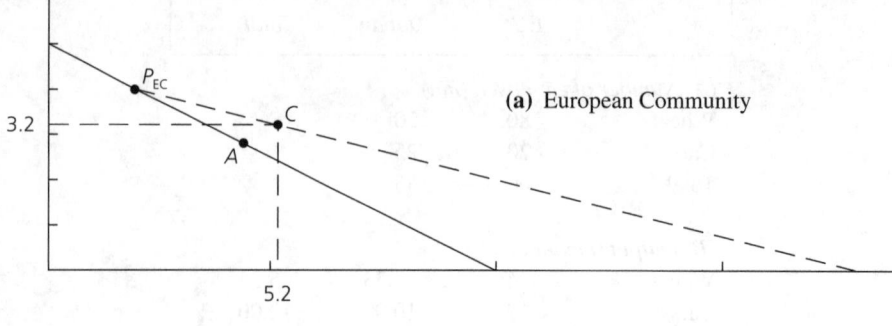

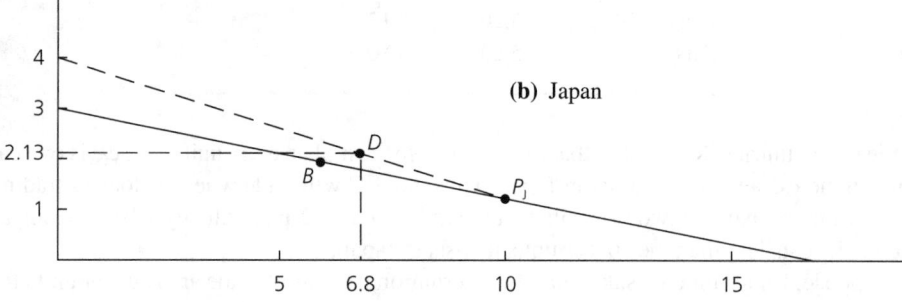

comes into the picture insofar as international financial transactions serve to facilitate and expand international trade. In this sense, the first benefits of international finance are clearly associated with the benefits derived from comparative and absolute advantage.

Investment enhancing and consumption smoothing

The welfare benefits of international finance are not limited to those derived from facilitating and expanding international trade. Cross-country financial flows also generate welfare benefits by contributing to a more efficient allocation of international resources. Such gains can be achieved due to the fact that the possibility of investing on an international scale creates the conditions for resources to be allocated on the basis of where they can be used most efficiently rather than on the basis of where they are the most abundant. This means that potentially high return projects in countries with low savings will not be neglected in favor of lower return projects in high saving countries simply because of where the saving is generated. Two examples relevant to current world conditions will make this clear.

The first example is straightforward and concerns two countries at the same technology level. Most western European countries, for instance, can be considered as being at the same technology level.[7] They are at the same stage of development, have similarly qualified labor forces, have the same standard of living and employ the same basic technologies in

---

[7] The differences that exist between economies at the same technology level can be ascribed to different techniques. The distinction between technique and technology is not always clear. One way to look at it is to consider technique as the different ways that a basic technology can be exploited. In this case, the technology curves can be interpreted as the envelope of the efficiency curves of the individual techniques within a given technology. See John Hicks, *Capital and Time* (Oxford: Clarendon Press, 1987).

Figure 1.3 Gains from improved resource allocation

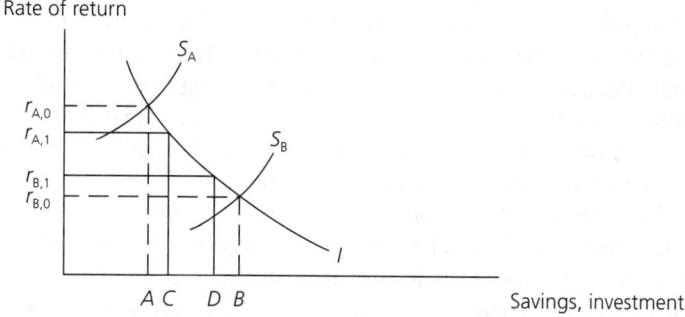

their productive processes. Figure I.3 illustrates the situation for countries A and B that are similar in size and technology. The I curve represents the marginal efficiency of capital schedule for both countries. The marginal efficiency of capital is the rate of return earned on each incremental ECU's worth of investment. It is the same for both countries because both are the same size and at the same technology level. It is downward sloping because as more is invested each additional project earns less. S_A and S_B represent the savings supply schedules for both countries. They indicate the amounts saved at different rates of return on savings. If there are no net capital flows between countries, the equilibrium rates of return are $r_{A,0}$ and $r_{B,0}$. Since country B saves more than country A and is obliged to invest all its savings domestically, its marginal efficiency of capital is lower than in country A.

It is clear that if capital flows between countries were possible, overall investment efficiency would be increased if investments with lower rates of return in country B were sacrificed in favor of the higher yielding projects in country A. For example, an extra ECU's worth of investment in country A on the part of country B would increase returns by $r_{A,0}$ in country A and reduce them by $r_{B,0}$ in country B for a net gain of $r_{A,0} - r_{B,0}$. The net gain would decrease with each incremental ECU transfer. After $AC = DB$ has been transferred, for example, the net gain would be $r_{A,1} - r_{B,1}$ and so on until the marginal efficiency of capital becomes equal in both countries.

The conclusion is the same if the special case of similar economies is extended to include economies of different sizes and with different marginal efficiency of capital schedules. This could be the case, for example, of a developing country undergoing structural transformation such as in a transition from subsistence farming to commercial agriculture, or an Eastern bloc country recovering from communism by replacing its outdated plants, machinery and methods with state of the art models employed in the developed countries. In Figure I.4, I_A and $I_{A'}$ are the marginal efficiency of capital schedules for the small economy in transition. I_A represents the new, more productive technology and $I_{A'}$ the outdated technology. I_B is the marginal efficiency of capital schedule for the large developed country. The higher returns in the upper left-hand side of I_A represent those investments associated with the structural transformation. S_A and S_B are the savings supply schedules for the two economies. We have drawn S_A so that domestic savings are inadequate even to assure the basic investments for the structural transformation. This is the case of most countries in a transitional situation. If the basic investments are not assured then the marginal efficiency of capital schedule will fall, to $I_{A'}$, for example, because the individual investment projects are complementary. The failure of one causes the failure of the other such as when incremental agricultural output is wasted because transport is inadequate for getting the produce to market. Thus, the gains from international financial flows are two-fold. First of all there is the gain from the return differential discussed in the preceding example. Secondly, there is the gain associated with moving from a lower to a higher marginal efficiency of capital schedule.

The two foregoing examples bring out the role of international financial flows in resource allocation and investment efficiency. Another, less obvious investment benefit associated with international financial flows are gains arising from diversification opportunities. Diversification is the principle of not putting all your eggs in one basket. In finance it means spreading a portfolio over a variety of assets so that either risk can be reduced without reducing returns or returns can be increased without increasing risk. Since economic performance can differ considerably from country to country, diversification benefits can be achieved by spreading a portfolio of assets across a number of countries. This is a subject that we will take up in more detail in a subsequent chapter.

International financial benefits are not limited to the investment side of the equation. Consumers can also gain. The consumers' gain is similar to the investor's diversification benefit insofar as the possibility of borrowing and lending makes it possible to smooth consumption levels and make them less uncertain. A simple example will make this clear.

Consider a country that needs to consume 75 units of goods per year in order to keep its residents healthy and happy. Anything less than 75 units will begin to cause ill-health and starvation while anything more will permit residents to begin to indulge themselves. The country's consumption good is agricultural and output depends on the weather. The weather pattern is such that there is a 50% chance of producing 50 units in any one year and a 50% chance of producing 100 units. Average output is thus 75 units, just what the country needs to be healthy and happy. However, in bad years there will be ill-health and starvation while in good years there will be indulgence. It is clear that the losses from ill-health and starvation are greater than the gains from indulgence and that the country would be better off if consumption could be guaranteed at the required 75 units to make its residents permanently healthy and happy. In the presence of international financial flows, this could be achieved by borrowing from abroad in bad years and lending abroad in good years.[8]

Current trends in international trade and finance

With all the purported gains from international trade and finance it should not be surprising to find widespread growth in both categories over the years. In fact, this is the case. In Table I.1 we showed the relative growth of imports in the total consumption of the world's major

---

[8] In this example consumers are risk-averse and hence their utility functions exhibit diminishing marginal utility. In other words, the first unit of consumption has more utility than the second unit and the second unit has more utility than the third unit and so on. In our example, a certain 75 units of consumption has more utility than a 50% chance of 50 units and a 50% chance of 100 units. If U represents the utility function this can be written as follows:

$$U(75) > 0.5U(50) + 0.5U(100).$$

The property of diminishing marginal utility can be shown by multiplying both sides by two and rearranging:

$$U(75) - U(50) > U(100) - U(75).$$

Going from 50 to 75 has more utility than going from 75 to 100. For a discussion of the notion of utility functions and risk-aversion see Edwin J. Elton and Martin J. Gruber, *Modern Portfolio Theory and Investment Analysis*, second edition (John Wiley & Sons, Inc., 1984).

Figure 1.4 Gains from facilitating structural transformation

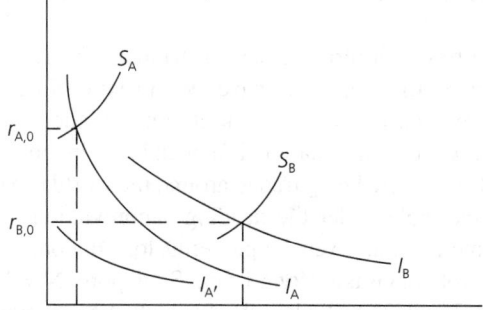

economies. In absolute terms the growth is just as impressive. Table I.4 shows the value of imports measured in constant US dollars. For the world as a whole they went from USD 518.1 billion in 1960 to USD 2583.1 billion in 1990, a multiple of almost five. Both the industrial and developing countries shared in the growth. The industrial countries increased their imports by over 5.3 times from USD 355.8 billion in 1960 to USD 1895.1 billion in 1990, while in the same period the developing countries increased theirs by over 4.4 times from USD 155.4 billion to USD 688 billion.

The growth in international financial activity is even more impressive than the growth in trade. Table I.5 is indicative of what was happening in international finance from the end of the 1960s to the present. It shows the evolution of the total external assets of banks reporting to the BIS between 1968 and 1990. They increased by a multiple of over 173 from

Table I.4 Imports in billions of constant US dollars (base 1980 = 100)

	1960	*1970*	*1980*	*1990*
World	518.1	1143.2	1946.3	2583.1
Industrial countries	355.8	862.7	1370.2	1895.1
Developing countries	155.4	268.1	556.4	688.0

Source: IMF, *International Financial Statistics*, several issues.

Table I.5 External assets of banks in countries reporting to the Bank for International Settlements* (in all currencies measured in US dollars)

1968	*1976*	*1985*	*1987*	*1989*	*1990*
37.7	305.3	2576.9	4207.9	5355.3	6528.1

*Includes Austria, Belgium, Luxembourg, Denmark, Finland, France, Germany, Ireland, Italy, Netherlands, Norway, Spain, Sweden, Switzerland, United Kingdom, Canada, Japan, United States, Bahamas, Bahrain, Cayman Islands, Hong Kong, Netherlands Antilles, Singapore and branches of US banks in Panama.
Source: BIS, *47th Annual Report* (June 1977) and *Evolution de l'Activité Bancaire et Financière Internationale*, several issues.

USD 37.7 billion to USD 6528.1 billion. Banks, however, were not the only players in the explosion of international financial activity. Over the same period the Eurobond and Euro-commercial paper markets were developed along with the globalization of the major domestic stock exchanges.

As new financial opportunities proliferated, new instruments were created to help manage the evolving risk–return profile. The 1980s have seen an explosion in the number of markets trading financial futures and options. A look at some of the products they are trading will give a good idea of what the international financial terrain looks like. Table I.6 shows some of the top contracts that were being traded around the world in May 1991. First of all, look at the bottom of the table under the heading "abbreviations". Twenty-eight exchanges are listed. They come from all over the globe: Oslo, London, Paris, Germany, The Netherlands, Switzerland, Tokyo, Osaka, Hong Kong, Singapore, New York, Chicago, Kansas City, New Zealand and Brazil. Then look at the products they are trading. They are trading interest rate futures and options ranging from Brazilian T-bonds to US municipals, German bunds, ECU bonds, French Pibors, Spanish Mibors, Australian bank bills and Japanese government bonds. They are also trading futures and options on stock indexes ranging from the United States to Japan, Sweden, The Netherlands, the United Kingdom, Denmark, Brazil and France. The list is only a sample of what is available. Besides the financial futures and options, there are other futures and options available on products like energy, metals, softs and agrics.

All these derivative products are being traded on a worldwide basis because the underlying instruments are being traded on a worldwide basis. They both offer definite opportunities and anyone involved in international trade or finance – exporters, importers, professional investors, company treasurers, bankers and portfolio managers – is at a

Table I.6 Financial futures and options trading

Contract	Exchange	Contract	Exchange
Interest rates		**Stock Indices**	
Brazilian T-bond	BM&F	XMI option	Ames
US T-bond	CBOT	XII	Amex
US T-bond option	CBOT	Ibovespa	BM&F
US T-note	CBOT	S&P 100 option	CBOE
US T-note option	CBOT	S&P 500 option	CBOE
US 5-yr T-note	CBOT	MMI maxi	CBOT
US Municipal bond index	CBOT	S&P 500	CME
Eurodollar	CME	S&P 500 option	CME
Eurodollar option	CME	Nikkei 225	CME
US T-bill	CME	Dutch stock index option	EOE
5-yr US T-note	Finex	Danish KFX index	Futop
Danish mortgage credit bond	Futop	Danish KFX index options	Futop
Danish mortgage bond option	Futop	Value line	KCBT
Long gilt	Liffe	FTSE 100	Liffe
3-month sterling	Liffe	FTSE 100 option	LTOM
German Bund	Liffe	Euro FTSE	LTOM
German Bund option	Liffe	CAC 40	Matif
Euromark	Liffe	CAP 40 option	Monep
Eurodollar	Liffe	Barclays index	NZFOE
US T-bond	Liffe	NYSE Composite	NYFE

Contract	Exchange	Contract	Exchange
10-yr French gov. bond	Matif	NYSE Composite option	NYA
10-yr French gov. bond option	Matif	Nikkei 225	Osaka
Pibor	Matif	Nikkei 225 option	Osaka
Pibor option	Matif	OBX option	OSE
ECU bond	Matif	Nikkei Dow	Simex
3-yr Spanish notional bond	Meff	All-Ordinaries	SFE
Mibor 90 days	Meff	SMI option	Soffex
Can. gov. bond	Montreal	Swedish OMX index	SOM
Can. gov. bond options	Montreal	TSE 35 option	Toronto
Can. Bankers' Acceptance	Montreal	Topix	TSE
5-yr NZ gov. bond	NZFOE	Topix option	TSE
90-day bank bill	NZFOE		
Notional bond option	OMI		
Mibor 90 option	OMI		
Eurodollar	Simex		
Euroyen	Simex		
10-yr Aus. gov. bond	SFE		
10-yr Aug. gov. bond option	SFE		
90-day bank bills	SFE		
Euroyen	Tiffe		
10-yr Japanese gov. bond	TSE		

Abbreviations

Amex	American Stock Exchange
ATA	Agricultural Futures Exchange Amsterdam
BFE	Baltic Futures Exchange
BM&F	Bolsa Mercantil & de Futuros
EOE	European Options Exchange
Finex	Financial Instrument Exchange
FUTOP	Guarantee Fund Danish Options & Futures
HKFE	Hong Kong Futures Exchange
KCBT	Kansas City Board of Trade
London Fox	London Futures & Options Exchange
LTOM	London Traded Options Market
Matif	Merché à Terme International de France
Meff	Mercados de Futuros Financieros
Monep	Marché des Options Negociables de la Bourse de Paris
NYCE	New York Cotton Exchange
NYFE	New York Futures Exchange
NZFOE	New Zealand Futures & Options Exchange
Osaka	Osaka Stock Exchange
OMI	OMI Iberica
OSE	Oslo Stock Exchange
SFE	Sydney Futures Exchange
Simex	Singapore International Monetary Exchange
Soffex	Swiss Options & Financial Futures Exchange
SOM	Stockholm Options Market
Tocom	Tokyo Commodity Exchange
TGE	Tokyo Grain Exchange
TSE	Tokyo Stock Exchange
WCE	Winnipeg Commodity Exchange

Source: *Futures and Options World*, Issue 240 (May 1991).

distinct disadvantage if he is not familiar with the products that are available and how they can be used. It should not be forgotten that the opportunities associated with international trade and finance also have their risks. Assets held in a foreign currency are subject to changes in value due to exchange rate fluctuations. Governments can also cancel debts, expropriate investments, impose exchange controls and do many other things with nefarious consequences for cross-border transactions. Other risks can arise from things such as unfamiliarity with local trading rules, high transaction costs, insider trading and the like. This is not to say that international investments are riskier than domestic invest-ments. In fact, many studies claim proof that investing internationally actually reduces risk per unit of return through diversification benefits.[9] It does mean, however, that risks can be different from those that are present in our domestic market. One of the goals of this book is to make it clear what these risks are and how they can be managed most effectively.

[9] See, for example, B. Solnik, "Why not diversify internationally rather than domestically", *Financial Analysts Journal* (July 1974); M. Adler, "Global fixed income portfolio management", *Financial Analysts Journal* (September–October 1983); H. Hana, "Why Americans should have diversified", *Euromoney* (March 1980); B. Noetzlin and B. Solnik, "Optimal international asset allocation", *Journal of Portfolio Management* (Fall 1982).

THE ECONOMICS OF INTERNATIONAL TRANSACTIONS

Balance of payments

The international financial environment is intimately related to the macroeconomic performance of the individual countries that participate in the world economy. This is because the concept of national sovereignty is a key element in the current structure of the international economic and financial system. Individual countries have the right to regulate transactions within the geographic area they control and are responsible for organizing domestic resource allocation and income distribution. Transactions between different national jurisdictions, however, fall outside the scope of the individual national authorities. On the international level resource allocation and income distribution across countries depend to a large extent on competitive forces. The outcome reflects the relative success of the different national economic policies in the international market-place and is measured by the economic and financial flows between countries, presented in a special account called "the balance of payments". Because cross-border economic and financial flows affect economic performance, such as output and employment, and financial variables, such as interest rates and exchange rates, it is important for financial decision making to understand how this process occurs. A good starting point is the balance of payments accounting equation.

This chapter shows what the balance of payments is and how it relates to the exchange rate and to overall economic activity. We begin with a general presentation of the balance of payments and the major transactions to which it refers. We examine the principles guiding its structure and the interpretation of each type of transaction that is included. Particular attention is paid to the fact that the balance of payments always balances, meaning that it always comes out to zero. We then consider the role of the monetary authorities and the different ways that this balance can be achieved. Finally, we look at the functional relationship between the balance of payments and the overall economy.

International transactions: The balance of payments

The **balance of payments** is the record of the economic and financial flows that take place over a specified time period between residents and non-residents of a given country. The time period itself is arbitrary but it is common practice to supply balance of payments data on a monthly, quarterly and yearly basis. The residents of a country comprise the general government, individuals, private non-profit bodies serving individuals, and enterprises, all defined in terms of their residential relationship to the territory of that economy.[1] Flows refer

---

[1] A detailed presentation of the distinction between residents and non-residents for balance of payments accounting can be found in *Balance of Payments Manual*, fourth edition (International Monetary Fund, 1977), p.p. 19–25.

to income and expenditure or changes in levels of outstanding assets and liabilities. They are recorded in a double entry system of credits and debits or sources and uses.

The best way to understand this definition is via some simple examples, but before these we should get a general idea of what the balance of payments includes. Table 1.1 shows a shorthand presentation of how the International Monetary Fund (IMF) portrays the balance of payments. It is divided into two major accounts, the **current account** and the **capital account**. Each general account is then subdivided into categories such as exports, imports, direct investment, portfolio investment, etc. When necessary, even more detail is available. In *Balance of Payments Statistics*, for example, the IMF regularly publishes member countries' balance of payments data divided into 112 different categories.

In order to make comparisons between different economies, a standardized method for compiling the accounts is important. The accepted practice is that the elements of both accounts should be recorded at **market prices** where possible. Market prices mean the amount of money that a willing buyer pays to acquire something from a willing seller, when buyer and seller are independent and when such an exchange is motivated only by commercial considerations. In this context, each transaction is priced individually according to the contract terms specific to that transaction. It is therefore conceivable that separate transactions, though identical in every way, could have different market prices. While most transactions lend themselves to this notion of a market price, many, such as direct barter, tax payments, transfers between affiliated enterprises and gifts do not. In cases like these it is necessary to estimate the actual market values.[2]

Table 1.1 Standard components of the balance of payments

Current account

	Exports fob
−	Imports fob
=	Trade balance
+	Exports of non-financial services
−	Imports of non-financial sservices
+	Investment income (credit)
−	Investment income (debit)
+(−)	Private unrequited transfers
+(−)	Official unrequited transfers
=	Current account balance

Capital account

+(−)	Direct investment
+(−)	Portfolio investment
+(−)	Other long-term capital
+(−)	Other short-term capital
+(−)	Net errors and omissions
+(−)	Counterpart items
+(−)	Total change in reserves
=	Capital account balance

[2] See *Balance of Payments Manual*, op. cit., p.p. 26–33 for a discussion of the practical valuation problems involved in balance of payments reporting.

With these general definitions in mind, we can move on to some concrete examples of how balance of payments accounting works.

The current account

The trade balance

As we saw in Table 1.1, the current account includes the **trade balance**, which comprises **merchandise** exports and imports fob. Merchandise refers to all movable goods such as cars, textiles and appliances, and "fob" means **free on board**. Free on board implies that distributive services like transport and handling performed on goods up to the customs frontier of the economy from which the goods are exported are classed as merchandise.

Transaction 1: A merchandise export

Suppose, for example, that a Californian vineyard sells 5000 bottles of wine to a Japanese retailer. The price of the wine when it leaves the vineyard is USD 250,000 and it costs USD 15,000 to ship the wine to the airport in Los Angeles from where it will be flown to Tokyo. The "fob" price of the wine will then be USD 265,000, which includes the ex vineyard price of USD 250,000 and the USD 15,000 transport cost of shipping the wine to Los Angeles. The US balance of payments will show a credit or a source of USD 265,000 of exports fob.

We mentioned earlier that balance of payments accounting is based on a double entry system. A credit or source of USD 265,000 implies a debit or use of an equal amount. In order to account for the debit we have to know how the export was financed. Suppose that the US exporter allows the Japanese retailer 60 days to pay for the wine. The US exporter now has a short-term claim of USD 265,000 on the Japanese retailer. Expressed in "T"-accounts the US balance of payments will look like this:

Exports fob

| | 265,000 |

Short-term claims

| 265,000 | |

where sources (credits) of external purchasing power are on the right and uses (debits) of external purchasing power are on the left. The merchandise export account shows an increase of external purchasing power of USD 265,000 while the short-term capital account shows an investment of USD 265,000 that represents a decrease of external purchasing power.

When working out balance of payments transactions in terms of T-accounts, it is helpful to remember that a source is generated when liabilities increase or when assets decrease and a use is generated when liabilities decrease or when assets increase. In the foregoing example, the sale of wine represents a reduction in US tangible assets (a source of external purchasing power) while the trade credit extended by the US exporter represents an increase in US financial assets (a use of external purchasing power).

Transaction 2: A merchandise import

Galeries Laffitte, a department store located in New York, buys USD 200,000 worth of textiles from a South Korean company. The merchandise is billed in US dollars and Galeries Laffitte pays for the merchandise with a check drawn on a New York branch of Citicorp.

In this case, the textile imports represent an increase in US tangible assets and is a use of external purchasing power. The check drawn by Galeries Laffitte on a New York branch of Citicorp represents an increase of short-term liabilities owed by residents of the United States to non-residents and is a source of external purchasing power. For the US balance of payments expressed in T-accounts, these transactions will appear as follows:

Imports fob
--- | ---
200,000 |

Short-term liabilities
--- | ---
| 200,000

From Transactions 1 and 2 we can calculate the US trade balance for the period which is equal to:

Trade balance = Exports fob – Imports fob = USD 265,000 – USD 200,000 = USD 65,000.

The offsetting entries in the accounts' short-term claims and short-term liabilities should not be forgotten. They represent how the merchandise transactions were financed. Their place in the balance of payments will become clear when we study the capital account.

Non-financial services

The next components of the current account are exports and imports of **non-financial services**. Non-financial services include such things as freight, insurance, passenger services and travel. Freight refers mainly to the carriage or transport of goods between economies. Insurance comprises insurance on movable goods during the course of shipment between economies as well as insurance on the carriers themselves and other types of insurance such as life insurance. The transportation of persons represents the largest component of passenger services but it also includes any other services for which passengers make expenditures on board carriers or for which they pay charges to carriers. Travel covers the goods and services acquired from an economy by non-resident travelers for their personal use during their stay in that economy. The most common goods and services are lodging, meals, entertainment and transportation within the economy, together with gifts, souvenirs and personal articles that travelers take out of the economies visited.

Transaction 3: An export of a non-financial service
Jean Pierre de la Martingale is a Frenchman who lives in Paris, France. He decides to spend his two-week vacation traveling around the United States. He buys a round trip ticket on American Air Lines for the equivalent of USD 7000 and spends an extra USD 100 for head-phones and drinks while on the plane. His US expenses for hotels, food, transportation and souvenirs comes to the equivalent of USD 14,900. He pays American Air Lines in cash with euros and obtains the USD 14,900 that he spends in the United States by selling euros to a US branch of Citicorp.

The equivalent of USD 7100 that Jean Pierre de la Martingale pays American Air Lines will be credited to passenger services in the balance of payments and the USD 14,900 that he spends in the United States will be credited to travel for a total of USD 22,000 of exports of non-financial services for the US economy. On the other hand, American Air Lines increased its cash euro holdings by the equivalent of USD 7100 while Citicorp increased its cash euro holdings by the equivalent of USD 14,900 for a total increase of USD 22,000 for the US economy. For the US balance of payments expressed in T-accounts, these transactions will appear as follows:

Exports of non-financial services
|22,000

Short-term claims
22,000 |

The exports of non-financial services generate a source of USD 22,000 worth of external purchasing power. This is offset by an increase of USD 22,000 worth of cash euro holdings in the account "short-term claims". Remember that cash, as **legal tender**, is the shortest-term type of claim available.

Investment income

The next item in the current account is **investment income**, which comprises income derived from the ownership of foreign financial assets. It includes interest and dividends from portfolio investment but excludes the earnings of incorporated enterprises that are not formally distributed. If, for example, earnings per share on a portfolio investment are GBP 10 and a GBP 5 dividend is declared, only the GBP 5 dividend would be counted in the balance of payments. The same is not true for non-distributed earnings on direct invest-ments, which are treated as investment income. The distinction between portfolio investment and direct investment revolves around the investor's intentions concerning the management of the foreign company. When the investor's purpose is to have an effective voice in the management of the foreign enterprise, it is considered as a direct investment; when there is no such purpose it is considered as a portfolio investment. We will have more to say later on about this distinction.

Transaction 4: Investment income: The export of a financial service

Elepha, Inc., a wholly owned Nigerian subsidiary of the New York based Phi, Inc., has after-tax profits of the equivalent of USD 100,000 and declares a dividend of USD 50,000. Phi uses the dividend to purchase long-term bonds issued by the Nigerian government.

As a wholly owned subsidiary, Elepha represents a direct investment for Phi. Therefore, total profits of USD 100,000 including retained earnings and the declared dividend is counted as investment income for the US balance of payments and a source of external purchasing power. The uses of this external purchasing power can be divided into two categories – direct investment and portfolio investment. The non-distributed profits or retained earnings of USD 50,000 have effectively been reinvested in Elepha and represent a USD 50,000 increase of Phi's direct investment in Nigeria. Phi is a US resident enterprise and, hence, US residents' claims on non-residents have increased by USD 50,000. By the same token, the long-term government bonds purchased by Phi with the dividend represents a USD 50,000 increase in US resident portfolio investment. In T-accounts for the US balance of payments, these transactions will be recorded as follows:

Investment income

	100,000

Direct investment

50,000	

Long-term claims

50,000	

Unrequited transfers

The final components of the current account are **private unrequited transfers** and **official unrequited transfers**. Private unrequited transfers refer mainly to resident immigrant workers' remittances to their country of origin as well as gifts, dowries, inheritances, prizes, charitable contributions, etc. Official unrequited transfers include voluntary subsidies, military aid, voluntary cancellation of debt, contributions to international organizations, indemnities imposed under peace treaties, technical assistance, taxes and fines. Because of the non-market quality of unrequited transfers, adherence to the market price principle applied in the other accounts is often impossible. The general rule of thumb is that when unrequited transfers are offsets to real or financial resources, their value should be assumed to be the same as that of the real or financial resources to which they correspond. If these resources themselves have no actual market value, they should be valued at cost or some notional value determined by one of the parties to the transaction.[3]

Transaction 5: An unrequited transfer

Mohammed Hassan, who is a citizen of Algeria but has been a resident of the United States for several years, transfers USD 5000 from his account at a New York branch of Citicorp to his ageing father's account at an Algiers branch of the Algerian National Bank. There is no commercial quid pro quo involved in the operation and Mr Hassan's father is still a resident of Algeria. Thus, the transaction falls under the heading "immigrant worker's remittance" and represents an unrequited transfer and a use of external purchasing power for the US economy. The offsetting source of external purchasing power is the increase in Citicorp's short-term liabilities to the Algerian National Bank. These transactions will be recorded in the US balance of payments as follows:

Private unrequited transfers

5000	

Short-term liabilities

	5000

---

[3] See *Balance of Payments Manual*, op. cit., p.p. 113–117.

The current account as an income statement

This completes the components of the current account. We can see that the current account resembles the income statement of a private company. Exports of goods and non-financial services plus credits of unrequited transfers correspond to sales. Imports of goods and non-financial services plus debits of unrequited transfers correspond to non-financial expenses such as cost of goods sold, selling expense and general and administrative costs. Investment income corresponds to dividends and interest. One major difference does exist, however, in that there is no distinction between costs accruing to operations and costs associated with capital investment. Consequently, to the extent that there is no provision for depreciation and imports of non-financial goods and services can include investment expenditure, it is not clear from the balance of payments whether there is a profit or loss. This type of question can only be answered in the context of the overall economy, a problem we will take up in the following chapter.[4]

The current and capital accounts: The double entry system

Table 1.2 presents all the information resulting from Transactions 1 through 5. Although we were considering transactions related to the current account, the double entry system made it necessary to consider transactions related to the capital account as well. As we can see, at the end of Transaction 5 the United States had a current account surplus of USD 182,000. This surplus was offset by a USD 182,000 deficit in the capital account. In fact, because of the double entry system, the balance of the current and capital accounts will always be equal to zero. The importance of this fact will become clear when we analyze the effects of balance of payments transactions on other economic and financial variables. We can complete the presentation of balance of payments accounting by taking a close look at the capital account.

Table 1.2 US balance of payments after Transaction 5

	Current account	
	Exports fob	265,000
–	Imports fob	–200,000
=	Trade balance	= 65,000
+	Exports of non-financial services	+22,000
–	Imports of non-financial services	—
+	Investment income (credit)	+100,000
–	Investment income (debit)	—
+(–)	Private unrequited transfers	–5,000
+(–)	Official unrequited transfers	—
=	Current account balance	= +182,000
	Capital account	
+(–)	Direct investment	–50,000
+(–)	Portfolio investment	–50,000
+(–)	Other long-term capital	—
+(–)	Other short-term capital	–82,000
+(–)	Net errors and omissions	—
+(–)	Counterpart items	—
+(–)	Change in reserves	—
=	Capital account balance	= –182,000

[4] For an in depth discussion of this problem see Ephraim A. Clark, *Cross-Border Investment Risk* (Euromoney Books, 1991) Chapters 1 and 2.

The capital account

Direct investment and portfolio investment

As mentioned in the discussion of investment income, the difference between direct investment and portfolio investment revolves around whether or not the investor intends to take an active role in the management of the enterprise the assets of which are being acquired. In many cases there is no ambiguity. Bonds, debentures and the like are clearly portfolio investment insofar as they confer no management or voting rights on their owners. On the other hand, foreign branches, wholly owned subsidiaries and joint ventures are clearly direct investments. Although ownership of at least some voting stock is usually seen as a requirement for direct investment status, the distinction between direct investment and portfolio investment becomes increasingly difficult to establish as the proportion of foreign ownership falls or is dispersed among various owners and economies. Most countries solve the problem based on the percentage of foreign ownership by a single investor in the enterprise. If single investor foreign ownership is above a certain percentage, the investment is considered as a direct investment; below this percentage it is considered as portfolio investment.

Other capital

The next component of the capital account is referred to as "**other capital**", which is a residual category that groups all the capital transactions that have not been included in direct investment, portfolio investment and reserves. It is divided into long-term capital and short-term capital and, because of its residual status, can differ from country to country. Generally speaking, other long-term capital includes most non-negotiable instruments of a year or more like bank loans and mortgages. Other short-term capital includes financial assets of less than a year such as currency, deposits and bills.

In Table 1.2 we can see that although there was no net movement in the long-term capital account, there was a deficit of USD 82,000 in the short-term capital account. In other words, uses of short-term capital were USD 82,000 higher than sources. We can find this figure by looking at short-term capital movements in Transactions 1–5, which are summarized in the T-accounts below.

In Transaction 1 short-term claims increased when the US exporter extended a USD 265,000 trade credit to the Japanese importer. In Transaction 2 short-term liabilities increased when the South Korean exporter accepted the USD 200,000 check drawn on the US bank. In Transaction 3 short-term claims increased when American Air Lines and Citicorp accepted USD 22,000 worth of euros. Finally, in Transaction 5 short-term liabilities increased when the Algerian National Bank accepted the USD 5000 sight deposit at the New York branch of Citicorp. Total short-term sources in the form of short-term liabilities were USD 205,000 while total short-term uses in the form of short-term claims were USD 287,000. Taking the difference between sources and uses (205,000 – 287,000) shows a deficit of USD 82,000 in the short-term capital account.

	Short-term claims	
(1)	265,000	
(3)	22,000	
	287,000	

	Short-term liabilities	
		200,000 (2)
		5,000 (5)
		205,000

Change in reserves

A key element in international economic and financial analysis is the amount of international liquidity or "reserves" held by the central authority of individual countries. Reserves include **monetary gold**, **special drawing rights** (SDRs), the **reserve position in the Fund** and **foreign exchange**. Monetary gold is gold held by the authorities as a financial asset. SDRs are reserves created by the International Monetary Fund (IMF) as bookkeeping entries and credited to the accounts of IMF member countries according to their established IMF quotas. A decision to create SDRs requires the approval of a majority of the member countries holding 85% of the weighted voting power of the IMF. Once created they may be used in the settlement of balance of payments imbalances among countries participating in the Special Drawing Account administered by the IMF. More will be said about SDRs and the IMF when we look at the organization of the international financial system. The reserve position in the Fund is basically the difference between the member's quota plus other claims on the Fund less the Fund's holdings of that member's currency. Foreign exchange is by far the largest component of total international liquidity. It includes monetary authorities' claims on non-residents in the form of bank deposits, Treasury bills, short-term and long-term government securities, and other claims usable in the event of balance of payments need, including non-marketable claims arising from inter-central bank and inter-governmental arrangements, without regard to whether the claim is denominated in the currency of the debtors or the creditors.[5]

The evolution of international reserves in balance of payments accounting is recorded in the account called "**change in reserves**". This account differs from the other accounts in the balance of payments insofar as it is the only account that records transactions with residents as well as non-residents. First, let's look at a transaction with a non-resident.

Transaction 6: A reserve transaction with a non-resident

NatWest Bank in London pays USD 100,000 to buy GBP 62,500 from the Fed (the Federal Reserve Bank), the US central bank.

In this transaction the Fed's claims on non-residents decrease by GBP 62,500, the equivalent of USD 100,000. A decrease in assets is a source. Thus, a reduction of international reserves represents a source of external purchasing power. It is worth taking some time to think about this operation because our experience has been that, based on intuition, the contrary would seem to be true. The corresponding use of external purchasing power comes about through the replacement of a US short-term liability formerly owed to the British bank by a short-term liability now owed to the US central bank. The following T-accounts record these transactions:

Change in reserves	
	100,000

Short-term liabilities	
100,000	

---

[5] See introductory pages to *International Financial Statistics*, published monthly by the International Monetary Fund.

Transaction 7: A reserve transaction with a resident

A New York branch of Citicorp sells CHF 75,000 (i.e. Swiss francs) to the Fed for USD 50,000. In this transaction, claims on non-residents by Citicorp decrease by CHF 75,000, the equivalent of USD 50,000. The corresponding use is the CHF 75,000 increase of the Fed's foreign exchange reserves. These transactions are recorded as follows:

Change in reserves	
50,000	

Short-term claims	
	50,000

Table 1.3 summarizes the US balance of payments after the conclusion of Transaction 7. The current account has not changed. It is still in surplus by USD 182,000. The capital account has not changed either. It is still in deficit by USD 182,000. Although the overall capital account has not changed, two of the sub-accounts in the capital account have. The short-term capital account has moved from a deficit of USD 82,000 to a deficit of USD 132,000, while the change in reserves account has gone from zero to a surplus of USD 50,000 due to the reduction in foreign exchange holdings. When analyzing a country's external position, it is important to look at the individual accounts to see how the balance between the capital and current accounts was achieved.

Table 1.3 US Balance of payments after Transaction 7

	Current account	
	Exports fob	265,000
−	Imports fob	−200,000
=	Trade balance	= 65,000
+	Exports of non-financial services	+ 22,000
−	Imports of non-financial services	—
+	Investment income (credit)	+100,000
−	Investment income (debit)	—
+(−)	Private unrequited transfers	−5,000
+(−)	Official unrequited transfers	—
=	Current account balance	= +182,000
	Capital account	
+(−)	Direct investment	−50,000
+(−)	Portfolio investment	−50,000
+(−)	Other long-term capital	—
+(−)	Other short-term capital	−132,000
+(−)	Net errors and omissions	—
+(−)	Counterpart items	—
+(−)	Change in reserves	+ 50,000
=	Capital account balance	= − 182,000

Counterpart items

So far nothing has been mentioned about the accounts labeled **counterpart items** and **net errors and omissions**. Counterpart items are analogous to unrequited transfers in the current account. They arise because of the double entry system in balance of payments accounting and refer to adjustments in reserves owing to monetization or demonetization of gold, allocation or cancellation of SDRs and revaluation of the various components of total reserves.

When monetary authorities add to their holdings of monetary gold by acquiring newly mined gold or existing gold offered on the private market, their reserves increase which creates a debit or use on the capital account. The offsetting source for the same amount as the increase in reserves is applied to the counterpart account. When monetary authorities sell gold to the private sector (demonetization), the resulting source is offset by a use entry for the same amount in the counterpart account.

The same procedure holds for the allocation of SDRs. SDRs, as a pure creation by the IMF, give rise to a debit in the reserve account when they are allocated. The offsetting source is credited to the counterpart account. When SDRs are cancelled, the resulting source in the reserve account is offset by a debit in the counterpart account.

The floating exchange rate system, in place since the early 1970s, and the fact that an official gold price no longer exists means that in the absence of a fixed price unit of account the various reserve components can show valuation changes relative to each other. When the monetary authorities adjust the value of their reserves upwards or downwards in response to these changes, the offsetting credit or debit is applied to the counterpart account.

Net errors and omissions

The errors and omissions in balance of payments accounting arise in large part from the statistical difficulties involved in gathering balance of payments data. Because officials do not have the necessary information to make the double entries that we applied in the earlier examples, they make single entries based on the information available to them. This information often comes from multiple sources that vary in coverage and reliability. For example, merchandise trade figures are derived from customs documents, freight charges from reports by shipping organizations, and the resulting changes in international bank accounts from either banks' balance sheets or from transaction records compiled by banks or others. Short-term capital movements are particularly difficult to track, especially when there is an intent to evade exchange controls, taxes and other restrictions. Capital movements may also lead or lag the transactions they are meant to finance. For example, an export shipped in the month of November or December may not be paid for until January or February of the following year. The net errors and omissions account offsets the cumulated net difference in the other accounts.[6]

---

[6] On the world level net errors and omissions should cancel each other out, but in fact this is not the case. The cumulated discrepancy between 1977 and 1983 was USD 111 billion and since then it has increased consistently. A major study of this problem by the IMF (*Report on the World Current Account Discrepancy*), published in September 1987, found that besides the relatively specific and persistent statistical problems associated with recording merchandise trade, unrequited transfers and shipping, the overriding factor was the emergence of a large body of cross-border assets recognized by the debtor countries but not by the creditors.

Interpreting the balance of payments

The exchange markets

The different accounts in the balance of payments are like windows. They make it possible to see into the overall balance of payments to understand the forces at work. The possible number of accounts and resulting "balances" depend on the amount of detail used in compiling balance of payments data and the number of ways that the data can be grouped. For example, merchandise exports and imports can be broken down by product or product type. This is useful for determining how a country's balance of payments and overall economic performance will react to different situations. Oil exporting countries are sensitive to energy prices. Coffee exporters are sensitive to premature frosts in Brazil. Food importers are vulnerable to changes in the European Union's agricultural policy. Indebted countries are affected by international interest rates. Considerations such as these are indispensable for judicious economic and financial decision making. However, to refer to the balance of payments as being in surplus or deficit is meaningless unless the particular accounts that are being included in the calculation are specified. The balance of the overall balance of payments will always be equal to zero.

The principal sub-accounts

The examples in the first part of this chapter grouped the balance of payments into two accounts, the current account and the capital account. In this distinction we saw that the current account plays a role similar to a private company's income statement. It gives an idea of the country's economic performance vis-à-vis the rest of the world. The capital account shows how this activity was financed. Another popular grouping draws the line under "other long-term capital" to emphasize the role of economic performance and stable long-term financing. This is sometimes called the basic balance. One of the most important aspects of the balance of payments is its effect on the exchange rate. When this is the problem, a good place to draw the line is under counterpart items so that the account "change in reserves" can be isolated. The change in reserves account gives an idea of the imbalance between the supply and demand of local currency for foreign currency. Let's examine why this is so.

The balance of payments as the measure of the supply and demand of domestic currency for foreign currency

In the balance of payments accounting system described above, a credit entry gives rise to an increase in external purchasing power, which could also be described as a demand for local currency. Conversely, a debit that gives rise to a use of external purchasing power could be described as a supply of local currency. In Transaction 1, for example, the Japanese importer needed USD 265,000 to pay for Californian wine. Consequently, the demand for local currency is implicit in the export transaction because if there had been no trade credit the importer would have had to buy the dollars with foreign currency to pay for the wine. Because there was a trade credit, the demand for USD 265,000 that was implicit in the wine purchase was effectively supplied by the US exporter. Thus, the trade credit is the equivalent of a sale of dollars and a purchase of foreign currency. If the wine had been billed in Japanese yen, the argument is similar. The Japanese importer would supply the yen and the US exporter would sell the yen and buy US dollars. The demand for dollars is still implicit in the export transaction. The extension of a trade credit in yen is the equivalent of the exporter buying yen with dollars and then lending the yen to the Japanese importer.

Similar arguments could be made for all credits and debits. The purpose of approaching the balance of payments in terms of supply and demand of local currency for foreign currency is to bring out the relationship between the balance of payments and the exchange rate. In subsequent chapters of this book we will see that the exchange rate plays a prominent role in both international financial theory and practice. Consequently, a thorough understanding of how exchange rates are determined and what effects they have on other economic and financial variables is crucial for the study of international finance. The first step is to appreciate that the exchange rate results from the supply and demand of local currency for foreign currency and to understand that the supply and demand is reflected in the balance of payments.

The monetary authorities and the exchange rate

The **exchange rate** is the price of foreign currency in units of local currency or, conversely, the price of local currency in units of foreign currency. For convertible currencies, the price depends on the supply and demand of one for the other. Just as in any market, prices will adjust to equate supply with demand. If the *ex ante* supply and demand for local currency is not in balance, the exchange rate will change to restore equilibrium. This effectively means that certain transactions that were projected *ex ante* will not be realized *ex post* and others that were not projected *ex ante* will be realized *ex post*. The next chapter is devoted to studying this proposition in detail, but here we want to outline the role of the monetary authorities in determining the exchange rate.

Remember that to examine the relationship between the balance of payments and the exchange rate we decided to draw the line under the account "net errors and omissions". Everything above the line represents the combined supply and demand of local currency for foreign currency generated by private transactions. Below the line, the account "change in reserves" represents the supply and demand of local currency for foreign currency generated by the monetary authorities. If there is a disequilibrium above the line, the monetary authorities have two choices. They can either intervene through the account "change in reserves" to make up the difference or they can do nothing. Intervention has the effect of preventing the exchange rate from changing. Non-intervention means that the exchange rate will move to equate supply with demand.

Let's go back to Transaction 6 where NatWest Bank in London pays USD 100,000 to buy GBP 62,500 from the Fed. This implies that the exchange rate is USD 1.6/GBP 1. Suppose that this is the rate that the US authorities feel is most appropriate for their policy objectives. If the Fed had not intervened by selling the sterling to NatWest, the supply of dollars for pounds would have been greater than the demand and the dollar would have depreciated relative to the pound. The Fed prevented the dollar from depreciating relative to the pound by supplying the USD 62,500 at the rate of USD 1.6 for GBP 1.

The limits to this type of intervention are obvious. It can only last as long as reserves hold out. The limits to intervention designed to prevent currency appreciation are also obvious. They are determined by the willingness of the monetary authorities to accumulate foreign assets. Furthermore, both policies – intervention and non-intervention – are fraught with consequences for the overall economy. As we will see in the next chapter, a change in the exchange rate tends to change the quantities and types of merchandise that are produced and consumed in the economy, while intervention affects the economy through changes in the money supply.

Macroeconomic accounting discipline

Besides a direct link to the exchange rate, the balance of payments also plays a prominent role in an economy's overall performance. In its most general sense, this role is one of **macroeconomic accounting discipline**, by which we mean that an economy's consumption and investment of resources cannot be greater than the resources that it produces plus the resources that it borrows. We can appreciate how this accounting discipline is achieved if we examine how the external sector, reflected in the balance of payments, fits into the schema of overall economic performance.

Most economists refer to **gross domestic product** (GDP) or **gross national product** (GNP) as a measure of economic performance. GDP measures an economy's output defined as the total flow of goods and services produced by an economy over a specified time period. It is obtained by valuing the outputs of both final and investment goods and services at the market prices of the country in question and then aggregating. Intermediate goods are netted out but are implicitly included in the prices of the final goods.[7] GDP is usually broken down as follows:

+ Exports
− Imports
+ Private consumption
+ Government consumption
+ Gross fixed capital formation
+ Variation in stocks
= Gross domestic product

GNP measures an economy's total income. It is equal to GDP plus the income from abroad accruing to domestic residents minus income generated in the domestic market accruing to non-residents: i.e. GNP = GDP +(−) net factor payments abroad. Hence, GDP shows what can be produced with factors located within the country's geographic boundaries while GNP shows what can be earned with factors located domestically or abroad but owned by domestic residents.

Let's start with GDP. We can define GDP by the accounting identity:[8]

$$GDP = X - M + C + \Delta stk + I \tag{1.1}$$

where:

X = merchandise exports plus exports of all non-financial services plus unrequited transfers (credit)

M = merchandise imports plus imports of all non-financial services plus unrequited transfers (debit)

FS = net investment income (investment income (credit) minus investment income (debit))

F = net foreign capital not counting the change in reserves (capital account balance minus the change in reserves)

BP = the increase in reserves

C = private consumption plus government consumption

I = gross fixed capital formation

Δstk = change in inventory.

[7] The main international standard for a comprehensive and systematic framework for collecting and presenting the economic statistics of a nation is provided by the United Nations in, *A System of National Accounts, Studies in Methods*, Series No. 2, Rev. 3 (New York, 1968).

[8] For economies that are net borrowers, GDP is usually retained as the measure of economic performance. Here we define GDP to include unrequited transfers in exports and imports. The principles applied in compiling the balance of payments are generally the same as those governing the construction of the external segment of the national accounts. The major differences are outlined in the *Balance of Payments Manual*, op. cit., p.p. 177–180.

By the same token, the balance of payments accounting identity can be written:

$$BP = X - M + FS + F \qquad (1.2)$$

Note that BP refers to the account "change in reserves" where the change refers to an *increase* in reserves. In other words, if reserves increase, BP is positive and if reserves decrease, BP is negative.

If we compare Equations 1.1 and 1.2, it is clear that the role of the balance of payments is explicit in the overall economy. GDP is constrained by:

$$X - M = BP - FS - F.$$

Practically speaking, what this means is that an economy can only use more resources than it produces ($X < M$) to the extent of its foreign reserves ($\sum_{t=0}^{T} BP_t$), where T is the current period), its investment income (FS) or the willingness of the rest of the world to extend credit (F). An example will make this clear. Consider an economy with the following GDP:

Exports	GBP 10
Imports	GBP 10
Private and government consumption	GBP 70
Gross fixed capital formation	GBP 30
Change in inventory	GBP 0
= GDP	GBP 100

This economy exports only textiles and imports only oil, which, because it has no energy resources, represents all its energy needs. Given the economy's technology, GBP 1 worth of energy is required for every GBP 10 worth of output. There is no net investment so that the GBP 30 of gross fixed capital formation represents the replacement of worn out machinery necessary to maintain output at the current equilibrium level of GBP 100. The economy has no reserves and no external debt so that the balance of payments equation reduces to:

$$BP = X - M = \text{GBP } 0 = \text{GBP } 10 - \text{GBP } 10.$$

Suppose that an increase in domestic demand for textiles reduces textile exports from GBP 10 to GBP 5. In the absence of foreign capital, balance of payments discipline would make imports of oil fall to GBP 5. Because of the technical relationship between output and energy, this would in turn provoke a fall in output from GBP 100 to GBP 50. Think of it! A GBP 5 reduction of imports causes a GBP 50 reduction in output. Balance of payments discipline can have economic effects many times greater than the balance of payments figures themselves.

Suppose that to avoid this clearly unacceptable outcome the government borrows GBP 5 abroad at an annual rate of interest of 10%. The balance of payments would then look like this:

$$BP = X - M + F = \text{GBP } 0 = \text{GBP } 5 - \text{GBP } 10 + \text{GBP } 5.$$

With imports at GBP 10 output could be maintained at GBP 100. However, the composition of GDP will have changed:

Exports	GBP 5
Imports	GBP 10
Private and government consumption	GBP 75
Gross fixed capital formation	GBP 30
Change in inventory	GBP 0
= GDP	GBP 100

Consumption has increased by GBP 5 to the detriment of exports. This implies a rise in the standard of living. In the following year, however, interest of GBP 0.50 must be paid on the foreign loan. In the absence of new foreign capital and remembering that, in this case, $BP = X - M + FS$, consider two possible scenarios:

Scenario 1: GBP 5.50 of textiles are retired from domestic consumption and made available for export:

$$BP = X - M + FS$$

$$BP = GBP\ 10.50 - GBP\ 10.00 - GBP\ 0.50 = GBP\ 0$$

Scenario 2: Only GBP 5 of textiles are retired from domestic consumption and made available for export and imports are decreased by GBP 0.50.

$$BP = GBP\ 10.00 - GBP\ 9.50 - GBP\ 0.50 = GBP\ 0$$

Table 1.4 shows the effects on GDP.

Scenario 1 implies a voluntary reduction in domestic consumption in response to the economic reality of accounting discipline. In this case, the textiles freed by the GBP 5.50 reduction in consumption are exported and the proceeds used to maintain the equilibrium level of imports. This makes it possible for output to remain at its maximum equilibrium level of GBP 100. Still, the fall in consumption implies a fall in the standard of living from the original equilibrium level of GBP 70 and, other things being equal, this for as long as the loan remains outstanding.

Scenario 2 implies an involuntary reduction in consumption in response to the economic reality of accounting discipline. This could come about, for example, if, in order to maintain pre-loan levels of consumption, the money supply is allowed to expand. Instead of freeing GBP 5.50 worth of textiles from domestic consumption for export, only GBP 5 worth are freed. Balance of payments discipline ensures that oil imports fall to GBP 9.50. This is

Table 1.4 GDP under Scenarios 1 and 2

	Scenario 1 (GBP)	Scenario 2 (GBP)
Exports	10.50	10.00
Imports	10.00	9.50
Private and government consumption	69.50	64.50
Gross fixed capital formation	30.00	30.00
Change in inventory	00.00	00.00
GDP	100.00	95.00

insufficient to maintain output at its equilibrium level of GBP 100. Energy shortages cause output to fall by 5% and ultimately cause a fall in consumption of GBP 5.50. The reduction in output from its long-term equilibrium level of GBP 100 suggests an underemployment of resources as well as a reduced standard of living.

Without going into the transition process from one situation to another, which will certainly be more costly than the frictionless, idealized scenarios presented above, it is clear that balance of payments discipline is an important factor in determining an economy's output, consumption and employment performance. Furthermore, the magnitude of balance of payments induced effects on the overall economy is likely to be many times larger than the magnitude of the transactions figuring in the balance of payments itself.

Does this mean that foreign borrowing is always bad? The answer is clearly "no". Foreign borrowing can be justified if it is used in such a way that it creates at least as much foreign exchange value as it costs. This is another way of saying that the rate of return on the use of the borrowed resources must be at least as high as their cost. In the foregoing example this would entail an increase in the production of at least GBP 0.50 of export value, a cost saving of at least GBP 0.50 of import value for the same level of output, or a combination of the two of at least GBP 0.50.

Saving and investment

Another way of presenting balance of payments discipline is in terms of saving and investment. Let income be equal to GNP.

$$GNP = GDP + FS \tag{1.3}$$

Then saving is equal to income minus consumption:

$$\text{Saving} = GDP + FS - C = X - M + FS + \Delta stk + I \tag{1.4}$$

We recognize $(X - M + FS)$ as the current account balance and $(\Delta stk + I)$ as gross investment. Then, letting S = saving, $B_c = X - M + FS$ and $I_g = \Delta stk + I$ and rearranging:

$$S - I_g = B_c \tag{1.5}$$

The difference between saving and investment is equal to the current account balance. Remember that the current account balance is equal to the variation in official reserves less net foreign investment. Thus:

$$\text{Saving} - \text{Investment} = \text{Current account balance} = BP - F.$$

This is a basic relation between the external sector and the overall economy. Any excess in the current account balance is matched by an excess in domestic saving over domestic investment and this will be reflected in the capital account balance by an increase in reserves and net foreign lending. On the other hand, any deficit in the current account balance is matched by an excess in domestic investment over domestic saving and this will be reflected in the capital account balance by net foreign borrowing and a decrease in reserves.

Summary

1. The balance of payments is the record of the economic and financial flows that take place over a specified time period between residents and non-residents of a given country.

Positive flows such as exports are sources of external purchasing power and negative flows such as imports are uses of external purchasing power. Sources of external purchasing power generate demand for a country's currency while uses generate a supply of the currency.

2. Balance of payments accounting is based on the double entry system of bookkeeping. Every source has a corresponding use and vice versa. Thus, the overall balance of payments will always be equal to zero. Analyzing the performance of a country's external sector requires segregating the overall balance, which is equal to zero, into sub-accounts that explain how the balance was achieved.

3. The most common practice is to divide the balance of payments into the current account and the capital account. The current account includes exports and imports of all goods and non-financial services, investment income and unrequited transfers. The capital account includes direct investment, portfolio investment, other long and short-term capital and the change in official reserves. The current account resembles a private company's income statement in many respects but does not distinguish between costs accruing to operations and costs associated with capital investment. The capital account shows how the current account transactions were financed.

4. The exchange rate is determined by the supply and demand for a country's currency on the foreign exchange markets. A disequilibrium in supply and demand causes the exchange rate to vary. The monetary authorities can intervene in the foreign exchange markets to reduce or eliminate exchange rate variations. This activity will be reflected in the account "change in reserves". Thus, it is common practice to segregate the account "change in reserves" as a means of determining to what extent the monetary authorities intervened in the foreign exchange markets to offset a disequilibrium between supply and demand.

5. Intervention designed to offset currency depreciation can only last as long as reserves hold out. The limits to intervention designed to prevent currency appreciation are determined by the willingness of the monetary authorities to accumulate foreign assets.

6. To the extent that foreign resources are necessary for a country's economic activity, we say that balance of payments discipline imposes accounting discipline on the overall economy. This is another way of saying that an economy's saving can differ from its investment only insofar as non-residents are willing to lend the difference.

7. An economy's transactions with non-residents, reflected in the balance of payments, affect the economy's output, consumption and employment performance. The magnitude of balance of payments induced effects on the overall economy is likely to be many times larger than the magnitude of the transactions figuring in the balance of payments itself.

Questions

Solutions to the following questions are set out on the web site, details of which are included in the Preface.

1. Give an example of each of the major categories in the current account.

2. Give an example of each of the major categories in the capital account.

3. Why must the sum of the capital account and the current account be equal to zero? How are discrepancies accounted for?

4. Express the following operations on the Dutch balance of payments in T-accounts:

   a. An export billed for EUR 100,000 with credit terms of 90 days.

   b. An import billed for EUR 150,000 paid with a check drawn on a London bank.

   c. A Dutch company based in Rotterdam uses EUR 1 million that it was holding in a short-term deposit with its Rotterdam bank to purchase 10-year bonds issued by the German government.

   d. The Dutch central bank buys US dollars for EUR 500,000 from a London bank.

5. True or false: A credit entry in the balance of payments represents a demand for local currency whereas a debit entry represents a supply of local currency. Explain your answer.

6. Why does the central bank intervene in the foreign exchange markets? What happens if it does not intervene?

7. Explain the following statement: Accounting discipline is imposed on a national economy through the balance of payments.

8. What is the relationship between the current account balance and a country's saving and investment?

The exchange rate and economic adjustment

The external sector is the link between a national economy and the rest of the world. In Chapter 1 we saw that transactions between the national economy and the rest of the world are recorded in the balance of payments and reflect the supply and demand for the country's currency on the foreign exchange markets. Although transactions with the external sector ultimately end in a zero sum accounting equation, the various paths leading to this result have their own consequences on current and future economic performance. The consequences are not always desirable.

The problem is often presented in terms of conflict between domestic and external equilibrium. Domestic equilibrium refers to full employment and a certain standard of living. External equilibrium refers to the *ex ante* equality between the supply and demand of domestic currency on the foreign exchange markets. Because balance of payments discipline ensures that the *ex post* supply and demand of domestic currency will always be equal, any incompatibility between domestic and external equilibrium suggests that it will be domestic equilibrium that suffers. At the time of the gold standard or even fixed exchange rates, this meant a painful deflation where levels of output and consumption were reduced to the point where *ex ante* external equilibrium was restored. This can still be the case when the disequilibrium is minor or temporary. Since the advent of active nationalistic monetary policies, however, and especially since the last link between currencies and gold was cut by the United States in 1971, solutions to major fundamental external disequilibrium have usually revolved around a change in the exchange rate. On the surface, a change in the exchange rate seems to involve nothing more than a change in the price of one currency for another. In fact, the effects, with varying time lags, magnitudes and intensities, penetrate to the core of the economy and ultimately generate a new set of economic conditions with resulting consequences for the balance of payments, the supply and demand for foreign currency and the exchange rate. Understanding the forces and relationships involved is therefore indispensable for judicious international financial analysis.

In this chapter we examine the economic adjustment process caused by external disequilibrium. First, we look at the consequences of a devaluation on relative prices, incomes, and the composition of output and consumption. Next, we consider the consequences of external disequilibrium when a change in the exchange rate is avoided through offsetting transactions by the monetary authorities. Finally, we present the monetary approach to balance of payments analysis and develop the basic conditions for external equilibrium.

Exchange rate depreciation

Relative price effects: The elasticities approach

The elasticities approach to exchange rate depreciation (devaluation) considers the problem of devaluation and balance of payments adjustment in terms of the supply and demand of exports and imports. Exports are assumed to account for the only supply of foreign exchange and imports the only demand for foreign exchange. In other words, there are no capital flows between countries. The only way that foreign exchange can be obtained is by exporting and the only need for foreign exchange is to pay for imports. Figure 2.1 shows how this could look for the Danish economy if pounds sterling is the unit of account used to measure foreign exchange value. The x-axis represents the amount of foreign exchange and the y-axis represents the price of one unit of foreign currency in Danish kroner. At the spot exchange rate, S_0, the supply of foreign exchange is A. Because exports are assumed to account for the only supply of foreign exchange, A is calculated by multiplying the number of export units by the price per unit in foreign currency. At the same exchange rate, the demand for foreign currency is B, calculated by multiplying the number of import units by the price per unit in foreign currency. The current account balance is thus in disequilibrium by the amount $B - A$ and a devaluation is in order.

The goal of the devaluation is to bring the supply and demand for foreign exchange into equilibrium. In Figure 2.1 the supply of foreign exchange is equal to the demand at C when the exchange rate is at S_1. According to the elasticities approach, the key to the success of the devaluation depends on the **price elasticities** of demand for exports and imports. The price elasticities of demand can be defined as the percentage change in the quantity demanded divided by the percentage change in price. Suppose, for example, that when the price of imported cars rises by 1% the number of cars imported falls by 2%. The price elasticity of demand for imported cars is then:

$$-2\%/1\% = -2.$$

There is a minus sign before the price elasticity because for normal demand curves there is a negative relation between price and demand so that when price goes up the quantity demanded goes down and vice versa. A devaluation implies a fall in the price of exports in foreign currency and a rise in the price of imports in domestic currency. Thus, the higher the demand elasticities, the more exports should rise and the more imports should fall. The price elasticity of demand can be written algebraically as:

$$\text{Demand elasticity} = \frac{dQ/Q}{dP/P} \tag{2.1}$$

where Q is quantity and P is price.

Figure 2.1 The supply and demand for foreign currency

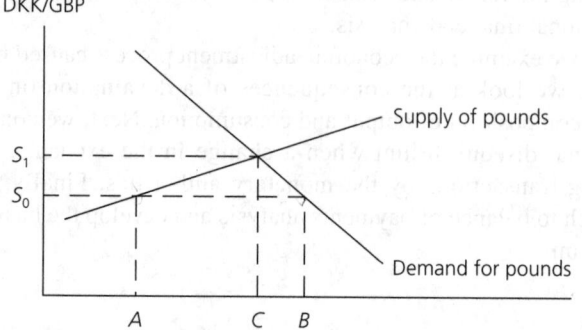

This brings up the issue of supply elasticities, which are similar to demand elasticities except that there is normally a positive relation between prices and the quantity supplied. In a devaluation the role of the supply elasticities is to determine the effects of the devaluation on the **terms of trade**. The terms of trade refer to the number of units of imports that one unit of exports will buy (or vice versa) and can be calculated by dividing the price of exports by the price of imports. If, for example, the price of one unit of exports in foreign currency is GBP 3 and the price of one unit of imports is GBP 1, the terms of trade are GBP 3/GBP 1 = 3. In other words, one unit of exports will buy three units of imports.

Suppose that supplies of exports can be increased without increasing costs in domestic currency and supplies of imports can be reduced without causing a fall in their foreign currency price. Then the price of exports in domestic currency will remain constant and their price in foreign currency will fall by the full amount of the devaluation while the foreign currency price of imports remains constant. In this case the terms of trade will deteriorate by the full amount of the devaluation. If, for example, the unit cost of exports is DKK 30 and the value of the krone goes from DKK 10 = GBP 1 to DDK 20 = GBP 1, the foreign currency value of an export unit goes from DKK 30/DKK 10 = GBP 3 to DKK 30/DKK 20 = GBP 1.5. With the foreign currency price of an import unit constant at GBP 1 the terms of trade fall from 3 to 1.5. Hence, the deterioration of the terms of trade due to a devaluation is maximum when supply elasticities are infinite – that is, when the exports and imports of the devaluing country are supplied at constant cost. It is minimum when the supply elasticities are zero – that is, when costs rise proportionately in the devaluing country or fall proportionately in the rest of the world.

Elasticity of supply of foreign exchange

The elasticity of the supply of foreign exchange depends on two things: the elasticity of foreign demand for domestic exports and the elasticity of the supply of domestic exports. If foreign demand is sensitive to price changes, a decline in export prices resulting from the devaluation will increase the quantities of goods that are exported. The actual decline in export prices depends on the supply elasticity of exports. Thus, the supply of foreign exchange will tend to increase because of the increase in export volume and decrease because of the fall in the foreign exchange price at which this volume can be sold.

Demand is considered elastic when the elasticity is greater than one and inelastic when the elasticity is less than one. In practice, whether or not exports are elastic depends on many things such as the type of product and the market share of the exporter, the affluence of the importer and trade restrictions. Consumer durables like automobiles sold in the United States, for example, are probably more demand elastic than rice exports to Bangladesh. In any case, trade restrictions, including tariffs, quotas, oligopolies and cartels, restrict competition and reduce the demand elasticities by reducing the role of prices in buying decisions.

It is also difficult to generalize about export supply elasticities, which also depend on many factors such as the type of product, its production function, stocks of intermediate and raw materials, and available qualified labor. It is probably safe to say that in the short run context of a devaluation, supply elasticities depend to a large extent on the domestic economy's position in the trade cycle. In a downturn increments in products available for export at little extra cost are more likely to be forthcoming than in the later stages of an expansion when inventories are low and factors of production are being used at close to full capacity.

Elasticity of demand for foreign exchange

The elasticity of the demand for foreign exchange depends on the elasticity of supply and demand for imports. Other things being equal, a devaluation raises the price of imports in domestic currency. In the preceding example, when the Danish krone falls from 10 to 20 per pound sterling, the domestic price of imports goes from GBP 1 × DKK 10/GBP 1 = DKK 10 to GBP 1 × DKK 20/GBP = DKK 20. If domestic demand is sensitive to price changes, an increase in domestic import prices resulting from the devaluation will decrease the quantities of goods that are imported. The actual rise in domestic import prices depends on the supply elasticity of imports. Thus, the demand for foreign exchange will tend to decrease because of the decrease in import volume. This decrease will be offset to the extent that supply elasticities are not infinite and the price of imports in foreign exchange tends to fall with the fall in demand.

Like export demand elasticities, import demand elasticities depend on the type of product and the affluence of the domestic market. Probably more important, however, is the supply of import substitutes produced by the domestic economy. When domestic products compete with imports, the higher prices of imported products should cause a switch from imports to domestic substitutes, thereby raising the import demand elasticity.

Where import supply elasticities are concerned, most countries are in the position of a "price-taker". In other words they are too small to have much effect on world prices. In this case supply elasticities, if not infinite, are likely to be very high. In the case of large, affluent countries like the United States that account for an important share of world trade in many products, the price-taking assumption is less likely to be valid.

The adjustment process: An example

Going back to Figure 2.1, we can see that external equilibrium is attained at C when the exchange rate moves from S_0 to S_1. Consider the following scenario for Denmark:

S_0 = DKK 10/GBP 1
S_1 = DKK 11/GBP 1
A = supply of foreign currency = GBP 500
B = demand for foreign currency = GBP 706
$P_{E,0}$ = the price of exports before the devaluation = DKK 10 = GBP 1
$P_{M,0}$ = the price of imports before the devaluation = DKK 20 = GBP 2

Elasticity of demand for exports = −3.53
Elasticity of demand for imports = −1.5
Elasticity of the supply of imports and exports = infinite
Current account deficit at $S_0 = A − B$ = GBP 500 − GBP 706 = −GBP 206.

Before the devaluation the exchange rate is DKK 10 for GBP 1 and there is a current account deficit of GBP 206. The domestic price of an export unit is DKK 10 and the foreign currency price of an import unit is GBP 2. At the exchange rate of DKK 10 for GBP 1 the foreign currency price of an export unit is GBP 1 and the domestic price of an import unit is DKK 20. Denmark's export products face stiff competition from other countries. Consequently, its price elasticity of demand for exports is very high at −3.53, which means that a 1% increase (decrease) in the foreign currency price causes a 3.53% decrease (increase) in the quantity demanded. Although lower than the price elasticity of demand for exports, competition on the domestic market between imports and import substitutes makes the price elasticity of demand for imports high also. It is −1.5, which means that a 1% increase (decrease) in the domestic price of imports causes a 1.5% decrease (increase) in the quantity demanded. Because Denmark is a small country accounting for only a marginal share of total world output of the products that it imports, changes in domestic demand for imports have little or no effect on world prices. Consequently, the price elasticity of supply of Danish imports is infinite. As far as exports are concerned, Denmark is in the initial stages of a recession. Inventories of exportable products are high, so in the short run at least, the price elasticity of the supply of exports is also infinite. Because of the current account deficit, which indicates a disequilibrium in the supply and demand of foreign currency, the krone is devalued from DKK 10 per pound to DKK 11 per pound.

Adjustment in the supply of foreign currency

From a disequilibrium of a GBP 206 deficit in the current account we can appreciate the adjustment in the supply of foreign currency by examining the devaluation induced changes in the prices and quantities of exports. Before the devaluation, the number of units of exports is equal to the supply of foreign exchange divided by the price per unit: GBP 500/GBP 1 = 500 units of exports.

We know that the export supply elasticity is infinite. This means that after the devaluation the krone price of exports will remain constant at DKK 10. Consequently, the foreign currency price of exports will fall by GBP 0.09 to GBP 0.91 (DKK 10, the domestic price, divided by DKK 11/GBP , the new exchange rate, equals GBP 0.91). Because the demand elasticity of exports is equal to –3.53, foreign demand will rise from 500 units of exports to 659 units. From Equation 2.1:

$$\text{Demand elasticity } \frac{dQ/Q}{dP/P} = -3.53 = \frac{dQ/500}{-0.09/1}$$

therefore, $dQ = 159$ units of exports.

The total number of units exported is equal to the price induced change, dQ, plus the initial quantity, Q:

$$dQ + Q = 159 + 500 = 659 \text{ total units of exports.}$$

At GBP 0.91 per unit, the supply of foreign currency will be equal to:

$$\text{GBP 0.91 price per unit} \times 659 \text{ units} = \text{GBP 600.}$$

Adjustment in the demand for foreign currency

Now let's examine what happens to imports. The number of units of imports before the devaluation is equal to the demand for foreign currency divided by the price per unit:

$$\text{GBP 706/GBP 2} = 353 \text{ units of imports.}$$

We know that the supply elasticity for imports is infinite. This means that the price of imports in foreign exchange remains constant at GBP 2. Consequently, after the devaluation the domestic price of imports will rise from DKK 20 to DKK 22 (GBP 2, the foreign currency price of imports, multiplied by DKK 11/GBP , the new exchange rate, equals DKK 22). Because the demand elasticity is equal to –1.50, the number of units of imports will fall from 353 to 300:

$$\text{Demand elasticity } = \frac{dQ/Q}{dP/P} = -1.50 = \frac{dQ/353}{2/20}$$

therefore, $dQ = -53$ units

The total number of units imported is equal to the price induced change, dQ, plus the initial quantity, Q:

$$dQ + Q = -53 + 353 = 300 \text{ total units of imports.}$$

Thus, the number of units imported falls from 353 units to 300 units. At GBP 2 per unit the total demand for foreign currency will be equal to:

$$\text{GBP 2 price per unit} \times 300 \text{ units} = \text{GBP 600.}$$

Hence, after the adjustment process induced by the devaluation the supply of foreign exchange is GBP 600, the demand for foreign exchange is GBP 600 and the balance of payments is in equilibrium. This corresponds to point C in Figure 2.1. The initial supply of foreign exchange was GBP 500 so the devaluation induced increase is GBP 100. The value of the krone fell by DKK 1 from DKK 10 per pound to DKK 11 per pound. Substituting this information into Equation 2.1, the elasticity of supply of foreign exchange is thus:

$$\text{Supply elasticity of foreign exchange} = \frac{\text{GBP 100/GBP 500}}{\text{DKK 1/DKK 10}} = 2$$

The demand for foreign exchange fell by GBP 106 from GBP 706 to GBP 600. Thus, the demand elasticity for foreign exchange is equal to:

$$\text{Demand elasticity for foreign exchange} = \frac{\text{GBP 106/GBP 706}}{\text{DKK 1/DKK 10}} = -1.5.$$

Another consequence of the devaluation is that Denmark's terms of trade have deteriorated. Before the devaluation the export price was GBP 1 and the import price was GBP 2. The terms of trade were thus:

$$\text{Terms of trade before the devaluation} = \text{GBP 1/GBP 2} = 0.5.$$

In other words, it took one unit of exports to buy a half unit of imports. After the devaluation, the terms of trade fall to 0.455:

$$\text{Terms of trade after the devaluation} = \text{GBP 0.91/GBP 2} = 0.455.$$

One unit of exports only buys 45.5% of a unit of imports. This, of course, is because we assumed infinite supply elasticities, which made the full impact of the devaluation fall on the terms of trade.

Elasticities and the balance of payments

In summary therefore, the elasticities approach underlines the price effects of exchange rate changes on the balance of payments. A devaluation makes imports more expensive in the domestic market and, depending on demand elasticity, this should cause imports to fall. The devaluation should also make exports cheaper on foreign markets and, again depending on demand elasticity, this should make exports rise. The extent to which the domestic price of imports rises and the foreign price of exports falls depends on the supply elasticities of the two types of products. The combined effects of the price elasticities will determine whether the devaluation will be successful in restoring external equilibrium.[1]

---

[1] The "Marshall-Lerner condition" is a more precise statement of the requirements for stable equilibrium in the foreign exchange market. Assuming infinite supply elasticities for imports and exports, it states that devaluation will always improve the trade balance if the *sum* of the demand elasticities for imports and exports is greater than one.

The empirical question of actually measuring these elasticities has never proceeded very far because of variations in the prices, quantities and types of products that are exported and imported.[2]

In spite of its empirical shortcomings, the elasticities approach is a theoretically sound short-term explanation of the reaction of the balance on current account to exchange rate changes. To the extent that these reactions do tend to occur, it has considerable analytical value. However, as we saw in the foregoing example, there is some confusion and inconsistency arising from the use of two units of account – national currency and foreign exchange – in the measurement of the relevant variables. Furthermore, it neglects devaluation induced effects on income and expenditure, and the absence of time lags and capital movements also limits its scope.

Income effects: The absorption approach

The shortcomings of the elasticities approach to devaluation analysis led to the development of what is called the absorption approach.[3] The absorption approach abandons the partial elasticities of the preceding section – that is, the effects of price variations on the quantities supplied and demanded when the other relevant variables remain unchanged – in favor of what it calls the "total elasticities", which are, the effects of price variations on the quantities supplied and demanded when the other relevant variables have been allowed to change. In other words, the absorption approach takes into consideration variations in income and consumption caused by the devaluation.

Income effects

There are three major devaluation induced effects on income or GDP. The first effect we have already considered. It concerns the terms of trade and depends on how much the supply elasticities cause the terms of trade to deteriorate. A deterioration in the terms of trade tends to reduce domestic income. The second effect depends on the demand elasticities and on whether or not the economy is working at full capacity. If the economy has excess capacity, the increased demand for exports and import substitutes should increase output and employment in industries producing these products. If the economy is working near full capacity, however, supply elasticities are likely to be low and the increased demand will translate into price increases. The third effect concerns resource allocation. Income should increase if the relative price changes induced by the devaluation improve resource allocation by transferring factors of production to sectors where they are more productive. For long-term external equilibrium, this is a key consideration.

Absorption effects

Absorption refers to the economy's total consumption of resources. It is equal to private and government consumption plus total gross investment ($C + \Delta stk + I$). The first and most important effect on absorption is the result of an income redistribution that takes place within the domestic economy. Producers of importables and exportables should experience an increase in income due to the elasticity effects discussed above. On the

---

[2] The IMF estimates demand elasticities for its world trade model. See Michael C. Deppler and Duncan Ripley, "The world trade model: Merchandise trade flows", *Staff Papers* (March 1978), p.p. 147–206.

[3] See S.S. Alexander, "Effects of a devaluation on a trade balance", *Staff Papers*, Vol. II, No. 2 (IMF, April 1952), p.p. 263–278.

other hand, consumers of importables and exportables should experience a reduction in real income due to the higher prices of these products. Importables and exportables refer to products actually imported and exported as well as their close substitutes produced domestically.

A second effect on absorption is caused by the desire of investors to maintain their real cash balances. The rise in prices following devaluation causes real cash balances to decline, and this causes investors to sell stocks and bonds in an effort to maintain those balances. A fall in bond prices means a rise in the rate of interest, which causes a reduction in investment and consumption. Finally, there may be other diverse effects deriving from devaluation such as anticipated price rises inciting immediate consumption or a high import content in investment goods causing a reduction in investment because of the higher cost of imports.

Combined effects of income and absorption

In this context the devaluation will improve the external balance on current account if the increase in income caused by the devaluation is greater than the devaluation induced increase in absorption. This can be written algebraically in terms of the national accounting equation. Remember from Equation 1.1 in Chapter 1 that GDP = $X - M + C + \Delta stk + I$, where GDP represents the nation's total output or income and $C + \Delta stk + I$ represents the nation's total absorption. From this we can see that a devaluation will improve $X - M$ when

$$\frac{dGDP}{dS_0} > \frac{d(C + \Delta stk + I)}{dS_0} \qquad (2.2)$$

The new exchange rate is the key to success.

The new exchange rate determines the volume of exports and the division of absorption between imports and domestic importables. In this way the exchange rate fixes the relative price of exports on foreign markets and the relative price of imports on domestic markets. Income and absorption, then, are two distinct functions of the exchange rate, with the long-term success of the devaluation depending on the ability of these functions to maintain income greater than, or at least equal to, the level of absorption. Let's examine some of the characteristics of these functions.

Relative price effects on income and absorption

The initial effects of a devaluation should increase the domestic price of importables and exportables relative to **non-tradables**. Non-tradables refer to goods and services produced and consumed domestically that are not close substitutes of exportables and importables. The actual amount of the price increases depends partly on supply elasticities and partly on demand elasticities. For exportables, a lower supply elasticity and a higher foreign demand elasticity will cause a larger increase in the domestic price. This is because the lower the supply elasticity, the greater the reduction in the supply of exportables to the domestic market as exports increase in response to the increased foreign demand. A lower supply in the face of an unchanged demand will cause prices to rise. For importables the domestic price increase will be greater the higher the supply and the lower the demand elasticities. Higher prices and increased demand for exportables should stimulate output. Higher prices and the substitution of domestic importables for imports should stimulate output in this sector as well. Therefore, there should be a switch in absorption from foreign to domestic importables and the increase in exports should increase domestic income. The ultimate increase will depend on the foreign trade income multiplier.[4]

Non-tradable goods

Because by definition, the demand for non-tradables is strictly domestic, its price is not directly affected by a devaluation. However, its cost is determined by the international markets directly, if imported intermediate products, investment goods and raw materials are direct inputs, and indirectly, if importable and exportable goods are consumed by the labor force. Higher prices for importables and exportables make direct inputs more expensive. They also reduce labor's real income and lead to demands for higher wages that raise costs.

The income redistribution resulting from the devaluation affects the demand for non-tradables. The winners in the redistribution are the producers of importables and exportables. If they are consumers of non-tradables, some of their incremental income will be spent on non-tradables, which will raise the demand for non-tradables. The losers in the redistribution are the consumers of importables and exportables. If they are also consumers of non-tradables, their loss of real income should reduce the demand for non-tradables. The net effect determines whether overall demand for non-tradables will increase or decrease. In fact, an overall decrease is the usual outcome. Thus, it is the reaction of the non-tradable sector during the period between devaluation and the response of the balance on current account that explains the apparent paradox of the devaluation causing a recession.[5]

Figure 2.2 illustrates the reaction of the non-tradable sector to a devaluation when consumers of non-tradables are net losers in the income redistribution. Before the devaluation, supply and demand schedules are represented by S_1 and D_1 and consumption of non-tradables is at A. The percent of importable and exportable goods in the total production cost of the non-tradable sector determines the rise in its price as a result of the devaluation. The supply curve shifts from S_1 to S_2. The fall in real income causes the demand curve to shift from D_1 to D_2. Consumption of non-tradables falls from A to B.

---

[4] The foreign trade income multiplier is equal to $1/(dS/dGNP + dM/dGNP)$ where $dS/dGNP$ is the marginal propensity to save and $dM/dGNP$ is the marginal propensity to import. This can be shown as follows. From Equation 1.5 saving is equal to the current account balance plus gross investment:

$$S = B_c + I_g$$

Let financial services be included in exports and imports so that $B_c = X - M$. Then:

$$X + I_g = S + M$$

A change in exports is a change in income equal to dX that will induce a change in savings and imports. Assume that I_g is unaffected. Then

$$dX = dS + dM$$

and dividing both sides into $dGNP$ gives

$$dGNP/dX = 1/(dS/dGNP + dM/dGNP).$$

[5] See I.F. Pearce, "The problem of the balance of payments", *International Economic Review*, Vol. II, No. 1 (January 1961), p.p. 1–28; and A.S. Gerakis, "Recession in the initial phase of a stabilization program: The experience of Finland", *Staff Papers*, Vol. XI, No. 1 (IMF, November 1964), p.p. 434–445.

Figure 2.2 Reaction of the non-tradable sector to a devaluation

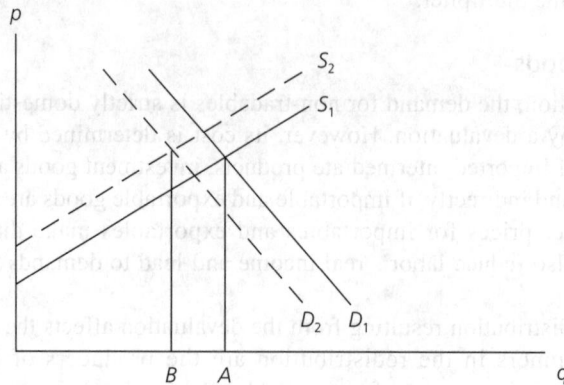

The wealth effect

For countries exporting raw materials, income can be influenced by the wealth effect. When the supply of exports is inelastic in the long term (limited by land, mineral deposits, etc.) or in the short term (limited by mines, wells, herds, etc.), a devaluation increases the wealth of the owners of these resources even if output does not increase. Resource allocation can be disturbed if the owners of the inputs count on the effects of relative price movements to increase their wealth rather than increasing it through investments that will raise output. This phenomenon occurred at the international level when oil producing countries limited their output but increased their wealth through higher prices that increased income and the value of their reserves underground.

The wealth effect can have serious consequences if the exportable products are also wage goods such as in Argentina where beef and wheat, besides being major export products, are also consumed in large quantities by the general population. The devaluation induced income redistribution depresses real income and standards of living while the wealth effect tends to perpetuate or prolong the situation.

Strategic imports

"Strategic imports" refer to intermediate goods necessary to maintain current levels of output, or investment goods necessary to maintain future output. If imports of intermediate goods for current output are reduced, current income will fall by several times the value of the reduction in imports, as we saw in Chapter 1. A reduction in imports of investment goods will reduce the economy's potential productive capacity and future output will be limited.

Time lags and the composition of exports

Although world supply elasticities may be considered as infinite or very high for a price-taking country, the supply elasticities of the country itself cannot usually be considered in the same way. Most products require a time lag before they can respond to demand signals. A prime example is agricultural products. The season has to be right and the plants take time to grow. Even industrial output requires an interval between the moment that increased demand manifests itself and production can be increased and distributed to meet this demand. Thus, in the short term exports can only increase at the expense of domestic consumption of exportable goods. This will be the case if the domestic prices of exportable goods rise faster than the incomes of those that consume them, thereby exacerbating the income transfer from consumers to producers of exportables.

Structural change

We have seen that the exchange rate plays an important part in how resources are allocated. It determines the economy's external terms of trade – that is, the relative prices of exports to imports. It also determines the economy's internal terms of trade, or the relative prices of tradable goods to non-tradable goods. These relative prices then determine the economy's structure of production and the composition of output and consumption. Thus, a variation in the exchange rate implies a change in the economy's structure of production as the modified relative price structure induces a reallocation of the economy's resources. Resource reallocations can take many forms. A temporary, more or less intensive use of labor and capital in the same basic processes, such as production cutbacks or overtime, are the forms likely to manifest themselves in the early phases of the devaluation. The later stages are likely to see resource shifts between sectors and the apparition of entirely new processes and technologies as well as the elimination of the production of certain products and the creation of processes for products not formerly produced. The reorganization process will have long and short-term consequences on levels of output and growth. In the case of idle resources and excess capacity, the beneficial effects should be felt relatively quickly. However, as is more likely to be the case, when it is necessary to make investments in order to create the required resources and incremental capacity, the beneficial effects will be longer in coming while the negative effects will be felt immediately. Furthermore, capital losses will appear in industries losing out in the devaluation. Many operations will become unprofitable and have to shut down.

Thus, there will be powerful forces working against the structural change. Losers in the income redistribution will fight to restore their standard of living while industries benefiting from tariffs, subsidies and controls will strive to maintain their privileges. If the income redistribution is allowed to progress and privileges are effectively eliminated, many producers will be forced out of business. The resulting layoffs and reduced output will create political and social pressures that cannot be resisted indefinitely. The time element, then, is crucial to the outcome. How long it takes for the beneficial effects of the resource reallocation to begin to offset the negative effects often determines whether the devaluation will be successful in establishing the conditions for the long-term equilibrium of the external sector.

The J-curve

How the balance on current account eventually reacts to the elasticities, income and absorption forces of the preceding sections depends on the time it takes for each one to make itself felt. Price elasticities may be smaller in the short run than in the long run. Income and absorption effects may take several years to work themselves through the economy. Structural adjustment may take much longer. Consequently, the time path of the current account balance can take different forms. One of the forms frequently observed is an initial worsening of the current account balance followed by a gradual improvement.[6] Figure 2.3 shows that a time path like this looks like a "J". Hence, it has become known as the "J-curve effect".

The J-curve effect is usually explained as the result of flexible prices and sticky quantities.[7] In other words, the external terms of trade deteriorate faster than quantities of exports and imports can adjust to them. It is not entirely clear exactly why this should be the case.

---

[6] Considerable attention was paid to this phenomenon when the massive depreciation of the US dollar between 1985 and 1988 was accompanied by a worsening of the US trade deficit.

[7] See Richard Baldwin and Paul Krugman, "The persistence of the US trade deficit", *Brookings Papers on Economic Activity*, No.1 (1987), p.p. 1–43; and Rudiger Dornbusch and Paul Krugman, "Flexible exchange rates in the short-term", *Brookings Papers on Economic Activity*, No. 3 (1976), p.p. 537–575.

Figure 2.3 The J-curve

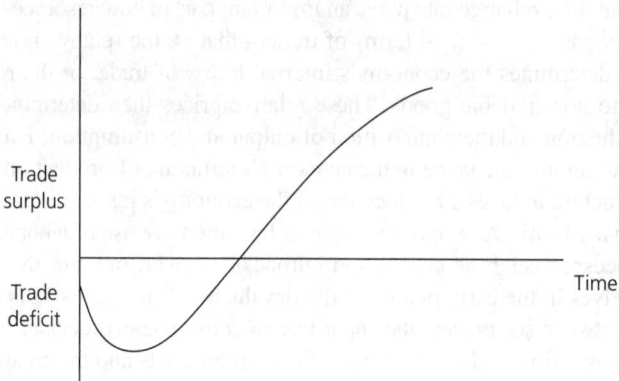

However, an interesting explanation of the phenomenon holds that immediately following a devaluation, the anticipation of higher prices for tradables causes a strong inter-temporal substitution effect between tradables and non-tradables. Anticipating price rises in tradables as a result of the devaluation, economic agents rush to make purchases before they occur, thereby causing a temporary reduction in exports and an increase in imports.[8]

There are many combinations of short and long-term supply and demand elasticities that can produce the J-curve effect. The important point to remember is that the J-curve effect depends on different time lags in the adjustment process set off by the devaluation. When it appears, it tends to increase the disequilibrium between the supply and demand for foreign currency.

Income and absorption adjustment: An example

The foregoing discussion might seem somewhat complicated, but a simple example will illustrate the most important arguments and help to put everything that has been said so far into perspective.

Consider a small price-taking country called Austrama, producing wheat, automobiles and construction. It exports wheat, imports automobiles and construction is the non-traded good. The peso (PES) is the national currency and its foreign exchange value is PES 1 equals USD 1. Because Austrama is a price-taking country, foreign demand elasticities for Austrama's exports and the supply elasticities of its imports are very high. On the other hand, as an agricultural product, Austrama's supply of exportables is completely inelastic in the short run. Hence, the only way that exports can be increased is by reducing domestic consumption of exportables. Before the devaluation, the situation is as follows.

Wheat industry: The wheat industry exports 80 units of wheat. The domestic price of wheat is PES 10 per unit and the international price is USD 10 per unit. The domestic demand for wheat is determined by the function:

$$Q_w = -2P_w + 100$$

[8] See Stefan Gelach, "Inter-temporal speculation, devaluation and the J-curve", *Journal of International Economics*, 27 (1989), p.p. 335–345.

where Q is the number of units consumed and P is the price per unit. Thus, domestic consumption of wheat is equal to:

$$Q_w = -(2 \times 10) + 100 = 80 \text{ units}$$

and the economy's total output of wheat is 80 units exported plus 80 units consumed domestically for a total of 160 units.

The domestic demand elasticity for exportables can be found from the demand function. First take the derivative with respect to price:

$$\frac{dQ_w}{dP_w} = -2.$$

Next, take the ratio of P_w to Q_w:

$$\frac{P_w}{Q_w} = \frac{10}{80}.$$

Then:

$$\text{Domestic demand elasticity for exportables} = \frac{dQ_w}{dP_w} \times \frac{P_w}{Q_w} = -2 \times \frac{1}{8} = -0.25.$$

Automobile industry: The foreign currency price of automobiles is USD 10, which means that the domestic price is PES 10. The economy produces 40 units of automobiles and the domestic demand for automobiles is determined by the function:

$$Q_a = -3P_a + 200.$$

Thus the total domestic demand for automobiles is:

$$Q_a = -(3 \times 10) + 200 = 170 \text{ units of automobiles.}$$

The economy's imports of automobiles is the 170 units of total domestic consumption less the 40 units that are produced domestically for a total of 130 units.

The domestic demand elasticity for importables can be calculated from the demand function:

$$\text{Domestic demand elasticity for importables} = \frac{dQ_a}{dP_a} \times \frac{P_a}{Q_a} = -3 \times \frac{10}{170} = -0.1763.$$

Construction industry: The price of one unit of construction is PES 10 and since this good is non-traded it has no international price. However, importables and exportables account for 50% of its production cost. The demand for construction depends on consumers' real income as well as on the price. Consumers' real income is a positive function of the quantities of exportables and importables that are effectively consumed by the economy. In other words, the higher the consumption of importables and exportables, the higher the consumers' real income. For Austrama the domestic demand for construction is determined by the equation:

$$Q_c = -1P_c + (Q_w + Q_a)$$

$$Q_c = -1P_c + (80 + 170) = 240 \text{ units.}$$

Table 2.1 Volume of output by sector before the devaluation

	Wheat	*Automobiles*	*Construction*	*Total*
Exports	80	0	0	80
Imports	0	130	0	130
Consumption	80	170	240	490
Output	160	40	240	440

Table 2.1 summarizes the economic situation before the devaluation. Austrama's income can be calculated by multiplying the price times the number of units produced in each sector and summing across sectors:

$$GDP = (160 \times PES\ 10) + (40 \times PES\ 10) + (240 \times PES\ 10) = PES\ 4400.$$

Absorption can be calculated by multiplying the price times the number of units produced in each sector and summing across sectors:

$$Absorption = (80 \times PES\ 10) + (170 \times PES\ 10) + (240 \times PES\ 10) = PES\ 4900.$$

The current account balance is equal to income minus absorption:

$$GNP - Absorption = PES\ 4400 - PES\ 4900 = -PES\ 500$$

or, what we have seen is the same thing, exports minus imports:

$$(80 \times PES\ 10) - (130 \times PES\ 10) = -PES\ 500.$$

The current account balance can also be calculated in US dollars:

$$(80 \times USD\ 10) - (130 \times USD\ 10) = -USD\ 500.$$

Austrama's current account balance is in deficit by PES 500 = USD 500. From this situation we are going to examine the effects of a devaluation on Austrama's economy in two phases. The initial phase looks at the effects on income and absorption before output can be increased to respond to the new price structure. The secondary phase looks at the effects on income and absorption after the economy has modified its production structure and changed its output in response to the new price structure.

Devaluation: The initial phase

Suppose that the current account deficit causes a depreciation in the value of the peso from PES 1 = USD 1 to PES 2 = USD 1. The high supply elasticities for Austrama's imports means that the domestic price of imports reflects the full effect of the devaluation and doubles to PES 20 for one unit of imports. The price of domestically produced automobiles follows the price of imports as domestic demand shifts from imports to domestic importables and producers have only to be marginally cheaper to maintain pre-devaluation sales levels. This means that Q_M, the quantity of imports, will continue to be equal to total demand for automobiles less domestic production.

$$Q_M = Q_A - 40 = -3P_a + 200 - 40.$$

Differentiating Q_M with respect to P_a gives:

$$\frac{dQ_M}{dP_a} = -3$$

and the demand elasticity for imports is equal to:

$$\frac{dQ_M}{dP_a} \times \frac{P_a}{Q_M} = -3 \times \frac{10}{130} = -0.231.$$

The low supply elasticities and the high demand elasticities for Austrama's exports means that the US dollar price of wheat changes little or not at all and the peso unit value of exports doubles from PES 10 to PES 20. The domestic price of wheat also rises as producers shift sales from the domestic market to the export market. The shift of sales from the domestic market to foreign markets is possible because of the high foreign demand elasticities for Austrama's wheat.

The price of construction is not directly affected by the devaluation and stays unchanged at PES 10 per unit.

The outcome of all this leaves the following domestic price structure:

P_w = PES 20
P_a = PES 20
P_c = PES 10

Domestic consumption becomes:

$Q_w = -(2 \times 20) + 100 = 60$ units
$Q_a = -(3 \times 20) + 200 = 140$ units
$Q_c = -(1 \times 10) + (60 + 140) = 190$ units.

The change in the domestic demand for wheat, automobiles and imports can be calculated directly by subtracting the original position from the new position. They can also be calculated from the formula for the elasticity of demand. By rearranging Equation 2.1:

$$dQ = \text{demand elasticity} \times Q \times \frac{dP}{P}.$$

The domestic demand elasticities calculated above were:

Domestic demand elasticity for wheat = –0.25
Domestic demand elasticity for automobiles = –0.1763
Domestic demand elasticity for imports = –0.231

and thus:

$dQ_w = -0.25 \times 80 \times 10/10 = -20$
$dQ_a = -0.1763 \times 170 \times 10/10 = -30$
$dQ_M = -0.231 \times 130 \times 10/10 = -30.$

By the same token, the change in demand for construction can be calculated by subtracting the original demand level from the new demand level:

$$dQ_c = 190 - 240 = -50$$

or by taking the total differential of Q_c:

$$dQ_c = dP_c + dQ_w + dQ_a$$

$$= 0 - 20 - 30 = -50.$$

Table 2.2 summarizes the economic situation at the end of the initial phase. GDP, absorption, and the current account balance in pesos are thus:

GDP = (160 × PES 20) + (40 × PES 20) + (190 × PES 10) = PES 5900
Absorption = (60 × PES 20) + (140 × PES 20) + (190 × PES 10) = PES 5900
Current account balance = PES 2000 – PES 2000 = 0.

Income equals absorption and exports equal imports. Supply and demand for foreign exchange are equal and the external sector is in equilibrium. It is interesting to note that although peso GDP rose by over 34% from PES 4400 to PES 5900, the volume of output fell by over 11% from 440 units to 390 units due to the fall in demand for construction. This is the recessionary effect described above when the losers in the devaluation are the consumers of non-tradables. The increase in peso GDP is entirely due to price rises.

The fall in absorption is even more impressive. Although nominal absorption increased from PES 4900 to PES 5900, real absorption fell by over 20% from 490 units before the devaluation to 390 units afterwards. This implies a drastic fall in living standards and represents a source of resistance to the adjustment forces unleashed by the devaluation.

Devaluation: The secondary phase

The secondary phase comes about as producers and consumers respond to the new price structure. In response to higher prices and profits, producers of exportables and importables are likely to make investments in order to expand their output. This will tend to increase GDP. The ultimate effect on GDP depends on the economy's investment income multiplier.[9] Consumption functions will also change as labor transfers from the non-tradable sector to the sectors producing importables and exportables and seeks to regain lost purchasing power by bidding up wages. The construction sector will benefit from the renewed economic activity. Its price will also have to change because exportables and importables account for 50% of its production costs. Suppose, then, that output of

Table 2.2 Volume of output by sector at the end of the initial phase

	Wheat	Automobiles	Construction	Total
Exports	100	0	0	100
Imports	0	100	0	100
Consumption	60	140	190	390
Output	160	40	190	390

[9] The investment income multiplier is the same as the foreign trade income multiplier but is generated by an autonomous increase in investment instead of exports.

exportables increases by 20 units and demand rises in all three sectors. The new domestic price-demand situation will look something like this:

$$Q_w = -2P_w + 110$$
$$Q_a = -3P_a + 230$$
$$Q_c = -1P_c + (Q_w + Q_a)$$

$$P_w = \text{PES } 20$$
$$P_a = \text{PES } 20$$
$$P_c = \text{PES } 15$$

The prices of wheat and cars are unchanged because they are determined by the foreign currency price of imports and the exchange rate. The price of construction rises by 50% to reflect its increased production costs (tradables account for 50% of production costs). In these conditions, Table 2.3 summarizes the economy's performance.

GDP, absorption and the current account balance in pesos and dollars are thus:

GDP = (180 × PES 20) + (70 × PES 20) + (225 × PES 15) = PES 8375
Absorption = (70 × PES 20) + (170 × PES 20) + (225 × PES 15) = PES 8175
Current account balance = PES 8375 – PES 8175 = PES 200
Current account balance in foreign exchange = (110 × USD 10) – (100 × USD 10) = USD 100.

The current account balance is now in surplus by PES 200 or USD 100 at the prevailing exchange rate and the supply of foreign currency is larger than demand. Nominal GDP has grown by over 90% from the pre-devaluation situation. However, most of this growth is due to price changes. Output volume has only grown by about 8%, from 440 units to 475 units, and absorption volume has fallen by over 5% from 490 units to 465 units.

It is important to note that not only the volume of output has changed, but also the composition of output. In Table 2.4 we can see that the relative importance of non-tradables

Table 2.3 Volume of output by sector at the end of the secondary phase

	Wheat	Automobiles	Construction	Total
Exports	110	0	0	110
Imports	0	100	0	100
Consumption	70	170	225	465
Output	180	70	225	475

Table 2.4 Percent of output by sector

	Pre (%)	Initial (%)	Final (%)
Wheat	36	41	38
Automobiles	9	10	15
Construction	55	49	47

fell from 55% of output before the devaluation to only 47% after the adjustment process. This implies a massive transfer of resources from the construction sector to the sectors producing wheat and automobiles.

The balance of payments, exchange rate, and money supply

Intervention in the exchange markets

Many governments would like to avoid the adjustment process outlined above and the economic, social and political consequences it implies. As we pointed out in Chapter 1, this can be done by using foreign reserves to make up the difference between the supply and demand of domestic currency on the foreign exchange markets. By intervening, the monetary authorities keep the exchange rate from changing and avoid the consequences of the adjustment process. Intervention, however, is not without its economic and financial consequences. To understand how they arise we have to look at the organization of a national monetary system and the creation of a country's money stock.

Money creation and destruction

Table 2.5 represents a national monetary system composed of the central bank (monetary authorities) and the deposit money banks. Each account within the system is numbered. Account 1, foreign assets, represents the country's official reserves. A change in this account indicates a change in the country's international reserves and will be reflected in the account "change in reserves" in the balance of payments format of Chapter 1. Account 2 represents the claims of the central bank on the central government, the deposit money banks and any industrial loans it has outstanding. When the central bank increases Accounts 1 and 2 by buying foreign currency or other types of securities such as government bonds or Treasury bills, it pays for them with a claim or check drawn on itself. In other words, it creates a liability. If the new liability it has created is owed to a domestic resident, Account 3, the **money base** or (M_o), will increase. The money base is composed of currency and coins outside the banking system plus liabilities to the deposit money banks. If the new liability is owed to a non-resident, Account 4, foreign liabilities, will increase.

Account 3, the money base, is the key to the money supply. Suppose that the central bank buys Treasury bills in the money market. Account 2, claims on the economy, will

Table 2.5 A national monetary system

Central bank (monetary authorities)

1. Foreign assets	3. Money base
2. Claims on the economy	4. Foreign liabilities

Deposit money banks

5. Reserves	8. Demand deposits
6. Foreign assets	9. Time deposits
7. Claims on the economy	10. Foreign liabilities

increase by the value of the bills. To pay for the bills, the central bank issues a check to the seller and Account 3 increases by that amount. The seller then deposits the check with its commercial bank (deposit money bank). The commercial bank credits the seller's account and owns a claim on the central bank. When the commercial bank credits the seller's account, Account 8, demand deposits, increases and the claim on the central bank increases Account 5, reserves.

The first measure of the money supply, M_1, is equal to demand deposits plus the currency and coins outside the banking system. Thus, the increase in Account 8 is an immediate increase in the money supply. The process does not stop here, however. The increase in Account 5, reserves, represents a claim by the commercial bank on the central bank (the corresponding liability by the central bank is found in Account 3). Because the commercial bank is required to hold reserves equal to only a fraction of its demand deposits, the increase in reserves enables the banking system as a whole to increase its demand deposits by a multiple of the increase in reserves. The multiple is equal to the reciprocal of the required reserve ratio (1/reserve ratio). Demand deposits and, therefore, the money supply, are increased by making loans.

Suppose, for example, that the reserve ratio is 10%. The demand deposit multiplier is equal to 1/0.1 = 10. An increase of USD 1000 in the commercial bank's reserves means that the banking system can increase its demand deposits by USD 10,000. It increases its demand deposits by making loans, and when it makes a loan, Account 7, claims on the economy, increases. When it credits its client's account with the product of the loan, Account 8, demand deposits, increases. A USD 10,000 loan could conceivably increase the banking system's claims on the economy and demand deposits by USD 10,000. In practice, this will not be the case because reserves leak out of the banking system in the form of bills and coins. The ultimate money and credit expansion due to the process of successive deposits and loans depends on the reserve ratio and the way the public divides its money holdings between bank deposits and cash. Let rr be the reserve ratio and c be the amount of cash per unit of bank deposits held by the public. Then for each unit of bank deposits the money supply will be equal to $1 + c$ and the percent of the total money supply held as cash will be equal to $[c/(1 + c)]$. An increase of USD 1 in the money base will lead to $[c/(1 + c)]$ being withdrawn as cash and $[1/(1 + c)]$ being deposited with the bank. Of the amount deposited in the bank $[rr/(1 + c)]$ will be held by the bank as reserves and $[(1 - rr)/(1 + c)]$ will be relent and $[1/(1 + c)] \times [(1 - rr)/(1 + c)] = [(1 - rr)/(1 + c)^2]$ will be deposited in the banking system. Of this amount $[(1 - rr)^2/(1 + c)^2]$ will be re-lent. This process generates a geometric series that will continue until there is nothing left to lend. The sum of this series indicates how much the money supply will increase for each dollar increase in the money base and is called the money supply multiplier:

$$\text{Sum} = 1 + \frac{1 - rr}{1 + c} + \frac{(1 - rr)^2}{(1 + c)^2} + \frac{(1 - rr)^3}{(1 + c)^3} + \dots$$

$$\text{Sum} = \frac{1 + c}{rr + c} \tag{2.3}$$

Going back to the earlier example, suppose that c = USD 0.25. Then the client that made the deposit wants to hold 20% of his money in cash, and thus he withdraws USD 200. The bank's deposits fall to USD 800 and, because cash constitutes part of the bank's reserves, reserves also fall to USD 800. The bank only needs to hold reserves equal to 10% of its deposits. Therefore, it holds USD 80 in reserves and lends USD 720, which is spent and deposited in another bank. If this client also wants to hold 20% of his money in cash, he will withdraw USD 144 and leave USD 576 in his account. The bank will be left with USD 576 in reserves but only needs to hold USD 57.6, so it lends the difference, USD 518.4, which is spent, deposited etc., until no reserves remain to be loaned. According to Equation 2.3, the money supply multiplier is equal to:

$$\text{Money supply multiplier} = \frac{1.25}{(0.1 + 0.25)} = 3.57.$$

Thus, the increase in the money supply resulting from a USD 1000 increase in the money base will be:

$$\text{Increase in the money supply} = \text{USD } 1000 \times 3.57 = \text{USD } 3570.$$

The important point to remember is that an increase in the money base leads to an increase in the money supply many times larger than the increase in the money base. On the other hand, a decrease in the money base leads to a decrease in the money supply many times larger than the decrease in the money base.

Money destruction

Suppose that the central bank sells Treasury bills on the open market. Claims on the economy, Account 2, decrease. The buyer of the bills pays by writing a check drawn on its commercial bank. The commercial bank debits the buyer's account (demand deposits decrease) and the central bank debits the commercial bank's account (Account 3). The money base and Account 5, reserves, decrease. Other things being equal, the lower level of reserves means that loans and demand deposits must be reduced by the corresponding money supply multiplier.

Table 2.6 summarizes the monetary situation resulting from central and commercial bank balance sheets presented in Table 2.5. Net foreign assets are equal to Account 1 plus Account 2 minus Account 4 minus Account 10. Foreign assets are considered net because we are measuring the domestic monetary situation. A foreign asset offset by a foreign liability has no effect on the domestic monetary aggregates. Domestic credit is equal to Account 2 plus Account 7. Money, M_1, is equal to Account 8 plus the portion of Account 3 in the form of currency and coins outside the banking system. The rest of Account 3 and its counterpart in Account 5 cancel each other out in the monetary survey. Their role, as we have seen, is to act as the generator for money creation. Quasi-money is equal to Account 9 and the second measure of money, M_2, is equal to M_1 plus quasi-money.

Economic effects of intervention in the exchange markets

By now it should be clear that intervention in the exchange markets affects an economy's domestic money supply. When foreign reserves are bought, Account 1 increases and the money supply increases by a multiple of the domestic currency value of the reserves. When foreign reserves are sold, Account 1 decreases and the money supply decreases by a multiple of the domestic currency value of the reserves. Hence, the economic effects of intervention are introduced through the monetary system and depend on how the quantity of money and changes in the quantity of money affect economic performance.

Table 2.6 Monetary survey

Net foreign assets	Money
Domestic credit	Quasi-money

Consider intervention aimed at preventing currency appreciation. Foreign reserves increase (*BP* is positive) and the money base increases. Other things being equal, an increase in the money base should increase credit to the economy and the money supply. According to the quantity theory of money, an increase in the money supply will cause prices to rise. The higher prices worsen the trade balance by attracting imports and diverting exportables from foreign markets to the domestic market.

At the same time, the increase in credit to the economy increases spending on investment and, through the investment income multiplier, causes an increase in overall income and expenditure. The ultimate magnitude of the increase depends on the investment income multiplier. Some of the incremental expenditure will be on imports and exportables, further worsening the trade balance. Furthermore, if the incremental money supply exceeds the demand for cash balances necessary to assure the increased economic activity, the excess will be used to purchase financial assets both domestic and foreign. An increase in the purchase of foreign assets worsens the capital account. Increased demand for domestic assets raises their price and lowers the domestic interest rate. A lower domestic interest rate stimulates investment, expenditure and the demand for imports and exportables. It also makes domestic assets less attractive relative to foreign assets and tends to further worsen the capital account. The ultimate outcome of all this depends on the economy's production possibility curve, its demand function for money, the marginal propensity to save and the marginal propensity to import. If, for example, the economy is operating at full capacity in all sectors, the increase in expenditure will fall disproportionately on imports and foreign assets. Any increase in expenditure on non-tradables will translate into price increases. If only one or two sectors are operating at full capacity, increased expenditure on their output will also raise their prices. In any case the effects of intervention will tend to bring the supply and demand for foreign currency into equilibrium and the adjustment process will affect income distribution, the level and composition of output, resource allocation and the price level.

Let's consider intervention aimed at preventing a depreciation of the currency. Foreign reserves decrease (*BP* is negative) and the money base decreases. Other things being equal, a decrease in the money base should lead to a reduction in credit to the economy and a corresponding decrease in the money supply. According to the quantity theory of money, a decrease in the money supply reduces demand and causes prices to fall. Lower demand and prices reduce imports and divert exportables from the domestic market to foreign markets.

The reduction in credit to the economy reduces investment and causes a reduction in overall income and expenditure. The ultimate magnitude of the reduction depends on the investment income multiplier. Because some of the reduction in expenditure will fall on imports and exportables, the trade balance should improve. Furthermore, if the reduction in the money supply exceeds the reduction in demand for cash balances due to the reduced level of transactions, domestic residents will rebuild them by selling financial assets both domestic and foreign. A decrease in the purchase of foreign assets improves the capital account. Reduced demand for domestic assets lowers their price and raises the domestic interest rate. A higher domestic interest rate discourages investment, expenditure and the demand for imports and exportables. It also makes domestic assets more attractive relative to foreign assets and tends to improve the capital account. The overall price level as well as relative prices will be affected. As before, the ultimate outcome of all this depends on the economy's production possibility curve, its demand function for money, the marginal propensity to save and the marginal propensity to import. In any case the effects of intervention will tend to bring the supply and demand for foreign currency into equilibrium and the adjustment process will affect income distribution, the level and composition of output, resource allocation and the price level.

Offsetting the monetary effects of intervention

It turns out that the adjustment process set off by changes in the money supply is just as traumatic as the adjustment process set off by the devaluation. Unfortunately, it is easy for governments to offset the effects of intervention and thereby postpone the adjustment process. For example, the sale of foreign currency by the monetary authorities (decrease in Accounts 1 and 3) can be offset by the purchase of domestic securities (increase in Accounts 2 and 3). On the other hand, the purchase of foreign currency can be offset by the sale of domestic securities. When the external disequilibrium is seasonal or temporary, no harm is done and some may even be avoided.

Seasonal disequilibrium occurs when the production and consumption of a nation's exports and imports vary seasonally and when the seasonal variation is not the same for both. Seasonal disequilibrium is usually short-lived and offsetting. France, for example, virtually closes down its industry for the month of August when most of its workforce goes on vacation. This causes a seasonal reduction in the demand for imports. On the other hand, as a major tourist attraction, French service exports are likely to increase, leading to a disequilibrium in the current account. The surge in economic activity and the reduction in tourism at the *rentrée* in September, however, offsets the August disequilibrium as service exports decrease and industrial imports increase.

Other, irregular or random disturbances may cause temporary external disequilibrium. Crop failure can reduce exports or make it necessary to increase imports of foodstuffs. Labor strikes and natural disasters such as floods and earthquakes can also upset the balance of payments. When these disturbances are such that they are self-correcting or one-off affairs and have no lasting effect on the economy, central bank intervention in the exchange markets and a compensating monetary policy can be justified as a means of avoiding the needless adjustment process that will be set in motion by a change in the exchange rate. However, when the external disequilibrium is caused by relative price distortions or structural shortcomings, the adjustment is necessary and this type of policy only puts off the inevitable and makes the adjustment all that more painful.

The monetary approach to the balance of payments

The preceding section established the link between the domestic monetary situation and the external sector. We saw that changes in the domestic monetary situation induced by disequilibrium in the external sector set in motion a self-correcting process as prices and cash balances adjust to the new situation. The monetary approach concentrates on the relationship between the money supply, prices and real cash balances to explain balance of payments equilibrium.

Remember that the total supply elasticities of the traditional approach to balance of payments discipline and devaluation theory recognize the importance of price differentials or relative rates of inflation between the devaluing country and the rest of the world. The traditional approach also recognizes the importance of real cash balances in determining balance of payments equilibrium. In these respects it resembles the monetary approach. Unfortunately, it concentrates on flow adjustments such as exports, imports, income and absorption and fails to consider stock adjustments. The monetary approach recognizes money as a stock concept and its importance for balance of payments equilibrium. Therefore, its analysis is conducted in terms of stock adjustments in the supply and demand for money. For example, a deficit in the balance of trade can be considered as a reduction in the level of cash balances in favor of goods and services beyond the domestic economy's productive capacity. A deficit on capital account can be considered as a reduction of cash balances in favor of other types of financial assets or as a level of outstanding credit in excess of the economy's capacity to save.

The monetary approach assumes a stable functional demand for money and considers the world economy as a closed system where optimal prices are those determined in the international market-place. Relative prices that deviate from those in the international market-place due to tariffs, subsidies and controls are viewed as sources of suboptimal resource allocation and impediments to balance of payments equilibrium. In Appendix 2.1 we develop a formal mathematical model of the monetary approach to the balance of payments but the essential elements of the approach can be summarized in four equations.[10]

The first equation is the balance of payments identity of Chapter 1 (Equation 1.2):

$$BP = X - M + FS + F \tag{2.4}$$

where, as before, BP is the increase in foreign reserves, X is exports, M is imports, FS is investment income and F is net foreign capital.

The second equation is the identity showing that the money supply is partially determined by the external sector, as we saw in the preceding paragraph:

$$\Delta MO = BP + \Delta D \tag{2.5}$$

where ΔMO represents the change in the money supply and ΔD represents the change in domestic credit (see Table 2.6).

The first behavioral equation reflects the assumption of a constant **velocity of money**. The velocity of money refers to the rate at which the stock of money circulates through the economy in order to finance transactions.[11] Suppose that Swiss GNP is CHF 1000 for 2001 and that the Swiss money supply is CHF 250. Then the velocity of money for 2001 is 1000/250 = 4. The assumption of a constant velocity of money can be written as follows:

$$GNP = vMO \tag{2.6}$$

where v represents the velocity of money.

The second behavioral equation explains imports in terms of national income in domestic currency:

$$M = mGNP \tag{2.7}$$

If we combine Equations 2.6 and 2.7 we have:

$$MO = \frac{M}{mv} \tag{2.8}$$

Equation 2.8 is the condition for monetary stability. It says that the money supply compatible with external equilibrium depends on the role of imports in the total economy and the economy's velocity of money. Imports are given by the balance of payments identity in Equation 2.4. Thus, everything necessary for external equilibrium is known. By

[10] See J.J. Polak and V. Argy, "Credit policy and the balance of payments", in International Monetary Fund, *The Monetary Approach to the Balance of Payments* (Washington DC: IMF, 1977), p.p. 205–225.

[11] For an excellent review of the history of monetary theory, see J. Marchal and J. Lecaillon, *Les Flux Monétaires* (Editions Cujas, 1967).

rearranging Equation 2.5, we can single out the policy variable that the authorities can use to assure external equilibrium:

$$\Delta D = \Delta MO - BP \qquad (2.9)$$

The policy variable that the authorities can use to assure external equilibrium is the amount of domestic credit. In Equation 2.9 we can see that domestic credit should be regulated with respect to the change in official reserves so that the money supply varies just enough to keep it at the equilibrium level defined in Equation 2.8. The mechanics of how this can be done were outlined in the preceding paragraph and in Tables 2.5 and 2.6.

When monetary equilibrium of Equation 2.8 is not respected, the consequences will fall on the price level because, according to the quantity theory of money on which the monetary approach is based, a nominal money supply that exceeds or falls short of the real cash balances demanded by domestic economic agents will affect the price level. An excess supply of money raises the price level and a shortage lowers it. Let's see why.

In its most primitive form the quantity theory of money postulates a strict proportional relationship between the price level and the supply of money. For example, suppose we divide nominal GNP into Y, the measure of the flow of real goods and services or real income, and P, the average price level. Then Equation 2.6 can be written:

$$PY = vMO \qquad (2.10)$$

and

$$P = \frac{v}{Y} MO \qquad (2.11)$$

Equation 2.10 is known as the Fisher equation after the economist Irving Fisher. It expresses the identity on which the quantity theory of money is based. Price times quantity equals the money supply times the rate at which it circulates through the economy. It is argued that both v and Y are constants, at least in the medium term: v is a constant determined by certain behavioral patterns and institutional features of the economy that only evolve slowly over time, while Y is a constant because of the hypothesis that the economy is at full employment and will remain there. Thus from 2.11 an increase in the money supply, MO, will increase prices by the proportion v/Y and the rate of increase in prices will be equal to the rate of increase of the money supply.

Suppose that $v = 5$, $Y = 100$, $P = 10$ and $MO = 200$. If the money supply increases by 10% to 220, then according to the quantity theory, the price level will rise to

$$P = 5/100 \times 220 = 11$$

an increase of 10%.

Thus when condition 2.8 is not respected – that is, when MO is not equal to M/mv – the consequences will be reflected in the domestic price level. We have already seen the effect of the exchange rate on prices and the important role that prices play in determining the level and composition of exports, imports, consumption and output. By focusing on the money supply, the monetary approach underlines the importance of the domestic price level for external equilibrium. In the following chapter we will take a long look at how prices or, more precisely, the price level affects external equilibrium and the exchange rate.

The monetary approach to the balance of payments is a powerful tool for international financial analysis. Where the traditional approach relies on knowledge of complicated micro and macroeconomic relationships as well as generally unmeasurable supply and demand elasticities, the monetary approach concentrates on one observable variable, the money supply, and the prospective performance of the economy's external sector can be judged by domestic monetary policy represented by domestic credit. Some caution is in order, however. First of all, except in the most unsophisticated financial systems, there is some confusion surrounding the financial aggregates corresponding to the definition of "money".[12] Secondly, the velocity of money is probably not a constant but rather a stable function of certain variables such as prices, interest rates and wealth.[13]

Summary

1. The exchange rate is determined by the supply and demand of domestic currency for foreign currency.

2. When the external sector is in fundamental disequilibrium, a change in the exchange rate is often necessary to restore equilibrium. In the case of a devaluation, restoration of equilibrium can be separated into two phases. (a) The initial phase refers to the period before supply and demand have had a chance to fully react to the new situation. A successful initial period depends in large part on the elasticities of demand for the devaluing country's exports and imports. The higher the demand elasticities, the more successful the devaluation. The supply elasticities in the initial period generally serve to determine the terms of trade. (b) The secondary phase refers to the period when all the economic variables have had a chance to change. This period is characterized by a redistribution of income and changes in the levels and composition of output and consumption.

3. The money supply is partially determined by the external sector.

4. Changes in the money supply due to disequilibrium in the external sector set off an adjustment process that causes a redistribution of income and changes in the levels and composition of output and consumption.

5. The domestic money supply is a key variable for external equilibrium. Insofar as domestic credit is a major determinant of the money supply and can be controlled by the authorities, it appears as the single most important policy variable for achieving external equilibrium.

Questions

Solutions to the following questions are set out on the web site, details of which are included in the Preface.

1. How do elasticities of supply and demand for imports and exports affect the supply and demand for foreign exchange?

2. Explain this statement: When supply elasticities of imports and exports are very high, a devaluation will cause a country's external terms of trade to deteriorate.

---

[12] See Michael T. Belongia and James A. Chalfant, "The changing empirical definition of money: Some estimates from a model for money substitutes", *Journal of Political Economy*, *97, 2*, (1989), p.p. 387–397; William A. Barnett, "New indices of money supply and the flexible Laurent demand system", *Journal of Business and Economic Statistics*, *1*, (January 1983), p.p. 7–23.

[13] See Milton Friedman, "The quantity theory of money: A restatement", in *Studies in the Quantity Theory of Money*, edited by M. Friedman (University of Chicago Press, 1956).

3. How are the level and composition of a country's output and consumption affected by a devaluation?

4. Explain why even the sector producing non-tradable goods is affected by a devaluation.

5. What is the J-curve effect?

6. How does central bank intervention in the foreign exchange market affect the money supply?

7. What are the economic effects of a change in the money supply?

8. Are there any situations when sterilizing the monetary effects of central bank intervention in the foreign exchange market might be justified?

9. According to the monetary approach to the balance of payments, what is the policy variable that the authorities can use to assure equilibrium in the supply and demand for foreign currency?

10. Where will a disequilibrium between the supply and demand for money manifest itself?

Appendix 2.1 – A mathematical model of the monetary approach to the balance of payments

In this appendix we present a formal mathematical model of the monetary approach to the balance of payments. Let

MO_{1d}	=	quantity of nominal money balances demanded
MO_{1s}	=	country's money supply
MO_0	=	$(D + F)$ = country's money base
D_0	=	domestic component of the country's money base
F	=	foreign component of the country's money base
P	=	domestic price level
Y	=	real output
r	=	interest rate
a	=	price elasticity of demand for money
b	=	income elasticity of demand for money
c	=	interest elasticity of demand for money
m	=	money multiplier
g_i	=	growth rate of variable i
ε	=	error term.

Remember that PY = GNP. Then start with the traditional assumption that the complete demand function for money has the following form:

$$MO_{1d} = \frac{P^a Y^b \varepsilon}{r^c} \qquad (A2.1.1)$$

The demand for money is positively related to GNP and inversely related to the interest rate.

As we saw in the section on the effects of exchange rate intervention on the money supply, the money supply is a multiple of the country's money base:

$$MO_{1s} = m(D_0 + F) \qquad (A2.1.2)$$

In equilibrium, money supply equals money demand:

$$MO_{1d} = MO_{1s}$$

or

$$\frac{P^a Y^b \varepsilon}{r^c} = m(D_0 + F) \tag{A2.1.3}$$

To get this equation into testable form, take the natural logarithm of both sides:

$$a\ln P + b\ln Y + 1\ln \varepsilon - c\ln r = \ln m + 1\ln(D_0 + F) \tag{A2.1.4}$$

Differentiate A2.1.4 with respect to time:

$$a\frac{1}{P}\frac{dP}{dt} + b\frac{1}{Y}\frac{dY}{dt} + \frac{1}{\varepsilon}\frac{d\varepsilon}{dt} - c\frac{1}{r}\frac{dr}{dt} = \frac{1}{m}\frac{dm}{dt} + \frac{D_0}{D_0+F}\frac{1}{D_0}\frac{dD_0}{dt} + \frac{F}{D_0+F}\frac{1}{F}\frac{dF}{dt} \tag{A2.1.5}$$

Remember that $D_0 + F = MO_0$, let

$$\frac{1}{P}\frac{dP}{dt} = g_p, \frac{1}{Y}\frac{dY}{dt} = g_y, \text{ etc.,}$$

and rearrange:

$$\frac{F}{M_0}g_F = ag_p + bg_y + g_\varepsilon - cg_r - g_m - \frac{D_0}{M_0}g_D \tag{A2.1.6}$$

Equation A2.1.6 is the general form of the equation usually used in empirical tests of the balance of payments. It says that the weighted growth rate of the country's international reserves,

$$\frac{F}{MO_0}g_F,$$

is a function of the growth rates and elasticities of the different variables.

It is interesting to note that the weighted growth rate of the country's reserves is negatively related to the weighted growth rate of the domestic component of the country's money base. In other words, other things being equal, a change in the central bank's credit to the economy, D_0, will produce an automatic equal and opposite change in F. Thus, under fixed exchange rates, a country can only determine the composition of the money base. It cannot control the size of the money base itself and, consequently, it has no control over its monetary policy.

International parity relations

The outcome of the supply and demand of one currency for another is reflected in the exchange rate. As we have seen, the exchange rate has major consequences on a country's economic well-being. It also has major consequences for non-residents investing in the country or doing business with it. Apparently profitable transactions can suddenly turn sour if the exchange rate moves in the wrong direction. The current system of floating exchange rates that replaced the Bretton Woods fixed rate system has focused attention on the importance of managing exchange rate risk. This involves forecasting exchange rates and taking measures to protect against potential unfavorable developments. Understanding the underlying forces that determine exchange rates and why they are likely to vary is a fundamental and indispensable tool for judicious financial decision making.

The international parity relations, embodied in the writings of J.M. Keynes, G. Cassel and I. Fisher, form the basis of most analysis of exchange rate behavior. They are an elegant set of simple equilibrium relationships between the prices of goods and services, interest rates, and the spot and forward exchange rates. Although they are highly stylized and depend on some demonstrably unrealistic assumptions, they constitute a powerful theoretical framework for understanding and explaining the international financial environment. Many of the subsequent chapters in this book draw on the relationships derived from the parity conditions that are developed in this chapter and, therefore, it is important that they be well understood.

Purchasing power parity

Of all the factors outlined in Chapter 2 that influence exchange rate movements and long-term external equilibrium, price increases or inflation stand out as particularly important. The theory linking inflation and exchange rate movements is known as **purchasing power parity** (PPP). The theory of purchasing power parity has its source in the mercantilist literature of the 17th century but it came into prominence through the writings of Gustav Cassel in the early part of the 20th century.[1] Since then it has come to occupy an important place in international economic and financial analysis. PPP, for example, is often the long-run equilibrium condition for the exchange rate in dynamic exchange rate models. In systems of fixed exchange rates it has been widely used by

[1] Gustav Cassel, "The present situation in the foreign exchanges", *Economic Journal* (1916), p.p. 62–65; "Abnormal deviations in international exchanges", *Economic Journal* (1918), p.p. 413–415.

monetary authorities for establishing new par values when the existing ones were clearly out of line. Money managers also commonly use PPP for forecasting exchange rates or for determining the currency composition of their portfolios.

The law of one price

The theory of PPP is based on the **law of one price**. The law of one price states that identical commodities or goods must have the same price in all markets. If this were not the case, profit-seeking entrepreneurs could exploit the situation by buying in the market with the lower price and selling in the market with the higher price. The increased demand in the market with the lower price would tend to raise the price in that market, while the increased supply in the higher priced market would tend to lower its price. This activity would continue until the prices in both markets equalized, thereby eliminating the potential for profit. Exploiting price differentials in this way is known as **arbitrage**.

Suppose, for example, that the price of gold in Zürich is USD 370 an ounce and in London it is USD 355 an ounce. Arbitragers will buy gold in London and simultaneously sell it in Zürich for a profit of USD 15 per ounce. As more and more gold is bought in London, its price will rise while the price in Zürich will fall as more and more gold is offered for sale. In a very short time the prices will become equal or at least close enough so that, when the costs associated with buying and selling are taken into consideration, the opportunity for arbitrage profits disappears.

Even without arbitrage, the law of one price should hold for internationally traded goods because outside buyers would only buy in the market with the lowest price. In practice, of course, it costs money and takes time to ship goods from one place to another and there are often restrictions of various forms on international trade. In this sense prices might differ somewhat. For example, a banana should cost more in Holland than in Honduras where it is produced because of the cost of shipping the banana from Honduras to Holland.

When only one currency is involved, the law of one price is easy to see. When more than one currency is involved, the law of one price states that when financial and commodity markets are perfect (no controls, delays, transaction or shipping costs, etc.), identical commodities or goods must have the same price in all markets when quoted in a common currency. For example, let p_{GBP} and p_{USD} be the price of natural gas in the United Kingdom and the United States respectively and $S_0(GBP/USD)$ be the number of pounds it takes to buy one dollar at time 0. Then, by the law of one price: [2]

$$p_{GBP} = p_{USD} S_0 \text{ (GBP/USD)} \qquad (3.1)$$

or conversely:

$$p_{USD} = \frac{p_{GBP}}{S_0 \text{ (GBP/USD)}} \qquad (3.2)$$

---

[2] When financial and goods markets are not perfect, relations 3.1 and 3.2 will hold within the financial magnitude of market imperfections and transaction costs. This can be written:

$$|p_{GBP} - p_{USD} \times S(GBP/USD)| < T$$

where T represents the financial magnitude of market imperfections and transaction costs.

Thus, if the price of natural gas in the United States is USD 5.00 a cubic meter and it takes GBP 2 to buy USD 1, by Equation 3.1 the price of natural gas in the United Kingdom should be:

$$p_{GBP} = USD\ 5.00 \times 2(GBP/USD) = GBP\ 10$$

In other words, the price of natural gas should be the same in the United Kingdom and in the United States when quoted in the same currency. If the price is GBP 10 in the United Kingdom, by Equation 3.2 the price in the United States should be:

$$p_{USD} = \frac{GBP\ 10}{2(GBP/USD)} = USD\ 5.00$$

The price is the same in the United Kingdom and the United States whether it is quoted in dollars or pounds.

Absolute and relative PPP

PPP describes the relation between *average price levels* in each country and the equilibrium exchange rate. Suppose that the law of one price holds for all goods and services. According to Equation 3.1, the same basket of goods and services in both countries should have the same price. Let $P(0)$ represent the price of the basket of goods and services at time 0. Then

$$P_{GBP}(0) = P_{USD}(0)S_0(GBP/USD) \tag{3.3}$$

This relation represents the absolute form of PPP and is very restrictive. It can only be valid if goods and financial markets are perfect and the same commodities appear in the same proportions in each country's market basket. This is an unrealistic proposition insofar as it ignores the effects of market imperfections, transaction costs, product differentiation, and restrictions on international trade such as quotas and tariffs.

The relative form of PPP, more commonly used today, is less restrictive than the absolute form. It states that in comparison to a period when exchange rates were in equilibrium, changes in the ratio of domestic to foreign prices indicate the appropriate adjustment in the exchange rate. Let $S_0(GBP/USD)$, $P_{GBP}(0)$, $P_{USD}(0)$ be the base period equilibrium exchange rate and price levels, and rearrange Equation 3.3:

$$S_0(GBP/USD)\frac{P_{GBP}(0)}{P_{USD}(0)} \tag{3.4}$$

At time t the corresponding relation is:

$$S_t(GBP/USD) = \frac{P_{GBP}(t)}{P_{USD}(t)} \tag{3.5}$$

Dividing 3.5 by 3.4 gives the relative form of PPP:

$$\frac{S_t(GBP/USD)}{S_0(GBP/USD)} = \frac{P_{GBP}(t)\big/P_{GBP}(0)}{P_{USD}(t)\big/P_{USD}(0)} \tag{3.6}$$

Equation 3.6 is usually expressed in terms of rates of inflation. Let i_{GBP} and i_{USD} be the US and UK rates of inflation respectively. Then

$$\frac{P_{GBP}(t)}{P_{GBP}(0)} = 1 + i_{GBP}$$

and

$$\frac{P_{USD}(t)}{P_{USD}(0)} = 1 + i_{USD}$$

Substituting these values into Equation 3.6 gives the relative form of PPP in terms of inflation rates:

$$\frac{S_t(GBP/USD)}{S_0(GBP/USD)} = \frac{1 + i_{GBP}}{1 + i_{USD}} \qquad (3.7)$$

Relative PPP can also be presented as the percentage change in the exchange rate over the period by subtracting 1 from both sides of Equation 3.7:

$$\frac{S_t(GBP/USD) - S_0(GBP/USD)}{S_0(GBP/USD)} = \frac{i_{GBP} - i_{USD}}{1 + i_{USD}} \qquad (3.8)$$

This is the most usual presentation of relative PPP. When inflation rates are low, Equation 3.8 can be approximated as the difference between the two countries' rates of inflation:

$$\frac{S_t(GBP/USD) - S_0(GBP/USD)}{S_0(GBP/USD)} = i_{GBP} - i_{USD} \qquad (3.9)$$

To take an example of the relative form of PPP, suppose that the US consumer price index rises from 100 to 105 in the period from 31 December 2000 to 31 December, 2001 and the UK consumer price index increases from 200 to 225 over the same period. If the exchange rate was in equilibrium on 31 December 2000, according to Equation 3.4 it would have been equal to

$$S_{2000}(GBP/USD) = \frac{200}{100} = 2(GBP/USD).$$

The UK rate of inflation can be calculated as

$$i_{GBP} = \frac{P_{GBP}(2001)}{P_{GBP}(2000)} - 1 = 1.125 - 1 = 0.125$$

or 12.5% and the rate of inflation in the United States as

$$i_{USD} \frac{P_{USD}(2001)}{P_{USD}(2000)} - 1 = 1.05 - 1 = 0.05$$

or 5%. Then, according to Equation 3.7, the equilibrium exchange rate on 31 December 2001 would be

$$S_{2001}(GBP/USD) = 2(GBP/USD) \times \frac{1.125}{1.05} = GBP\ 2.1429\ for\ USD\ 1.$$

From Equation 3.8 the percentage change in the exchange rate would be

$$\frac{(0.125 - 0.05)}{1.05} = 7.14\%$$

which means that according to the relative form of PPP it should take 7.14% more pounds to buy one dollar on 31 December 2001 than it did on 31 December 2000.

If we use the approximation in Equation 3.9, the percentage change in the exchange rate is equal to

$$12.5\% - 5\% = 7.5\%$$

which is close to the exact figure of 7.14% obtained with Equation 3.8.

The empirical evidence

Whether or not PPP holds is an ongoing controversy. The reasons why it might not hold are numerous. The strictest form of PPP requires that:

1. financial markets are perfect with no controls, taxes, transaction costs, etc;
2. goods markets are perfect with international shipment of goods able to take place freely, instantaneously and without cost;
3. there is a single consumption good common to everyone; or
4. the same commodities appear in the same proportions in each country's consumption basket.

These assumptions are clearly unrealistic. Goods and financial markets are not perfect. Goods cannot be shipped instantaneously, transport costs are high and import restrictions of various forms are widespread. Taxes, transaction costs and controls are present in the financial markets. There are also many types of consumption goods, and economic agents throughout the world have different tastes and preferences so that a common basket of consumption goods does not exist. Furthermore, the PPP hypothesis designates relative inflation differentials as the only source of exchange rate variations. We saw in Chapter 2 that, at least in the short run, other non-monetary phenomena such as changes in relative prices as well as changes in the level and composition of output and consumption influence the supply and demand for foreign currency and thus the exchange rate. With all these qualifications, the question is, then, to what extent purchasing power parity exists as a real world phenomenon.

Some studies find little support for the PPP hypothesis. Studies by J.D. Richardson, P. Isard, and I.B. Kravis and R.E. Lipsey find substantial deviations from the law of one price in the commodities markets.[3] If the law of one price does not hold, then PPP is not likely to hold either. However, another series of studies finds that PPP does hold but with a considerable time lag.[4] H.J. Galliot tested PPP between the United States and Canada, Great Britain, France, West Germany, Italy, Japan and Switzerland from 1900 to 1967.[5] H.J. Edison tested the dollar/pound exchange rate between 1890 and 1978.[6] Both authors found that PPP is often violated in the short run but holds up well in the long run.

[3] J.D. Richardson, "Some empirical evidence on commodity arbitrage and the law of one price", *Journal of International Economics* (May 1978), p.p. 342–351; P. Isard, "How far can we push the law of one price?", *American Economic Review* (December 1977), p.p. 942–948; I.B. Kravis and R.E. Lipsey, "Price behavior in the light of balance of payments theory", *Journal of International Economics* (May 1978), p.p. 193–246.

[4] J. Hodgson and P. Phelps in, "The distributed impact of price level variation on floating exchange rates", *Review of Economics and Statistics* (February 1975), p.p. 58–64 found that differential inflation rates precede the change in exchange rates by up to 18 months. In an attempt to forecast exchange rates, W.R. Folks, Jr. and S.R. Stansell, "The use of discriminant analysis in forecasting exchange rate movements", *Journal of International Business Studies* (Spring 1975), p.p. 71–81 found that exchange rates only adjust differential rates of inflation after a long lag.

[5] H.J. Galliot, "Purchasing power parity as an explanation of long-term changes in exchange rates", *Journal of Money, Credit and Banking* (August 1971), p.p. 348–357.

[6] H.J. Edison, "Purchasing power parity in the long run: A test of the dollar/pound exchange rate (1890–1978)", *Journal of Money, Credit and Banking* (August 1987), p.p. 376–387.

Traditional regression techniques have been replaced by the now well known cointegration technique, which states that if PPP holds as a long-term equilibrium, the exchange rate and the price level should be cointegrated. Abuaf and Jorion, analyzing annual data over the period 1900–1972 found that deviations from PPP, although substantial in the short term, take about three years to be reduced by half.[7] Most of the testing carried out since the inception of floating exchange rates at the beginning of the 1970s either rejects or provides only weak support for PPP, while tests done on longer periods or on high inflation economies provide stronger support for PPP.[8] Despite disagreements over some specific points, the consensus emerging from the vast literature on the subject is that PPP in its relative form is generally valid, at least in the long run.[9]

The evidence is also growing that PPP is more than a long-run phenomenon. R.J. Rogalski and J.D. Vinso, studying a period of floating exchange rates in the early 1920s and mid-1950s, found that freely floating markets react immediately or almost immediately to changes in relative inflation rates, and noted that their finding is consistent with both PPP and the **efficient markets theory**.[10] The efficient market hypothesis holds that all relevant information is fully and immediately reflected in a security's market price.[11] R. Roll has applied the efficient markets hypothesis to PPP by assuming that the current spot rate reflects anticipated exchange-adjusted inflation differentials rather than a slow adjustment to past inflation differentials.[12] His results on 252 pairs of countries over the period 1957 through 1976 strongly support this hypothesis and suggest that for most countries, and for all the largest trading nations, the adjustment duration is less than one month.

[7] N. Abuaf and Philippe Jorion, "Purchasing power parity in the long run", *Journal of Finance* (March 1990), p.p.157–174.

[8] See, for example, R. McKnown and M. Wallace, "National price levels, purchasing power parity and cointegration: A test of four high inflation countries", *Journal of International Money and Finance, 8* (December 1989); K. Phylaktis, "Purchasing power parity and cointegration: The Greek evidence from the 1920s", *Journal of International Money and Finance, 11* (October 1992); W. Enders, "ARIMA and cointegration tests of PPP under fixed and flexible exchange rate regimes", *Review of Economics and Statistics, 70* (August 1988); N. Mark, "Real and nominal exchange rates in the long run: An empirical investigation", *Journal of International Economics, 28* (February 1990); M.K. Pippenger, "Cointegration tests of purchasing power parity: The Swiss case", *Journal of International Money and Finance, 12* (February 1993).

[9] For extensive coverage of the PPP issues and literature, see M. Adler and B. Dumas, "International portfolio choice and corporation finance: A synthesis", *Journal of Finance* (June 1983), p.p. 925–984; A.C. Shapiro, "What does purchasing power parity mean?", *Journal of International Money and Finance* (1983), p.p. 295–318; B. Solnik, *International Investments* (Addison-Wesley Publishing Co., Inc., 1996).

[10] R.J. Rogalski and J.D. Vinso, "Price variations as predictors of exchange rates", *Journal of International Business Studies* (Spring–Summer 1977), p.p. 71–83.

[11] The efficient market hypothesis is usually divided into the strong form where the information set includes all currently known information, the semi-strong form where the information set includes all publicly available information, and the weak form where the information set includes the previous prices of securities. See E. Fama, "Efficient capital markets: A review of theory and empirical work", *Journal of Finance* (May 1970).

[12] R. Roll, "Violations of purchasing power parity and their implications for efficient commodity markets", in M. Sarnat and G. Szego (Eds.) *International Finance and Trade* (Cambridge, Mass.: Ballinger 1979). The efficient markets form of PPP is expressed by writing Equation 3.7 in terms of expected values:

$$\frac{E[S_t(\text{GBP/USD})]}{S_0(\text{GBP/USD})} = \frac{1 + E(i_{\text{GBP}})}{1 + E(i_{\text{USD}})} \qquad (3.7')$$

where E represents the expectations operator.

Reasons for divergence from short-term PPP

The asset market approach

Besides the practical considerations of market imperfections and heterogeneous market baskets, there are also some theoretical arguments for short-run departures from PPP. Building on the efficient markets hypothesis, the asset market approach to exchange rate determination argues that currencies are assets and that the present value of an asset depends on what it is expected to be worth in the future. An exchange rate is simply the relative price of two assets – the two currencies – and is determined in the same way as the prices of other assets such as stocks and bonds. Hence, because the present value of a currency is today's exchange rate, today's exchange rate depends on the expected future exchange rate. The expected future exchange rate depends on what is expected to happen in the overall economy and how this will be reflected in the supply and demand for foreign currency. In other words, the current spot exchange rate contains all relevant information about the future and is the market's best estimate of how the exchange rate is likely to evolve. New information that can change the outlook for the future is arriving all the time and is just as likely to be favorable as it is to be unfavorable. Thus, the evolution of the exchange rate is likely to exhibit an element of randomness. The randomness may or may not be related to PPP because the information relevant to the expected future exchange rate includes more than just inflation differentials. Elections, natural catastrophes and wars, among many other things, can also influence exchange rates.

The asset market approach is not inconsistent with PPP. On the contrary, it recognizes the importance of inflation differentials on the evolution of the exchange rate. Furthermore, by considering the random element associated with expectations about the future it offers a theoretical explanation of how spot rates can diverge from their PPP equilibrium in the short run.

Overshooting

Another popular explanation for significant short-term deviations from PPP is the Dornbusch theory of overshooting.[13] This theory marries the concepts of PPP, "sticky prices" and the asset market approach. Suppose that PPP holds in the long run but the prices of non-traded goods are sticky and adjust slowly to their new equilibrium level after a disturbance such as a unilateral increase in the domestic money supply. Eventually prices will rise in proportion to the increase in the money supply, and the nominal exchange rate, driven by changes in PPP, will depreciate in proportion to the change in prices. In the short term, however, the price level increases less than the money supply due to the sticky prices for non-traded goods. The resulting excess supply of money will be spent at least partially on bonds, thereby causing bond prices to rise and interest rates to fall. Because investors have rational expectations and anticipate the eventual depreciation of the currency, they require higher interest rates to offset the depreciation. This is because total expected returns include interest plus or minus the expected appreciation or depreciation of the currency. But current interest rates are lower than before. Thus, in order for investors to buy domestic assets the currency must overshoot or depreciate to a point below its long-term PPP equilibrium level, from where it is then expected to appreciate. In this way its anticipated appreciation will compensate for the lower interest rates.

[13] See R. Dornbusch, "Expectations and exchange rate dynamics", *Journal of Political Economy* (December 1976), p.p. 1161–1176.

The portfolio balance approach

Another explanation of exchange rate determination adds demand functions and equilibrium conditions for bond markets to the traditional monetary approach.[14] This approach, called the portfolio balance approach, assumes that investors desire diversified portfolios and, hence, will hold both domestic and foreign assets. Whereas the monetary approach assumes that bond markets always clear, the portfolio balance approach, through supply and demand functions for bonds and equilibrium conditions setting bond supply equal to demand, shows how bond markets clear. With this modification, the effects of changing bond supplies and demands can have consequences on interest rates and the exchange rate that differ in the short run from what is forecast in the monetary approach.

Suppose, for example, that the central bank buys domestic bonds on the market. From Chapter 2 we know that this will increase the money base and, through the reserve ratio multiplier, cause an increase in the domestic money supply. Other things being equal, the primitive formulations of the monetary approach predict that the exchange rate will depreciate by the percentage increase in the money supply. The portfolio approach argues that by reducing the supply of bonds in circulation, the central bank has created an excess demand that will raise bond prices and lower interest rates. Lower interest rates have well known consequences on investment, output and prices that will affect the exchange rate. This implies that at least in the short run the exchange rate can stray from its long-run PPP equilibrium. In Appendix 3.1 at the end of this chapter we present the mathematical model of the portfolio balance approach to the balance of payments.

Besides the many explanations of short-run departures from classical PPP, some of the observed departures may be due to the statistical problems of evaluating PPP. Price indexes, for example, vary substantially across countries. The goods and services included are not always the same and when they are the same they are not always given the same weight. Changes in the relative prices of the goods that make up the indexes will cause differently constructed indexes to react differently, thereby sending false signals of departure from PPP.

In summary, then, in spite of the evidence of significant short-term departures from PPP, it is clear that there is a strong correspondence between relative rates of inflation and changes in the exchange rate. However, because PPP is not a complete theory of exchange rate determination, the correspondence is not perfect and there is no theoretical imperative to associate departures from PPP with market disequilibrium.

Interest rate parity

Interest rate parity is the cornerstone to most if not all of today's international financial transactions. As a theory it was first developed by J.M. Keynes in 1930.[15] Like purchasing power parity, interest rate parity is based on the law of one price. However, where PPP refers to the law of one price in the market for goods and services, interest rate parity refers to the law of one price in the securities market. When quoted in a common currency, identical securities should have the same price in all markets.

Consider a one-year US dollar deposit with a branch of Barclays in New York paying 12% and an equivalent one-year Swiss franc deposit with a branch of Barclays in Zürich paying 8%. With the interest rate higher in New York than in Zürich, investors

[14] See P.J.K. Kouri and M.G. Porter, "International capital flows and portfolio equilibrium", *Journal of Political Economy* (May–June 1974), p.p. 443–467.

[15] J.M. Keynes, *A Treatise on Money* (London: Macmillan 1930).

would be tempted to move funds from Zürich to New York. In order to do so they must sell Swiss francs and buy dollars. The spot exchange rate, $S_0(CHF/USD)$, is CHF 2 for USD 1. However, when they move from Swiss francs into dollars the investment in New York is not identical to the Swiss franc deposit because the exchange rate could change over the year of the investment. This means that they are exposed to **exchange risk**. A change in the value of the Swiss franc versus the US dollar would change the number of francs they receive when they convert their dollar investment into francs at the end of the year. An appreciation of the Swiss franc (the number of Swiss francs it takes to buy one dollar declines) would reduce the number of francs they receive, while a depreciation of the Swiss franc (the number of Swiss francs it takes to buy one dollar increases) would increase it. In order to render the two investments identical, the exchange risk must be eliminated. This can be done by making a deal to sell the proceeds of the dollar investment in the **forward market**. The forward market is where currencies are traded for future delivery and the **forward exchange rate** is the current price of one currency for another for delivery at a specified date in the future.[16] Suppose that the forward rate for delivery in one year, noted as $F_{0,1}(CHF/USD)$, where the first subscript denotes the transaction date and the second subscript denotes the maturity date, is the same as the spot rate, that is, CHF 2 = USD 1. With the forward transaction the two investments are comparable and the return in Swiss francs on the dollar deposit can effectively be calculated.

Consider a USD 1000 deposit. The Swiss investor pays CHF 2000 at the spot rate of CHF 2 = USD 1 and deposits the USD 1000 with Barclays in New York. At the end of the year he knows he will receive USD 1120 so he sells USD 1120 forward at the rate of CHF 2 = USD 1. When the loan matures at the end of the year, he surrenders the USD 1120 and receives CHF 2240 (CHF2/USD 1 × USD 1120 = CHF 2240) for a percentage gain in Swiss francs of:

$$\frac{2240-2000}{2000} = 12\%.$$

If financial markets are efficient, this situation cannot last for long because of what is known as **covered interest arbitrage**. Covered interest arbitrage involves borrowing in one currency, selling the borrowed currency on the spot market, investing the proceeds of the sale, and simultaneously buying back the borrowed currency on the forward market. Using the data of the foregoing example, a covered interest arbitrage transaction is illustrated in Table 3.1.

In this transaction shown in the table there was no investment on the part of the arbitrager. His investment was made with borrowed money. On the other hand, his profit of CHF 80 was guaranteed because all the prices were known and agreed upon from the beginning. Arbitrage transactions of this type have the effect of raising the interest rate of the borrowed currency, lowering the interest rate of the loaned currency, appreciating the spot rate and depreciating the forward rate and thereby eliminating the opportunity for guaranteed profit.

Interest rate parity theory develops from the foregoing discussion. Suppose that financial markets are perfect with no controls, transaction costs, taxes and so forth. Let r_{CHF} and r_{USD} be the interest rate on the Swiss franc and the dollar respectively. If one Swiss franc is borrowed, $1 + r_{CHF}$ must be paid back at the end of the investment period. The possibility for covered interest arbitrage disappears when the Swiss franc cost of borrowing is just equal to

[16] See Chapter 6 for a detailed discussion of the forward currency market.

Table 3.1 An example of a covered interest arbitrage transaction

Operation	Cash flow
Borrow CHF 2000	+CHF 2000
Sell Swiss francs spot	–CHF 2000
	+USD 1000
Lend dollars	–USD 1000
Sell USD 1120 forward	0
Receive interest and principal in dollars	+USD 1120
Deliver dollars for Swiss francs	–USD 1120
	+CHF 2240
Pay interest and principal in Swiss francs	–CHF 2160
Net gain	+CHF 80

the Swiss franc gain from lending in dollars. If one Swiss franc is borrowed, $1/S_0(\text{CHF/USD})$ dollars will be invested and this will yield $(1 + r_{USD})/S_0(\text{CHF/USD})$ dollars at the end of the investment period. With the forward transaction the Swiss franc value of the investment will be.

$$\frac{(1 + r_{USD})F_{0,t}(\text{CHF/USD})}{S_0(\text{CHF/USD})}$$

If there is to be no possibility for covered interest arbitrage, this must be equal to the $(1 + r_{CHF})$ that must be paid back on the franc loan. From this equality the interest rate parity relation can be written:

$$\frac{F_{0,t}(\text{CHF/USD})}{S_0(\text{CHF/USD})} = \frac{(1+r_{CHF})}{(1+r_{USD})}. \tag{3.10}$$

Subtracting 1 from each side gives:

$$\frac{F_{0,t}(\text{CHF/USD}) - S_0(\text{CHF/USD})}{S_0(\text{CHF/USD})} = \frac{r_{CHF} - r_{USD}}{(1+r_{USD})}. \tag{3.11}$$

The interest parity relation states that on perfect money markets the forward discount or premium on the foreign exchange market is equal to the relative difference between the two interest rates. When r_{USD} is low, the forward discount or premium can be approximated by:

$$\frac{F_{0,t}(\text{CHF/USD}) - S_0(\text{CHF/USD})}{S_0(\text{CHF/USD})} = r_{CHF} - r_{USD}. \tag{3.12}$$

Going back to our example we can use 3.10 to find the forward exchange rate compatible with interest rate parity. From 3.10:

$$\frac{F_{0,1}(\text{CHF/USD})}{S_0(\text{CHF/USD})} = \frac{1.08}{1.12}$$

$$F_{0,1}(\text{CHF/USD}) = \text{CHF } 1.9286.$$

The forward rate should be CHF 1.9286 for each dollar. Otherwise, riskless arbitrage opportunities would exist.

From 3.11 we can calculate the percentage discount on the dollar:

$$\frac{F_{0,1}(\text{CHF/USD}) - S_0(\text{CHF/USD})}{S_0(\text{CHF/USD})} = \frac{0.08 - 0.12}{1.12} = -0.0357 = -3.57\%.$$

In other words, for interest rate parity to hold, the forward rate should be 3.57% lower (it should take 3.57% fewer francs to buy one dollar) than the spot rate. Using the first-order linear approximation in Equation 3.12 gives:

$$\frac{F_{0,1}(\text{CHF/USD}) - S_0(\text{CHF/USD})}{S_0(\text{CHF/USD})} = 0.08 - 0.12 = -0.04 = -4\%.$$

Figure 3.1 is a graphic representation of the relationship between the interest rate differential and the spot and forward exchange rates. The vertical axis represents the interest rate differential from Equation 3.11 and the horizontal axis represents the forward discount (negative) or premium (positive) on the dollar. The interest parity line joins the points where the forward exchange rate is in equilibrium with the interest rate differential. For example, point A represents the equilibrium rate calculated above where the dollar is at a 3.57% discount to the Swiss franc. Point B indicates a situation where the premium on the dollar is not high enough to offset the interest rate differential between the franc and the dollar. The interest rate differential in favor of the Swiss franc is 5% while the premium on the dollar is only 4%. In this case capital would flow into Switzerland.

Figure 3.1 Interest rate parity

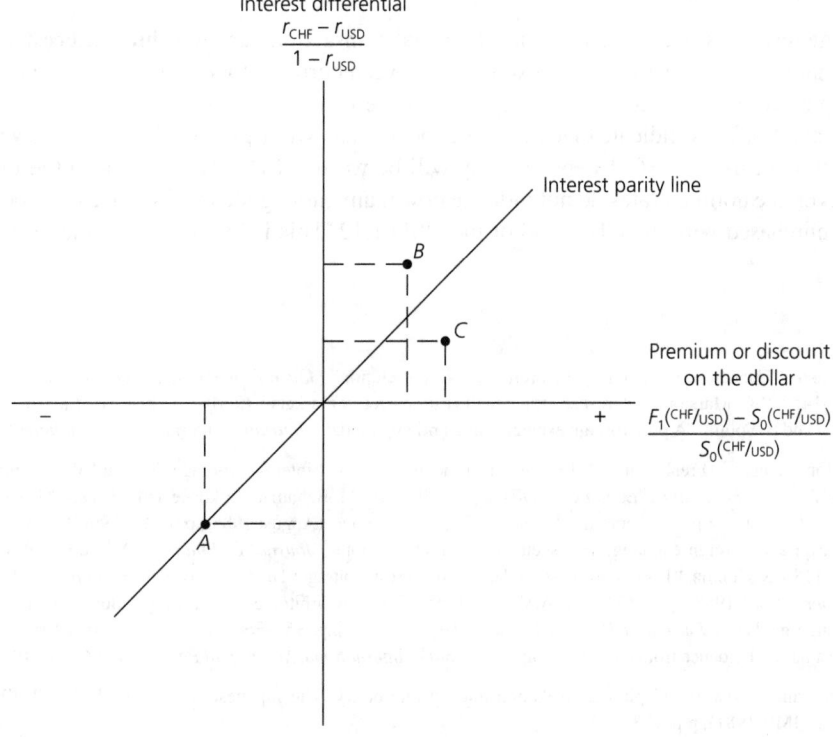

Point *C* indicates a situation where the interest rate differential in favor of the Swiss franc is too low for the premium on the dollar. The interest rate differential is only 1% and the premium on the dollar is 3%. In this case, funds would flow from Switzerland to the United States.

Empirical evidence

The evidence for the validity of interest rate parity in the Eurocurrency markets is convincing. Three studies, one by R. Aliber, one by R.C. Marston and the third by R. Roll and B. Solnik, concluded that it holds almost perfectly in the Eurocurrency markets.[17] This not surprising, because, as we shall see in Chapter 6, the Eurocurrency markets come close to the condition of perfect financial markets: they have very low transaction costs and they are devoid of taxes and controls. When transaction costs are considered, the conclusion is much the same. They do not contribute substantially to departures from interest rate parity. The literature on the subject is extensive, but it is generally recognized that uncovered or one-way interest arbitrage is the reason for this. One-way interest arbitrage as opposed to covered interest arbitrage is just another way of saying that people will borrow where they get the lowest rate and lend where they get the highest rate.[18] When controls exist, however, the conclusion is different. I. Otani and S. Tiwari found that Japanese capital controls caused the interest rate parity relation to break down in the Tokyo market.[19]

The general consensus is that interest rate parity holds nicely in the integrated and unregulated Eurocurrency markets. In markets where there seems to be substantial departure from interest parity, this can be attributed to transaction costs, taxes and other types of controls.

The international Fisher relation

The Fisher relation

The interest rates used in day-to-day financial transactions are **nominal interest rates**. Nominal rates express the rate of exchange between current money and future money. For example the interest rates that we quoted in the example for interest rate parity were nominal rates. They indicate that a CHF 1 deposit today will be worth CHF 1.08 one year in the future, or that a USD 1 deposit today will be worth USD 1.12 one year in the future. However, the nominal rates do not indicate how many more goods and services will be able to be purchased with the CHF 1.08 or the USD 1.12. This is because the value of money

[17] R. Aliber, "The interest rate parity theorem: A reinterpretation", *Journal of Political Economy*, (1973), p.p. 1451–1459; R.C. Marston, "Interest arbitrage in the Eurocurrency markets", *European Economic Review*, (1976); R. Roll and B. Solnik, "A pure foreign exchange asset pricing model", *Journal of International Economics* (1977).

[18] See, for example J. Frenkel and R. Levich, "Transaction costs and interest arbitrage: Tranquil versus turbulent periods", *Journal of Political Economy* (1977), p.p. 1209–1226; M. Bahamani Oskooee and S.P. Das, "Transaction costs and the interest parity theorem", *Journal of Political Economy* (August 1985), p.p. 793–799; P. Callier, "One way arbitrage, foreign exchange and securities markets: A note", *Journal of Finance* (December 1981), p.p. 1177–1186; K. Clinton, "Transaction costs and covered interest arbitrage: Theory and evidence", *Journal of Political Economy* (April 1988), p.p. 358–370; A.V. Deardorff, "One-way arbitrage and its implications for the foreign exchange markets", *Journal of Political Economy* (April 1979), p.p. 351–364; H. Popper, "Long-term covered interest parity: Evidence from currency swaps", *Journal of International Money and Finance, 12* (August 1993).

[19] I. Otani and S. Tiwari, "Capital controls and interest rate parity: The Japanese experience 1978–1981", *Staff Papers*, (IMF, 1981), p.p. 793–815.

may change over the course of time. In fact, a changing value of money over time is the rule rather than the exception.

The value of money changes when prices change. Lower prices mean that money gains in value because more goods and services can be purchased with the same amount of money. Higher prices mean that money loses in value because fewer goods and services can be purchased with the same amount of money. In the recent past higher prices, known as inflation, are by far the more common phenomenon. We have already considered the role inflation plays in determining the exchange rate. In this context, we could say that the theory of purchasing power parity explains what happens to the exchange rate as a consequence of the changing values of the two monies (currencies).

What is important to investors, then, is not the number of dollars or pounds or francs that they own but rather what goods and services that those dollars, pounds and francs will purchase for them. Therefore, it is the **real interest rate** and not the nominal rate that interests the investor. The real interest rate represents the rate at which current goods and services are being transformed into future goods and services.

Irving Fisher suggested that because investors are concerned with the real interest rate, the nominal interest rate should be composed of two elements: the real interest rate that we can call the real required rate of return ρ and the expected rate of inflation $E(i)$.[20] Suppose, for example, that the real required rate of return in the United Kingdom is 3% and the rate of inflation over the year is expected to be 5%. If, at the end of the year, the rate of inflation was effectively 5%, the purchasing power of the pound will be

$$GBP\ 1\ /\ 1.05 = GBP\ 0.9524.$$

In other words, at the end of the year GBP 1 will only purchase 95.24% of what it can purchase today, a loss of 4.76%. The investor requires his real purchasing power to be 3% higher at the end of the year than today to induce him to lend. Thus, the nominal rate that he will demand will be

$$GBP\ 0.9524 \times (1 + r) = 1.03,\ r = 0.0815 = 8.15\%.$$

With a 3% real required rate of return the investor will demand a nominal interest rate of 8.15%, a rate 5.15% higher than the real rate, to compensate for the expected 5% rate of inflation that will cause a loss of 4.76% in the value of his purchasing power.

Stated formally, this relation is known as the **Fisher relation** and can be written:

$$1 + r = (1 + \rho)(1 + E(i)) \tag{3.13}$$

where E is the expectations operator.

The international Fisher relation

Where more than one currency is involved, the Fisher relation can be generalized. Take the dollar and the pound, for example, and apply 3.13:

$$\frac{1 + r_{GBP}}{1 + r_{USD}} = \frac{[1 + \rho_{GBP}][1 + E(i_{GBP})]}{[1 + \rho_{USD}][1 + E(i_{USD})]} \tag{3.14}$$

---

[20] Irving Fisher, *The Theory of Interest* (New York: Macmillan, 1930).

This is called the international Fisher relation or the **Fisher open condition**, where "open" refers to an open economy. It gives the ratio of nominal investment values in terms of relative real rates of interest and expected rates of inflation. It should not be forgotten that this relation is not a market arbitrage condition like PPP and interest rate parity. It is a general equilibrium condition derived from first-order optimality conditions from individuals' utility optimization.

Arbitrage conditions can be applied, however, to generate other forms of the international Fisher relation. It is often argued that if expected real returns on identical assets were higher in one country than another, arbitrage would cause capital to flow from the country with the lower real return to the country with the higher real return. Assuming perfect markets, this arbitrage would continue until real returns became equal. In this case, Equation 3.14 would become:

$$\frac{1 + r_{GBP}}{1 + r_{USD}} = \frac{[1 + E(i_{GBP})]}{[1 + E(i_{USD})]} \tag{3.15}$$

The right-hand side of Equation 3.15 corresponds to the efficient markets formulation of PPP so that 3.15 could be written: [21]

$$\frac{E[S_t(GBP/USD)]}{S_0(GBP/USD)} = \frac{1 + r_{GBP}}{1 + r_{USD}}. \tag{3.16}$$

This form of the international Fisher relation explains the expected future spot rate in terms of relative nominal interest rates. Another common presentation of the international Fisher relation is derived by subtracting 1 from both sides of Equation 3.16:

$$\frac{E[S_t(GBP/USD)] - S_0(GBP/USD)}{S_0(GBP/USD)} = \frac{r_{GBP} - r_{USD}}{1 + r_{USD}} \tag{3.17}$$

which explains the expected percentage change in the exchange rate in terms of the relative interest rate differential. When r_{USD} is not too high, Equation 3.17 can also be approximated:

$$\frac{E[S_t(GBP/USD)] - S_0(GBP/USD)}{S_0(GBP/USD)} = r_{GBP} - r_{USD} \tag{3.18}$$

Empirical evidence

The historical evidence is consistent with the Fisher relation. It seems that most if not all the variation in nominal interest rates can be attributed to changing inflationary expectations. Most countries show a strong correlation between inflation and nominal interest rates. Whether or not real interest rates are stable and equal across countries is a more difficult proposition. E. Kane and L. Rosenthal studied the Eurocurrency market for six major currencies over the period 1974–79 and found support for this argument.[22]

F.S. Mishkin, on the other hand, found evidence that real interest rates are somewhat variable over time and differ across countries.[23] The problem, of course, is that verification

---

[21] Remember that the efficient markets form of PPP is expressed by writing Equation 3.7 in terms of expected values. See footnote 12.

[22] E. Kane and L. Rosenthal, "International interest rates and inflationary expectations", *Journal of International Money and Finance* (April 1982).

[23] F.S. Mishkin, "Are real interest rates equal across countries? An empirical investigation of international parity relations", *Journal of Finance* (December 1984).

requires a measure of expected inflation. Because expected inflation cannot be observed directly, the validity of the conclusions depends to a large extent on how well the estimated expected inflation approximates to the actual figure. In any case it is hard to believe that real interest rate differentials could last for very long in fully integrated international financial markets. Most economists agree that the increasingly integrated nature of today's financial markets and the vast supply of liquid capital that nourishes them are causing real interest rates to converge in most of the major economies.

Some caution is in order. The limit to this type of convergence depends on the risk characteristics of the different countries. A country with an economy that is inherently riskier than another will incite foreign investors to demand a higher real rate of return to compensate for the incremental risk. The incremental risk can derive from the economy's structural organization, its financial position, its political or social situation, etc. For example, an economy exporting only primary products, with a high level of foreign debt, is likely to represent a riskier investment environment than an economy with low foreign debt exporting a diversified variety of manufactured products, raw materials and agricultural goods. E. Clark has shown that there are wide discrepancies in risk levels even between the major industrialized countries.[24] We will come back to the question of cross-border investment risk in Part IV of this book.

The relation between the exchange rate and nominal interest rate differentials (Equations 3.16, 3.17 and 3.18) also seems to have some weak support. The first observable fact is that currencies with high rates of inflation and high nominal interest rates have a tendency to depreciate. In Mexico, for example, between 1982 and 1988 the Treasury bill rate averaged in excess of 67% and, over the same period, the peso exchange rate went from MXN 96.5 per US dollar to MXN 2281, for a loss of value of over 95%. The same phenomenon can be observed in other high inflation countries like Argentina, Brazil, Israel, etc. In an interesting empirical study, however, R. Cumby and M. Obstfeld reject a predictable relationship between the nominal interest rate differential and the exchange rate.[25] On the other hand, other empirical studies indicate that interest differentials correctly anticipate exchange rate changes, which implies that currencies with relatively high nominal rates can be expected to depreciate vis-à-vis currencies with relatively low nominal rates.[26]

Here again some caution is in order. Nominal interest rates are composed of the real interest rate and expected inflation. If expected inflation is the cause of the nominal interest rate differential, the exchange rate can effectively be expected to depreciate. However, if the nominal interest rate differential is caused by a change in the real interest rate, the opposite will occur. Suppose, for example, that the differential widens because the real interest rate increases relative to other countries. The exchange rate will then appreciate as investors buy the currency in order to take advantage of the higher real interest rate. The Dornbusch theory of overshooting that we mentioned earlier also relies on the mechanism of temporary shifts in the real interest rate to explain seemingly excessive fluctuations in the exchange rate.

In summary, then, there does not seem to be conclusive evidence for a stable, predictable relationship between changes in the nominal interest rate differential and movements in the exchange rate.

[24] E. Clark, *Cross-Border Investment Risk: Applications of Modern Portfolio Theory* (Euromoney Publications, 1991).

[25] R. Cumby and M. Obstfeld, "A note on exchange rate expectations and nominal interest differentials: A test of the Fisher hypothesis", *Journal of Finance* (1981), p.p. 697–703.

[26] See, for example, R.A. Aliber and C.P. Stickney, "Accounting measures of foreign exchange exposure: The long and the short of it", *The Accounting Review* (January 1975), p.p. 44–57; I.H. Giddy and G. Dufey, "The random behaviour of flexible exchange rates", *Journal of International Business Studies* (Spring 1975), p.p. 1–32.

Forward rate parity

Foreign exchange expectations

The **forward rate parity hypothesis** states that the forward exchange rate quoted at time 0 for delivery at time t is equal to what the spot rate is expected to be at time t. This hypothesis is based on the important role that expectations play in financial decision making and the close link between the forward and spot rates through interest rate parity. It is usually written:

$$F_{0,t}(\cdot) = E[S_t(\cdot)] \tag{3.19}$$

This relation can also be stated in terms of a forward discount or premium relative to the current spot rate. Subtracting S_0, the current spot rate which is known with certainty, from both sides of the equation and dividing by S_0, gives:

$$\frac{F_{0,t}(\cdot) - S_0(\cdot)}{S_0(\cdot)} = \frac{E[S_t(\cdot)] - S_0(\cdot)}{S_0(\cdot)} \tag{3.20}$$

where the left-hand side of the equation is the forward discount or premium.

If the future spot rate were known with certainty this relation would have to hold. Otherwise there would be an opportunity for riskless arbitrage. Suppose the forward rate on the Danish kroner is DKK 5.25 = USD 1 and the expected future spot rate, which is known with certainty, is DKK 5.00 = USD 1. Arbitragers would sell dollars at the forward rate, wait until the forward contract matures, receive DKK 5.25 for each dollar, and immediately sell the kroner for dollars on the spot market, paying only DKK 5.00 per dollar for a profit of DKK 0.25 per dollar. The transaction is riskless and requires no investment on the forward contract. Such a sweet deal could not last for long because everybody would do it until buying pressure pushed the forward rate to DKK 5.00/USD 1, the level of the expected future spot rate.

All this depends on the certainty assumption concerning the future spot rate. It is a well known fact, of course, that the future spot rate is not known with certainty. It is often argued, however, that forward parity will still hold in the presence of uncertainty because the forward rate is an unbiased predictor of the future spot rate. Others argue that the forward rate is a biased predictor of the future spot rate because risk-averse investors will demand a risk premium for bearing foreign exchange risk and therefore Equation 3.19 will not hold.[27]

Suppose, for example, that the expected future spot rate in the preceding case was not known with certainty. Then risk-averse economic agents with a large exposure in Danish krone might be willing to pay the DKK 0.25 difference between the forward rate and the expected future spot rate as protection against the rate going even higher than DKK 5.25/USD 1.

A risk premium of this type is a common feature of modern portfolio investment theory. In modern portfolio theory, however, only risk that cannot be eliminated through diversification is rewarded with a premium. A major argument against the existence of a risk premium in the forward exchange market is that currency risk can be diversified away. If this is true, a risk premium on the foreign exchange market is unnecessary and

[27] See, for example, B. Solnik, "An equilibrium model of the international capital market", *Journal of Economic Theory* (August 1974); R. Roll and B. Solnik, "A pure foreign exchange asset pricing model", *Journal of International Economics* (May 1977); M. Adler and B. Dumas, "International portfolio choice and corporation finance: A synthesis", *Journal of Finance* (June 1983).

the forward exchange rate will indeed be an unbiased predictor of the expected future spot exchange rate.

Another problem with forward rate parity stems from a technical problem called "Siegel's Paradox" which states that if

$$F_{0,t}(\cdot) = E[S_t(\cdot)]$$

is true for one currency, it cannot be true for the other currency[28]

$$\frac{1}{F_{0,t}(\cdot)} < E\left[\frac{1}{S_t(\cdot)}\right].$$

An example will make this clear. Suppose that the number of euros to the dollar (EUR/USD) one year in the future has a 50% chance of being 1.15 and a 50% chance of being 0.85. In this case, $E[S_1] = 1$. If forward rate parity holds, $F_{0,1} = 1$ as well. However, if we take the rate as the number of dollars for euros (USD/EUR), we get

$$\frac{1}{F_{0,t}(\text{EUR/USD})} = 1$$

and

$$E\left[\frac{1}{S_t(\text{EUR/USD})}\right] = 0.5 \times \frac{1}{1.15} + 0.5 \times \frac{1}{0.85} = 1.023,$$

a considerable difference of 2.3% between the two. Although Siegel's paradox is often dismissed as being insignificant in the short run, we can see from this example that in the longer run this is not true[29] and, even in the short term, forward rate parity is nothing more than an approximation. Ultimately, the forward rate parity hypothesis boils down to an empirical issue rather than a theoretical one.

Empirical evidence

The literature on the relation between forward and future spot rates is extensive. First of all, it seems that since the inception of floating exchange rates in 1973 the forward exchange rate has had a very inefficient predictive performance. One study comparing the US dollar to the British pound, the Japanese yen and the German mark from April 1975 to June 1985 found that losses from a forward transaction averaged 5% per year and that from early 1980 to February 1985 annual losses averaged 15%. Furthermore, regressions linking the one-month percentage change in the spot dollar price of these foreign currencies to the corresponding one-month forward premium from the previous month had less than 3% explanatory power (R^2) and tended on average to mispredict the direction in which the dollar exchange rate would move during the subsequent month.[30]

---

[28] This is an application of what is known as "Jensen's inequality" which states that the expected value of a convex function is greater than the function of the expected value of its argument. For a proof see H. Tucker, *A Graduate Course in Probability* (New York: Academic Press, 1967), p. 217.

[29] Siegel's paradox also has important implications for international hedging. See F. Black and R. Litterman, "Global portfolio optimization", *Financial Analysts Journal, 48(5)*, (1992), p.p. 28–43.

[30] G. Kaminsky and R. Peruga, "Can a time varying risk premium explain excess returns in the forward market for foreign exchange?", *Journal of International Economics* (1990).

Other tests have been performed to determine whether the forward exchange rate is an unbiased and efficient predictor of the future spot rate. One approach has been to calculate the average error of the difference between $F_{0,1}(\cdot)$ and $S_1(\cdot)$.[31] According to these results, the mean forecast error is not statistically different from zero, thereby suggesting a zero risk premium. However, when the sample is divided in half so that the risk premium could take two values over the whole observation period, evidence of a non-zero risk premium is present.

Another approach has been to search for serial correlation in the prediction error. There is evidence that the exchange rate forecast errors are serially correlated, which implies that there is a risk premium that fluctuates between positive and negative values.[32]

Other researchers use survey data polled from exchange specialists who are asked to provide short-term forecasts for the major currencies. These studies tend to conclude that market participants are irrational, the markets are inefficient or that the specialists' forecasts are erroneous.[33]

The upshot of most studies that seem to confirm the presence of a risk premium is that the risk premium, if it exists, seems to change signs. Sometimes it is positive, sometimes it is negative and it usually averages close to zero. Many studies fail to find evidence for the existence of any risk premium at all. Therefore, in the absence of a more precise econometric model, it seems perfectly acceptable to adopt the forward parity hypothesis and treat the forward rate as an unbiased estimator of the future spot rate.

Forecasting exchange rates

International parity relations linkages

The international parity relations are an elegant set of simple equilibrium relationships between the prices of goods and services, interest rates, and the spot and forward exchange rates. Although they are highly stylized and depend on some demonstrably unrealistic assumptions, they constitute a powerful theoretical framework for understanding and explaining the international financial environment and the underlying forces that determine exchange rates and why they vary. For this reason they form the basis for much of the economic analysis involved in exchange rate forecasting. Understanding and interpreting the relationships among them are an important part of the exercise.

[31] A.C. Stockman, "Risk, information and forward exchange rates", in J.A. Frenkel and H.G. Johnson (Eds.), *The Economics of Exchange Rates* (Reading, MA,: Addison-Wesley, 1978); J.A. Frenkel, "Test of rational expectations in the forward exchange market", *Southern Journal of Economics* (1980), p.p. 1083–1101.

[32] J. Geweke and E. Feige, "Some joint tests of the efficiency of markets for forward exchange", *Review of Economics and Statistics* (1979), p.p. 334–341; R. Cumby and M. Obstfeld, "A note on exchange rate expectations and nominal interest differentials: A test of the Fisher hypothesis", *Journal of Finance* (1981), p.p. 697–704; L.P. Hansen and R.J Hodrick, "Risk-averse speculation in the forward exchange market: An econometric analysis of linear models", in J.A. Frenkel (Ed.), *Exchange Rates and International Macroeconomics* (Chicago: University of Chicago Press, 1983).

[33] See J.A. Frankel and K. Froot, "Using survey data to test standard propositions regarding exchange rate expectations", *American Economic Review, 77* (March 1987); S. Tagaki, "Exchange rate expectations: A survey of surveys studies", IMF *Staff Papers* (June 1991); P.C. Liu and G.S. Maddala, "Rationality of survey data and tests of market efficiency in the foreign exchange market", *Journal of International Money and Finance, 11* (August 1992); S. Cavaglia, W.F.C. Verschoor and C.P. Wolff, "Further evidence on exchange rate expectations", *Journal of International Money and Finance, 12* (February 1993).

In Table 3.2 we have reproduced the four international parity relations, for clarity presenting them in the form of their first-order approximations. Because the efficient markets form of PPP is more consistent with financial theory and the empirical evidence, PPP is presented in this way in Equation 3.7′.

A comparison of the equations shows some interesting relationships. For example, combining the equations for interest rate parity (3.12) and the international Fisher relation (3.18) yields the forward rate parity relation (3.20). Combining forward rate parity (3.20), purchasing power parity (3.7′) and interest rate parity (3.12) yields:

$$r_{GBP} - r_{USD} = E(i_{GBP}) - E(i_{USD})$$

which is the first-order linear approximation of Equation 3.15, another form of the international Fisher relation. Combining the international Fisher relation (3.18) with forward rate parity (3.20) yields interest rate parity (3.12). The relation between the forward rate and expected rates of inflation can be found by combining forward rate parity and purchasing power parity. Figure 3.2 summarizes the relationships among the variables. The lines connecting the boxes in the north, south, east and west represent the equations linking the variables in each box. The whole figure is divided into halves in two different ways, each way forming two triangles. The northern triangle, for example, is formed by the lines linking boxes $[E(i_{GBP}) - E(i_{USD})]$, $[r_{GBP} - r_{USD}]$ and $\dfrac{E[S_t\,(GBP/USD)] - S_0\,(GBP/USD)}{S_0\,(GBP/USD)}$. The equation on any line can be generated by combining the equations of the other two lines in the triangle.

Forecasting techniques

The simplest technique for forecasting exchange rate movements is to trust the market and use the forward rate as a forecast of the future spot rate. We have seen that the forward rate is just as likely to overestimate as it is to underestimate the future spot rate and, consequently, is an unbiased estimator of the future spot rate. However, we have also seen that it explains only a very small percentage of actual exchange rate movements. Furthermore, the percentage that it does explain tends to diminish as the forecasting period is lengthened. Nevertheless, currencies selling at a forward discount do tend to depreciate while those selling at a premium tend to appreciate.

Since widespread forward rates only exist on maturities for up to a year, longer-term forward rates have to be deduced from the interest rate differential. This can be done by

Table 3.2 The international parity relations

$$\frac{E[S_t(GBP/USD)] - S_0(GBP/USD)}{S_0(GBP/USD)} = E(i_{GBP}) - E(i_{USD}) = \text{Efficient markets form of PPP} \qquad (3.7')$$

$$\frac{F_{0,t}(GBP/USD) - S_0(GBP/USD)}{S_0(GBP/USD)} = r_{GBP} - r_{USD} = \text{Interest rate parity} \qquad (3.12)$$

$$\frac{E[S_t(GBP/USD)] - S_0(GBP/USD)}{S_0(GBP/USD)} = r_{GBP} - r_{USD} = \text{International Fisher relation} \qquad (3.18)$$

$$\frac{F_{0,t}(\cdot) - S_0(\cdot)}{S_0(\cdot)} = \frac{E[S_t(\cdot)] - S_0(\cdot)}{S_0(\cdot)} = \text{Forward rate parity} \qquad (3.20)$$

Figure 3.2 International parity relations: First-order linear approximations

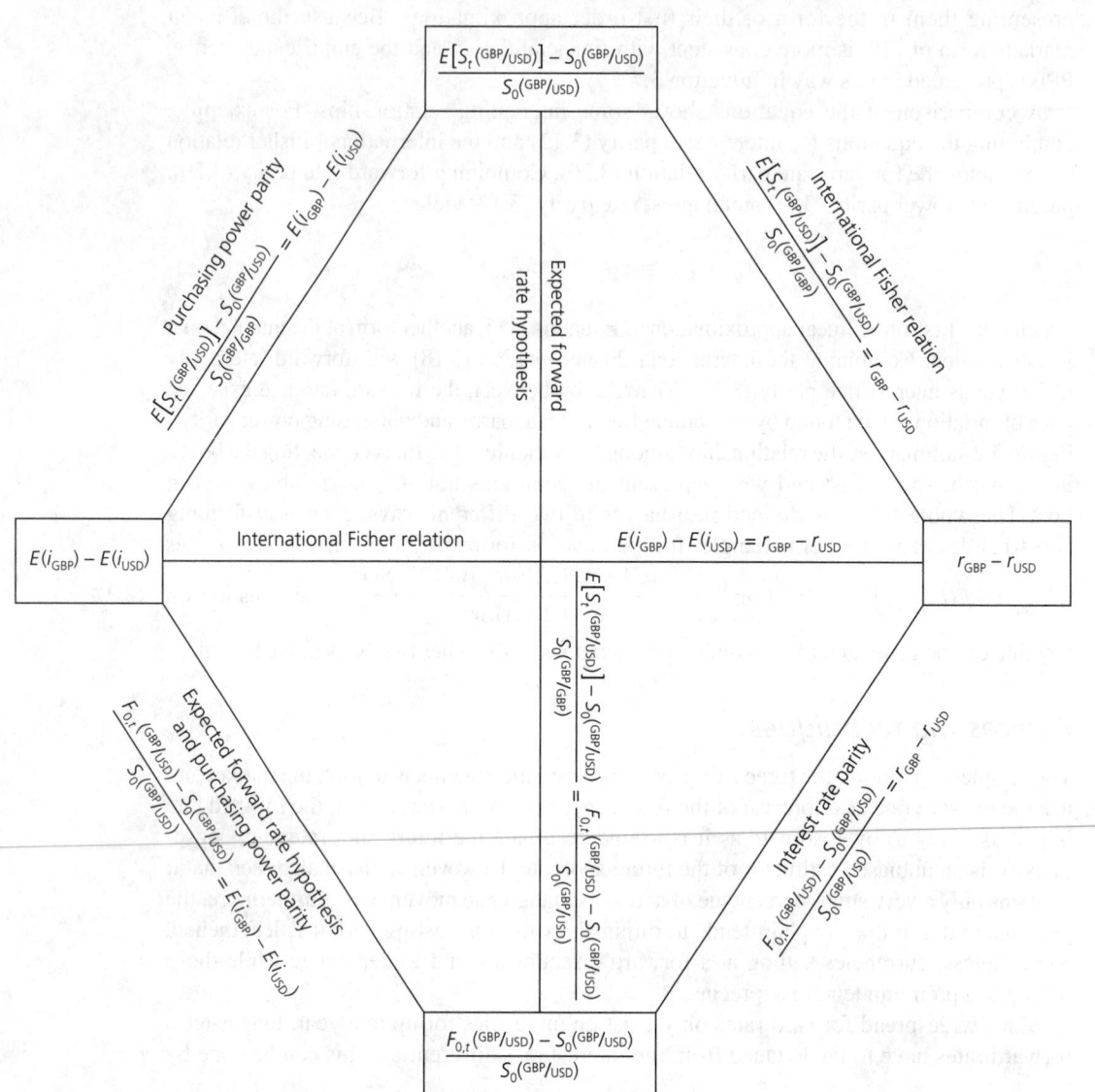

extending the single period interest rate parity relation presented in Equation 3.10 to include several periods. Let $r_{GBP,n}$ and $r_{USD,n}$ be the annual interest rate on a zero coupon loan lasting n years. Because of compounding over n periods, at the end of n years the loans will be worth $(1 + r_{GBP,n})^n$ and $(1 + r_{USD,n})^n$ respectively. The same arbitrage argument holds in the multi-period case as in the single-period case. It should not be possible for an investor to make a profit by borrowing in one currency, selling the currency spot for another currency, lending the second currency and buying the first currency back in a forward transaction. Thus, the multi-period forward rate implied by interest rate parity can be written:

$$\frac{F_{0,n}(GBP/USD)}{S_0(GBP/USD)} = \frac{(1 + r_{GBP,n})^n}{(1 + r_{USD,n})^n} \tag{3.21}$$

Suppose the USD/GBP spot rate is USD 2 = GBP 1, $n = 5$ years, $r_{USD,5} = 10\%$ and $r_{GBP,5} = 15\%$, then applying this information in Equation 3.21, gives:

$$\frac{F_{0,5}(GBP/USD)}{S_0(GBP/USD)} = \frac{(1.10)^5}{(1.15)^5}$$

$$F_{0,5}(USD/GBP) = USD\ 2 \times \frac{(1.6105)}{(2.0114)} = USD\ 1.6014$$

The five-year forward exchange rate implied by the interest rate differential is USD 1.6014 for GBP 1.

Although the forward rate seems to indicate trends in exchange rates, it's short-term inaccuracy makes it a poor predictor of future spot rates. **Fundamental analysis** is an alternative approach to the market-based forward rate for exchange rate forecasting. Fundamental analysis involves examining the macroeconomic variables and policies that are likely to influence a currency's performance. The relevant variables are numerous and the functional relationships among them are complex so that one of the problems facing the forecaster is to develop a model complex enough to mirror reality but simple enough that it can be understood. The basic variables relevant to fundamental analysis are those found in the international parity relations: spot and forward exchange rates, relative interest rates and rates of inflation. Interpreting these variables depends on the analyst's model of exchange rate determination.

The literature on exchange rate determination is vast but the theories currently being used can generally be broken down into two categories: a balance of payments flow adjustment model and an asset market stock adjustment model.

Balance of payments flow adjustment model

The balance of payments flow adjustment model focuses on macroeconomic flows and their impact on the balance of payments. Through macroeconomic analysis the forecaster attempts to determine the imbalances that will occur in the various sub-accounts in the balance of payments identity in order to estimate the overall supply and demand for foreign currency as well as the exchange rate where supply just equals demand.

In Chapter 2 the elasticities-absorption approach to balance of payments theory outlined the relationships between macroeconomic flows, interest rates and prices. The relationships are complex and depend on such things as supply and demand elasticities, marginal rates of saving and investment, interest rate differentials and the economy's structural organization. Using these tools for exchange rate forecasting involves determining the relevant relationships and then estimating the direction and magnitude of their effects on the supply and demand for foreign currency.

Asset market stock adjustment model

The asset market stock adjustment model rejects the view that the exchange rate is determined in flow markets. As we saw above, the asset market approach considers exchange rates as asset prices traded in an efficient market. Like other asset prices, today's price depends on expectations about the future. When expectations change, investors rebalance their portfolios, which causes a change in the prices of the stock of outstanding assets. Thus, a change in the exchange rate represents a change in the value of an economy's stock of assets. Using the asset market stock adjustment model to forecast exchange rates involves macroeconomic analysis aimed at estimating the values of variables that are likely to influence asset prices, such as profits, real interest rates and rates of inflation.

Purchasing power parity

The monetary approach to balance of payments theory concentrates on one type of asset – money – in exchange rate determination. It assumes that all the other asset markets clear and that monetary phenomena are the only source of price disturbances.[34] Combined with the efficient markets form of purchasing power parity, the monetary approach to exchange rate determination supplies the forecaster with a policy variable – domestic credit – that can be used to predict exchange rates by estimating the future rate of inflation.

This use of the efficient markets form of PPP contrasts with the traditional form of PPP forecasting that assumes that a lag exists between price level changes and exchange rate changes. If, for example, it takes three months for an increase in prices to work its way through to the exchange rate, PPP will be useful in predicting the future exchange rate. It should be remembered, however, that there is an inherent conflict between the efficient markets concept and the predictive power of any lagged variable.

Forecasting models

Forecasting models can be subjective, econometric or a combination of the two. The goal of some models is to discover divergence between actual market rates and a set of theoretical exchange rates derived from fundamental analysis on the assumption that the divergence will be quickly corrected by market forces. Other models in the efficient markets tradition assume that currencies are correctly priced and attempt to forecast the variables that are likely to affect their values in the future.

Different approaches to exchange rate determination can lead to different conclusions about a currency's future value. The balance of payments flow adjustment approach, for example, often concludes that economic growth will cause a balance of trade deficit by increasing imports and decreasing exports and will therefore lead to currency depreciation. On the other hand, the asset market approach often concludes that economic growth will lead to currency appreciation caused by foreign capital inflows attracted by expected higher returns.[35] The issues involved were discussed in Chapter 2 where we presented the major cause–effect relationships linking economic activity, monetary policy, balance of payments discipline and exchange rate determination. The relationships are complex, often differing in magnitude and direction and with varying time lags. The outcome depends on a process of stock adjustments to economic and financial flows as well as flow adjustments to changes in economic and financial stocks. An example of a change in a financial flow could be an increase in GDP. One of the stock adjustments that this might cause could be a reduction in money holdings in favor of increased equity holdings. The effects on the balance of payments of an increase in GDP might be a decrease in exports and an increase in imports, thereby putting downward pressure on the exchange rate. On the other hand, the rise in equity prices that the stock adjustment implies might attract foreign capital, thereby putting upward pressure on the exchange rate.

Most models of fundamental analysis incorporate one or both sides of this adjustment process. Understanding these relationships and using them to forecast exchange rates is a difficult proposition. Subjective fundamental analysis risks lacking objectivity and often

---

[34] John Hicks has shown that even in conditions of monetary equilibrium and full employment, real economic phenomena can cause price disturbances. See John Hicks, *Capital and Time: A Neo-Austrian Theory* (Oxford: Clarendon Press, 1987).

[35] Care must be taken when associating financial qualities with economic growth. A study by R. Barro and X. Sala i Martin (*World Real Interest Rates*, NBER Working Paper 3317), for example, found that economic growth tends to lower the real interest rate by increasing saving while expected increases in profitability increase the demand for capital and raise the real rate of interest.

suffers from the limits on the complexity it can attain. Econometric models, even when they are theoretically sound, suffer from the fact that their accuracy depends on forecasts of key exogenous variables such as the central bank's monetary policy or the government's fiscal policy. These exogenous variables are no easier to forecast than the model's endogenous variables. Furthermore, structural relationships can and do change over time, thereby making it necessary to re-estimate the model. However, since models are estimated with historical data, it might take a while before the new structural relationships become statistically significant enough to appear in the coefficients.

Technical analysis

Another popular method of exchange rate forecasting is based on **technical analysis,** so named because it makes no use of the economic and financial fundamentals deemed relevant to exchange rate determination. It focuses on prices and seeks to detect repetitions of past price patterns. The two primary methods for detecting these patterns are **chartism** and **trend analysis**. Chartism relies on the study of charts to find recurring price patterns. Trend analysis uses mathematical calculations or computer-based models such as moving averages, filters, or momentum to identify turning points or trends. If it is effective at all, technical analysis is only useful for very short-term forecasting (from several days to several weeks). This is because it is designed to detect trends, which, due to the competitive nature of the markets, tend to disappear rapidly.

The effectiveness of foreign exchange forecasting

Foreign exchange forecasting services are many and varied, covering market models, subjective and econometric models based on fundamental analysis, as well as numerous methodologies based on chartism and trend analysis.[36] Just how effective any of these services are at forecasting future spot rates is very doubtful. First of all, reliable statistics are hard to come by. Secondly, it is not clear how the performance of these forecasts can be judged. Should the forecasting model be compared in magnitude to the forward rate, should it be judged on the percentage of the number of times that the forecast rate is on the correct side of the forward rate, or should some type of rate of return on an investment strategy based on the forecast be calculated? Euromoney magazine began running an annual survey on the performance of foreign exchange forecasting in August 1978.[37] It shows that over the years the performance of the advisory services has been irregular. In 1983, for example, no single service was able to beat the Treasury bill rate and their percentage of correct signals was only 44.9%.[38] In other years some services had outstanding results while others were big losers. No services had consistently outstanding results over all years. *Euromoney* concluded that it is difficult to judge whether or not on the whole the advisory services bring any value added to the problem of exchange rate determination because all the services do not participate in the survey each year, most have changed forecasting methods over the years and the figures used in the survey were provided by the forecasters themselves, very few of which were audited.[39]

---

[36] The types of foreign exchange forecasting services available range from fundamental subjective analysis to econometric models to technical analysis. See "An A to Z guide of the services", *Euromoney* (August 1987), p.p. 127–130.

[37] Because of difficulties in determining a common set of evaluation criteria, the rating was suspended in 1986, restarted in 1987 in a less rigorous format and abandoned again on a pessimistic note in 1988.

[38] *Euromoney* (August 1984).

[39] See *Euromoney* (August 1986), p.p. 198–201; (August 1987), p.p. 121–124; (August 1988), p.p. 99–104.

Summary

1. Purchasing power parity is based on the law of one price. It states that the exchange rate between one currency and another is in equilibrium when the domestic purchasing powers of each currency are equivalent at that rate. The empirical evidence suggests that although short-term deviations from PPP are frequent, there is a strong tendency for it to hold in the long run.

2. Interest rate parity states that on free money markets the forward discount or premium on the foreign exchange market is equal to the relative difference between the interest rates on the two currencies. The empirical evidence shows that there is a strong tendency for interest rate parity to hold and that on the Eurocurrency markets it is equivalent to a technical fact.

3. The Fisher relation states that the nominal interest rate is composed of expected inflation and the real interest rate. Contrary to PPP and interest rate parity, it is not an arbitrage condition. It is an equilibrium condition derived from first-order optimality conditions of individuals' utility maximization. Assuming that real interest rates are stable and equal across countries, the international Fisher relation suggests that exchange rates move because of the relative expected inflation differential reflected in the nominal interest rates. The empirical evidence supports the relationship between the nominal interest rate, the real interest rate and expected inflation but there is no strong evidence to support the hypothesis that real interest rates are stable and equal across countries.

4. The forward rate parity hypothesis states that the forward exchange rate quoted at time 0 for delivery at time t is equal to the spot rate that is expected at time t. Based on the available evidence, it seems perfectly acceptable to adopt the forward parity hypothesis and treat the forward rate as an unbiased estimator of the future spot rate.

5. The international parity relations form the basis for most fundamental analysis associated with exchange rate forecasting.

6. The theories currently being used in fundamental analysis can generally be broken down into two categories: a balance of payments flow adjustment model and an asset market stock adjustment model. The forecasting models used to apply these theories can be subjective, econometric or a combination of the two. The goal of some models is to discover divergence between actual market rates and a set of theoretical exchange rates derived from fundamental analysis on the assumption that the divergence will be quickly corrected by market forces. Other models in the efficient markets tradition assume that currencies are correctly priced and attempt to forecast the variables that are likely to affect their values in the future.

Questions

Solutions to the following questions are set out on the web site, details of which are included in the Preface.

1. Given the following information, what would you do and why?

   $S(\text{CHF/GBP}) = 4.0000$

   Price of gold in London = GBP 100 per ounce

   Price of gold in Switzerland = CHF 500 per ounce.

2. Explain the relationship between the law of one price and PPP.

3. Given PPP and the following information, what should the exchange rate be at the end of the year?

$S_0(\text{CHF/GBP}) = 4.0000$

Rate of inflation in the Switzerland = 2% per year

Rate of inflation in the United Kingdom = 10% per year.

4. What are some of the reasons for short-term divergence from PPP?

5. Given the following information, what would you do and why?

$S_0(\text{CHF/GBP}) = 4.0000$

$F_1(\text{CHF/GBP}) = 4.1000$

One-year interest rate on Swiss francs = 10%

One-year interest rate on sterling = 5%.

6. Explain the international Fisher relation.

7. True or false: The forward rate parity hypothesis denies the existence of a risk premium for foreign exchange risk based on the argument that currency risk can be diversified away.

8. What is the difference between fundamental analysis and technical analysis?

Appendix 3.1: A mathematical model of the portfolio balance approach to the balance of payments

Let

W	=	country's wealth
B	=	demand for domestic bonds
SB^*	=	demand for foreign bonds in domestic currency
S	=	the exchange rate (number of units of domestic currency for one unit of foreign currency
MO_{1d}	=	the demand for money
r	=	domestic interest rate
r^*	=	foreign interest rate
$h, i,$ and j	=	the percent of wealth held in each type of asset with $h + i + j = 1$.

The model can be summarized in four equations:

$$MO_{1d} = h(r,r^*)W \qquad\qquad (A3.1.1)$$

$$B = i(r,r^*)W \qquad\qquad (A3.1.2)$$

$$SB^* = j(r,r^*)W \qquad\qquad (A3.1.3)$$

$$W = MO_{1d} + B + SB^* \qquad\qquad (A3.1.4)$$

The first three equations postulate that the proportions of wealth held as money, domestic bonds and foreign bonds are functions of the domestic and the foreign interest rates. MO is inversely related to both the domestic and foreign interest rates. B is directly related to the domestic interest rate and inversely to the foreign interest rate. SB^* is directly related to the foreign interest rate and inversely to the domestic interest rate.

According to the portfolio balance approach, equilibrium occurs when the quantity demanded of each financial asset equals the quantity supplied. Assuming that each financial market is in equilibrium, we can solve for SB^*:

$$SB^* = W - M_{1d} - B = W - i(r,r^*)W - h(r,r^*)W$$

$$SB^* = W[1 - i(r,r^*) - h(r,r^*)] \qquad (A3.1.5)$$

and

$$S = \frac{W}{B^*}[1 - i(r,r^*) - h(r,r^*)] \qquad (A3.1.6)$$

From Equation A3.1.6 we can postulate that the exchange rate is directly related to W and r^* and inversely related to B^* and r. An increase in wealth resulting from an increase in savings increases the demand for all three financial assets. As the country exchanges domestic currency for foreign currency to purchase the foreign bonds, the domestic currency will depreciate. The same goes for a rise in the foreign interest rate. As the country exchanges domestic currency for foreign currency to purchase the foreign bonds, the domestic currency will depreciate. On the other hand, an increase in the supply of the foreign bond will lower its price and reduce the wealth of domestic residents, which causes them to reduce their holdings of all financial assets. As they sell the foreign bonds and exchange foreign currency for domestic currency, the value of the domestic currency appreciates. The same thing happens if the domestic interest rate rises.

ORGANIZATION OF THE
INTERNATIONAL FINANCIAL SYSTEM

The international monetary system

4

The international monetary system is the framework within which countries borrow, lend, buy, sell and make payments across political frontiers. The framework determines how balance of payments disequilibrium is resolved and the consequences that the adjustment process will have on the countries involved. Numerous frameworks are possible and most have been tried in one form or another. Today's system is a combination of several different frameworks.

In this chapter we look at some of the major frameworks, understand how they operate and point out their principal strengths and weaknesses. We also discuss what frameworks have been tried in the past and how they succeeded or why they failed. Finally, we outline the major characteristics of today's ongoing framework.

Alternative exchange rate systems

Given the importance of exchange rates in determining international flows of goods and capital and levels of economic well-being, the framework providing for adjustments of balance of payments disequilibrium is a centerpiece of the international financial system. Many frameworks have been tried, ranging from the original gold standard to the hybrid gold exchange standard to today's system of flexible exchange rates. All have their advantages and disadvantages, which we are going to look at in this section. In so doing it is important to keep in mind that the economic and accounting principles established in Chapters 1, 2 and 3 remain valid no matter what exchange rate system is in place. What changes with the system is the way that these principles manifest themselves in the economic variables such as output, consumption, prices and interest rates.

Fixed exchange rates systems

Under **fixed exchange rate** systems governments are committed to maintaining a target exchange rate. The gold standard and the gold exchange standard are the two fixed rate systems that have been adopted in the recent past.

The gold standard

Under the **gold standard** each country pegs its money to gold. For example, if the Swiss central bank fixes the price of gold at CHF 100 per ounce, it effectively stands ready to buy and sell gold at this rate. The same goes for the United States if the US Federal Reserve (the Fed) fixes the price of gold at USD 20 per ounce. The exchange rate, then, is simply the ratio of the two prices: CHF 100 / USD 20 means an exchange rate of CHF 5 for USD 1, or USD 20 / CHF 100 for an exchange rate of USD 0.20 for CHF 1. If it were different, arbitrage opportunities would exist.

If, for example, the exchange rate were CHF 4 for USD 1, an arbitrager could pay CHF 80 for USD 20, buy an ounce of gold in the United States, and sell the gold in Switzerland for CHF 100 for a profit of CHF 20. Everyone would be buying dollars but no one would be selling dollars. The excess demand for dollars would make the exchange rate increase to CHF 5 for USD 1, the point at which the arbitrage opportunity disappears.

Under the gold standard, external disequilibrium is corrected through a process known as **price specie flow**. Price specie flow means that balance of payments disequilibrium will be adjusted through adjustments in the country's money supply. Suppose, for example, that the United Kingdom has a deficit in its balance of payments accounts up to but not including the central bank's reserve account. In the terminology of Chapter 1, this involves taking the current account balance plus the capital account balance without the account "change in reserves". In other words, the line for determining the balance is drawn after the account "net errors and omissions". Remember that the overall balance of payments must equal zero. From Chapter 2 we know that a balance of payments deficit reflects an excess supply of domestic currency or, what amounts to the same thing, an excess demand for foreign currency. In the case of the gold standard this means an excess demand for gold. Because the overall balance of payments must equal zero, the UK central bank makes up the difference by selling gold from its reserves. In Chapter 2 we saw that a reduction in central bank foreign assets has the effect of reducing the money supply. Thus, when the central bank sells gold it reduces the excess supply of money that was causing the balance of payments deficit.

The adjustment process to a reduction in the money supply proceeds as outlined in Chapter 2. The decrease in the money supply implies a reduction in credit to the economy, reduces demand and causes prices to fall. Lower prices make British goods relatively cheaper and foreign goods relatively more expensive. Domestic demand for imports and exportables falls and foreign demand for British exports increases, thereby improving the trade balance. The reduction in credit to the economy also reduces investment and causes a reduction in overall income and expenditure. The ultimate magnitude of the reduction depends on the investment income multiplier. Since some of the reduction in expenditure will fall on imports and exportables, the trade balance should improve further. The ultimate outcome of all this depends on the economy's production possibility curve, its demand function for real cash balances (money), the marginal propensity to save and the marginal propensity to import. In any case, the adjustment process will affect income distribution, the level and composition of output, resource allocation and the price level.

For a country with a balance of payments surplus, the reverse process occurs. A surplus reflects an excess demand for domestic currency. When the central bank buys gold, it simultaneously increases the money supply, thereby satisfying the excess demand that was causing the balance of payments surplus. An increase in the money supply implies an increase in credit to the economy, increases demand and raises prices. Higher prices make British goods relatively more expensive and foreign goods relatively cheaper. Domestic demand for imports and exportables rises and foreign demand for British exports falls, thereby worsening the trade balance. The increase in credit to the economy also increases investment and, through the investment income multiplier, causes an increase in overall income and expenditure. The ultimate magnitude of the increase depends on the investment income multiplier. Since some of the incremental expenditure will be on imports and exportables, the trade balance should improve further. As before, the ultimate outcome of all this depends on the economy's production possibility curve, its demand function for money, the marginal propensity to save and the marginal propensity to import. The adjustment process will affect income distribution, the level and composition of output, resource allocation and the price level.

Thus, the gold standard is based on the principle that the domestic money supply is determined by the government's supply of gold. Governments must acquire more gold before they can issue more money. In this way the world money supply and for that matter, price level, are effectively determined by the supply of gold.

By linking the world money supply directly to the supply of gold, the gold standard has the advantage of limiting the scope of politicians for financial mismanagement through unrestrained money creation. It also reduces most of the uncertainty surrounding the exchange rate. Nevertheless, adjustment through price specie flow has all the painful side effects on income distribution, the level and composition of output, resource allocation and the price level that were discussed in Chapter 2. Furthermore, it makes international liquidity dependent on the production of gold, since gold is the basic medium of exchange in international transactions. This means that the supply of international liquidity is inelastic and unable to expand to meet the needs of expanding volumes of output and cross-border trade.

The gold exchange standard

The depression of 1929–33 eventually ended the gold standard. It was replaced by the **gold exchange standard** in the Bretton Woods agreement of 1944. The gold exchange standard involved the United States pegging the US dollar to gold and other countries pegging their currencies to the dollar. Under this agreement the price of gold was fixed at USD 35 per ounce and the United States promised to exchange dollars for gold at this price. Other countries promised to exchange their currencies for dollars at an official, fixed exchange rate. The countries that pegged their exchange rates to the dollar were obliged to keep the market rate within 1% of the official parity rate. Maintaining the market rate within plus or minus 1% of official parity required the central banks to intervene in the foreign exchange markets by buying and selling domestic currency for dollars whenever market forces started to push the rate outside the permitted range.

Suppose that the official parity rate for the Swiss franc is CHF 5 for USD 1. The permitted range would be between CHF 5.05 and CHF 4.95. If the market tends to push the rate higher than CHF 5.05, this signals an excess supply of francs and the central bank has to buy francs with its dollar reserves. If the market tends to push the rate lower than CHF 4.95, this signals an excess demand for francs and the central bank has to sell francs and buy dollars.

The adjustment process to balance of payments disequilibrium under the gold exchange standard is similar to the process under the gold standard. Central bank intervention to keep the dollar below CHF 5.05 involves reducing official reserves and the money supply. Central bank intervention to keep the dollar above CHF 4.95 involves increasing official reserves and the money supply. The increase or decrease in the money supply triggers the adjustment process outlined above.

By maintaining a fixed rate system, the gold exchange standard kept the advantage of limiting the scope of non-US politicians for financial mismanagement. It also freed the world money supply from the gold standard straightjacket of the supply of gold. Unfortunately, it increased the scope for financial mismanagement on the part of US monetary authorities, even though they are supposed to be independent of the politicians, and made the world money supply dependent on US economic policy. Although the adjustment process is essentially the same as under the gold standard, the gold exchange standard made it theoretically possible to regulate the adjustment process in times of international disequilibrium by expanding or contracting the supply of international liquidities through changes in US monetary policy.

Weakness of fixed rate systems

The weakness of fixed rate systems should be obvious. They depend on the willingness of the monetary authorities to follow the rules. Because of the painful economic consequences of playing by the rules implied by the adjustment process, many governments try to avoid it. As we saw in Chapter 2, this can be done by having the central bank neutralize the reduction (increase) in the money base with an increase (decrease) in credit to the economy. This, of course, only postpones the inevitable. Neutralizing the decrease in the money supply means perpetuating the balance of payments deficit and can only be continued as long as the central bank's reserves (gold in the gold standard and gold and dollars in the gold exchange system) hold out. Neutralizing the increase in the money supply means perpetuating the balance of payments surplus and can only be continued as long as the government is willing to accumulate reserves. The problem is usually one of reserves running out. Therefore, fixed rate systems tend towards what is often called an **adjustable peg** – that is, relatively long periods of constant rates punctuated by sharp devaluations.

It has also been argued that even in the absence of neutralization, neither system could work. It is said that the gold standard won't work because prices are rigid downwards, thereby blocking the self-correcting adjustment process.[1] Although it is true that downward price rigidity would hamper the adjustment, it would by no means block it. First of all, in the absence of price reductions, the adjustment to a lower level of demand would be effected through a reduction in the quantities produced and consumed. Secondly, as we have seen in the purchasing power parity hypothesis, it is the relative price levels across countries that determine the exchange rate not the absolute levels. Therefore, even if the deficit country's price level does not decline, if the surplus country's price level increases, the system is self-correcting.

The argument against the gold exchange standard held that if the stock of international reserves (dollars) were to grow along with world trade, the United States would have to run a continual balance of payments deficit because these deficits are the means by which other countries accumulate dollar reserves. However, the larger the deficits the more the holders of dollars would doubt the ability of the Federal Reserve to convert dollars into gold at the official price.[2] First of all, the argument is technically unsound. From Chapter 1 we know that the balance of payments is an accounting equation and must sum to zero. The United States is no different from any other country in this respect. As a matter of fact the United States ran a current account surplus in most years up to 1977. The real problem was keeping the price of gold at or below the official price of USD 35 per ounce, in other words, a US monetary policy of zero or negative world dollar inflation. First of all, this requires knowing what to do. Secondly, it requires the discipline to follow through on the policy. Working out and following through on an effective monetary policy for a single domestic economy is difficult enough. For the world it looks impossible.

The amount of US gold reserves compared to the total amount of US foreign liabilities might eventually have been a problem because under the gold exchange standard this ratio is comparable to the reserve ratio of a commercial bank in a domestic banking system. If it became too small, doubts about conversion might have cropped up even in the absence of dollar inflation. Thus, ultimately, in addition to a policy of zero world dollar inflation, for the system to work the United States would have had to manage its monetary policy in

---

[1] R. Triffin, "The myth and realities of the so-called gold standard", *The Evolution of the International Monetary System: Historical Reappraisal and Future Perspective*, (Princeton University Press, 1964).

[2] R. Triffin, *Gold and the Dollar Crisis* (Yale University Press, 1960).

relation to its gold stocks. Even under the gold exchange standard, world liquidity was constrained by the supply of gold.

Flexible exchange rate systems

To function effectively, fixed exchange rate systems rely on the automatic adjustment process set off by changes in the money supply. If exchange rates are allowed to adjust freely to the supply and demand of one currency for another, there is no need for an economy to undergo the painful adjustment process set in motion by a decrease or increase in the money supply. Thus, flexible exchange rates were seen by enthusiasts of the monetary approach as a simple means of escape from the constraints that balance of payments discipline so clearly imposes on macroeconomic policy making. The basic argument for flexible exchange rates is that they would allow a high degree of autonomy in the application of domestic economic policy while automatically guaranteeing balance of payments equilibrium. An incipient disequilibrium, for example, would be immediately reflected in a change in the exchange rate with no consequences on prices, output, resource allocation and consumption. From Chapter 2 we know that this argument is untrue. A change in the exchange rate causes relative price changes, a redistribution of income, resource reallocation and changes in the level and composition of output and consumption. Flexible exchange rates do have the advantage of perhaps making the cause and effect of bad economic policy less transparent. They do not free the economy from balance of payments discipline and the consequences of bad economic policy.

Another argument for flexible exchange rates is that they protect the domestic economy from bad economic policy in the rest of the world. Suppose, for example, that France, a major trading partner of Germany in a fixed exchange rate system, allows excess growth in its money supply that causes a French balance of trade deficit with Germany. Other things being equal, Germany should be affected by France's profligacy. Its corresponding trade surplus should cause an increase in the German money supply and set off the adjustment process. It is argued that a flexible exchange rate would spare Germany from this outcome. In fact, what happened when France actually pursued such a policy at the beginning of the 1980s was that France was obliged to devalue the franc and rein in its monetary policy. Instead of exporting its inflation and bad monetary policy to Germany, Germany exported its good monetary policy and price stability to France.

Two other points can be made in favor of flexible exchange rates. The first is that because flexible exchange rates diminish the need for foreign reserves, they offer the possibility of reducing the cost of holding reserves. The second is that flexible rates offer the possibility of reducing controls on international trade such as tariffs, subsidies, quotas and the like. The rationale is that they will not be needed because external equilibrium will always be guaranteed.

The arguments against flexible rates concern the instability of exchange rates, uncertainty and speculation. However, exchange rate instability is caused by the same forces of supply and demand that would exist in a fixed rate system, and the exchange risk can be covered in the forward market. Thus, short-term speculative profits would actually be reduced because the spot rate could move with the forward rate. Nevertheless, forward cover is expensive and not always practical, such as with long-term contracts. Flexible rates also expose the economy to cyclical pressures and overshooting phenomena that could make the economy seem much riskier than it is and, therefore, reduce the economy's access to foreign capital or at least raise the price that must be paid for it.

The most powerful argument against floating exchange rates flows from the principle on which floating exchanges are founded, that is, autonomy in the application of domestic economic policy. But a flexible rate offers autonomy only to a diversified economy with a relatively small external sector. The less diversified an economy and the larger its external sector, the less the utility of domestic currency is derived from its internal purchasing power. In the classic example of a small banana republic, the currency is more useful if it is stable in terms of its command over foreign goods than if it is stable in terms of its command over bananas.

Other exchange rate systems

Even in today's generalized system of flexible exchange rates, governments have not been able to resist the temptation to actively intervene in the exchange markets in pursuit of their policy objectives. When they do, the outcome is somewhere between fixed and flexible.

Managed float

The **managed float**, sometimes called a "dirty float", is employed by governments to preserve an orderly pattern of exchange rate changes and is designed to eliminate excess volatility. Rather than resist the underlying market forces, the authorities occasionally intervene by buying or selling domestic currency to smooth the transition from one rate to another. At other times they intervene to moderate or counteract self-correcting cyclical or seasonal market forces. The rationale for the managed float is to improve the economic and financial environment by reducing uncertainty. The problem is to define just what is meant by "excess volatility". It is also highly questionable that governments are more capable than market professionals at distinguishing between what is fundamental and what is temporary and self-correcting.

Crawling peg

The **crawling peg** is an automatic system for revising the exchange rate. It involves establishing a par value around which the rate can vary up to a given percentage. The par value is revised regularly according to a formula determined by the authorities. Once the par value is set the central bank intervenes whenever the market value approaches a limit point. Suppose, for example, that the par value of the Mexican peso is MXN 10 for USD 1 and can vary plus or minus 2% around this rate between MXN 10.2 and MXN 9.8. If the dollar approaches the rate of MXN 10.2 the central bank intervenes by buying pesos and selling dollars. If the dollar approaches MXN 9.8, the central bank intervenes by selling pesos and buying dollars. If it hovers around a limit point too long causing frequent central bank intervention, a new par value closer to this point is established. Suppose the dollar was hovering around MXN 10.2. The government might then establish the new par value at MXN 10.2 with the new limit points at MXN 10.404 and MXN 9.996.

Fixed rates with wider bands

Fixed rates with wider bands increase the intervention limits around official parity. They are supposed to reduce the magnitude and frequency of government intervention by discouraging speculation and allowing the exchange rate fluctuations themselves to accomplish some of the necessary adjustments. When the Bretton Woods gold exchange standard was breaking down in the early 1970s, for example, the members of the International Monetary Fund decided on a new set of parity rates and the conditions for maintaining them at a meeting on 18 December 1971 at the Smithsonian Institute in Washington, DC. It was agreed that currencies were to be allowed to fluctuate within a band of plus or minus 2.25% around parity rather than the previous limits of plus or minus 1%. By the middle of March 1973 this regime had been abandoned and the major currencies were allowed to float freely in relation to the US dollar.

Fixed rate system with controls

Many governments attempt to achieve exchange rate stability by imposing exchange controls. Exchange controls short circuit the allocation function of the foreign exchange market. One widespread practice is to impose restrictions on imports. Another has been to prohibit residents from holding bank accounts in foreign currency. This, in effect, means that all foreign exchange must be turned over to the monetary authorities who, in turn, decide how the foreign exchange will be allocated, usually on the basis of government priorities. Two-tiered exchange rates are another popular measure. In this system, different exchange rates are applied to different transactions. For example, the official fixed rate, which is usually overvalued, is applied to transactions associated with the current account while the market rate is applied to capital transactions.

Governments have been particularly creative in inventing foreign exchange controls, as can be seen in Exhibit 4.1, which lists some of the most frequently used measures. Exchange controls distort prices and resource allocation and are a major source of risk for corporations and individuals doing business in countries where they already exist or might be imposed.

Historical overview of the international financial system

The current international monetary system has its roots in a series of decisions that were taken by the authorities of the allied powers towards the end of World War II and its immediate aftermath. Exhibit 4.2 outlines some of the most important decisions and how they

Exhibit 4.1 Examples of foreign exchange controls

1. Import controls
2. Prohibition on holding bank accounts in foreign currency
3. Multiple exchange rates
4. Limits on direct investments abroad
5. Restrictions on certain types of remittances such as dividends and royalties.
6. Restrictions on portfolio investment and bank lending
7. Prohibition or restriction of prepayments for imports
8. Government export monopolies
9. Export taxes
10. Interest-free deposits for a specified period tied to certain transactions such as imports and dividends.
11. Minimum amounts of currency to be exchanged at the official rate on incoming travelers
12. Maximum amounts of currency to be exchanged for outgoing residents
13. Taxes on foreign-owned bank accounts
14. Limits on incoming direct investment
15. Limits on incoming portfolio investment or bank borrowing.

were followed up. Many of the decisions taken then were in response to perceived mistakes that had been made in the past. A short historical overview will make it possible to put those decisions and today's system into context and shed some light on how it might evolve.

Exhibit 4.2 International monetary system timeline

1944	The conference at Bretton Woods establishes the gold exchange standard and creates the **International Monetary Fund** (IMF) and the **International Bank for Reconstruction and Development** (IBRD), better known as the World Bank.
1948	The Bill appropriating funds for the reconstruction of Europe, the Marshall Plan, is signed.
1949	Devaluation of the currencies of the major European and many other countries.
1950	The European Payments Union (EPU) is created by recipients of the Marshall Plan.
1958	The **European Economic Community** (EEC) is established and the EPU is abolished. Most European countries restore convertibility of their currencies into dollars and gold for non-residents.
1960	A run on gold causes the creation of the London gold pool by the major central banks in order to hold down the price of gold.
1961	Revaluation of the German mark and Dutch guilder. The Organization for Economic Cooperation and Development (OECD) comes into existence. The original member countries were Austria, Belgium, Canada, Denmark, France, the Federal Republic of Germany, Greece, Iceland, Ireland, Italy, Luxembourg, The Netherlands, Norway, Portugal, Spain, Sweden, Switzerland, Turkey, the United Kingdom and the United States. The following countries became members subsequently: Japan (28 April 1964), Finland (28 January 1969), Australia (7 June 1971) and New Zealand (29 May 1973).
1962	The French begin selling dollars for gold.
1963	United States levies the interest equalization tax on non-resident borrowers.
1965	United States imposes "voluntary" controls on foreign investment by US residents.
1967	A world monetary crisis follows the devaluation of the British pound.
1968	Voluntary controls on foreign investment become mandatory. A new run on gold forces governments to abandon the London gold pool and adopt a two-tiered gold market where central banks trade at the official price and private transactions take place at the market price.
1969	The French franc devalues. The German mark revalues after a short float.
1970	Special drawing rights (SDRs) are created.
1971	The United States runs its first trade deficit of the century and a massive balance of payments deficit on a liquidity basis. The US gold stock falls below USD 10 billion. On 15 August convertibility of the dollar is suspended and the dollar is allowed to float. On 17 December the Smithsonian Agreement devalues the dollar against gold and fixes new parities with wider bands (plus or minus 2.25% instead of 1%). Dollar convertibility into gold is not reinstated.
1972	The EC countries, Denmark and Great Britain agree to maintain a narrow band of 1.125% among themselves while maintaining the band of 2.25% versus the dollar.
1973	The dollar is devalued and many currencies are allowed to float. The oil producing countries establish an embargo.
1974	United States eliminates restrictions on capital outflows. France withdraws from the joint float. The IMF redefines the value of the SDR. Instead of reflecting the value of the dollar, it reflects a basket of 16 currencies.

1975	In November at Rambouillet, France, the leaders of the major countries acknowledge the need for a flexible exchange rate system.
1976	A new international monetary system of floating exchange rates is agreed on in Jamaica. Gold is demonetized.
1978	The IMF's articles of agreement are amended.
1979	On 13 March the **European Monetary System** (EMS) is established. On 10 October the Fed announces its new anti-inflation monetary policy that will focus on the money supply rather than interest rates.
1980	The IMF simplifies the value of the SDR. Instead of 16 currencies it will be based on a basket of the five currencies with the largest exports of goods and services between 1975–79: the US dollar, German mark, French franc, Japanese yen and British pound.
1981	Adjustments are made in the par values of the EMS to relieve downward pressure on the French franc.
1982	In February there is a new realignment of the EMS currencies. In August Mexico closes its foreign exchange markets and is unable to meet payments on its foreign debt.
1983	The IMF raises its quotas from SDR 61.03 billion to SDR 90 billion.
1985	The Group of Five announce policies to push down the value of the dollar.
1987	**The Single European Act** is established to eliminate all remaining barriers on goods, labor and capital within the EC by 1992.
1990	The first step towards European economic and monetary union (EMU) called for in the Maastricht Treaty.
1994	The second step towards EMU begins with the creation of the European Monetary Institute, which is the precursor of the European Central Bank.
1995	On 31 May the European Commission adopts the Green Book (the reference scenario for the common currency). On 15–16 December, the European Council of Madrid adopts the name "euro" for the common currency. The technical details and timetable for the introduction of the euro in 1999 are also established.
1996	The Council of Dublin fixes the practical details for the transition to the euro, including its legal status and the relationship between the "ins" and the "pre-ins".
1998	Designation by the governments of the 11 countries in the euro-zone, creation of the European Central Bank and nomination of its directors. The European Central Bank System begins issuing bills in euros.
1999	The third phase of European and Monetary Union begins on 1 January. The final conversion rates of the participating currencies are fixed, the euro is born and the ECU ceases to exist.
1999–2002	The European Central Bank System exchanges individual currencies at the official rate established on 1 January 1999 and prepares for the transition to the euro.
2002	Bills and coins denominated in euros are issued and substituted for the individual currencies of the participating countries. By 1 July transition to the euro is complete and the individual currencies of participating members cease to exist as legal tender.

The gold standard era, 1880–1931

By 1880 most of the major trading nations were on the gold standard. The period between 1880 and 1914, when World War I brought an end to the gold standard, was marked by free flows of labor, capital and goods across borders, rapid economic growth, and stable prices and exchange rates. In spite of two depressions and several recessions it is remembered as a time of prosperity.

Following the war there was a period of flexible exchange rates but by 1926 the gold standard was reinstated in an attempt to bring down the inflation that was savaging the world economy and reverse the protectionism and competitive devaluations that accompanied it. Unfortunately, many governments were not up to the discipline that the gold standard implied and failed to obey the rules. When, in 1931, France announced that it would no longer accept sterling and would convert its existing sterling holdings into gold, Britain had no choice but to make sterling inconvertible. The other countries holding sterling followed suit and, because the basis of the gold standard is the ability to exchange currencies for gold at a fixed rate, for all practical purposes the gold standard was dead.

The subsequent period saw a return to flexible exchanges and **beggar-thy-neighbor** policies of competitive devaluations and increased protective barriers. Since the great depression of the 1930s was followed by World War II, no new system was able to emerge until after the war.

Bretton Woods and the gold exchange standard, 1944–73

The Bretton Woods system negotiated by the allied powers towards the end of the World War II in 1944 created the gold exchange standard described above. The goal of the allies was to prevent a return to the years following the previous war when the international financial system was characterized by protectionism, inflation and competitive devaluations. To this end the **International Monetary Fund** was created to oversee exchange rate changes and serve as a reserve base for deficit countries. The IMF was empowered to collect and distribute reserves in order to promote international monetary cooperation, facilitate the growth of trade, promote exchange rate stability, establish a system of multilateral payments and create a reserve base.

As we have seen, the linchpin of the system was the decision to make the US dollar freely convertible into gold with the other currencies fixed in terms of dollars. This required the United States to maintain a sizeable stock of gold reserves. Furthermore, for the system to succeed, it also required the United States to manage its monetary policy with a zero or negative rate of inflation so that the dollar price of gold would remain at or below USD 35 per ounce. Bretton Woods collapsed because the US monetary authorities failed in this duty.

Low but persistent dollar inflation was present from the outset and was undermining the system. As usual, France was the first to sniff out problems, and by 1962 it was exchanging dollars for gold. Meanwhile, the United States was trying everything to maintain the official gold price of USD 35. It pressured governments not to convert, restricted overseas investment, abolished private gold redemption, prohibited US citizens from holding gold abroad as well as at home, and issued non-marketable securities in lieu of redeeming gold. It did everything but restrict the supply of dollars, the one and only measure that could have saved the system. By 1968 the run on gold reached the point where it was necessary to establish a two-tiered system for gold pricing. The official price was reserved for official transactions between central banks and the private market price would be allowed to find its own level.

Before long the private market price was far above the official price of USD 35 and the so-called "run" on the dollar continued until, on 15 August 1971, President Nixon terminated dollar convertibility even for central banks. This announcement was followed by the Smithsonian Agreement in December under which the dollar was devalued to USD 38 per ounce of gold, other currencies were revalued relative to the dollar, and the intervention bands were increased from plus or minus 1% to plus or minus 2.25%. By 1973 even this system was no longer tenable and the world entered the realm of flexible exchange rates.

Flexible exchange rates, 1973–85

Flexible exchange rates and higher oil prices combined to make the 1970s the inflation decade. When the oil shock hit the world economy with a quadrupling of oil prices between the end of 1973 and 1974, most governments had already freed themselves from the monetary discipline of fixed exchange rates. Nevertheless, some countries such as Japan and Germany accepted the reduction in living standards mandated by the deterioration of their external terms of trade (more units of exports to acquire one unit of imported oil). Others responded with characteristic laxity. One of these was the United States, which postponed the economic adjustments in living standards and resource allocation implied by the radical relative price shake-up by keeping the domestic price of oil artificially low. As a major oil producer and beneficiary of the higher oil price, the consequences were not too drastic for the US economy. Other, less endowed countries that tried the same thing fared far worse.

These countries, many of them poor and developing, postponed the inevitable and financed their balance of payments deficits by borrowing massive sums on the international financial markets that were recycling the OPEC (**Organization of Petroleum Exporting Countries**) balance of payments surpluses. These were the seeds of what was to become the international debt crisis of the 1980s.

In 1978 the IMF ratified the de facto system of flexible exchange rates that had begun to emerge in 1971 and gold was officially demonetized. Half the IMF's gold was to be returned to its members and the other half was to be sold, with the proceeds to be used for development in the poor countries. In an effort to promote exchange rate stability among their currencies, the countries of the European Community created the **European Monetary System** (EMS) in 1979. The EMS was a fixed rate system with an accounting unit called the **European Currency Unit** (ECU), a cocktail of the participating countries' currencies with specific weights.

Meanwhile, the United States was pursuing an expansive monetary policy that was out of step with the other major currencies. From the end of 1976 to the end of 1978 the dollar lost 12% of its value compared to the SDR (special drawing right: see Chapter 1). Finally, in October 1979 the Fed announced that its focus would henceforth be on controlling the money supply rather than on stabilizing interest rates, which had been its central aim up to that point. Its goal was to curb inflation, which by then was close to 12% a year.

The goal was achieved. Inflation subsided substantially and the dollar rebounded against the major currencies. From the end of 1979 to the end of 1984 the dollar gained over 34% against the SDR and dollar inflation fell to close to 4%.

The turnaround was not without consequences. As dollar inflation fell, dollar interest rates remained high. This put a double squeeze on the developing countries that had borrowed heavily in the 1970s. Most of these countries depended on a limited number of primary products for most of their foreign exchange earnings and the world disinflation was causing the prices of these products to fall. Unfortunately, most of their loans were in dollars where interest rates remained high. Consequently, a higher percentage of their supply of foreign exchange went to service their foreign debt, leaving less to buy the imports necessary to keep their economies running. Furthermore, through decades of incoherent economic and financial administration using taxes, controls, tariffs, subsidies, credit allocation and monetary policy, the crisis countries had created the economic conditions guaranteed to generate inefficiency and massive wastage of resources. When foreign credit slowed down, this reality struck home. In August 1982, Mexico (a major oil exporter, it should not be forgotten) announced that it could not meet payments on its USD 100 billion of foreign debt. Brazil and Argentina quickly followed suit and, within a year, 47 countries were negotiating with their creditors to reschedule their debt.

1985 to date: The era of the managed float

By March 1985 the dollar had hit its peak. The US current account deficit was at the unheard of level of over USD 100 billion a year. Most economists agreed that the dollar was far above its long-term PPP equilibrium level. The arguments of why this was so ranged from the Dornbusch sticky price hypothesis to fiscal irresponsibility to the reassuring argument that the high exchange rate was a sign of confidence in the US economy. Whatever the reason, it was decided that the dollar had to come down in order to defuse protectionist sentiment in the US Congress that was mounting with the mounting trade deficit.

Intervention in the foreign exchange markets was the method to be used to achieve this goal. In September 1985 the Group of Five – the United States, France, Japan, Great Britain and West Germany – came up with the Plaza Agreement, named after the Hotel in New York where they met. This was essentially a coordinated program to force down the value of the dollar against the other major currencies.

The policy worked like a charm. In fact, it worked too well. The dollar fell like a stone, losing close to 11% of its SDR value in 1985. The Group of Five reversed field and began to support the dollar in 1986, to no avail. The dollar lost another 10% in 1986. The Group of Five plus Canada and Italy, now called the Group of Seven (G-7), reconvened in February 1987 in Paris and negotiated the Louvre Accord. It called for the G-7 countries to slow the dollar's fall by coordinating their economic policies and supporting the dollar on the exchange markets within some undisclosed target range.

This seemed to work for a while. The United States promised to cut the budget deficit and reduce the rate of growth of the money supply while Japan and Germany promised to stimulate their economies. Although the United States did manage to reduce the rate of growth of the money supply, the budget cuts were not forthcoming, and neither did Germany and Japan come through with their promised stimulatory measures. When worldwide stock markets crashed in October 1987 all pretense of policy coordination collapsed. The Fed flooded the markets with dollars and the dollar fell nearly 10% against the SDR in the last quarter of 1987.

Current international financial system

Where is the international financial system today? The answer to this question revolves around three facts: (a) the dollar is still the principal currency used in international transactions but its unchallenged dominance is no longer taken for granted; (b) the European Community is gaining importance as an economic and financial force; and (c) Bretton Woods is dead but its child, the IMF, has evolved with the times and is more important than ever as watchdog and arbiter of balance of payments disequilibrium.

International Monetary Fund

One of the most important players in the current international financial system, the IMF was created to administer a code of fair exchange practices and provide compensatory financial assistance to member countries with balance of payments difficulties. The role of the IMF was clearly spelled out in its articles of agreement:

1. To provide international monetary cooperation through a permanent institution that provides the machinery for consultation and collaboration on international monetary problems.

2. To facilitate the expansion and balanced growth of international trade, and to contribute thereby to the promotion and maintenance of high levels of employment and real income

and to the development of the productive resources of all members as primary objectives of economic policy.

3. To promote exchange stability, to maintain orderly exchange arrangements among members, and to avoid competitive exchange depreciation.

4. To assist in the establishment of a multilateral system of payments in respect of current transactions between members and in the elimination of foreign exchange restrictions that hamper the growth of world trade.

5. To give confidence to members by making the Fund's resources available to them under adequate safeguards, thus providing them with the opportunity to correct maladjustments in the balances of payments without resorting to measures destructive of national or international balances of payments of members.

When a member entered the IMF, it was obliged to submit a par value of its currency in gold or in US dollars. Once that value was established it could only vary by 1% either way and any changes required the permission of the IMF. All transactions with other members were then exercised at that rate.

The resources of the IMF came from the subscriptions of member countries. Subscriptions were determined on the basis of the member's relative economic size, 25% of the quota was to be paid in gold and the rest in the member's domestic currency. The size of the quota was important because it determined the member's voting power and the amount it could borrow. In practice, members could borrow up to the first 25% of their quota, which was called the "gold tranche". Beyond the gold tranche, the IMF imposed conditions.

Although the goals and ground rules for membership are still the same, the IMF has changed considerably since its creation. Its capital has been increased several times. The gold tranche has become the "first credit tranche" and other "upper credit tranches" have been added. In 1969 it created the first SDRs. As we mentioned in Chapter 1, SDRs are pure accounting creations that qualify as reserves because of the commitment of member countries to accept them for convertible currencies.[3] In 1978 the IMF ratified the demonetization of gold and in the 1980s it played an active role in resolving the ongoing "debt crisis".

The IMF has evolved with the perceived problems of the times. In 1963 it introduced the Compensating Financing Facility to help countries with temporarily inadequate foreign exchange reserves resulting from events such as crop failure. In 1974 it set up the Oil Facility to help oil importing developing countries. It also set up the Extended Fund Facility for countries with structural difficulties, created the Trust Fund of 1976 to allow the sale of gold for the development of third world countries and in the 1980s it negotiated special standby facilities for countries with foreign debt problems. Exhibit 4.3 shows outstanding IMF credit by facility available in the 1980s.

The prestige and importance of the IMF have grown over the years and today it plays a key role in the international financial system. Coming to terms with the IMF has become a condition *sine qua non* for troubled countries seeking incremental funding from the commercial banks. For example, at the height of the Mexican peso crisis, the IMF along with the United States and other OECD countries guaranteed a USD 50 billion credit line to Mexico that enabled it to avoid a debt default. During the South-East Asian meltdown of 1997, the IMF played a major role in avoiding a breakdown of the international financial system, although many observers judged its performance as "too little, too late and wrong-headed".

---

[3] They must only be accepted up to a limit of three times the accepting country's own SDR allocation.

Exhibit 4.3 Types of financial assistance provided by the IMF as of 1988

First credit tranche: No conditions. Repurchases made in 3.25 – 5 years.

Upper credit tranches: The member must have a substantial and viable program to re-establish balance of payments equilibrium. Resources are provided as standby arrangements with purchases in installments on performance criteria. Repurchases made in 3.25 – 5 years.

Extended Fund facility: Medium-term program aimed at structural reform. A program is usually for three years but can be extended to four. A program states policies and measures in detail for the first 12 months. Resources are provided in the form of extended arrangements that include performance criteria and drawings in installments. Repurchases made in 4.5 – 10 years.

Enlarged access policy: Used to augment resources available under standby and extended arrangements. Policies on conditionality, phasing, and performance are the same as under the credit tranches and the extended Fund facility. Repurchases made in 3.5 – 7 years and charges based on the IMF's borrowing costs.

Compensatory and contingency financing facility: The compensatory element provides resources to a member for an export shortfall and an excess in cereal import costs that are beyond the member's control. The contingency element extends assurance to help members with IMF-supported adjustment programs in order to maintain the momentum of adjustment efforts in the face of unanticipated, adverse external shocks. Repurchases made in 3.25 – 5 years.

Buffer stock financing facility: Resources to help finance a member's contribution to an approved international buffer stock. Repurchases made in 3.25 – 5 years.

Structural adjustment facility: Resources are provided on favorable terms to low-income countries facing long-term balance of payments problems, in support of medium-term macroeconomic and structural adjustment programs. With the aid of the IMF and the World Bank, the member develops and updates a medium-term policy framework for a three-year period, which is set out in a policy framework paper. Detailed annual programs are formulated prior to disbursement of annual loans. They include benchmarks to assess performance. Repurchases are made in 5.5 – 10 years.

Enhanced structural adjustment facility: Basically the same as the structural adjustment facility. Differences relate to monitoring and funding. A policy framework paper and detailed annual program are prepared each year. Arrangements include quarterly benchmarks, semi-annual performance and a mid-year review. Loans are disbursed semi-annually and repurchases made in 5.5 – 10 years.

European economic and monetary union

The European Union

The European Union (EU), formerly the European Community (EC), has become a major economic and financial force. It ranks with the United States and Japan as a giant of world trade. Excluding trade among themselves, by 1990 the then 12 member countries accounted for about 20% of world exports while the United States accounted for only 15%. By 2000 this position was consolidated and reinforced, and combined EU GDP was larger than that of the United States. EU stock markets and bourses are among the most sophisticated and fastest growing in the world and EU banks are among the largest and most active in international financial markets.

The EU grew from the post-war recognition of the necessity for European economic cooperation if further catastrophes were to be avoided. The first step on the road to cooperation came with the creation in 1948 of the Organization for European Economic Cooperation (OEEC) to administer the Marshall Plan. The next step was the establishment by Belgium, France, Italy, Luxembourg, The Netherlands and West Germany in 1952 of the European Coal and Steel Community (ECSC) to create a common market in steel and coal. However, the first big initiative on the road to today's economic integration was the Treaty of Rome – signed on 25 March 1957 by the same six countries – which created the European Economic Community (EEC) since shortened to the European Community.

The Treaty of Rome made it possible to organize the six signatories into a **customs union** and a **common market**. A customs union involves the erection of a common external tariff and the abolition of all restrictions on trade among members. A common market permits the free movement of capital and labor as well as all goods and services. By July 1968 all internal import duties had been abolished and the common external tariff established, and by 1969 common market workers could move freely from one country to another in response to employment opportunities. By 1989 most capital controls had been abolished.

Over the years, the EC has grown from the original six member countries to the current 15. Great Britain, Ireland and Denmark joined in 1973, Greece in 1981, Spain and Portugal in 1986, and Austria, Finland and Sweden in 1995. It looks set to grow further with Turkey, the former Eastern bloc countries, and most of the European Free Trade Association (EFTA) countries keen to get in.

The **Single European Act** (SEA) of 1987 affirmed the EC's intention to make the transition from a common market to a full **economic union** by 1992. An economic union involves the free movement of capital, labor and all goods and services, as well as the harmonization and unification of social, fiscal and monetary policies. Full economic union implies the transfer of economic and financial sovereignty to the EC's supranational institutions. It means that tax systems must be harmonized by reducing the existing rate differentials across countries and that non-tariff barriers to trade, such as national technical standards, must be eliminated. It also means that sensitive services such as banking, insurance and telecommunications must be liberalized.

Considerable progress has been made. An EC directive in 1988 requires the elimination of all remaining restrictions on capital movements within the EC. The principle of "mutual recognition", which holds that certification provisions in one country must be recognized as equivalent to the provisions in force in another country, will make it possible for banks to operate EC-wide without prior harmonization of banking regulations across countries. The principle will be extended to many other sectors. The most important progress, however, has been made in the domain of harmonization of economic and monetary policy enshrined in the single currency, the euro, the notes and coins for which were officially introduced on 1 January 2002.

The European Monetary System

After the collapse of the Bretton Woods system in 1971, the EC countries, together with the United Kingdom and Denmark, who were to join the EC in 1973, agreed to maintain their currencies within a narrower band (2.25%) than the 4.5% permitted by the Smithsonian Agreement. This arrangement was referred to as the "snake in the tunnel" because the EC currencies floated as a group against outside currencies such as the US dollar or the yen. The turmoil of the 1970s reduced the snake from eight to four participants (West Germany, The Netherlands, Belgium and Denmark) and it was decided in 1978 that a new effort to achieve monetary cooperation was necessary.

Led by West Germany and France, the European Monetary System (EMS) was launched in 1979. The goal of the EMS was to create a zone of monetary stability in Europe. Its major features were:

1. A system of bilateral exchange rates defining par values and limiting variations to a band of 2.25% around the par value.

2. The creation of the **European Currency Unit** (ECU), a weighted average of each of the EMS currencies plus the Greek drachma, as the special unit of account that was used in all intra-system balance of payments settlements (Table 4.1 shows the weights as of 21 September 1989).

3. Establishment of the European Monetary Cooperation Fund (EMCF), which allocated ECUs to members' central banks in exchange for 20% of those central banks' gold and dollar holdings.

4. The provision of credit facilities for compensatory financing of balance of payments deficits.

A central feature of the EMS system of fixed exchange rates was that the central banks of both of the currencies involved in the rate were obliged to intervene if the market rate approached a limit point. Suppose, for example, that the French franc was approaching its lower limit on the parity grid (a square matrix showing the par value as well as the upper and lower limits of each pair of currencies). The French authorities would be required to buy French francs and the German authorities to sell German marks. The difference between this system and the gold exchange standard is that in the gold exchange standard the required intervention was only on one side. If, for example, the French franc was approaching its lower limit with the dollar, the French authorities were required to intervene by buying francs. There was no requirement on the part of the US authorities to cooperate by selling dollars.

The advantages of bilateral intervention are obvious. The adjustment process is spread across both countries. When the French central bank buys francs, the money supply falls and sets the adjustment process of lower prices, investment and output in motion. When the German central bank sells marks, the money supply increases and sets in motion the adjustment process of higher prices, investment and output. Since both countries are participating simultaneously, the adjustment should be swifter and less painful than if one of the two had intervened alone.

The success of the EMS was mixed. Up to 1988 there had been 11 realignments in spite of some heavy intervention. The values of the German mark and the Dutch guilder rose

Table 4.1 Composition of the ECU by individual currency weights as of 21 September, 1989

Currency	Weight (%)
German mark	30.10
French franc	19.00
Pound sterling	13.00
Italian lira	10.15
Netherlands guilder	9.40
Belgian franc	7.60
Spanish peseta	5.30
Danish krone	2.45
Irish punt	1.10
Greek drachma	0.80
Portuguese escudo	0.80
Luxembourg franc	0.30

spectacularly while the French franc and the Italian lira flopped. It is said that defending the franc in 1983 cost the French socialist government over USD 5 billion in two weeks. After that, France reined in its monetary policy and fell in behind Germany. The system was successful enough, however, to encourage the countries of the Community to proceed towards full economic and monetary union.

Economic and monetary union: The euro

The single currency came to life in the Treaty of Maastricht, which was signed in February 1992 and became law on 1 November 1993. Phase 1 of economic and monetary union (EMU) had actually begun in July 1990 when capital movements within the EU were liberalized. In January 1994 Phase 2 began with the creation of the European Monetary Institute and the policy of economic and monetary convergence. In 1998 the European Central Bank (ECB) was established, its directorate named, the European System of Central Banks (ESCB) started issuing euros and the ECB began to put in place a common monetary policy. Finally, Phase 3 was implemented on 1 January 1999 when the exchange rates of the 11 countries that had qualified for membership in 1998 were irrevocably fixed. These countries comprised Belgium, Germany, Spain, France, Ireland, Italy, Luxembourg, The Netherlands, Austria, Portugal and Finland, while Greece was admitted two years later. Phase 3 marked the end of the ECU as a basket currency and the establishment of the euro as a fully fledged currency.

From 1999 to 2002 the currencies of EMU members were exchanged at the irrevocable exchange rate fixed on 1 January 1999 and preparations were made for the replacement of individual currencies with the euro, which, for all practical purposes, was completed on 1 July 2002.

Current system of exchange rates

Sources of international liquidity

It should be becoming clear by now that the current international system of exchange rates is really a mixture of all the systems discussed above. Before we get into the details of that, however, it might be a good idea to review the different instruments that can be used to settle international debts. Remember that in Chapter 1 we listed four sources of international liquidity: monetary gold, special drawing rights (SDRs), the reserve position in the Fund and foreign exchange. The sources of international liquidity can be summarized as follows:

- Monetary gold is gold held by the authorities as a financial asset.

- SDRs are reserves created by the IMF as bookkeeping entries and credited to the accounts of IMF member countries according to their established IMF quotas. The value of the SDR is determined daily by the IMF on the basis of a basket of currencies, with each currency assigned a weight in the determination of that value. In the derivation of the SDR value the currencies of the basket are valued at their market exchange rates for the US dollar, and the US dollar equivalents of each of the currencies are summed to yield the rate of the SDR in terms of the US dollar. The number and weights of the SDR basket have changed over time. From 1 January 1986 the SDR valuation basket consisted of the five members having the largest exports of goods and services during the period 1980–84, i.e. the US dollar 42%, the German mark 19%, the Japanese yen 15%, the French franc 12% and the pound sterling 12%.[4]

- The reserve position in the Fund is the difference between each member's quota plus other claims on the Fund less the Fund's holdings of that member's currency.

[4] IMF, *International Financial Statistics* (November 1989) p. 7.

- Foreign exchange comprises monetary authorities, claims on non-residents in the form of bank deposits, Treasury bills, short-term and long-term government securities, and other claims usable in the event of balance of payments need, including non-marketable claims arising from inter-central bank and inter-governmental arrangements, without regard as to whether the claim is denominated in the currency of the debtors or the creditors.

With this in mind we can now summarize the current situation of exchange rate arrangements. The basic system is one of flexible exchange rates. We know that since 1985 the US dollar, the most important reserve currency, has been in the throes of a managed float against the other major currencies. Within this system, for reasons discussed in previous chapters, many countries have decided to peg their currencies to another currency or a basket of currencies. As of March 1997, 21 currencies were pegged to the US dollar, two were pegged to the SDR, 14 were pegged to the French franc and 20 currencies were pegged to various baskets of currencies other than the SDR. The 12 EMS countries had their currencies pegged to the ECU. The gulf countries of Bahrain, Qatar, Saudi Arabia and the United Arab Emirates had their currencies targeted to the dollar but allowed a certain amount of flexibility. Finally, 48 countries were on a managed float and 51 countries allowed their currencies to float freely.

Summary

1. To function effectively fixed exchange rate systems require strict fiscal and monetary discipline on the part of the authorities. The failure of governments to respect this discipline was the weakness that killed both the gold standard and the gold exchange standard.

2. Flexible exchange rate systems require less fiscal and monetary discipline and therefore offer more latitude for financial and economic mismanagement on the part of the authorities. Furthermore, flexible exchange rates only make sense for large well diversified economies with relatively small external sectors.

3. Hybrid exchange rate systems that are part fixed and part flexible such as the adjustable peg, the crawling peg, wider bands, and the managed float are evidence of the recognized necessity for exchange rate stability and the difficulty of achieving it.

4. Although the gold exchange standard disappeared, the US dollar has remained the central currency for international transactions.

5. The IMF, another vestige of the gold exchange standard, has survived the demise of Bretton Woods and emerged as the watchdog and arbiter of the international monetary system and balance of payments problems.

6. The European Union and its monetary creation, the euro, are becoming an important force in international economic and financial affairs.

7. The current international monetary system has the major currencies floating against each other with most of the minor currencies pegged or targeted against a major currency or basket of currencies.

Questions

Solutions to the following questions are set out on the web site, details of which are included in the Preface.

1. What is the difference between the gold standard and the gold exchange standard? Explain the practical weaknesses of these two systems.

2. What are the arguments for and against a flexible exchange rate system?

3. What is the difference between an adjustable peg, a crawling peg and a managed float?

4. Explain the economic and financial effects of foreign exchange controls.

5. What was the exchange rate system negotiated in the Bretton Woods agreement? Why did the system fail?

6. True or false: The seeds of the debt crisis in the 1980s were the bad economic policies pursued by many governments after the oil shocks of the 1970s. Explain. What else contributed to the crisis?

7. What is the current role of the International Monetary Fund? How has its role changed since Bretton Woods and why?

8. What is the goal of the Single European Act signed in 1987?

9. What are the current major sources of international liquidity?

10. Describe the current situation of exchange rate agreements.

International banking and the Eurocurrency market

5

Interntional institutions and agreements have evolved over the years in response to the growth in cross-border trade and capital flows as well as the revolution in communications and information processing. The same forces were at work in the evolution of the private component of the international financial system. Nowhere has this been more pronounced than in the domain of international banking. The traditional system of correspondent banking, where banks maintain deposits, subject to local regulations, in the domestic currency of the country where they are located, has been overtaken by today's system of banks taking and holding deposits in any currency, regardless of the banks' location. Deposits of this type are outside the jurisdiction of the monetary authorities where the currencies are legal tender. They can be bought and sold, borrowed and loaned, with little or no interference from politicians and regulators. Any interference in one location only has the effect of chasing business to another where there is no interference. Furthermore, the development of communications networks and data processing has increased the speed and efficiency of transfer and settlement to the point where geographic location is almost irrelevant.

For the international financial system the consequences have been revolutionary. International liquidity, interest rates, and the magnitude and direction of capital flows have all undergone profound changes. Even domestic banking systems have been influenced because they are cross-linked through the offshore operations in their currencies.

In this chapter we examine this offshore international banking system, called the Eurocurrency market, and see what it is, how it developed and how it functions. We will see how funds are transferred through the system and how international liquidities are created and destroyed in the process. We will study its links to individual domestic banking systems and how it influences the balance of payments, the exchange rate and the magnitude and direction of trade and capital flows.

The Eurocurrency market

Market characteristics

A **Eurocurrency** is any freely convertible currency, such as a dollar or a pound, deposited in a bank outside its country of origin. Thus, a pound held on deposit with a bank in Paris is a Europound and a dollar held on deposit with a bank in London is a Eurodollar. It is the residency of a bank and not its nationality that determines the "Euro" nature of the deposit so the Europound could be held with a Paris branch of a British bank and the Eurodollar could be held with a London branch of a US bank. "Eurocurrency" also refers to this type of deposit held in non-European financial centers, although the term "offshore currency" is sometimes used in its place.

Eurocurrency deposits are typically conventional **term deposits** of one day to one year's duration. Conventional term deposits are non-negotiable bank deposits with a fixed term where the interest rate is fixed for the duration of the deposit. In Eurocurrency transactions the currency that is used is always a foreign currency to at least one of the two parties and one of the two parties is always a bank. The other party can be another bank, a central bank, a government or a large corporate entity. In fact, transactions between banks and other financial institutions constitute the core of the Eurocurrency market. This interbank Eurocurrency market is organized as an international over-the-counter market whose members are linked electronically. Access to this market is reserved to top quality institutions. The sums involved are huge, with USD 1 million the usual minimum transaction size. Eurocurrency markets are outside the jurisdiction of any single regulatory authority and interest rates are determined by pure supply and demand.

Origins and development

The Eurocurrency market is not a new phenomenon. Before and after World War I banks in most European countries accepted deposits in many different currencies. The origin of today's Eurocurrency market, however, is usually credited to countries of the former Soviet bloc who, during the height of the Cold War, feared that their dollar reserves might be frozen if held in the United States. This was the heyday of the gold exchange standard and the Soviet bloc countries were obliged to accept dollars if they wanted to do business with the West. To avoid having their dollar balances blocked by the Americans, they held them with banks located in England and France.

The threat of sanctions may have created the post-World War II Eurodollar market, but it was the reality of regulations that made it prosper. Two US Federal Reserve Board regulations – Regulation Q and Regulation M – were especially influential in the development of the Eurodollar market. Regulation Q set interest rate ceilings on deposits in the United States. European banks, of course, were not subject to this regulation and, consequently, could pay higher rates for dollar deposits than American banks. This made it attractive to deposit dollars in the European markets where the rates were higher. In fact, many US banks set up overseas branches to take these funds.

As we mentioned in Chapter 2, a major instrument of monetary policy is the reserve ratio that requires commercial banks to hold a proportion of their deposits in an account with the central bank. Regulation M established the reserve ratio requirement for the US banking system. Reserves pay no interest and, hence, represent a high cost for banks. Consider, for example, a situation where the reserve ratio is 5% and the interest rate on deposits is 10%. If a bank receives a deposit of USD 1000, it pays interest on the full USD 1000. However it only has effective use of USD 950 because 5% of the deposit must be held without interest with the central bank. Thus, the total cost of the funds is 10.53%, the USD 100 of interest divided by USD 950, the amount that it can effectively use. European banks were under no obligation to maintain fractional reserves on dollar deposits. This lowered their costs relative to domestic banks and made it possible for them to pay higher rates of interest to attract deposits.

Two other regulations that contributed to the development of the Eurodollar market came about as a result of the failing gold exchange standard. In Chapter 4 we mentioned that the US monetary authorities refused to take the painful step of reining in the US money supply in order to save the gold exchange standard. Instead they tried regulations as a means of improving the capital account:

- To discourage non-residents from borrowing in the United States the interest equalization tax was passed in 1963. It was a tax on US residents' earnings on foreign securities. To compensate for the tax, foreign borrowers were obliged to pay higher interest rates, which made it costly for foreign firms and governments to borrow in the United States. Many turned to the Eurodollar market where no such restrictions existed.

- To discourage US corporations from lending overseas, restrictions were placed on non-domestic uses of domestically generated funds. The voluntary restrictions of 1965 on borrowing funds in the United States for reinvestment abroad became mandatory in 1968. Under these restrictions many US firms with plans for overseas projects simply shifted their financing requirements to the Eurodollar market.

Special regulations were not the only reason for the development of the Eurocurrency market. By the mid-1970s Regulation Q was inoperative, the interest equalization tax was abolished and most restrictions on overseas investment had been lifted. Still, as we can see in Table 5.1, the Eurocurrency market continued to grow by leaps and bounds. Its nature is such that some cost savings are inherent. As a wholesale market dealing in large quantities, economies of scale can be achieved, which lower costs. Because the participants are also all professionals, costly regulatory supervision and consumer protection such as deposit insurance are unnecessary. Furthermore, Eurocurrency transactions are simply more convenient in today's global economy. The development of cross-border commercial trans-actions has generated multiple currency cash flows that corporate treasurers are obliged to manage. It is impractical to deal with a different bank in a different country for each separate currency. Alternatively, dealing with one bank would also be costly and inefficient if it meant systematically converting all foreign currency cash flows into domestic currency when they arrive, only to reconvert into foreign currency when payments must be made. The Eurocurrency market makes it possible to deal with an easily accessible, well known bank that can handle all currency needs.

Thus, factors of cost and convenience are behind the emergence and growth of all the Eurocurrencies. Depositors want to receive the highest yield while borrowers want to pay the lowest cost, and the nature of the Euromarket and the absence of restrictions make it possible to fulfill these requirements.

Eurocurrency interest rates

As we have suggested, Eurocurrency rates are closely related to the rates in the currency's home market but, because of lower costs, **spreads** are lower. Spreads refer to the difference between borrowing rates and lending rates. Tighter spreads mean that the Eurocurrency markets offer slightly higher interest rates to lenders and slightly lower

Table 5.1 Size of the Eurocurrency market (bank liabilities in foreign currencies, USD bn), 1968–99

1968	33.71	1989	4186.30	1995	5883.98
1976	310.65	1990	4936.70	1996	6094.48
1985	1980.60	1991	4950.00	1997	6858.53
1986	2526.90	1992	4880.85	1998	6365.36
1987	3230.60	1993	4815.31	1999	6159.52
1988	3505.20	1994	5398.65		

Source: Bank for International Settlements.

rates to borrowers than are available in the home market. Figure 5.1 shows how the smaller spread in the Eurocurrency market makes it possible for banks to offer better borrowing and lending rates than the domestic market. Notice that the trend of the Eurocurrency rates follows the trend of domestic interest rates without being perfectly parallel. Because of arbitrage, interest rates in the domestic and Eurocurrency markets can only differ insofar as there are additional costs, controls or risks involved in moving funds between one market and the other. Otherwise, arbitragers would borrow in the market where funds were cheaper and lend them where they are dearer, thereby causing the difference to disappear.

Because the cost of shifting funds from one market to another is negligable, substantial interest rate differentials between the domestic market and the Euromarket suggest the presence of differences in perceived risk or effective controls. For many years Eurofranc rates were considerably higher than domestic rates due to French restrictions on loaning abroad combined with domestic credit controls. With the supply limited, credit-starved French borrowers dodging the domestic controls maintained the differential by borrowing Eurofrancs whenever the interest rate began to fall. On the other side of the coin, Euromark and Euro Swiss franc rates have seen periods when they were considerably lower than domestic rates because of measures seeking to discourage capital inflows. One such measure was minimum reserves on certain types of non-resident deposits, which raised the cost of funds for domestic banks borrowing abroad. This caused them to lower the rate they were willing to pay for foreign funds to bring their total cost into line with the cost of domestic funds. In both cases controls caused considerable interest rate differentials between the two markets. Controls designed to restrict capital outflows will tend to push the Eurocurrency rate above the domestic rate while controls designed to restrict capital inflows will tend to push the Eurocurrency rate below the domestic rate.

Anticipating controls that do not yet exist can also cause an interest rate differential. If there is a possibility that at some future date funds will be unable to cross the border,

Figure 5.1 Domestic and Eurocurrency borrowing and lending rate spreads

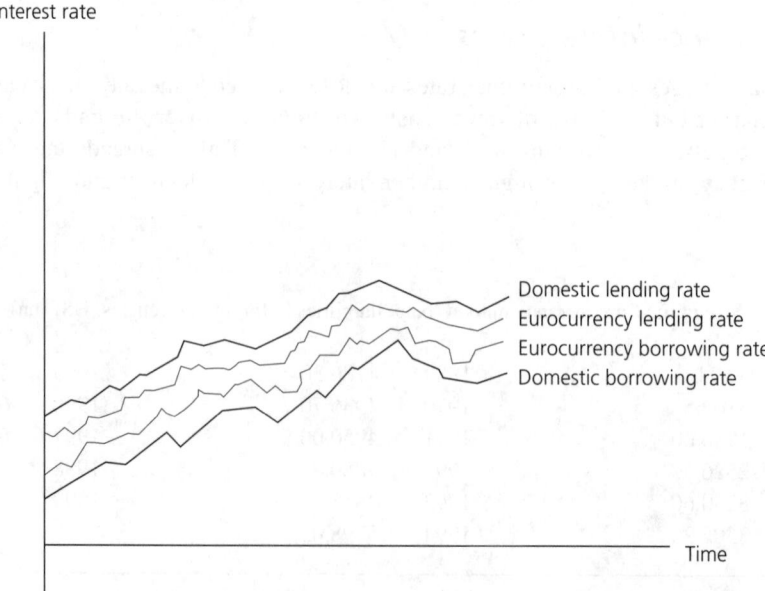

investors will require a premium for holding assets in the domestic market.[1] In this case the interest rate differential is due to higher perceived risk on assets held in the domestic market.

Quotes and spreads

Table 5.2 shows some Eurocurrency interest rates as reported in the *International Herald Tribune*. These rates refer to the interbank market and are quoted as a bid–ask spread. For example, the interest rate on six-month Eurosterling is quoted $10\frac{3}{4}$–$10\frac{7}{8}$. The first figure, $10\frac{3}{4}$, refers to the rate that banks are willing to pay another bank to borrow sterling for six months. The second figure, $10\frac{7}{8}$, refers to the rate that banks charge to lend sterling to another bank for six months. The difference of $\frac{1}{8}$% between the two rates, the spread, is the banks' gain.

If a trader gives a quotation such as the $10\frac{3}{4}$–$10\frac{7}{8}$ above, it means that his bank is ready to borrow from, or lend to, any institution of good standing at those rates. Table 5.2 indicates that the rates shown refer to deposits of USD 1 million or the foreign exchange equivalent, which is the usual minimum transaction size in the interbank market. Banks generally set maximums to limit their risks.

A non-member of the interbank club, such as a corporation or investor wishing to lend into this market, will be given a quote of the bid rate less a commission. Because of fierce competition among banks, commissions on lending are typically very low. In the example above, if the commission is $\frac{1}{16}$%, a customer would be able to lend six-month sterling to the bank at $10\frac{3}{4}$% less $\frac{1}{16}$% = $10\frac{11}{16}$%. On the other hand, a customer wishing to borrow from the market will be quoted the ask or offer rate plus a commission that includes a risk premium. The risk premium depends on the customer's creditworthiness. The more doubtful the customer's creditworthiness, the higher the premium. A good quality customer might be able to borrow at $\frac{3}{8}$% over the ask rate. In the example above the customer would then have to pay $10\frac{7}{8}$% + $\frac{3}{8}$% = $11\frac{1}{4}$%. Quotes for Eurocurrency loans are often given in terms of **Libor** (London interbank offered rate) or **Pibor** (Paris interbank offered rate) plus the risk-adjusted commission. Libor rates are calculated as the averages of the lending rates in the respective currencies of six leading London banks. Pibor rates

Table 5.2 Eurocurrency interest rates

Period	US dollars	German mark	Swiss franc	UK sterling	French franc	Japanese yen
1 month	$5\frac{13}{16}$–$5\frac{15}{16}$	9–$9\frac{1}{8}$	$7\frac{11}{16}$–$7\frac{13}{16}$	$10\frac{13}{16}$–11	$9\frac{5}{16}$–$9\frac{1}{2}$	$7\frac{5}{16}$–$7\frac{1}{2}$
2 months	$5\frac{13}{16}$–$5\frac{15}{16}$	$9\frac{1}{8}$–$9\frac{1}{4}$	$7\frac{3}{4}$–$7\frac{7}{8}$	$10\frac{13}{16}$–11	$9\frac{5}{16}$–$9\frac{1}{2}$	$7\frac{3}{8}$–$7\frac{9}{8}$
3 months	$5\frac{13}{16}$–$5\frac{15}{16}$	$9\frac{1}{4}$–$9\frac{3}{8}$	$7\frac{3}{4}$–$7\frac{7}{8}$	$10\frac{13}{16}$–11	$9\frac{3}{8}$–$9\frac{9}{16}$	$7\frac{5}{16}$–$7\frac{1}{2}$
6 months	6–$6\frac{1}{8}$	$9\frac{7}{16}$–$9\frac{9}{16}$	$7\frac{13}{16}$–$7\frac{15}{16}$	$10\frac{3}{4}$–$10\frac{7}{8}$	$9\frac{1}{2}$–$9\frac{11}{16}$	$7\frac{1}{16}$–$7\frac{1}{4}$
1 year	$6\frac{1}{4}$–$6\frac{3}{8}$	$9\frac{1}{2}$–$9\frac{5}{8}$	$7\frac{3}{4}$–$7\frac{7}{8}$	$10\frac{5}{8}$–$10\frac{13}{16}$	$9\frac{9}{16}$–$9\frac{3}{4}$	$6\frac{7}{8}$–$7\frac{1}{16}$

Source: *International Herald Tribune* (5 August 1991).
Rates applicable to interbank deposits of USD 1 million minimum (or equivalent).

[1] R.Z. Aliber, *Exchange Risk and International Corporate Finance* (London: Macmillan, 1978); "The interest rate parity theorem: A reinterpretation", *Journal of Political Economy* (1973), p.p. 1451–1459.

are the averages of the lending rates of the 14 top Parisian banks in the respective currencies where the three highest and the three lowest rates are eliminated.

For borrowing maturities of over a year, a "floating" interest rate is usually charged. Floating interest rates mean that periodically (every six months, for example) the loan is rolled over and the interest rate is revised according to current Libor. In the example above, suppose that the customer negotiated a five-year sterling loan at Libor plus $\frac{3}{8}\%$ revisable every six months. As we saw, he would have to pay $11\frac{1}{4}\%$ for the first six months. Suppose that at the end of six months sterling rates have fallen so that six-month sterling Libor is at $10\frac{5}{8}\%$. The customer will then have to pay $10\frac{5}{8}\% + \frac{3}{8}\% = 11\%$ for the next six months.

It is interesting to note that Libor and Pibor are losing some of their importance as the benchmarks for lending in the Euromarket. This is because as a result of bad management and bad loans, banks themselves are perceived as inferior credit risks to many other borrowers. These borrowers can borrow at rates below Libor and Pibor and thus bypass the banks. The rapid growth of the Eurobond market, which we will examine in a later chapter, can be attributed to this phenomenon.

International funds transfer and credit expansion through the Eurocurrency system

In Chapter 2 we saw that the borrowing and lending activity of banks has the effect of expanding or contracting the money supply in domestic markets. The limit to the expansion or contraction is determined by the reserve ratio. The lower the reserve ratio the higher the possible multiplicative effect. The same principle was applied to the Eurocurrency market and it was argued that since the Eurocurrency markets were outside the jurisdiction of the regulatory authorities, the reserve ratio is zero and therefore the money supply multiplier is infinite or at least very high.[2] Other authors criticized this view.[3] They pointed out that the reserve ratio multiplier works in a domestic market because the domestic market is essentially a closed circuit, and they argued that the Eurocurrency system is not a closed system. Potential borrowers and lenders have the choice between the Eurocurrency market and the domestic market. In order for the Eurocurrency market to increase its transactions, it has to offer advantages in price and service. Otherwise, funds will leak out of the system and the multiplier will break down. The general conclusion is that although money and credit expansion through the Eurocurrency system is possible, it is incorrect to suppose that the expansion will occur through a fixed multiplier.

The question is interesting because it highlights the fundamental characteristics of the Eurocurrency system, its interaction with the individual domestic markets and the international transfer of funds.

Money expansion through the Eurocurrency markets

The best way to illustrate how the Eurocurrency market functions is with an example. We can start with a commercial transaction.

---

[2] For a discussion of this point of view see M. Friedman, "The Eurodollar market: Some first principles", *Morgan Guaranty Survey* (October 1969); F. Machlup, "Eurodollar creation: A mystery story", *Banca Nazionale del Lavoro Quarterly Review* (September 1970); G. Carli, "Eurodollars: A paper pyramid", *Banca Nazionale Quarterly Review* (June 1971).

[3] A.D. Crockett, "The Eurocurrency market: An Attempt to clarify some basic issues", *Staff Papers*, (IMF, July 1976); J. Hewson and E. Sakakibara, "The Eurodollar multiplier: A Portfolio approach", *Staff Papers*, (IMF, July 1974); F. Klopstock, "Money creation in the Eurodollar market: A note on Professor Friedman's views", *Monthly Review*, Federal Reserve Bank of New York (January 1970).

Transaction 1

Suppose that Burberry's, a British clothes-maker, sells US Corporation, an American importer, USD 1 million worth of merchandise. The goods are billed in dollars and US Corporation pays with a check drawn on its New York bank. Burberry's has an account at Citicorp in New York and deposits the check there. Citicorp's external position (its position vis-à-vis non-residents) as a result of this transaction will be as follows:

Citicorp	
	Demand deposit owed to Burberry's
	USD 1 million

Transaction 2

Burberry's needs dollars for working capital purposes but wants to earn interest and decides to put the USD 1 million into a seven-day time deposit. Its London bank, NatWest, is paying higher rates than Citicorp so Burberry's instructs Citicorp to transfer the USD 1 million to NatWest in London. This transaction will be recorded by the two banks as follows:

Citicorp		NatWest	
Demand deposit owed to Burberry's – USD 1 million	Demand deposit held at Citicorp + USD 1 million	Time deposit owed to Burberry,s + USD 1 million	
Demand deposit owed to NatWest + USD 1 million			

The USD 1 million time deposit owed to Burberry's is a Eurodollar deposit that NatWest has created by borrowing from Burberry's. Although the time deposit is in US dollars, NatWest is outside the jurisdiction of the US authorities and the conditions of the loan are not subject to any US regulations on bank deposits, interest rates and the like. Notice that Citicorp's total external position is unchanged. It still has a total of USD 1 million in demand liabilities vis-à-vis non-residents. The only thing that has changed for Citicorp is that the demand liability is owed to NatWest instead of to Burberry's.

Transaction 3

The funds that NatWest is holding with Citicorp in New York are earning lower interest than the interest it is paying to Burberry's on the time deposit. This is very costly, so if there were no commercial borrowers available, NatWest would deposit the funds in the interbank market. Fortunately, Honda, a Japanese automaker, has approached NatWest about a six-month, USD 1 million loan. Because Honda is a high-quality customer, NatWest agrees to the loan at Libor plus $\frac{1}{2}\%$.

When the loan is extended the funds are initially made available to Honda in the form of a demand deposit at NatWest. The transactions for the two banks will be recorded as follows:

Citicorp		NatWest	
	Six-month loan to Honda + USD 1 million	Demand deposit owed to Honda + USD 1 million	

Notice that Citicorp is not affected by the transaction because there is no transfer of funds. However, NatWest has effectively created USD 1 million in the form of a demand deposit owed to Honda. This is the type of operation that those who feared unlimited money supply multiplication were referring to. There are now USD 2 million of liabilities owed by non-US banks backed by only USD 1 million of claims on US banks.

Transaction 4

Honda wants the proceeds of the loan transferred to the Sumitomo Bank in Japan where the money will earn interest in a time deposit until used. NatWest sends a telex to Citicorp in New York, instructing it to transfer USD 1 million to Honda's account with Sumitomo in Japan. This transaction will be recorded with the three banks as follows:

Citicorp		NatWest		Sumitomo
Demand deposit owed to NatWest – USD 1 m	Demand deposit at Citicorp – USD 1 m	Demand deposit owed to Honda –USD 1 m	Demand deposit at Citicorp + USD 1 m	Time deposit owed to Honda + USD 1 m
Demand deposit owed to Sumitomo + USD 1 m				

There are still USD 2 million of Eurodollars, only now Sumitomo has acquired dollar balances. Citicorp's external position is still USD 1 million of demand liabilities, owed now to Sumitomo.

Transaction 5

Sumitomo is in the same position that NatWest was in when it took the time deposit from Burberry's. It is paying higher interest on the time deposit than its demand deposit held with Citicorp is earning. Sumitomo has no loan prospects in sight so it decides to place the money in the interbank market. After casting around for quotes, it finds that Swiss Bank Corp. in Switzerland is offering the best rate. Sumitomo instructs Citicorp to credit its account with Swiss Bank Corp. The transactions for the four banks will be recorded as follows:

Citicorp	NatWest	Sumitomo	Swiss Bank Corp.
Demand deposit owed to Sumitomo – USD 1 m	Demand deposit at Citicorp – USD 1 m	Demand deposit at Citicorp + USD 1 m	Time deposit owed to Sumitomo + USD 1 m
Demand deposit owed to Swiss Bank Corp. + USD 1 m	Time deposit at Swiss Bank Corp. + USD 1 m		

A new Eurodollar deposit has been created in the form of a time deposit that Sumitomo is holding with Swiss Bank Corp. There are now USD 3 million worth of Eurodollars in the system. Citicorp's external position is still the same: only the owner of the deposit has changed. If Swiss Bank Corp. decides to leave its dollars with Citicorp, no more Eurodollars will be created. The same is true if Swiss Bank Corp. decides to transfer its dollar claim to another US bank. When dollars are redeposited in the United States the multiplicative process comes to an end. This is the first way that funds can "leak" out of the Eurocurrency system and bring the multiplicative process to an end.

We can consolidate the foregoing transactions and see how the balance sheet of each bank will look at the end of Transaction 5:

Citicorp		NatWest		Sumitomo		Swiss Bank Corp.
Demand deposit owed to Swiss Bank Corp. USD 1 m	Six-month loan to Honda USD 1 m	Time deposit owed to Burberry's USD 1 m	Time deposit at Swiss Bank Corp. USD 1 m	Time deposit owed to Honda USD 1 m	Demand deposit at Citicorp USD 1 m	Time deposit owed to Sumitomo USD 1 m

Citicorp has USD 1 million in external liabilities and there are USD 3 million in Eurodollar liabilities. This balance sheet is the result of the three basic operations involved in the Eurocurrency market. After the commercial transaction (Burberry's export to the United States) they were successively:

1. A private loan to the banking system (Burberry's time deposit with NatWest).

2. A commercial loan to the non-bank sector (NatWest's six-month loan to Honda).

3. An interbank loan (Sumitomo's loan to Swiss Bank Corp.).

Most of these transactions involve a bank in the currency's domestic market. In our case Citicorp was involved in most of the transactions. For a short period of time it was not involved in the Honda transaction and if Honda had decided to hold its deposit with NatWest, it would not have become involved. However, this situation can only be shortlived. Borrowers borrow to make payments. When payments are made and recipients do not bank at NatWest, Citicorp will be involved in the transfer of funds to the different banks receiving payments.

It seems that Eurodollar expansion is limitless, stopping only when some bank decides to hold its funds in the United States. In fact, reality is far more reassuring. In the first place, if a Eurobank makes a Eurodollar loan and the proceeds are transferred or spent in the United States, the multiplication will also be ended. This is the second way that dollars can "leak" from the Eurocurrency system. For example, in Transaction 4 if Honda had transferred its funds to Citicorp instead of to Sumitomo, Citicorp's external liability would have disappeared from the Eurobanking system and no more Eurodollars would have been created. Furthermore, Eurodollar creation does not depend just on the ability of Eurobanks to offer slightly better rates than US banks. Dollars must compete with other currencies for borrowing and lending purposes. If borrowers and lenders find that that they are better off borrowing and lending in another currency, they will sell dollars for the other currency, thereby reversing the multiplicative process.

Transaction 6

Suppose, for example, that when Honda's time deposit matures, the company decides that sterling is a better investment than dollars. Honda thus sells dollars for pounds at the rate of

USD 2 = GBP 1 and leaves its sterling in a demand deposit with Sumitomo. This transaction will be recorded by Sumitomo as follows:

	Sumitomo
	Dollar demand deposit owed to Honda −USD 1 million
	Sterling demand deposit owed to Honda +GBP 500 000

The first thing to notice is that the outstanding amount of Eurodollars has been reduced by USD 1 million. A sale of dollars for another currency is thus the third way that dollars can "leak" from the system and reverse the multiplicative process. The second thing to notice is that Sumitomo now has a liability in sterling and an asset in dollars. Such an unbalanced position leaves Sumitomo exposed to a loss if the value of the dollar falls with respect to the pound. In practice Eurobanks try to stay well hedged, which means that they generally try to balance their assets and liabilities in terms of currencies. Consequently, Sumitomo is likely to try to balance its position by selling dollars for pounds, which will reduce the outstanding amount of Eurodollars by USD 1 million more.

Thus, redepositing or spending Eurodollars in the United States stops the multiplicative process and sales of Eurodollars reverses it. Estimates of the actual multiplicative power of the Eurocurrency markets varies. Klopstock argues that leakage from the system is such that the multiplier is barely larger than 1.[4] Clendenning and Meyer find that leakage is seriously reduced insofar as central banks redeposit their reserves in the Eurocurrency market.[5] Following this reasoning, Hewson and Sakakibara,[6] estimate the multiplier at between 3 and 7.

Swoboda estimates its value at about 2.[7] We ourselves find that the multiplier is 3.091 with a one-year lag.[8]

The Eurocurrency market and balance of payments disequilibrium

The central role of the Eurocurrency system in the international transfer of funds raises the question of its effects on an individual country's balance of payments and exchange rate. From a technical point of view, the answer is straightforward. Except when a central bank is involved, Eurocurrency transactions – i.e. the short-term borrowing and lending of

---

[4] F. Klopstock, op. cit., 1970.

[5] E.W. Clendenning, "Eurodollar and credit creation", *International Currency Review* (March–April 1971); H. Meyer, "Multiplier effects and credit creation in the Eurodollar market", *Banca Nazionale del Lavoro Quarterly Review* (September 1971).

[6] J. Hewson and E. Sakakibara, op. cit., 1974.

[7] A.K. Swoboda, "The Eurodollar market: An interpretation", *Essays in International Finance, No. 64,* Princeton University Press, 1968.

[8] Estimations of the equation presented in E.A. Clark, "Le système monétaire international: Liquidités privées et reserves officielles", *Eurépargne* (Septembre 1978).

foreign currencies – have no effect on the balance of payments. If we go back to Transaction 2 in the previous section when Burberry's transferred its dollar deposit from Citicorp to NatWest, we can see that the US balance of payments was unaffected. The amount of external liabilities was unchanged: only the owner changed. The UK's balance of payments was also unaffected. The increase in short-term claims by NatWest on Citicorp was offset by the reduction in short-term claims on Citicorp by Burberry's. The supply and demand of foreign exchange was equal and neither the balance of payments nor the exchange rate were affected.

The same goes for Transaction 3. NatWest's increase in short-term claims as a result of the six-month loan to Honda was offset by the increase in short-term liabilities in the demand deposit owed to Honda. When Honda transferred the demand deposit to Sumitomo in Transaction 4, the supply and demand of foreign currency for all three countries involved in the transaction was perfectly matched. For the United States, the reduction in the demand deposits owed to NatWest was offset by the increase in the demand deposits owed to Sumitomo. For the United Kingdom, the decrease in demand deposits owed to Honda was offset by the decrease in demand deposits held at Citicorp. For Japan, the increase in demand deposits held by Sumitomo at Citicorp was offset by the decrease in demand deposits held by Honda at NatWest.

When a central bank is involved in a transaction, we might isolate the account "change in reserves" and say that the supply and demand of foreign exchange is in equilibrium but the balance of payments is affected. Suppose in Transaction 5 that Sumitomo had loaned to the Swiss central bank rather than to Swiss Bank Corp. The supply and demand of foreign currency would have been equal for Switzerland with the increase in time deposits owed to Sumitomo offset by the increase in demand deposits held at Citicorp. In the balance of payments accounts, however, the time deposit owed to Sumitomo would be found on the source side of short-term liabilities and the demand deposit at Citicorp would show up as an increase in reserves.

Financing balance of payments disequilibrium through the Eurocurrency markets

While it is true that Eurocurrency transactions in themselves have no effect on the balance of payments or the exchange rate, in the overall role of intermediation played by the Eurobanks, Eurocurrency transactions do have an effect. In Transaction 4, if Honda had used its Eurodollar loan to purchase goods in the United States instead of lending to Sumitomo, both the US and the Japanese balance of trade would have been affected. If the loan had been used to purchase securities in the United States, both the US and the Japanese capital accounts would have been affected. If it had been used to purchase goods, services or securities in a third country, that country's balance of payments would also have been affected. Thus, financial intermediation through the Eurocurrency markets influences both the magnitude and direction of trade and capital flows.

This should not be surprising because that is the fundamental role of banks. Banks collect funds from lenders who have a temporary excess of funds and distribute them to borrowers who have a temporary shortage. An excess of funds means a temporary excess of purchasing power. A shortage of funds means an immediate need to purchase and a shortage of purchasing power. Bank intermediation makes it possible to transfer purchasing power to where it is needed. If the banks are doing their job right, they will not only transfer purchasing power to where it is needed, they will also see to it that it is transferred to where it can be used most productively. In the process they transform the maturities and conditions associated with the funds to suit the needs of borrowers and lenders. Many lenders, for example, prefer short-term maturities and conditions that permit access to funds on short notice. Many borrowers prefer longer maturities and conditions that assure access to the funds for as long as they need them. Without the banks the two parties might never come to an agreement. Bank intermediation makes it possible to satisfy the two and avoid wasting purchasing power.

In the Eurocurrency system, bank intermediation plays a key role in the international adjustment of balance of payments disequilibrium by taking deposits from surplus countries and lending to deficit countries. One of the best, or worst, examples of this role came in the wake of the first oil shock in 1973–74. The oil exporting countries were unable to transform all their oil revenues into purchases of goods and services. They therefore had a tremendous trade surplus. The oil importing countries had a corresponding trade deficit. The surplus countries were unwilling to lend directly to many of the deficit countries and much of the proceeds of their surplus was held as foreign exchange reserves in the Eurocurrency market. To the Eurobanks everlasting regret, they performed their role of intermediation with extreme efficiency. They channeled hundreds of billions of what were called "petrodollars" from the oil exporting countries to the oil importing countries, many of them among the poorest and most economically inefficient in the world. Unfortunately, the banks failed to appreciate the risks they were taking by indiscriminately recycling the oil exporting countries' balance of trade surplus, and this came back to haunt them in the 1980s in the form of the "debt crisis".

The Eurocurrency market and exchange rate adjustment

Thus, while Eurocurrency transactions in themselves have no effect on any country's balance of payments, they act as the conduit for the forces that determine the magnitude and direction of trade and capital flows. Given the relation between a country's balance of payments and its exchange rate, it follows that they also act as the conduit for the forces that determine a country's exchange rate.

First let's consider a country whose currency is used on the Euromarkets. In Transaction 6 Honda sells its US dollar deposit to Sumitomo for a sterling deposit. Because both Honda and Sumitomo are Japanese residents, the Japanese balance of payments and exchange rate are not affected by the sale of dollars. The transaction does not affect the US or UK balance of payments directly either. However, it does affect the dollar/sterling exchange rate by putting downward pressure on the dollar. If the initial sale is followed by Sumitomo balancing its foreign exchange position by selling dollars, the dollar will undergo further downward pressure. Furthermore, Swiss Bank Corp. will have an unbalanced position with a liability in sterling and an asset in dollars. If it decides to balance its position, the dollar will fall further. In fact, every dollar that has been created in the Eurocurrency system can be sold (or bought) and it will have the same effect on the exchange rate as if a dollar created in the United States had been sold (or bought).

This has some interesting implications for the domestic monetary policy of a country whose currency is used on the Euromarkets. Notice that the downward pressure on the dollar was not generated by a change in the US price level or balance of payments. In fact, nothing connected with the US economy or financial system was involved. It was generated by a preference for sterling over dollars. This means that a disequilibrium between the supply and demand of a currency used on the Euromarkets can be reflected in the exchange rate before it is reflected in domestic prices or the balance of payments. This contrasts with the scenario that we developed in Chapter 2 where a monetary disequilibrium provoked a price change, which, depending on the exchange system in use, was reflected either in the balance of payments or the exchange rate. In the current scenario the disequilibrium first causes a change in the exchange rate, which, we know from Chapter 2, will affect prices, output, income distribution and consumption.

The situation is somewhat different for a country whose currency is not used on the Euromarkets. Since the currency is not borrowed and lent outside the domestic market, most transactions with the Eurocurrency market involve a foreign currency transaction and affect either the balance of payments or the exchange rate.[9] Consider a bank that borrows on the Eurocurrency market and lends to a firm to pay for imports. There is no sale of foreign exchange but the balance of trade is affected. If a firm borrows on the Eurocurrency market to finance domestic operations, there is a sale of foreign exchange and the exchange rate is affected. If a firm buys foreign currency to lend on the Eurocurrency market, the exchange rate is affected. As we mentioned before, when the central bank borrows on the Eurocurrency markets, the balance of payments is affected because foreign reserves increase. However, if the central bank transfers a part of its reserves from a domestic market like the United States to the Eurocurrency market, neither the balance of payments nor the exchange rate is affected.

International banking: structure and instruments

Organization of the international banking system

The transactions described in the foregoing paragraphs imply the existence of a well developed communications network and an organized system of financial cooperation. This, in fact, is the case. Banks are linked by telephone and telex, and most use a special satellite communications network called **SWIFT** (Society for Worldwide Interbank Financial Telecommunications). SWIFT, based in Belgium, connects over 1800 banks, brokerage firms and non-banking financial institutions worldwide and makes it possible to transmit financial messages in a standardized format that reduces errors that might crop up due to different languages and banking customs. Financial cooperation is achieved through informal arrangements with **correspondent banks** or the more formal formats of representative offices, agencies, and **foreign branches** and **subsidiaries**.

Correspondent banking

A correspondent bank is a bank located in another city, state or country that provides a service for another bank. Correspondent banking originally developed to facilitate long-distance payments, both domestic and foreign. In return for this service, client banks kept relatively large, interest-free balances with the correspondent bank. The term "correspondent" refers to the days before telecommunications when the mail and the telex were used for settling accounts. Today, as we mentioned, these have largely been replaced by SWIFT and computerized international clearing houses such as **CHIPS** (Clearing House Interbank Payments System).

International correspondent banking has evolved over the years as it has become more competitive. Cross-border funds transfers are still the largest single area of international correspondent banking, although services can extend to granting loans, setting up business contacts and giving advice. While interest-free demand balances remain the glue that holds

---

[9] Some countries whose currencies are not Eurocurrencies are centers for Eurocurrency transactions. Singapore, for example, is growing in size and sophistication as a Eurocurrency center (sometimes referred to as an Asiacurrency center). For these countries, their Eurocurrency dealings have no effect on the balance of payments except insofar as profits earned by resident banks on their Eurocurrency activities affect the current account balance. Otherwise, transactions between the Eurocurrency market and the domestic market have the same effect on the exchange rate and the balance of payments as they have for countries that are not Eurocurrency centers.

the banks together and represents the main way that banks pay for correspondent services, fees have assumed a certain importance. Banks can now opt to pay by fee or a combination of fees and interest-free balances. When balances represent payment, they are now more rigorously enforced than they were in the past.

Most smaller banks have correspondents in countries where they do business and large banks have correspondent arrangements in most countries where they do not have an office of their own. Correspondent banking has the advantage of offering a range of international banking services while making it possible to scale costs to the amount of service required in a given area. The disadvantage is that correspondents are not likely to give top priority to another bank's clients.

Representative offices

Representative offices are a way to establish a formal presence in foreign markets. They are not authorized to perform banking services such as effecting transfers and taking deposits. The purpose of these offices is to provide information on local business practices and markets, supply financial contacts with host country institutions and commercial contacts for the bank's home customers, as well as to offer them assistance with local rules and regulations. They are also useful in expediting the services of the local correspondent bank. Although they have the advantage of on-the-spot supervision, they are relatively costly and difficult to staff with competent people because of their lowly status in the banking hierarchy.

Foreign branches and subsidiaries

Foreign branches are banks, just like local banks, and can offer the same types of services. They are subject to the same rules and regulations as local banks but many countries also impose other restrictions on deposit taking and local expansion.

Foreign branching has grown dramatically with the growth of international banking in general. The European Union has also seen a proliferation of cross-border branches of other Union members as well as the growth of Union member branches in the United States and Asia. Japan's banks have followed its commercial successes and established branches in most of the major financial centers. Most countries have at least one or two banks with a network of branches in the major financial centers.

Foreign branching has grown for many reasons. First of all, commerce has become intrinsically international in nature. It is rare for a medium-sized company to be isolated from foreign suppliers and customers and many of the larger companies do more business abroad than they do in their home markets. Establishing a foreign branch was a way of keeping clients that might otherwise have been lost. Secondly, a foreign branch affords access to foreign money markets. This access is indispensable to the larger banks that have funding needs in many currencies. It also offers them investment opportunities that might be unavailable in the domestic market. Finally, foreign branching is a way to diversify cash flows. Economic expansion and contraction varies across countries. A downturn in Japan might accompany an expansion in the EU or the United States. Since banking activity is closely tied to economic activity, a diversified geographical presence should give a diversified range of cash flows.

While foreign branching has been widespread, its growth has been curtailed because most countries restrict branch banks' activities in order to protect local banks from aggressive competition. This was true in many EU countries where local banks grew bloated and inefficient. The United Kingdom has been comparatively liberal in allowing foreign banks to operate, and it owes its position as a major financial center partly to that. Banking restrictions for EU member banks came down in 1992 and this caused a flurry of merger activity as local banks positioned themselves for a competitive onslaught. The

International Banking Act of 1978 provides for the regulation and supervision of foreign banks in the United States. They may be granted a license in states where this is allowed but are restricted to that one state. They have access to Federal Reserve services and must respect reserve requirements and provide deposit insurance.

Rather than establish branches, some banks decide to create a subsidiary. A subsidiary differs from a branch insofar as the branch is part of a company that is incorporated elsewhere whereas the subsidiary is incorporated locally and owned either completely or partially by a foreign parent. Generally speaking, a subsidiary is indistinguishable from a locally owned bank. Most major countries provide some scope for foreign subsidiary banking.

Branches and subsidiaries have the advantage of expanding a bank's presence and offering a wider range of international services to its home clients as well as the possibility of cultivating local clients. On the other hand, branches and subsidiaries are costly to start up and run. They need to generate a considerable amount of business to make them worthwhile and it may take years before they establish a presence. For this reason many banks try to enter a local market through a merger or acquisition.

Mergers and acquisitions make it possible to "hit the ground running". An existing bank is a going concern. It has an ongoing deposit base, a functioning management team knowledgeable in the customs and culture of the home country, and a network of contacts and clients. For these same reasons, mergers and acquisitions are expensive. Furthermore, they don't always work. In fact, they often fail and failures are costly both financially and in terms of reputation.

An overview of the system

The international banking system has its roots in the domestic monetary systems of each individual country. Banks in the domestic monetary systems include foreign branches and subsidiaries and are supervised by the domestic monetary authorities. They are linked by the domestic communications system and domestic transactions are cleared by the domestic clearing system.

Besides transactions with domestic financial institutions, banks also deal with foreign financial institutions. For these transactions a foreign intermediary is necessary. The most common relationship is a correspondent agreement, whereby domestic banks undertake transfers on behalf of the clients of foreign banks. Transfers between the correspondent bank and the foreign bank's client are cleared on the domestic clearing system. Transfers between the foreign bank and its correspondent are cleared either bank to bank or through the domestic system of the currency that is being transferred. Communications between correspondent and foreign bank are carried out by telephone, telex, fax, mail and more commonly through the specialized SWIFT network.

Banks that require a higher level of service maintain representative offices or agencies in foreign countries. An even higher level of service can be achieved by establishing a branch or a fully fledged subsidiary. Communications between branch or subsidiary and parent are closer than correspondent–foreign bank communications but they are basically carried out on the same systems.

International banks have developed an offshore network of transactions that are outside the jurisdiction of any single regulatory authority. These transactions routinely use both domestic and international communications systems and clearing facilities. Operations are conducted from financial centers with a developed domestic financial system such as London, Paris or New York, and they are also conducted from centers with relatively small domestic financial systems specializing in international transactions such as the Cayman Islands, Singapore, and the Channel Islands of Jersey and Guernsey.

Communications and information processing have evolved to the point that geographical distance has almost become irrelevant. The well developed network of correspondent arrangements and physical presence in the form of representatives, agencies, branches and subsidiaries ensure that the communications possibilities are exploited intensely and in increasingly inventive ways. The result is a highly integrated system where it is often difficult to discern where one market begins and the other ends.

Instruments of Eurobank financing

Term deposits

As we mentioned, Eurocurrency liabilities are typically conventional term deposits of one day to one year's duration. Conventional term deposits are non-negotiable bank deposits with a fixed term where the interest rate is fixed for the duration of the deposit. Maturities can vary from one day to several years but most Eurocurrency term deposits are in the range of seven days to six months. Although the term of the deposit is fixed at the outset, under certain conditions and after payment of a penalty on the rate of interest, most banks offer the possibility to make an early withdrawal. Early withdrawals are not widespread, however. Investors seem to prefer to keep their maturities short and if they find themselves in need of cash, rather than cash in their deposit, they use it for collateral.

Certificates of deposit

A growing proportion of Eurobank liabilities are in the form of **certificates of deposit** (CDs). Certificates of deposit are negotiable instruments that can be traded on the secondary market. This makes them more liquid or closer to cash than a conventional term deposit, which has a penalty for early withdrawal. Because of their greater liquidity CDs usually pay a lower rate of interest than a term deposit. The difference is normally between 6 and 15 **basis points** (a basis point is 0.01%). In spite of the lower rate of return, they are popular with company treasurers because of the flexibility they offer.

Most Eurocurrency CDs are denominated in dollars or sterling issued by London or New York banks. They can pay as much as 50 basis points or more above the rate on a comparable domestic CD but 20–25 basis points is the norm. Although they can be purchased in denominations as low as USD 25,000, rates tend to be lower on smaller denominations.

The secondary market for Eurocurrency CDs is liquid and active. Because they are issued to "bearer", trading is facilitated by the lack of documentation. Several London banks act as market-maker and always stand ready to buy or sell. Compensation is effected between banks in London.

Floating rate notes

Floating rate notes (FRNs) are generally medium-term CDs where the interest rate is fixed at a percentage above Libor (usually 15 to 30 basis points). Adjustments are made at regular intervals (every three or six months) according to the prevailing Libor. Some FRNs guarantee a minimum interest rate. The secondary market is liquid and the relatively high yields make them attractive investments.

Summary

1. A Eurocurrency is any freely convertible currency, such as a dollar or a pound, deposited in a bank outside its country of origin. It is the residency of a bank and not its nationality that determines the Eurocurrency nature of the deposit. Sometimes the term "offshore currency" is used instead.

2. Eurocurrency deposits are typically conventional term deposits of one day to one year's duration. In Eurocurrency transactions the currency that is used is always a foreign

currency to at least one of the two parties, and one of the two parties is always a bank. The other party can be another bank, a central bank, a government or a large corporate entity.

3. The interbank market is the core of the Eurocurrency market. This interbank Eurocurrency market is organized as an international over-the-counter market, the members of which are linked by telephone and telex. Access to this market is reserved to top quality institutions. The sums involved are huge with USD 1 million the usual minimum transaction size.

4. Eurocurrency markets are outside the jurisdiction of any single regulatory authority and the interest rates are determined by pure supply and demand. As a wholesale market dealing without costly regulations, the Eurocurrency market can offer attractive rates and certain services that are unavailable in the domestic markets. Factors of cost and convenience are behind the emergence and growth of all the Eurocurrencies.

5. Interest rates in the Eurocurrency markets are closely related to interest rates in the domestic markets. Large differentials indicate controls, incremental risk or both.

6. Banks quote bid–ask spreads to each other. Non-banks are usually quoted the bid rate less a small commission when lending, and Libor or Pibor plus a commission that reflects its creditworthiness when borrowing.

7. Money and credit expansion through the Eurocurrency system is possible but limited because of "leaks" from the system. Leaks occur through redepositing or spending Eurocurrencies in their domestic markets or when the currency is sold.

8. Except when a central bank is involved, Eurocurrency transactions have no effect on the balance of payments. The role of financial intermediation played by banks through the Eurocurrency markets does, however, influence both the magnitude and direction of trade and capital flows.

9. Eurocurrencies are more difficult for their domestic monetary authorities to manage than non-Eurocurrencies.

10. The international banking system is linked by a sophisticated system of telecommunications. It is organized around informal correspondent agreements and outright physical presence involving representative offices, agencies, branches or subsidiaries.

11. The major source of funds for Eurobanks is the non-negotiable term deposit, but the negotiable CD is popular with corporate treasurers and growing in importance.

Questions

Solutions to the following questions are set out on the web site, details of which are included in the Preface.

1. Describe the Eurocurrency market.

2. Why can the Eurocurrency markets offer more attractive borrowing and lending rates than the domestic markets for the same currencies?

3. Translate the following information on Eurocurrency interest rates into words:

   a. One-month USD: $5\frac{13}{16} - 5\frac{15}{16}$

   b. Two-month EUR: $9\frac{1}{8} - 9\frac{1}{4}$

   c. Three-month CHF: $7\frac{3}{4} - 7\frac{7}{8}$

   d. Six-month GBP: $10\frac{3}{4} - 10\frac{7}{8}$

   e. One-year EUR: $9\frac{9}{16} - 9\frac{3}{4}$

4. What is Libor and Pibor and what role do they play in quoting interest rates?

5. Use T-accounts to record the following transactions for Citicorp, NatWest and BNP:

    a. US Corp. pays British Petroleum USD 1 million with a check drawn on Citicorp;

    b. BP instructs Citicorp to transfer USD 1 million to its account with NatWest in London;

    c. NatWest lends USD 1 million for six months to BNP in Paris;

    d. BNP makes a five-year USD 1 million loan to France Télécom.

Show the position of these banks at the end of the last transaction.

6. In the light of the fact that there are no reserve requirements in the Eurocurrency markets, what limits the multiplicative process generated by successive deposits and loans?

7. Do Eurocurrency transactions in themselves create a disequilibrium in the supply and demand of one currency for another? What role does the Eurocurrency market play in balance of payments and exchange rate adjustments?

8. What alternatives are open to domestic banks for clients with international activities?

9. Describe the international banking system.

The foreign exchange market

Most international financial transactions sooner or later involve an exchange of one currency for another. This is why the exchange rate and exchange rate determination play such an important role in international financial theory. How theory comes out in reality, however, depends on the systems and procedures that are effectively used for executing the exchange. Costs and delays in execution can be the determining factors in whether or not certain operations can be profitably undertaken. Hence, the efficiency of the international financial system and its degree of integration with the individual national financial systems depends to a large extent on how cheaply and quickly foreign exchange transactions can be effected.

The foreign exchange market is where currencies are bought and sold. In this chapter we look at the foreign exchange market from a technical point of view, examining how the market is organized, how exchange rates are quoted and how trades are actually made. We will also see how delivery and settlement is achieved between agents in different countries. An important element in the discussion is the link between the foreign exchange market and the Eurocurrency market. In fact, we will see that it is this link that determines the limits on costs in foreign exchange transactions, ensures financial efficiency and generates the conditions for the integration of the individual national financial markets.

Organization of the foreign exchange spot market

The interbank market

Foreign exchange transactions involve buying and selling one currency for another. In reality bills and coins rarely change hands and what is involved is exchanging a demand deposit denominated in one currency for a demand deposit denominated in another currency. The transactions can be made for immediate delivery on the spot market or for future delivery on the forward market. The core of the foreign exchange market is the interbank market, which is closely linked to the Eurocurrency interbank market described in Chapter 5. It is an informal, over-the-counter, around-the-clock market that includes the major commercial banks and some specialized brokers located in the principal financial centers throughout the world. They are linked by telephone and telex, and most use the special satellite communications network called SWIFT.

Foreign exchange trading can be a hectic existence. Traders have their control panel of display monitors, telex machines and several telephones that generate a continuous flow of current information. The continuous transmission of indicative rates via international database services such as Reuters and Telerate as well as direct online quotes from numerous financial institutions and constant telephone contact among market participants ensure that exchange rates react quickly to new developments and traders have to be alert. Competition is fierce and spreads are narrow, often below 0.1% of the value of a contract.

The interbank market is composed of traders and brokers. The roles of the trader and the broker are essentially different. Traders usually operate out of the foreign exchange trading room of a major bank, and essentially they are **market-makers** standing ready to buy and sell foreign currencies on a more or less continuous basis. They take buying and selling positions based on their assessment of the market and on orders from their clients.

Actual trading is accomplished through an informal and straightforward procedure. When a trader is contacted by another trader for a quote, the latter does not reveal the amount of the transaction he has in mind or whether he wants to buy or sell. The trader who has been contacted will give the caller two prices, the price at which he will buy the currency in question and the price at which he will sell it. This is the same system as in the Eurocurrency market and the difference between the two prices is the spread. These prices apply to minimum quantities of USD 1 million or its foreign exchange equivalent, although standard transactions are up to about USD 3 million in the interbank market. Once the caller has the trader's quote he only has about a minute to decide what he wants to do. After that, convention has it that the trader has the right to change the quote. If the caller decides to deal, the trader is bound to honor his quote and the caller will tell the trader whether he wants to buy or sell and the amount of the transaction. Written confirmation of the trade follows the oral agreement, and it is important that traders establish a reputation for honesty and reliability.

Bank traders cannot always locate a counterparty to the trades they want to make and sometimes find it necessary or convenient to employ a broker. When a trader calls a broker, he does not have to hide his position. He can tell the broker whether he wants to buy or sell, the amount involved and the rate he is willing to pay. The broker thus has knowledge of what is available in the market and this he communicates to other traders until he matches a buy and a sell. Once the match is made, the trade takes place. The broker keeps the names of his customers secret so, before the deal is made, neither of the counterparties knows who they are dealing with. Once the trade is finalized the broker supplies the names of the counterparties and collects a fee from both sides. The fee makes dealing through a broker more expensive than direct dealing but has the advantage of dealing at the desired price and keeping the trader's identity secret until the trade is made.

Thus, the broker serves three important purposes. First of all, he is a precious source of information for the traders in markets where one or two basis points can mean a difference of thousands of dollars on a contract. Secondly, he brings buyers and sellers together and contributes to market efficiency. Thirdly, he makes it possible for traders to remain anonymous when revealing their identity would put them at a disadvantage. Suppose, for example, that a trader has a comfortable long position in sterling and sterling is on the rise. He feels that the rise is almost over and would like to undo his position. However, the other traders recognize him as the current "specialist" in sterling and are watching his quotes and whether he buys or sells. If he enters the market directly as a seller, he might reverse the rising trend of sterling and cause himself some heavy losses in the process. In this situation he might find it advantageous to contact a broker and quote some buy and sell prices for sterling without divulging whether he wants to buy or sell, but quoting prices that are more likely to attract a buyer than a seller. His anonymity protected by the broker, he can undo his position without divulging his intentions to the market.

Spot quotations

Direct dollar quotes

Exchange rates can be quoted in two ways: (a) the number of units of domestic currency for one unit of foreign currency; or (b) the number of units of foreign currency for one unit of domestic currency. Most financial centers use the first method and quote the number of units of domestic currency for one unit of foreign currency. Thus, in the euro-zone the spot exchange rate between the dollar and the euro will be quoted:[1]

$$S_0(EUR/USD) = EUR\ 1.10000$$

which means that it takes EUR 1.1 to buy USD 1. In Switzerland the sport exchange rate will be quoted:

$$S_0(CHF/USD) = CHF\ 2.0000$$

which means it takes CHF 2 to buy USD 1. If we want to know how many dollars it takes to buy one euro or one Swiss franc, we simply take the reciprocal of the dollar rate:

$$S_0(USD/EUR) = \frac{1}{S_0(EUR/USD)} = USD\ 0.9091$$

which means it takes 90.91 US cents to buy one euro and

$$S_0(USD/CHF) = \frac{1}{S_0(CHF/USD)} = USD\ 0.5000$$

which means it takes 50 US cents to buy one Swiss franc.

Unfortunately all countries do not respect this convention. In the United Kingdom and Ireland, among others, quotes are made in the number of units of foreign currency it takes to buy one unit of domestic currency. Starting in 1979 New York banks also went on what is called European terms, which involves giving the number of units of foreign currency it takes to buy one dollar. American terms refer to giving the number of dollars it takes to buy one unit of foreign currency. French-speaking countries call quotes in the number of units of domestic currency for one unit of foreign currency as the "*incertain*" and quotes in the number of units of foreign currency for one unit of domestic currency as the "*certain*". In any case, what is important is to know which currency is in the denominator because the currency in the denominator is the unit currency. You will have noticed that our notation, although somewhat cumbersome, makes that clear. When reading foreign currency tables, however, care must be taken to avoid errors. For example, Table 6.1 quotes rates published in the *Financial Times* on 27 December 2000. The rates are in European terms (i.e. the number of units of each currency it takes to buy one dollar). However, on close inspection the footnote reveals that the pound sterling and the euro are quoted the other way around, as the number of dollars for the other currency.

The rates set out in Table 6.1 are interbank rates and the column labeled "Closing mid-point" refers to the spot rate taken towards the end of London trading. Notice in the column labeled "Bid/offer spread" that there are two rates for each currency. The first rate refers to the bid rate and the second to the ask rate. Banks were willing, for example, to buy dollars and pay CHF 1.6374 per dollar. On the other hand they would sell dollars and charge

[1] In fact, quotes are usually given in the form USD: EUR1.1000, meaning that it takes EUR 1.1 euros to buy USD 1. We will not adopt this method because it does not lend itself to ease of use in equations.

Table 6.1 Selected US dollar spot and forward rates, 27 December 2000

	Closing mid-point	Bid/offer spread	One month	% p.a.	Three months	% p.a.
Denmark	8.0179	163–195	8.0084	1.4	7.9962	1.1
Switzerland	1.6377	374–380	1.6330	3.4	1.6255	3.0
United Kingdom	1.4886	883–888	1.4895	–0.7	1.4908	–0.6
Euro	0.9306	303–308	0.9321	–1.9	0.9342	–1.5
Canada	1.5107	104–110	1.5095	1.0	1.5079	0.7
Australia	1.7920	908–931	1.7916	0.2	1.7912	0.2
Japan	114.170	140–200	113.58	6.2	112.535	5.7
South Korea	1258.50	700–000	—	—	—	—

Note: Bid/offer spreads in the dollar spot column show only the last three decimal places. The UK pound and the Euro are quoted in US currency.
Source: *Financial Times*.

CHF 1.6380 per dollar. The difference is the spread and represents the banks' gain. In this case we can see that it is very small, at less than 0.04%.

Spreads make it a little more complicated when going from European to American quotes or from the "*certain*" to the "*incertain*" by taking the reciprocal as we did above. Just remember that foreign exchange quotes are symmetrical. Buying one is the same as selling the other. For example, buying dollars for Swiss francs is the same as selling Swiss francs for dollars. Hence, the reciprocal of the bid price for dollars is the *ask* price for francs:

$$S_0(\text{USD/CHF})_{\text{ask}} = \frac{1}{S_0(\text{CHF/USD})_{\text{bid}}} \tag{6.1}$$

By the same token, selling dollars for francs is the same thing as buying francs for dollars. Therefore, the reciprocal of the ask price for dollars is the *bid* price for francs:

$$S_0(\text{USD/CHF})_{\text{bid}} = \frac{1}{S_0(\text{CHF/USD})_{\text{ask}}} \tag{6.2}$$

We can use these two formulae to calculate the bid–ask dollar rates on the Swiss franc from the information in Exhibit 6.1.

$$S_0(\text{USD/CHF})_{\text{bid}} = \frac{1}{S_0(\text{CHF/USD})_{\text{ask}}} = \frac{1}{1.6380} = 0.6105$$

$$S_0(\text{USD/CHF})_{\text{ask}} = \frac{1}{S_0(\text{CHF/USD})_{\text{bid}}} = \frac{1}{1.6374} = 0.6107$$

Thus, the bid–ask dollar rates on the Swiss franc would be 0.6105–0.6107.

One last remark is in order. Professional traders have a shorthand way of quoting prices. Rather than quote the rate as 0.6105–0.6107, or even 0.6105–07, they will only quote the last two digits, 05–07. For non-traders quotes like this seem somewhat mysterious. However, because traders follow the market continuously, they know what the missing figures are. Just to make sure that there is no confusion, we shall continue to give the full quote.

Cross rates

For currencies that are traded frequently like the US dollar, the Swiss franc and the Japanese yen, the system is fairly straightforward. But what about the rate of the Vanuatu vatu (VUV) for the Vietnamese dong (VND), or the Malawi kwacha (MWK) for the Maldivian rufiyaa (MVR)? The IMF records exchange rates for 152 countries, which means that there are $(152 \times 151)/2 = 11\ 476$ different pairs of currencies and the same number of possible exchange rates. Most of these possibilities are likely never to come up for a trade and many only once in a blue moon. If they do come up, however, how can the trader arrive at a price?

The answer is that all currencies are quoted against the US dollar. Knowing the price of any two currencies against the dollar means that the price of one currency for the other can easily be found. The exchange rate between two currencies not involving the dollar is called the **cross rate**.

Let's forget about the spread for a moment and take a simple example. Suppose the following information is available:

$$S_0(CHF/USD) = CHF\ 2.0000$$

$$S_0(JPY/USD) = JPY\ 120.000$$

The number of Japanese yen for Swiss francs or the number of francs for yen can easily be found. If you had yen and wanted francs, you could pay JPY 120 and get USD 1. Then you could sell the dollar and buy CHF 2. For each franc you would have paid JPY 120/CHF 2 = JPY 60. Conversely, if you had Swiss francs and wanted yen, you could sell CHF 2 and receive USD 1. Then you could sell the dollar and buy JPY 120. For each yen you would have paid CHF 2/JPY 120 = CHF 0.0167

Suppose, then, that you have USD 1 million and the following information:

In New York USD 1 = CHF 2.0000
In London USD 1 = JPY 120.000
In Tokyo CHF 1 = JPY 59.000.

Something is wrong in Tokyo. You know that the JPY/CHF rate should be JPY 60 but it is only 59. As an astute trader, you could sell your dollars and buy JPY 120 million in London. You could sell your yen for CHF 2,033,898 in Tokyo and then use them to buy USD 1,016,949 in New York, making a profit of USD 16,949. This is called "triangular arbitrage" and in an efficient market should keep the exchange rates from getting out of line. Buying yen in London would raise the price of yen for dollars. Selling yen in Tokyo would lower the price of yen for Swiss francs and buying dollars in New York would lower the price of francs for dollars. This would continue until the arbitrage opportunity disappeared. In today's world of sophisticated telecommunications and round-the-clock trading, arbitrage opportunities such as this should be short-lived.

When spreads are involved, the reasoning is the same but the calculations are a little more complicated. Suppose you are a trader and you are asked for a quote on Philippine pesos for the Norwegian krone. This is a combination that you don't see too often and is not being quoted directly. Therefore, you get the quotes of pesos for dollars and kroner for dollars, which are:

Philippine peso (PHP): 49.9000–50.0000
Norwegian krone (NOK): 6.8475–6.8525

You then make the following argument. If my client wants to buy pesos, he could obtain pesos for kroner by first buying dollars and paying NOK 6.8525 and then selling the dollars and receiving PHP 49.90. The price per krone would then be 49.90/6.8525 = PHP 7.2820 per krone. My bid price can't be any lower than this, otherwise my client will by-pass me and take this route. On the other hand, if he wants kroner, my client could obtain kroner for pesos by buying dollars with pesos for PHP 50.00 per dollar and then selling the dollars for NOK 6.8475. The price of each krone will then be 50.00/6.8475 = PHP 7.3019 per krone. My ask price cannot be any higher than this, otherwise my client will by-pass me and take this route. Thus my direct quote has to be somewhere between the limits of:

$$S_0(\text{PHP/NOK}): 7.2820\text{--}7.3019.$$

The reason that it could be somewhere between the two limit quotes is because calculating the cross rate from the bid–ask price effectively includes the transaction cost of both a buy and a sell against the dollar. Some banks may want to buy or already be holding pesos or kroner or both, and thus be willing to reduce their spread. Consequently, a better situation than the limit quotes is likely to exist, especially with a bank that is a market-maker in the direct exchange under consideration. When dealing in cross rates, it will probably pay to shop around for a price better than the limit quotes.

Retail rates and settlement procedures

The spreads on the exchange rates that the banks charge their customers are different from the spreads that are found in the interbank market. Spreads on the interbank market are based on the breadth and depth of a market for a given currency as well as on the currency's volatility. Currencies that are more volatile or less widely traded usually have higher spreads. Spreads also tend to widen in times of financial or economic turbulence. Because of competition, spreads to bank customers reflect the spreads on the interbank market but include a commission. The commission depends on the size of the transaction. Generally speaking, the larger the transaction the lower the spread. Let's see what happens in a typical transaction.

On Wednesday, 28 August, a dollar-based money manager from Renco, a US mutual fund, has USD 1 million that he wants to invest with Barclays in London in a one-year certificate of deposit in Danish krone yielding 10%. A comparable deposit in the United States would only yield 6%. The interbank rate is 5.0100–5.0120. The money manager calls around to several banks for quotes without indicating whether he wants to buy or sell kroner. The best quote is from Citicorp, at 5.0000–5.0220. Citicorp is taking a one øre commission between the interbank bid rate and the rate it is charging the money manager, which works out to 0.2%. For a lower dollar amount the money manager would have had to pay a higher commission. However, he would have paid a lower commission if he had decided to buy the certificate of deposit in a currency that is traded more heavily than the Danish krone.

When the agreement is reached between the money manager and Citicorp, telexes are exchanged to confirm. Citicorp requests the details of where the krone are to be paid and Renco gives Citicorp the information on Barclays in London. Citicorp then notifies Barclays on the day of the sale via SWIFT of the impending transfer of Danish kroner from Renco. In foreign exchange transactions funds are not usually actually transferred until two business days after the deal was initiated. Thus, two business days later, on Friday 30 August, Citicorp debits Renco's account for USD 1 million, Barclays credits Renco's account for DKK 5 million and Barclays and Citicorp settle between themselves for DKK 5 million. If the transaction had been initiated on Thursday 29 August, the transfer would not have taken place until Monday 2 September, because Saturday and Sunday are not counted as business days.

Renco's settlement with Barclays is a straightforward bank transaction similar to that in a domestic transaction. The international aspect of the settlement between Citicorp and Barclays, however, makes it worth examining in more detail. It can take two forms. If the two banks maintain correspondent accounts with each other, we know from Chapter 5 that the transaction described above will be reflected in the banks' accounts as follows:

Citicorp			Barclays
Demand deposit held at Barclays −DKK 5,000,000	Demand deposit owed to Renco −USD 1,000,000		Demand deposit owed to Citicorp −DKK 5,000,000
			Certificate of deposit owed to Renco + DKK 5,000,000

Fund transfers through clearing houses

If Citicorp does not hold a correspondent account in Danish kroner, it will have to buy the kroner and have them transferred to Barclays. This implies the necessity for some kind of clearing system whereby banks can settle accounts among themselves. Let's see how an international clearing system works.

Suppose that Citicorp buys DKK 5 million from NatWest, which has no correspondent agreement with Citicorp but which is a member of CHIPS (Clearing House Interbank Payments System). CHIPS is a computerized network for international transfers of dollar funds that links depository institutions with offices in New York City. The system is owned and operated by the New York Clearing House Association whose members comprise 12 New York money center banks. It currently handles around 90% of international interbank transfers involving US dollars.

As soon as Citicorp buys Danish kroner from NatWest, it instructs NatWest to transfer the kroner to its account at Barclays. The transfer will be effected two business days later on Friday 30 August. Payment to NatWest for the kroner will be made through CHIPS and Citicorp immediately enters its identity code, NatWest's identity code, and the amount to be transferred into its CHIPS terminal where the message is stored in the CHIPS central computer. NatWest does the same.

On 30 August when the CHIPS network closes down at 4.30p.m. (16.30) Eastern Standard Time, the CHIPS computer sends out a settlement report for the net amounts to be paid or received that day. If Citicorp had no other transactions with CHIPS on 30 August, it has to settle for the dollar value of the DKK 5,000,000. Remember that the interbank rate was 5.0100–5.0120. Applying Formula 6.1, the ask rate for Danish kroner was 1/5.0100 = 0.1996. Thus Citicorp owes 0.1996 × 5,000,000 = USD 998,004 and has until 5.45p.m. (17.45) to settle. This it does by sending a message via **Fedwire** to the Federal Reserve Bank of New York to debit its account there by that amount in favor of the CHIPS settlement account. The Fedwire system is operated by the Federal Reserve (the Fed) for domestic money transfers between institutions that have accounts at the Federal Reserve banks. CHIPS will then send the messages via Fedwire instructing the Fed to credit the accounts of the net creditors out of the CHIPS settlement account. If NatWest is a creditor as a result of its transaction with Citicorp, its account with the Fed will increase by USD 998,004. The whole process is usually completed by 6:00p.m. (18.00).

Other clearing systems for international payments also exist. **CHAPS** (Clearing House Automated Payments System), for example, is a computerized clearing system for sterling funds that began operations on 9 February 1984. It includes 14 member banks and nearly 450 participating banks, and is one of the clearing companies within the Association for Payment Clearing Services (APACS) structure.

Whereas CHIPS is a centralized system, CHAPS is a two-tiered system whereby the member clearing banks operate the core clearing system but offer agency agreements with a wide variety of other financial institutions that allow them access to it. Consider a bank in Hong Kong that has been instructed to make a payment of GBP 1 million to a non-clearing UK bank. The Hong Kong bank sends the payment instruction, including the identification of the clearing bank where its non-clearing UK customer holds its account, via SWIFT or some other mutually acceptable medium, to the UK clearing bank where it holds its own account. After verification, this clearing bank then creates the payment message in the CHAPS format and sends it through its access to the central CHAPS system, called a Gateway. The Gateway, having accepted and acknowledged the payment message, delivers it via British Telecom Packet Switching Service (PSS) to the Gateway of the correct receiving clearing bank for onward transmission to the non-clearing UK bank that is the beneficiary. After verification, the receiving clearing bank acknowledges receipt of the payment, which is passed on to the CHAPS payment process within its own network. At the close of the day's normal business (3.10p.m.) the clearing banks calculate the net difference that has arisen between them as a result of the day's transactions. The debtor clearing banks then send CHAPS payment messages to the Bank of England, which is itself a clearing bank and which holds the settlement accounts, in favor of the clearing banks that are owed money. If, for instance, the day's only transaction between the two clearing banks was the USD 1 million in our example, the clearing bank for the Hong Kong bank would instruct the Bank of England to debit its account by USD 1 million in favor of the receiving clearing bank.

The forward foreign exchange market

Spot exchange rates are quoted for delivery two business days after the transaction is concluded. Foreign exchange traders in the interbank market also quote exchange rates for delivery further than two days in the future. As we mentioned in Chapter 3, deals like this are called forward contracts. The rates and the amounts are agreed on today but settlement occurs sometime later than two days in the future. Contracts can be negotiated for just about any maturity but most banks supply regular quotes on maturities of 30, 60, 90, and 180 days.

Forward quotes

Discounts and premiums

When we looked at interest rate parity in Chapter 3 we established the relationship between the spot and forward exchange rates and the interest rate differential. Equation 3.11, reproduced here for convenience, stated that relationship:

$$\frac{F_{0,t}(\text{CHF/USD}) - S_0(\text{CHF/USD})}{S_0(\text{CHF/USD})} = \frac{r_{\text{CHF}} - r_{\text{USD}}}{(1 + r_{\text{USD}})} \quad (3.11)$$

We said that the left-hand side of the equation represented the forward premium or the forward discount. It is useful, as we shall see, to present the premium or discount as an annual percentage in order to compare it with interest rates which are also presented this way. This can be done by dividing the discount by the number of years or fraction of a year of the forward contract's duration:

$$\text{Forward discount (premium)} = \frac{F_{0,t}(\text{CHF/USD}) - S_0(\text{CHF/USD})}{t S_0(\text{CHF/USD})} \qquad (6.3)$$

where t represents the number of years to the contract's settlement. Thus $F_{0,1}$ means the contract will be settled in one year, $F_{0,2}$ means it will be settled in two years and $F_{0,1/4}$ means the contract will be settled in one-fourth of a year or 90 days.

Let's take a simple example where no transaction costs are involved. Suppose that the South Korean won (KRW) spot rate versus the dollar is KRW 1308.00 and that the forward rate for delivery 90 days later is KRW 1327.50. On a 360-day year basis, 90 days is one-quarter of one year. We can apply Formula 6.3 to calculate the premium as an annual percentage that must be paid in South Korean won to buy one dollar today for delivery 90 days in the future:

$$\frac{F_{0,1/4}(\text{KRW/USD}) - S_0(\text{KPW/USD})}{\frac{1}{4}S_0(\text{KRW/USD})} = \frac{1327.50 - 1308.00}{\frac{1}{4}(1308.00)} = 0.0596 = 5.96\%.$$

Thus, it will cost 5.96% more won to buy a dollar for delivery 90 days forward than it does to buy a dollar for delivery in two days. This is what is meant by a forward premium. We knew it was a premium because the forward rate is higher than the spot rate. If the forward rate had been lower than the spot rate we would have said that there was a forward discount concerning the amount of South Korean won that must be paid for the dollar 90 days forward.

Care must be taken when talking about discounts and premiums on forward foreign exchange contracts. Because buying one currency is the same as selling the other, there can be some ambiguity about which currency is being sold at a discount or premium. For example, some people would say that a 5.96% premium for the 90-day forward dollar is the same as a 5.96% discount for the 90-day forward won. In fact, this is exactly how it is shown in Table 6.1. We can work through an example to see how discounts and premiums are often presented in the financial press.

In the column labeled "Closing mid-point" we can see that the Japanese yen is quoted spot as 114.170. This rate was calculated by using the bid/offer spread to calculate the bid/ask rate: 114.140–114.200. Taking the sum of the bid and the ask and dividing by two gives the closing mid-point. In the column labeled "one month" we see that the mid-point rate for a one-month forward contract is 113.58. We know that the US dollar is at a discount to the yen because the dollar buys fewer yen for delivery in one month than it does for spot delivery. In the first column labeled "% p.a." we see 6.2, which means that the premium on the yen vis-à-vis the dollar is 6.2%. The premium of 6.2% was calculated by using the average forward and spot rates in Equation 6.3 to calculate the discount on the dollar:

$$\frac{113.58 - 114.17}{\frac{1}{12}(114.17)} = -6.2\%.$$

Because the discount on the dollar is approximately equal to the premium on the yen, it is reported as the premium on the yen. In fact, the premium on the yen is higher than 6.2%. Taking the reciprocals of $S_0(\text{JPY/USD})$ and $F_{0,1/12}(\text{JPY/USD})$ to get the (USD/JPY) rates gives a premium on the yen of

$$\frac{\frac{1}{113.58} - \frac{1}{114.17}}{\frac{1}{12}\left(\frac{1}{114.17}\right)} = 6.233\%.$$

This having been said, in order to reduce the opportunities for confusion, we will always speak of the discount or premium in terms of the currency that is in the denominator of the exchange rate. Thus, if we give the CHF/USD exchange rate, we will speak of the discount or premium on the dollar or say the dollar is at a forward discount or premium. If it takes more Swiss francs to buy a dollar forward than it does to buy a dollar spot, we will say that there is a premium on the dollar or the dollar is at a premium. If it takes fewer Swiss francs to buy one dollar forward, we will say that there is a discount on the dollar or the dollar is at a discount.

Conventions in forward quotations

There are basically two methods of expressing forward exchange rates. The first method is to quote the rate "outright" and is similar to spot quotes. It involves giving the number of units of one currency that it takes to buy one unit of another currency for delivery in the future. The second method presents the forward rate as a discount or premium on the spot rate and is called the **swap rate**. Table 6.1, for example, quotes the forward rates outright.

When forward rates are quoted as a swap instead of outright, the spot rate is given and then the forward rate is given as a number of points that must be added or subtracted from the spot rate. Consider, for example, the rates set out in Table 6.2. On the USD/GBP rates, the bid points are larger than the ask points (80 > 78 and 213 > 210). This tells us that the pound is selling at a discount and that to obtain the outright forward rate we must subtract the bid–ask points from the spot rate. The reasons for this are simple. First of all, the spread on the forward rate should increase as the maturity of the contract increases. This is so partly because longer maturities are riskier than shorter maturities. To the extent that banks do not offset all their forward positions, they will demand a larger spread. The market also thins out as maturities increase, which makes it more difficult for banks that have contracted at a given rate to take an offsetting position. To compensate for this risk they will also require a larger spread. Secondly, the bid price must always be lower than the ask price. Hence, when bid points are higher than ask points, the only way to ensure that spreads will increase with maturity and that the bid price will always be lower than the ask price is to subtract. Table 6.3 shows the outright quotes for the USD/GBP exchange rate. Notice that the spread increases with the maturity of the forward contract.

Table 6.2 Example spot and forward rates

	Spot	One-month	Three-months
USD/GBP	1.6715–25	80–78	213–210
CAD/USD	1.1435–45	27–31	83–88

Table 6.3 Bid–ask rates, USD/GBP

	Bid	Ask	Spread	%
Spot	1.6715	1.6725	0.0010	0.0598
One-month	1.6635	1.6647	0.0012	0.0721
Three-months	1.6502	1.6515	0.0013	0.0788

The same reasoning goes for the CAD/USD exchange rate except that the bid points are smaller than the ask points (27 < 31 and 83 < 88). This tells us that the US dollar is at a forward premium and that the points should be added to the spot rate to obtain the outright forward quote. Table 6.4 shows the outright quotes for the CAD/USD rate. The relatively higher spreads on the CAD/USD indicate that if the Canadian dollar is not considered as more volatile than the pound sterling, they are due to a thinner market.

Forward cross rates

Forward cross rates can be calculated in the same way as spot cross rates. Using the information in these tables, we can calculate the three-month CAD/GBP rate. First we have to get the GBP/USD rate. Remember that $[GBP/USD_{bid}]$ is equal to the reciprocal of $[USD/GBP_{ask}]$ and that $[GBP/USD_{ask}]$ is equal to the reciprocal of $[USD/GBP_{bid}]$. Thus:

Three-month GBP/USD: 0.6055 – 0.6060.

The three-month CAD/GBP cross bid rate can be obtained by selling pounds for dollars three months forward and paying GBP 0.6060, while simultaneously selling dollars three months forward and receiving CAD 1.1518. The bid rate will then be 1.1518/0.6060 = CAD 1.9007. Similarly, the three-month cross ask rate can be obtained by selling Canadian dollars for US dollars three months forward and paying CAD 1.1533 per US dollar, while simultaneously selling the US dollars three months forward and receiving GBP 0.6055 per dollar. The ask rate will then be 1.1533/0.6055 = CAD 1.9047.

While it is possible to calculate forward exchange rates in the foregoing manner, in practice there is a much easier method based on the interest rate parity hypothesis. We will look at this method in detail later on in the chapter.

Reasons for using forward contracts

Regular quotes on forward contracts are limited to a relatively small number of currencies. The euro, the Japanese yen and the British pound make up a large part of the whole market, although the Swiss franc and the Canadian dollar also account for considerable volume. Much of the activity comes from banks offsetting positions that they have taken in other transactions. As we mentioned, banks tend to trade on even multiples of 30 days such as one month, two, months, three months, etc. However, when dealing with customers, banks stand ready to organize forward contracts for any period from three days to several years.

Another source of activity is from interest rate parity arbitraging if the forward premium or discount is out of line with the interest rate differential.

A common use of forward contracts is to eliminate uncertainty in commercial contracts arising from possible changes in the exchange rate. For example, an exporter who bills in

Table 6.4 Bid–ask rates, CAD/USD

	Bid	Ask	Spread	%
Spot	1.1435	1.1445	0.0010	0.0875
One-month	1.1462	1.1476	0.0014	0.1221
Three-months	1.1518	1.1533	0.0015	0.1302

foreign currency needs to know how many units of domestic currency he will receive for his goods. There is often a long lag between the time the sale is made and when the merchandise is delivered and paid for. In men's and women's apparel, for example, orders are placed six to nine months before delivery of the merchandise and payment is often made two to three months after delivery. A lot can happen in six months to a year so many firms take on a forward position to lock in their income in domestic currency.

Suppose that on 1 September Simay Ltd., a producer of stylish sportswear, takes an order for jogging suits to be delivered to its Danish client on 25 February of the following year. The order is for DKK 1,000,000 to be paid on delivery. The current exchange rate between the krone and the pound is DKK 10 = GBP 1. If the rate is the same on 25 February, Simay will receive GBP 100,000. If it goes to DKK 9.85 Simay will receive GBP 101,522.84, but if it falls to DKK 10.15 Simay will only receive GBP 98,522.17. The 177-day forward rate is DKK 10.02 and Simay decides to sell the DKK 1,000,000 forward and be sure to receive GBP 99,800.40. Figure 6.1 illustrates Simay's situation. The line that bisects the right angle represents Simay's position if it does not sell forward. Each øre increase in the exchange rate represents an øre loss for Simay and each øre fall represents an øre gain. The horizontal line is Simay's position with the forward contract. No matter what happens to the exchange rate Simay's position remains the same. If, on 25 February, the exchange rate is DKK 10.02, Simay neither gains nor loses from the forward transaction. If the exchange rate is higher than 10.02, Simay avoided a loss. The shaded area to the right of point P represents the implicit gain associated with avoiding the loss. On the other hand, if the exchange rate is below 10.02, Simay forfeited a potential gain. The shaded area to the left of point P represents the implicit loss associated with the forfeited gain.

The same reasoning can be applied to investors who make forward contracts to lock in returns in domestic currency. Sometimes, however, forward transactions are undertaken to preserve the domestic currency value of an asset that will not be sold or cashed in over the life of the contract.

Figure 6.1 Forward cover for a commercial transaction

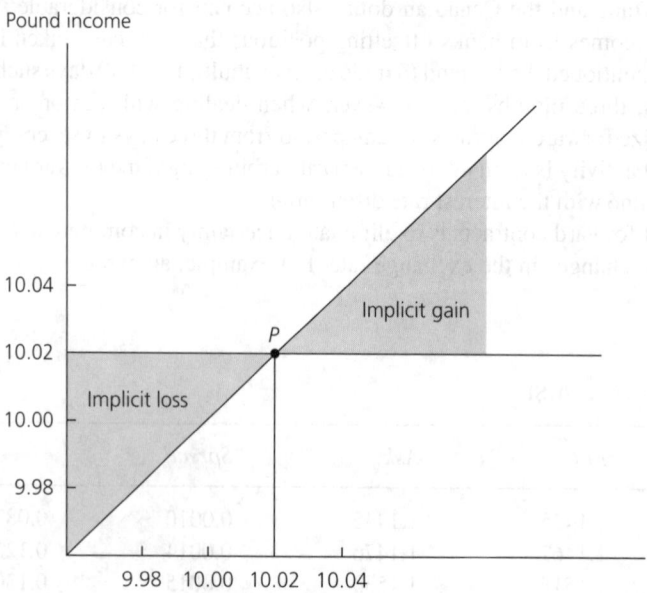

The foreign exchange and Eurocurrency markets

There is a close relationship between the foreign exchange market and the Eurocurrency market. The theoretical relationship is derived from the interest rate parity hypothesis derived in Chapter 3 that links the spot and forward exchange rates to the interest rates of the two currencies. In practice, the relationship is closest in the interbank markets where regulation is minimal and transaction costs are low. The participants in both markets are the same and quotes for foreign exchange and Eurocurrency interest rates are carried on the same communications network. The Eurocurrency markets are also a ready source of funds for financing foreign currency purchases and a convenient depository for placing the proceeds of foreign currency sales. In fact, the two markets are so thoroughly integrated that forward cross rates are often calculated from the interest rate differential. Suppose, for example, that the following information is available:

> Interest rate on three-month Japanese yen = $6\frac{3}{4}$–7
> Interest rate on three-month South Korean won = $11\frac{1}{2}$–$11\frac{3}{4}$
> Spot KRW/JPY = 9.5390–9.5490

If a trader is asked for a quote on the three-month forward KRW/JPY exchange rate, in the absence of KRW/USD and JPY/USD forward rates, he could apply the interest parity relation in Equation 3.10 to come up with a quote. First, he would calculate the average bid–ask quotes for the interest rates and the spot exchange rates:

> Average won interest rate: (11.50 + 11.75)/2 = 11.625%
> Average yen interest rate: (6.75 + 7.00)/2 = 6.875%
> Average spot KRW/JPY exchange rate: (9.5390 + 9.5490)/2 = 9.5440

The average interest rates are annualized and must be scaled to the period of three months. Three months is one-fourth of a year (3 months/12 months). Thus the interest rates appropriate to the interest parity relation are found by taking $\frac{1}{4} \times$ the annualized rate:

> won rate = $r_{KRW} = \frac{1}{4}$ (11.625%) = 2.90625%
> yen rate = $r_{JPY} = \frac{1}{4}$ (6.875%) = 1.71875%

Applying this information to the interest rate parity relation gives:

$$\frac{F_{0,\frac{1}{4}}(KRW/JPY)}{S_0(KRW/JPY)} = \frac{(1+r_{KRW})}{(1+r_{JPY})} = \frac{F_{0,\frac{1}{4}}(KRW/JPY)}{9.5540} = \frac{1.0290625}{1.0171875}$$

$$F_{0,\frac{1}{4}} = 9.6554$$

Thus, the mid-point three-month forward rate would be KRW 9.6554 for one yen. To get from this rate to his quote, he would subtract points to get the bid rate and he would add points to get the ask rate. Bid and ask quotes add a new dimension to the interest rate parity relation because they add extra costs to the arbitrage operations on which it depends. The lower the costs, the more precisely the relation holds and the closer the links between the foreign exchange market and the Eurocurrency market. The question that comes to mind, then, is what determines the forward bid–ask spread. One way of looking at the answer is in terms of how many points can the trader add or subtract and still continue to do business.

Covered interest arbitrage does not tell us much on this score. Remember from Chapter 3 that covered interest arbitrage involves borrowing in one currency, selling the borrowed currency on the spot market, investing the proceeds of the sale, and simultaneously buying back the borrowed currency on the forward market. Four spreads are present in this type of operation:

1. the interest rate spread on currency 1.
2. the interest rate spread on currency 2.
3. the spread on the spot exchange rate.
4. the spread on the forward exchange rate.

Widening the spread on the forward exchange rate will only make covered interest arbitrage less likely to occur and, in the absence of any other countervailing forces, could provoke wide deviations from interest rate parity. Fortunately, there are other less costly arbitrage transactions that establish limits on the forward exchange rate spread. They are usually called "one-way arbitrage" because, rather than starting and ending in the same currency, they start in one currency and end in the other. Their effect is to reinforce the close integration of the Eurocurrency and foreign exchange markets.

Take, for example, someone who will be receiving won in three months but will have to make a payment in yen. Because arbitrage conditions are usually determined by the lowest cost arbitragers, who, as we know, are the participants in the interbank market, this could be the situation of a bank that has loaned in won and borrowed in yen, or a financial institution that has sales income in won and accounts payable in yen, or some other participant in the interbank market. Starting in the top right-hand corner with the inflow of won, Figure 6.2 shows that there are two choices. The first choice is to cover his position directly by selling won forward for yen at the three-month forward KRW/JPY ask rate. This route takes him directly from the top right-hand corner to his destination in the bottom right-hand corner. If he decides to do this, at the end of the operation he will have:

$$\frac{1}{F_{0,\frac{1}{4}}(KRW/JPY)_{ask}} \text{ yen for each won.}$$

Alternatively, he could cover his position by borrowing won at the ask rate $[r_{KRW,ask}]$, buying yen spot at the ask rate and lending yen at the bid rate $[r_{JPY,bid}]$. Thus, starting in the top right-hand corner, for each won that he will receive in three months, he borrows $1/(1 + r_{KRW,ask})$, which moves him to the top left-hand corner. The won inflow in three months will be used to pay off the loan. From the top left-hand corner he buys yen spot at the ask rate, which moves him to the bottom left-hand corner. From the bottom left-hand corner he

Figure 6.2 One-way covered interest arbitrage: A long route

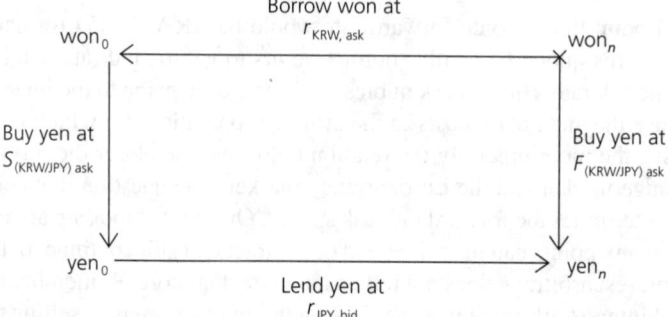

loans yen at the bid rate, which moves him to his destination in the bottom right-hand corner. The number of yen for each won that he will end up with is:

$$\frac{1}{1+r_{KRW,ask}} \times \frac{1}{S_0(KRW/JPY)_{ask}} \times (1 + r_{JPY,bid}) \text{ yen.}$$

Investors will choose the route that will leave them with the most yen at the end of three months. If the trader's forward ask rate is too high no one will trade with him so his limit forward ask rate can be found just where the two alternative routes yield the same amount of yen:

$$\frac{1}{F_{0,\frac{1}{4}}(KRW/JPY)_{ask}} = \frac{1}{1+r_{KRW,ask}} \times \frac{1}{S_0(KRW/JPY)_{ask}} \times (1+r_{JPY,bid})$$

and rearranging:

$$F_{0,\frac{1}{4}}(KRW/JPY)_{ask} = \frac{(1+r_{KRW,ask}) \times S_0(KRW/JPY)_{ask}}{(1+r_{JPY,bid})} \tag{6.4}$$

Substituting the data on the won and the yen into 6.4 gives the limit forward won/yen ask rate:

$$F_{0,\frac{1}{4}}(KRW/JPY)_{ask} = \frac{(1+\frac{0.1175}{4}) \times 9.5490}{(1+\frac{0.0675}{4})} = 9.6664.$$

The same kind of argument could be made for someone who was expecting income in yen and payments in won. Figure 6.3 shows the two alternatives. Starting from the bottom right-hand corner, he could take the direct route and buy won forward. This would leave him with $F_{0,\frac{1}{4}}(KRW/JPY)_{bid}$ won for each yen. On the other hand, he could take the long route by borrowing $1/(1 + r_{JPY,ask})$ yen. This would move him from the bottom right-hand corner of Figure 6.3 to the bottom left-hand corner. Then he could sell the yen spot and receive $S_0(KRW/JPY)_{bid}$ won for each yen. This would move him from the bottom left-hand corner to the top left-hand corner. Finally, he could lend the won at $r_{KRW,bid}$ for three months, which will bring him to the top right-hand corner. At the end of the operation he will have:

$$\frac{1}{1 + r_{JPY,ask}} \times S_0(KRW/JPY)_{bid} \times (1 + r_{KRW,bid}) \text{ won.}$$

Figure 6.3 One-way covered interest arbitrage: Another long route

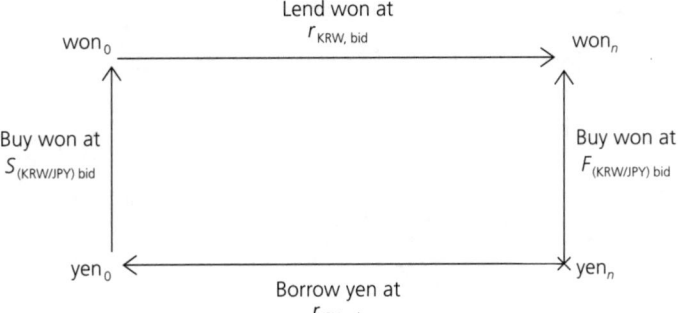

Investors will choose the route that will leave them with the most won at the end of three months. If the trader's forward bid rate is too low, no one will trade with him so his limit forward bid rate can be found just where the two alternative routes yield the same amount of won:

$$F_{0,\frac{1}{4}}(KRW/JPY)_{bid} = \frac{1}{1 + r_{JPY,ask}} \times S_0(KRW/JPY)_{bid} \times (1 + r_{KRW,bid}) \tag{6.5}$$

Substituting the data for won and yen into Equation 6.5 gives:

$$F_{0,\frac{1}{4}}(KRW/JPY)_{bid} = \frac{1}{1 + \frac{0.07}{4}} \times 9.5390 \times (1 + \frac{0.115}{4}) = 9.6445.$$

The trader's three-month forward KRW/JPY bid rate could not be any lower than 9.6445. Otherwise, no one would buy forward and everyone would take the long route to get to won three months in the future. Thus the limit quote for three-month KRW/JPY would be:

$$9.6445 - 9.6664.$$

This quote depends on the ease with which funds can be borrowed and lent in both currencies and illustrates why the Eurocurrency and foreign exchange markets have achieved their high degree of integration. The quote represents a spread of 0.0219 which, although narrow, is still considerably wider than the spot spread of 0.01. The forward spread is wider than the spot spread because in addition to the spot spread of 0.01 it includes the spreads on the yen and won interest rates. The reason for this is that the arbitrage includes borrowing at the ask rate and lending at the bid rate. This could be a source of weakness in the integration of the two markets. However, other forces are at work that should reduce the spread even further.

Consider someone who has won but will need yen three months in the future. Figure 6.4 shows the two routes he can take. Starting at the top left-hand corner, he could lend his won for three months at the bid rate $[r_{KRW,bid}]$. This brings him to the top right-hand corner where he sells his won forward at the ask rate $[F_{0,1/4}(KRW/JPY)_{ask}]$. This will leave him with:

$$\frac{1 + r_{KRW,bid}}{F_{0,\frac{1}{4}}(KRW/JPY)_{ask}} \quad \text{yen for each won.}$$

Figure 6.4 One-way covered interest arbitrage: A short route

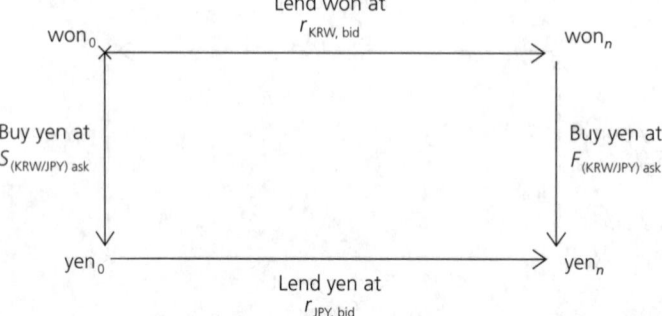

Alternatively, he could buy yen at the spot ask rate $[S_0(\text{KRW/JPY})_{\text{ask}}]$ which will bring him to the lower left-hand corner. Then he could lend the yen at the bid rate $[r_{\text{JPY,bid}}]$ to get to his destination in the lower right-hand corner. At the end of the operation he will have:

$$\frac{1 + r_{\text{JPY,bid}}}{S_0(\text{KRW/JPY})_{\text{ask}}} \text{ yen for each won.}$$

The investor will choose the route that yields the largest amount of yen. Thus arbitrage should ensure that both routes yield the same amount of yen so that:

$$\frac{1 + r_{\text{KRW,bid}}}{F_{0,\frac{1}{4}}(\text{KRW/JPY})_{\text{ask}}} = \frac{1 + r_{\text{JPY,bid}}}{S_0(\text{KRW/JPY})_{\text{ask}}}$$

and rearranging:

$$F_{0,\frac{1}{4}}(\text{KRW/JPY})_{\text{ask}} = S_0(\text{KRW/JPY})_{\text{ask}} \times \frac{(1 + r_{\text{KRW,bid}})}{1 + r_{\text{JPY,bid}}} \qquad (6.6)$$

Substituting the data for won and yen into Equation 6.6 yields:

$$F_{0,\frac{1}{4}}(\text{KRW/JPY})_{\text{ask}} = 9.5490 \times \frac{(1 + \frac{0.1150}{4})}{(1 + \frac{0.0675}{4})} = 9.6605.$$

The same type of argument can be used to obtain the three-month forward KRW/JPY bid rate. Consider an investor who will receive yen three-months in the future but who needs won now. Figure 6.5 shows the two routes he can take to get from future yen to present won. Starting in the bottom right-hand corner, he can buy won three months forward at the bid rate. For each yen he will receive $F_{0,\frac{1}{4}}(\text{KRW/JPY})_{\text{bid}}$ won. This will bring him to the top right-hand corner where he borrows won at the ask rate $[r_{\text{KRW,ask}}]$. Because he will use the proceeds from the forward sale of yen to pay off the loan, he borrows $1/(1 + r_{\text{KRW,ask}})$ for each won he will receive in the forward transaction. At the end of the operation he will have:

$$\frac{F_{0,\frac{1}{4}}(\text{KRW/JPY})_{\text{bid}}}{1 + r_{\text{KRW,ask}}} \text{ won for each yen.}$$

The second route he can take to get from future yen to present won is to borrow yen at the ask rate $[r_{\text{JPY,ask}}]$. Because he will use the yen he will receive in the future to pay off the loan,

Figure 6.5 One-way covered interest arbitrage: Another short route

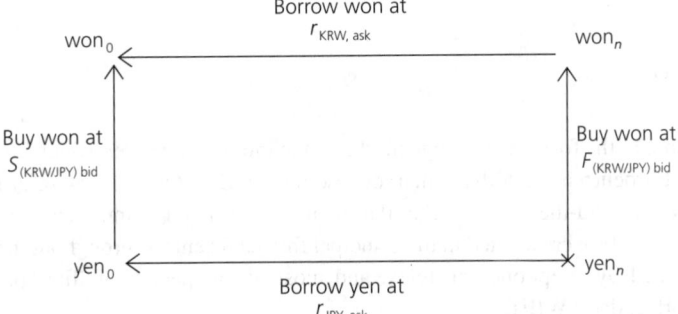

he borrows $1/(1 + r_{JPY,ask})$ for each future yen. This brings him to the lower left-hand corner. He then sells the yen at the spot bid rate $[S_0(KRW/JPY)_{bid}]$, which brings him to his destination in the top left-hand corner. At the end of the operation he will have:

$$\frac{S_0(KRW/JPY)_{bid}}{1 + r_{JPY,ask}} \text{ won for each yen.}$$

Since the investor will choose the route that yields the largest amount of yen, arbitrage should ensure that both routes yield the same amount of yen so that:

$$\frac{F_{0,\frac{1}{4}}(KRW/JPY)_{bid}}{1 + r_{KRW,ask}} = \frac{S_0(KRW/JPY)_{bid}}{1 + r_{JPY,ask}}.$$

Rearranging yields:

$$F_{0,\frac{1}{4}}(KRW/JPY)_{bid} = S_0(KRW/JPY)_{bid} \times \frac{(1 + r_{KRW,ask})}{(1 + r_{JPY,ask})} \tag{6.7}$$

Substituting the won/yen data into Equation 6.7 yields:

$$F_{0,\frac{1}{4}}(KRW/JPY)_{bid} = 9.5390 \times \frac{(1 + \frac{0.1175}{4})}{(1 + \frac{0.0700}{4})} = 9.6503.$$

If this type of arbitrage holds, the three-month KRW/JPY forward quote would be:

9.6503–9.6605.

The spread is only 0.0102, much lower than the limit quotes, and reflects the fact that the interest rate spreads were irrelevant in the arbitrage operations. A look at Equations 6.6 and 6.7 show that this is because the arbitrage was effected with bid/bid and ask/ask interest rates. There was no problem of borrowing at a higher rate and lending at a lower rate. The whole forward spread is just a reflection of the spot spread and the interest rate differential.

In summary, then, we can say that in order for arbitrage to be effective, it is necessary to have access to large sums of diverse currencies that can be mobilized quickly and cheaply. The Eurocurrency markets fill this role and this is why the foreign exchange and Eurocurrency markets are so closely integrated. Domestic financial markets cannot offer the same service. Because of regulations and controls, they carry higher transaction costs. Furthermore, even where regulations or controls do not already exist, the possibility that they could one day be imposed raises the risks, and thus the costs, associated with domestic markets.

Summary

1. The core of the foreign exchange market is the interbank market, which is closely linked to the Eurocurrency interbank market described in Chapter 5. It is an informal, over-the-counter, around-the-clock market that includes the major commercial banks and some specialized brokers located in the principal financial centers throughout the world. They are linked by telephone and telex, and most use a special satellite communications network called SWIFT.

2. The interbank market is composed of traders and brokers. The role of the trader and the broker is essentially different. The trader usually operates out of the foreign exchange trading room of a major bank and is essentially a market-maker, standing ready to buy and sell foreign currencies on a more or less continuous basis. The broker is an intermediary between traders, bringing buyers and sellers together and contributing to market efficiency. Brokers also serve as a source of information for traders and make it possible for traders to remain anonymous when revealing their identity would put them at a trading disadvantage.

3. Exchange rates can be quoted in two ways: (a) the number of units of domestic currency for one unit of foreign currency, or (b) the number of units of foreign currency for one unit of domestic currency. Most financial centers use the first method and quote the number of units of domestic currency for one unit of foreign currency. The United Kingdom and, increasingly, Europe (for the euro) and the United States quote the number of units of foreign currency for one unit of domestic currency.

4. Costs on foreign exchange transactions are in the form of bid–ask spreads. They are generally very low on interbank transactions and higher on retail transactions depending on the size of the trade and the currencies traded.

5. The exchange rate of all currencies is given against the US dollar. The exchange rate between two currencies not involving the dollar is called the cross rate. Indicative cross rates can be calculated from the individual dollar exchange rates. Because of transaction costs, cross rates calculated in this way only indicate the range within which the cross rates must fall.

6. When banks do not maintain correspondent accounts, they use clearing houses to settle balances among themselves. Most foreign exchange transactions involving dollars are settled through CHIPS. Most sterling transactions are settled through CHAPS.

7. The forward market provides for buying and selling currencies at a predetermined rate for delivery in the future. Forward contracts can be for any maturity but they rarely exceed one or two years. The interbank market concentrates on maturities of multiples of 30 days (30 days, 60 days, 90 days, etc.).

8. Forward exchange rates can be quoted in two ways. The first way is to quote the rate outright and is similar to spot quotes. It involves giving the number of units of one currency that it takes to buy one unit of another currency for delivery in the future. The second method presents the forward rate as a discount or premium on the spot rate and is called the swap rate.

9. Forward contracts are valuable to importers, exporters and cross-border investors for offsetting risks that could result from moves in the spot exchange rate.

10. There is a close relationship between the foreign exchange market and the Eurocurrency market, especially the interbank segments of these markets where regulation is minimal and costs are low. The relationship is generated by the interest rate parity hypothesis and the arbitrage conditions that surround it. In practice, quotes for foreign exchange and Eurocurrency interest rates are carried on the same communications network and the Eurocurrency markets are a ready source of funds for financing foreign currency purchases and a convenient depository for placing the proceeds of foreign currency sales.

11. Because of transaction costs, covered interest arbitrage opportunities are probably rare and contribute less to the close integration of the foreign exchange and Eurocurrency markets than one-way arbitrage. By keeping transaction costs to a minimum, one-way arbitrage imposes tight limits on the forward bid–ask spread.

Questions

Solutions to the following questions are set out on the web site, details of which are included in the Preface.

1. What is the difference between a trader and a broker?

2. How do most financial centers quote exchange rates? Name some exceptions to this convention.

3. Translate the following exchange rate quotes into words:

   a. $S(USD/GBP)$: 1.6715–1.6725

   b. $S(EUR/GBP)$: 1.7525–1.7535

4. Using the information in Question 3, what would the $S(GBP/USD)$ and $S(USD/EUR)$ quotes be?

5. Using the information in Question 3, calculate the $S(GBP/EUR)$ and the $S(EUR/USD)$ quotes.

6. What is the difference between the CHIPS and CHAPS clearing systems?

7. Given:

   a. $S(CHF/USD)$: 1.9720–1.9730

   b. three-month forward: 1.9600–1.9650

   Calculate the discount (premium) of the Swiss franc against the dollar.

8. You are an English producer of candy expecting a USD 2,000,000 payment in 30 days from your US client. The exchange rate is $S(USD/GBP)_{ask}$ = 1.6725. What will your income in sterling be if the rate goes to 1.6500? If $F_{1/12}(USD/GBP)_{ask}$ = 1.6647 and you sell forward, what will your income be?

9. Given:

   a. $S(DKK/USD)$: 10.0000–10.0040

   b. interest rate on three-month krone: $10–10\frac{1}{4}$

   c. interest rate on three-month dollars: $6–6\frac{1}{4}$

   Use one-way arbitrage to determine the limit quote for the three-month forward exchange rate.

DERIVATIVE MARKETS, INSTRUMENTS AND TECHNIQUES

Futures markets and instruments

Organized futures markets originated in the middle of the 19th century in Chicago, Illinois. The Chicago Board of Trade was created in 1848 and around 1865 the first "modern" futures contracts were developed. Although forward contracts had existed for hundreds of years – Japan and Holland, for example, were trading forward-type contracts two centuries earlier – the first formalized futures contract originated in Chicago. Since then it has spread all over the world, although Chicago remains the world's leading futures center.

The development and growth of futures markets did not come about by chance. Chicago in the 19th century, for example, was already at the heart of a fertile agricultural region. Transportation, however, was somewhat hazardous, especially in winter when the rivers would freeze over. This entailed serious risks for the farmers. If the farmers sold at harvest time when supply was abundant, prices were often low. If they waited for winter, prices were often higher but the ability to deliver was chancy due to the effects of the weather on the transportation system. If they waited till spring, prices would be high or low depending on the size of the harvest and how much was held back. In these conditions, farmers were never certain how much they would receive for their produce. Futures markets made it possible to overcome this problem.

The same type of phenomenon was behind the development of futures markets in Great Britain at the end of the 19th century. London and Liverpool, where the first futures markets opened up in copper and wool among other commodities, were not production centers for these products. They were, however, the gateways for imports and centers of production and consumption of products that used them as inputs. The international trade cycle of economic expansion and contraction combined with the nature of producing many raw materials gave rise to a situation where prices could fluctuate violently from one period to another.[1,2] British

[1] The trade cycle refers to regular oscillations in the level of business activity over a number of years. Most explanations of the existence and nature of the trade cycle are based on *ex ante* disequilibrium between savings and investment that can be caused or aggravated by monetary phenomena and the interaction of the multiplier process and the acceleration principle of derived demand. See F. Hayek, *The Pure Theory of Capital* (London: Routledge and Kegan Paul, Ltd., 1941); F. Hayek, *Monetary Theory and the Trade Cycle*, trans. N. Kaldor and H.M. Croome (London: Jonathan Cape, 1933); F. Hayek, *Prix et Production*, trans. Tradecom (Vienne: Calmann-Levy, 1975); J. Hicks, *Capital and Time: A Neo-Austrian Theory* (Oxford: Clarendon Press, 1987); J. Hicks, *A Contribution to the Theory of the Trade Cycle* (Oxford: Clarendon Press, 1950).

[2] Wide price fluctuations are often associated with the production of perishable raw materials in what is known as the "cobweb effect"– the graphic representation of conditions that may exist in a competitive market when the sale of a perishable good, requiring a period of time to produce, is confined to a short but fairly constant seasonal demand. The seasonal sales period is too short and the time required for production too long to permit changes in the supply by any producer after sales have begun. This tends to cause price oscillations from year to year with a relatively high price and short supply or a relatively low price and plentiful supply.

industrialists were therefore exposed to considerable uncertainty concerning the price they would pay for their imported inputs. Futures markets for these products enabled them to eliminate, or at least control, this uncertainty.

From these two historical examples we can see that commodity futures markets developed for basic products subject to wide price fluctuations. They originated where there was large-scale trade in the basic products themselves due either to the fact that the region was a production center for the products or that it was a center where the basic products were transformed into more elaborate consumer goods. It is interesting to note that if one of these two conditions disappears, the futures market will die. This was the case, for example, with the European raw wool futures markets when the European wool industries disappeared.

Another condition for the creation of a commodity futures market is that the underlying commodity be homogeneous enough to permit contract standardization. Product differentiation makes delivery too complicated and kills the market. For example, no futures markets have ever developed for sophisticated manufactured products with varied technical characteristics. They have developed, however, for a wide range of agricultural products, industrial metals, precious metals and energy that lend themselves to standardization and that exhibit a high degree of price volatility. Table 7.1 illustrates the range of commodity futures contracts available in the world today.

The same conditions associated with the commodities markets led to the development of futures contracts on financial products. On 16 June 1972 the Chicago Mercantile Exchange (CME) opened the market for futures contracts on the pound sterling, the Canadian dollar, the German mark, the yen, the Mexican peso, the Swiss franc and the Italian lira. It later introduced contracts on the French franc, the Dutch guilder, the Australian dollar and the ECU. In October 1975 the Chicago Board of Trade (CBOT) was the first to offer a futures contract directly related to the long-term interest rate. The underlying security, reflecting the American mortgage market, was issued by the Government National Mortgage Association (GNMA), called "Ginnie Mae". GNMA is a wholly owned US government corporation whose object is to support the housing market.

In August 1977 the CBOT launched a contract on US Treasury bonds, the success of which went beyond all expectations. Since then, contracts on long-term interest rates have spread to other continents and other exchanges, such as the Matif in Paris, Liffe in London, Tiffe in Tokyo and the SFE in Sydney. Liquid interest rate futures are now available on a wide range of instruments both long and short term in US dollars, the British pound and the Australian dollar, as well as on Swiss francs, Canadian dollars, Japanese yen and European euros. Financial futures are also available on most major stock indices. Table 7.2 lists some of the most popular contracts on financial futures.

For a futures market to function correctly, a competitive spot market in the underlying asset is indispensable. By competitive we mean that there exists an indeterminate number of traders all dealing in the same product, and where no one trader can offer or demand a quantity sufficiently large to materially affect the market price. In other words, monopolistic and monopsonistic markets do not lend themselves to futures trading.[3] For example, as long as OPEC (the Organization of Petroleum Exporting Countries) dominated the oil market, no market in petroleum futures ever emerged.

From this introduction we can see why futures markets developed and how they spread from a limited range of raw materials to a wide range of agricultural products, industrial metals, precious metals, energy, currencies, interest rates and stock indices. The keys to an

---

[3] A monopoly is where one supplier dominates the market and a monopsony is where one buyer dominates it.

Table 7.1 Examples of commodity futures contracts

Contract	Exchange	Size
Grains and oil-seeds		
Corn	CBT	5000 bushels
Oats	CBT	5000 bushels
Soybeans	CBT	5000 bushels
Soybean meal	CBT	100 tons
Soybean oil	CBT	60 000 pounds
Wheat	CBT, KC, MPLS	5000 bushels
Wheat	WPG	20 metric tons
Canola	WPG	20 metric tons
Barley-Western	WPG	20 metric tons
Livestock and meat		
Cattle-feeder	CME	50 000 pounds
Cattle-live	CME	40 000 pounds
Hogs-lean	CME	40 000 pounds
Pork bellies	CME	40 000 pounds
Food and fiber		
Cocoa	NYBOT	10 metric tons
Cocoa	Liffe	Lots of 10 tons
Coffee	NYBOT	37 500 pounds
Coffee	Liffe	Lots of 10 tons
Sugar	NYBOT	112 000 pounds
Sugar	Liffe	Lots of 50 tons
Cotton	NYBOT	50 000 pounds
Orange Juice	NYBOT	15 000 pounds
Metals and petroleum		
Copper	CMX	25 000 pounds
Gold	CMX	100 troy ounces
Platinum	NYM	50 troy ounces
Silver	CMX	5000 troy ounces
Crude oil	NYM	1000 bbls.
Heating oil	NYM	42 000 gallons
Gasoline	NYM	42 000 gallons
Natural gas	NYM	10 000 MMBtu.
Brent crude	IPE	1000 bbls.
Gas oil	IPE	100 metric tons

Key: CBT = Chicago Board of Trade; CME = Chicago Mercantile Exchange; CMX = Commodity Exchange, New York; IPE = International Petroleum Exchange; KC = Kansas City Board of Trade; Liffe = London International Financial Futures Exchange; MPLS = Minneapolis Grain Exchange; NYBOT = New York Board of Trade; NYM = New York Mercantile Exchange; WPG = Winnipeg Commodity Exchange.
Source: *Wall Street Journal Europe*, 6 October 2000.

Table 7.2 Examples of financial futures contracts

Contract	Exchange	Size
Interest rates		
Treasury bonds	CBT	USD 100,000
Treasury bonds	MCE	USD 50,000
Treasury notes	CBT	USD 100,000
Ten-year agency notes	CBT	USD 100,000
Five-year Treasury notes	CBT	USD 100,000
Two-year Treasury notes	CBT	USD 200,000
30-day Federal Funds	CBT	USD 5 mn
MUNI Bond Index	CBT	USD 1,000 times Bond Buyer MBI
Treasury bills	CME	USD 1 mn
One-month Libor	CME	USD 3 mn
Eurodollar	CME	USD 1 mn
Euroyen	CME	JPY 100 mn
Short sterling	Liffe	GBP 500,000
Long gilt	Liffe	GBP 50,000
Three-month Euribor	Liffe	EUR 1 mn
Three-month Euroswiss	Liffe	CHF 1 mn
Canadian bankers' acceptance	ME	CAD 1 mn
Ten-year Canadian government bonds	ME	CAD 100,000
Ten-year euro notional bond	Matif	EUR 100,000
Three-year Commonwealth T-bonds	SFE	AUD 100,000
Euroyen	SGX	JPY 100 mn
Five-year German euro government bond	Eurex	EUR 100,000
Ten-year German euro government bond	Eurex	EUR 100,000
Two-year German euro government bond	Eurex	EUR 100,000
Currencies		
Japanese yen	CME	JPY 12.5 mn
Deutschmark	CME	DEM 125,000
Canadian Dollar	CME	CAD 100,000
British Pound	CME	GBP 62,500
Swiss Franc	CME	CHF 125,000
Australian Dollar	CME	AUD 100,000
Mexican Peso	CME	MXN 500,000
Euro FX	CME	EUR 125,000
Indices		
Share price index	SFE	AUD 25 times index
CAC-40 Stock Index	Matif	EUR 10 times index
DAX-30 Stock Index	Eurex	EUR 25 per DAX index point
FT-SE 100 Index	Liffe	GBP 10 per index point
DJ Euro Stoxx Index	Eurex	EUR 10 times index
DJ Stoxx 50 Index	Eurex	EUR 10 times index

Key: CBT = Chicago Board of Trade; CME = Chicago Mercantile Exchange; Liffe = London International Financial Futures Exchange; Matif = Marché à Terme International de France, Paris; ME = Montreal Exchange; MCE = MidAmerica Commodity Exchange; SFE = Sidney Futures Exchange.
Source: *Wall Street Journal Europe*, 6 October 2000.

effectively functioning futures market are a competitive spot market, product homogeneity and price volatility.

Organization of the futures exchanges

Forwards versus futures

As discussed in Chapters 3 and 6 with respect to currencies, a forward contract is an agreement to buy or sell an asset at a certain future time for a certain future price, whereas a spot contract is an agreement to buy or sell an asset today. Forward contracts are traded in the over-the-counter market and usually involve a financial institution on one side of the deal and either a client or another financial institution on the other side of the deal. One party to the deal takes a long position and agrees to purchase the asset, while the other party takes a short position and agrees to sell the asset. The agreed price in the forward contract is called the delivery price, which is chosen so that the value of the contract to both sides is equal to zero. Consequently, it costs nothing to enter into a forward agreement.

A futures contract is very similar to a forward contract. It is an agreement between two parties to buy or sell an asset at a certain time for a certain price. Futures contracts are traded on organized exchanges. To facilitate trading the exchange specifies certain standardized features of the contract and trading takes place in such a way that the exchange is the ultimate counterparty to each transaction. Futures contracts differ from forward contracts in two other ways. First of all, payments are made over the life of the contract in what is called marking to market.[4] Secondly, most futures contracts are closed out before maturity.

Thus, the organized futures markets have four important features: (a) the contracts are standardized; (b) trading is organized and centralized either in one physical location, such as the trading pit, or in a virtual location such as a computerized order book; (c) contracts are settled through the exchange's clearing house; and (d) contracts are **marked to market** each day, which means that they are revalued according to their market value.

Standardized contracts

Contract standardization is a key feature of organized exchanges facilitating market liquidity. For example, when the Chicago Mercantile Exchange (CME) opened the International Money Market to trade foreign exchange futures, these contracts were patterned after the futures contracts for the commodities it had been trading for over 100 years. The success of this format led to its widespread adoption by other exchanges. Hence, contrary to the workings of the interbank currency market, trading in currency futures conforms strictly to the exchange's internal rules. The traded currencies are limited in number. Maturities are based on a quarterly cycle of March, June, September, and December, and each contract has a precise delivery date, typically the third Wednesday of March, June, September and December or the first business day following one of these Wednesdays. Trading stops two business days before the expiration date and delivery takes place on the second business day after the expiration date. Each contract also corresponds to a given amount of foreign exchange. For example, the CME's yen contract is for JPY 12,500,000, the pound contract for GBP 62,500 and the Swiss franc contract for CHF 125,000.

---

[4] Marking to market and its effects are discussed below.

Public and competitive trading procedures

Only commission houses registered as member firms are allowed to trade on the exchange. Anyone else who seeks access to the market must do so through a commission house by opening an account. All orders are then executed through the commission house. In the United States, for example, opening an account is subject to strict rules. Before opening an account, clients must read a number of documents and declare that they have understood them. This is designed to ensure that the client appreciates the risks associated with the futures markets. Furthermore, opening an account is also subject to certain financial guarantees such as a deposit of cash or marketable securities.

When a client wants to trade, he transmits his order to the "registered representative" who manages his account for the clearing house. Different types of conditions can be attached to the order. The order can be limited to a certain period of time, or to a certain price range, or both. When the registered representative receives the order, he transmits it directly to the offices of the clearing house in the city where the futures market is located. From there it is sent to the commission house's order desk or the trading floor and a messenger takes it to the commission house's trader. At each stage of the operation the order is time stamped so as to control the speed of execution and serve as proof in the case of a complaint.

Futures trading is organized around a centralized market that matches supply and demand. One method of matching supply and demand that is popular in continental Europe is to centralize limit orders in a computerized limit order book. Under this system, brokers are linked through a computer network that makes it possible for them to electronically post and delete their own orders or fill orders posted by others on the screen. Another method of centralizing supply and demand is by open outcry. In this system, transactions take place either around a ring or inside a pit. The traders, either from the different commission houses or independent speculators, take their places around the ring or on different steps of the pit based on the maturity date of the commodity being traded. The messengers bring them orders for execution and large electronic panels flash information that keeps them constantly informed of what is happening in the market. Trading is carried out via an auction system of open outcry where any trader is free to take the opposite side of a trade. Voices are combined with a particular sign language to communicate prices, quantities and buys or sells. If, for example, a trader wants to buy 20 February contracts at FRF 1.05 per kilo, he signals this to the other traders. Any trader can answer and if several do, the fastest to respond is the one who gets the deal. If no one responds, the trader knows that his price is unacceptable. He either has to wait to execute his order or has to offer a better price. This system guarantees that at any particular moment there is only one price in the market.

Exchange employees permanently monitor what is going on in each pit or ring. After each order is executed they enter the price in the computer system. In this way all exchange members are kept informed of market developments. Some exchanges link their computer systems to outside networks and the internet for public distribution of the information.

Once an order has been executed, the floor broker uses a messenger to transmit the information to his desk. The desk then informs the client and transmits the information to the commission house's accounting services where the appropriate entries are recorded. Recording requirements do not end here, however. The clearing house, which is the ultimate counterparty to each trade, must also be informed. For this purpose, floor brokers are obliged to fill in a "trading card" for each transaction indicating the type of contract, its maturity, the number of contracts, the price, the commission houses' code numbers and the initials of the floor broker. These procedures are shown in Figure 7.1.

Figure 7.1 Trading procedures

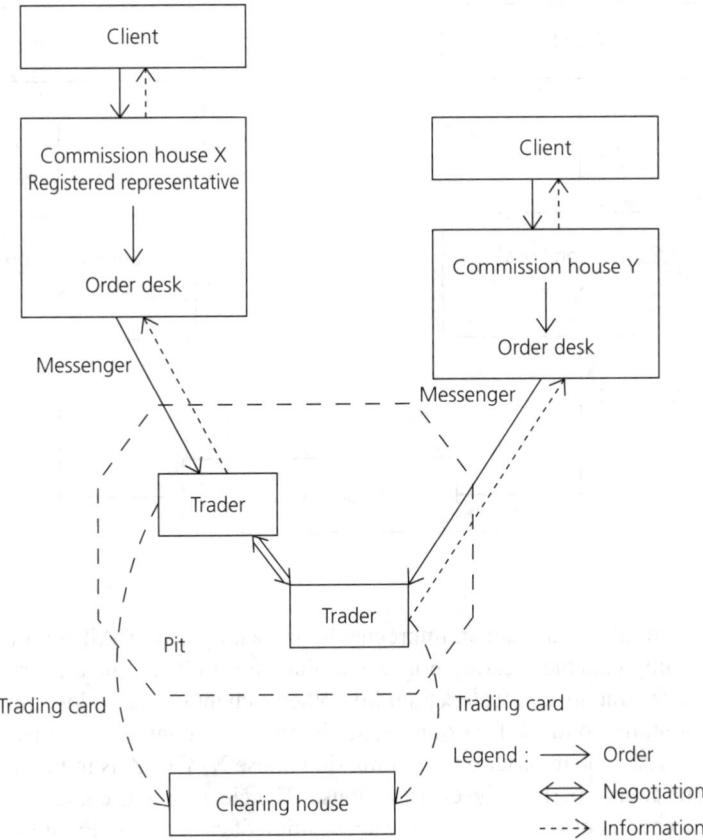

Role of the clearing house

The role of the clearing house is three-fold: it records the existence of the contract; it manages settlement of day-to-day operations; and it guarantees delivery at the contract's maturity. Thus, there is no individual counterparty risk because all clients have the clearing house as the ultimate counterparty.

The modern system of clearing used today by almost all futures markets was developed in the United States in about 1920. Most clearing houses are specific to each exchange, although some clearing corporations, such as ICCH in London, act on behalf of several markets. Their role is always the same. They act as third party guarantors to all futures contracts and they manage the financial implications associated with their guarantee.

Once a trade has been completed, the commission houses on either side of the trade do not have an obligation to each other. They each have an obligation to the clearing house. Thus, as we can see in Figure 7.2, the commission house on the buy side of a trade has an obligation to the clearing house to buy. The commission house on the sell side of a trade has an obligation to the clearing house to sell, and the clearing house has an obligation to sell to the buyer and an obligation to buy from the seller.

The role of the clearing house is essential for a smooth functioning futures market. Clients do not have to worry about the solvency of the commission house, nor do commission houses have to worry about the solvency of other exchange members. The only risk is the solvency of the clearing house itself, and this risk is minimal because the clearing

Figure 7.2 Commission houses and the clearing house

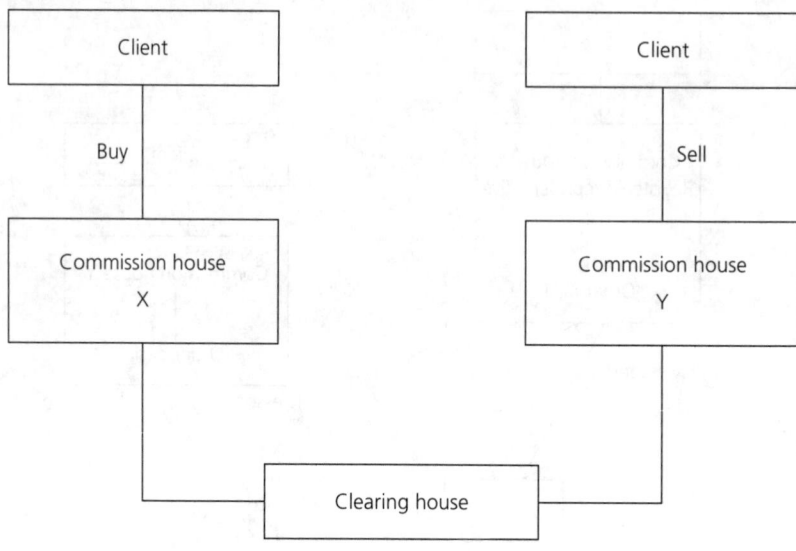

house is required to maintain an impregnable financial position. All contracts are with the financially impregnable clearing house and, thus, for a given type are strictly equivalent. This facilitates trading and fosters liquidity. When a client wants to close out a position on a purchased futures contract, for example, he simply sells a contract to someone else. No one cares who makes the transaction – commission house X, Y or Z as in Figure 7.3 – because the ultimate counterparty is the clearing house. The clearing house keeps its accounts with each member and knows at all times the net position of each one. In Figure 7.3, for example, commission house X has a net position of zero, since the buys and sells cancel out. Commission house Y is a net purchaser and commission house Z is a net seller.

Because of its role as ultimate counterparty, the clearing house is at risk from all the members with whom it does business. Consequently, it requires certain guarantees from each one. One of the most important guarantees of an exchange's financial system is the strict "clearing margin" imposed on members. A clearing margin is a deposit in the form of cash, government issued securities, stock in the clearing corporation, or letters of credit issued by an approved bank that clearing members lodge with the clearing house. The size of the deposit is fixed by the clearing house based on the member's net position, or on its long and short positions, and it can be revised upward or downward at any time depending on how the clearing house views market developments. Clearing margins are calculated every day in an exercise similar to the way that clients are marked to market, and they must be large enough to cover maximum fluctuations in futures prices. Because prices vary from day to day, initial margins may become inadequate if prices move strongly against one or more members and, in this case, the clearing house can make a margin call against the deficient members. They then have one hour to effect a wire transfer of funds, which will be included in the end-of-day settlement procedures when all accounts are marked to market. It is clear that much care is taken to ensure the exchange's solvency and that the clearing house wields extensive power over its members.

Margin calls and marking to market

As would be expected, member commission houses demand the same type of guarantees from their clients that the clearing house demands of them. In fact, the margins that

Figure 7.3 Closing out a position

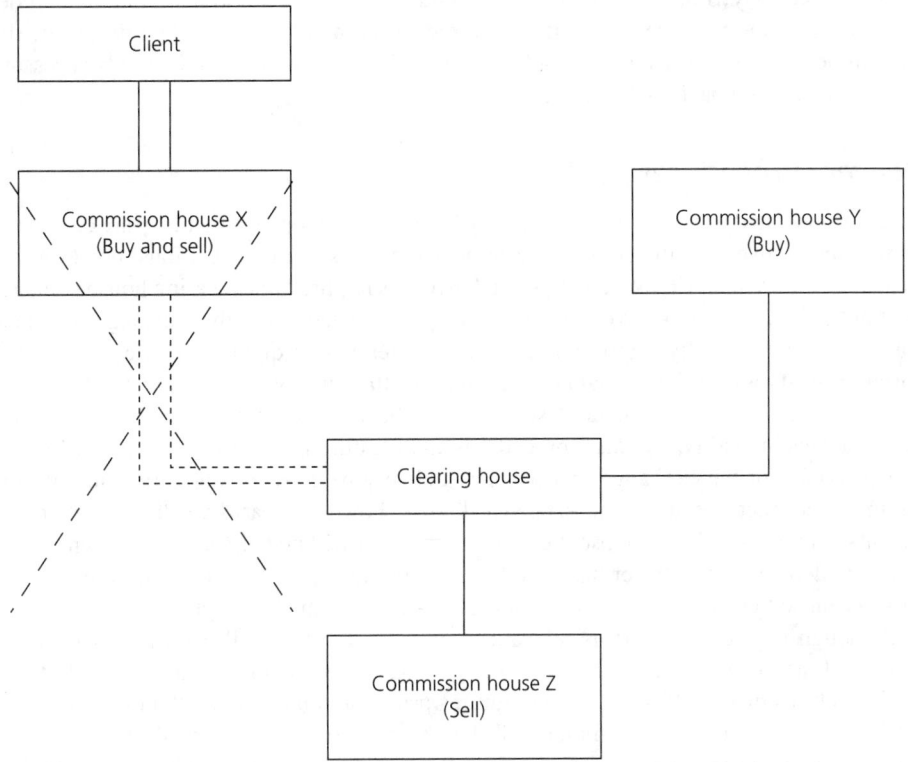

commission houses require of their clients are often higher than the margins required by the clearing house, although the deposits represent only a small proportion of the total contract and are virtually cost-free because interest-bearing Treasury bonds can be used. Clients' accounts are marked to market at the end of each day and clients are subject to margin calls if their position deteriorates. Margins and daily marking to market make client defaults a rare occurrence and reinforce the overall financial soundness of the exchange.

Marking to market means that profits and losses are paid every day at the end of trading and is equivalent to closing out a contract each day, paying off losses or receiving gains, and writing a new contract. The procedure can best be illustrated by an example. On Monday morning an investor takes a long position in a euro futures contract at a price of USD 0.70. At the end of the day the price has risen to UDS 0.705. The amount of the contract is EUR 125,000 and therefore the investor's gain is:

$$(USD\ 0.705 - USD\ 0.700) \times 125,000 = USD\ 625.$$

The investor receives USD 625 and is the owner of a contract the price of which is now USD 0.705. On Tuesday evening the price has fallen to USD 0.695 and therefore the investor has to pay:

$$(USD\ 0.705 - USD\ 0.695) \times 125,000 = USD\ 1250$$

and now owns a contract the price of which is USD 0.695.

The margin procedure is straightforward. An initial **margin** is deposited when a position is taken on a futures contract. This initial margin is usually set high enough so that the cost and inconvenience of frequent small payments can be avoided as the futures price is marked to market each day. Small losses are simply deducted from the initial margin until a predetermined minimum, called the **maintenance margin**, is reached. At this point, the commission house issues a margin call requesting the client to deposit the funds necessary to bring the margin back to the initial level.

Delivery procedures

Except for isolated exceptions, futures positions that remain open at maturity are closed out by physical delivery of the commodity in question. Most futures positions, however, are closed out before maturity. When physical delivery is required, the clearing house manages the transaction. It assigns buyers to sellers and fixes exactly how the exchange is to take place. This is especially important for commodities where quality can vary and transportation costs are high. Exchange rules specify the quality of the merchandise to be delivered, where it is to be delivered, storage and other costs, compensation differentials for discrepancies in quality, appraisal procedures and conditions for refusal by the buyer. It is indispensable for the exchange that physical delivery be effected smoothly and with the minimum conflict possible. The exchange knows, however, that the seller maintains an advantage in being able to choose the merchandise that will be delivered and, often, where it will be delivered. The buyer has little latitude and must pay the price determined as the most recent settlement price. We will come back to this theme in Chapters 18 and 19.

Although physical delivery is relevant to only 1% to 3% of all contracts, it is nevertheless a fundamental element of the arbitrage operations that ensure an efficiently functioning futures market. If, for example, futures prices are much higher than spot prices as the maturity date approaches, traders will be able to earn a riskless profit by buying the commodity on the spot market, stocking it, selling a futures contract, and making physical delivery at maturity. The difference in price, of course, has to be large enough to cover the storage costs and the financial opportunity cost of buying spot. On the other side of the coin, if futures prices are too low, traders can sell the commodity short, make a futures purchase and take delivery at maturity. The commodity can then be resold at a profit or consumed directly. Thus, the possibility of physical delivery ensures that the spot and futures prices will converge as maturity approaches and the futures market is linked directly to the reality of the spot market in the underlying commodity. For futures contracts that involve cash settlement rather than physical delivery, such as those on stock indices, the settlement price is often taken as the closing spot price of the underlying asset as a means of guaranteeing convergence.

Futures information

The financial press contains regular information on many of the currency futures traded on the different exchanges. Table 7.3, for example, shows data on euro contracts traded on the Chicago Mercantile Exchange (CME) as reported in the *Wall Street Journal Europe* on Friday, 6 October 2000.

Each CME contract is for EUR 125,000 and prices are given in US dollars per euro. The first column gives the maturity month of each contract, and the three active contracts shown are those expiring in December 2000, March 2001 and September 2001 respectively. Column two (headed "Open") gives the price at the start of trading on Thursday, 5 October 2000; column 3 (headed "High") gives the highest transaction price during that day and column 4 (headed "Low") gives the lowest transaction price during the same day. Column 5 (headed "Settle") shows the price representative of transactions near the market's close. It is this price that is used in the process of marking to market. For example, the settlement price

Table 7.3 Information on euro futures (contract EUR 125,000; USD per euro)

	Open	High	Low	Settle	Change	Lifetime high	Lifetime low	Open interest
Dec 00	.8770	.8816	.8709	.8721	−.0057	1.0572	.8501	66,686
Mar 01	.8780	.8845	.8743	.8757	−.0057	.9999	.8554	784
Sep 01	....	....	....	.8823	−.0057	.8962	.8616	165

Note: Estimated volume 15 633; volume Wednesday 8 983; open interest 67 662 (+66).
Source: *Wall Street Journal Europe*, 6 October 2000.

for the March contract was USD 0.8757. Column 6 (headed "Change") shows the change in the settlement price between Wednesday and Thursday. For the March contract the settlement price fell by USD 0.0057. Thus, on Thursday, 5 October 2000 the owner of this contract made a loss of USD 0.0057 × 125,000 = USD 712.50 and the seller made a gain of an equal amount. It is interesting to note that although the September contract did not trade on October 5, there is a reported settlement price of USD 0.8823 for a fall of USD 0.0057. In fact, when a contract does not trade, the CME fixes the settlement price based on reported bid–ask quotes. Columns 7 and 8 (headed "Lifetime high" and "Lifetime low") show the highest and lowest observed prices for each contract since its inception. As might be expected, the longer a contract has traded, the wider will be the high–low spread. Thus, the spread on the December contract is wider than the spread on the March contract, which is wider than the spread on the September contract. Column 9 (headed "Open interest") reports the number of outstanding contracts. Again, the longer a contract has been traded, the higher the number of outstanding contracts. Consequently, the December maturity has 66 686 contracts outstanding while the September contract has only 165. The note to the table shows that the total number of contracts traded on Thursday was 15 633, that the total number of contracts traded on Wednesday was 8 983, and that the total number of contracts outstanding at the end of trading on Thursday was 67 662, an increase of 66 over Wednesday's close.

Basis and effective hedging

Although spot and futures prices converge at maturity, they can and do differ significantly before maturity. The difference between the futures price and the spot price is called the **basis:**[5]

$$\text{Basis} = F_{t,T} - S_t \tag{7.1}$$

The basis and how it varies through time are important elements in hedging strategies that use the organized futures exchanges.

The flexibility afforded by the possibility of closing out a futures position at any time before the contract's maturity is an important element for such strategies. Suppose, for example, that in May a Swiss chocolate manufacturer forecasts a need for USD 4 million to purchase sugar at the end of June. It feels that the dollar is likely to rise in the interim and

[5] The alternative definition is Basis = $S_t - F_{t,T}$. We use the definition in Equation 7.1.

wants to cover itself. A hedge can be constructed with a futures contract having a different maturity than the date on which the company must make the payment in dollars. This brings up the question of basis risk. In this section we will first look at the conditions for choosing the maturity of the futures contract. We will then look at what determines the basis on the commodities markets.

Choosing the maturity of the futures contract

Futures delivery dates, being relatively infrequent, will often not correspond perfectly with the maturity of the risk to be hedged. Consequently, the hedge might not eliminate all risk. This is because, although the futures price and spot (cash) price will converge at maturity, before maturity they can and do differ significantly.[6] Thus, the choice of a maturity date will affect the effectiveness of the hedge. This can be illustrated with an example.

Suppose that on 16 May the spot price for sugar is USD 286.50 per ton. At the same time, an August futures contract on the Paris exchange is selling at USD 279.50 per ton. To cover itself, the Swiss manufacturer decides to purchase eight August contracts (each contract is for 50 tons). On 20 June it purchases 400 tons of sugar from its regular suppliers at a price of USD 327.50 per ton and simultaneously closes out its futures position at USD 325 per ton for a gain of:

$$(USD\ 325 - USD\ 279.50) \times 8 \times 50 = USD\ 18,200.$$

The cost of purchasing the 400 tons of sugar was:

$$USD\ 327.50 \times 400 = USD\ 131,000.$$

Including the gain on the futures contract the net cost was:

$$USD\ 131,000 - USD\ 18,200 = USD\ 108,800$$

or a price of USD 282 per ton.

The chocolate manufacturer's hedging operation turned out to be extremely effective insofar as the spot price of sugar on the purchase date was USD 327.50 and it only paid USD 282. This outcome is due to the fact that the futures price followed an evolution parallel to the spot price. The spot price went from USD 286.50 to USD 327.50, for a gain of USD 41, while the futures price went from USD 279.50 to USD 325, for a gain of USD 45.50. As long as the two prices evolve in a parallel fashion, it does not matter too much if the maturity dates differ.

We can also see that the hedge made it possible to get a better price than was available on 16 May, i.e. USD 282 instead of USD 286.50. The reason for this is that the forward price went up by more (USD 45.50) than the spot price (USD 41). The USD 4.50 difference explains the difference between the USD 282 and USD 286.50. This brings up the question

---

[6] P.A. Samuelson, "Proof that properly anticipated prices fluctuate randomly", *Industrial Management Review*, Vol. 6 (1965), 41–49, showed that futures prices will become more volatile as they approach maturity. D. Rutledge, "A note on the variability of futures prices", *Review of Economics and Statistics*, Vol. 58 (1976), 118–120 found empirical support for this law. Other studies supporting Samuelson's Law are R. Anderson. "Some determinants of the volatility of futures prices", *Journal of Futures Markets*, Fall (1985) 331–348; N. Milonas, "Price variability and the maturity effect in futures markets", *Journal of Futures Markets,* Spring (1986), p.p. 443–460. This means that the volatility of the basis for a particular contract may tend to increase as the contract approaches maturity.

of the basis. Remember that the basis is the difference between the futures price and the spot price. On 16 May the basis was

$$USD\ 279.50 - USD\ 286.50 = -USD\ 7.$$

On 20 June the basis was:

$$USD\ 325 - USD\ 327.50 = -USD\ 2.50.$$

The basis increased by USD 4.50 from – USD 7 to – USD 2.50 and this is what explains the difference between the spot price of USD 286.50 on 16 May and the USD 282 effective cost of the sugar on 20 June.

Unfortunately, there is no reason why the basis should always increase. It could also decrease. Suppose that instead of USD 325 the futures price had been USD 317.50 on 20 June. The basis would have been

$$USD\ 317.50 - USD\ 327.50 = -USD\ 10$$

for a fall of USD 3. The gain on the futures contracts would have been

$$USD\ 317.50 - USD\ 279.50 = USD\ 38\ per\ ton.$$

The net cost of the sugar would have been

$$USD\ 327.50 - USD\ 38 = USD\ 289.50\ per\ ton,$$

USD 3 higher than the spot price on 16 May. The USD 3 fall in the basis is responsible. A hedger purchasing futures benefits from a rise in the basis and suffers from a fall. An imperfect hedge using futures contracts like the one above where the maturities do not match is called a **delta hedge**. In practice, a delta hedge will never eliminate all the risk. Basis risk will always exist insofar as the futures price is not perfectly correlated with the spot price. Choosing the maturity of the futures contract is therefore important for the effectiveness of the hedge and depends on how the price of the futures contract is expected to evolve relative to the spot price. The expected evolution of the basis, then, is the key to choosing the maturity of the hedging instrument.

Before examining the factors that determine the basis we should remember that all hedgers, both buyers and sellers, are subject to basis risk. Whereas buyers benefit when the basis increases and lose when the basis decreases, sellers benefit when the basis decreases and lose when the basis increases. This is only logical because they are on opposite sides of the fence, with buyers hedging against a rise in the spot price and sellers hedging against a fall.

Determining the basis: Financial assets

The evolution of the basis is crucial for the effectiveness of the hedge. Consequently, it is important to understand what determines the basis. The basis in financial futures is straightforward. Resting on the principle of efficient markets and no arbitrage, it generally depends on the difference between the interest rate and the payout on the underlying asset. To see this, start with the following notation:

T = delivery date of the futures contract (years)
t = current date (years)

$\tau = T - t$

$F_{t,T}$ = price of a futures contract at time t for delivery at time T

S_t = Spot (cash) price at time t

K = present value of storage costs or other known intermediate payouts such as interest or dividends

r = riskless rate of interest

k = proportional cost of storage

c = convenience yield

δ = dividend yield

r_B = the bond yield

r^* = the riskless rate on foreign currency.

No intermediate payments

First we consider an underlying asset with no intermediate cash payments and no storage costs such as a pure discount bond or a stock that pays no dividends. If there are no intermediate payments, the no-arbitrage relationship between the futures price and the spot price is:

$$F_{t,T} = S_t e^{r\tau} \tag{7.2}$$

If this were not true and $F_{t,T} > S_t e^{r\tau}$ it would be possible to sell a futures contract (cash flow = 0), borrow S_t (cash flow = $+S_t$) and buy the underlying asset (cash flow = $-S_t$). At maturity take delivery and pay off the loan. The riskless profit is equal to $F_{t,T} - S_t e^{r\tau}$. If $F_{t,T} < S_t e^{r\tau}$, it would be possible to purchase a futures contract (cash flow = 0), sell the asset short (cash flow = $+S_t$) and lend the proceeds of the sale at the riskless rate (cash flow = $-S_t$). At maturity use the proceeds from the loan to take delivery and return the borrowed asset. The riskless profit is equal to $S_t e^{r\tau} - F_{t,T}$. The only way that riskless arbitrage profits can be eliminated is if Equation 7.2 holds.

Intermediate cash payments

Consider a security such as a currency, a coupon-paying bond or a stock with a known dividend. Suppose that the present value of these payments is equal to K. The no-arbitrage relationship between F and S must be:

$$F_{t,T} = (S_t - K)e^{r\tau} \tag{7.3}$$

If this were not true and $F_{t,T} > (S_t - K)e^{r\tau}$, it would be possible to make an arbitrage profit by selling F, borrowing S at the riskless rate and using the proceeds to purchase the underlying at the cost of S. The income that is received from the security over the life of the contract is invested in the riskless asset. At maturity we would take delivery and use F plus the proceeds from the income invested in the riskless asset to pay off the loan. The profit would be $F_{t,T} - (S_t - K)e^{r\tau}$. If $F_{t,T} < (S_t - K)e^{r\tau}$, the arbitrager can purchase F, sell S short and use the proceeds to invest in the riskless asset for maturities corresponding to the intermediate cash payouts and the maturity date. At maturity he would use the proceeds from the investment in the riskless asset to take delivery. The profit would be $(S_t - K)e^{r\tau} - F_{t,T}$.

Known dividend yields

Consider a security such as a stock that pays a known, constant yield equal to δ expressed as a percentage of the security price. The no-arbitrage relationship between F and S is:

$$F_{t,T} = S_t e^{(r-\delta)\tau} \tag{7.4}$$

To prove this, set up a portfolio by first selling a futures contract (cash flow = 0), secondly borrowing $F_{t,T}e^{-r\tau}$ (cash flow = $+F_{t,T}e^{-r\tau}$), and thirdly buying $S_t e^{-\delta\tau}$ (cash flow = $-S_t e^{-\delta\tau}$). If payouts are reinvested in the asset, at maturity we will have:

$+S_T$ from the purchases of the asset,
$-F_{t,T}$ from paying off the loan, and
$+F_{t,T} - S_T$ from the futures contract.

This is equal to zero. The value of a portfolio with a certain zero outcome is equal to zero. Thus, $Fe^{-r\tau} - Se^{-\delta\tau} = 0$. Rearranging gives Equation 7.3.

Currency futures

If the security in question is a foreign currency, using the same arguments, 7.4 becomes:

$$F_{t,T} = S_t e^{(r-r^*)\tau} \qquad (7.5)$$

where r^* is the riskless rate on foreign currency.

Long-term interest rate futures

If the security in question is a long-term bond, using the same arguments, 7.4 becomes:

$$F_{t,T} = S_t e^{(r-r_B)\tau} \qquad (7.6)$$

where r_B is the bond yield.

Determining the basis: Commodities

The relationship between the futures and spot prices of financial assets is straightforward because the underlying instruments on the financial futures markets have no supply problems associated with production costs, weather and the like; nor do they have inventory problems related to storage facilities, damage and obsolescence. The underlying instruments on the commodity futures markets do suffer from these problems, which makes the determination of the basis more complicated.

First of all, we have seen that when the maturity of the futures contract and the commodity transaction are the same, arbitrage ensures that the basis will tend to zero as the maturity date approaches. Convergence is never perfect, however, because arbitrage transactions are costly. Transport costs, insurance against litigation and eventual differences in the quality of the merchandise, among other factors, can be the source of differences between the futures price and the spot price at maturity. Nevertheless, on the whole, convergence is satisfactory for most commodities. If it were not, commodities futures would lose their attraction for professional traders and eventually die out.

When the maturity date is somewhere in the future, there is no reason for the basis to be equal to zero. On the contrary. In practice it can be either positive or negative. When it is positive, it is referred to as **contango**, and when it is negative it is called **backwardation**. There are two major factors that explain the existence of a positive or negative basis. The first is the cost of setting up an arbitrage operation, called the carrying cost, and the second is the expected evolution of the spot market.

When the commodity in question is stockable (grain, gold, oil, etc.), the no-arbitrage relationship between the futures price and the spot price should verify the following inequality:

$$F_{t,T} \leq (S + K)e^{r\tau} \qquad (7.7)$$

It is easy to see that if $F_{t,T} > (S_t + K)e^{rt}$, a trader could make a riskless profit by selling a futures contract, borrowing $S+K$ and using the proceeds of the loan to purchase the commodity on the spot market and pay storage costs. On the maturity date, physical delivery would be made and the loan would be paid off out of the proceeds. The arbitrager's riskless profit would be $F_{t,T} - (S_t - K)e^{rt}$. Consequently, the upper limit of the futures price is determined by the carrying cost of the arbitrage transaction. In certain commodity markets, relation 7.7 is particularly binding. On the gold market, for example, where storage costs are low and stable, it is almost an equality.

While this arbitrage relation is important, it has some practical shortcomings. First of all, it only defines the upper limit of the futures price. It tells us nothing about how low the price can go. Secondly, it supposes that storage costs are easily observable. Thirdly, it is entirely inapplicable to commodities such as cattle on the hoof that are not stockable.

Convenience yield

H. Working was the first to provide a partial answer to the first two shortcomings.[7] He demonstrated in a formalized argument that storage costs cannot be considered as fixed. They depend on the level of stocks as depicted in Figure 7.4. The explanation is straightforward. In the weeks following a harvest, the silos are full and storage space is rare and costly. As time goes on, stocks are run down, storage space becomes available and its cost falls.

Working's analysis of storage costs explains why the basis is higher or lower, depending on the maturity in question. It also explains how the basis can be negative. In practice, the basis is often negative for certain commodities. During the Iraq–Kuwait crisis of 1990, for example, the spot price of crude oil rose to over USD 40 a barrel while the futures price hovered at about USD 24 per barrel. With such a large negative basis it is hard to understand why traders would continue to hold stocks. It seems like it would be better to sell spot and assure future supplies at a lower price by buying a futures contract. The fact that this does not always happen proves that there must be certain advantages in holding stocks. The advantages come in the form of the planning benefits of having a secure supply and the elimination of costs associated with stock-outs or avoiding stock-outs when it looks like they might occur. Benefits of this type are

Figure 7.4 Storage costs and level of stocks

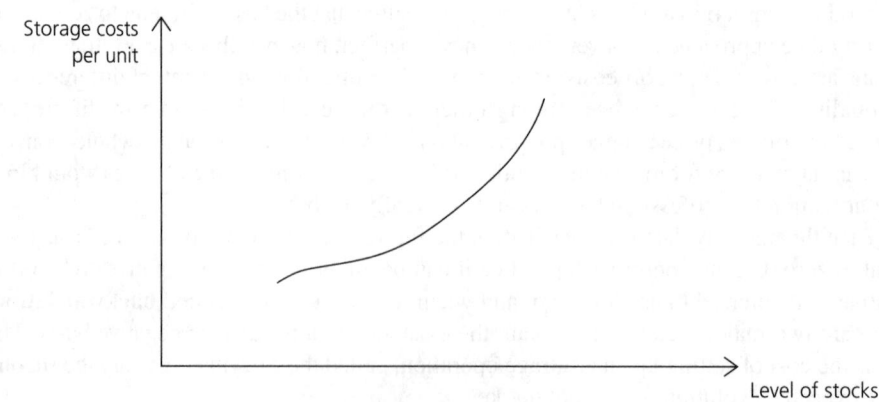

Storage costs per unit

Level of stocks

[7] H. Working, "Price of cash wheat and futures at Chicago since 1883", *Wheat Studies of the Food Research Institute* (November 1934); S. Hoss and H. Working, "Wheat Futures Prices and Trading at Liverpool since 1886", *Wheat Studies of the Food Research Institute* (November 1938).

referred to as **convenience returns or yields**. Lower stocks make a stock-out more likely and raise the convenience yield. Figure 7.5 completes Figure 7.4 with the notion of convenience yields. At high levels of stocks, convenience yields are negligible or non-existent. At low stock levels, convenience yields rise rapidly and push down the price of the futures contract.

No-arbitrage relationships with storage costs and convenience yields

We can summarize the no-arbitrage determination of the basis for commodities as follows. When stocks are high and expected to remain adequate, convenience yields are non-existent and the carrying cost of arbitrage determines the futures price at a level above the spot price. On the other hand, when stocks are very low or expected to get very low, convenience yields rise and storage costs fall. The futures price is determined by the difference between convenience yields and carrying costs. Convenience yields higher than carrying costs can push the futures price below the spot price and make the basis negative.

Using the no-arbitrage arguments above, this gives the relationships between the futures and spot prices for commodities detailed in the following sub-sections.

Non-proportional storage costs

Suppose that the present value of storage costs are equal to K. The no-arbitrage relationship between F and S must be:

$$F_{t,T} \leq (S_t + K)e^{r\tau} \tag{7.8}$$

If this were not true and $F_{t,T} > (S_t + K)e^{r\tau}$, it would be possible to make an arbitrage profit by selling F, borrowing $S+K$ at the riskless rate, using the proceeds to first purchase the underlying at the cost of S and secondly to invest in the riskless asset for maturities corresponding to payments for storage costs. Over the life of the contract we use the proceeds of the investments in the riskless asset to pay off the storage costs as they come due. At maturity we take delivery and use F to pay off the loan. The profit would be $F_{t,T} - (S_t + K)e^{r\tau}$. If $F_{t,T} < (S_t + K)e^{r\tau}$, the problem is more complicated because it is usually not possible to short the commodity in

Figure 7.5 Storage costs, convenience yield and level of stocks

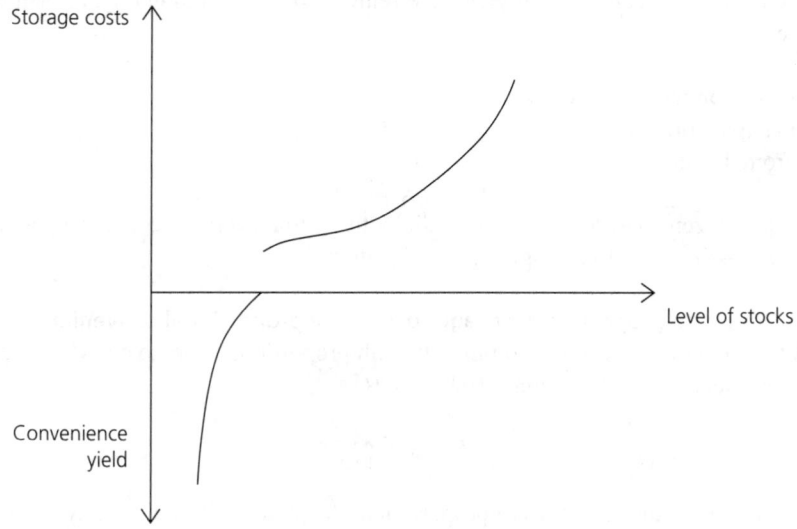

such a way that the storage costs are paid to the short position. Thus, the strategy of buying the futures contract and shorting the commodity will not work. For precious metals like gold and silver that are held as investments as well as for consumption, however, an arbitrage profit could be made by those holding the commodity as an investment. This could be done by purchasing F, selling S out of stocks (thereby saving K in storage costs, which for expository purposes we can assume are invested in the riskless asset) and using the proceeds to invest in the riskless asset. At maturity we would use the proceeds from the investment in the riskless asset to take delivery. The profit with respect to the original position would be $(S_t + K)e^{r\tau} - F_{t,T}$.

Non-proportional convenience yield

Suppose that the present value of the convenience yields is equal to K. The no-arbitrage relationship between F and S must be:

$$F_{t,T} = (S_t - K)e^{r\tau} \tag{7.9}$$

If this were not true and $F_{t,T} > (S_t - K)e^{r\tau}$, it would be possible to make an arbitrage profit by selling F, borrowing S at the riskless rate and using the proceeds to purchase the underlying at the cost of S. The convenience yields received over the life of the contract are invested in the riskless asset. At maturity we would take delivery and use F plus the proceeds from the income invested in the riskless asset to pay off the loan. The profit would be $F_{t,T} - (S_t - K)e^{r\tau}$. If $F_{t,T} < (S_t - K)e^{r\tau}$, the arbitrager can purchase F, sell S short and use the proceeds to invest in the riskless asset for maturities corresponding to the intermediate convenience yield payouts. At maturity we would use the proceeds from the investment in the riskless asset to take delivery. The profit would be $(S_t - K)e^{r\tau} - F_{t,T}$.

Commodities with a proportional convenience yield

Consider a commodity that pays a known, constant convenience yield equal to c expressed as a percentage of the commodity price. The relationship between F and S is:

$$F_{t,T} = S_t e^{(r-c)\tau} \tag{7.10}$$

To see this, set up a portfolio by first selling a futures contract (cash flow = 0), secondly borrowing $F_{t,T}e^{-r\tau}$ (cash flow = $+F_{t,T}e^{-r\tau}$) and thirdly buying $S_t e^{-c\tau}$ of the commodity (cash flow = $-S_t e^{-c\tau}$). If the convenience yields are reinvested in the commodity, at maturity we will have:

$+S_T$ from the commodity purchase,
$-F$ from paying off the loan, and
$+F - S_T$ from the futures contract.

This is equal to zero. The value of a portfolio with a certain zero outcome is equal to zero. Thus, $F_{t,T}e^{-r\tau} - S_t e^{-c\tau} = 0$. Rearranging gives Equation 7.10.

Commodities with proportional storage costs and a proportional convenience yield

If the futures contract refers to a commodity with proportional storage costs and a proportional convenience yield, Equation 7.10 becomes:

$$F_{t,T} = S_t e^{(r+k-c)\tau} \tag{7.11}$$

where k represents storage costs as a proportion of the price of the commodity.

Normal backwardation

Another theory of the determination of the basis borrows from expectations theory and the role of the speculator. Don't forget that spot and futures prices should converge at maturity. Furthermore, it is reasonable to assume that today's futures price represents the market's expectation of what the spot price will be on the maturity date of the futures contract. This assumption, as we saw in Chapter 3, is called the forward rate parity hypothesis. It can be written:

$$F_{t,T} = E(S_T) \tag{7.12}$$

where E is the expectations operator. Equation 7.12 represents forward rate parity and says that today's future rate for maturity T is the best estimate of what the spot rate will be on that date. If it is true, this is a valuable statistic. Unfortunately, it is not compatible with the presence of speculators in the market, at least according to Keynes.[8] In fact, if a speculator holds his position until maturity, his expected gain will be zero: $F_{t,T} - E(S_T) = 0$. Because there are many speculators in the market and since they have to make a profit on the average in order to stay in business, something else must be at work. Keynes' solution to the problem is the hypothesis of "normal backwardation", whereby the rate of profit for a speculator with a long position in futures should be positive. The hypothesis can be written as follows:

$$E(S_T) - F_{t,T} = \lambda \tag{7.13}$$

where λ represents the level of remuneration necessary for the speculator to finance the margin requirements, transaction costs and profits necessary to keep him in business. A negative basis reflects all these elements when the expected spot price at time T is just equal to the current spot price. This proposition is important because it fixes a lower limit to the futures price. The futures price cannot fall below the expected spot price at time T less the premium λ. Otherwise, speculators will all take up long positions. The same type of argument can be made for speculators with short positions. The futures price cannot exceed the sum of the expected spot price at maturity plus the speculator's premium. Otherwise, all speculators would sell futures in order to benefit from the excessively high expected profits, thereby lowering the futures price.

Systematic risk and return

Modern portfolio theory leads to the conclusion that there are two types of risk in the economy: risk that can be eliminated through diversification, called unsystematic risk, and risk that cannot be eliminated through diversification, called systematic risk.[9] Because unsystematic risk can be eliminated, investors should not worry about it. Systematic risk arises from correlations of returns across all assets or, as in the capital asset pricing model (CAPM), from the correlation between returns on the investment and the market as a whole. Since this risk cannot be diversified away, investors should require a return above the riskless rate of interest for taking on positive amounts of systematic risk. They should also be prepared to accept a return below the riskless rate if their systematic risk is negative. Equations 7.12 and 7.13 can be interpreted in this context.

---

[8] J.M. Keynes, *A Treatise on Money* (London: Macmillan, 1930), Vol. 2, p.p. 142–144.

[9] For an excellent, in depth presentation of modern portfolio theory see, for example, E.J Elton, and M.J. Gruber, *Modern Portfolio Theory and Investment Analysis*, fifth edition (New York: John Wiley & Sons, 1995).

Consider an investor who purchases a futures contract for $F_{0,T}$ at time 0 for delivery at T and invests the amount $F_{0,T}e^{-rT}$ in the riskless asset. On the delivery date, the proceeds from the loan are used to pay off the futures contract and take delivery of the underlying asset, which is then sold for its market price. The cash flows of this investment at maturity are $S_T - F_{T,T}$, the price received for the underlying asset less the futures price. If the capital markets are in equilibrium, the present value of this investment at time 0 is:

$$E(S_T)e^{-RT} - F_{0,T}e^{-rT} = 0$$

where R is the required rate of return on the underlying asset necessary to compensate investors for its systematic risk. This can be written as:

$$F_{0,T} = E(S_T)e^{T(r-R)} \qquad (7.14)$$

Thus, R depends on the systematic risk of the underlying asset: if it has positive correlation with the market, $R > r$, which suggests that $F_{0,T} < E(S_T)$; if it has negative correlation, $R < r$, and $F_{0,T} > E(S_T)$; if it is uncorrelated with the market, $R = r$, and $F_{0,T} = E(S_T)$.

The basis on commodities markets: Summary

It is clear that there are two types of participants on the futures markets. There are those who trade for the purpose of hedging and those who trade for the purpose of speculating. Some are short; others are long. Taken together, their actions determine the basis. The elements that motivate their actions can be summarized as follows:

- the expected evolution of the spot price
- carrying costs
- convenience returns
- the speculators' premium
- the systematic risk premium

All these elements are not necessarily present simultaneously at all times. There are times when simple arbitrage will determine the basis, and there are other times when convenience yields and the speculators' premium will come into play. The fact is that although the basis converges to zero at maturity, in practice its evolution can be erratic. Basis risk is real. For this reason hedging operations require technical expertise and should be undertaken carefully.

Hedging with futures

Hedging with futures is similar to hedging with forwards. To cover a short position, a futures contract can be bought. To cover a long position, a futures contract can be sold. Because the contracts are standardized and guaranteed by the clearing house, they are liquid and represent no counterparty risk. Hence, futures are generally cheaper than forwards and positions can be closed out or rolled over more easily and cheaply than they can with forwards. A short position in futures can be closed out by a purchase of the same contract. It can be rolled over by a simultaneous purchase of the same contract and the sale of a similar contract with a later maturity date. A long position in futures can be closed out by a sale of the same contract. It can be rolled over by a simultaneous sale of the same contract and purchase of a similar contract with a later maturity date.

The ease of opening and closing out positions makes it possible to manage relatively small levels of exposure on a continuous basis. This is especially attractive to commercial customers who have a fairly regular stream of payments and receipts. Furthermore, arbitrage ensures that pricing advantages between futures and forward markets should be negligible. It is true, though, that because of marking to market, forward and futures prices can theoretically differ, with the difference between the futures price minus the forward price depending on the correlation of the riskless interest rate with the futures price.[10] If the futures price falls when the riskless interest rate rises and vice versa, the correlation is negative and the futures price will be below the forward price. If the futures price rises when the riskless interest rate rises and vice versa, the correlation is positive and the futures price will be higher than the forward price. The reason is straightforward. Marking to market generates interim cash flows. A negative correlation between the futures price and the riskless rate means that for the buyer of a futures contract, on average, financing costs of interim outflows when interest rates rise and futures prices fall will be higher than interest gains on interim inflows when interest rates fall and futures prices rise. For example, financing a USD 1000 loss on a futures contract when the interest rate goes from 8% to 10% costs the annual equivalent of USD 100. A USD 1000 gain on a futures contract when the interest rate goes from 8% to 6% only brings in an annual equivalent of USD 60. The expected return on the interim cash flows is negative. Consequently, to compensate for the expected losses on the interim cash flows, the buyer's price is lower than it would be for a forward contract that has no interim cash flows. For the seller of the futures contract, losses and gains are reversed and he is willing to accept a lower price than he would for a forward contract.

If the correlation between the futures price and the riskless interest rate is positive, financing costs and gains are reversed and marking to market is an advantage for the buyer and a disadvantage to the seller, thereby causing the price of the futures contract to rise above that of the forward contract. In the case where the correlation is zero, futures and forward prices are the same. All this having been said, comparisons of futures and forward prices in the foreign exchange market have consistently revealed the absence of a significant difference between the two.[11] Consequently, for all practical purposes, the prices of futures contracts can be determined as if they were forward contracts.

Although futures contracts exhibit definite advantages over forwards in transaction costs and ease of use because of standardization and liquidity, they also have some definite disadvantages:

- Futures contracts are only available for short maturities. The maximum maturity is one year and markets are usually thin for maturities exceeding six months. Hence, for long-term hedging the futures markets are not a viable alternative to the forward and swap markets.

- The fixed contract size makes it difficult to make an exact match with the position to be hedged. As we mentioned, however, the size of the contracts is small enough that most users' needs can be approximated quite well.

- The infrequent maturity dates make it unlikely that the futures contract will correspond perfectly with the maturity of the cash flow to be hedged. In this case, hedging with futures requires the setting up of what is called a minimum variance delta hedge, discussed below.

---

[10] See J. Cox, J. Ingersoll, Jr., and S. Ross, "The relation between forward prices and futures prices", *Journal of Financial Economics*, Vol. 9 (1981), p.p. 321–346.

[11] See B. Cornell and M. Reinganum, "Forward and futures prices: Evidence from the foreign exchange markets", *Journal of Finance*, Vol. 36 (1981), p.p.1035–1045; H.Y. Park and A.H. Chen, "Difference between futures and forward prices: A further investigation of marking to market effects", *Journal of Futures Markets*, Vol. 5 (1985), p.p. 77–88; C.W. Chang and J.S.K. Chang, "Forward and futures prices: Evidence from the foreign exchange markets", *Journal of Finance*, Vol. 45, (1990), p.p. 1333–1336.

- The liquidity requirement on futures contracts limits them to a few, high turnover underlying assets. However, because many of the untraded, lower turnover assets are highly correlated with one of the high turnover assets that are traded, a traded asset can be used as a proxy to hedge a cash flow in an untraded asset. Using a futures contract in one asset to hedge a cash flow in another asset requires the setting up of what is called a minimum variance cross hedge, discussed below.

Minimum variance delta hedge

Consider the foreign currency market. As we saw in Equation 7.5, it is the interest rate differential that determines the basis in currency markets. Because the infrequent maturity dates on futures contracts make it unlikely that the maturity of the futures contract will correspond perfectly with the maturity of the cash flow to be hedged, basis risk must be taken into consideration when setting up a hedging strategy. To see how this can be done, consider the situation of a dollar-based agent expecting an inflow of GBP C at time 1. His hedge involves selling N futures contracts of size GBP Q that mature at time 2. Ignoring the interest rate risk associated with marking to market, at time 1 when the GBP C arrive, the agent will receive the dollar equivalent of GBP C converted at the spot exchange rate less N times the difference between the futures price at time 1 and the futures price contracted at time 0 multiplied by GBP Q, the size of the contract. The problem is to determine the optimum number of futures contracts to be sold. To answer this question let

S_1 = the spot exchange rate at time (the number of dollars to purchase GBP 1)
$F_{0,2}$ = the futures price of GBP 1 at time 0 for delivery at time 2
$F_{1,2}$ = the futures prices of GBP 1 at time 1 for delivery at time 2.

Converting the pound into dollars at the maturity date's spot exchange rate gives

$$S_1 \times C \text{ dollars.}$$

The difference between the futures prices gives

$$-N(F_{1,2} - F_{0,2}) \times Q \text{ dollars.}$$

Thus the dollar value of the portfolio will be

$$S_1 C - N(F_{1,2} - F_{0,2})Q \tag{7.15}$$

Divide by C and define the hedge ratio as $\beta = \dfrac{NQ}{C}$ and Equation 7.15 can be written as

$$S_1 - \beta(F_{1,2} - F_{0,2}) \tag{7.16}$$

The idea is to choose β so that the variance of Equation 7.16 is minimized. Since $F_{0,2}$ is known, the variance of Equation 7.16 is

$$Var(S_1) - 2\beta Cov(S_1, F_{1,2}) + \beta^2 Var(F_{1,2}) \tag{7.17}$$

Taking the derivative of Equation 7.17 with respect to β and setting it equal to zero gives

$$-2Cov(S_1, F_{1,2}) + 2\beta Var(F_{1,2}) = 0$$

which implies that

$$\beta = \frac{Cov(S_1, F_{1,2})}{Var(F_{1,2})} \qquad (7.18)$$

Thus, the optimal number of contracts is equal to

$$N = \beta \frac{C}{Q} \qquad (7.19)$$

Example of a minimum variance delta hedge

Starting with the following information:

C = GBP 3,125,000 to be received in one month
Q = GBP 62,500
maturity date of the futures contract = two months

we want to find N, the optimal number of futures contracts to be sold. The first step is to estimate β. Going back to Equation 7.18, we can see that β is equal to the slope coefficient in the equation

$$S_1 = \alpha + \beta F_{1,2} + \varepsilon \qquad (7.20)$$

In theory, 7.20 should be estimated as a forecast. In practice, because the data necessary for making a reliable forecast is generally unavailable, 7.20 is usually estimated in a time series regression using historical data.[12] Using monthly historical data over a five-year period we find $\beta = 0.895$. Hence, the number of contracts to be sold is

$$N = 0.895 \frac{3,125,000}{62,500} = 44.75.$$

Rounded to the closest full contract, N = 45. If there were no basis risk N would be equal to 50. Remember that basis risk is due to variations in the interest rate differential and that the effect of an interest rate differential increases with a contract's time to maturity. Thus, for currencies with historically large and volatile interest rate differentials, optimal hedge N will be considerably different from the N for the perfect riskless hedge, and the difference will increase with the difference between the hedged cash flow date and the date of the futures contract.

Minimum variance cross hedge

Because futures contracts are only available for a few high turnover currencies, a cross hedge must be constructed to hedge cash flows in currencies with no futures contracts. The problem is similar to that of a maturity mismatch, except here the disparity arises because the spot price of the hedged currency and the futures price of the proxy currency are likely

---

[12] For technical reasons due to problems of stationarity, it might be necessary to estimate β based on changes in the spot and futures rates rather than on the actual rates themselves. Stationarity and related topics such as cointegration are routinely explained in standard econometrics texts. See, for example, Damodar N. Gujarati, *Basic Econometrics*, third edition (New York: McGraw-Hill, Inc. 1995), p.p. 709–733.

to differ at maturity. The objective is to minimize the difference between the two. The first and most obvious step is to choose a proxy currency with a close relationship to the currency to be hedged. The second step is to adjust the hedge for likely divergences.

To see how this can be done, consider the situation of a dollar-based agent expecting an inflow of C Danish kroner (DKK) at time 1. Given the close relationship between the Danish and European economies, their exchange rates are highly correlated. In the absence of a futures contract on the krone, the futures contract on the euro will be the hedging vehicle. The agent's hedge involves selling N futures contracts of size EUR Q that mature at time 1, the same time as the krone inflow. Ignoring the interest rate risk associated with marking to market, at time 1 when the DKK C arrive, the agent will receive the dollar equivalent of DKK C converted at the spot exchange rate less N times the difference between the futures price of EUR 1 on a contract maturing at time 1 and the futures price contracted at time 0 multiplied by EUR Q, the size of the contract. The problem is to determine the optimum number of euro futures contracts to be sold. To answer this question let

S_1 (USD/DKK) = the spot exchange rate at time 1 (the number of dollars to purchase DKK 1)
$F_{0,1}$ (USD/EUR) = the futures price of EUR 1 at time 0 for delivery at time 1
$F_{1,1}$ (USD/EUR) = the futures price of EUR 1 at time 1 for delivery at time 1.

Converting the kroner into dollars at the maturity date's spot exchange rate gives

$$S_1(\text{USD/DKK}) \times C \text{ dollars.}$$

The difference between the futures prices gives

$$-N[F_{1,1}(\text{USD/EUR}) - F_{0,1}(\text{USD/EUR})] \times Q \text{ dollars} \tag{7.21}$$

At maturity, the futures price converges to the spot price so that Equation 7.21 becomes

$$-N[S_1(\text{USD/EUR}) - F_{0,1}(\text{USD/EUR})] \times Q \text{ dollars} \tag{7.22}$$

Thus the dollar value of the portfolio will be

$$S_1(\text{USD/DKK})C - N[S_1(\text{USD/EUR}) - F_{0,1}(\text{USD/EUR})]Q \tag{7.23}$$

Divide by C and define the hedge ratio as $\beta = \dfrac{NQ}{C}$ and Equation 7.23 can be written as

$$S_1(\text{USD/DKK}) - \beta[S_1(\text{USD/EUR}) - F_{0,1}(\text{USD/EUR})] \tag{7.24}$$

As with the delta hedge, the idea is to choose β so that the variance of 7.24 is minimized. Since $F_{0,1}$ is known, the variance of 7.24 is

$$Var(S_1(\text{USD/DKK}) - 2\beta Cov(S_1(\text{USD/DKK}), S_1(\text{USD/EUR})), + \beta^2 Var(S_1(\text{USD/EUR}))$$

Taking the derivative with respect to β and setting it equal to zero gives

$$\beta = \frac{Cov[S_1(\text{USD/DKK}), S_1(\text{USD/EUR})]}{Var(S_1(\text{USD/EUR}))} \tag{7.25}$$

Thus, the optimal number of contracts is equal to

$$N = \beta \frac{C}{Q} \qquad (7.26)$$

Example of a minimum variance cross hedge

Starting with the following information:

C = DKK 9,375,000 to be received in one month
Q = EUR 125,000

we want to find N, the optimal number of futures contracts to be sold. The first step is to estimate β. Going back to Equation 7.25, we can see that β is equal to the slope coefficient in the equation

$$S_1(\text{USD/DKK}) = \alpha + \beta S_1(\text{USD/EUR}) + \varepsilon \qquad (7.27)$$

Bearing in mind the econometric problems associated with time series regressions, suppose that a time series regression using monthly historical data over a five-year period yields $\beta = 1.15$. The number of contracts to be sold is

$$N = 1.15 \frac{9,375,000}{125,000} = 86.25.$$

Rounded to the closest full contract, $N = 86$. In the absence of basis risk, $\beta = 1$ and the optimum hedge would be $N = 75$.

Minimum variance delta cross hedge

Having solved the problems of the maturity and currency mismatches, it is easy to solve the problem when both mismatches occur simultaneously. To see how this can be done, we can go back to the situation of a dollar-based agent expecting an inflow of C Danish kroner at time 1. The euro futures contract will still be his hedging vehicle. Because there is no contract that matures on the date of his krone inflow, his hedge involves selling N futures contracts of size EUR Q that mature at time 2, the closest maturity date to the krone inflow. This information can be summarized as follows

$S_1(\text{USD/DKK})$ = the spot exchange rate time 1 (the number of dollars to purchase DKK 1)
$F_{0,2}(\text{USD/EUR})$ = the futures price of EUR 1 at time 0 for delivery at time 2
$F_{1,2}(\text{USD/EUR})$ = the futures price of EUR 1 at time 1 for delivery at time 2

Proceeding as in the previous examples, we seek to determine the optimum number of euro futures contracts to be sold. The dollar value of the cash flow at time 1 is equal to

$$S_1(\text{USD/DKK}) - \beta \left[F_{1,2}(\text{USD/EUR}) - F_{0,2}(\text{USD/EUR}) \right] \qquad (7.28)$$

and the minimum variance hedge ratio is found by estimating the equation

$$S_1(\text{USD/DKK}) = \alpha + \beta F_{1,2}(\text{USD/EUR}) + \varepsilon \qquad (7.29)$$

Using

C = DKK 9,375,000 to be received in one month
Q = EUR 125,000

and estimating

$$\beta = \frac{Cov[S_1(\text{USD/DKK}), F_{1,2}(\text{USD/EUR})]}{Var(F_{1,2}(\text{USD/EUR}))} = 1.20,$$

the optimal number of contracts is equal to

$$N = 1.20 \times \frac{9{,}375{,}000}{125{,}000} = 90 \text{ contracts.}$$

Other hedging strategies

In the foregoing examples the hedge ratio

$$\beta = \frac{NQ}{C}$$

is found by minimizing the variance of the portfolio. This methodology is consistent with modern portfolio theory that seeks to maximize expected utility. Other objectives, however, are also possible.

The traditional strategy is to choose the hedge ratio equal to one so that the principal value of the futures contract is equal to the principal value of the spot position. Another popular strategy is to build a futures position so that its dollar market value is equal to the market value of the position in the underlying asset. In this strategy the hedge ratio differs from one if the futures price is different from the spot price. We will come back to this issue in the chapters dealing with hedging the risks associated with specific assets.

Summary

1. A futures contract is very similar to a forward contract. It is an agreement between two parties to buy or sell an asset at a certain time for a certain price. Futures contracts are traded on organized exchanges. To facilitate trading, the exchange specifies certain standardized features of the contract and trading takes place in such a way that the exchange is the ultimate counterparty to each transaction. Futures contracts differ from forward contracts in two other ways. First of all, payments are made over the life of the contract in what is called marking to market. Secondly, most futures contracts are closed out before maturity. Thus, the organized futures markets have four important features: (a) the contracts are standardized; (b) trading is organized and centralized either in one physical location such as the trading pit or in a virtual location such as a computerized order book; (c) contracts are settled through the exchange's clearing house; and (d) contracts are marked to market each day, which means that they are revalued according to their market value.

2. Contract standardization means traded assets are limited in number with standardized maturities and amounts of the underlying asset.

3. The role of the clearing house is three-fold. It records the existence of the contract; it manages settlement of day-to-day operations; and it guarantees delivery at the contract's maturity. Thus, there is no individual counterparty risk because all clients have the clearing house as the ultimate counterparty.

4. Marking to market means that profits and losses are paid every day at the end of trading and is equivalent to closing out a contract each day, paying off losses or receiving gains, and writing a new contract.

5. Except for isolated exceptions, futures positions that remain open at maturity are closed out by physical delivery of the commodity in question. Most futures positions, however, are closed out before maturity. When physical delivery is required, the clearing house manages the transaction. It assigns buyers to sellers and fixes exactly how the exchange is to take place. This is especially important for commodities where quality can vary and transportation costs are high. Exchange rules specify the quality of the merchandise to be delivered, where it is to be delivered, storage and other costs, compensation differentials for discrepancies in quality, appraisal procedures and conditions for refusal by the buyer.

6. Although spot and futures prices converge at maturity, they can and do differ significantly before maturity. The difference between the futures price and the spot price is called the "basis". The basis and how it varies through time are important elements in hedging strategies that use the organized futures exchanges. The evolution of the basis is crucial for the effectiveness of the hedge. Consequently, it is important to understand what determines the basis. The basis in financial futures is straightforward. Founded on the principle of efficient markets and no arbitrage, it generally depends on the difference between the interest rate and the payout on the underlying asset. For commodities the basis is more complicated. It depends on: the expected evolution of the spot price; carrying costs; convenience returns; the speculators' premium; and the systematic risk premium. All these elements are not necessarily present simultaneously at all times. There are times when simple arbitrage will determine the basis, and there are other times when convenience yields and the speculators' premium will come into play. The fact is that although the basis converges to zero at maturity, in practice its evolution can be erratic. Basis risk is real. For this reason hedging operations require technical expertise and should be undertaken carefully.

7. Although futures contracts exhibit definite advantages over forwards in transaction costs and ease of use because of standardization and liquidity, they also have some distinct disadvantages:

   • Futures contracts are only available for short maturities. The maximum maturity is one year and markets are usually thin for maturities exceeding six months. Hence, for long-term hedging the futures markets are not a viable alternative to the forward and swap markets.

   • The fixed contract size makes it difficult to ensure an exact match with the position to be hedged. However, the size of the contracts is small enough that most users' needs can be approximated quite well.

   • Infrequent maturity dates make it unlikely that the futures contract will correspond perfectly with the maturity of the cash flow to be hedged. In this case, hedging with futures requires setting up what is called a minimum variance delta hedge.

Option markets and instruments

Organized options markets are another major feature of the international financial landscape. The forward and futures markets make it possible to set up a fixed hedge, which enables the investor to avoid a loss when the spot price moves against him but it also eliminates the possibility of making a gain if it moves in his favor. A fixed hedge strategy is appropriate when the investor assigns a strong probability to a move against him and a weak probability for a move in his favor. It is less appropriate, however, in cases where the investor feels that there is an equally strong chance for favorable and unfavorable moves. The reason for this is that the advantage of avoiding the loss is offset by the disadvantage of missing out on the gain. The fixed hedge is still useful but its usefulness is considerably diminished, and another type of coverage in the form of an option might be preferable. Options make it possible to take advantage of potential gains while limiting downside risk. Proper use of options requires a clear understanding of their nature and the elements that determine their price. In this chapter we start with a presentation of options, their characteristics and the markets where they are traded. We then develop the basic option pricing formulas and show how options can be used in international risk management. Finally, we present the tools for managing options.

Option features and markets

Introduction to options

An option is a contract that gives its owner the right for a given period of time to buy or sell a given amount of an underlying asset at a fixed price, called the **exercise price** or the **strike price**. The underlying asset can be a financial security such as a stock or a bond, a financial commodity such as an interest rate or currency, or a physical commodity such as oil, gas, coffee or potatoes. If the right can be exercised at any time during the life of the option it is called an **American option**. If the right can be exercised only at the option's expiration date, it is called a **European option**. The right to buy is called a **call**, while right to sell is called a **put**. The buyer of the option pays the seller, or "writer", a certain sum, called the **option premium**, for the right to buy or sell at the prescribed price. The characteristic elements of an option contract can be summed up as follows:

- the nature of the transaction (call or put)
- the underlying asset

- the amount of the underlying asset
- the strike or exercise price
- the expiration date
- the premium.

Consider a European call option on 100 shares of ATT with a maturity of 15 January, and a strike price of USD 25. It gives the buyer the right to buy 100 shares of ATT at the price of USD 25 per share on 15 January. The underlying asset is the share of ATT, the amount is 100 shares, the strike price is USD 25, and the expiration date is 15 January. If the premium is USD 0.50, this means that the buyer has to pay the writer 100 shares × USD 0.50 = USD 50 at the outset.

A European put option on GBP 500,000, a strike price of 1.45, and a maturity of six months gives the buyer the right to sell GBP 500,000 at the rate of USD 1.45 per pound in six months. If the premium is 2%, the buyer has to pay the writer GBP 10,000 (GBP 500,000 × 2%) at the outset. The premium can also be expressed in dollars by using the spot exchange rate. If, for example, the spot bid rate is 1.50, the premium will be USD 15,000 (GBP 10,000 × 1.50).

Option contracts are listed according to the underlying asset, the expiration date and the strike price. The two types of option are calls and puts, and all options of the same type in the same underlying asset constitute an option "class". All options in the same class with the same expiration date and the same strike price constitute an option "series".

Over-the-counter markets

In the over-the-counter (OTC) market, options are written by financial institutions. This market is similar to the forward market described in Chapters 3 and 6. Like forward contracts, OTC options can be made to order with the expiration date, contract size and strike price determined at the buyer's discretion. OTC options, however, can be more liquid than forward contracts because the institutions that write these contracts often quote regular bid–ask prices and stand ready to buy them back at any time. This is the case in the foreign currency options market, for example, but the increased liquidity has a cost in that bid–ask spreads are relatively high.

In the absence of buyer preference, it is customary in the OTC market to write options with the strike price equal to the spot price of the moment and to quote the premium to clients as a percentage of the underlying value. The norm for quoting strike prices is two decimal places. Among themselves, traders do not usually quote a price but instead quote volatility from which the price can be inferred. Later on in this chapter we will see why this is so.

Organized options markets

Organized options markets share many features with the futures markets described in the previous chapter. First of all, contracts are standardized. On the Philadelphia Stock Exchange, for example, all currency options are American style and expire on the third Wednesday of March, June, September or December. Early exercise is possible until the last Saturday of the option's life. Each currency has a standard contract size (e.g. JPY 6,250,000), with strike prices conforming to prearranged formulas depending on the currency (e.g. multiples of 1 US cent for the GBP). Premiums are quoted in US cents per unit of foreign currency.

Organized options exchanges also utilize a **clearing house** that records transactions concluded by members. Each member also has an obligation to keep records of its clients' accounts. Just as in the futures markets, the role of the clearing house is essential. It guarantees the execution of all contracts negotiated on the exchange and effectively becomes the counterparty to both sides of the transaction. The role of the clearing house and contract standardization facilitate trading and make the market more liquid as the exchanges continually write new options and close out ongoing positions. An investor who has written an option can close out his position by buying an equivalent option, while an investor who has bought an option can close out his position by selling an equivalent option. Because the contracts are standardized and the clearing house is the counterparty to both sides of the contract, all options in the same series are equivalent no matter who the end buyers and sellers are.

Options are also used in the futures markets. In this case, the buyer of a call has the right to buy a given futures contract on the exchange at a price equal to the option's strike price. The buyer of the put has the right to sell a given futures contract at a price equal to the option's strike price. If a call futures option is exercised, the buyer acquires a long position in the underlying futures contract plus a cash amount equal to the difference between the most recent futures settlement price and the strike price. If a put futures option is exercised, the buyer acquires a short position in the underlying futures contract plus a cash amount equal to the difference between the strike price and the most recent futures settlement price. Options on futures contracts are more attractive to investors than options on the underlying asset when it is cheaper or more convenient to deliver a futures contract on the underlying asset than the underlying asset itself. This is true of many physical commodities and, in fact, most options on physical commodities are options on futures contracts. For example, it is cheaper, easier and more convenient to make or take delivery of a pork belly futures contract than it is to make or take delivery of the pork bellies themselves. Thus, exercise of a futures option does not normally lead to delivery of the underlying asset because most futures contracts are closed out before delivery.

Information on traded options is published daily in the financial press and Table 8.1 provides an example of data on currency futures options from the *Wall Street Journal Europe*. The table headings tell us that the table is divided into information on calls and puts. Column 1 gives the strike price. Columns 2, 3 and 4 give the prices for calls

Table 8.1 Information on GBP futures options (contract GBP 62,500, quoted in cents per pound)

Strike Price	Calls-Settle			Puts-Settle		
	Oct	Nov	Dec	Oct	Nov	Dec
1430	1.86	2.66	3.28	0.04	0.84	1.48
1440	0.98	2.04	2.72	0.16	1.22	1.90
1450	0.36	1.50	2.16	0.54	1.68	2.34
1460	0.16	1.06	1.72	1.34	2.24	2.90
1470	0.04	0.76	1.40	2.22	2.94	...
1480	0.08	0.52	1.10	3.18	...	4.24

Note: Estimated volume 1182; Wednesday 242 calls 126 puts; open interest Wednesday 12 091 calls 10 108 puts.
Source: *Wall Street Journal Europe,* 6 October 2000.

expiring in October, November and December, and columns 5, 6 and 7 give the prices for puts expiring in October, November and December. For example, the last traded price of a put with a strike price of USD 1.460 expiring in December was 2.90 US cents. The table notes detail the trading volume and the number of options outstanding. The estimated volume for Thursday 5 October was 1182 contracts. The preceding day's (Wednesday's) volume was 242 calls and 126 puts, while open interest was 12 091 calls and 10 108 puts.

Tables 8.2 and 8.3 provide an idea of some of the traded options that are available around the world.

Table 8.2 Examples of commodity option contracts on futures

Commodity options on futures	Exchange	Size
Grains and oil-seeds		
Corn	CBT	5000 bushels
Soybeans	CBT	5000 bushels
Soybean meal	CBT	100 tons
Soybean oil	CBT	60 000 pounds
Wheat	CBT	5000 bushels
Livestock and meat		
Cattle-feeder	CME	50 000 pounds
Cattle-live	CME	40 000 pounds
Hogs-lean	CME	40 000 pounds
Food and fiber		
Cocoa	NYBOT	10 metric tons
Coffee	NYBOT	37 500 pounds
Sugar	NYBOT	112 000 pounds
Cotton	NYBOT	50 000 pounds
Orange juice	NYBOT	15 000 pounds
Metals and petroleum		
Copper	CMX	25 000 pounds
Gold	CMX	100 troy ounces
Silver	CMX	5000 troy ounces
Crude oil	NYM	1000 bbls.
Heating oil	NYM	42 000 gallons
Gasoline	NYM	42 000 gallons
Natural gas	NYM	10 000 MMBtu.
Brent crude	IPE	1000 bbls.
Gas oil	IPE	100 metric tons

Key: CBT = Chicago Board of Trade; CME = Chicago Mercantile Exchange; CMX = Commodity Exchange, New York; IPE = International Petroleum Exchange; NYBOT = New York Board of Trade; NYM = New York Mercantile Exchange.
Source: *Wall Street Journal Europe,* 6 October 2000.

Table 8.3 Examples of options on financial futures contracts

Financial options	Exchange	Size
Interest rates		
Treasury bonds	CBT	USD 100,000
Treasury notes	CBT	USD 100,000
Five-year Treasury notes	CBT	USD 100,000
MUNI Bond Index	CBT	USD 1,000 times Bond Buyer MBI
Eurodollar	CME	USD 1 mn
Long gilt	Liffe	GBP 50,000
Euribor	Liffe	EUR 1 mn
Ten-year German euro-government bond	Eurex	EUR 100,000
Currencies		
Japanese Yen	CME	JPY 12.5 mn
Deutschmark	CME	DEM 125,000
Canadian dollar	CME	CAD 100,000
British pound	CME	GBP 62,500
Swiss franc	CME	CHF 125,000
Mexican peso	CME	MXN 500,000
Indices		
FT-SE 100 Index	Liffe	GBP 10 per index point
DJ Industrial Average	CBT	USD 100 times index
S&P 500 Stock Index	CME	USD 250 times

Key: CBT = Chicago Board of Trade; CME = Chicago Mercantile Exchange; Liffe = London International Financial Futures Exchange.
Source: *Wall Street Journal Europe*, 6 October 2000.

Valuing options

Option pricing theory is one of the most important contributions to the theory and practice of finance over the past 50 years. Much of the credit goes to F. Black, M. Scholes and R. Merton for the development of a workable option pricing formula for European calls and puts on non-dividend paying stocks.[1] Since then, option pricing has been extended to a myriad of instruments including, among many others, dividend-paying stocks, indexes, interest rates, currencies, commodities and futures. It has even been extended into the realm of what are called "real options" as a tool for strategic management and capital budgeting.[2] In this chapter we will develop the option pricing methodology in a general framework that includes intermediate payouts such as dividends on stocks, interest on currencies and convenience yields on commodities. This will enable us to understand the OTC products that are discussed in Chapter 9.

[1] For the original option pricing formula, see F. Black and M. Scholes, "The pricing of options and corporate liabilities", *Journal of Political Economy*, (June, 1973), p.p. 637–659.

[2] See, for example, A.K. Dixit, and R.S. Pindyck (1994), *Investment Under Uncertainty* (Princeton: Princeton University Press) and L. Trigeorgis (1996), *Real Options* (Cambridge, Mass: The MIT Press).

Elements of option value

The value of an option depends, first of all, on the value of the underlying asset and its volatility. Secondly, it depends on the specific characteristics of the option contract itself concerning the strike price and the expiration date. Finally, it depends on the level of the risk-free interest rate.

Premium and the spot price: European options

The premium on a call option is higher when the price of the underlying asset is higher. This is easy to understand. If the current spot price of a stock is USD 14, an investor will be willing to pay more for the right to purchase the stock at USD 12 than if the current spot price were USD 10. On the other hand, the premium on a put will be higher when the spot price of the underlying asset is lower. An investor will be willing to pay more for the right to sell a stock for USD 12 if the current spot price is USD 10 than if it is USD 14.

No matter what the value of the underlying asset is, the premium on a call or a put will always be positive, although sometimes it might be very small. This is because there is always at least a remote possibility that something will happen to make the option profitable. Even if the spot price is USD 10.00 and the strike price on a call with a week to expiration is USD 25, some exceptional event like a new discovery, a huge contract, a takeover bid, etc. could possibly take place before the option expires that would push the value of the stock above USD 25. If it does not take place, the option expires worthless but still only costs the investor the premium that he paid for it. The right to a possible gain with no chance of a loss is clearly worth something.

When the spot price is very high compared to the strike price, the probability that the call option will be exercised is also very high. Because exercise uncertainty decreases with the rise in the spot price, the value of a European call will tend to approach the value of the spot price minus the strike price (multiplied by the nominal amount of the contract). In this situation the option starts to resemble a fixed forward contract where the strike price is the forward price. Similarly, when the spot price is very low compared to the strike price, the probability that a European put option will be exercised becomes very high. Its value approaches the difference between the strike price and the spot price. Again, because of the high probability of exercise, the option begins to resemble a fixed forward contract.

Figures 8.1 and 8.2 summarize the relationship between the value of European calls and puts respectively and the spot price of the underlying security. The solid line in Figure 8.1 represents the difference between the spot price and the strike price. The broken line represents the value of the call. At very high levels of the spot price, the value of the call comes close to this line. At very low levels of the forward rate, the value of the option approaches zero.

In Figure 8.2 the solid line represents the difference between the strike price and the spot price. At very low levels of the forward rate, the value of the option comes very close to this line. At very high levels of the spot price, it approaches zero.

Premium and the strike price

The higher the strike price, the lower the value of a call and the higher the value of a put. On the other hand, the lower the strike price, the higher the value of a call and the lower the value of a put. The reason is straightforward. A call is the right to buy at a given price. The lower the strike price, the more chance there is that the market price of the underlying asset will surpass it for a profit. A put is the right to sell a given price. The higher the strike price, the more chance there is that the market price of the underlying asset will fall below it for a profit. At a lower strike price, the results are reversed.

Figure 8.1 The relationship between the value of a European currency call and the spot exchange rate

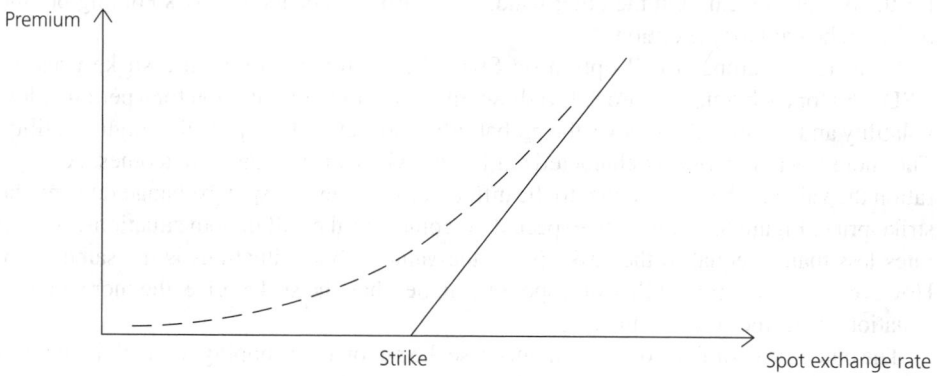

Figure 8.2 The relationship between the value of a European currency put and the spot exchange rate

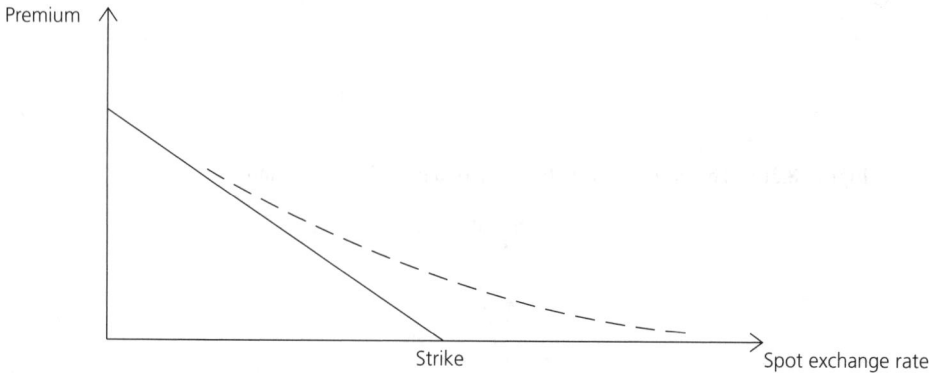

When the strike price is higher than the spot price, the value of a call is due entirely to the possibility that the spot price will rise above the strike price before the option expires. The call is then said to be **out-of-the-money** and its value is called "time value". On the other hand, if the strike price is lower than the spot price, there is an immediate gain equal to the difference between the spot price and the strike price. The option is said to be **in-the-money**. Since the option buyer acquires the right to this gain, called the **intrinsic value**, he must pay for it. Besides the in-the-money value, though, the possibility that the price could go higher before the option expires still exists. Hence, the value of an in-the-money option is equal to its intrinsic value plus its time value. When the spot price and the strike price are equal, the option is said to be **at-the-money**.

The same expressions are used to qualify puts. If the strike price is higher than the spot price, there is an immediate gain for the buyer insofar as the writer contracts to pay a higher price than the current market price. The put is in-the-money. Conversely, if the strike price is lower than the spot price, the put has only time value and is said to be out-of-the-money. When the spot price and the strike price are equal, the put is at-the-money.

Premium and volatility

The volatility of the underlying asset is an important factor in determining the time value of an option. The higher the volatility of the price of the underlying asset, the higher is the probability that a strong rise or fall will occur. As we have seen, this is exactly what the buyer of the option is hoping for. A sharp rise in the spot price will be extremely profitable for the owner of a call. On the other hand, if a sharp fall occurs, he loses nothing but the premium he paid for the option.

Consider a European call option on Swiss francs for dollars with a strike price of USD 0.60 for each franc. Figure 8.3(a) shows the probability distribution for a period of low volatility and Figure 8.3(b) shows the probability distribution for a period of high volatility. The more volatile period is characterized by the wider dispersion of outcomes. At expiration the value of the call is equal to the difference between the spot exchange rate and the strike price. Figure 8.4 shows the expected outcomes for the call in both situations. At spot rates less than or equal to the strike price, the value in both situations is the same, zero. However, at a given probability of a spot rate higher than the strike price, the more volatile situation yields the better results.

The outcome is similar for a put. In this case the put owner is hoping for a fall in the spot price. The larger the fall, the greater is his gain. On the other hand, if there is no fall or even a sharp rise, the option expires worthless and he only loses the premium he paid to buy it. The value of a put increases with the volatility of the spot price.

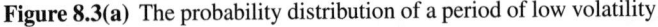

Figure 8.3(a) The probability distribution of a period of low volatility

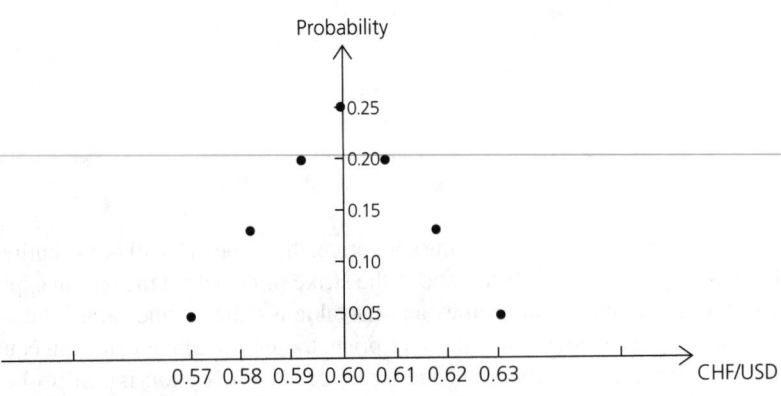

Figure 8.3(b) The probability distribution of a period of high volatility

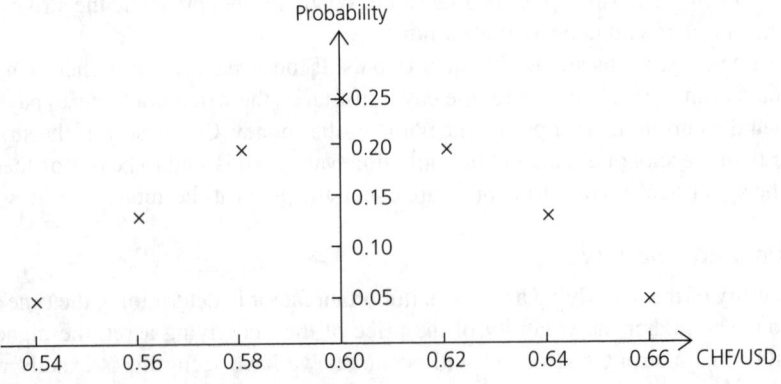

Figure 8.4 The expected outcomes for a European call option with a strike price of USD 0.60 in both situations

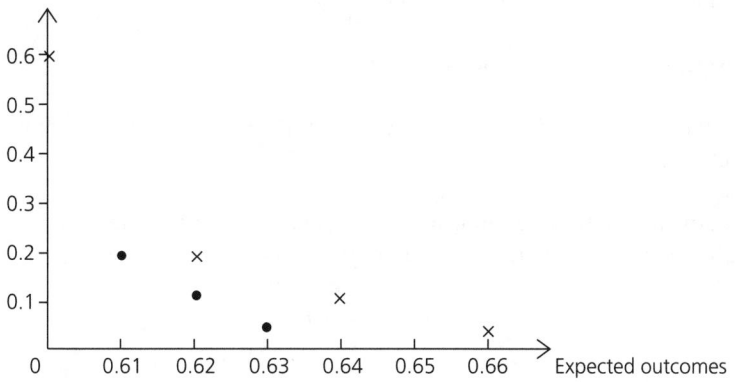

Premium and the expiration date

The expiration date plays an important role in determining the value of an option. When the time to expiration is longer, the chances for fluctuations in the spot price of the underlying asset are increased. Thus, all other things being equal, an option that expires in six months is worth more than an option that expires in three months.

It is interesting to note that an option's time value is not proportional to its time to expiration. In fact, as far back as 1900, Bachelier showed that it is the square root of the time to expiration that influences an option's time value. Exactly why this is so is the subject of the next section.

Binomial approach to option pricing

Option prices, also called premiums or values, reflect all the complex interrelationships among the elements discussed in the preceding section as well as all the factors that could possibly affect the judgement of the participants in a free market. Professional traders and arbitragers, who have very low transaction costs, have developed pricing rules derived from the law of one price that they use in their day-to-day operations. Theorists have summarized their experiences in a number of pricing models that are useful tools for effective risk management. The binomial model is the simplest and easiest to understand.

Example of a one-period European style option

The binomial option pricing model is a simple approach to option pricing that makes it possible to understand the basic principles involved. The binomial model assumes that, given the current value of the underlying asset, there are only two values for the next period's price – an upward move or a downward move. Hedging is then combined with borrowing and lending to determine the option's value. The following numerical examples will show how the binomial model works for an underlying asset with a proportional payout such as a dividend-paying stock, a currency or a commodity with a proportional convenience yield.

We start with the following notation:

C_t = the value of the call on one unit of the underlying asset after t moves
u = an upward move equal to 1 plus a percentage gain

d = a downward move equal to 1 minus a percentage loss
δ = the proportional payout on the underlying asset
r = the riskless interest rate in domestic currency
$R = 1 + r$
r^* = the riskless interest rate in foreign currency
X = exercise price
Δ = delta: the number of units of the underlying asset to be held per option shorted to create a riskless hedge.

For the sake of simplicity, we assume that u, d, δ and the domestic interest rate are constant over time. In order to rule out risk-free arbitrage profits, we also have the constraint that

$$d < \frac{1+r}{1+\delta} < u.$$

Valuing a one-period call

Now consider the following information:

S = 100
u = 1.20
d = 0.80
δ = 0.03
r = 0.10
$1 + \delta$ = 1.03
R $= 1 + r = 1.10$
X = 100.

Figure 8.5(a) shows the stock price movements with probability $q = 0.5$ of an up move and probability $1-q = 0.5$ of a down move. Figure 8.5(b) shows the value of the option if the price of the underlying asset moves up or down. Notice that the probabilities q and $1-q$ are absent from Figure 8.5(b). This is because the procedure for option valuation eliminates the need to make assumptions about the probability distribution of the price of the underlying asset.

The problem is to determine the value of a call option with one period until expiration during which the asset price can either move up to uS or down to dS. The evaluation process includes four steps.

First, build a portfolio by selling a call on one unit of the asset and simultaneously purchasing Δ units of the same asset. When we sell the call, we receive C_0 and we pay ΔS when we purchase the asset. If the asset price moves up to uS, the call will be worth 20, the difference between the asset price and the exercise price. Since we sold the call, we have to pay this amount. We receive ΔuS, the value of our investment in the asset, plus $\delta \Delta uS$, the

Figure 8.5 (a) Asset price in a one-step binomial tree; (b) Call price

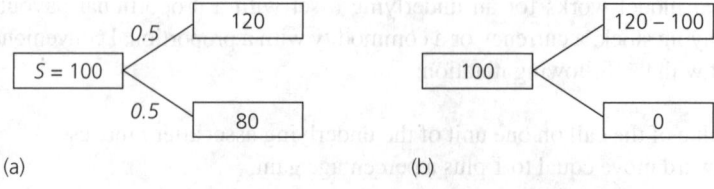

(a)   (b)

payout, which is proportional to the asset price. From Table 8.4 we can see that this is equal to $\Delta 123.6$ for a net inflow of $\Delta 123.6 - 20$. If the asset price moves to dS, the call expires worthless and we receive $\Delta 82.4$, the value of the investment in the asset plus the proportional payout from the investment in the asset.

The second step is to make the portfolio risk-free. To do this, we choose Δ so that the outcome will be the same whether the price moves up or down. Setting the two possible outcomes in period 1 equal gives $\Delta 123.6 - 20 = \Delta 82.4$ and $\Delta = 0.4854$. Thus, if we purchase 48.54% of one unit of asset, the outcome of the portfolio will be the same whether the price moves up or down.

In step three we expand the portfolio by borrowing an amount that will yield a net cash flow of zero in period 1. This amount is equal to $0.4854 \times 82.4 = 40$ (or $0.4854 \times 123.6 - 20 = 40$ since they are equal) discounted back to the present. Table 8.4 shows the flows associated with this portfolio.

In step four, we find the value of the call by applying the well known fact that the value of an investment with zero net cash flows is equal to zero. Thus:

$$+C_0 - \Delta S + \frac{\Delta dS(1 + \delta)}{1 + r} = 0.$$

Substituting the values for S, r and Δ gives the price of the call:

$$C_0 = 12.18.$$

The one-period binomial formula

Using the same methodology as above we can derive a simple formula for one-period binomial option pricing. Table 8.5 shows the cash flows. To find the value of Δ that makes both outcomes independent of the move in the exchange rate, set the two possible period 1 outcomes equal and solve. This gives:

$$-C_u + \Delta uS(1 + \delta) = -C_d + \Delta dS(1 + \delta)$$

$$\Delta = \frac{C_u - C_d}{S(u - d)(1 + \delta)} \tag{8.1}$$

Table 8.4 One-period cash flows with borrowing

		Flows at period 1	
	Flows at period 0	uS = 120	dS = 80
Write a call	$+C_0$	$-C_u = -20$	0
Purchase Δ units of asset	$-\Delta S =$ $-0.4854 \times 100 = -48.54$	$+\Delta uS(1 + \delta) =$ $0.4854 \times 123.6 = 60$	$+\Delta dS(1 + \delta) =$ $0.4854 \times 82.4 = 40$
Borrow	$+\dfrac{\Delta dS(1 + \delta)}{1 + r} =$ $(0.4854 \times 82.4)/(1.1) =$ $^{40}/_{1.10}$	$-(60 - 20) = -40$	-40
Total	$+C_0 - 48.54 + {}^{40}/_{1.10}$	0	0

Table 8.5 Cash flows

	Flows at period 0	Flows at period 1	
		uS	dS
Write a call	$+C_0$	$-C_u$	$-C_d$
Purchase Δ units of the asset	$-\Delta S$	$+\Delta uS(1+\delta)$	$+\Delta dS(1+\delta)$
Borrow	$\dfrac{(-C_d + \Delta dS(1+\delta))}{R}$	$C_u - \Delta uS(1+\delta)$	$C_d - \Delta dS(1+\delta)$
Total	$+C_0 - \Delta S + \dfrac{-C_d + \Delta dS(1+\delta))}{R}$	0	0

We then borrow

$$\frac{-C_d + \Delta dS(1+\delta)}{R}$$

so that the net outcomes in period 1 are zero. Since the investment generates zero net cash flows, its value is zero as well. Thus

$$C_0 - \Delta S + \frac{-C_d + \Delta dS(1+\delta)}{R} = 0 \tag{8.2}$$

Substituting the value of Δ from Equation 8.1 and rearranging gives:

$$C_0 = \frac{C_u \left[\dfrac{\dfrac{R}{1+\delta} - d}{u - d} \right] + C_d \left[1 - \dfrac{\dfrac{R}{1+\delta} - d}{u - d} \right]}{R} \tag{8.3}$$

This seemingly complicated formula can be simplified. Define

$$P = \frac{\dfrac{R}{1+\delta} - d}{u - d}$$

and substitute this definition into Equation 8.3. This gives

$$C_0 = \frac{C_u P + C_d [1 - P]}{R} \tag{8.4}$$

Delta and risk neutral valuation

Delta was defined as the number of units of the underlying asset to be held (shorted) per option shorted (held) to create a riskless hedge. The creation of the riskless hedge then made it possible to derive Equation 8.4. It is important to notice that the original probabilities given in Figure 8.5a are absent from this equation. In fact, we were able to price the option without making any assumptions at all about the probabilities of up and down moves in the asset price. However, we can interpret P as the probability of an up move in a world without risk and 1-P as the probability of a down move in a world without risk.[3] The risk was eliminated when we chose Δ so that the outcome of the portfolio was the same whether there was an up move or a down move in the underlying asset. The absence of risk makes it possible to discount and compound the expected cash flows at the riskless rate.

This result is an example of what is called risk-neutral valuation. It means that we can correctly value an option by using the risk-neutral probabilities and pretending that investors are neutral to risk. This is an application of what is known as the "Girsanov Theorem". The new probabilities change the mean but leave the volatility structure intact. The answers obtained in this way are valid in all worlds, not only in the risk-neutral world.[4]

In practice, the construction of a binomial tree involves defining the volatility of the price of the underlying security σ so that $\sigma\sqrt{dt}$ is the standard deviation of the return on the security over a short period of time. We then choose the parameters u and d to match the volatility of the asset price. The values for u and d suggested by Cox, Ross and Rubenstein (1979) are:

$$u = e^{\sigma\sqrt{dt}}$$
$$\text{and}$$
$$d = e^{-\sigma\sqrt{dt}}.$$

The multi-period model

Valuing a two-period call

Valuing a call with more than one period to expiration involves the same procedure as before, although the calculations are more complicated. We start at the option's value on the expiration date and work backwards to the present. Figure 8.6(a) shows the different possible values of the asset price in a two-period binomial tree and Figure 8.6(b) shows the corresponding value of the option at each period. There are three steps to the valuation procedure:

1. Use C_{u2} and C_{ud} to calculate C_u, the value of the option if the asset price makes one upward move. C_{u2} is the terminal value of the option if the asset price makes two upward moves and C_{ud} is the terminal value of the option if it makes one upward and one downward move.

---

[3] We can verify that $E(S_1)$ is equal to

$$S_0 \frac{R}{(1+r)} = PuS_0 + [1 - P]dS_0$$

by substituting the value of P.

[4] For a more detailed discussion of this point see Hull (2000) and Neftci (1996).

Figure 8.6 (a) Asset price in a two-step binomial tree; (b) Call price

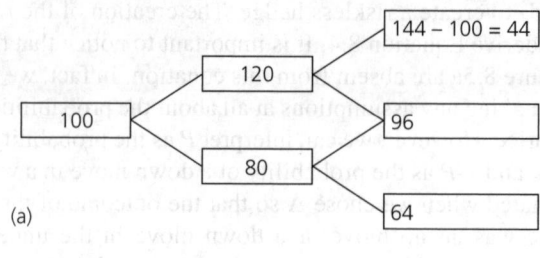

(a)

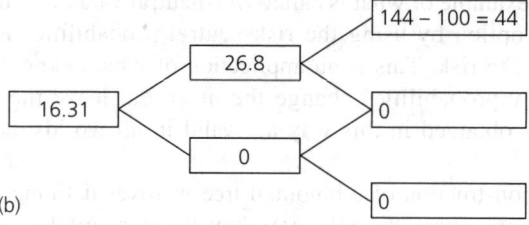

(b)

2. Use C_{ud} and C_{d2} to calculate C_d, the value of the option if the asset price makes one downward move. C_{d2} is the terminal value of the option if the asset price makes two downward moves.

3. Use the calculated values of C_u and C_d to calculate the value of C_0.

In step one we proceed as we did for a one-period option. Table 8.6 consolidates the information from Figures 8.6a and 8.6b necessary to calculate the value of C_u. First we find Δ by equating the cash flows for the two possible outcomes and solving:

$$-44 + \Delta 148.32 = \Delta 98.88$$

$$\Delta = 0.89$$

Table 8.6 Two period cash flows

	Flows at period 1	Flows at period 2	
		$u^2S = 144$	$udS = 96$
Write a call	$+C_u$	$-C_{u2} = -44$	$-C_{ud} = 0$
Purchase Δ units of asset	$-\Delta uS$	$+\Delta u^2S(1+\delta) =$ $0.89 \times 148.32 = 132$	$+\Delta udS(1+\delta) =$ $0.89 \times 98.88 = 88$
Borrow	$\dfrac{(-C_{ud} + \Delta udS(1+\delta))}{R}$	$C_{u2} - \Delta u^2S(1+\delta) =$ $44 - 0.89 \times 148.32 =$ -88	$C_{ud} - \Delta udS(1+\delta) =$ $0 - 0.89 \times 98.88 \, 0 =$ -88
Total	$+C_u - \Delta uS +$ $\dfrac{-C_{ud} + \Delta udS(1+\delta)}{R}$	0	0

Next, we borrow

$$\frac{0.89 \times 98.88}{1.10}$$

so that net cash flows are equal to zero in period 2. Since the net cash flows are zero the value of the investment is also zero. Thus:

$$+C_u - \Delta uS + \frac{-C_{ud} + \Delta udS(1 + \delta)}{R} = 0$$

$$C_u = 0.89 \times 120 - 80$$

$$C_u = 26.8.$$

In step two, $C_d = 0$ because both C_{ud} and C_{d^2} are equal to zero. Since we know C_u and C_d, step three boils down to calculating the value of a one-period option. First we find Δ using Equation 8.1:

$$\Delta = \frac{26.8 - 0}{100 \times (1.03) \times (1.2 - 0.8)}$$

$$\Delta = 0.65.$$

Next, we borrow

$$\frac{0.65 \times 80 \times 1.03}{1.10} = 48.69$$

so that net cash flows will equal zero. Finally, we set the investment in period 0 equal to zero and find that

$$C_0 = 0.65 \times 100 - 48.69$$

$$C_0 = 16.31.$$

The general n-period binomial pricing formula for European calls

Starting from Equations 8.4 and 8.5, it is easy to develop the general binomial option pricing formula. Rather than go through the steps of hedging and borrowing, we use the formula expressed in Equation 8.4 to value C_u:

$$C_u = \frac{C_{u2}P + C_{ud}[1 - P]}{R} \tag{8.5}$$

For C_d, we have

$$C_d = \frac{C_{ud}P + C_{d^2}[1 - P]}{R} \tag{8.6}$$

Substituting Equations 8.5 and 8.6 into 8.4 gives

$$C_0 = \frac{P\left[\dfrac{C_{u^2}P + C_{ud}[1-P]}{R}\right] + (1-P)\left[\dfrac{C_{ud}P + C_{d^2}[1-P]}{R}\right]}{R}.$$

Simplifying

$$C_0 \frac{P^2 C_{u^2} + 2P(1-P)C_{ud} + (1-P)^2 C_{d^2}}{R^2} \tag{8.7}$$

where $C_{i,j}$ = the value of the call at expiration if there are i up movements and j down movements. Using the same recursive strategy, we can find the option value after 3, 4 or n moves. In Appendix 8.1 we show that starting from the option's value after n moves and working backwards in the foregoing manner we arrive at the general binomial pricing formula

$$C_0 = S(1 + \delta)^{-n} \Phi(a,n,P') - XR^{-n}\Phi(a,n,P) \tag{8.8}$$

where $\Phi(a,n,P)$ is the probability of realizing at least a upward moves when the probability at each trial is P and $\Phi(a,n,P')$ is the probability of obtaining at least a upward moves when the probability at each trial is P' where

$$P' = Pu\frac{1+\delta}{R}$$

Valuing European puts

The same recursive methodology used to value European calls can be used to value European puts. We build a riskless portfolio composed of the put and Δ units of the underlying asset, borrow the appropriate amount and end up with the equivalent of Equation 8.4 where p represents the value of the put:

$$P_0 = \frac{p_u P + p_d[1 - P]}{R} \tag{8.9}$$

Starting with the information as above, consider a one-period European put with a strike price of 100. If the spot price moves up to 120, the put expires worthless. If the spot price falls to 80, the put will be worth 20. Thus $p_u = 0$, $p_d = 20$ and

$$P = \frac{\dfrac{1.10}{1.03} - 0.8}{1.20 - 0.8} = 0.67$$

$$P_0 = \frac{(0 \times 0.67) + (20 \times 0.33)}{1.10}$$

$$P_0 = 6.$$

Valuing American style options

The difference between European and American style options is that American style options can be exercised at anytime over the option's life whereas European style options can only be exercised on maturity. This added flexibility makes the American style option more valuable than the European style option. Unfortunately, it also makes it more complicated to compute the price, and an extra step must be added in the price computation of an American style option. The steps are:

1. Start from the right-hand side of the binomial tree as before and compute the expiration values of the option.

2. Work towards the left using the expiration values and the risk-neutral probabilities to compute the option value if it is not exercised.

3. Compute the option's value if it is exercised.

4. Compare the two values and choose the higher of the two.

5. Return to step two and repeat this process until the initial period is reached.

Consider the following information which is the same as before except that $\delta = 15\%$ instead of 3%:

$S = 100$
$u = 1.20$
$d = 0.80$
$\delta = 0.15$
$r = 0.10$
$X = 100$

Figure 8.7 shows the value of the European style option in ordinary type and the value of the American style option in bold type. In the upper middle node we can see that the option is worth 15.65 alive. It is worth 20 if it is exercised. Since the value of the option is higher if it is exercised, it will be exercised. Thus, to compute the value of the American style option at the initial period, the value of the option in the first period after an up move will be 20 rather than 15.65. The value of the American style option is considerably higher than the equivalent European style option (7.83 versus 5.57).

Binomial valuation of european options on assets with different yields

The foregoing binomial model can be used to value options on assets with different types of yields. All we need to know are the yields to calculate the probabilities P and P'. Remember that

$$P = \frac{\dfrac{R}{1+\delta} - d}{u - d} \text{ and } P' = Pu\,\frac{1+\delta}{R}.$$

Thus, to value an option on an asset with no yield, $\delta = 0$ so that

$$P = \frac{R - d}{u - d} \text{ and } \frac{P' = Pu}{R}$$

Figure 8.7 American call price (in bold) and European call price

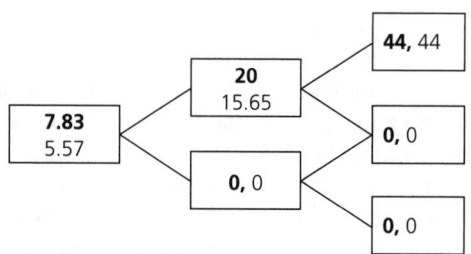

and the value of the option is

$$C_0 = S\Phi(a,n,P') - XR^{-n}\Phi(a,n,P)$$

(8.10)

To value a currency option the yield on the foreign currency is r^* so that

$$P = \frac{\frac{R}{1+r^*} - d}{u - d} \text{ and } P' = Pu\frac{1+r^*}{R}$$

and the value of the option is

$$C_0 = S(1 + r^*)^{-n} \Phi(a,n,P') - XR^{-n}\Phi(a,n,P)$$

(8.11)

To value an option on a commodity the convenience yield is c so that

$$P = \frac{\frac{R}{1+C} - d}{u - d} \text{ and } P' = Pu\frac{1+c}{R}.$$

and the value of the option is

$$C_0 = S(1 + c)^{-n}\Phi(a,n,P') - XR_d^{-n}\Phi(a,n,P)$$

(8.12)

The yield on a futures contract is equal to the riskless rate r so that

$$P = \frac{1 - d}{u - d} \text{ and } P' = Pu$$

and the value of the option is

$$C_0 = SR^{-n}\Phi(a,n,P') - XR^{-n}\Phi(a,n,P)$$

(8.13)

As we mentioned earlier, because of the convenience and low cost of delivery of a futures contract relative to the underlying asset, options on most physical commodities are options on futures contracts relating to the underlying asset rather than on the underlying asset itself. With this important practical consideration in mind, we will spend some time developing the relationship between the cash and futures markets in the following sections and derive the Black-Scholes style continuous time option pricing model.

Continuous time options pricing formulas

The binomial model refers to a limited number of discrete time periods. When the time period is reduced so that it becomes infinitely small, we are working in what is called "continuous time" and the foregoing binomial pricing formulas reduce to their continuous time equivalents. The methodology for pricing these instruments is the same as for the binomial formula: set up a riskless hedge and constitute a portfolio the value of which is zero. In Appendix 8.2 we show how this can be done for a European style call option on an underlying asset with no intermediate payouts. In Appendix 8.3 we then show how the call formula can be obtained by computing the true expectation of the option value at maturity.

Pricing an asset with no intermediate payouts

The original Black-Scholes option pricing formula refers to a European style call option on an underlying asset with no intermediate payouts. In Appendix 8.2 we show how to derive the original Black-Scholes partial differential equation. In Appendix 8.3 we show how to compute the Black-Scholes formula starting with the knowledge that on the expiration date the option will be worth either $S_T - X$ or 0, whichever is higher: $[Max(S_T - X,0)]$. This involves computing the present value of the expected value of the option at expiration:

$$C_t = e^{-r(T-t)}E[Max(S_T - X,0)] \tag{8.14}$$

which gives

$$C_t = S_t N(d_1) - Xe^{-r(T-t)}N(d_2) \tag{8.15}$$

and

$$p_t = Xe^{-r(T-t)}N(-d_2) - S_t N(-d_1) \tag{8.16}$$

where $N(d)$ = the value of the cumulative normal distribution evaluated at d:

$$d_1 = \frac{\ln(S_t / X) + (r + \sigma^2 / 2)(T - t)}{\sigma\sqrt{T - t}}$$

$$d_2 = \frac{\ln(S_t / X) + (r - \sigma^2 / 2)(T - t)}{\sigma\sqrt{T - t}}$$

T is the expiration date of the option and σ is the standard deviation of the percentage change in the value of the underlying asset.

Pricing an asset with a continuous yield[5]

This model refers to assets such as stocks with proportional dividend yields or commodities with proportional convenience yields and was first proposed by Robert Merton in 1973.[6] It can be written as

$$C_t = S_t e^{-\delta(T-t)}N(d_{1\delta}) - Xe^{-r(T-t)}N(d_{2\delta}) \tag{8.17}$$

and

$$p_t = Xe^{-r(T-t)}N(-d_{2\delta}) - S_t e^{-\delta(T-t)}N(-d_{1\delta}) \tag{8.18}$$

[5] When the yield is discrete, the option can be valued by subtracting the present values of payouts that are forecast over the life of the option from the current spot price and then using the formula with no intermediate payouts (Equations 8.15 and 8.16). See Hull (2000), p.p. 257–258.

[6] See R. Merton (1973), "Theory of rational option pricing", *Bell Journal of Economics and Management Science*, Vol 4 p.p. 141–183.

where

$$d_{1\delta} = \frac{\ln(S_t / X) + (r - \delta + \sigma^2 / 2)(T - t)}{\sigma\sqrt{T - t}}$$

$$d_{2\delta} = \frac{\ln(S_t / X) + (r_d - \delta - \sigma^2 / 2)(T - t)}{\sigma\sqrt{T - t}}$$

Pricing currency options

The pricing formula for a currency option was developed by Garman and Kohlhagen[7] in 1983 and can be written as

$$C_t = S_t e^{-r^*(T-t)} N(d_{1r^*}) - X e^{-r(T-t)} N(d_{2r^*}) \qquad (8.19)$$

and

$$p_t = X e^{-r(T-t)} N(-d_{2r^*}) - S_t e^{-r^*(T-t)} N(-d_{1r^*}) \qquad (8.20)$$

where

$$d_{1r^*} = \frac{\ln(S_t / X) + (r - r^* + \sigma^2 / 2)(T - t)}{\sigma\sqrt{T - t}}$$

$$d_{2r^*} = \frac{\ln(S_t / X) + (r - r^* - \sigma^2 / 2)(T - t)}{\sigma\sqrt{T - t}}$$

Pricing an option on a futures contract

This model was developed by Fisher Black[8] in 1976 and can be written as

$$C_t = e^{-r(T-t)} [F_{t,T} N(d_{1F}) - X N(d_{2F})] \qquad (8.21)$$

and

$$p_t = e^{-r(T-t)} [X N(-d_{2F}) - F_{t,T} N(-d_{1F})] \qquad (8.22)$$

where

$$d_{1F} = \frac{\ln(F_{t,T} / X) + \sigma^2 / 2(T - t)}{\sigma\sqrt{T - t}}$$

$$d_{2F} = \frac{\ln(F_{t,T} / X) - \sigma^2 / 2(T - t)}{\sigma\sqrt{T - t}}$$

[7] M. Garman, and S. Kohlhagen, "Foreign currency options values", *Journal of International Money and Finance* (December 1983), p.p. 231–237.

[8] See F. Black (1976), "The pricing of commodity contracts", *Journal of Financial Economics*, Vol. 3, p.p. 167–179.

Using the continuous time model

Calculating the premium: An example of a currency option

In spite of the apparent complexity of the formula, using the model to derive the theoretical value of an option is quite simple. All that is necessary is a table giving the values for $N(d)$ and a hand calculator. Consider the following information concerning the Swiss franc versus the US dollar exchange rate (note that the domestic currency is the Swiss franc):

$S(CHF/USD) = 1.50$
$r_{USD} = 4\%$
$r_{CHF} = 9\%$
$T-t = 6$ months $= 0.5$ years
$\sigma = 10\%$
$X = 1.55$.

Substituting this information into Equation 8.19 for d_{1r^*} and d_{2r^*}, the calculation is straightforward:

$$d_{1r^*} = \frac{\ln(1.50/1.55) + (0.09 - 0.04 + \frac{0.01}{2})0.5}{0.1\sqrt{0.5}} = -0.0748$$

$$d_{2r^*} = \frac{\ln(1.50/1.55) + (0.09 - 0.04 - \frac{0.01}{2})0.5}{0.1\sqrt{0.5}} = -0.1455.$$

By looking up these values in the cumulative normal curve tables we find:

$$N(d_{1r^*}) = N(-0.0748) = 0.4702$$

$$N(d_{2r^*}) = N(-0.1455) = 0.4584.$$

Thus:

$$C = 1.50e^{-0.04(0.5)}0.4702 - 1.55e^{-0.09(0.5)}0.4584 \cong 0.0121.$$

Thus, the investor must pay CHF 0.0121 per dollar. If he wants to calculate the premium in dollars rather than francs, all he has to do is divide by the spot rate. In this case $0.0121/1.50 = 0.81\%$.

American style options

Although the Black-Scholes model and its extensions are easy to use, it has a number of shortcomings. First of all, it can only be used for European options. Because of the possibility of early exercise, we have seen that American options are worth more than European options. Black (1975) suggests a simple procedure for evaluating an American style call option.[9] It can be shown that in most circumstances the only date that needs to be considered for the early exercise of an American call option is the final payout date. With

[9] F. Black, "Fact and fantasy in the use of options", *Financial Analysts Journal* (1975), p.p. 36–72.

this in mind, Black's procedure involves using Equation 8.15 to calculate the option value at maturity T and at the last payout date $T–i$ and then setting the American option price equal to the higher of the two.[10] An example will make this clear.

Consider an American call option on a stock with dividend dates in two months and five months. The dividend on each date is expected to be USD 1.00 and the current stock price is USD 80.00. The expiration date is six months, the exercise price is USD 80.00, the stock price volatility is 40% and the riskless rate is 8%. First we calculate the value of the option on the expiry date. We start by calculating the present value of the dividends:

$$\text{PV of dividends} = \text{USD}1e^{-0.08\times2/12} + \text{USD}1e^{-0.08\times5/12} = \text{USD } 1.9540.$$

We then subtract this from the current stock price:

$$\text{USD } 80 - \text{USD } 1.9540 = \text{USD } 78.0460.$$

Using this price in Equation 8.15 with $T = 6/12 = 0.5$ and $S = \text{USD } 78.046$ gives:

$$C = \text{USD } 78.046 \times N(d_1) - \text{USD } 80e^{-0.08\times6/12}N(d_2) = \text{USD } 9.3306.$$

We now calculate the value of the option if it is exercised just before the last dividend pay-out. First, we calculate the present value of the dividend that will be paid in two months:

$$\text{USD}1e^{-0.08\times2/12} = \text{USD } 0.9868$$

and subtract this from the current stock price:

$$\text{USD } 80 - \text{USD } 0.9868 = \text{USD } 79.0132.$$

Using this price in Equation 8.15 with $T = 5/12 = 0.4167$ and $S = \text{USD } 79.0132$ gives:

$$C = \text{USD } 79.0132 \times N(d_1) - \text{USD } 80e^{-0.08\times5/12}N(d_2) = \text{USD } 8.8737.$$

Thus, according to Black's approximation, the value of the American call option is USD 9.3306, the higher of the two.

There is no equivalent approximation for American style put options. It should be noted, however, that intermediate payouts make it less likely that an American style put option will be exercised early.

Implied volatility

Another practical difficulty resides in the choice of the volatility parameter, σ. One possible solution is to estimate volatility using past values of the exchange rate. Unfortunately, experience has shown that volatility is not stable and tends to fluctuate considerably over time. Instead of past volatility, the volatility estimate necessary for the Black-Scholes model is volatility expected over the life of the option. This variable is not directly observable, of course, because it depends on the expectations of all the

[10] Roll (1977), Geske (1979 and 1981) and Whaley (1981) suggest an alternative procedure.

participants in the foreign exchange market. Consequently, investors have developed another use for the model. Rather than using it to determine the theoretical price of an option, they take the price observed on the market and use the model to determine the volatility that the market price implies. In fact, professional options traders do not quote a price for an option. Instead they quote a level of volatility from which the price can be deduced.

Take, for example, a call on US dollars for Swiss francs that expires in six months with a strike price of 1.50 and quoted at CHF 0.0694 per dollar. The investor can substitute the value 0.0694 into Equation 8.19:

$$0.0694 = 1.50e^{-0.04(0.5)}N(d_{1r^*}) - 1.55e^{-0.09(0.5)}N(d_{2r^*})$$

and solve for σ. The only unknown in the equation is σ in the formulas for $N(d_{1r^*})$ and $N(d_{2r^*})$. There is no explicit solution to the equation but an iterative trial and error method can get the job done quickly. In fact, 12% is the solution to this problem, which means that 12% is the value of σ that makes it possible to find the market price of 0.0694. This is called **implied volatility**.

Because there are numerous calls with different strike prices and expiration dates quoted on the same currency, implied volatility can be used in several ways. First of all, it can be used as a gauge of the relative expensiveness of the different calls. Those with the highest volatility are the most expensive and to be avoided by buyers. Secondly, if we make the assumption that market expectations only evolve slowly, the best estimation of anticipated risk is the weighted average of all the different implicit volatilities. In fact, this use seems to give the best results.

Option management tools

The usefulness of the Black-Scholes model goes beyond the limited scope of pricing European call options. The model expresses in a relatively simple manner the relationships between the price of the option and the principal variables, namely the spot price, volatility, time, and domestic and foreign interest rates. It allows investors to anticipate the effects of a change in one of these variables on the value of the overall position. There are five basic tools, called the "Greeks", to be derived from the model: the delta (Δ), the gamma (Γ), the theta (Θ), the vega and rho, the sensitivity to the interest rate. Although not strictly a greek letter, vega is included among the "Greeks". In deriving these parameters we will use Equations 8.17 and 8.18, the most general formula that we have presented. The "Greeks" for the other formulas can be derived by substituting for δ. For example, for currency options r^* replaces δ, for futures options r replaces δ and for options with no intermediate payouts $\delta = 0$.

Delta

We have seen that when the spot price is higher, the option premium is also higher. Mathematically, we can say that the option premium is an increasing function of the spot price. The Black-Scholes model makes it possible to state the relationship precisely. In fact, we can use the first partial derivative of the option premium with respect to the spot exchange rate. It is equal to

$$\Delta = \frac{\partial C}{\partial S} = e^{-\delta(T-t)}N(d_{1\delta}) \tag{8.23}$$

and is referred to by professionals as the call's **delta**.[11] A call's delta is always positive and measures the sensitivity of the premium to a small change in the spot price. For the writer of a call wanting to hedge his exposure, it represents the number of units of the underlying asset to be bought spot. For the owner of a call wanting to hedge his exposure, it represents the number of units of the underlying asset to be sold. When an investor has accumulated a position composed of calls with different strike prices and expiration dates, he would like to know how sensitive his overall position is to changes in the spot price. Individual call deltas can be used for this purpose.

The investor's overall position can be defined as the weighted sum of the value of the premiums of all the calls he has bought or written. Let Y be the overall position. then:

$$Y = \Sigma x_i C_i \tag{8.24}$$

where x_i is the number of calls in series i that have been bought if $x>0$ and the number of calls that have been written if $x<0$. The sensitivity of his overall portfolio to a change in the price of the underlying asset, ΔY, will then be the weighted average of the sensitivities of the different calls:

$$\Delta = \Sigma x_i \Delta_i \tag{8.25}$$

The investor can evaluate how well he is covered by comparing the delta of his overall position in calls with his exposure to the underlying asset. This technique is frequently used by professional investors.

For a put option:

$$\Delta = \frac{\partial p}{\partial S} = e^{-\delta(T-t)}(N(d_{1\delta}) - 1) \tag{8.26}$$

It is negative. Therefore, a long position in a put option should be hedged by a long position in the underlying asset and a short position in a put option should be hedged by a short position in the underlying asset.

Gamma

Delta only measures the sensitivity of the premium to changes in the price of the underlying asset in the vicinity of the actual price. If the price undergoes a large change, the delta will change considerably. Hence, if options are used to hedge risk, the level of exposure would automatically change if there is a large move in the asset price. The rate at which delta changes, then, is an important factor in the riskiness of the investor's

---

[11] When deriving the "Greeks", keep in mind that $Se^{-\delta(T-t)}N'(d_{1\delta}) = Xe^{-r(T-t)}N'(d_{2\delta})$. To see this, take the logs of both sides:

$$\ln S - \delta(T-t) + \ln \frac{1}{\sqrt{2\pi}} - \frac{d^2_{1\delta}}{2} = \ln X - r(T-t) + \ln \frac{1}{\sqrt{2\pi}} - \frac{d^2_{2\delta}}{2}$$

$$\Rightarrow \ln S - \ln X + (r-\delta)(T-t) = 1/2[d^2_{1\delta} - (d_{1\delta} - \sigma\sqrt{T-t})^2]$$

$$\Rightarrow \ln(S/X) + (r - \delta + \sigma^2/2)(T-t) = d_{1\delta}\sigma\sqrt{T-t}$$

which is true by definition.

position. **Gamma**, which is the second partial derivative of C or p (gammas for calls and puts are the same) with respect to S, measures the rate of change in delta:[12]

$$\Gamma = \frac{\partial \Delta}{\partial S} = \frac{\partial^2 C}{\partial S^2} = e^{-\delta(T-t)} \frac{1}{\sigma S \sqrt{2\pi(T-t)}} e^{-\frac{(d_1)^2}{2}} \tag{8.27}$$

As with delta, the gamma of the overall position can be calculated by taking a weighted average of all the calls:

$$\Gamma_Y = \sum_i x_i \Gamma_i \tag{8.28}$$

Because the x_i can be negative (calls sold), the gamma of a portfolio can be negative as well. Negative gammas can be dangerous in the case of a wide swing in the price of the underlying asset. A negative gamma will make hedging a short position with sold puts less and less effective in the case of a rise in the asset price because delta will fall as the price rises. Covering a long position in the underlying asset with sold calls is also less and less effective when the asset price falls because delta will decrease as the price falls. Furthermore, in the case of opposite moves, the position will immediately show a tendency to be over-hedged, which is costly. Some professional investors speak of "negative gamma hell".

Theta

The value of an option is indisputably a function of the time to expiration. The first partial derivative of the value of an option with respect to time is called **theta**. For a call it is

$$\Theta = \frac{\partial C}{\partial t} = -\frac{SN'(d_{1\delta})\sigma e^{-\delta(T-t)}}{2\sqrt{T-t}} + \delta Se^{-\delta(T-t)}N(d_{1\delta}) - rXe^{-r(T-t)}N(d_{2\delta}) \tag{8.29}$$

For a put it is

$$\Theta = \frac{\partial p}{\partial t} = -\frac{SN'(d_{1\delta})\sigma e^{-\delta(T-t)}}{2\sqrt{T-t}} - \delta Se^{-\delta(T-t)}N(-d_{1\delta}) + rXe^{-r(T-t)}N(-d_{2\delta}) \tag{8.30}$$

Normally, the value of an option diminishes as time passes and it usually diminishes faster as the expiration date approaches. Therefore, theta is usually negative. Theta is not the same type of hedge parameter as delta or gamma. Delta and gamma refer to hedging against uncertainty about changes in the underlying asset price. Since there is no uncertainty about the passage of time, it does not make sense to hedge against it. It is useful as a descriptive statistic.

---

[12] The value of gamma can be worked out as follows:

$$\frac{\partial^2 C}{\partial S^2} = e^{-\delta(T-t)} \frac{\partial N(d_{1\delta})}{\partial d_{1\delta}} \frac{\partial d_{1\delta}}{\partial S}$$

Where from the normal distribution

$$\frac{\partial N(d_{1\delta})}{\partial d_{1\delta}} = \frac{1}{\sqrt{2\pi}} e^{-\frac{(d_{1\delta})^2}{2}}$$

$$\frac{\partial d_{1\delta}}{\partial S} = \frac{1}{\sigma S \sqrt{(T-t)}}$$

Putting these together yields the derivative in the text.

Vega

The value of an option is a direct function of the volatility of the spot price. Higher volatility raises the value of the option. On the organized exchanges, most options positions are closed out before expiration. Consequently, the price of the option comes into play twice, once when it is bought and once when it is sold. It is thus important for an investor to have an idea of what the effect of an anticipated change in the volatility of an option will have on its premium. For example, a fall in volatility will cause a fall in the call's premium.

The relationship between the option's premium and volatility can be expressed as **vega** the first partial derivative of C or p (vega is the same for calls and puts) with respect to σ:[13]

$$\frac{\partial C}{\partial \sigma} = S\sqrt{T - t}\,\frac{1}{\sqrt{2\pi}}\,e^{\frac{(d_{1a})^2}{2}}\,e^{-\delta(T-t)} \tag{8.31}$$

It measures the increase in the premium for a small change in volatility. As with the other parameters, vegas can be added to calculate a global position consisting of different calls.

Interest rate sensitivity: Rho

To show the sensitivity of the option premium to small changes in the interest rate, we can do as we have done for the other parameters and take the first partial derivative of C and p with respect to the interest rate:

$$\frac{\partial C}{\partial r} = (T - t)Xe^{-r(T-t)}N(d_{2a}) \tag{8.32}$$

$$\frac{\partial p}{\partial r} = -(T - t)Xe^{-r(T-t)}N(-d_{2a}) \tag{8.33}$$

The result shows that for a call a higher interest rate has a positive effect on the premium. A higher interest rate lowers the present value of the strike price

$$[e^{-r(T-t)}X]$$

and increases the difference with the current asset price, thereby increasing the premium. For a put the effect is the opposite.

Pricing european puts and put-call parity

By using the same arbitrage arguments as with the call, we have shown that it is possible to derive a model for pricing European puts. It is also possible to derive the put formula from the **put-call parity** relationship. Consider a currency option. On the futures and options markets a distinction is usually made between hedging, speculation and arbitrage. Arbitrage operations are undertaken by professionals and involve establishing a riskless position that generates a net profit. We have shown that positions like this are hard to come by insofar as the markets are extremely competitive. They require low transaction costs and constant vigilance on the part of the arbitragers in the markets. The put-call parity relation is a well known example. It is interesting to study because it illustrates the relationships between calls and puts and all the other positions that incorporate calls and puts.

---

[13] The other member of the derivative disappears because $S(t)e^{-\delta(T-t)}N'(d_{1a}) - Xe^{-r(T-t)}N'(d_{2a}) = 0$.

Consider the following operations undertaken at time 0:

Buy a call on CHF 1
Sell a put on CHF 1
Sell CHF 1 forward.

The cash flows generated by these operations and their outcomes at time 1 can be summarized as shown in Table 8.7.

We can see that the cash flows generated by the portfolio are the same for all possible outcomes of S. Since the outcome of the portfolio is certain, the investment should earn the riskless rate in domestic currency. The investment is equal to $C - p$ and the investment return is $F - X$. Thus, when t is the time to expiration:

$$(C - p)e^{r(T-t)} = F - X \tag{8.34}$$

This means that the compounded value of the put premium less the compounded value of the call premium is equal to the difference between the forward rate and the strike price.

From interest rate parity we know that:

$$F = S \frac{e^{r(T - t)}}{e^{r*(T - t)}}$$

Substituting this value for F in Equation 8.34 and dividing by $e^{r(T - t)}$, gives the put-call parity equation

$$p - C = -Se^{-r*(T - t)} + Xe^{-r(T - t)} \tag{8.35}$$

Then substituting the Garman Kohlhagen formula for C and combining terms gives Equation (8.20).

Summary

1 An option is a contract that gives its owner the right for a given period of time to buy or sell a given amount of an underlying asset at a fixed price, called the exercise price or the strike price. The underlying asset can be a financial security such as a stock or a bond, a financial commodity such as an interest rate or a currency, or a physical commodity such

Table 8.7 Example cash flows and outcomes

Operation	Cash flow at time 0	Outcome if S>X	Outcome if S<X	Outcome if S=X
Buy call	$-C$	$-K + CHF\ 1$	0	0
Sell put	$+p$	0	$-K + CHF\ 1$	0
Sell forward	0	$+F - CHF\ 1$	$+F - CHF\ 1$	$+F - CHF\ 1$
Buy spot	—	—	—	$-S + CHF\ 1$
Result	$p - C$	$F - X$	$F - X$	$F - S = F - X$

as oil, gas, coffee or potatoes. If the right can be exercised at any time during the life of the option it is called an American option. If the right can be exercised only at the option's expiration date it is called a European option. The right to buy is called a call. The right to sell is called a put. The buyer of the option pays the seller, or the writer, a certain sum, called the premium, for the right to buy or sell at the prescribed price.

2. Contracts for future delivery of foreign exchange can be made in the over-the-counter markets or on the organized exchanges. There are fundamental differences between the two. In the over-the-counter bank market, maturities are variable. Although maturities of three or six months are customary, it is possible to find options with maturities from a day or a week up to a year or more. On the organized exchanges such as the Philadelphia Stock Exchange, expiration dates are standardized; for example, the Saturday that precedes the third Wednesday in the months of March, June, September and December.

   On the organized exchanges a clearing house records the transactions concluded by each of its members. The role of the clearing house is essential. It guarantees the execution of all contracts negotiated on the exchange and effectively becomes the counterparty to both sides of the transaction. The role of the clearing house and contract standardization facilitate trading and make the market more liquid. In the over-the-counter market, transactions take place on a person-to-person, deal-by-deal basis. There is no standard contract and no unique counterparty. Consequently, there is no real secondary market that would enable an investor to make low-cost, rapid or frequent changes in his position.

3. The value of an option depends, first of all, on the underlying asset, or, more precisely, on the price of the asset and its volatility. Secondly, it depends on the characteristics of the contract itself concerning the strike price and the expiration date. Finally, it depends on the level of the short-term interest rate and the yield on the underlying asset.

4. The premium on a call option is higher when the price of the underlying asset is higher. On the other hand, the premium on a put will be higher when the spot price of the underlying asset is lower.

5. The higher the strike price, the lower will be the value of a call and the higher the value of a put. On the other hand, the lower the strike price, the higher will be the value of a call and the lower the value of a put.

6. Higher volatility raises the value of both calls and puts.

7. A longer time to expiration raises the value of both calls and puts.

8. The option pricing models developed by theorists are based on certain basic rules of arbitrage practiced by professional traders.

9. Because of the possibility of early exercise, American options can never be worth less and can sometimes be worth more than European options with the same characteristics.

10. The Black-Scholes model (and its extensions) is an exact pricing formula for European style options. In spite of its seeming complexity, the model is simple and easy to use. One of the uses is a straightforward application of the model to determine the theoretical price of an option. It can also be used to determine the volatility of the underlying asset that is implied by current option prices.

11. There are five basic tools to be derived from the Black-Scholes model that can be used for option management: the delta, the gamma, the theta, the vega, and the sensitivity to the interest rate. The delta measures the sensitivity of the options price to changes in the price of the underlying asset. Gamma measures the sensitivity of delta to changes in the price of the underlying asset. Theta measures the sensitivity of the options price to the passage of time and vega measures its sensitivity to changes in volatility.

Appendix 8.1: The binomial option pricing model with known, proportional payouts

Remembering that the option's expiration value after j upward moves and n-j downward moves is equal to $Max[0, u^j d^{n-j} S - E]$, thus, n periods before its expiration date, the value of the call is

$$C_0 = \frac{\sum_{j=0}^{n} \frac{n!}{j!(n-j)!} P^j (1-P)^{n-j} Max\left[0, u^j d^{n-j} S - X\right]}{R^n} \tag{A8.1.1}$$

This expression can be simplified by defining a as the minimum number of upward moves in the asset price for the option to finish in-the-money. This will be the case when $u^a d^{n-a} S - X > 0$. Taking logs gives

$$a > \ln \frac{X}{Sd^n} \bigg/ \ln \frac{u}{d}$$

When there are fewer than a upward movements, the call will not be exercised and it will expire worthless. The maximum can then be written as $u^j d^{n-j} S - X$ over $j = a...n$. With these changes we can write Equation A8.1.1 as

$$C_0 = \frac{\sum_{j=a}^{n} \frac{n!}{j!(n-j)!} P^j (1-P)^{n-j} [u^j d^{n-j} S - X]}{R^n} \tag{A8.1.2}$$

Rearranging

$$C_0 = S(1+\delta)^{-n} \sum_{j=a}^{n} \frac{n!}{j!(n-j)!} \frac{(1+\delta)^n (Pu)^j ((1-P)d)^{n-j}}{R^n}$$

$$- XR^{-n} \sum_{j=a}^{n} \frac{n!}{j!(n-j)!} P^j (1-P)^{n-j} \tag{A8.1.3}$$

The second summation is the binomial formula with P as the probability. The first summation is also the binomial formula with

$$P' = Pu \frac{1+\delta}{R}$$

as the probability if

$$(1 - P') = (1 - P)d \frac{1+\delta}{R}.$$

This is indeed the case because

$$(1-P')=1-Pu\frac{1+\delta}{R}=1-u\frac{1+\delta}{R}\left[\frac{\dfrac{R}{1+\delta}-d}{u-d}\right]=1-\frac{u\dfrac{R}{1+\delta}-ud}{u\dfrac{R}{1+\delta}-d\dfrac{R}{1+\delta}}=\frac{u\dfrac{R}{1+\delta}-d\dfrac{R}{1+\delta}-u\dfrac{R}{1+\delta}+ud}{u\dfrac{R}{1+\delta}-d\dfrac{R}{1+\delta}}$$

$$=\frac{d}{\dfrac{R}{1+\delta}}\left[\frac{u-\dfrac{R}{1+\delta}}{u-d}\right]=\frac{d}{\dfrac{R}{1+\delta}}\left[\frac{u-d-\dfrac{R}{1+\delta}+d}{u-d}\right]=\frac{d(1+\delta)}{R}\left[1-\frac{\dfrac{R}{1+d}-d}{u-d}\right]$$

which is what we wanted to show. Thus, we can write the general binomial foreign currency option pricing model as

$$C_0 = S(1+\delta)^{-n}\Phi(a,n,P') - XR^{-n}\Phi(a,n,P) \tag{A8.1.4}$$

where $\Phi(a,n,P)$ is the probability of realizing at least a upward moves when the probability at each trial is P and $\Phi(a,n,P')$ is the probability of obtaining at least a upward moves when the probability at each trial is P'.

Appendix 8.2: Derivation of the Black-Scholes pricing model

In this appendix we develop the model for a European style option on an underlying asset that has no intermediate cash flows: the classic Black-Scholes option pricing formula.

A Weiner process

Suppose that the percentage change of the price of the underlying asset in the time interval dt follows a continuous stochastic process of the type

$$dS(t) = \mu S(t)dt + \sigma S(t)dz(t) \tag{A8.2.1}$$

where S refers to the price of the asset, μ is the expected percentage change in the asset price, called the drift, σ is the volatility and $dz(t)$ is a standard Weiner process sometimes referred to as Brownian motion. A Weiner process is a particular type of stochastic process, called a Markov process, where only the present value of the variable is relevant for predicting its future evolution. The major properties of a standard Weiner process are as follows:

1. $dz = \varepsilon\sqrt{dt}$ where ε is a standardized random variable following the normal law with a mean of 0 and variance of 1: $N(0,1)$.
2. The values of dz for any two different short time intervals are independent.
3. $E(dz) = 0$.
4. $E(dzdt) = 0$.
5. $E(dz^2) = dt$.
6. The variance of $dz^2 = 0$.

7. $E[(dzdt)^2] = 0.$

8. The variance of $dzdt = 0.$

Ito's lemma

Equation A8.2.1 is a generalized We(...)er process known as geometric Brownian motion with drift equal to μ and volatility (...) σ. It is also referred to as an Ito process after the mathematician who discovered (...) result on stochastic processes, which is called "Ito's lemma". Ito's lemma (...) on of an Ito process is itself an Ito process.

Let $C(S,t)$ represent (...) (...)nit of the underlying asset. To apply Ito's lemma, expand C in (...)

$$(...) dS^2 \qquad\qquad (A8.2.2)$$

In (...) (...) in ordinary calculus even (...)lly distributed random

$$(A8.2.3)$$

(...) properties 4 and 8, $dzdt$ (...) o, $dz^2 = dt$ so that Equation

$$(A8.2.4)$$

We (...) (...) creating a portfolio of one call and Δ units of the asset:

$$V = C + \Delta S \qquad\qquad (A8.2.5)$$

Choose Δ so that the (...) (...) in the value of the portfolio over a short period of time will be equal to zero. To do thi(...), we take the derivative of V with respect to S and set it equal to zero:

$$\frac{\partial V}{\partial S} = \frac{\partial C}{\partial S} + \Delta = 0$$

$$\rightarrow \Delta = -\frac{\partial C}{\partial S}.$$

The portfolio will be riskless when

$$\Delta = -\frac{\partial C}{\partial S}.^{14}$$

---

[14] This is the continuous time equivalent to the binomial

$$\Delta = \frac{C_u - C_d}{S(u - d)}.$$

Since we are now in a risk-neutral world, r, the riskless rate, replaces μ in Equation A8.2.1.[15]
Now differentiate Equation A8.2.5:

$$dV = dC - \frac{\partial C}{\partial S} dS \qquad \text{(A8.2.6)}$$

Substitute A8.2.2 and A8.2.4 into A8.2.6

$$dV = \frac{\partial C}{\partial t} dt + \frac{1}{2} \frac{\partial^2 C}{\partial S^2} \sigma^2 S^2 dt \qquad \text{(A8.2.7)}$$

Because V is riskless, it should earn the riskless rate through time. Thus

$$r(C - \frac{\partial C}{\partial S} S)dt = \frac{\partial C}{\partial t} dt + \frac{1}{2} \frac{\partial^2 C}{\partial S^2} \sigma^2 S^2 dt \qquad \text{(A8.2.8)}$$

Rearranging and simplifying gives the Black-Scholes differential equation

$$\frac{1}{2} \frac{\partial^2 C}{\partial S^2} \sigma^2 S^2 + r \frac{\partial C}{\partial S} S - rC + \frac{\partial C}{\partial t} = 0 \qquad \text{(A8.2.9)}$$

The solution to this equation depends on the boundary conditions. For a European call option the boundary conditions are

$$C(S_T, T) = Max(S_T - X, 0) \qquad \text{(A8.2.10)}$$

$$C(0, t) = 0 \qquad \text{(A8.2.11)}$$

Solving the differential equation and using the boundary conditions yields an exact analytical solution.[16]

Appendix 8.3: Derivation of the expected expiration value of the call option

In this appendix we derive the expected expiration value of the call option. This involves solving the equation

$$C = e^{-r(T-t)} E[Max(S_T - X, 0)] \qquad \text{(A8.3.1)}$$

[15] Equation A8.2.1 becomes:
$$dS(t) = rS(t)dt + \sigma S(t)dz(t) \qquad \text{(A8.2.1')}$$

[16] See, for example, Wilmott, Howison and Dewynne (1998).

We know that S is lognormally distributed. Applying the lognormal distribution to A8.3.1 gives

$$C = e^{-r(T-t)} \int_{\ln X}^{\infty} \frac{1}{\sqrt{2\pi\sigma^2(T-t)}} \frac{1}{S_T} e^{-(\ln S_T - m)^2/2\sigma^2(T-t)} dS_T [S_T - X]$$

$$= e^{-r(T-t)} \left[\frac{1}{\sqrt{2\pi\sigma^2(T-t)}} \int_{\ln X}^{\infty} e^{-(\ln S_T - m)^2/2\sigma^2(T-t)} dS_T - X \frac{1}{\sqrt{2\pi\sigma^2(T-t)}} \int_{\ln X}^{\infty} \frac{1}{S_T} e^{-(\ln S_T - m)^2/2\sigma^2(T-t)} dS_T \right]$$

$$\text{(A8.3.2)}$$

where m is the mean of S_T.

First we evaluate the second interval on the RHS of Equation A8.3.2. Let

$$\varepsilon = \frac{\ln S_T - m}{\sigma\sqrt{T-t}}$$

and make the change of variable, knowing that

$$\frac{d\varepsilon}{dS_T} = \frac{1}{S_T\sigma\sqrt{T-t}}.$$

This gives

$$-X \frac{1}{\sqrt{2\pi}} \int_{\frac{\ln X - m}{\sigma\sqrt{T-t}}}^{\infty} e^{-\varepsilon^2/2} d\varepsilon \qquad \text{(A8.3.3)}$$

Equation A8.3.3 is X multiplied by the probability that $S_T > X$. This probability can be visualized as the area under the standard normal curve to the right of the cut-off point. The convention in option pricing is to use areas to the left of the cut-off point. This translation is easy to achieve, since the standard normal curve is symmetrical around zero. The probability that

$$\varepsilon > \frac{\ln X - m}{\sigma\sqrt{T-t}}$$

is the same as the probability that

$$\varepsilon < \frac{m - \ln X}{\sigma\sqrt{T-t}}.$$

Making this transformation gives

$$-X \frac{1}{\sqrt{2\pi}} \int_{\infty}^{\frac{m - \ln X}{\sigma\sqrt{T-t}}} e^{-\varepsilon^2/2} d\varepsilon \qquad \text{(A8.3.4)}$$

and, since we are in a risk-neutral world we also know that S follows the process

$$dS(t) = rS(t)dt + \sigma S(t)dz(t) \qquad \text{(A8.3.5)}$$

To find the parameters for the log of S, let

$$y = \ln S \qquad \text{(A8.3.6)}$$

Apply Ito's lemma

$$dy = \frac{1}{S}dS - \frac{1}{2S^2}dS^2$$

$$dy = \frac{1}{S}(rSdt + \sigma Sdz) - \frac{1}{2S^2}\sigma^2 S^2 dt$$

$$dy = (r - \frac{\sigma^2}{2})dt + \sigma dz \qquad\qquad (A8.3.7)$$

Integrate Equation A8.3.7

$$y_T = y_t + (r - \frac{\sigma^2}{2})(T - t) + \sigma\varepsilon\sqrt{T - t} \qquad\qquad (A8.3.8)$$

The mean of the $\ln S$ is

$$y_t + (r - \frac{\sigma^2}{2})(T - t)$$

and the variance is $\sigma^2(T - t)$. Thus Equation A8.3.3 is evaluated at

$$d_2 = \frac{\ln\frac{S_t}{X} + \left(r - \frac{\sigma^2}{2}\right)(T - t)}{\sigma\sqrt{T - t}} \qquad\qquad (8.3.9)$$

To evaluate the first integral on the RHS of A8.3.2 we proceed as before. Let

$$\varepsilon = \frac{\ln S_T - m}{\sigma\sqrt{T - t}}$$

and make the change of variable, knowing that

$$\frac{d\varepsilon}{dS_T} = \frac{1}{S_t\sigma\sqrt{T - t}}.$$

This gives

$$\frac{1}{\sqrt{2\pi}}\int_{\frac{\ln X - m}{\sigma\sqrt{T-t}}}^{\infty} S_T e^{-\varepsilon^2/2}\, d\varepsilon \qquad\qquad (A8.3.10)$$

Substituting Equation A8.3.8 into S_T gives

$$\frac{1}{\sqrt{2\pi}} S_t e^{\left(r - \frac{\sigma^2}{2}\right)(T - t)}\int_{\frac{\ln X - m}{\sigma\sqrt{T-t}}}^{\infty} e^{\sigma\varepsilon\sqrt{T-t}} e^{-\varepsilon^2/2}\, d\varepsilon \qquad\qquad (A8.3.11)$$

Add

$$\frac{\sigma^2(T-t)}{2} - \frac{\sigma^2(T-t)}{2}$$

to the exponents in the integral to complete the square. This gives

$$\frac{1}{\sqrt{2\pi}} S_t e^{\left(r-\frac{\sigma^2}{2}\right)(T-t)+\frac{\sigma^2}{2}(T-t)} \int\limits_{\frac{\ln X - m}{\sigma\sqrt{T-t}}}^{\infty} e^{-\frac{1}{2}(\varepsilon^2 - 2\sigma\varepsilon\sqrt{T-t}+\sigma^2(T-t))} \, d\varepsilon \qquad (A8.3.12)$$

Make the change of variables

$$\omega = \varepsilon - \sigma\sqrt{T-t}$$

to give

$$\frac{1}{\sqrt{2\pi}} S_t e^{r(T-t)} \int\limits_{\frac{\ln X - m}{\sigma\sqrt{T-t}} - \sigma\sqrt{T-t}}^{\infty} e^{-\frac{w^2}{2}} \, d\omega \qquad (A8.3.13)$$

Substituting the value for m and translating from the right of the cut-off point to the left gives

$$\frac{1}{\sqrt{2\pi}} S_t e^{r(T-t)} \int\limits_{-\infty}^{d_1} e^{-\frac{w^2}{2}} \qquad (A8.3.14)$$

where

$$d_1 = \frac{\ln \dfrac{S_t}{X} + \left(r + \dfrac{\sigma^2}{2}\right)(T-t)}{\sigma\sqrt{T-t}} \qquad (A8.3.15)$$

Substituting A8.3.4, A8.3.9, A8.3.14 and A8.3.15 into A8.3.2 gives the solution in the text:

$$C = S_t N(d_1) - X e^{-r(T-t)} N(d_2) \qquad (A8.3.16)$$

where

$N(d)$ = the value of the cumulative normal distribution evaluated at d.

$$d_1 = \frac{\ln(S_t/X) + (r + \sigma^2/2)(T-t)}{\sigma\sqrt{T-t}}$$

$$d_2 = \frac{\ln(S_t/X) + (r - \sigma^2/2)(T-t)}{\sigma\sqrt{T-t}}.$$

Exotic options and other over-the-counter instruments

9

Besides the over-the-counter (OTC) products we studied in Chapters 3 and 6, the OTC market has a virtually unlimited range of instruments that can be used for hedging the risks encountered in international financial and business transactions. In this chapter we look at the most popular of these instruments, examining how they are priced and how they can be used. Subsequent chapters that deal specifically with exchange risk, interest rate risk and supply risk on the commodity markets will go into more detail on how OTC instruments can be applied to each individual type of risk.

Forward rate agreements

In a forward rate agreement (FRA), one party guarantees the other party an interest rate for a given time period on a given notional amount of principal. For example, suppose a bank makes a deal with a company whereby it guarantees an interest rate of 10% on a principal amount of USD 1 million for a one-year loan that begins in one year. The reference rate for the one-year loan is designated as Libor. In practice, interest rates are set to the compounding period of the time period in question. Thus, the 10% interest rate refers to annual compounding because the time period is one year. They are also usually set where the guaranteed rate is equal to the forward rate corresponding to the loan period so that there is no payout on the date the FRA is initiated. On the settlement date at the end of one year, the prevailing one-year Libor is compared with the guaranteed rate. If it is higher (lower), the company receives (pays) the present value of the difference between the two rates multiplied by the principal amount multiplied by the day count factor corresponding to the loan period. In this example the loan period is one year such that the day count factor is equal to one.[1] Thus, if the prevailing one-year Libor was 11% at the agreement's maturity, the company would receive

$$e^{-0.10436} \times [0.11 - 0.10] \times \text{USD } 1,000,000 \times 1 = \text{USD } 9009.01.$$

---

[1] If the loan period was three months, the day count factor would be about 0.25. If it was six months the day count factor would be about 0.5. The exact day count factor depends on the exact number of days of the loan and the day count convention of the market in question.

Note that the discounting was done at the continuous rate of 10.436%, which is equal to the 11% rate with annual compounding. If the prevailing one-year Libor was 9% at the agreement's maturity, the company would pay

$$e^{-0.0862} \times [0.09 - 0.10] \times USD\ 1,000,000 \times 1 = USD\ 9,174.31.$$

Again, the discounting was done at the continuous rate of 8.62%, which corresponds to the 9% rate with annual compounding.

Swaps

As we saw in Chapters 3 and 6, a swap is an agreement between two institutions to exchange cash flows in the future. The agreement specifies the dates when the cash flows are to be paid and the way that they are to be calculated. A forward contract is a simple example of a swap. Whereas a forward contract leads to the exchange of cash flows on only one future date, swaps typically involve exchanges of cash flows on several future dates.

Historical background

The precursor to today's swap was the "parallel loan" developed in the United Kingdom in the 1970s as a means of avoiding the premium on investments outside the country. At the time, exchange controls required that all purchases of foreign currency for the purpose of foreign investment be made at a premium over the spot rate. To get around this regulation, the UK company would make a sterling loan to the UK subsidiary of a company in another country. In return, the foreign company would lend the equivalent amount in another currency to the foreign subsidiary of the UK company. These parallel loans had several disadvantages: (a) it was difficult to find a partner to do the deal with; (b) the credit risk was with the subsidiary and not the mother company; and (c) both groups' outstanding liabilities were increased.

Successive refinements on the parallel loan led to the first swap in 1976, organized by two US banks, Continental Illinois and Goldman Sachs. It was a currency swap between the Dutch firm Bos Kallis and the British firm ICI Finance. Since then, the market has grown by leaps and bounds, thanks to banks' inventiveness and the development of the bond market. Currency swaps, for example, grew from almost nothing at the end of the 1970s to over USD 500 billion of total notional principal value outstanding at the end of 1990. By the same token, interest rate swaps grew from almost nothing to over USD 3 trillion of notional principal value outstanding at the end of 1991. Since then the growth has been nothing short of phenomenal. The International Swaps and Derivatives Association (ISDA) reports that, measured in notional principal outstanding amounts, interest rate swaps, currency swaps and interest rate options, as reported by member organizations totaled USD 60.366 trillion as at 30 June 2000.[2]

Although using swaps as vehicles for funding primary operations is a relatively new phenomenon, foreign exchange traders have been employing the principle for years. Remember from Chapter 6 that when a foreign exchange dealer receives an order to sell foreign exchange forward, he covers himself by borrowing in domestic currency, purchasing foreign currency spot, and lending the foreign currency. In this operation, he effectively swaps a liability in foreign currency for a liability in domestic currency. The

[2] www.isda.org (8 August 2001).

swap market is an extension of the foreign exchange trader's basic technique to a wide range of financial instruments.

Why use swaps?

There are three basic reasons why companies include swap transactions in their funding operations:

- market constraints
- cost advantages
- hedging.

Market constraints are a major incentive to swap transactions. They can involve technical constraints such as non-availability of longer maturities in certain markets or a lack of liquidity for primary borrowing in a particular market. Swapping makes it possible to transfer the desired liquidity and maturity from the markets where they exist to the markets where they are needed. Market constraints can also involve informational and political obstacles that can affect access or lack of access to funding in a particular currency. A company unknown in a market, for example, would find it difficult to borrow there. On the other hand, some credits, such as export credits, might be available to domestic borrowers in domestic currency when the need is to fund in another currency.

Cost advantages can also inspire swap transactions. An example will illustrate the issues involved. Let's take the case of Achtung AG with an investment grade credit rating that enables it to borrow on the fixed rate bond market. At the moment, however, it prefers to borrow at a variable rate. Its chief financial officer is told by the company's banker that an investment grade credit rating carries more weight on the fixed rate market than it does on the variable rate market where interest rate spreads are less sensitive to the quality of the borrower. The banker suggests that Achtung might be able to exploit its credit rating by means of an interest rate swap. Remember that an interest rate swap is a contractual agreement between two parties to exchange a series of payments – usually a floating rate payment for a fixed rate payment – for a stated period of time. The banker says he has another client, Ausgang AG, that would like to borrow at a fixed rate but has a lower credit rating, which makes fixed rate borrowing expensive. The banker has market information on the cost of borrowing for the two companies as set out in Table 9.1.

After careful study, he proposes a deal under which he will act as intermediary but as an exceptional offer of goodwill to strengthen relations with both companies will not take a commission. In the deal he proposes, Achtung will borrow at a fixed rate of 8.6%, while Ausgang will borrow at a floating rate of Libor plus 0.6%. A swap will be arranged so that Ausgang will pay the bank a fixed rate of 9.4%, 0.4% lower than if it had borrowed fixed

Table 9.1 The cost of borrowing for Achtung AG and Ausgang AG

	Fixed rate	Variable rate
Achtung	8.6%	Libor + 0.2%
Ausgang	9.8%	Libor + 0.6%

outside the swap. Achtung will pay the bank Libor less 0.2%, 0.4% lower than if it had borrowed variable directly.

The bank thus receives:

$$9.4\% + \text{Libor} - 0.2\%.$$

It pays Achtung 8.6% so that Achtung can pay off its fixed rate loan. It pays Ausgang Libor plus 0.6% so that Ausgang can pay off its floating rate loan. The bank thus pays out:

$$8.6\% + \text{Libor} + 0.6\%.$$

Its net position is:

$$9.4\% + \text{Libor} - 0.2\% - (8.6\% + \text{Libor} + 0.6\%) = 0.$$

The bank comes out even and both companies are 0.4% better off. The flows are summarized in Figure 9.1.

The swap made it possible for both companies to borrow more cheaply than if they had borrowed directly. The reason is that spreads are lower on the variable market than on the fixed market. On the variable market the difference is 0.4% in favor of Achtung while on the fixed market it is 1.2% in favor of Achtung. There is a possible net gain of 0.8% (1.2% less 0.4%) and Achtung has an absolute advantage in both markets because of its superior credit rating. Achtung has a comparative advantage in the fixed rate market but Ausgang has a comparative advantage in the variable rate market. By specializing in the markets where they have a comparative advantage and trading (swapping), both companies come out ahead.[3] In the example, we split the total gain equally between the two companies and assumed a benevolent bank that required no commission. In practice, there is no reason for the benefits to be divided equally between the two swappers and it is highly unlikely that the bank would not take a commission. Still, the example outlines the major elements of the forces at work generating swaps.

Swap characteristics

The major swap types are interest rate swaps, currency swaps and commodity swaps.

Interest rate swaps

The most common type of interest rate swap is the exchange of fixed rate interest payments on a given principal amount for floating rate interest payments on the same principal amount for a given number of years. The notional amount itself is not exchanged and serves only to calculate the interest payments. In this sense, it is equivalent to a series of FRAs where the fixed rate is the guaranteed rate and the floating rate is the designated spot rate

Figure 9.1 Cash flows on a hypothetical interest rate swap

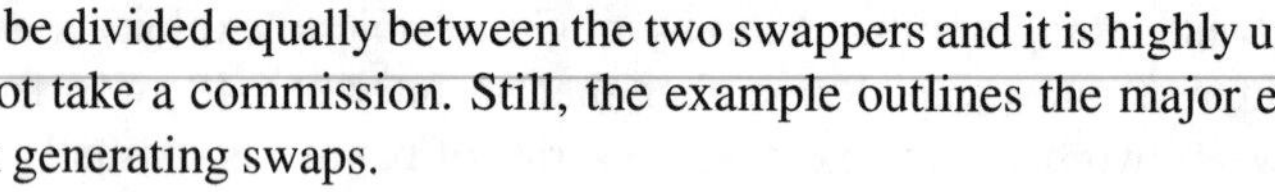

Achtung AG	← 8.6%	Bank	← 9.4%	Ausgang AG
	→ Libor – 0.2%		→ Libor + 0.6%	

[3] See the Introductory Chapter for a development of the theory of comparative advantage in international trade.

prevailing at the agreement's maturity. In the foregoing FRA example, the fixed rate was 10% and the floating rate was one-year Libor. Thus, a five-year swap agreement with the same terms would involve five exchanges. The amount of each exchange would be calculated using the same procedure applied in the example of the FRA.

Swaps are quoted in relation to the fixed interest rate applicable to the "fixed leg" of the swap. The fixed leg refers to the series of fixed interest rate payments. The "variable leg" of the swap refers to the series of variable interest rate payments and is usually determined by six-month Libor. For certain currencies, however, the reference for the variable leg will not be Libor. On the Canadian dollar, for example, the reference will be bankers' acceptances because Libor on the Canadian dollar does not exist. When setting up the swap, traders express their position in relation to whether they pay or receive the fixed interest.

In a US dollar interest rate swap, for example, fixed rates are equal to the rates on the Treasury yield curve for the corresponding maturity plus a spread expressed in basis points as a bid/ask quote. Thus, if the yield on a ten-year Treasury bond is 6%, the swap dealer's quote on a ten-year swap will be: UST+62–65 bp. This means he is willing to write a ten-year swap where he pays a fixed rate of 62 basis points over the yield of a ten-year US Treasury bond, in this case 6.62%, and receive six-month Libor. Alternatively, he is willing to receive a fixed rate of 65 basis points over the yield on a US Treasury bond, in this case 6.65%, and pay six-month Libor. The convention of quoting the fixed leg as US Treasury yield plus a spread gives stability to the quotes because the spreads change infrequently whereas the Treasury yield changes continuously over time as bond prices change.

Fixed interest payments are made either annually or every six months. Sterling, US dollar and yen fixed interest payments are made every six months, for example. Several important dates figure in the swap agreement. First of all, there is the "trade date" that corresponds to the date when the parties make the swap deal. Secondly, there is the "effective date" corresponding to the precise moment that interest starts to be calculated. Calculation normally starts two working days after the trade date but can be chosen in any way agreeable to the two parties, and can even be applied retroactively. Thirdly, the "termination date" specifies the date that the swap agreement ends.

The amounts that each party is obligated to pay are either specified directly or determined according to an explicit formula. In either case, each of these amounts will be payable with respect to a calendar period called a calculation period. The parties to a rate swap may make payments based on the same set of calculation periods or on a different set of calculation periods. For example, the fixed leg of the swap may be paid once a year on 15 January and the variable leg twice a year on 30 June and 31 December.

Calculation periods are measured by period-end dates, which may, but need not be the same as the days on which the payments are due, called payment dates. Each calculation period runs from (and includes) one period-end date to (but excludes) the next period-end date.

When payment dates fall on non-working days, one of three conventions is usually adopted:

1. *Following day*: interest is paid on the first working day following the payment date.

2. *Preceding day*: interest is paid on the last working day preceding the payment date.

3. *Modified following business day*: interest is paid according to the following day format if it falls in the same month as the payment date. Otherwise, interest is paid according to the preceding day format.

The amount of interest to be paid by each party is calculated according to the following formula:

Interest payment = (notional amount) × (interest rate) × (day count fraction).

There are several ways to calculate the day count fraction:

- The actual number of days from the beginning of the calculation period to the end divided by 360 ("Actual/360"); the actual number of days in a year is usually 365 except in a leap year when it is 366.

- The actual number of days from the beginning of the calculation period to the end divided by 365 ("Actual/365").

- The actual number of days from the beginning of the calculation period to the end divided by the actual number of days in the year ("Actual/Actual").

- The number of 30-day months from the beginning of the calculation period to the end divided by 360 ("30n/360").

Thus, a calculation period that begins on 10 January and ends on 15 April of a leap year will have the following day count fractions according to the different bases:

Actual/360 = 96/360
Actual/365 = 96/365
Actual/Actual = 96/366
30n/360 = 95/360.

Currency swaps

A currency swap involves the exchange of a loan in one currency for a loan in another currency and both principal and interest payments are exchanged. The exchange of the notional amount always takes place at the termination of a currency swap and usually at the beginning as well. When the notional amount is exchanged at the beginning and at the end, neither party is exposed to foreign exchange risk. This is not true when the notional amounts are not exchanged at the beginning.

The interest rates on the loans in the currency swap can both be fixed. In this case we speak of a fixed-to-fixed currency swap. If they are both variable we speak of a floating-to-floating currency swap. If one is fixed and the other is floating, we speak of a fixed-to-floating currency swap.

Currency swaps are larger on average than interest rate swaps because they are usually backed by a Eurobond issue, which traditionally varies between amounts of USD 100 million and USD 1 billion. They also always pass through the US dollar no matter what currencies are involved. For example, a fixed-to-fixed currency swap of euros for yen would be constructed of a swap of fixed euros for dollar Libor and dollar Libor for fixed yen. Any fixed rate currency swap against floating US dollar Libor payments is called a **circus swap**. In other words, currency swaps are composed of two circus swaps. The reason for this is that dollar Libor serves as a common denominator between fixed euros and fixed yen. It is extremely doubtful that counterparties in francs and guilders could be found with exactly the same maturities and amounts. However, since virtually all banks and most multinationals that participate in the swap market have access to interbank Libor funds, it is highly probable that one party could be found for the swap of guilders for Libor and another party for the swap of Libor for francs.

Commodity swaps

Commodity swaps are direct descendants of interest rate swaps. In an interest rate swap one party agrees to pay the other a fixed interest rate on a given notional amount at certain specified dates while the other party agrees to pay the first party a floating interest rate – Libor, for example – on the same notional amount at the same specified dates. In a commodity swap, one party agrees to pay the other a fixed price for a given quantity of a commodity at certain specified dates in the future while the other party agrees to pay the first party a variable price – the ongoing spot price or the futures price, for example – for the same quantity of the commodity on the same specified dates.

An example would be an airline company that consumes 40 000 tons of kerosene per month hedging against a price rise by making a deal with the bank whereby it agrees to pay the bank USD 190 per ton on the first day of every month for the next 12 months. In return the bank agrees to pay the company the price recorded on the Rotterdam spot market on the last working day of the preceding month. Thus, on the first of every month, the company owes USD 190 × 40 000 tons = USD 7,600,000. The bank's liability will depend on the spot price. Suppose that on the last working day of the first month the spot price on the Rotterdam market is USD 205. The bank will owe USD 205 × 40 000 tons = USD 8,200,000. The bank will pay the company the difference between the two liabilities: USD 8,200,000 – USD 7,600,000 = USD 600,000. If on the last working day of the second month, the Rotterdam spot price is USD 185, the company must pay the bank (USD 190 – USD 185) × 40 000 tons = USD 200,000. No kerosene changes hands. The company obtains its kerosene on the Rotterdam market where its effective price is always USD 190 no matter what the spot price of the moment happens to be.

A swap can also be used to hedge against a price fall. An example would be a small oil producer with 10 000 barrels of oil per month hedging by making a deal with the bank whereby it agrees to pay the bank on the first working day of every month for the next 24 months the spot price on the last working day of the preceding month reported by Platt's for Brent crude. In return the bank agrees to pay the company USD 20 per barrel for 10 000 barrels on the first working day of every month. Thus on the first working day of the month the company would receive (USD 20 – Spot) × 10 000. If the spot price was USD 18, it would receive (USD 20 – USD 18) × 10 000 = USD 20,000. Its total income from the oil plus the contract would be (USD 18 × 10 000 + USD 20,000 = USD 200,000. If the spot price rises to USD 30 per barrel in the next month, its total income would still be USD 200,000. It would receive USD 300,000 from the sale of the oil on the spot market but would have to pay the bank USD 100,000 on the difference between the fixed price and the flexible price.

Commodity swaps started off with petroleum products but have since branched out into most commodities including gas, precious metals non-ferrous metals and the soft commodities. They are especially effective for commodities such as kerosene that do not have a functioning futures market. Although cross hedging is possible (see Chapter 7), this type of hedge is risky because the price correlations with the hedging instruments are not necessarily stable. In many cases it might be preferable to enter into a swap agreement to avoid the spread risk in a cross hedge or the volatility of the spot price, in spite of the often costly nature of a swap.

Swaps can be arranged for any commodity that has a reliable reference price. These prices can be futures prices or spot prices reported by a reliable specialist organization such as Platt's. Professionals prefer futures prices on the organized exchanges because they are public and cannot be manipulated. Furthermore, the futures markets offer the hedging instrument that the floating price payer can use to offset his risk.

Other types of swaps

Although the standard interest rate swap consists of exchanging fixed interest payments for floating interest payments, it is also possible to organize a "basis swap" that consists of exchanging floating interest payments on one reference interest rate for floating interest payments on another reference rate. In the United States, for example, swaps of commercial paper rates for Libor rates are common. In France, several reference rates are swapped

(T4M, TAM, TME, etc.), although the market is fairly narrow. In fact, most industrialized countries offer opportunities for basis swaps.

A **zero coupon swap** allows a zero coupon debt issuer to convert a zero coupon liability into a conventional floating or fixed rate liability. When the effective date of a swap is fixed at some time in the future, we speak of a forward swap. An option to undertake a given type of swap is called a **swaption**, which we will examine below. In some cases the option clause is dependent on an external event such as a given interest rate. In this case we speak of a contingent swap. Another type of swap that was popular in the 1980s and early 1990s as a result of the "debt crisis" is the **debt–equity swap** where a country's outstanding foreign debt is bought at a discount on the secondary market and traded to the central bank for domestic currency that will be used to make an investment in the country. In fact, we can imagine all kinds of conditions that could be tacked on to the traditional swap contract. However, when undertaking a swap, it is important to understand the costs, benefits and risks associated with it. The more complicated and elaborate the conditions and operations involved in the swap, the more difficult it is to evaluate it.

Pricing a swap

A swap is a contract between two known parties. However, it can be undone by annulment with the original counterparty or by trading to a third party. In fact, the secondary swap market is developing rapidly, although it is far from being as liquid as the market for stocks and bonds. The decision on whether to trade or terminate a swap depends to a large extent on what the swap is worth. Consequently, the swap must be priced. The pricing procedure involves constructing a reference swap based on current market conditions and then comparing the reference swap with the actual swap to be traded or terminated. Although the basic procedure for pricing a swap is the same as that for any other financial asset, there are some particularities that merit closer inspection. An example will make it possible to highlight the major issues.

Suppose that an interest rate swap has been contracted on 15 September 2000 between Caswell SA and Citicorp where Caswell is the fixed rate payer. The conditions of the swap are as follows:

Currency: US dollars
Amount: 5 million
Effective date: 15 September 2000
Fixed rate: 7.5% (Actual/360)
Variable rate: Six-month Libor (Actual/360)
Six-month Libor on 15 September 2000: 6.4%.
Maturity: three years.

On 15 November 2000 the chief financial officer of Caswell decides he wants to reverse his position and undo the swap. He asks Citicorp to make him an offer to terminate the swap. The problem for Citicorp is to price the swap undertaken two months earlier in light of the current market conditions shown in Table 9.2.

We need to know the actuarial interest rates reflected in the rates given in Table 9.2. To find this out, the first step is to calculate the interest rates based on a 365-day year. For example, the one-month rate can be adjusted to 365 days as follows:

$$6.30 \times \frac{365}{360} = 6.3875\%.$$

Table 9.2 Example market information on 15 November 2000

Maturity	Yield (%) (Actual/360)	Maturity	Yield (%) (Actual/360)
1 month	6.30	2 year	7.20
3 month	6.50	3 year	7.30
6 month	6.70	4 year	7.40
1 year	7.00	5 year	7.50

This rate is the annual rate proportional to a one-month loan based on a 365-day year. The interest received each month will be equal to 0.063875/12 = 0.0053229. To arrive at the effective yearly interest rate, monthly interest has to be compounded for 12 months:

$$\left[1 + \frac{0.063875}{12} \right]^{12} - 1 = 6.5779\%$$

Applying the two foregoing steps to all the interest rates gives the effective yields to maturity presented in Table 9.3.

We now need to know the term structure of interest rates in order to discount the swap cash flows at the appropriate rate. As we will see in Chapter 18, correct valuation of future cash flows involves discounting them at the spot interest rate on a zero coupon basis. The interest rates for more than one year in Table 9.3 are on a coupon basis. To convert them to a zero coupon basis, a simple method can be applied.[4] We start by assuming that each interest rate is associated with a straight bullet bond issued at par and trading at par. We then line up the cash flows for the one-year bond and solve for r_1, the yield on a bond with only one cash flow. The cash flow is equal to the interest payment of 7.0972 plus the principal payment of 100:

$$100 = \frac{7.0972 + 100}{1 + r_1}$$

$$r_1 = 0.070972.$$

Table 9.3 Example yield to maturity

Maturity	Yield (%)	Maturity	Yield (%)
1 month	6.5779	2 year	7.3000
3 month	6.7549	3 year	7.4014
6 month	6.9084	4 year	7.5028
1 year	7.0972	5 year	7.6042

---

[4] See: Miron and Swannell (1990).

For the two-year interest rate, the cash flows are the interest payment of 7.3 the first year, and the interest payment of 7.3 the second year plus the principal repayment. Since the zero coupon interest rate for one year is known, only r_2 is unknown. We solve for r_2

$$100 = \frac{7.30}{1.070972} + \frac{7.30 + 100}{(1 + r_2)^2}$$

$$r_2 = 0.073074.$$

For the three-year bond we do the same thing. The interest payments are 7.4014 for each year plus the principal repayment at the end of the third year. With r_1 and r_2 known, we solve for r_3:

$$100 = \frac{7.4014}{1.070972} + \frac{7.4014}{(1.073074)^2} + \frac{7.4014 + 100}{(1 + r_3)^3}$$

$$r_3 = 0.074141.$$

The process can be applied to calculate r_4 and r_5. The set of zero coupon interest rates is given in Table 9.4.

From the zero coupon interest rates we can calculate the discount factors that will be applied to the cash flows on the swap. For example, carefully counting the days between 15 November and 15 December, the one-month discount factor is calculated as follows:

$$\frac{1}{(1.065779)^{30/365}} = 0.99478$$

and the three-month discount factor as:

$$\frac{1}{(1.067549)^{90/365}} = 0.98366.$$

Table 9.5 gives the whole set of discount factors:

The effective date for the swap was 15 September 2000 and the interest payments will be made every six months starting from that date – 15 March 2001, 15 September 2001, etc. – until the last payment on 15 September 2003. However, the evaluation of the swap is taking place on 15 November, two months later. Thus, the first cash flow will be paid in four months' time, the second cash flow in ten months' time, and so on, and the discount factors

Table 9.4 Example spot interest rates on a zero coupon basis

Maturity	Zero coupon rate (%)	Maturity	Zero coupon rate (%)
1 month	6.5779	2 year	7.3074
3 month	6.7549	3 year	7.4141
6 month	6.9084	4 year	7.5245
1 year	7.0972	5 year	7.6386

Table 9.5 Example discount factors

Maturity	Discount factors	Maturity	Discount factors
1 month	0.99478	2 year	0.86844
3 month	0.98366	3 year	0.80689
6 month	0.96742	4 year	0.74812
1 year	0.93373	5 year	0.69209

must be adjusted accordingly. The most straightforward method commonly used is simple linear interpolation, which assumes that the discount factors are proportional to time.[5] For example, the difference between the one-year and two-year discount factor is:

$$0.86844 - 0.93373 = -0.06529.$$

The proportion is 10/12, so the discount factor will be:

$$\frac{10}{12} \times (-0.06529) + 0.93373 = 0.87932.$$

Applying the appropriate proportions to all the discount factors, we obtain the factors shown in Table 9.6.

Now we have to determine the forward Libor rates reflected in the current market information in order to calculate the payments expected to be made on the variable leg of the swap.

In Chapter 18 we will show that the long-term interest rate can be calculated as a geometric average of the current short-term rate and the other short-term rates that are expected in the future. This makes it possible to write

$$(1 + {}_0r_{0,t})^t (1 + {}_tr_{t,T})^{T-t} = (1 + {}_0r_{0,T})^T \tag{9.1}$$

where ${}_0r_{0,t}$ is the spot interest rate from time 0 to time t on a zero coupon basis, ${}_tr_{t,T}$ is the spot interest rate on a zero coupon basis expected to prevail at time t on a loan from time t to time T and ${}_0r_{0,T}$ is the spot interest rate from time 0 to time T on a zero coupon basis. Taking the reciprocal of both sides gives the discount factors:

Table 9.6 Example modified discount factors

Maturity	Modified discount factors	Maturity	Modified discount factors
15/03/01	0.97855	15/09/02	0.87932
15/09/01	0.94496	15/03/03	0.84792
15/03/02	0.91197	15/09/03	0.81715

[5] Exponential interpolation, which supposes that the discount function is a negative exponential function of time, is another method commonly used. See Miron and Swannell (1990).

$$\frac{1}{(1+_0r_{0,t})^t} \frac{1}{(1+_tr_{t,T})^{T-t}} = \frac{1}{(1+_0r_{0,T})^T} \tag{9.2}$$

For example, if we want to calculate the discount factor expected to prevail between 15 March 2001 and 15 September 2001 we can use the information from Table 9.6 in Equation 9.2:

$$0.97855 \; \frac{1}{(1+_{\frac{120}{365}}r_{\frac{120}{365},\frac{304}{365}})^{T-t}} = 0.94496$$

where 0.97855 is the discount factor on the cash flow due on 15 March 2001 and 0.94496 is the discount factor on the cash flow due on 15 September 2001. There are 120 days between 15 November 2000 and 15 March 2001 and 184 days between 15 March 2001 and 15 September 2001. The subscripts around r represent the fractions of the year accounted for by these days. The variable

$$_{\frac{120}{365}}r_{\frac{120}{365},\frac{304}{365}}$$

is the expected zero coupon interest rate on a 184-day loan that will be contracted 120 days in the future. Rearranging the equation gives:

$$(1+_{\frac{120}{365}}r_{\frac{120}{365},\frac{304}{365}})^{T-t} = \frac{0.97855}{0.94496}$$

If we go back through the steps where we calculated the spot interest rates on a zero coupon basis, we see that this is equal to:

$$1 + (\text{Actual}/360) \times \text{Libor}.$$

The actual number of days is 184, so we can calculate Libor from the equation:

$$1 + \frac{184}{360} \times \text{Libor}_{15/03-15/09} = \frac{0.97855}{0.94496}$$

$$\text{Libor}_{15/03-15/09} = 0.069547.$$

Using this method for all the periods, we find the forward Libor rates in Table 9.7.

Now we have to construct the cash flows of the reference swap that will be used to evaluate the outstanding swap. The first step is to calculate the expected cash flows of the variable leg of the reference swap. For the payment due on March 15 2001 we can use the discount factor of 0.97855 for this date and its relation to Libor:

$$\frac{1}{1 + \frac{120}{360}\text{Libor}_{15/11-15/03}} = 0.97855.$$

Table 9.7 Estimated forward Libor rates

Period	Forward Libor %
15/03/01 to 15/09/01	6.9547
15/09/01 to 15/03/02	7.1949
15/03/02 to 15/09/02	7.2648
15/09/02 to 15/03/03	7.3250
15/03/03 to 15/09/03	7.3673

Solving for Libor yields:

$$\text{Libor}_{15/11-15/03} = 0.06576$$

6.576% is the Libor on a 120-day loan implied by the current market conditions. Thus, according to the Actual/360 formula in the swap agreement, the 15 March 2001 payment on the reference swap will be:

$$\text{USD } 5,000,000 \times 0.06576 \times \tfrac{120}{360} = \text{USD } 109,600.$$

For the payment due on 15 September 2001 we can use the forward Libor in Table 9.7 and the Actual/360 formula of the swap agreement:

$$\text{USD } 5,000,000 \times 0.069547 \times \tfrac{184}{360} = \text{USD } 177,731.$$

All the subsequent payments can be calculated in the same way. Table 9.8 shows the variable leg cash flows for the reference swap.

If the reference swap is correctly priced, the present value of the variable leg cash flows will be equal to the present value of the fixed rate cash flows. Thus, remembering that the fixed rate interest payment is equal to

$$\text{USD } 5,000,000 \times \text{Fixed rate} \times \text{Actual/360,}$$

Table 9.8 Variable leg cash flows of the reference swap

Maturity	Cash flows of the variable leg (USD)	Present value (USD)
15/03/01	109,600	107,249
15/09/01	177,731	167,949
15/03/02	180,872	164,950
15/09/02	185,656	163,251
15/03/03	185,158	156,999
15/09/03	188,275	153,848
Total	**1,027,292**	**914,246**

we can calculate the fixed rate that will yield this equality by applying the appropriate discount factor to each payment and solving for r, the fixed interest rate:

$$\text{USD } 5,000,000 \times r \times [(\tfrac{304}{360} \times 0.94496) + (\tfrac{365}{360} \times 0.87932) + \tfrac{365}{360} \times 0.81715] = \text{USD } 914,246$$

$$r = 0.0726168.$$

The fixed interest payment on the reference swap is

$$\text{USD } 5,000,000 \times 0.0726168 \times 365/360 = \text{USD } 368,127.$$

Since the first payment period corresponds to only 304 days from 15 November 2000 to 15 September 2001, the first payment is equal to:

$$304/365 \times \text{USD } 368,127 = \text{USD } 306,605.$$

The value of the outstanding swap will be equal to the present value of the difference between its cash flows and the cash flows of the reference swap. We know that the fixed interest payment of the outstanding swap is equal to:

$$\text{USD } 5,000,000 \times 365/360 \times 0.075 = \text{USD } 380,208.$$

Except for the first payment, the variable leg cash flows of the outstanding swap are the same as those of the reference swap. The interest for the first payment has been accruing since 15 September 2000 at the rate of 6.4%, so on 15 March 2001 it will be equal to:

$$\text{USD } 5,000,000 \times 181/360 \times 0.064 = \text{USD } 160,889.$$

Table 9.9 compares the cash flows of the two swaps.

Taking the difference between the cash flows of the outstanding swap and the reference swap and applying the appropriate discount factors yields the values shown in Table 9.10.

Citicorp is the payer of variable interest and the receiver of fixed interest. Thus, the value of its position is USD 39,858. If Caswell wants to reverse its position and undo the swap, it will have to pay Citicorp USD 39,858.

Table 9.9 Comparison of cash flows (in US dollars) of the outstanding swap and the reference swap from the perspective of the fixed rate receiver

Maturity	Outstanding swap		Reference swap	
	Fixed	Variable	Fixed	Variable
15/03/01		−160,889		−109,600
15/09/01	+380,208	−177,731	+306,605	−177,731
15/03/02		−180,872		−180,872
15/09/02	+380,208	−185,656	+368,127	−185,656
15/03/03		−185,158		−185,158
15/09/03	+380,208	−188,275	+368,127	−188,275

Table 9.10 Present value (in US dollars) of cash flow differences between the outstanding swap and the reference swap

Maturity	Difference in cash flows (outstanding minus reference)	Present value
15/03/01	−51,289	−50,189
15/09/01	+73,603	+69,552
15/03/02		
15/09/02	+12,081	+10,623
15/03/03		
15/09/03	+12,081	+ 9,872
Total		**+39,858**

In fact, pricing the outstanding swap is even less complicated than the foregoing example suggests. Construction of the reference swap is not really necessary. The same result could have been obtained by taking the difference between the present values of the fixed leg and the variable leg of the outstanding swap as we have done in Table 9.11. However, since interest rate swaps are quoted in relation to the fixed interest rate applicable to the fixed leg of the swap, construction of the reference swap is necessary for calculating the fixed interest rate that reflects the prevailing market conditions as of 15 November 2000.

Pricing currency swaps

In a currency swap, each leg of the initial swap is denominated in a different currency. In the Caswell case, for example, the fixed leg might have been denominated in Swiss francs and the variable leg in US dollars. Finding the value of a currency swap follows the same procedure outlined above. The difference is that it requires estimating the present values of each leg based on the interest rate structure in each currency. The repayment of the swap

Table 9.11 Present values of the cash flows of the outstanding swap

Maturity	Present value of the fixed leg cash flows (USD)	Present value of the variable leg cash flows (USD)
15/03/01		157,438
15/09/01	359,281	167,948
15/03/02		164,950
15/09/02	334,325	163,251
15/03/03		156,999
15/09/03	310,687	153,849
Total	**1,004,293**	**964,435**
Difference		**39,858**

amount at maturity creates no complication. It is treated as just another cash flow. Once the present values of both legs have been found, one of the two present values is converted into the other currency at the prevailing spot exchange rate. The value of the swap is the difference between this converted value and the present value of the other leg.

Risk and exposure of swap transactions

The rapid development of swap products and their relative complexity raise many questions about the risks they present. From the standpoint of a bank the risks vary according to whether the bank is an arranger or a principal. As an arranger the bank simply brings the two parties together and assists in the negotiations. There is no risk involved. As a principal in the transaction, however, it assumes a number of specific risks, the most important of which are credit risk, market risk and mismatch risk.

Credit risk reflects the counterparty's credit standing and its ability to meet its obligations in the swap agreement. As an intermediary between the two principal counterparties, the bank assumes the credit risk of both principals. **Market risk** reflects the difficulty in reversing positions due to market illiquidity. Longer maturities have thinner liquidity and are more difficult to dispose of in the market. Furthermore, longer maturities are more sensitive to interest rate changes (see Chapter 18 on duration) and are also associated with greater uncertainty about the behavior of interest rates in the future. **Mismatch risk** reflects the difficulty of precise matching in terms of payment dates and amounts when laying off positions in the market.

Of the three major risks, credit risk is the most important. Credit risk in swap transactions differs considerably from credit risk in traditional loan transactions, because swaps are not exposed to the full extent of the amounts exchanged. They are exposed only to the possible gain or loss involved in reversing the swap in case of non-performance by one of the swap's counterparties. The magnitude of the exposure depends on the market conditions concerning interest rates, exchange rates and liquidity at the time of default. Thus, in the case of a bank intermediated transaction, the banks exposure to non-payment by one party is not the principal amount due. It is the cost of setting up a position to offset its obligations to the non-defaulting party.

Interest rate swaps

As we saw in the pricing of an interest rate swap, the risk is associated with variations in the value of the swap due to movements of fixed interest rates over the life of the transaction. The same is true in the case of default by one party to the swap. If one party ceases its payments, the bank will stop its payments to the defaulting party. The exposure to the bank is the cost of entering into a new matched position vis-à-vis the non-defaulting party. It will depend on the interest rate differential between the current and contract fixed rate of interest at the time of default. The only floating rate that is affected is the short-term rate up to the end of the ongoing calculation period at the time of the default.

Going back to the pricing example discussed earlier, suppose that Caswell had defaulted and Citicorp, as intermediary, had a position with another company where it paid fixed and received floating interest. When Caswell defaults on its fixed interest payments, Citicorp will stop its floating rate payments but, to offset its interest rate risk, it wants to replace the Caswell side of the swap. The cost to Citicorp for replacing the swap arrangement it had with Caswell would be the USD 39,858 value of the outstanding swap. In other words, Citicorp lost the cash flows associated with the Caswell deal that were worth USD 39,858 and replaced them with a series of cash flows with a net present value of zero.

Defaults can generate gains as well as losses. Suppose that instead of Caswell, the variable rate payer had defaulted. The cost of replacing that side of the swap would be a gain of USD 39,858. Citicorp would effectively be replacing a series of cash flows with a negative net present value of USD 39,858 with another series of cash flows with a net present value of zero.

Several conclusions can be drawn. First of all, the bank will realize a gain or a loss depending on which party defaults, when the default occurs and the level of fixed interest rates at the time. Secondly, as the maturity of the swap reduces, exposure decreases. This is because the gain or loss is derived from the current and contract fixed interest differential. A shorter maturity means there will be fewer fixed payments and, therefore, reduced exposure.

Currency swaps

Besides risk arising from fluctuations in the interest rate, currency swaps are exposed to risk resulting from variations in the exchange rate. The magnitude of the exposure depends on the type of instruments that are swapped. Fixed-to-fixed swaps are exposed to interest rate changes in both currencies as well as to changes in the exchange rate. Fixed-to-floating currency swaps are exposed to interest rate changes in the fixed rate currency and to changes in the exchange rate. There is little or no exposure to changes in the floating rate. Floating-to-floating currency swaps are exposed only in terms of changes in the exchange rate. Fixed-to-fixed currency swaps, then, generate maximum exposure.

Consider a fixed-to-fixed currency swap on a notional amount of USD 50 million where the bank pays fixed dollars of 10% to A and receives fixed Swiss francs of 5% from A. From B the bank receives fixed dollars at 10% and pays fixed francs at 5%. If A defaults, the bank will have to borrow USD 50 million at the prevailing interest rate, buy francs at the current spot rate and invest the proceeds in fixed francs for the remaining life of the swap. If the prevailing dollar interest rate is lower than the contract dollar rate of 10%, the bank gains. In the opposite case the bank loses. If the dollar has appreciated since the contract's effective date, the bank will gain. If it has depreciated the bank will lose. If the prevailing Swiss franc interest rate is higher than the contract rate of 5%, the bank gains. If it is lower, the bank loses. If B defaults, the bank will borrow francs, buy dollars spot with the proceeds and lend dollars for the remaining life of the swap. The bank gains if the franc rate is lower than 5% and loses if it is higher. The bank gains if the dollar has depreciated and loses if it has appreciated. The bank gains if the dollar rate is higher than 10% and loses if it is lower.

The magnitude of the gain or the loss thus depends on which party defaults, when the default occurs, the levels of US dollar and Swiss franc interest rates, and the prevailing exchange rate.

Hybrid or package options

So-called hybrid options are packages or portfolios of other standard vanilla options. As such they can be priced with the pricing formulas used to price standard options.

Caps

A **cap** is an option offered by financial institutions in the over-the-counter market that permits hedging against a rise in the interest rate, the exchange rate or a commodity price. It is designed to provide insurance against the price of the underlying asset rising above a certain level, known as the cap price. It is similar to a swap in that it concerns a series of cash flows. In the swap, the floating price is reset periodically according to a predefined formula. The time between resets is called the "tenor", which could be monthly, quarterly, biannually, etc. If, for example, the tenor is monthly, the floating price will be reset every month. The cap differs from a swap in that a payment will be made only if the floating price rises above the cap price.

Consider a company with a floating rate loan, whose interest payments are based on three-month Libor. Rather than purchasing a swap to hedge against a rise in Libor, the company could purchase a cap with the same reset conditions. On each reset date the company would compare the floating price with the cap price. If it is lower than the cap price, the option would not be exercised and the interest rate on the loan would be determined by the spot Libor rate. If, however, Libor is higher than the cap price, the company will exercise the option and receive the difference between the two prices adjusted for the three-month duration multiplied by the size of the contract (the principal amount). Suppose, for example, that the cap rate is 6%, the principal amount is USD 5 million and Libor is 7% on the first reset date. Remembering that the tenor is three months or 25% of one year,[6] the payout would be

$$0.25 \times (0.07 - 0.06) \times \text{USD } 5,000,000 = \text{USD } 12,500.$$

It is important to note that the payout does not occur on the reset date. It occurs three months later to reflect the fact that interest is paid at the end of the borrowing period. On each reset date the same procedure would apply. If Libor is below the cap rate of 6%, the option is not exercised. If it is above, the option is exercised and the payout is calculated as above.

The cap as a series of call options

From the foregoing example we can see that the cap is a contract composed of a series of call options where:

X = cap price
S_t = the price of the underlying asset at time t
Q_i = the amount of the contract (if it is on interest rates it represents the notional principal multiplied by the day count factor)
F_{t,T_i} = the forward price of S at time t on a contract with maturity T_i.

Each individual option is called a **caplet**. On the exercise dates $T_1, T_2 \ldots T_n$ the payout will be:

$$Q_i Max(S_{T_i} - X, 0); i = 1, 2 \ldots n \tag{9.3}$$

To value each caplet we assume risk neutrality so that $E(S_{T_i}) = F_{t,T_i}$ and that S_{T_i} has a lognormal distribution.

$$C_t^i = Q_i e^{-r(T_i - t)} EMax(S_{T_i} - X, 0) \tag{9.4}$$

We then compute the true expectation (see Chapter 8, Appendix 8.3) and make the substitution $E(S_{T_i}) = F_{t,T_i}$. This gives the Black formula:

$$C_t^i = Q_i e^{-r(T_i - t)}[F_{t,T_i} N(d_1) - X N(d_2)] \tag{9.5}$$

[6] In practice, the calculation uses the exact number of days between the reset dates.

where

$$d_1 = \frac{\ln(F_{t,T_i}/X) + \sigma^2/2(T_i - t)}{\sigma\sqrt{T_i - t}}$$

$$d_2 = \frac{\ln(F_{t,T_i}/X) - \sigma^2/2(T_i - t)}{\sigma\sqrt{T_i - t}} = d_1 - \sigma\sqrt{T_i - t}$$

The total value of the cap is

$$Cap = \sum_{i=1}^{n} C_t^i \tag{9.6}$$

Suppose, for example, that a company purchases a contract that caps the interest rate on a USD 5 million loan for the next five years at 6%. The first reset date is in three months. To price the first caplet we have the following information:

X = the quarterly compounded cap rate = 6%
$F_{0,T}$ = the quarterly compounded forward rate on a three-month period starting in three months = 5.5%
Q = the notional principal multiplied by the day count factor = USD 5,000,000 × 0.25
r = the current continuously compounded six-month interest rate = 6%
σ = 20%.

To price this caplet we first calculate

$$d_1 = \frac{\ln(0.055/0.06) + 0.04/2 \times (0.25)}{0.20 \times \sqrt{0.25}} = -0.8201$$

$$d_2 = d_1 - 0.1 = -0.9201.$$

We then apply Equation 9.5:

USD 5,000,000 × 0.25 × 0.9704 × [0.055 × $N(-0.8201)$ − 0.06 × $N(-0.9201)$] = USD 736.9.

Floors

A **floor** is similar to a cap except that it is designed to provide insurance against the price of the underlying asset falling below a certain level, known as the floor price. Thus, the floor is equivalent to a series of put options, called **floorlets**. Using the same assumptions and notation as in the previous sub-section, each floorlet can be valued with the following equation:

$$p_t^i = Q_i e^{-r(T_i - t)}[XN(-d_2) - F_{t,T_i} N(-d_1)] \tag{9.7}$$

where d_1 and d_2 are defined as above.

The value of the floor is:

$$Floor = \sum_{i=1}^{n} p_t^i \tag{9.8}$$

Collars

A **collar** is an instrument designed to guarantee that the price of the underlying asset always lies between two given levels. A collar consists of a long position in the cap and a short position in the floor when hedging against price rises. It consists of a short position in the cap and a long position in the floor when hedging against price falls. A collar is usually constructed so that the price of the cap is initially equal to the price of the floor. In this case the initial cash outlay of entering into the collar is zero. Although there is no cash outlay, the collar is not free. The cost comes in the potential gains that have been surrendered in the option that was sold.

Swaptions

European options on swaps, or **swaptions**, are another increasingly popular innovation in the international financial and commodities markets. They give the holder the right to enter into a swap at a given time in the future. If it is a call swaption, the holder acquires the right to pay the fixed price. In a put swaption the holder acquires the right to pay the floating price.

Most swaptions refer to options on interest rate swaps. As an example of how a swaption can be used, consider the treasurer of a company who knows that in six months time he will have to finance a large investment with five-year floating rate notes but will want to swap into fixed interest rate payments. To guarantee the fixed interest rate he will have to pay, the treasurer could enter into a swaption giving him the right to receive six-month Libor and pay UST 6.25% + 75 bp for a total fixed rate of 7% for five years starting in six months. If the fixed rate for a five-year interest rate swap in six months is higher than 7% he will exercise the option and obtain the swap for 7%. If it is lower he will let the swaption expire and enter into the swap on the current terms.

Swaptions can also be useful for hedging on the commodities markets. Consider a manufacturer bidding on a long-term supply contract. The contract is to begin in six months and last for three years. If it is signed, it will generate the need for 40 000 tons of aluminum per quarter. The current price is USD 1500 per ton and the company feels that it can make a competitive bid based on this price. However, if the price rises much above USD 1500 the contract will become unprofitable. The company could organize a deferred swap (a swap that begins on a future date) with its bank, but if it is not successful in its bid the swap will not be needed. Furthermore, the price of aluminum might also fall. If it does, the company would like to take advantage of the lower price. Thus, it decides to purchase a call option on a swap on 40 000 tons of aluminum per quarter with the fixed price equal to USD 1500. If the price of aluminum has risen in six months time, the company will exercise the option and enter into the swap with the fixed price equal to USD 1500. If, however, the price has fallen, the option will not be exercised and the company can negotiate a swap based on the improved market conditions.

Valuation of swaptions

The swap price for a given maturity at a given time is the fixed price that would be exchanged for the floating price in a newly issued swap. Consider a swaption where we have the right to pay X and receive S on a swap that will last n years beginning in T_0 years. There are m payments per year and the amount of the swap is Q. For an interest rate swap, Q is equal to the notional amount of the swap divided by the number of payments per year:

$$Q = \frac{notional\ principal}{m}.$$

On the exercise date at time T_0, the contracted swap price X will be compared with the swap price that could be obtained on a similar swap initiated at that time. If it is higher than X, the option will be exercised and the holder obtains a swap with the rate equal to X. If it is lower than X, the option will expire worthless and the holder will negotiate the swap at the lower swap price. Thus, the holder of the swaption owns a series of options where the payoff is calculated from the value of the variable at time T but where the payoff is made at a later date determined by the reset dates. Let T_0 represent the date on which the payoff is calculated, $T_1, T_2 \ldots T_{mn}$ the other dates on which the payments are made (a payment may or may not be made at T_0) and X_{T_0} the swap price on the date when the payoff is calculated. The expected payoff from each call is discounted from T_i rather than T_0 and each call can be evaluated as:

$$C_t^i = Qe^{-r(T_i-t)}EMax(X_{T_0} - X,0) \tag{9.9}$$

Substituting the futures price at time t for delivery at time T_0 for $E(X_{T_0})$, $F_{t,T_0} = E(X_{T_0})$, we can evaluate Equation 9.9 using the Black formula on a futures contract:

$$C_t^i = Qe^{-r(T_i-t)}[F_{t,T_0}N(d_{1F}) - XN(d_{2F})] \tag{9.10}$$

$$d_{1F} = \frac{\ln(F_{t,T_0}/X) + \sigma^2/2(T_0-t)}{\sigma\sqrt{T_0-t}}$$

$$d_{2F} = \frac{\ln(F_{t,T_0}/X) - \sigma^2/2(T_0-t)}{\sigma\sqrt{T_0-t}} = d_{1F} - \sigma\sqrt{T_0-t}.$$

The total value of the call swaption is:

$$\sum_{i=0}^{mn} C_t^i = Q[F_{t,T_0}N(d_{1F}) - XN(d_{2F})]\sum_{T_i=T_0}^{T_{mn}} e^{-r(T_i-t)} \tag{9.11}$$

As an example, suppose the Libor yield curve is flat at a continuously compounded rate of 7% per year. The discrete rate is thus equal to $e^{0.07} = 0.0725$. Consider a swaption that gives the buyer the right to pay 7.25% in a three-year swap starting in one year. The volatility of the swap rate is 20%, payments are made every six months and the notional principal is USD 100 million.

X = 7.25%
S_0 = the current swap rate = 7.25%
m = 2
Q = the amount of the contract = USD 100 million/2 = USD 50 million
σ = 20%
$F_{0,1}$ = 7.25% (because the yield curve is flat).

From Equation 9.11 the total value of the call swaption is:

$$\sum_{i=1}^{3} C_0^i = \frac{USD\ 100}{2} \times [0.0725N(d_{1F}) - 0.0725e^{-0.07}N(d_{2F})] \times$$

$$[e^{-1.5\times0.07} + e^{-2\times0.07} + e^{-2.5\times0.07} + e^{-3\times0.07} + e^{-3.5\times0.07} + e^{-4\times0.07}]$$

$$= \text{USD } 50 \times 0.00577 \times 4.9582 = \text{USD } 1.43 \text{ million.}$$

The equivalent price of a put swaption (the right to receive the fixed price) can be calculated in the same way. The value of each put is:

$$p_t^i = Qe^{-r(T_i - t)}[XN(-d_{2F}) - F_{t,T_0}N(-d_{1F})] \tag{9.12}$$

and the total value of the put swaption is:

$$\sum_{i=0}^{mn} p_t^i = Q[XN(-d_2) - F_{t,T_0}N(-d_1)] \sum_{T_i=T_0}^{T_{min}} e^{-r(T_i - t)} \tag{9.13}$$

Consider the producer of 10 000 barrels of oil per month who purchases a put swaption on his output with a maturity date of one year. The swap involves payouts on the first day of months 14, 15 and 16 (there is no payout at T_0 = the first day of month 13). The yield curve is flat at the continuously compounded rate of 5%. The other pertinent information is:

X = USD 25 per barrel
S_0 = the current spot price = USD 25.
Q = the amount of the contract = 10 000 barrels
σ = 20%
c = the convenience yield = 2%
k = proportional storage costs = 2%
$F_{0,1}$ = $e^{(0.05+0.02-0.02)\times 1} \times S_0$ = USD 26.28.

From Equation 9.13 the value of the put swaption is:

$$\sum_{i=1}^{3} p_0^i = 10\,000 \times \text{USD } 1.46545 \times \sum_{T_i=1.08333}^{1.25} e^{-0.05 \times T_i} = \text{USD } 28,303.16.$$

Exotic options

Exotic options, which are sometimes referred to as second generation options, can generally be defined as standard options modified in one way or another to serve a special purpose or specific client need. There are many kinds of exotic options. Some, such as Asian options, barrier options, lookback options and forward start options, depend on the path of the underlying security over the life of the option. These are called "path dependent". Others depend on correlations with other assets such as spread options, exchange options, quanto options and basket options, to mention only a few.[7] As well as these, there are binary options, compound options, chooser options, power options, rainbow options and many others. In this section we will look at some of the most widely used exotic options and show how they can be priced.

---

[7] Although most exotic options are the exclusive preserve of the OTC market, some are popular enough to trade on the exchanges. The American Stock Exchange, for example, trades quantos and the Chicago Mercantile Exchange trades spread options.

Spread options

Spread options are options written on the difference between two indices, prices or rates. Where interest rates are concerned, for example, one popular spread is a long-term Treasury rate minus a shorter-term Treasury rate. The popular yield curve options are written on two-year to ten-year, two-year to 30-year, and ten-year to 30-year spreads. Another popular spread is three-month Libor over three-month US Treasury bills. Where commodities are concerned, one popular spread option is the spread between refined and crude oil prices. It can be used by oil refiners to hedge their risks on gross profits. To hedge against the spread falling and thereby squeezing profits the refiner could purchase puts. Alternatively, to hedge against missing out on a rise in the spread the refiner could purchase calls.

Given that some spreads can take negative as well as positive values, pricing spread options can be complicated. When the spread is liable to take on negative as well as positive values, Monte Carlo simulations or numerical methods are often used to price the spread option. However, when the spread is always positive, such as the spread on the difference between Libor and the equivalent US Treasury bill rate or the difference between refined and crude oil prices, it is reasonable to assume that it is lognormal at the option's maturity. If this is the case, the spread can be considered as an individual asset price, albeit an imaginary one, and Equations 8.17 and 8.18 can be used to evaluate the option's value. This method for valuing spread options is called the one-factor model.[8]

Asian options

Asian options, which are also called average price or average rate options, are path-dependent options, whose payoff depends on the average price of an asset, an index or rate calculated over a predetermined part of the option's life. Since an average price is generally less volatile than the price itself, Asian options are normally cheaper than corresponding vanilla options.[9] Consequently, they offer reasonably priced hedging instruments adapted to periodic cash flows resulting from commercial transactions. For example, a company with regular cash flows in foreign currency spread evenly over the year is likely to be interested in ensuring that the average exchange rate is below some level. An Asian call option can achieve this more cheaply and effectively than a series of vanilla call options on each cash flow.

The two types of Asian options are the average price option and the average strike option. For the average price option the strike price is fixed and the payoff depends on the average price of the underlying instrument. Payoffs for average price options are $Max(S_{ave} - X, 0)$ for a call and $Max(X - S_{ave}, 0)$ for a put. For the average strike option, the strike price is determined by the average price of the underlying asset. Thus, a treasurer with regular purchases of foreign currency can purchase a call to guarantee that the average rate he pays will not be higher than the strike price. If he has regular sales of foreign currency, he can purchase a put to guarantee that his average price will be no lower than the strike price.

---

[8] The one-factor model has the limitation in that the correlation coefficient between the two assets involved in the spread does not play an explicit role in the pricing formula. Another limitation is that the volatilities of the individual spread assets do not figure explicitly in the pricing formula. Thus, it is not possible to determine the sensitivity of the option price to changes in the individual volatilities. To overcome these shortcomings, two-factor models have been developed that use numerical methods for their solution.

[9] Because the payoff depends on an average, these options are also less susceptible to possible spot price manipulation on the settlement date.

Payoffs for average strike options are $Max(S_T - S_{ave}, 0)$ for a call and $Max(S_{ave} - S_T, 0)$ for a put. Average strike calls can be used to guarantee that over a given time period the average price paid for an asset in frequent trading is not greater than the final price. Average strike puts can be used to guarantee that over a given time period the average price received for an asset in frequent trading is not less than the final price.

Kemna and Vorst (1990) developed a pricing formula for average price options when the underlying asset is lognormally distributed and the average price in question is a geometric average. The key to the solution is that a geometric average of a set of lognormally distributed variables is also lognormally distributed. In a risk-neutral world, the probability distribution of the geometric average over a predetermined time period is the same as the distribution of the stock price at the end of the period with a growth rate equal to $\frac{1}{2}(r - \delta - \sigma^2/6)$ and volatility equal to $\sigma/\sqrt{3}$. Thus, average price options can be valued using Equations 8.17 and 8.18 with $(r - \delta)$ and σ replaced by $\frac{1}{2}(r - \delta - \sigma^2/6)$ and $\sigma/\sqrt{3}$ respectively. This gives[10]

$$C = S_t e^{-(r+\delta+\sigma^2/6)(T-t)/2} N(d_{1A}) - X e^{-r(T-t)} N(d_{2A}) \qquad (9.14)$$

and

$$p = X e^{-r(T-t)} N(-d_{2A}) - S_t e^{-(r+\delta+\sigma^2/6)(T-t)/2} N(-d_{1A}) \qquad (9.15)$$

where

$$d_{1A} = \frac{\ln\dfrac{S_t}{X} + (r - \delta + \dfrac{\sigma^2}{6})\dfrac{(T-t)}{2}}{\sigma\sqrt{\dfrac{T-t}{3}}}$$

$$d_{2A} = \frac{\ln\dfrac{S_t}{X} + (r - \delta - \dfrac{\sigma^2}{2})\dfrac{(T-t)}{2}}{\sigma\sqrt{\dfrac{T-t}{3}}}.$$

In practice, most Asian options are on arithmetic rather than geometric averages. Because the distribution of the arithmetic average of a set of lognormal distributions does not have analytically tractable properties, there are no analytical pricing formulas for arithmetic averages. It is, however, approximately lognormal, which makes it possible to generate an approximate analytical solution. One methodology involves calculating the first two moments of the probability distribution of the arithmetic average in a risk-neutral world and then assuming that the distribution is lognormal.[11] The option can then be priced as an option on a futures contract in Equations 8.21 and 8.22. Another methodology involves calculating an approximation coefficient that adjusts for the difference between the arithmetic and geometric means.[12]

---

[10] The dividend payout is equal to $r - \dfrac{1}{2}(r - \delta - \dfrac{\sigma^2}{6}) = (r + \delta + \sigma^2/6)/2$.

[11] See Turnbull, and Wakeman (1991). In this section we follow Hull (2000), p.p. 468–469.

[12] See Zhang (1998), p.p. 135–154.

To give an application of the moment methodology mentioned above, consider a just-issued Asian option with maturity at time T based on the arithmetic average from 0 to T with n observations. The first moment M_1 and the second moment M_2 of the average in a risk-neutral world calculated between time 0 and T are equal to[13]

$$M_1 = \frac{1}{n} \sum_{i=1}^{n} F_{0,T_i}$$ (9.16)

and[14]

$$M_2 = \frac{1}{n^2} \left[\sum_{i=1}^{n} F_{0,T_i}^2 e^{\sigma_i^2 T_i} + 2 \sum_{i<j} F_{0,T_i} F_{0,T_j} e^{\sigma_i^2 T_i} \right]$$ (9.17)

The variance of the arithmetic average can thus be approximated as:

$$\hat{\sigma}^2 = \frac{1}{T} \ln \frac{M_2}{M_1^2}$$ (9.18)

The option can be priced using Equations 8.21 and 8.22 where

$$F_{t,T} = \frac{M_1}{n} \text{ and } \sigma = \hat{\sigma}.$$

Basket options

Basket options are written on portfolios or "baskets" of risky assets. The payoff of a basket option depends on the value of a portfolio of assets. Because the assets are imperfectly correlated, basket options have lower volatility and therefore cost less than straight options. They also make it possible to worry about the forest, so to speak, without worrying about

---

[13] The equivalent moments for continuous sampling are

$$M_1 = \frac{e^{(r-\delta)T} - 1}{(r-\delta)T} S_0$$

and

$$M_2 = \frac{2 e^{[2(r-\delta)+\sigma^2]T} S_0^2}{(r-\delta-\sigma^2)(2r-2\delta+\sigma^2)T^2} + \frac{2 S_0^2}{(r-\delta)T^2} \left[\frac{1}{2(r-\delta)+\sigma^2} - \frac{e^{(r-\delta)T}}{r-\delta+\sigma^2} \right].$$

[14] Remember that

$$V = \sum_{i=1}^{n} S_{T_i} \text{ and } V^2 = \sum_{i=1}^{n} \sum_{j=1}^{n} S_{T_i} S_{T_j}. \quad E(S_{T_i} S_{T_j}) = F_{0,T_i} F_{0,T_j} e^{\rho_{ij}\sigma_i\sigma_j \sqrt{T_i T_j}}.$$

When

$$i < j, \rho_{ij} = \sigma_i \sqrt{T_i} / \sigma_j \sqrt{T_j}$$

so that

$$E(S_{T_i} S_{T_j}) = F_{0,T_i} F_{0,T_j} e^{\rho_{ij}\sigma_i T_i}.$$

each individual tree. Index options, for example, are a form of basket option. Thus, they are popular with fund managers managing portfolios containing many stocks or company treasurers with cash flows in numerous currencies. In fact, index options are the most actively traded options on most exchanges. Basket options can also be useful for manufacturers and processors that use a wide range of raw materials in their products. Food processors, for example, make regular purchases of a wide range of agricultural products such as corn, oats, wheat, barley, soybeans, meat, cocoa, coffee, sugar and orange juice. The purchase of a basket call hedges against a rise in the cost of the basket and the purchase of a basket put hedges against a fall in its price.

Basket options can be priced in a manner similar to the Asian option methodology explained in the preceding sub-section. The methodology involves calculating the first two moments of the probability distribution of the value of the basket at maturity in a risk-neutral world and then assuming that the distribution is lognormal. The option can then be priced as an option on a futures contract using Equations 8.21 and 8.22.

Let V represent the value of the basket. Then

$$M_1 = \sum_{i=1}^{n} F_i \tag{9.19}$$

where F_i is the futures price of the ith asset maturing at time T. We also know that:

$$V^2 = \sum_{i=1}^{n} \sum_{j=1}^{n} S_i S_j.$$

From the properties of the lognormal distribution:

$$E(S_i S_j) = F_i F_j e^{\rho_{ij}\sigma_i\sigma_j T}.$$

Using the relation

$$\rho_{ij} = \sigma_i \sqrt{T} / \sigma_j \sqrt{T}$$

gives

$$M_2 = \sum_{i=1}^{n} F_i^2 e^{\sigma_i^2 T} + 2\sum_{i<j} F_i F_j e^{\sigma_i^2 T} \tag{9.20}$$

Consequently, the variance of the basket can be approximated as

$$\hat{\sigma}^2 = \frac{1}{T}\ln\frac{M_2}{M_1^2} \tag{9.21}$$

Lookback options

A **lookback option** is an option the payoff on which depends on the maximum or minimum price of the underlying asset within the life of the option. For a call the payoff is $Max[S_T - S_{min}, 0]$ and for a put it is $Max[S_{max} - S_T, 0]$. For competitive purposes, it is often desirable for a manufacturer or a processor to purchase commodity inputs at the lowest price or, for commodity producers, to sell at the highest price. For this reason, the underlying asset in lookback options is often a commodity. Purchasing a lookback call option lets the holder pay the lowest price for the commodity over the life of the option.

Purchasing a lookback put option lets the holder sell the commodity at the highest price over the life of the option.

Goldman, Sosin and Gatto (1979) developed a lookback pricing formula that Garman (1989) extended to currency options. The price of a European lookback call at time zero is

$$C = S_0 e^{-\delta T} N(d_{1LBC}) - S_0 e^{-\delta T} \frac{\sigma^2}{2(r-\delta)} N(-d_{1LBC}) - S_{\min} e^{-rT} \left[N(d_{2LBC}) - \frac{\sigma^2}{2(r-\delta)} e^{y_{LBC}} N(-d_{3LBC}) \right] \quad (9.22)$$

where

$$d_{1LBC} = \frac{\ln(\frac{S_0}{S_{\min}}) + (r - \delta + \frac{\sigma^2}{2})T}{\sigma\sqrt{T}}$$

$$d_{2LBC} = \frac{\ln(\frac{S_0}{S_{\min}}) + (r - \delta - \frac{\sigma^2}{2})T}{\sigma\sqrt{T}}$$

$$d_{3LBC} = \frac{\ln(\frac{S_0}{S_{\min}}) + (-r + \delta + \frac{\sigma^2}{2})T}{\sigma\sqrt{T}}$$

$$y_{LBC} = \frac{2(r - \delta - \sigma^2/2)\ln(S_0/S_{\min})}{\sigma^2}$$

and

$$p = S_{\max} e^{-rT} \left[N(d_{1LBp}) - \frac{\sigma^2}{2(r-\delta)} e^{y_{LBp}} N(-d_{3LBp}) \right] + S_0 e^{-\delta T} \frac{\sigma^2}{2(r-\delta)} N(-d_{2LBp}) - S_0 e^{-\delta T} N(d_{2LBp}) \quad (9.23)$$

where

$$d_{1LBp} = \frac{\ln(\frac{S_{\max}}{S_0}) + (-r + \delta + \frac{\sigma^2}{2})T}{\sigma\sqrt{T}}$$

$$d_{2LBp} = \frac{\ln(\frac{S_{\max}}{S_0}) + (-r + \delta - \frac{\sigma^2}{2})T}{\sigma\sqrt{T}}$$

$$d_{3LBp} = \frac{\ln(\frac{S_{\max}}{S_0}) + (r - \delta - \frac{\sigma^2}{2})T}{\sigma\sqrt{T}}$$

$$y_{LBC} = - \frac{2(r - \delta - \sigma^2/2)\ln(S_{\max}/S_0)}{\sigma^2}$$

To derive the foregoing formulas, it is assumed that the asset price is observed continuously. In fact, as with Asian options, the price is sensitive to how frequently the price is observed for computing the maximums and minimums. To account for this, these formulas can be adjusted to take the observation frequency into account.[15]

---

[15] See Broadie, Glasserman and Kou (1998).

Binary options

Binary options, also known as digital options, are options with discontinuous payoffs. The payoff is usually either a fixed amount of cash (cash or nothing option), an asset (asset or nothing option), or the difference between the price of a given asset and a pre-specified level, which can be different from the strike price (gap option). Binary options can be useful for hedging ordinary swaps or "exotic" swaps, which possess knock-in or knock-out properties that depend on whether the price of the underlying commodity exceeds a pre-specified level on some pre-specified date. Consider, for example, a swap based on Libor. There are many exotic swaps in the market with knock-in or knock-out properties, depending on whether Libor exceeds a given trigger rate on a pre-specified date. In these swaps Libor is like the measurement instrument in a correlation binary option and the floating leg can be considered as the payoff asset.

Cash or nothing options

Cash or nothing options pay a fixed amount of cash if the price of the underlying ends up above the strike price for a call or below the strike price for a put. If it ends up below the strike price for a call or above the strike price for a put, it pays nothing. Although a straight vanilla call has more upside potential, a cash or nothing call might be preferred to a straight vanilla call if the price of the underlying is expected to go above a certain level but not by much. By the same token, a cash or nothing put would be purchased by someone expecting only a modest fall in the price of the underlying. Cash or nothing options are useful for hedging contracts that have a payout that depends on whether or not a specified level is reached.

Pricing a cash or nothing is straightforward. From Appendix 8.3 in Chapter 8 we know that in a risk-neutral world the probability that the asset price ends up above the strike price is $N(d_2)$. The probability that it ends up below the strike price is $N(-d_2)$. Thus, if the cash amount is equal to Q, the value of a cash or nothing call is $Qe^{-r(T-t)}N(d_2)$ and the value of a cash or nothing put is $Qe^{-r(T-t)}N(-d_2)$.

Gap options

Gap options pay the difference between an asset price and a pre-specified level (the level is different from the strike price) if the asset price is above the strike price for a call and below the strike price for a put. Otherwise it pays nothing. At maturity, the payoff of a gap option is equal to $Max[S_T - G, 0]$, where G is the pre-specified level, called the gap parameter. With this in mind it is easy to value a gap option. The factor by which the present value of contingent receipt of the asset price, contingent on exercise, exceeds the current value of the asset is $N(d_1)$, the same as for the asset or nothing option. The probability that the asset price ends up above the strike price is $N(d_2)$, the same as for the cash or nothing option. Putting these two together along with the payoff at maturity gives the value of the call as

$$S_t N(d_1)e^{-\delta(T-t)} - Ge^{-r(T-t)}N(d_2)$$

and the value of the put as

$$Ge^{-r(T-t)}N(-d_2) - S_t e^{-\delta(T-t)}N(-d_1).$$

Comparing these formulas with Equations 9.11 and 9.12, we can see that they are the same as those for straight calls and puts with X replaced by G.

Asset or nothing options

Asset or nothing options pay an amount of cash equal to the price of the underlying security if the price of the underlying security ends up above the strike price for a call.[16] If it ends up below the strike price, it pays nothing. Contrary to cash or nothing options, there is no limit to the upside potential. The payout at maturity is $Max(S_T,0]$, higher than the straight vanilla call. In fact, an asset or nothing option is like a gap option where $G = 0$. Thus, from the preceding sub-section we can see that the value of an asset or nothing call option is equal to

$$S_t N(d_1)e^{-\delta(T-t)}.$$

Correlation binary options

Correlation binary options involve two assets or indices.[17] One is called the measurement instrument and the other is called the payment instrument. As we mentioned earlier, correlation digitals can be useful for hedging certain kinds of swaps. They can also be useful for hedging situations where events in one market trigger actions that must be undertaken in another market. Consider the situation of an investor who has decided to sell his shares in ATT if the price reaches USD 25 at the end of the year and invest the proceeds in short-term government Treasuries, but wants to obtain a return of at least 8% on the Treasuries. The measurement asset is the share price of ATT with a strike price of USD 25. The payment asset is the futures price of the short-term interest rate where the gap parameter is 100% – 8% = 92%. Thus, if at maturity the share price is above USD 25 and interest rates have fallen to 6% so that the interest rate futures price is 100% – 6% = 94%, he exercises the option and obtains the bonds at the price of 92%.

In our notation, S is the payment asset and M is the measurement asset. At maturity, the payoff of a European style correlation binary option is $[S_T - G]$ if $M_T \geq X$ and 0 otherwise. Suppose that both S and M follow risk-neutral geometric Brownian motion

$$dS = (r-\delta)Sdt + \sigma Sdz \qquad (9.24)$$

$$dM = (r-\delta_M)Mdt + \sigma_M Mdz_M \qquad (9.25)$$

and the correlation between the two processes is ρdt. Applying the joint lognormal probabilities to the payoff function and discounting at the riskless rate gives

$$C_{CB} = S_t e^{-\delta(T-t)}N_2(d_1,a_1,\rho) - Ge^{-r(T-t)}N_2(d_2,a_2,\rho) \qquad (9.26)$$

where d_1 and d_2 are defined above, $N_2(\cdot)$ is the cumalative bivariate normal distribution function and

$$a_1 = \frac{\ln\dfrac{M_t}{X} + (r-\delta_M+\dfrac{\sigma_M^2}{2})(T-t)}{\sigma_M\sqrt{T-t}}$$

$$a_1 = \frac{\ln\dfrac{M_t}{X} + (r-\delta_M-\dfrac{\sigma_M^2}{2})(T-t)}{\sigma_M\sqrt{T-t}}$$

---

[16] Asset or nothing puts are not relevant.

[17] See Zhang (1998), p.p. 410–422 for a full discussion of correlation binary options.

This pricing formula in Equation 9.26 is very general. As we mentioned, if the payoff and measurement instruments are the same, it gives the formula for an ordinary gap option. If $S = M$ and $G = X$, it gives Equation 8.17, the formula for an ordinary European call option. If $S = M$ and $G = 0$, it gives the formula for an assets or nothing option. When we let $G = 0$, we get the value of an asset or nothing option where the payoff is the other asset. This is called "another asset or nothing" option.

Other popular exotics

The range of exotic instruments is so vast that anything more than a sketch of the most popular and useful types is outside the scope of this book.[18] Up to now we have tried to present the best known and most widely used instruments. We end this chapter with a brief description of three other popular instruments that could be useful for international risk management: **forward start options**, **barrier options** and **compound options** (an option on an option).

Forward start options

Forward start options become effective some time after they are bought or sold. They start sometime in the future with the strike price set to be the underlying asset price at the time that the option starts. Thus, they begin life at-the-money and the payoff is $Max[S_T - S_{t_1}, 0]$ for a call and $Max[S_{t_1} - S_T, 0]$ for a put, where t_1 is the time in the future when the option becomes valid. Because they start at-the-money we can substitute S_{t_1} for X in Equations 8.17 and 8.18 to get the value of the option at t_1.

$$C_{t_1} = S_{t_1} e^{-\delta(T-t_1)} N(d_{1FS}) - S_{t_1} e^{-r(T-t_1)} N(-d_{2FS}) \qquad (9.27)$$

and

$$p_{t_1} = S_{t_1} e^{-r(T-t_1)} N(-d_{2FS}) - S_{t_1} e^{-\delta(T-t_1)} N(-d_{1FS}) \qquad (9.28)$$

where δ represents the payout rate and

$$d_{1FS} = \frac{(r - \delta + \frac{\sigma^2}{2})(T - t_1)}{\sigma \sqrt{T - t_1}}$$

$$d_{2FS} = \frac{(r - \delta - \frac{\sigma^2}{2})(T - t_1)}{\sigma \sqrt{T - t_1}}.$$

In a risk-neutral world

$$E(S_{t_1}) = S_{t_0} e^{(r-\delta)t_1}.$$

The value of the option at t_0 is the present value of the option at t_1 discounted at the riskless rate

$$e^{-rt_1} C_{t_1}.$$

[18] For an in-depth, comprehensive treatment of exotic options in general, see Zhang (1998).

Substituting this information into Equations 9.27 and 9.28 gives the price of the forward start as

$$C_{t_0} = S_{t_0}e^{-\delta t_1}[e^{-\delta(T-t_1)}N(d_{1FS}) - e^{-r(T-t_1)}N(d_{2FS})] \qquad (9.29)$$

and

$$P_{t_0} = S_{t_0}e^{-\delta t_1}[e^{-r(T-t_1)}N(-d_{2FS}) - e^{-\delta(T-t_1)}N(-d_{1FS})] \qquad (9.30)$$

Barrier options

Barrier options are options where the payoff depends on whether the price of the underlying asset reaches a pre-specified level over a given time period. In fact, barrier options are one of the oldest types of exotic options, having traded in the United States as far back as 1967. One advantage of these options is that they are cheaper than corresponding standard calls and puts. Another advantage is that the barriers make it possible for users to restrict their hedging to price ranges that they consider feasible. Thus, risk managers can hedge their exposures without paying for price ranges that they believe are unlikely to occur.

Barrier options can be classified as either knock-out or knock-in. A knock-out option ceases to exist when the price of the underlying asset reaches a barrier. A knock-in option comes into existence when a barrier is reached. The standard knock-out option entitles its owner to receive a rebate when a barrier is hit and a European option payout if it is not hit. The standard knock-in option entitles its owner to receive a European option if a barrier is hit and a rebate at expiration if it is not hit. The price of the option depends on whether the barrier is hit from above or below. Depending on whether the price of the underlying asset is above or below the barrier, there are basically four kinds of barrier options for calls and for puts: down-and-outs, down-and-ins, up-and-outs, and up-and-ins.

Barriers can be added to almost any kind of option. Thus, besides the standard barrier options, there are Asian barriers, forward start barriers, dual barriers, correlation binary barriers, spread barriers, lookback barriers and so on. The common feature of all these barrier options is that their payoffs depend on whether or not one or more barriers are breached during the life of the option. The diversity of this family of options makes it impossible to go into much detail on pricing formulas.[19] However, to get an idea of how the barriers and rebates can affect the price of the option, we can look at a standard down-and-out barrier European call option with no yield where R represents the rebate and H represents the barrier with $H < X$.[20]

$$C_B = S_t N(d_{1B}) - Xe^{-r(T-t)}N(d_{2B})$$

$$- \left[S_t \left[\frac{S}{H}\right]^{-2\varepsilon} N(d_{3B}) - Xe^{-r(T-t)} \left[\frac{S}{H}\right]^{-2\varepsilon+2} N(d_{4B}) \right] +$$

$$+ R\left[\left[\frac{S}{H}\right]^{-2\varepsilon+1} N(d_{5B}) + \left[\frac{S}{H}\right] N(d_{6B}) \right] \qquad (9.31)$$

[19] See Zhang (1998), p.p. 203–335 for an in-depth examination of barrier options.

[20] See Cox and Rubenstein (1985), p.p. 410–411.

where

$$d_{1B} = \frac{\ln\frac{S_t}{X} + (r + \frac{\sigma^2}{2})(T-t)}{\sigma\sqrt{T-t}}$$

$$d_{2B} = \frac{\ln\frac{S_t}{X} + (r - \frac{\sigma^2}{2})(T-t)}{\sigma\sqrt{T-t}}$$

$$d_{3B} = \frac{\ln\frac{H^2}{S_t X} + (r + \frac{\sigma^2}{2})(T-t)}{\sigma\sqrt{T-t}}$$

$$d_{4B} = \frac{\ln\frac{H^2}{S_t X} + (r - \frac{\sigma^2}{2})(T-t)}{\sigma\sqrt{T-t}}$$

$$d_{5B} = \frac{\ln\frac{H}{S_t} + (r + \frac{\sigma^2}{2})(T-t)}{\sigma\sqrt{T-t}}$$

$$d_{6B} = \frac{\ln\frac{H}{S_t} + (r - \frac{\sigma^2}{2})(T-t)}{\sigma\sqrt{T-t}}$$

$$\varepsilon = \frac{r}{\sigma^2} + \frac{1}{2}$$

We can see that the down-and-out call has been written as the sum of three terms: (a) the value of a standard European call, (b) minus the reduction in value due to the early cancellation feature of the barrier, (c) plus the value of the rebate.

Compound options

A compound option is an option on an option. In this case the underlying instrument is itself an option. This kind of instrument is useful for managing risks associated with conditional cash flows. The four main types of compound options are: a call on a call, a call on a put, a put on a call, and a put on a put. Compound options have two separate exercise dates and two separate strike prices. The first exercise date and strike price refer to the compound option itself. The second exercise date and strike price refer to the option that is the underlying instrument.

Consider, for example, a European call option with an expiry date of six months and a strike price of USD 0.20 on a call option on GBP 62,500 with a strike price of USD 1.50 and an expiry date of 12 months. On the first exercise date six months later, if the premium on the call option on GBP 62,500 with an exercise date six months in the future is greater than USD 0.20, the option will be exercised. Otherwise it will expire worthless. In the case of exercise, the purchaser of the compound option will then own the option on GBP 62,500 with an exercise price of USD 1.50 and an exercise date six months in the future.

The original formulas for European style compound calls and puts were developed by Robert Geske.[21] In our usual notation they can be written as[22]

$$C_{cc} = S_0 e^{-\delta T_2} N_2(d_{1cc}, a_{1cc}, \sqrt{T_1/T_2}) - X_2 e^{-rT_2} N_2(d_{2cc}, a_{2cc}, \sqrt{T_1/T_2}) - e^{-rT_1} X_1 N(d_{2cc}) \quad (9.32)$$

where

S = the price of the underlying asset on which the underlying option is written (e.g. the stock price, the exchange rate, the commodity price, etc.)

X_1 = the exercise price on the compound option

X_2 = the exercise price on the underlying option

T_1 = the exercise date on the compound option

T_2 = the exercise date on the underlying option

$N_2(\cdot)$ = the cumulative bivariate normal distribution function.

$$d_{1cc} = \frac{\ln \frac{S_0}{S} + (r - \delta + \frac{\sigma^2}{2})T_1}{\sigma \sqrt{T_1}}$$

$$a_{1cc} = \frac{\ln \frac{S_0}{X_2} + (r - \delta + \frac{\sigma^2}{2})T_2}{\sigma \sqrt{T_2}}$$

$$d_{2cc} = d_{1cc} - \sigma \sqrt{T_1}$$

$$a_{2cc} = a_{1cc} - \sigma \sqrt{T_2}.$$

The variable $\overline{S}$ is the price of the underlying asset at T_1 for which the option price at T_1 equals X_1. Thus, $\overline{S}$ must satisfy the equation

$$\overline{S} e^{-\delta(T_2-T_1)} N(d_1) - X_2 e^{-r(T_2-T_1)} N(d_2) - X_1 = 0 \quad (9.33)$$

where

$$d_1 = \frac{\ln \frac{\overline{S}}{X_2} + (r - \delta + \frac{\sigma^2}{2})(T_2 - T_1)}{\sigma \sqrt{T_2 - T_1}}$$

and

$$d_2 = d_1 - \sigma \sqrt{T_2 - T_1}$$

Obtaining Equation 9.32 involves solving Equation 9.33 by trial and error to obtain $\overline{S}$ and then applying the bivariate normal density function to the payoff at T_1, the exercise date of the compound option. With similar methodology and notation, the formula of a European style put on a call is

$$P_{pC} = X_2 e^{-rT_2} N_2(-d_{2cc}, a_{2cc}, -\sqrt{T_1/T_2}) - S_0 e^{-\delta T_2} N_2(-d_{1cc}, a_{1cc}, -\sqrt{T_1/T_2}) + e^{-rT_1} X_1 N(-d_{2cc}) \quad (9.34)$$

[21] Geske (1979b),

[22] See Zhang (1998) for a clear derivation of the formulas.

The value of a European style call on a put is

$$C_{Cp} = X_2 e^{-rT_2} N_2(-d_{2cc}, -a_{2cc}, \sqrt{T_1/T_2}) - S_0 e^{-\delta T_2} N_2(-d_{1cc}, -a_{1cc}, \sqrt{T_1/T_2}) - e^{-rT_1} X_1 N(-d_{2cc}) \quad (9.35)$$

The value of a European put on a put is

$$P_{pp} = S_0 e^{-\delta T_2} N_2(d_{1cc}, -a_{1cc}, -\sqrt{T_1/T_2}) - X_2 e^{-rT_2} N_2(d_{2cc}, a_{2cc}, -\sqrt{T_1/T_2}) + e^{-rT_1} X_1 N(d_{2cc}) \quad (9.36)$$

Summary

1. The development of the swap market has had a profound impact on the evolution of the international financial markets in providing a bridge between different markets, different currencies and different financial instruments. As a result, the principles of comparative advantage, long applied to the markets for goods and services, is relevant to financial services. Governments, companies and institutions can now borrow where they have a relative cost advantage.

2. The three basic reasons why companies include swap transactions in their funding operations are market constraints, cost advantages and hedging.

3. In a standard interest rate swap the goal of the two parties is to exchange fixed rate interest payments for floating rate interest payments on a notional amount. The notional amount itself is not exchanged and serves only to calculate the interest payments. The swap agreement itself is explicit concerning the notional amount, reference interest rates, interest payment formulas, payment dates and calculation periods.

4. A currency swap involves the exchange of a loan in one currency for a loan in another currency and both principal and interest payments are exchanged. The exchange of the notional amount always takes place at the termination of a currency swap and usually at the beginning as well. When the notional amount is exchanged at the beginning and at the end, neither party is exposed to foreign exchange risk. This is not true when the notional amounts are not exchanged at the beginning. The interest rates on the loans in the currency swap can both be fixed. In this case we speak of a fixed-to-fixed currency swap. If they are both variable we speak of a floating-to-floating currency swap. If one is fixed and the other is floating, we speak of a fixed-to-floating currency swap.

5. A secondary swap market is developing rapidly, although it is far from being as liquid as the market for stocks and bonds. The pricing procedure involves constructing a reference swap based on current market conditions and then comparing the reference swap with the actual swap to be traded or terminated.

6. There are generally three basic risks associated with swap transactions: credit risk, market risk and mismatch risk. Of these three major risks, credit risk is the most important. Credit risk in swap transactions differs considerably from credit risk in traditional loan transactions, because swaps are not exposed to the full extent of the amounts exchanged. They are exposed only to the possible gain or loss involved in reversing the swap in case of non-performance by one of the swap's counterparties. The magnitude of the exposure depends on the market conditions concerning interest rates, exchange rates and liquidity at the time of default. Thus, in the case of a bank intermediated transaction, the bank's exposure to non-payment by one party is not the principal amount due. It is the cost of setting up a position to offset its obligations to the non-defaulting party.

7. Exotic options are standard options modified in some way to serve a special purpose or specific client need. Consequently, they are more complicated to price than standard

options. There are many kinds of exotic options, including spread options, Asian options, basket options, lookback options, binary options, forward start options and barrier options. Although this sample is relatively small, it is representative of the exotic options that are the most popular and potentially the most useful for hedging risk on the international commodity, currency and capital markets. Some of the options examined can be priced using straightforward extensions of the methods developed in Chapter 8. Others can be priced analytically using more complicated formulas and techniques. Finally, others require Monte Carlo simulations or numerical techniques.

INTERNATIONAL RISK ASSESSMENT

Country and political risk analysis

10

The internationalization of the financial landscape over the past half century is by now a well established fact, the effects of which are felt at all levels of economic activity. It is rare that even a small or medium-sized company has no foreign clients or suppliers. Their transactions involving different markets and currencies have to be negotiated, financed and settled. The financial transactions of most larger companies are even more international because besides foreign clients and suppliers they also have access to foreign financing and many have direct investments abroad. Banks have followed their clients and now routinely borrow and lend on a worldwide basis, while portfolio investors look to markets around the globe to enhance their returns.

This trend shows no signs of abating. On the contrary, it seems likely to accelerate as borrowers and lenders alike become more aware of the potential opportunities for the lower costs, increased returns and diversification benefits to be gained from an international approach to finance. Experience has shown, however, that financial transactions involving residents of different countries are subject to risks that would not otherwise be present. Besides cultural differences in institutions, legal and financial traditions, information sources and the like, there are other serious constraints such as legal barriers, transaction costs and discriminatory taxation that can affect the outcome of a cross-border financial operation. Furthermore, each country represents a distinct set of economic and financial conditions based on its dotation in human and natural resources and the way these resources are managed. Since international economic and financial activity is organized around the concept of national sovereignty where each country has its own economic, financial, political and legal organization that determines resource allocation and income distribution within the geographic area it controls, events or anticipated events at the national level have a profound effect on the performance of individual resident economic and financial agents. For example, a looser monetary policy by the European Central Bank (ECB) will tend to lower interest rates and raise the current value of outstanding financial obligations such as stocks and bonds of companies resident in the European Union (EU).

This is not the whole story, however. Events or anticipated events at the national level will also affect the relative performance of resident economic and financial agents vis-à-vis the rest of the world. Other things being equal, the looser ECB monetary policy that lowers interest rates and raises the current value of outstanding financial obligations will also tend to lower the value of the euro relative to other currencies, thereby reducing the foreign currency value of these same financial obligations.

The analysis can be further extended to include political, social, geographic and strategic considerations likely to affect returns of resident economic assets to non-resident investors. Expropriations, revolutions, natural catastrophes and wars are some of the most obvious examples that come to mind.

As a concept, then, international or cross-border risk is vast and complex. It refers to the volatility of returns on international investments caused by events associated with a particular country as opposed to events associated solely with a particular economic or financial agent. In the preceding chapters we developed the technical and theoretical relations linking economic performance to balance of payments discipline and the exchange rate. We also presented the international economic and financial framework. In this chapter we will look at the conditions specific to individual countries that can influence the outcome of a cross-border transaction and see how their effects can be analyzed.

Definitions and methods in cross-border risk assessment

Sources of cross-border risk

The sources of cross-border risk, often called **political risk** or **country risk** (see Exhibit 10.1), are many and varied. They include all aspects of a country's economic, financial, social and political organization as well as its geographic location and strategic importance. Take, for example, the comprehensive checklist of risk sources worked out by Pancras Nagy (in *Country Risk*, Euromoney Publications, 1984). It details almost every situation that could conceivably occur in a given country. The major headings include:

- war
- occupation by a foreign power
- civil war, revolution, riots, disorders
- takeover by an extremist government
- politically motivated debt default, renegotiation or rescheduling
- unilateral change in debt service terms
- state takeover of the enterprise
- indigenization (forced relinquishment of control by foreign owners of enterprises)
- natural calamities
- depression or severe recession
- mismanagement of the economy
- credit squeeze
- long-term slowdown in real GNP growth
- strikes
- rapid rise in production costs
- fall in export earnings
- sudden increase in food and/or energy imports
- over-extension in external borrowing
- devaluation or depreciation of the currency.

Each major heading in Nagy's list is followed by detailed situations to which a probability of "yes" or "no" or "very", "fairly", or "not at all" is assigned. For example, the situation list under the heading "Civil war, revolution, riots, disorders" has over 30 entries, a sample of some of which is presented in Exhibit 10.2.

Exhibit 10.1 A brief history of country risk analysis

The concept of country risk evolved in the 1960s and 1970s in response to the banking sector's efforts to define and measure its exposure to loss in cross-border lending. As a term, it has been shrouded in conceptual confusion from the beginning, often referring indiscriminately to transfer risk, sovereign risk, political risk, economic risk, financial risk or any other type of risk that could conceivably affect the ability or willingness of an economy or government to honor its financial obligations. In fact, the confusion existed because it was unclear what exactly was supposed to be measured.

At one time before the advent of widespread international lending, country risk was synonymous with **transfer risk**, the risk that a government might impose restrictions on debt service payments abroad. When governments themselves became major bank borrowers, the concept of **sovereign risk** appeared on the scene. Sovereign risk is broader than transfer risk insofar as it includes the idea that even if the government is willing to honor its external obligations, it might not be able to do so if the overall economy cannot generate the necessary foreign exchange. Taking a page from the multinational corporations that had a long history of direct cross-border investment, some analysts began referring to sovereign risk as "political risk". Political risk is a term used by industrial firms to describe adverse events outside their particular market sector. The events can be traced to macroeconomic, social, political or strategic factors. Political risk itself is a concept so broad that it has become virtually meaningless.

The end of the heyday of "country risk analysis" came with Mexico's financial default in 1982 followed by other "crisis countries" that left the banks' balance sheets in a shambles. The fact that traditional country risk analysts had failed so generally and for so long in their mission was certainly a contributing factor in their demise. A more important factor, however, was the globalization of financial markets and the growth of portfolio investment that brought in its wake the widespread application of the powerful tools of modern portfolio theory. It became clear that a significant part of what the country risk analysts had concentrated on was unsystematic risk that could be diversified away, and much of the rest was unsuitable in its content or presentation for portfolio building. Emphasis shifted to diversification and hedging techniques, including formal model building and increasingly sophisticated statistical analysis. Today the term country risk is out of style, having been replaced by, for example, "cross-border risk" or "international business risk", terms no more precise but which at least are unencumbered by the historical baggage of definitional ambiguities and (as yet) unsullied by association with failure. Chapter 12 examines this subject, which we call "political risk", in detail.

Potential entries in a list like this are virtually limitless. It is also clear that this kind of list can only be prepared by an analyst with in-depth knowledge of the country in question. In fact, given the heterogeneous nature of the information, it is not likely that any one analyst will have the expertise in all the fields involved and, in order to be effective, the analysis will have to be prepared by a team of experts with in-depth knowledge of the country, representing skills in economics, finance, political science, sociology, geology, etc. Furthermore, there is the problem of how to digest this menu of diverse information. Even if the analytical assessment is entirely accurate, it is far from clear how this can be translated into a comprehensible statement of the consequences for a financial transaction.

Later on in this chapter we will deal separately with the risk factors of a purely political nature, such as legal barriers, tax laws, strikes, environmental protests and legislation, expropriations, revolutions, wars, terrorism and the like. In this section we will concentrate

Exhibit 10.2 Sample situations for estimating the risk associated with civil war, revolution, riots and disorders

The tension, discontent and antagonism is high:

- the government is:
  1. weak and, therefore, unable to control the situation
  2. unsuccessful in its efforts to defuse the tension through appropriate reforms
- The discontented groups are:
  1. vocal
  2. well organized
  3. well armed
  4. under the influence of leaders who are able, fanatical, impulsive or irresponsible
  5. effectively supported, financially or otherwise, from abroad
- the drain on the country's resources will be substantial:
  1. the riots and disorders will paralyze production
     a. on a large scale
     b. for a long period
  2. there will be substantial destruction of productive capacity
  3. there will be capital flight on a large scale
  4. there will be loss on a large scale of entrepreneurial, managerial and/or technical expertise.

Source: P. Nagy, *Country Risk* (Euromoney Publications, 1984), p.p. 153–173.

on those factors associated with a country's economic and financial situation. They refer to economic and financial risk and depend on a country's dotation in human and natural resources and how these resources are managed. Their importance stems from the fact that they reflect the country's ability to honor its external financial obligations and that, to a large extent, this is often the determining factor in whether or not they are honored. Many of the other risk sources associated with political or sovereign risk are simply manifestations of the underlying economic and financial problems.

In Nagy's list, for example, mismanagement of the economy and over-extension in external borrowing should be analyzed in terms of their effects on the economic and financial situation. By the same token, the economic and financial situation will ultimately play a major role in determining many of the political variables such as politically motivated debt default, renegotiation and rescheduling, or unilateral changes in debt service terms. The reason is clear. A reputation as a poor payer would restrict the country's access to international financial markets, a penalty severe enough economically and socially to ensure that these "political" measures are usually only taken as a last resort. Witness Peru, where real GDP fell by 6.62% between 1984 and 1990, Argentina with a decline of 3.69% between 1984 and 1989, and Mexico with a decline of 6.9% between 1994 and 1995. In fact, most of the crisis countries of the 1980s have come to grips with their restricted access to the international financial markets by making the painful economic adjustments necessary to restore their creditworthiness. Governments and investors alike have come to realize that ability to pay is far more important than the political concept of "willingness" to pay.[1] This was clearly manifested in the Asian crisis of 1997 and the Russian default of 1998. Thus, many "political" variables associated with cross-border risk analysis are really economic and financial variables and, therefore, should be analyzed as such.

Variables and ratios for economic risk assessment

A country's **economic risk** refers to developments in the national economy that can affect the outcome of an international financial transaction. For instance, a currency devaluation in a country where an investment is held will reduce the value of the cash flows and returns from the investment in the investor's home currency. A recession or slowdown in the country will reduce the cash flows and returns to the investor in foreign currency.

Economic risk analysis involves an assessment of the country's ongoing and prospective economic situation as well as an estimate of the accuracy of the assessment itself. The economic variables currently used in assessing cross-border economic risk are those that are commonly used for domestic macroeconomic analysis. They can be divided into variables associated with the domestic economy and variables associated with the balance of payments (see Chapter 1 for the relationship between these two sets of variables). The principal domestic economic variables are:

- GNP or GDP
- gross domestic investment
- gross domestic fixed investment
- private and public consumption
- gross domestic savings (remember from Chapter 1, Equation 1.4, that gross domestic savings are equal to GNP minus total domestic consumption)
- the "resource gap", defined as the difference between gross domestic savings and gross domestic investment (remember from Chapter 1, Equation 1.5, that this is equal to the current account balance)
- the money supply
- the government budget deficit
- the GNP deflator (a Paasche index)[2]
- the consumer price index (a Laspeyre index).[3]

---

[1] Clark and Zenaidi (1999) show that "willingness to pay" can be measured as the value of the government's option to default. They show that it is a significant explanatory variable in determining the secondary market discount on sovereign debt for the 21 countries in the study. On average it explains about 4.1% of the discount ranging from a high of 16.77% for Mexico to a negligible 0.003% for Zaire.

[2] A Paasche price index is weighted by current consumption patterns. Thus, if p stands for price per unit and q for the number of units, with superscripts referring to the individual goods and subscripts referring to time, a Paasche price index can be expressed as follows:

$$\frac{\sum_{j} p_t^j q_t^j}{\sum_{j} p_0^j q_t^j}.$$

Most introductory statistics textbooks deal with the different types of index numbers.

[3] A Laspeyre index is weighted by comsumption patterns of the base year. Using the same notation as in the previous footnote, a Laspeyre price index can be expressed as follows:

$$\frac{\sum_{j} p_t^j q_0^j}{\sum_{j} p_0^j q_0^j}.$$

The principal variables associated with the balance of payments are:

- exports of goods and services in dollars or SDRs (X)
- imports of goods and services in dollars or SDRs (M)
- the trade balance
- the current account balance
- the export price index in dollars or SDRs
- the import price index in dollars or SDRs
- the exchange rate
- foreign reserves (RES).

Standard economic risk assessment consists of combining these two sets of variables to generate a number of ratios considered as significant indicators of the ongoing and prospective economic situation. One set of ratios aims at assessing the prospects for long-term growth in GDP or GNP. It includes:

- gross domestic fixed investment / GDP (or GNP)
- gross domestic savings / GDP (or GNP)
- marginal capital / output (the number of dollars of increase in investment necessary to increase output by one dollar)
- net capital imports / gross domestic fixed investment
- gross domestic savings / gross domestic fixed investment.

The ratio of gross domestic fixed investment / GDP measures the economy's propensity to invest. It is usually assumed that a higher rate of investment will lead to increased output and higher rates of growth of GDP. The extent to which this is true depends on the marginal capital / output ratio. The marginal capital / output ratio is supposed to measure the marginal productivity of capital. It is usually calculated by dividing gross fixed domestic investment in one period by the increase in GDP one or two periods later. A lower ratio signifies a higher productivity of capital and the higher the productivity of capital, the better the outlook for GDP growth. The net capital imports / gross domestic fixed investment ratio indicates the extent to which GDP growth is dependent on goods produced abroad. The higher the ratio the more dependent the economy. Combined with the gross domestic savings / gross domestic fixed investment ratio, it indicates how dependent the economy is on foreign resources. The lower domestic savings to domestic investment, the more dependent the economy. Dependence on foreign resources is usually interpreted as a negative insofar as economic risk assessment is concerned. Whether or not this is true is another question. For example, the resource gap can be large due to profitable investment opportunities and the willingness of foreigners to lend. It is hard to see why this should be a negative. On the other hand, in the absence of profitable investment opportunities, the resource gap can also be large due to a high propensity to consume. This, of course, is a negative because it signals that current consumption is being financed with foreign borrowing and that the rate of return on domestic investment is lower than the cost of the foreign resources.

Another set of ratios are used as indicators of price stability:

- government budget deficit / GDP (or GNP)
- percentage increase in the money supply.

Since price instability is considered undesirable, the outlook for price stability and economic performance should be more favorable when both the government budget deficit and the growth in the money supply are smaller.

The principal ratios for assessing the evolution of the balance of payments are:

- percentage change in exports / percentage change in world GDP (or the GDP of the main customer countries), which represents the income elasticity of demand for exports (see Chapter 2 for a discussion of the role of income and price elasticities)

- percentage change in imports / percentage change in GDP, which represents the income elasticity of demand for imports

- imports / GDP

- commodity exports / total exports

- official reserves / imports.

A high income elasticity of the demand for exports and a low income elasticity of the demand for imports is usually considered as favorable for the balance of payments. On the other hand, a high ratio of imports to GDP is considered as unfavorable. Because of the well known volatility of commodity prices, a high ratio of commodity exports to total exports is also considered unfavorable, while a high ratio of reserves to imports is favorable.

Variables and ratios for financial risk assessment

A country's **financial risk** refers to the ability of the national economy to generate enough foreign exchange to meet payments of interest and principal on its foreign debt. The debt crisis of the developing countries in the 1980s is an excellent example of financial risk. Because of over-borrowing and unproductive use of the resources that were borrowed, the crisis countries were unable to honor their debts to the banks that had lent to them, thereby causing massive losses for the banks and economic sacrifices from the defaulting countries.

Financial risk analysis involves an assessment of the country's foreign financial obligations compared to its ongoing and prospective economic situation. The variables currently used in assessing cross-border financial risk include those presented in the previous subsection that are commonly used for domestic macroeconomic analysis. They also include information on the country's foreign debt and interest:[4]

- total external debt (EDT), which can be broken down into:
  a. long-term public and publicly guaranteed outstanding and disbursed (DOD)
  b. long-term private non-guaranteed
  c. short-term
  d. use of IMF credit

- total debt service (TDS) which can be broken down into:
  a. interest payments (INT)
  b. principal payments.

---

[4] In *Global Development Finance,* formerly the *World Debt Tables,* the World Bank publishes detailed statistics on the foreign debt of over 110 developing countries. The information includes undisbursed debt, commitments, disbursements, principal repayments, net flows, interest payments, net transfers, debt service, average terms of new commitments, debt restructurings and debt service projections. The information is broken down by type of creditor and type of loan.

"Long-term external debt" refers to debt that has an original or extended maturity of more than one year and that is owed to non-residents and repayable in foreign currency, goods, or services.[5] It has three components – public debt, publicly guaranteed debt and private, non-guaranteed external debt.

- Public debt is an external obligation of a public debtor, including the national government, a political subdivision or agency of either, and autonomous public bodies.

- Publicly guaranteed debt is an external obligation of a private debtor that is guaranteed for repayment by a public entity.

- Private non-guaranteed external debt is an external obligation of a private debtor that is not guaranteed by a public entity.

"Short term external debt" refers to debt that has a maturity of one year or less and includes no distinctions between public and private non-guaranteed short-term debt. "Use of IMF credit" refers to repurchase obligations to the IMF with respect to all uses of IMF resources, excluding those resulting from drawings in the reserve or first credit tranche. "Total debt service" is the sum of (1) principal repayments and interest payments on long term debt, (2) repurchases and charges on use of IMF resources and, (3) principal and interest payments on short-term debt.

Information on a country's external debt can be combined with the economic and balance of payments variables to generate a number of ratios considered as significant indicators of the ongoing and prospective financial situation. Some of the most common financial ratios are (see, for example, *Global Development Finance*, published by the World Bank):

- total external debt / exports (EDT / X)

- total external debt / GNP (EDT / GNP)

- official reserves / total external debt (RES / EDT)

- official reserves / imports (RES / M)

- long-term public and publicly guaranteed outstanding and disbursed / exports (DOD / X)

- long-term public and publicly guaranteed outstanding and disbursed / GNP (DOD / GNP)

- total debt service / exports (TDS / X)

- total debt service / GNP (TDS / GNP)

- interest payments / exports (INT / X)

- interest payments / GNP (INT / GNP)

- official reserves / long-term public and publicly guaranteed outstanding and disbursed (RES / DOD).

In corporate finance, **financial leverage** plays a major role in determining financial risk. Financial leverage is measured by the extent to which the assets of the firm are financed with debt. It shows up as interest expense, causing variability in net income over and above the variability in operating income caused by operating risk. Where macroeconomic financial risk is concerned, the same type of effect is present. Financial leverage shows up as interest expense, causing variability in GDP or GNP over and above the variability caused by economic risk. However, in the absence of a macroeconomic balance sheet, GNP

---

[5] These definitions are those given by the World Bank: see *World Debt Tables, 1989–1990, vol. 2* (Washington D.C.: The World Bank, 1989), p.p. xii–xvi.

and exports are used as proxies for determining financial leverage. Thus, ratios such as EDT / X, EDT / GNP, DOD / X, and DOD / GNP can be interpreted as a measure of the economy's financial leverage. The lower these ratios, the better the economy's financial position. How reliable these ratios are in signaling an economy's financial position depends on how accurately the variables X and GNP reflect the state of the economy's balance sheet. Later in this chapter we will see that GDP and the traditional presentation of its component parts can be very misleading regarding the state of an economy's health. Consequently, these ratios should be used with caution.

Other types of leverage ratios used in corporate finance, such as times interest earned and cash flow coverage, seek to determine the extent to which current obligations are covered by current income. The times interest earned ratio relates earnings before interest and taxes to current interest charges while the cash flow coverage ratio relates earnings before interest and taxes to total current financial obligations including payments for interest and principal. Thus, INT / X and INT / GNP resemble a times interest earned ratio and TDS / X and TDS / GNP resemble a cash flow coverage ratio. Lower ratios indicate a better financial position.

These latter leverage ratios are probably more reliable than the former proxy balance sheet ratios for determining a country's financial health. Nevertheless, they are conceptually different from the corresponding ratios in corporate finance, where the starting point is earnings net of operating costs. The country ratios use exports and GNP, which are gross of costs and do not reflect the net flows such as earnings or net exports $(X - M)$ that the economy can generate and make available to honor its external financial obligations.

The ratio RES / M complements the leverage ratios and resembles a **liquidity ratio** in corporate finance. Liquidity ratios measure the firm's ability to meet its maturing short-term obligations. The RES / M ratio measures a country's ability to maintain import levels with current cash in hand.

Political risk[6]

The concept of political risk has been widely analyzed. In 1971 S. Robock was one of the first to address it.[7] By 1979 – the eve of the debt crisis, the literature was extensive.[8] More recently, in the light of the debt crisis, T. Brewer has explored new directions for research while D. Roddock undertook an investigation at the corporate level.[9] In spite of the widespread coverage of the subject, however, political risk has not received a clear cut definition. For Robock and Simmons, for instance, "political risk in international investment exists when discontinuities occur in the business environment, when they are difficult to anticipate, and when they result from political change".[10] F. Root makes a distinction between transfer risks (potential restrictions on the transfer of funds,

---

[6] In this chapter we follow E. Clark and B. Marois (1996).

[7] S. Robock, "Political risk: Identification and assessment", *Colombia Journal of World Business*, Vol. 6, No. 4 (July 1971).

[8] For an exhaustive review of the subject, see S. Kobrin, "Political risk: A review and reconsideration", *Journal of International Business Studies*, Vol. X, No. 1 (Autumn 1979).

[9] See T. Brewer, *Political Risk in International Business: New Directions for Research, Management and Public Policy* (New York: Praeger, 1985); D. Roddock, *Assessing Corporate Political Risk* (Totowa, NY: Rowman and Littlefield Publishers, 1986).

[10] S. Robock and K. Simmons, *International Business and Multinational Enterprise* (Homewood: R. Irwin, 1973).

products, technology and people), operational risks (uncertainty about policies, regulations or governmental administrative procedures which would hinder results and management of operations in the foreign country) and, finally, risks on control of capital (discrimination against foreign firms, expropriation, forced local shareholding, etc.).[11] In fact, as we mentioned earlier, there is no general agreement on exactly what political risk assessment is supposed to measure.

To throw some light on the problem, it is interesting to look at some of the distinctions that are often drawn. A first distinction is usually made between global political risk, which is related to a firm with several foreign subsidiaries, and specific political risk, which is inherent to one particular investment in a given country. A second distinction opposes macro-risk to micro-risk. Macro-risk is sometimes called country risk and includes all events or measures likely to affect foreign investment in general. These measures are often divided into "soft" and "hard". For instance, blacklisting, ecological protest movements, strikes in a particular industry or the incorporation of a competing firm by the public authorities can be considered as soft political risk. On the other hand, expropriations or nationalizations would be considered hard political risk. Micro-risk concerns a particular firm in a given country. It depends on factors such as the nationality of the foreign firm, its previous history in the country, its sector of activity, etc. Some authors make a further distinction between political risk and country risk where country risk refers to loans made by commercial banks to developing countries and political risk refers to direct foreign investments.

Although the foregoing distinctions are often useful for analyzing a particular problem, they can confuse the subject when a more general discussion is in order. Consequently, in this book, we adopt the definition of political risk as "the probability of politically motivated change that affects the outcome of foreign-based transactions". In this sense, some effects will be direct and explicit such as expropriations, nationalizations and strikes. Others, such as taxes and monetary policy, will be indirect, manifesting themselves in macroeconomic performance, foreign debt levels and currency fluctuations.

Sources and effects

Sources of political risk

From the foregoing definition it is clear that political risk covers a wide field. Some authors like to distinguish between political events such as war, revolution, riots, strikes, etc., and political decisions in the form of laws or decrees. Political events can be sudden and unpredictable and, therefore, difficult to forecast, whereas political decisions that alter the business environment are often more gradual and easier to assess. Two kinds of definition can be given to political decisions of this type. The first reduces them to measures taken by the public authorities. The second broadens the definition to include the activities of various groups such as pressure groups, political parties, lobbies and revolutionaries.[12]

The motivating factors behind political risk are also diverse. Ideology, for example, is a major motivation. It generated the Soviet expropriation of foreign investors to turn Russia and its captive countries into planned economies and was a major source of world conflict during the years of the Cold War. Another series of nationalizations came from sociological

---

[11] F. Root, "Analyzing political risks in international business", in Kapoor and Grub (Eds.), *Multinational Enterprise in Transition* (Princeton: Darwin Press, 1973).

[12] For instance, D.W. Zinc describes it this way: "The state is the main channel through which an enterprise is put under pressure". See: D.W. Zinc, *The Political Risks for Multinational Enterprise in Developing Countries*, (New York: Praeger, 1973). Robock and Simmons, op. cit., 1973, adopt the broader definition.

causes as newly independent countries sought to assert their sovereignty over local resources by expropriating foreign investors. Similarly, sociological considerations are behind the ethnic and religious strife that undermine the overall economic atmosphere and can culminate in the destruction of human and material assets. Rwanda, Israel/Palestine, the former Yugoslavia and Northern Ireland are some of the most prominent recent examples. The psychology of political leaders is another major factor in risk generating political decisions. Saddham Hussein's invasion of Kuwait, Ayatollah Khomeini's xenophobic economic policy and Kim Il Jong's saber-rattling are some of the most notorious recent examples. Finally, economic constraints can explain many of the political strains on foreign firms. Lack of hard currency will cause restrictions on remittances abroad, while recession can lead to conservative policies concerning transfer of funds, recruitment of foreigners, production standards, taxation and price controls.

Effects of political risk: Direct investment

To summarize the foregoing discussion, we can put the measures and events affecting foreign operations into three general categories: hard political risk, administrative or soft political risk and social risk. As we mentioned, the first group includes expropriation, confiscation, nationalization, forced local shareholding, etc.; the second group covers decisions such as control of prices, foreign exchange, remittances, etc.; and, finally, social risk encompasses strikes, lack of experienced labor force, war, ethnic strife, etc.

The usual effects of soft measures are to reduce profitability. For example, taxes and price controls reduce net income; capital controls delay cash flows, thereby reducing the project's internal rate of return; indigenization of management increases training costs and often reduces efficiency. The usual effects of hard measures are often the partial or total loss of the foreign operation. The post World War II years were particularly noted for this. In Iran in the 1950s, Mossadegh nationalized the multinational petroleum companies. The North African and Middle Eastern countries followed suit in the 1960s and early 70s. Chile's Allende carried out numerous expropriations in 1972. Between 1956 and 1972, foreign investments were nationalized or expropriated by at least 40 LDC governments to the tune of 25% of the outstanding stock of foreign-owned capital invested in LDCs at the end of 1972.[13] As we can see in Table 10.1, radical change does, however, seem to have been taking place. Between 1970 and 1975, 336 acts of expropriation have been identified versus 87 between 1976 and 1979, 15 from 1980 to 1985, and only one between 1986 and 1992.[14] As for geographic trends, Africa was the area with the highest number of nationalizations in the 1960s and 1970s whereas Latin America and Asia were more active in the 1980s. The most popular sectors for expropriation were agriculture and the oil industry. According to Kobrin, the main reasons for the decline in mass nationalizations seem to have been the growing capacity of new independent states to manage their economies, the highly desirable investment flows at a time of reduced supply of bank credit, the attractiveness of privatizations, and the initiatives of the international organizations such as the IMF and the World Bank to protect private investors.

In recent years expropriation has become more insidious with countries using local laws and dubious financial maneuvers to dispossess foreign partners. For example, in October 1999 a Russian court in Saint Petersburg ruled that the 255-year-old Lomonosov porcelain

[13] M. Williams, "The extent and significance of the nationalization of foreign-owned assets in developing countries", *Oxford Economic Papers*, Vol. 27 (1975) p. 260.

[14] S. Kobrin, "Expropriations as an attempt to control foreign affiliates, 1960–1979", *International Studies Quarterly*, Vol. 3, (September 1984), p.p. 329–348; M. Minor, "The demise of expropriation as an instrument of LDC policy, 1980–1992", *Journal of International Business Studies*, Vol. 25, No. 1 (1994), p.p. 177–188.

Table 10.1 Expropriation acts 1970–92

Year	Number of acts
1970–1975	336
1976–1979	87
1980–1985	15
1986–1992	1

Source: M. Minor, "The demise of expropriation as an instrument of LDC policy, 1980–1992", *Journal of International Business Studies*, Vol. 25, No. 1, p. 180.

factory be renationalized. The ruling annulled a majority stake held by executives of a prominent Wall Street buyout firm, Kohlburg, Kravis, Roberts & Co., and a US financed investment fund, United States–Russia Investment Fund. Financial shenanigans include issuing large numbers of shares to insiders that dilute foreign shareholdings and the transfer or sale of valuable assets to companies controlled by insiders at drastically reduced prices. The result leaves the foreign shareholders with a reduced stake in a valuable company or with a stake in a worthless shell company with no assets of any value. In a celebrated case, British Petroleum was outmaneuvered by an aggressive and well connected rival, Tyunmen Oil of Russia, that forced Sidanko, a Russian oil company in which BP held a hefty stake, into bankruptcy and then picked off the valuable assets.

Besides the consequences on ownership and profits, political risk can also affect the security of physical assets, intellectual property and personnel. In fact, these issues are becoming more important in the assessment of foreign investment risk. Physical and intellectual assets must be protected or insured against damage and destruction. Factories, offices and cars can be burned, bombed, battered and damaged in many ways. Intellectual property is especially vulnerable to damage and loss. Patent and license abuses, pirated merchandise, imitations and fakes, not to mention industrial espionage and computer viruses, are some of the most obvious examples that come to mind. Personnel security is perhaps the most difficult problem of all, with kidnapping a major issue. Blackmail and extortion are not far behind, while civil disorder, natural disasters and epidemics can also put personnel at risk. Events such as these are difficult (probably impossible) to forecast and their consequences are difficult to estimate in terms of dollars and cents. Nevertheless, when they do happen, their effects are often disastrous for the outcome of the investment.

Political risk can also have a positive connotation when it means "incentives to invest". Germany, for instance, has set up some interesting programs for firms wishing to invest in the eastern part of the country. Indeed, after reunification, the German authorities sought to attract foreign enterprises to the former East Germany in order to make the transition to the market economy easier for the new "Lander". Thus, direct subsidies from the federal government can reach 12% of the total investment and financial incentives from the state authorities 23% more for a total discount of 35%. Air Liquide, the world leader in the gas industry, bought 40% of the existing equipment in this sector in what was formerly East Germany. Besides the direct subsidies of 35% offered by the central government and the states, it also took advantage of an income tax deferral and a first-year depreciation rate of 50%. As a result, market share of Air Liquide in united Germany rose from 6% to 12% on an annual turnover of DEM 300 million in 1991.

Political (country) risk: cross-border loans

As we mentioned above, many analysts make a distinction between political risk and country risk, where political risk is associated with direct investment and country risk is used by bankers to distinguish between foreign and domestic loan risk. Both foreign and domestic loans can suffer default by the borrower but only the foreign loan can incur a risk of transfer, due either to economic constraints or to political expediency. Following this line of reasoning, country risk is often defined as the probability that economic, political or social factors within a country will create a situation in which borrowers in that country will be unable to service or repay their debts to foreign lenders in a timely manner. This definition, however, makes it clear that the distinction between political and country risk based on whether direct investments or bank loans are at stake is artificial and confuses the issue. In fact, a more appropriate distinction is the one we have adopted in this book between what we have defined as economic, financial and currency risk. Political risk is common to both types of investment. In this context, bank loans are primarily affected by a country's financial risk represented by the economy's capacity to generate enough foreign exchange to maintain the required level of imports and service the external debt, whereas direct investments are affected by economic and currency risk as well as financial risk. Although the specific decisions and events affecting each one may differ, both direct investments and cross-border loans are vulnerable to political considerations.[15]

If a country does default, loans are either rescheduled or renegotiated. Figure 10.1 outlines this situation. Loans by public authorities or state agencies are renegotiated in the framework of the Paris Club where the borrowing government meets its lenders and tries to arrange for a rescheduling of its debt. Loans by commercial banks take a different route. The banks set up a "steering committee" in charge of negotiating the rescheduling, which takes place in the London Club framework.

Political risk: Portfolio investment

Besides the economic, financial and currency risk associated with cross-border portfolio investment, political risk is also a major consideration. The political authorities typically monitor and regulate the financial markets in their geographical jurisdiction. Thus, they have a major say in who participates in the markets; the types of instruments available to investors; the transactions, settlement and delivery procedures; the brokerage fees, stamp duties and other costs for a foreign investor; and the taxation and other regulations affecting foreign investors. Their response to different situations can have a major effect on the outcome of an investment.

Taxes, commissions and transaction costs are the most obvious example. After the performance of the security itself, tax effects are probably the single most important factor in determining the investor's ultimate rate of return. Commissions and other transaction

---

[15] The evolution of country risk analysis is reflected in the literature. In the 1970s the long-term debt service capacity of a borrower was the main variable in the evaluation process. See, for example, C. Frank and W. Cline,"Measurement of debt servicing capacity: An application of discriminant analysis", *Journal of International Economics*, No. 1 (1971), p.p. 327–344; G. Feder and R. Just, "A study of debt service capacity applying logic analysis", *Journal of Developing Economics*, Vol. 4 (1976), p.p. 25–39. In the 1980s scholars tried to distinguish between solvency, liquidity and default risks. See J. Eaton, M. Gersovitz and J. Stiglitz, "The pure theory of country risk", *European Economic Review*, Vol. 30 (1986), p.p. 481–513 and P. Krugman "Internal debt strategies in an uncertain world", in G. Smith and J. Cuddington (Eds.), *International Debt and the Developing World*, (Washington DC: World Bank, 1985) who show that debt default can result from a debtor's cost–benefit analysis. Finally, in the recent past, some authors have tried to introduce political risk into the analysis of country creditworthiness. See T. Brewer and P. Rivoli, "Politics and perceived country creditworthiness in international banking", *Journal of Money, Credit and Banking*, Vol. 22 (3) (1990), p.p. 357–369 and J.C. Cosset and J. Roy, "The determinants of country risk rankings", *Journal of International Business Studies*, Vol. 22 (1) (1991), p.p. 135–142.

Figure 10.1 The rescheduling process

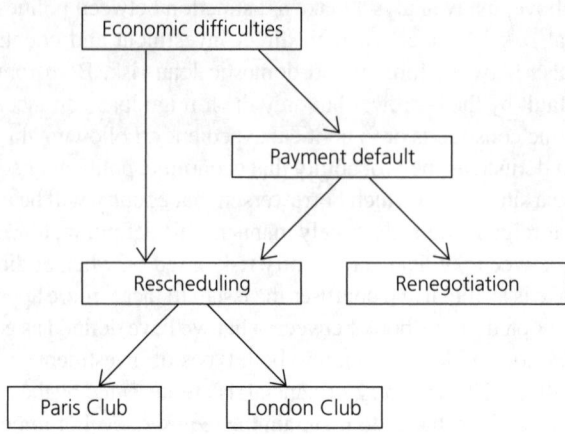

Source: E. Clark and B. Marois, *Managing Risk in International Business* (London: Thomson Learning, 1996).

costs can also significantly affect an investment's rate of return. Politically motivated changes in the tax, commission or transaction cost structure will consequently affect the outcome of a foreign portfolio investment.

Another consideration arises from the structure of share ownership. Share ownership across different categories of investors differs widely from country to country. In South Korea, for example, 68% of shares are held by private individuals while in Australia they hold only 4%. Institutional investors dominate the US and Japanese markets, holding 46% and 47% respectively. In The Netherlands 50% of equity is held by foreigners.

Different patterns of shareholdings lead to different political responses to changing market conditions. The recent fall in the Korean market caused widespread protests by individual investors and sparked government attempts to prop up prices, while the Asian crisis of 1997 caused the Hong Kong authorities to intervene directly in the stock market. It is said that complicity between the Japanese Ministry of Finance and the financial institutions that own 47% of Japanese equity buoyed stock prices in the massacre of October 1987. This sort of collusion would be impossible in the United States because commercial banks are prohibited by law from participating in their clients' equity. On the other hand, equity holdings by Japanese banks is a double-edged sword when prices continue to fall in spite of efforts to prop them up. In the early 1990s Japanese banks were finding it difficult to meet minimum BIS capital requirements in the face of a declining stock market, thereby causing them to restrain lending to their clients which further exacerbated falling stock prices.

At the least, these considerations can have a significant short-term effect on share prices and represent another source of risk that the foreign investor should consider before undertaking an investment. In fact, the structure of the stock market may make it more or less susceptible to political manipulation. Other things being equal, the public stock markets of France, Belgium, Spain, Italy, Greece and some Latin American countries are more highly regulated and susceptible to political control than the private stock exchanges found in the United States, Japan, Canada, Australia, South Africa and the United Kingdom, or the Germanic bankers' exchanges found in Germany, Austria, Switzerland, Scandinavia and The Netherlands. Although subject to some government regulation, the private exchanges are probably the most independent of the three types. Bankers' bourses have the disadvantages associated with concentration of power in the hands of a narrow interest group.

Government regulations on foreign participation in domestic financial markets can also have an important effect on the cost of, and returns from cross-border portfolio investment. Many emerging markets, for example, restrict foreign participation in their equity markets to officially approved funds. Consequently, approved funds often trade at a premium to the value of the securities they own. A change in the regulations can have dramatic effects on the price funds. If, for example, the government decides to expand foreign participation by accrediting more funds, the price of existing funds is likely to fall.

Switzerland is the classic case of government restrictions on foreign equity holdings causing substantial price changes. Until 1988 the Swiss equity market was divided into three categories: bearer shares, registered shares and participation certificates. Registered shares, which carried voting and certain other rights, were restricted to Swiss nationals and traded at a considerable discount to the bearer shares available to foreign investors. Since Nestlé's decision in November 1988 to make its registered shares available to foreigners, the distinction between registered and bearer shares has changed considerably and caused a sharp reduction in the price differential between the two types of security.

Political risk analysis

Political risk has a long history as an important input in international business decision making. Nevertheless, as we have already mentioned, there is no real consensus on the exact definition of political risk. In general, most would agree that it concerns the effects of non-economic variables on business transactions that are undertaken abroad. Just exactly what political risk analysis can achieve is also open to question. In contrast to the hard data of economic and financial analysis, the political world appears as a vast quagmire of nebulous, subjective terrain. This perceived intractability has been reinforced by the inability of political risk analysts, ranging from individual consultants to large consulting firms, to deliver on the promises they make when promoting their services. In fact, the impression is often given that with the right methodological framework or the key, well placed contact, political risk in a given country can be accurately forecast. It can't! The reality is just too complex. What can be achieved, however, is a guide for reducing some of the uncertainty surrounding the foreign political and social developments that can affect foreign business transactions. In the following section, we address the issue of how and to what extent political risk can be assessed.

Methods and techniques

Comparative techniques

The aim of the comparative techniques in political risk analysis is to compare all countries or some subset of them, such as the LDCs, according to an analytical grid based on a set of relevant parameters. Because of the nature and scope of political risk, the set of what is deemed to be the relevant parameters is wide ranging and often includes elements that are difficult to measure with any precision. The comparison itself can be achieved either through an ordinal rating system or a mapping exercise on a two-axis space.

Rating systems

Quite a few specialized think tanks such as the Business Environment Risk Index (BERI), Business International and the Economist Intelligence Unit have adopted the rating approach, which proceeds in two stages. First, each country is graded on the parameters selected as judgemental criteria. Secondly, the resulting data is weighted into a global rating that makes it possible to compare all the countries on the same scale. The success of the operation depends, of course, on the relevance of the judgemental parameters and the weights assigned to each, as well as on the accuracy of the grading exercise.

To illustrate this presentation we can describe the method adopted by one of these forecasting firms, Credit Risk International, whose system is summarized in Exhibit 10.3. It designates four parameters to assess the degree of a country's riskiness:

1. market prospects and flexibility in coping with changes
2. financial risks
3. political instability
4. the business environment.

Various criteria and subcriteria are selected in determining the score for each parameter. For example, their parameter number 4, the business environment, is based on three criteria:

1. the economic management of the country, which counts for 40% of the parameter's value
2. the foreign investment climate, which counts for 40% of the parameter's value
3. working conditions, which counts for 20% of the parameter's value.

The foreign investment climate, criterion 11 in Exhibit 10.3, is divided into 11 subcriteria:

1. market share of foreign direct investment in the local economy (7%)
2. legal restrictions to foreign control of local firms (5%)
3. legal restrictions to capital flows (remittances of dividends) (3%)
4. stability of business law (3%)
5. frequency of intervention of local government in business life (3%)
6. availability and cost of local financing (4%)
7. cost of labor (4%)
8. cost of local transportation (3%)
9. cost of energy (3%)
10. price level of local real estate (3%)
11. degree of modernity of distribution channels (2%).

In all, there are 100 subcriteria.

To assess each criterion, Credit Risk International follows the "Delphi technique". This methodology involves submitting a series of identical questions to a group of experts. The experts, who remain anonymous to each other, receive continual feedback on the responses of the other members of the group. The goal of the exercise is to reach a group position on a particular issue. In the Credit Risk International process, a group of experts on each country gives its feeling on each subcriterion, which is then translated into a grade between one (the worst grade) and seven (the best grade). Once each subcriterion has been assessed, the overall, weighted rating is computed with a maximum of 700 and a minimum of 100. In the 1994–95 ratings, Singapore, for instance, was rated number one with a score of 628 points, Morocco 29th with 415 points and Zaire last with 168 points.

This global rating can be adjusted according to whether the risk is associated with an export transaction, a direct investment or a loan. Morocco, for example, was allocated 396 points and the 29th rank from the exporter's point of view, 456 points and the 27th rank when direct foreign investment was considered, and 394 points and the 29th rank as a borrower. Furthermore, these ratings can be translated into risk classes, from class seven (no risk) to class one (danger). Based on this rating, Credit Risk International

Exhibit 10.3 Credit Risk International's rating system

- **Parameter 1: Market prospects and flexibility in coping with changes**
  Criterion 1: economic size (weight: 30%)
  Criterion 2: level of economic development (40%)
  Criterion 3: standard of living (30%)

- **Parameter 2: Financial risks**
  Criterion 4: financial vulnerability (30%)
  Criterion 5: external debt (30%)
  Criterion 6: financial rating (40%)

- **Parameter 3: Political instability**
  Criterion 7: homogeneity of social fabric (30%)
  Criterion 8: government political regime stability (50%)
  Criterion 9: foreign relationships (20%)

- **Parameter 4: Business environment**
  Criterion 10: management of the economy (40%)
  Criterion 11: foreign investments (40%)
  Criterion 12: working conditions: (20%)

derives its decision-making rules. For a country belonging to class three (high risk), for instance, Credit Risk International suggests a risk premium of 75% of the risk-free rate of interest.[16]

Many other types of rating systems are in use and, like Credit Risk International's, include economic and financial indicators along with the estimates of political risk. For instance, *Euromoney* magazine publishes annual credit ratings assigning a 25% weight to economic data, 25% to political risk, 10% to financial data based on ratio analysis, 10% to default performance, 10% to credit ratings, and 5% each to access to bank financing, access to short-term finance, access to capital markets and access to forfaiting.[17] The economic score is compiled from a survey of 35 economists from leading banks, financial and economic institutions. The political risk score is compiled from a poll of risk analysts, risk insurance brokers and bank credit officers. The financial ratios are taken from the World Bank World Debt Tables and include the debt service to export ratio, the current account balance to GNP ratio and the external debt to GNP ratio. The default performance is measured by the amount of debt rescheduled or in default over the preceding three years. Credit ratings are obtained as the average of sovereign ratings from Moody's and Standard and Poor's. Unrated countries receive a score of zero and countries with only a short-term rating receive a score based on a rating of BBB. Access to bank finance is calculated from disbursements of long-term private non-guaranteed debt as a percentage of GNP. Access to short-term financing is calculated according to which OECD consensus group the country belongs to. Access to capital markets is based on an analysis by *Euromoney* of international bond and syndicated loan issues since 1989, plus a judgement of current accessibility. Access to forfaiting is scored from a combination of maximum tenor (up to seven years) and the forfaiting spread over the riskless countries.

[16] See Chapter 18 for a definition of the risk-free rate of interest.

[17] See *Euromoney* (September 1993), p.p. 363–368.

Institutions such as Moody's and Standard and Poor's produce country ratings but, in contrast to *Euromoney* and the other institutions, their weighting system is not transparent. They tend to rate specific financing instruments like Eurobonds or Euro-commercial paper using a scale from AAA to C, according to increasing solvency risk.

Insofar as rating systems go, it can be helpful to consider their evolution across time. In Table 10.2 we show *Institutional Investor's* rating for 29 countries between 1979 and 1991. It is interesting to note that only three countries had a better credit rating in 1991 than they did in 1979. It is also interesting to note that in 1979 Mexico, the country that introduced us to the debt crisis, had the second best credit rating after Venezuela. Argentina and Brazil, the two countries that defaulted on Mexico's heels were also among the best rated countries. In fact, just before the Asian crisis of 1997 erupted with devastating consequences for South Korea, Malaysia, Thailand and Indonesia, *Institutional Investor's* country risk rating still showed positive assessment of the Asian countries with South Korea and Malaysia standing ahead of Chile and Hong Kong, Thailand ahead of China, Greece and Israel, and Indonesia ahead of Poland, Hungary and Tunisia. This indicates how fast ratings and financial positions can change. To capture this effect in Table 10.2, we also show the average rating and standard deviation. This procedure adds a new dimension to the use of rating systems by casting the problem in mean-variance space. A high rating with a high standard deviation indicates that the rating is unstable and subject to wide fluctuations. On the other hand, more confidence could be placed in a high rating with a low standard deviation that indicates stability over time.

Other types of indirect ratings also exist. Interest rate risk premiums on Eurobond issues by government agencies calculated as the number of basis points over the benchmark (T-bonds for the dollar, Bunds for the mark) are one of these. The use of this method is relatively limited, however, because only high quality borrowers can tap the Eurobond market and the basis point premiums on the benchmark are often distorted by the issuing process whereby syndicate managers trade basis points for higher fees. Nevertheless, some market sentiment should still be reflected in this premium.

Mapping systems

The mapping approach is similar to the rating approach insofar as it uses a set of relevant parameters in the process of risk estimation. However, rather than an ordinal ranking of the countries under consideration, the analytical results are mapped on a two-dimensional graph divided into four quadrants separated by two axes. Each axis represents a distinct parameter or risk. For example, one axis might reflect political risk while the other reflects economic risk. In this case, the first quadrant will contain the countries with both high political and economic risk while quadrant three will contain the countries with both low political and economic risk. Quadrants two and four will contain the countries with high risk in one category and low risk in the other. In the early analysis done by Business International, the two axes identified risk and market prospects.

The weakness of comparative systems is obvious. First of all, there is no objective theoretical basis for the inclusion or exclusion of the numerous parameters employed in the different rating systems. Secondly, the process for attributing the respective weights given to the various parameters has no indisputable foundation. Different weights might give different results. Third, the same grid is applied to all countries, whatever their regional location or specific characteristics. Moreover, "extreme" situations (e.g. the Iranian revolution or the Gulf War) cannot be anticipated from comparative approaches. Nevertheless, comparative methods can be useful as a screening process designed to eliminate the countries that are completely unacceptable. It seems that US firms are keener on accepting the comparative techniques than are their European and Japanese counterparts.

Table 10.2 Mean and standard deviation (in parentheses) of credit ratings published by *Institutional Investor*, 1979 to 1991[a]

	1979–1991	1979	1986	1991
Global average	42.73 (5.70)	55.7	40.5	37.9
Countries included in the study				
1. Algeria	48.99 (8.71)	58.6	50.4	34.2
2. Argentina	32.67 (17.26)	62.4	24.9	20.2
3. Bolivia	13.78 (7.49)	31.6	8.0	15.0
4. Brazil	37.92 (12.54)	64.9	35.2	26.5
5. Cameroon	33.55 (5.04)[b]	35.0[c]	38.4	23.1
6. Chile	37.64 (12.16)	54.9	25.1	41.1
7. Colombia	45.50 (9.93)	60.7	39.2	36.6
8. Costa Rica	22.05 (10.44)	44.7	17.0	22.5
9. Ecuador	31.10 (13.50)	53.2	26.7	19.6
10. Egypt	30.03 (5.92)	33.9	29.5	23.4
11. Greece	52.66 (6.26)	62.6	47.6	47.2
12. India	47.66 (3.60)	54.2	50.7	38.4
13. Indonesia	50.05 (4.57)	53.2	47.6	50.4
14. Ivory Coast	30.98 (9.99)	48.2	27.5	17.2
15. Korea	61.55 (5.52)	71.2	58.4	68.1
16. Malaysia	64.60 (6.76)	70.3	59.9	62.0
17. Mexico	43.89 (17.08)	71.8	30.8	38.7
18. Morocco	29.57 (7.32)	45.5	23.1	28.3
19. Nigeria	32.42 (15.17)	54.1	22.8	19.5
20. Peru	22.86 (11.99)	30.7	14.9	12.2
21. Philippines	30.63 (11.08)	53.7	21.4	24.5
22. Portugal	55.19 (5.04)	52.0	51.8	63.3
23. Sudan	8.43 (3.81)	18.5	7.3	6.1
24. Thailand	55.05 (3.96)	54.7	53.3	62.5
25. Tunisia	42.02 (5.72)	50.0	39.7	37.5
26. Turkey	30.78 (11.43)	14.8	38.6	42.7
27. Uruguay	32.78 (5.64)	41.0	27.8	31.2
28. Venezuela	45.99 (15.07)	72.4	38.1	37.2
29. Yugoslavia	34.87 (10.68)	57.5	31.4	24.5

[a]The range of credit ratings is from 0 to 100, where 100 represents the most creditworthy country.
[b]Credit rating for Cameroon starts in year 1982.
[c]The number represents credit rating in year 1982.

Source: Lee, S.H. (1993) "Relative importance of political instability and economic variables on perceived country creditworthiness", *Journal of international Business Studies*, Vol. 24(4), p. 803.

Analytical techniques

Whereas comparative approaches encompass all the countries at the same time, the analytical techniques focus on one country at a time. Among these, we have the "special report" approach, the "probabilistic" approach, the "sociological" approach based on dynamic segmentation, and finally the "expert systems" approach.

Special report approach

The special report approach to political risk analysis is the most descriptive of the analytical approaches. It involves one or several experts who examine the key variables that are supposed to describe a given country's main characteristics and who then communicate their findings in the form of a special report. Thus, for each country under study, the report usually contains an analysis of the political, social and economic outlook that explicitly takes into account the specificities of the local environment. As an example, before the end of apartheid, a French company specializing in political and economic risk assessment acknowledged eight special features pertaining to the South African Republic, namely:

- the production and export of gold
- the impact of embargo and its consequences
- the "borderline" with Namibia, Angola, etc.
- the evolution of apartheid, the institutional framework
- the policies of white minorities
- the policies of black parties
- the Zulu factor.

The special reports themselves usually sum up a country's overall strengths and weaknesses and focus on such aspects as the country's political life, the major characteristics of the current regime, the degree of stability of the domestic currency, the tax system, regulations pertaining to foreign investment, the social structure and climate, and the country's economic prospects.

The advantages of the special report are its ability to focus on the particularities of each country, its low cost and speed of production. Its main drawbacks are its subjectivity, lack of scientific analysis and relative partiality. In fact, the quality of any special report basically depends on the capabilities and intuition of the analyst.

Probabilistic approach

Using the decision tree process, the probabilistic approach is based on computing various alternative outcomes, each one receiving a certain probability of occurrence and implying specific measures with regard to foreign investment. For example, the outcome of a definitive election in an African country might be depicted by two scenarios: the current government remains in power or the opposition takes over. Each scenario might have a different probability, such as 65% for the current regime and 35% for the opposition, but the probabilities must sum to 100%. Once the government is elected, it will be faced with several choices. Probabilities are then assigned to the possibility of each choice occurring. For example, if the current government remains in power, its choices might be a subsidy for foreign investment with a 60% probability or the status quo with a 40% probability. If the opposition wins, its choices might be an increased tax on foreign operations with a 70% probability or expropriation with a 30% probability. The effects of each choice are then calculated. The subsidy might make the investment worth USD 110, the status quo USD 100, the increased tax USD 85 and expropriation USD 10. All this information is summarized in Figure 10.2 where we can find the value of the investment by multiplying the joint probability by the value of each outcome and summing. Hence, the investment is worth USD 90.775.

The same methodology can be applied to more complicated situations with several steps and numerous possible outcomes but the obvious difficulty is calculating the different probabilities and estimating the effect that the different measures will have on the outcome of the investment.

Figure 10.2 The probabilistic approach

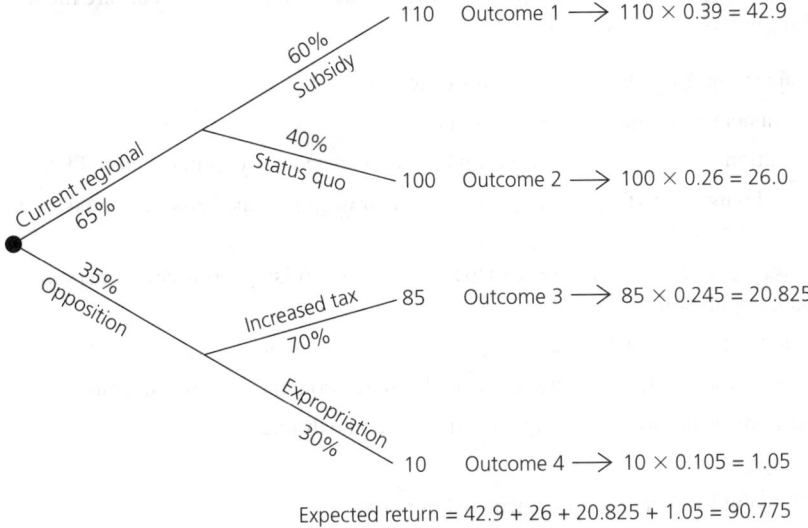

Expected return = 42.9 + 26 + 20.825 + 1.05 = 90.775

Source: E. Clark and B. Marois, *Managing Risk in International Business* (London: Thomson Learning, 1996).

Sociological approach

In its most general form, the sociological approach to political risk analysis seeks to identify a set of variables that can be specific to each country as a means of apprehending the country's "degree of stability". The variables can range from the realities of state hegemony and political terrorism to such concepts as a democratic tradition and the capacity to live in peace. Each country gives rise to a new set of variables and a distinct methodology. The advantage of this approach is its tailor-made nature that makes it possible to individualize the analysis. The disadvantage is that it lacks scientific rigor and is difficult to apply in a comparative context.

One of the oldest and most respected techniques of the sociological approach is the "dynamic segmentation" methodology, known as the ALLY method, which seeks to analyze the fundamental trends of a country that are likely to influence the relationship between the investing company and the political powers.

Dynamic segmentation divides a society into various behavior-homogeneous groups, called segments. A segment can be socio-economic or ethnic. Power in the society is based on the coalition of a number of these segments while the segments outside the coalition form the opposition. Over a long period, some new segments may appear and others disappear but most of them continue to exist no matter what coalitions come to power. It is recognized that demographic, economic and social developments in a given country can, in the space of a few years, substantially modify the relative importance of the individual segments. However, certain segments occupy a pivotal position, thereby guaranteeing them a place in all possible power coalitions. It is, therefore, essential to focus information gathering on the medium-term developments and short-term fluctuations affecting these pivotal segments.

Some segments have natural or historic ties that make it possible to identify the coalitions of segments that are likely to wield power. From these, the coalition of maximum homogeneity and importance is selected and its future evolution is assessed by answering such questions as will it stay in power or when will it be replaced by another coalition. Based on these forecasts, the investing foreign corporation will attempt to take advantage of the situation by modifying its policy.

As an illustration of the dynamic segmentation methodology we can take the case of Morocco. In step one, a group of qualified experts designates what it feels are the ten fundamental segments in Moroccan society:

- the palace (the King, his family and his officers)
- the technocracy (trained mostly in Europe)
- the traditional bourgeoisie (the *fassi*), who originate generally from the city of Fez
- the new bourgeoisie (the *soussis*), who trace their origins to the berber elements of the Souss region in the south
- the rural "notables", who are a dispersed elite exercising political leadership over the peasant population
- the intelligentsia, a small group
- the urban proletariat, a growing segment, due to the country's industrialization
- the peasants, who, so far, display great fidelity to the throne
- the army
- the "Muslim Brothers", a fundamentalist minority.

In step two, the various segments are mapped as circles of varying sizes on two axes, where the y-axis represents political power and the x-axis economic power. The size of each circle is proportional to the importance of the given segment. The distance between the circles is determined by indices of affinity between the segments taken two by two. The experts then estimate the affinity indices by analyzing how each segment behaves vis-à-vis the others. Closer affinity means closer proximity on the graph. From the mapping, different coalitions are ascertained and their strengths and weaknesses are analyzed. Consider, for example, three possible outcomes forecast for the year 2010. Coalition One is composed of all the segments except the intelligentsia, the proletariat and the Muslim Brothers. It represents a kind of status quo. Coalition Two includes only the technocrats, the palace, the rural notables and the peasants. Thus it is more unstable due to the fact that the army and the bourgeoisie are either neutral or in opposition. Coalition Three includes the palace, the technocrats and the bourgeoisie, the army again remaining neutral. It is clear that Coalition One is the most favorable to foreign investors as far as the political stability of Morocco is concerned because it is the broadest and includes the army. The two other coalitions are narrower and imply a possibly destabilizing reinforcement of the fundamentalist influence. Once the different coalitions have been identified, the final step involves estimating the probability of each coalition occurring and analyzing the implications.

Expert systems approach

The expert systems approach is adapted to analyses in conditions of uncertainty. It essentially requires a database and an inference paradigm. The database includes quantitative information such as population, economic growth, current account balance, etc., as well as symbolic information that ranges from management definitions and rules to the description of international institutions (the IMF, World Bank, etc.), national institutions (the government, the central bank, armed forces, etc.) and private agents (multinational firms, domestic firms, etc.). The inference paradigm replicates the thinking of an expert through chains of causality such as event x causes effect y which causes effect z. For example, the Institut Français de Polémologie has set up a system to examine the potential consequences of a blockage of the Straight of Hormuz on the economic situation in certain European countries. Chains of causality are drawn from the effects of this blockage on the world oil supply and prices to the effects on the energy equilibrium of each European country and from this to the effects on inflation, economic growth and employment. In a parallel exercise, experts are interviewed to explain their vision of possible military events in the wake of a blockage of the Straight of Hormuz. Thus, the Institut's expert system enables potential users to ponder real consequences of a political event (the blockade) on a series of different actors.

Another organization, Coface, the official French insurer of cross-border transactions, has developed three expert systems, one to estimate country-specific economic risk, another to estimate country-specific political risk and the third associated with the legal aspects of cross-border commercial transactions.

Econometric techniques

Econometric techniques for political risk estimation have concentrated on debt default and rescheduling. In contrast to the techniques discussed above, the econometric approach is completely objective. It starts from the assumption that certain economic indicators such as growth rates, debt ratios and the current account balance have predictive value. During the late 1970s and early 1980s many banks began to develop their own econometric models. The World Bank and several central banks, including the Bank of England, also experimented with them. Although the shortcomings of econometric forecasting are well known, it is widely accepted that econometric analysis can be a powerful complement to the comparative and analytical techniques described above. The two most popular econometric techniques have been discriminant analysis and logit models.

Discriminant analysis

Discriminant analysis is a statistical technique that makes it possible to classify an observation into one of several a priori groupings. In the case of political risk analysis, the idea is to classify countries according to whether they are likely to default or not. Basically, three steps are involved:

1. Establish mutually exclusive group classifications. Each group is distinguished by a probability distribution of the characteristics.
2. Collect data for each of the groups.
3. Derive the linear combinations of the characteristics that best *discriminate* between the groups. "Best" in this sense means the discriminations that minimize the probability of misclassification.

Consider, for example, the case where two variables, x_1 and x_2 are used to discriminate between two types of countries – defaulters, and non-defaulters. Let x_1 stand for the country's growth rate and x_2 for the ratio of debt to exports. Let

$$Z = a_1 x_1 + a_2 x_2 \tag{10.1}$$

be a linear combination of x_1 and x_2. The problem is to establish a criterion and use past data in order to determine the values of a_1 and a_2 that will make Z useful for discriminating between members of the two groups. The idea, then, is to minimize the number of misclassifications. In a perfect model, there would be no misclassifications. In order to minimize the number of misclassifications, we maximize the function

$$G = \frac{(\bar{Z}_1 - \bar{Z}_2)^2}{\sum_{i=1}^{2} \sum_{j=1}^{n_i} (Z_{ij} - \bar{Z}_i)^2} \tag{10.2}$$

where the numerator represents the separation of the two groups and the denominator is a measure of the variation of Z within the groups. Z_{ij} is the Z value for the jth country in the ith group ($i = 1, 2$), while n_i is the number of countries in group i and $\bar{Z}_i$ is the mean of the Z values in group i. The values a_1 and a_2 can be found by partial differentiation.

Once the values of a_1 and a_2 have been found, the Z values for each country can be calculated and compared in order to determine the cutoff value. A cutoff value is necessary because there will usually be a "zone of ignorance" where some defaulting countries will have higher Z values than some non-defaulting ones. Suppose, for example, that the zone of ignorance lies between Z values of 1.81 and 2.67. The point of minimum misclassification might lie at 2.05. Thus, $Z > 2.05$ classifies a country as non-defaulting and $Z < 2.05$ classifies a country as defaulting.

As an example of how discriminant analysis can be used, suppose that Chase Manhattan is contemplating a sizeable loan to the Philippine government. To see if the Philippine government is statistically likely to default or reschedule over the life of the loan, the analyst assigned to the Philippines uses the bank's in-house model to compute the country's Z value. He finds that the Z value is substantially lower than the cutoff point and that the Philippines is classified as a country that is likely to default. With this classification in mind, he then proceeds with his own in-depth analysis of the country's economic, financial, social and political outlook, which shows that the Philippines is effectively relatively risky compared with other countries in the region. This conclusion, combined with the country's default classification derived from the discriminant analysis, leads the analyst to recommend that the loan be refused.

Frank and Cline published the first systematic empirical study of debt rescheduling.[18] Their fundamental unit of analysis was a country year. They examined data from 26 countries over a period of nine years but, because of holes in the data, they only had 145 country years with 13 reschedulings in their sample. Their original analysis included eight macroeconomic variables and they found that three of these – the lagged ratio of debt to export trend, the ratio of imports to international reserves, and the reciprocal of the maturity of the country's foreign debt – had significant explanatory power to discriminate between cases of rescheduling and cases of normal payment. Since the Frank and Cline study, many other models have been developed and the list of relevant explanatory variables has grown with them.

Logit analysis

The logit model is similar to discriminant analysis insofar as it describes an either-or proposition. Either the country defaults or it doesn't. The dependent variable y_i can be defined as

$$y_i = \begin{cases} 1 & \text{if default occurs} \\ 0 & \text{if it does not occur} \end{cases}$$

Let x_i be a $k \times 1$ vector of independent variables and a a $k \times 1$ vector of coefficients. The logit model assumes that the conditional probability that y_i equals 1 is

$$\frac{1}{(1+e^{-x_i' a})}.$$

The a coefficients can be calculated using iterative techniques such as maximum likelihood methods. One drawback of the logit model is that its power to discriminate is most

---

[18] See: C.R. Frank and W.R. Cline, "Measurement of debt servicing capacity: An application of discriminant analysis", *Journal of International Economics*, Vol. 1 (1971), p.p. 327–344.

sensitive near the mid-point when the probability is equal to 0.5. As the probability moves away from 0.5, changes in the independent variables have less and less impact on the probability that y_i equals 1.

One way of using logit analysis in cross-border lending decisions is to assign a maximum default probability above which no loans will be granted. As we mentioned, however, it is more common to use the data from logit analysis as a complement to other analytical techniques.

Feder and Just were the first to use a logit model for studying debt rescheduling.[19] Like Frank and Cline their analytical unit was the country year. Their sample spanned 41 countries and eight years but, because of incomplete data, it only included 238 country years with 21 cases of rescheduling. In fact, they experienced some difficulties in determining just when an episode of rescheduling had occurred. They ended up finding six macroeconomic variables that were statistically significant in explaining a country's likelihood of rescheduling debt:

- per capita income
- the rate of growth of exports
- the ratio of imports to foreign exchange reserves
- the ratio of debt service payments to total exports
- the ratio of capital inflows to debt service payments
- the ratio of amortization to the outstanding stock of total foreign debt.

Conclusions

The foregoing methodologies yield a number of rating systems, some more rigorous than others. Survey-based approaches that combine expert opinion with a weighting system to generate country scores are probably the least rigorous.[20] Rating systems highlighting political risk also seem vulnerable to a lack of rigor, although some progress is being made in this field. Alesina and Tabellini, for example, have developed a formal economic model linking political instability to the accumulation of public external debt, private capital outflow, income distribution, restrictions on capital outflows and repudiation of external debt, while Johnson, Srinivasan and Bolster present a formal judgemental model for assigning sovereign debt ratings.[21]

Although statistical approaches are considerably more objective and usually more rigorous than the politico-judgemental systems, they are not necessarily more reliable.[22] They suffer from conceptual and statistical shortcomings and are based on the dubious premise that historical data has significant value for predicting future outcomes.

[19] See: G. Feder and R.E. Just, "A study of debt servicing capacity applying logit analysis", *Journal of Development Economics*, Vol. 4 (1976), p.p. 25–39.

[20] See F.T. Haner, *Business Environment Risk Index*, BERI Ltd. system for selected countries (August 1981) p. 9; C.R. Kennedy Jr., "Multinational corporations and political risk in the Persian gulf", *International Journal of Middle East Studies* (August 1984), p.p. 391–403.

[21] A. Alesina and G. Tabellini, "External debt, capital flight and political risk", *Journal of International Economics*, Vol. 27 (1989), p.p. 199–220; R.A. Johnson, V. Srinivasan and P.J. Bolster, "Sovereign debt ratings: A judgemental model based on the analytic hierarchy process", *Journal of International Business Studies* (1990), p.p. 95–117.

[22] For a survey of some of the work in the field, see P.S. Bates and K.G. Saini, "A survey of the quantitative approaches to country risk analysis", *Journal of Banking and Finance* (1984) p.p. 341–356.

Furthermore, none of the foregoing methodologies are adapted to efficient portfolio building. The problem has long been recognized.[23] However, little progress seems to have been made. The two published papers applying the theory of mean-variance efficient portfolios to international banking tend to confirm this conclusion. Laurie Goodman's 1981 paper in the *Federal Reserve Bank of New York Quarterly Review* concludes that the risks on US bank loans to developing countries over the period 1960–79 were diversifiable.[24] Harold Cataquet's 1987 paper to the annual meeting of the Applied Econometrics Association is even more explicit.[25] It covers all OECD-BIS banks using monthly data for 26 countries from January 1972 through April 1984 and concludes that although banks do seem to seek mean-variance efficient portfolios, they behave as if the returns across countries were uncorrelated and thus their portfolios are inefficient. This means that by rearranging their exposure, banks could obtain a higher rate of return for the same amount of risk or lower risk for the same rate of return.

Overall, country rating systems have been unsuccessful. Given the quantity and the high quality of human and material resources devoted to cross-border risk analysis, its dismal track record is somewhat surprising. A consensus is forming among analysts and academics alike that the problem lies not with the individual analyses, which on the whole seem satisfactory, but rather in the way that these analyses are exploited. In other words, while each analysis may accurately describe individual country risk, they are not effectively combined in a systematic process designed to maximize the risk–return tradeoff in the context of an overall portfolio. The final section of this chapter proposes a methodology that makes it possible to overcome this problem.

Applications

Measuring exposure in direct investments

Three factors determine the extent of the foreign investor's exposure to political risk:

- the strategic dimension of the investment
- the bargaining power of the foreign firm
- the foreign firm's relation with the host country.

The strategic dimension of the investment is related to the size of the subsidiary and the industrial sector it belongs to. Several studies have shown that size is synonymous with high visibility and hence with political risk.[26] The larger the investment, the more critical the risk becomes. Some industries are also more vulnerable to political risk than others. For

---

[23] See, for example, P. Bennett, "Applying portfolio theory to global bank lending", *Journal of Banking and Finance* (1984), p.p. 153–169; E.A. Clark, "Country risk analysis in globalized financial markets", *The Business Economist*, Vol. 19, No. 1 (Winter 1987); E.A. Clark, "L'Analyse du risque-pays des années 70 à la période actuelle", *Revue Banque*, No. 477 (Novembre 1987).

[24] L. Goodman, "Bank lending to non-OPEC LDCs: Are risks diversifiable?", *Federal Reserve Bank of New York Quarterly Review* (Summer 1981), p.p. 25–45.

[25] H. Cataquet, *Bank Lending to Developing Countries and the Capital Asset Pricing Model: How Diversifiable are the Risks?*. Paper presented at the annual meeting of the Applied Econometrics Association in Lille, France, 9–11 December 1987.

[26] See, for example, J. Poynter, "Government intervention in less developed countries: The experience of multinational companies", *Working Paper No. 238*, University of Ontario (March 1980).

example, between 1960 and 1974, the heyday of expropriation, banks and insurance companies were especially vulnerable to nationalization.

The bargaining power of the foreign firm depends on two variables. First there is the degree of complexity of the foreign subsidiary. This complexity can result either from the sophistication of the technical process embedded in the factory or from the manufacturing process and the international division of production in which each subsidiary is linked to other subsidiaries of the same multinational in various countries, buying from them and selling to them components and parts of the final products. For example, in Toyota's organization of its Asian operations, the five subsidiaries of this Japanese automotive firm in Thailand, Malaysia, the Philippines, Indonesia and Singapore are closely linked by cross-purchases and sales of different components. A more complex, interdependent system reduces exposure. In fact, firms that integrate their production at a world or region-wide level make any form of nationalization useless. A similar method would consist of making foreign subsidiaries dependent on the parent company's technology. A 1992 study, however, shows that in order to effectively reduce exposure it is important that the host country understands to what extent the local investment is dependent on parent technology or integrated production in order to avoid self-damaging expropriations.[27]

The second determinant in the bargaining power of the foreign firm with the host country is the net added value it brings to the economy. If the foreign investor brings hard currencies, new jobs, regional development, transfers of technology and executive training, it increases its bargaining power and reduces its exposure.

The firm's relationship with the local authorities is more ambiguous. The behavior of the host country's authorities will probably differ, depending on whether the foreign investor is a new entrant or, on the contrary, has been active in the host country for a long time. Long time investors might hope to get better treatment than newcomers except, of course, if they have been too involved with local political parties. Because political power can and does change hands, it is probably better to stay out of local politics as much as possible. Many companies have ignored this cautious view. ITT in Chile and United Fruit in Guatemala, for example, which were identified with reactionary governments, suffered a backlash from new governments when the former regimes were toppled.

The behavior of the host country's authorities will also probably differ depending on the nationality of the investor. For example, US companies in Cuba were all expropriated when Fidel Castro took over, while Swedish firms fared much better. Usually, the current attitude of the local government relates to its past experience with regard to the foreign investor as well as to the foreign investor's country.

The first task, then, of a company going abroad is to identify its potential exposure to political risk by determining what the main threats to its project are and how to improve security. First, the political risk relating to the project's environment must be assessed. This involves an application of one or more of the techniques described above. As a first step, for example, the rating approach could be used to screen countries on a comparative basis to determine a shortlist of potential host countries. The special report method could then be used to contribute to the final decision on the country or countries that are selected. Before a final decision can be made, however, the political risk associated with the investment itself must be assessed and exposure estimated. The exposure estimation involves an appreciation of the strategic positioning and bargaining power mentioned above. It also involves an appreciation of the political risks at the local level, which can be significantly different to those of the central authority. The capacity for interference by local authorities must be

---

[27] See H. Raff, "A model of expropriation with asymmetric information", *Journal of International Economics*, Vol. 33 (1992), p.p. 245–265.

appraised and the reliability of local partners assessed. In this context, the quality and reliability of local banks, suppliers and clients is particularly important. Once the investment has
been completed, ongoing analysis is necessary to monitor events and ensure the protection
of physical and non-physical assets as well as the individual security of personnel. The
initial and ongoing political risk analysis can be conducted in-house or with the aid of
specialized institutions such as the Control Risks Group, which offers a wide range of
services from security forecasts, training and support to crisis management, planning and
problem solving.

Measuring political risk

If they are to have any practical use, the political risk assessments presented in the foregoing paragraphs must be integrated into the capital budgeting process. The orthodox
theory of capital budgeting and investment under uncertainty taught in most business
schools and economics departments revolves around the net present value (NPV) rule. The
theoretical superiority of the NPV rule to other approaches such as the payback period, the
accounting rate of return or the internal rate of return explain its widespread acceptance in
practice.[28] According to this rule, expected flows of income and expenditure are estimated
for each period and discounted at the appropriate rate. The present values for expenditure
are then subtracted from the present values of income to find the NPV. Positive NPV indicates that the investment should be accepted, negative NPV that it should be rejected. In
Chapter 21 we will examine the question of capital budgeting techniques and how they can
be applied to international investing. For the moment we take a look at how political risk
estimates can be integrated into the traditional NPV capital budgeting process.

Adjusting the discount rate

One way to include political risk in NPV analysis is to adjust the discount rate to reflect the
incremental political risk. Let

κ = a risk factor that depends exclusively on the country in which the investment is to be
located. It can be interpreted as the premium required to compensate the investor for
the political risk

CF_t = the net cash flow for period t

r = the project's required rate of return per period in the absence of the country-specific
political risk.

In the absence of country-specific political risk, the risk-adjusted discount factor is equal to
$(1 + r)$. With country-specific political risk, the discount factor is adjusted to $1 + r + \kappa$. The
project's NPV adjusted for political risk can thus be expressed as:

$$NPV = \sum_{t=0}^{n} CF_t(1 + r + \kappa)^{-t} \tag{10.3}$$

NPV will be smaller because the discount factor is larger.

The drawback to this procedure is that there is no theory for determining κ and,
therefore, the choice of κ is completely arbitrary.

---

[28] See for example, T.E. Copeland and J.F. Weston, *Financial Theory and Corporate Policy* (Reading, Mass.:
Addison-Wesley Publishing Company, 1988), p.p. 17–76.

Adjusting the expected cash flows

A more theoretically sound method of accounting for political risk involves adjusting the cash flows to reflect the country-specific political risk. Let

u_t = a risk factor for year t that depends exclusively on the country where the investment is to be located with $0 < u < 1$. It can be interpreted as the probability that something bad will not happen.

In the absence of country-specific political risk, the expected net cash flow for year t is CF_t. With country-specific risk, the expected cash flow is reduced by $(1 - u_t)CF_t$ and the expected cash flow will be $u_t CF_t$. The project's NPV adjusted for political risk can thus be expressed as:

$$NPV = \sum_{t=0}^{n} u_t CF_t (1 + r)^{-t} \tag{10.4}$$

The theoretical difficulty with this method is that it assumes that political risk has no effect on the project's cost of capital. The practical difficulty with the method is how the u coefficients can be determined. However, its advantage lies in associating a specific coefficient to each period. This makes it possible for the analysis to reflect the specific time profile of the country's political, social and economic cycles. For example, the u's in election years or renegotiation years for union contracts might be adjusted downwards while years when international agreements take effect might be adjusted upwards.

Monte Carlo simulations

Monte Carlo simulations are another well known and widely used approach to capital budgeting under uncertainty. Basically, they use a table of random numbers to generate the possible probabilities. The whole process involves three steps.

1. The first and most important step in the simulation process is to give the computer a precise model of the project under consideration. This requires identifying the relevant variables and their interdependencies across time. The complete model would include a set of equations for each variable describing their evolution over time. The more complete the model, the more complex the system of equations.

2. The probabilities for forecast errors must be drawn up for each variable.

3. The computer samples from the distribution of forecast errors, calculates the resulting cash flows for each period and records them. After a large number of simulations, accurate estimates of the probability distributions of the project's cash flows are obtained.

In a Monte Carlo simulation the effects of political risk are estimated directly and the role of the political risk analyst is to identify the relevant variables and the probabilities for forecast errors. The Hertz method is particularly well adapted to this task.[29] Under the Hertz method the decision maker is not required to assign specific probabilities to the individual variables, but is only required to choose:

1. the pertinent variables

2. the expected value of each variable

---

[29] See D.B. Hertz, "Uncertainty and investment selection" in J.F. Weston and M.B. Goudzwaard (Eds.), *The Treasurer's Handbook* (Homewood, IL.: Dow Jones-Irwin, 1976) Chapter 18, p.p. 376–420.

3. the upper estimate of each variable

4. the lower estimate of each variable.

Thus, this system only requires what a good political risk analyst is likely to know or be able to estimate with some accuracy. The Monte Carlo simulation is then used to generate the required probability distributions.

The Monte Carlo method also permits assignment of values that reflect differing degrees of dependence between some events and other subsequent events. For example, the project's expected sales and prices might be determined by the intensity of competition in conjunction with the total size of market demand and the country's growth rate. A further advantage of the Hertz technique is that by separating the individual factors that determine profitability, the separate effects of each factor can be estimated and the sensitivity of profitability to each factor can be determined. If the effects of a particular factor on the final results are negligible, it is not necessary for management to spend time on analyzing that factor. Thus, certain aspects of the myriad possible sources of political risk can be ruled out at the beginning, thereby simplifying the analysis.

Despite some serious drawbacks such as cost, complexity, and difficulty in estimating the interrelationships between variables and their underlying probability distributions, the Monte Carlo method can be a valuable tool for assessing a project's riskiness and determining its NPV.

Advanced techniques: Measuring political risk as an insurance premium

Clark (1997 and 1998) has developed an approach for measuring the effect of political risk on the outcome of foreign direct investment projects that overcomes the theoretical shortcomings of the traditional methods. It uses the tools of option pricing theory to solve the problem of the determination of the discount rate for political risk: the no-arbitrage argument makes it possible to discount at the riskless rate.[30] It also explicitly defines the evolutionary process of political risk and incorporates the stochastic element in its evolution as well as the timing of the political events that generate losses.[31]

The approach involves measuring the effects of political risk on the outcome of a foreign direct investment as the value of an insurance policy that reimburses all losses resulting from the political event or events in question. It adopts the very broad definition of political risk as the probability of politically motivated change that affects the outcome of foreign direct investment, but makes a distinction between explicit events and ongoing change. Explicit events take the form of legislation or decrees such as expropriations, nationalizations, devaluations, etc. or the form of direct actions such as strikes, boycotts, terrorist acts, etc. The nature of explicit events is that they arrive intermittently at discrete intervals and that they generate an actual loss. Explicit events can be represented by a "Poisson jump" process. Ongoing change takes the form of continuous activity such as macroeconomic management and monetary policy, legislation, or social and political evolution that affects some or all aspects of the FDI's overall environment. Thus, in this model, ongoing change impacts on the level of what can be lost in the case of an explicit

[30] See, for example, E. Kasanen and L. Trigeorgis, 1994, "A market utility approach to investment valuation", *European Journal of Operational Research* (Special Issue on Financial Modeling) Vol. 74, No. 2, 294–309 and S.P. Mason and R.C. Merton, 1985, "The role of contingent claims analysis in corporate finance", in E. Altman and M. Subrahmanyam (Eds.), *Recent Advances in Corporate Finance* (Homewood, IL: Richard D. Irwin), 7–54.

[31] See: E. Clark, "Valuing political risk as an insurance policy", *Journal of International Money and Finance*, Vol. 16 (1997), p.p. 477–490 and E. Clark, "Political risk in Hong Kong and Taiwan: Pricing the China factor", *Journal of Economic Integration*, Vol. 13, No. 2 (1998), p.p. 278–293.

event and can be represented by geometric Brownian motion. As an example of the distinction between explicit events and ongoing change, take the case of an over-expansive monetary policy with a fixed exchange rate. The over-expansive monetary policy generates the ongoing changes that affect what will be lost if the explicit event of a devaluation takes place. On the other hand, with a floating exchange rate, changes in the value of the host country's currency would be considered ongoing change and not an explicit event. Another example of ongoing change would be social agitation for excessive increases in worker benefits. The amount at risk would vary as the social dialogue ebbs and flows. The actual loss would come about as the result of an explicit event such as a strike or an unfavorable government-imposed settlement.

To see how this works, let x follow geometric Brownian motion and represent the exposure to loss in the case of an explicit political event:[32]

$$dx(t) = (\alpha + \beta)x(t)dt + \sigma x(t)dz(t) \tag{10.5}$$

where

α = the rate of growth of the intensity of political risk with $\alpha < 0; \alpha > 0; \alpha = 0$. It measures the intensity of the political environment surrounding the particular risk in question. The interpretation of α is that as the intensity of the political risk increases, the severity or cost of the measures undertaken will be increased when an explicit event does occur. If $\alpha < 0$, the intensity of the political risk in question is expected to be declining on the average; if $\alpha > 0$, it is expected to be increasing on the average; if $\alpha = 0$, it is expected to remain the same.

β = the rate of growth of the investment and depends on the investment's internal rate of return and the rate of reinvestment out of profits.

$dz(t)$ = a Wiener process with zero mean and variance equal to dt.

σ^2 = the variance of $dx(t)/x(t)$ due to political risk. σ^2 can be interpreted as the level of the political risk.

Equation 10.5 says that exposure to political risk is expected to change at a rate of $\alpha + \beta$, the rate of growth of political intensity plus the rate of growth of the value of the investment, with a standard deviation due to political risk of σ times the random element in ongoing change represented by the Wiener process, $z(t)$.

Suppose that political events occur at random times according to a Poisson arrival process where q is a random variable that increases by steps of u every time a Poisson event occurs and λ is a constant intensity parameter such that:

$$dq(t) = \begin{cases} 1 \text{ with probability } \lambda dt \\ 0 \text{ with probability } 1 - \lambda dt. \end{cases}$$

This means that losses arrive at a rate of λdt and that λ is the political risk probability parameter, that is, the probability that a loss-causing political event will actually occur over the interval dt. If $x(t)$ represents the potential loss when a Poisson event occurs, the expected loss per interval dt is equal to $\lambda x(t)dt$.

Let V represent the value of an insurance policy covering the investment against losses arising from the political risk, so that when losses occur they are reimbursed by the

---

[32] See Chapter 8 for a presentation of Brownian motion and the basic mathematics involved.

insurance. The typical direct investment involves setting up a subsidiary in the host country or purchasing all or part of an already existing company in the host country. Legislation in most countries is such that either there is no specified life span for a company or when the life span is specified, such as in France, it can be renewed indefinitely. Consequently, the typical direct investment can be viewed as a perpetual claim. Because of the perpetual nature of the typical direct investment, V is also a perpetual claim and, consequently, its value does not depend on time. Thus, V is a function of the exposure to losses arising from political risk: $V = V(x(t))$ = value of the insurance policy covering the investment against losses arising from political risk.

The expected total return on the insurance policy is equal to $E(dV)$ plus the expected cash flow generated by the explicit event, $\lambda x(t)dt$. Assume that the world economy is risk neutral and that the risk-free interest rate is constant at r, apply Ito's lemma and take expectations. This gives the following differential equation:

$$\frac{1}{2}\sigma^2 x(t)^2 V''(x(t)) + V'(x(t))(\alpha + \beta)x(t) - rV(x(t)) + \lambda x(t) = 0 \qquad (10.6)$$

where the primes denote first and second derivatives.

The solution to this equation depends on the values of the various parameters and the boundary conditions associated with each investment. For example, if we rule out speculative bubbles and assume that the policy has no value when there is nothing at risk, the value of the policy covering a series of losses is

$$V = \frac{\lambda x(t)}{r - (\alpha + \beta)} \qquad (10.7)$$

The value of a policy covering expropriation is

$$V = \frac{\lambda x(t)}{r + \lambda - (\alpha + \beta)} \qquad (10.8)$$

Once political risk quantified as the value of the insurance policy has been estimated, it can be integrated into the capital budgeting process in a two-step methodology:

1. Estimate the NPV of the project in the absence of political risk.

2. Subtract the value of the insurance policy from the project's NPV in the absence of political risk. This gives NPV $-$ V, the net present value of the investment adjusted for political risk.

This methodology has the advantage of being theoretically consistent with modern portfolio theory. It also avoids the difficulty of forecasting risk parameters far into the future. In its more advanced forms, the policy can be valued to reflect various options available to managers, such as the option to abandon the project if things go badly. It can also be valued to reflect the change from one level of political risk to another, such as the case of South Africa from white to black rule or Hong Kong from British to Chinese rule.[33] The political risk parameter, λ, can also be modeled to reflect uncertainty about the risk parameter itself and to be re-estimated in an endogenous Bayesian updating process.[34]

[33] See Clark (1998, 1999).

[34] See E. Clark and R. Tunaru, "Valuing and managing multiple political risks", *Middlesex University Business School, Discussion Paper Series*, No. 4, May 2000.

Example: Labor strife in Poland

Consider the case of labor strife in the manufacturing sector in Poland. A US manufacturer is considering building a factory in Poland for a total outlay of USD 200 million. The US manufacturer has no intention of increasing the size of his investment in the country and, consequently, all profits will be repatriated ($\beta = 0$). Net cash flows are estimated at USD 35 million per year, comprising USD 45 million in cash income less USD 10 million of variable operating costs. Suppose that analysis shows that there is a 5% chance of a strike or other related actions ($\lambda = 0.05$) and that the level of political risk is equal to 0.14 ($\sigma^2 = 0.14$).

The US manufacturer estimates that in the case of a strike in the immediate future the company would lose USD 7.5 million ($x(0) = $ USD 7.5 million and evolves according to Equation 10.5). Further analysis shows that closer relations with the EU should increase the country's economic performance, that the domestic political situation should continue to improve as the country becomes wealthier and more familiar with capitalism, that external relations, especially with the EU, should improve, but that social agitation due to increasing economic inequities will increase. It is decided that, taken together, these phenomena will cause a gradual decline in political intensity at the rate of 3% per year ($\alpha = -0.03$). Table 10.3 summarizes the foregoing information. Applying it in Equation 10.7 gives the cost of this political risk:

$$V = \frac{0.05 \times \text{USD } 7.5}{0.06 + 0.03} = \text{USD } 4.17 \text{ million.}$$

Suppose that the company's cost of capital for an equivalent project in the United States is 12%. In the absence of the cost of Polish political risk the NPV of the project is USD 8.33 million ($^{\text{USD } 45}/_{0.12} - {^{\text{USD } 10}}/_{0.06} - \text{USD } 200 = \text{USD } 8.33$). To calculate the project's NPV adjusted for political risk, subtract the cost of political risk from the project's NPV in the absence of political risk: NPV adjusted for political risk = USD 8.33 – USD 4.17 = USD 4.16 million.

Summary

1. The sources of cross-border risk, often called country risk, are many and varied. They include all aspects of a country's economic, financial, social and political organization as well as its geographic location and strategic importance. In its broadest sense it includes almost every situation that could conceivably occur in a given country.

2. Many of the risk factors can actually be managed quite easily through straightforward means such as research and expert advice, diversification, or by employing locals as principals or consultants.

3. The most important factors to assess and incorporate into the analysis are those associated with a country's economic and financial situation. They depend on a

Table 10.3 Parameter summary for the case of labor strife in Poland

α	β	σ^2	λ	r	x_o	C	x^*	γl
–0.03	0	0.14	0.05	0.06	USD 7.5	USD 25	119.91	1.8836

country's human and natural resources and how these resources are managed. One of the main difficulties is the lack of pertinent information.

4. Conventional cross-border economic and financial analysis relies on traditional macroeconomic analysis complemented by some specific ratios designed to relate the exercise to the needs of the international economic agent.

5. Cross-border risk analysis for portfolio investment is far ahead of what has been done in the banking sector, especially where theory is concerned. Emphasis has been on diversification to offset market risk and on hedging techniques to offset exchange risk.

6. The concept of political risk can generally be defined as *"the probability of politically motivated change that affects the outcome of foreign-based transactions"*.

7. The measures and events affecting foreign operations can be grouped into three general categories: hard political risk, administrative or soft political risk, and social risk. The first group includes expropriation, confiscation, nationalization and forced local shareholding; the second group covers decisions such as control of prices, foreign exchange and remittances; and, finally, social risk encompasses factors like strikes, lack of an experienced labor force, war, ethnic strife and environmental protests.

8. Political risk affects all types of foreign transactions including direct investment, portfolio investment, cross-border loans and commercial transactions.

9. Traditional methods for assessing political risk range from the comparative techniques of rating and mapping systems to the analytical techniques of special reports, dynamic segmentation, expert systems and probability determination, to the econometric techniques of model building and discriminant and logit analysis. Although all are aimed at assessing political risk, the individual methods differ drastically as regards the type of information they supply. In a rating exercise each country is graded and ranked based on a set of parameters selected as judgemental criteria. A special report involves one or several experts that examine the key variables that are supposed to describe a given country's main characteristics and who communicate their findings in the form of a special report. Dynamic segmentation seeks to analyze the fundamental trends of a country by dividing a society into various behavior-homogeneous groups, called segments, and then forecasting the most likely coalitions of these segments and how the coalitions are likely to influence the relationship between the investing company and the political powers. The probabilistic approach involves computing various alternative outcomes, each one being allocated a certain probability of occurrence and implying specific measures with regard to foreign investment. The econometric methods rely on historical data to forecast economic variables or group countries according to whether or not they will do something such as default on debt obligations or expropriate.

10. Traditional methods for integrating political risk analyses into the capital budgeting process involve using the analyses to estimate a risk premium or a cash flow adjustment factor that is then pasted on to the traditional NPV equation. Neither approach, however, is theoretically satisfactory. The choice of a risk premium (or risk premia if the discount rate is allowed to vary) is completely arbitrary whereas the choice of a cash flow adjustment factor requires the unrealistic assumption that political risk is completely diversifiable and thus has no effect on the investment's cost of capital. Furthermore, the foregoing methods do not address the diverse nature of the political risks in question or the fact that the frequency and intensity of the political risks can change randomly through time.

11. Using techniques borrowed from option pricing theory, more recent work addresses the theoretical and practical shortcomings of the traditional methods. It involves measuring the cost of political risk as the value of a hypothetical insurance policy that pays off all

losses resulting from political events. The contingent claims methodology overcomes the arbitrariness that makes the traditional methods for integrating political risk into the capital budgeting process theoretically deficient. More specifically, the well known techniques applied in contingent claims analysis solve the problem of determining risk-adjusted discount rates by making it possible to discount at the riskless rate. This, in turn, makes it possible to treat cash flows associated with political risk independently of the investment's cash flows in the absence of political risk. Political risk is then incorporated in the capital budgeting framework in a three-step process. First, the net present value (NPV) of the investment in the absence of political risk is estimated. Secondly, the cost of political risk is estimated. Thirdly, the cost of political risk is subtracted from the investment's NPV to obtain the NPV adjusted for political risk.

Questions

Solutions to the following questions are set out on the web site, details of which are included in the Preface.

1. Define cross-border risk.

2. What are some of the shortcomings of traditional country risk and political risk analysis?

3. What is meant by a country's economic risk and what are some of the major variables used in assessing it?

4. What is meant by a country's financial risk and what are some of the major variables used in assessing it?

5. Discuss the concept of political risk.

6. Explain how rating systems work and how they can be used to assess political risk.

7. What information does a special report include?

8. What econometric techniques can be used for political risk analysis?

9. What are the three methods for incorporating political risk in the capital budgeting decision?

10. What are the advantages of the method that uses a hypothetical insurance policy to measure political risk in foreign direct investments?

The benefits and risks of international portfolio investment

Certain aspects of portfolio investment are peculiar to the international arena. They are present on a theoretical and practical level and are caused by the necessity of comparing risk and return across countries with different markets, customs and consumer preferences, as well as distinct currencies, legal systems and tax codes. In this chapter we look first at the major theoretical issues involved in international portfolio building and examine how they square with the empirical evidence. We then turn to the practical issues associated with international portfolio management and see how they affect the investment process.

The nature of risk

Expected return and standard deviation

Before examining the specifics of risk associated with international financial transactions, it is important to develop a precise definition of what exactly is meant by the word "risk". Risk has different meanings in different contexts. It is generally defined as the probability of unfavorable outcomes. In finance we are interested in the effects of risk on the valuation of financial assets and liabilities. Thus, one measure of risk might be the probability that the return on an investment will fall below a certain level. We might say, for example, that there is a 30% probability that the return on an investment in Microsoft shares will fall below 12%. As a risk measure, it is better than nothing but still is not very informative. It would be better if we knew by how much the return was likely to be below 12%. Our perception of the riskiness of the investment would certainly be different if the return could fall as low as –20% instead of +10%. A more complete way to look at risk would be to associate a probability to each possible outcome. This **probability distribution** would make it possible to calculate the most likely outcome as well as by how much the real outcome is likely to diverge from the most likely outcome.

Suppose that the return on an investment (Asset 1 in Table 11.1) depends on economic conditions. If economic conditions are good, the investment will show a return of 32%. If economic conditions are average, it will show a return of 20%. If economic conditions are bad, it will only show a return of 8%. Research reveals that there is an equally likely probability (1/3) of any one of the three economic situations actually happening. In these conditions, what is the return that the investor should expect? In fact, expected return means the arithmetic average, and is calculated by multiplying each possible outcome by the probability that the outcome will occur and summing. The expected return for Asset 1 can thus be calculated as:

$$(1/3 \times 32\%) + (1/3 \times 20\%) + (1/3 \times 8\%) = 20\%.$$

Table 11.1 summarizes the foregoing information for Asset 1.

The investor now knows what to expect from the investment. How risky it is depends on how much it is likely to diverge from its expected value. The **standard deviation** is the simplest statistical measure of how much a variable is likely to diverge from its expected value. It is sometimes referred to as "volatility" and in finance it is often used to indicate the riskiness of an asset, a portfolio of assets or a market. The standard deviation is the square root of the variance.

The variance of a variable is the arithmetic average of the squares of the deviations around the variable's arithmetic average. Using the information in Table 11.1, the variance of Asset 1 can be calculated by taking the difference between each possible outcome and the average outcome, squaring it, multiplying the squared difference by the probability of the outcome occurring, and summing:

$$(32 - 20)^2 \times 1/3 + (20 - 20)^2 \times 1/3 + (8 - 20)^2 \times 1/3 = 96.$$

The variance of the returns on Asset 1 is 96. Variance is converted into the original units of percentages by taking the square root. The square root of 96 is about 9.8, so the standard deviation of Asset 1 is 9.8%. It measures how much actual returns are likely to diverge from the expected return. In the case of Asset 1, it is plus or minus 9.8%. Consequently most actual returns should fall between 10.2% and 29.8%. The Greek letter sigma (σ) is often used to denote standard deviation.

Mean-variance analysis

To summarize, then, we can say that standard deviation is an estimate of the probable divergence of an actual return from an expected return. It measures the degree of uncertainty. Expected return and standard deviation or variance as parameters for financial decision making are often referred to as the mean-variance criterion. Combined with two entirely plausible assumptions about investor preferences, mean-variance analysis is a powerful tool in modern financial theory. The first assumption is that investors prefer more return to less return. The second assumption is that they prefer less risk to more risk. In other words, they are risk averse. The implication is that there is a trade-off between risk and return such that riskier securities require higher returns than less risky ones. Let's see how this works.

In Table 11.1, Assets 1 and 2 both have the same return. However, Asset 2 has a higher standard deviation. This indicates that Asset 2 is riskier than Asset 1. Therefore, since less risk is preferred to more risk, for the same level of return, Asset 1 is preferred to Asset 2. If

Table 11.1 Expected return and standard deviation

Economic conditions	Probability	Return on Asset 1 (%)	Return on Asset 2 (%)	Return on Asset 3 (%)
Good	1/3	32	2	38
Average	1/3	20	20	20
Bad	1/3	8	38	6
Expected return		20	20	21.33
Standard deviation		9.8	14.7	13.1

two assets have the same standard deviation but one asset has a higher return than another, the asset with the higher return will be preferred. The situation is more complicated when there is no clear-cut advantage.

Consider Asset 3 in Table 11.1. Its expected return is higher than that of Asset 2 and its standard deviation is lower. It is clearly preferable to Asset 2. However, compared to Asset 1, there is a problem. Asset 3's expected return is higher than Asset 1"s but Asset 1"s standard deviation is lower. One procedure that can be used to compare them is to standardize the risk per unit of expected return by dividing the standard deviation by the expected return. This concept is called the coefficient of variation:

$$CV = \frac{\sigma}{E(R)}$$

For Asset 1, $CV = 9.8/20 = 0.49$. For Asset 3, $CV = 13.1/21.33 = 0.614$. Asset 1 has less risk per unit of return than Asset 3 and thus is preferred to Asset 3.

Some comments on risk

In the strict sense of modern financial theory, volatility and standard deviation are usually considered an acceptable measure of risk. In this book, this is the sense that is implied when we refer to risk. Building on this definition, many analyses even assume that returns follow a particular probability distribution. Much of modern financial theory, for example, is based on the assumption of a normal probability distribution (or log normal when the continuously compounded rate of return is used) represented by the well known bell-shaped curve. This assumption is also present in much of what follows in later chapters. Risk analysis, however, is more than choosing probability distributions and calculating standard deviations. It requires identifying potential sources of risk and analyzing their impact on the financial variables under consideration. In the following section we present the principle of diversification and outline the major analytical frameworks and techniques used for portfolio construction and risk management. We then extend the analysis to include the risks associated with portfolio building and trading in an international environment.

International diversification

The benefits of diversification

The main argument for international portfolio investment is based on the principle of diversification. Diversification means reducing risk by not putting all your eggs in one basket. In finance it means reducing risk by not putting all your wealth into one asset. In modern portfolio theory it can be shown that by spreading wealth over a variety of assets selected on the basis of their expected returns and the correlations between the individual expected returns, portfolio risk can be reduced for a given level of expected return, or, conversely, expected portfolio return can be increased for a given level of risk. Table 11.2 shows an example of how this works.

Assets 1 and 2 are perfectly negatively correlated. They both have an expected return of 20% and relatively high levels of risk measured by their standard deviations.[1] If the two assets

---

[1] Terms such as expected return, variance, standard deviation, covariance and correlation are commonly used in discussing modern portfolio theory. Students should see a standard textbook on statistics for a more complete presentation of these concepts.

are combined into a portfolio comprising 60% of Asset 1 and 40% of Asset 2, the expected return of the combination is unchanged at 20% but the standard deviation falls to zero. Generally speaking, the lower the correlation the greater the benefits of diversification.

In the preceding section we introduced the concept of mean-variance analysis based on expected returns and standard deviations. The foregoing example extends the mean-variance analysis to include the concepts of correlation and covariance. The covariance between two variables is the arithmetic average of the products of deviations around each variable's arithmetic average. Using the information from Table 11.2, for example, the covariance between Assets 1 and 2 can be calculated as follows:

$$(32\% - 20\%)(2\% - 20\%) \times 1/3 + (20\% - 20\%)(20\% - 20\%) \times 1/3 + (8\% - 20\%)$$
$$(38\% - 20\%) \times 1/3 = -144.$$

The covariance between two random variables is related to the correlation between them. In fact, covariance is equal to the correlation coefficient multiplied by the standard deviation of each of the two variables. The correlation coefficient can take values between +1.0 and −1.0. A correlation coefficient of +1.0 means that the two variables are perfectly synchronized in their movements, while a correlation coefficient of −1.0 means that the variables move in opposite directions. The correlation coefficient can be calculated by dividing the covariance by the product of the standard deviations of each variable. From Table 11.2, for instance, the standard deviations of Assets 1 and 2 are 9.8 and 14.7 respectively. Thus, the correlation between the two assets is:

$$-144/(9.8 \times 14.7) = -1,$$

which means that the two assets are perfectly negatively correlated.

Armed with the concepts of correlation and covariance, we can extend the principle of diversification to include *n* assets. The expected return on a portfolio of *n* assets is equal to the sum of the expected returns of each asset weighted by the percent of the portfolio invested in the asset:

$$E(R_p) = \sum_{i=1}^{n} x_i E(R_i) \tag{11.1}$$

Table 11.2 Diversification benefits by combining two negatively correlated assets

Economic conditions	Probability	Return on Asset 1 (%)	Return on Asset 2 (%)	Return on portfolio of 60% Asset 1 and 40% Asset 2 (%)
Good	1/3	32	2	20
Average	1/3	20	20	20
Bad	1/3	8	38	20
Expected return		20	20	20
Standard deviation		9.8	14.7	0.0

where:

x_i = percent of funds invested in asset i
R_{ij} = jth return on asset i
R_p = return on the portfolio
E = expectation operator
σ_i^2 = variance of returns on asset i
σ_{ik} = covariance of returns between assets i and k.

The variance of the portfolio can be calculated as follows:

$$\sigma_p^2 = E[R_p - E(R_p)]^2$$

$$= E[x_1R_{1j} + x_2R_{2j} + \ldots + x_nR_{nj} - x_1E(R_1) - x_2E(R_2) - \ldots - x_nE(R_n)]^2$$

$$= \sum_{i=1}^{n} x_i^2\sigma_i^2 + \sum_{\substack{i=1 \\ i \neq k}}^{n} \sum_{k=1}^{n} x_i x_k \sigma_{i,k} \tag{11.2}$$

Equation 11.2 shows that the variance of a portfolio can be divided into two parts. The first part is the sum of the variances of the individual assets weighted by the square of the weight of each asset in the portfolio. The second part is the sum of the covariances of all the pairs of assets weighted by the product of the weights of both assets in the portfolio.

Suppose that the same amount is invested in each asset. Since there are n assets, $1/n$ will be invested in each one, so that Equation 11.2 becomes:

$$\sigma_p^2 = \sum_{i=1}^{n} \frac{1}{n^2}\sigma_i^2 + \sum_{\substack{i=1 \\ i \neq k}}^{n} \sum_{k=1}^{n} \frac{1}{n^2}\sigma_{i,k} \tag{11.3}$$

The single summation has n terms and the double summation has $n(n-1)$ terms. If we factor $1/n$ from the single summation and $(n-1)/n$ from the double summation, what remains in the summations are averages. The single summation is the average of the variance terms of all the individual assets and the double summation is the average of all the covariance terms:

$$\sigma_p^2 = \frac{1}{n}\sum_{i=1}^{n} \frac{1}{n}\sigma_i^2 + \frac{n-1}{n}\sum_{\substack{i=1 \\ i \neq k}}^{n} \sum_{k=1}^{n} \frac{1}{n(n-1)}\sigma_{i,k} \tag{11.4}$$

Hence, as n tends to infinity (as more and more assets are added to the portfolio), $1/n$ tends to zero and the contribution of the variance of the individual assets to the variance of the portfolio tends to zero. However, as n tends to infinity, $(n-1)/n$ tends to 1 and the variance of the portfolio tends to the average of the covariance terms. The lower the covariance terms, the lower the variance of the portfolio. This means that in the context of a portfolio, the riskiness of the individual assets is less important than the correlation of its returns with the returns of the other assets. Individually risky assets with low correlation may be better additions to a portfolio than less risky assets with higher correlation.

The Markowitz optimization of the diversification principle suggests that the risk-averse investor can diversify over a security universe by selecting those securities that provide portfolios with maximum expected return for a given level of risk or minimum risk for a given level of expected return.[2] The family of portfolios having the greatest expected return for a given level of risk forms the curve of the "efficient frontier". Depending on his risk–return trade-off, the investor can select his desired portfolio from this group. The shaded portion of Figure 11.1 represents all the feasible portfolios of risky assets and the concave envelope represents the efficient frontier. Portfolios M and A, for example, have the same risk measured at σ_1 on the x-axis. However, portfolio M, which is on the efficient frontier, has a higher return measured at R_M on the y-axis than portfolio A, the return on which is only R_A.

Capital asset pricing model

Equilibrium pricing of individual assets draws on the diversification principle and mean-variance Markowitz optimization presented above. Before we go on to look at diversification and asset pricing in an international context, however, it is useful to review the theory of asset pricing in the domestic context in order to have a clear idea of the issues involved.

The capital asset pricing model (CAPM) is the first well known and widely used model of market equilibrium. Its objective is to project a simplified view of the world that captures all the most important aspects of reality. The simplification is necessary because the real world is too complex to analyze down to its last detail. The complexities of the real world are simplified in the CAPM by making certain restrictive assumptions that can be summarized as follows:

- Investors are concerned only with risk and return. They prefer higher expected returns and lower risk.

- Every investor has the same information that he analyzes and processes in the same way, which means that everyone agrees about future prospects for securities.

- An individual investor cannot affect the price of a stock by his buying and selling.

- All assets, including human capital, are marketable.

- There are no transaction costs or taxes.

- There exists a riskless rate of interest and investors can borrow or lend any amount of funds at this rate.

The introduction of a "riskless" asset into the family of portfolio possibilities greatly simplifies the problem of optimal portfolio selection. By definition, the portfolio composed

Figure 11.1 The efficient frontier

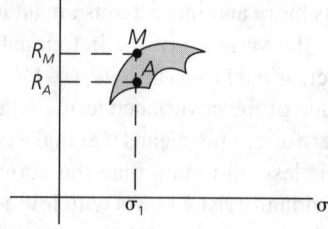

[2] H. Markowitz, *Portfolio Selection: Efficient Diversification of Investments* (New York: John Wiley & Sons, 1959).

only of the riskless asset has a standard deviation of zero. In Figure 11.2 we represent the return on the riskless asset by R_F on the y-axis. Line R_FMZ represents all the combinations of the riskless asset with portfolio M, the portfolio attained where the line R_FZ is tangent to the efficient frontier. This line is called the capital market line and portfolio M is called the market portfolio. Any portfolio of risky assets other than M would yield lower returns for a given level of risk than portfolios on the capital market line. For example, portfolio C on the efficient frontier has the same risk as portfolio B on the capital market line but its return is lower. Therefore, all investors who believed they faced the efficient frontier and the riskless lending and borrowing rate shown in Figure 11.2 would hold the same portfolio of risky assets, portfolio M. The more risk averse would combine the riskless asset with portfolio M and find themselves somewhere between R_F and M on the capital market line. The less risk averse would borrow and invest the funds in M and find themselves between M and Z on the capital market line. The ability to determine the optimum portfolio without having to know anything about the investor except that he is risk averse is known as the **separation theorem**. From here it is just a short step to equilibrium pricing of individual securities.

The expected return on the market portfolio can be written as:

$$E(R_M) = R_F + [E(R_M) - R_F]$$ (11.5)

where $[E(R_M) - R_F]$ is the market premium for risk. It can be shown that in equilibrium the required rate of return on a given asset is a linear function of the market premium for risk:[3]

$$E(R_i) = R_F + \beta_i[E(R_M) - R_F]$$ (11.6)

where β is the covariance of the returns on asset i with the returns on the market portfolio divided by the variance of the returns on the market portfolio:

$$\beta_i = \frac{\sigma_{i,M}}{\sigma_M^2}$$

Equation 11.6 is called the **security market line** (SML). β measures the risk that each asset or portfolio of assets contributes to the market as a whole. This is the risk that cannot be eliminated through diversification and is known as **systematic risk**. The implications of the CAPM for returns on individual securities or portfolios of securities is illustrated in Figure 11.3. The figure shows expected return on the y-axis and the degree of systematic risk, β, on the x-axis. The security market line maps the expected

Figure 11.2 The capital market line

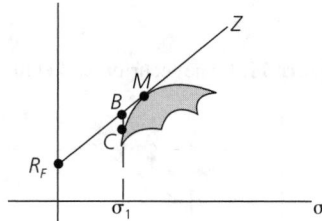

[3] For the derivation and explanation of the capital asset pricing model see E.J. Elton and M.J. Gruber, *Modern Portfolio Theory and Investment Analysis*, 5th edition (John Wiley & Sons, 1995).

rate of return that is required for taking different amounts of systematic risk. For example, a security with no systematic risk ($\beta = 0$) will only offer the riskless rate of return. A security with the same systematic risk as the market portfolio has a beta of one and offers the same return as the market portfolio. A security with an expected return above the security market line, like security A, will be recognized by investors as a bargain. Demand for security A will rise, causing its price to rise and its expected return to fall until it reaches equilibrium on the SML. A security with an expected return below the security market line, like B, will be recognized by investors as a loser. Investors will sell the security, causing its price to fall and its expected return to rise until it reaches equilibrium on the SML.

The conclusions of the CAPM are that in equilibrium all investors should hold the same portfolio of risky assets and that each individual asset or portfolio of assets will offer an expected rate of return equal to the risk-free interest rate plus a risk premium that is linearly related to the risk that the asset or portfolio of assets contributes to the market as a whole.

Value at risk

Wilmott (1998a, p. 547) defines value at risk (VaR) as "an estimate, with a given degree of confidence, of how much one can lose from one's portfolio over a given time horizon". VaR uses the principles of mean-variance analysis that underlie the CAPM but concentrates on the negative tails of the distributions rather than the overall distribution. It is an attempt to provide a simple measure that summarizes the overall risk of a portfolio in a single number. It has become popular with senior management and corporate treasurers as well as with financial institutions and regulators and figures prominently in the BIS 1998 capital requirements for market risk.

For a more formal definition of VaR, let c represent the degree of confidence and δV the change in the value of a portfolio over a given period. Then VaR can be written as

$$\text{Prob} \, [\delta V \leq - VaR] = 1 - c \tag{11.7}$$

Suppose that VaR is USD 20 million and the degree of confidence is 99%, then if the time horizon is ten days, Prob $[\delta V \leq \text{USD } 20 \text{ million}] = 1 - 0.99 = 0.01$ means that there is a 1% probability that the portfolio could lose USD 20 million or more over the next ten days.

VaR is calculated assuming normal market conditions, meaning that extreme market conditions are not considered. Extreme conditions are considered separately. In the simplest situation the assumption is that the movement of the components of the portfolio are random and drawn from a normal distribution. For short time periods it is also customary to assume

Figure 11.3 The security market line

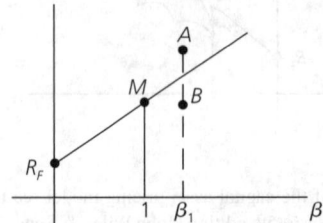

that the expected change in the price of the variable is zero. More complicated assumptions can also be accommodated, usually at the cost of time and/or tractability.[4]

VaR for a single-asset portfolio

We start by estimating VaR for a single asset. Consider a portfolio of USD 50 million worth of shares in Microsoft. Since the BIS 1998 time horizon is ten days, assume that this is the relevant time period. The confidence level is 99%, the annualized volatility of Microsoft shares is 47.5% and there are 250 trading days in the year. First, we calculate the standard deviation of the portfolio over the ten-day horizon:

$$\sqrt{\delta t} \times \sigma_{year} = \sqrt{\frac{10}{250}} \times 0.475 = 0.095.$$

Secondly, we find the 99% confidence interval of the cumulative normal curve corresponds to 2.33 standard deviations from the mean. Thus, the ten-day 99% VaR on a portfolio of USD 50 million worth of Microsoft shares can be calculated as

$$0.095 \times 2.33 \times \text{USD 50 million} = \text{USD 11.0675 million.}$$

VaR for a two-asset portfolio

Next consider a USD 50 million portfolio with 50% in Microsoft shares and 50% in Conagra shares. Assume as before that the time horizon is ten days, the confidence level is 99%, the annualized volatility of Microsoft shares is 47.5% and there are 250 trading days in the year. Assume further that the annualized volatility of Conagra shares is 47.5% and the correlation between the two companies' shares is –0.5. First we estimate the annual volatility of the portfolio using Equation 11.3:

$$\sigma_p = \sqrt{\sigma_p^2} = \sqrt{\sum_{i=1}^{2} \frac{1}{n^2} \sigma_i^2 + \sum_{\substack{i=1 \\ i \neq k}}^{2} \sum_{k=1}^{2} \frac{1}{n^2} \sigma_{i,k}}$$

$$= \sqrt{0.5^2 \times 0.475^2 + 0.5^2 \times 0.475^2 + 2 \times 0.5^2 \times 0.475^2 \times (-0.5)} = 0.2375.$$

Next, we calculate the volatility of the portfolio over the ten-day horizon:

$$\sqrt{\frac{10}{250}} \times 0.2375 = 0.0475.$$

Thus, the ten-day 99% VaR on a USD 50 million portfolio with equal amounts in Microsoft and Conagra can be calculated as:

$$0.0475 \times 2.33 \times \text{USD 50 million} = \text{USD 5.53375 million.}$$

---

[4] For more on VaR, see www.jpmorgan.com.

The reduction in the VaR is due to the diversification effects associated with the low correlation between the two companies' share prices. Extensions of VaR to portfolios containing *n* assets is straightforward.

Other methods for estimating VaR

There are many other methods for calculating VaR. The two most popular involve simulations using either the Monte Carlo method, described in some detail in Chapter 10, or "bootstrapping".

Monte Carlo simulations

The Monte Carlo method applied to VaR involves using numbers drawn from the normal distribution to build a distribution of future scenarios. For each of these scenarios the pricing model is applied to calculate the value of the portfolio and estimate the VaR directly. The advantage of the Monte Carlo simulation is that it can accommodate intermediate payoffs as well as any stochastic process. Thus, it can be used to value portfolios that include many types of derivative products. The drawback is that it is computationally time consuming.

Bootstrapping

Whereas Monte Carlo simulations are based on the generation of normally distributed random numbers, bootstrapping uses actual asset price movements taken from historical data. The popularity of bootstrapping is due to the well documented observation that the distributions of daily changes in many market variables do not seem to be normal. They generally have fatter tails than the normal distribution and are often skewed. The bootstrapping method captures the features of the historical distributions when estimating the VaR.

The method involves collecting daily data for the assets in the portfolio over a relatively long period. Four years of daily data is usually an adequate minimum. The data is then organized into vectors of daily returns that include all the assets for each day. Each vector of daily returns is given a number, which can be selected randomly from the uniform distribution. For example, if there are 1000 vectors of daily returns, a number from one to 1000 is drawn randomly and the daily returns corresponding to the vector with this number are used to calculate the portfolio's value for the first day of the simulation, which is added to or subtracted from the portfolio's value on the preceding day. The process is repeated until the appropriate time horizon is reached: for a ten-day horizon there will be ten draws. This process is repeated many times to obtain a distribution of the portfolio's returns from which the VaR can be inferred.

The main drawbacks to this approach are that it requires a lot of historical data and that the data in question may not correspond to the economic and financial conditions of the time period they are supposed to simulate.

Arbitrage pricing model

The CAPM and VaR models have their basis in mean-variance analysis. In these models all the investor requires to make optimal investment choices are the investment's expected return and its variance. Ross (1976) has proposed a different approach to asset pricing, called arbitrage pricing theory (APT). It is based on a mechanism that derives asset prices from arbitrage arguments, once a pre-specified return generating process has been given. In other words, it is based on the law of one price and does not need strong assumptions on utility theory that are necessary in deriving the CAPM. In this sense it is more general than the CAPM in that influences other than means and variances can affect asset pricing.

There are basically two assumptions in the derivation of APT: (a) all investors have the same expectations about asset prices, and (b) the process generating security returns is known. APT requires that returns on any stock be linearly related to a set of indices as follows:

$$R_i = a_i + b_{i1}I_1 + b_{i2}I_2 + \ldots + b_{ij}I_j + e_i \qquad (11.8)$$

where

a_i	= the expected return on stock i if all indices are equal to zero
I_j	= the value of the jth index that affects the return on stock i
b_{ij}	= the sensitivity of stock i's return to the jth index
e_i	= a random error with mean equal to zero and variance equal to σ_{ei}^2
$E(e_ie_k)$	= 0 for $i \neq k$
$E(e_i(I_j - \bar{I}_j))$	= 0 for all stocks and indices where the bar indicates expectations.

What we have in Equation 11.8 is a multi-index model. APT shows how to go from a multi-index model to a description of equilibrium. When the arbitrage arguments are applied we get

$$\bar{R}_i = R_f + b_{i1}(\bar{R}_{I_1} - R_f) + \ldots + b_{ij}(\bar{R}_{I_j} - R_f) \qquad (11.9)$$

The terms in parentheses represent the excess expected return or the market price of risk on the individual indices.

Without entering into a detailed discussion on the merits and demerits of APT with respect to the CAPM, several important comments are in order.[5] First of all, APT is not necessarily inconsistent with the CAPM. Secondly, although APT is very general, it requires a price-generating process that is known in order to describe equilibrium. Unfortunately, it has nothing to say about what the appropriate price-generating process actually is. This makes it difficult to interpret tests of APT and implement it in practice. This having been said, APT and multi-index models are becoming popular with practitioners because they make it possible to identify specific types of risk that can be monitored and controlled on an individual basis.

The factors used in practical applications of APT have to be common factors that affect a large number of assets. Three types of factors are being used in practice:

1. *Statistical factors*. Using an historical database of asset returns, a set of factors can be extracted from the data using what is known as factor analysis or principal component analysis. The weakness of this method is that it lacks a theoretical underpinning, which makes it difficult to interpret the results. The in-sample correlations are often spurious and unstable over time.

2. *Macroeconomic factors*. These factors can be selected based on a theoretical macroeconomic model. There are many models to choose from and we saw many logical candidates for explanatory factors such as growth, inflation, interest rates and investment in the preceding chapter. One popular factor in the international models is the exchange

---

[5] See E.J. Elton and M.J. Gruber, *Modern Portfolio Theory and Investment Analysis*, 5th edition, (John Wiley & Sons, 1995) Chapter 16 for a derivation of APT and a discussion of its strengths and weaknesses.

rate. The problem with the macroeconomic variables is that they often suffer from significant measurement error and long publication lags.

3. *Microeconomic factors.* These factors relate to company attributes such as its industry grouping, size, leverage ratio and earnings volatility. A common criticism of the microeconomic factors is that they are often chosen without an underlying theoretical rationale.

Once the factors have been determined, managers can use the model to identify and quantify the various risks embedded in a portfolio. They can also use it along with professional forecasts and personal analysis to tilt the portfolio to take advantage of expected developments.

Benefits of international diversification

Based on the foregoing discussion, the risk–return benefits to be derived from international diversification depend to a large extent on the correlation of the price behavior of the world's various capital markets. Table 11.3 shows the correlation of monthly returns in US dollars of some of the world's major stock markets from 1971–94. For example, the correlation coefficient between Switzerland and the United Kingdom is 0.55 and for the United States and Japan it is 0.27. Overall, the correlations indicate a high degree of independence across the various stock markets. This is true even for markets with economies that are closely related. Canada and the United States for example, close neighbors and major trading partners, have a correlation of only 0.68 and for West Germany and the United Kingdom, both members of the European Union, the correlation is only 0.43.

The situation is similar for bonds. Table 11.4 shows that US government bonds have a low correlation with other bond markets over the period 1971–94. In fact, the relationship ranges from 0.65 for Canada to as low as 0.21 for Swiss franc bonds. The correlation between the other foreign bond markets is also very low.[6]

Table 11.3 Stock market correlation of monthly returns in US dollars, 1971–94

	West Germany	United Kingdom	Switzerland	Australia	Japan	Canada	United States
West Germany	1.00						
United Kingdom	0.43	1.00					
Switzerland	0.69	0.55	1.00				
Australia	0.29	0.45	0.37	1.00			
Japan	0.39	0.35	0.40	0.24	1.00		
Canada	0.31	0.51	0.45	0.57	0.27	1.00	
United States	0.36	0.51	0.47	0.47	0.27	0.68	1.00

Source: B. Solnik, International Investments (Exhibit 4.3, p.p. 94–5). © 1996 Addison Wesley. Reprinted by permission of Pearson Education, Inc.

[6] See: K. Chollerton, P. Pieraerts and B. Solnik, "Why invest in foreign currency bonds?", *Journal of Portfolio Management* (Summer 1986).

Table 11.4 Bond market correlation of monthly returns in US dollars, 1971–94

	West Germany	United Kingdom	Switzerland	Japan	Canada	United States
West Germany	1.00					
United Kingdom	0.46	1.00				
Switzerland	0.78	0.44	1.00			
Japan	0.60	0.46	0.57	1.00		
Canada	0.32	0.35	0.26	0.28	1.00	
United States	0.31	0.25	0.24	0.25	0.65	1.00

Source: B. Solnik, International Investments (Exhibit 4.5, p.p. 97). © 1996 Addison Wesley. Reprinted by permission of Pearson Education, Inc.

This evidence suggests, and studies confirm, that the potential benefits from international diversification are considerable. In one of the earliest and most widely cited studies, Bruno Solnik showed that the risk of a portfolio can be reduced significantly by including foreign securities.[7] He computed the risk of portfolios of US stocks, increasing the number of stocks in the portfolio as he went along. He found, unsurprisingly, that by increasing the number of stocks in the portfolio, he could reduce the risk. After 40 or 50 stocks, however, addition of more domestic stocks had only a negligible effect on risk reduction. When he added foreign stocks to the purely domestic portfolios, he found not only that risk fell much faster but that it reduced overall risk to less than half that of a purely domestic portfolio of comparable size.

Many other studies have since confirmed these initial results. Hunter and Coggin found that international stock diversification could have reduced investment risk over the period 1970–86 to about 56% of the level achievable using only national diversification.[8] Bailey and Stultz examined Pacific Basin stocks from 1977 to 1985 and found that a US investor holding the S&P 500 Index could have reduced the standard deviation of his portfolio by a third by also investing in Pacific Basin stocks.[9]

The potential gains are not limited to risk reduction. International diversification also makes it possible to achieve higher returns. Over the period 1971 to 1994 the average annual returns of the world stock index in US dollars outperformed the US stock index by 12.2% versus 11% with volatility of only 14.6% versus 15.5% for the US index. The Morgan Stanley Capital International EAFE Stock Index also outperformed the US stock index by 14.6% versus 11% and its rate of return per unit of risk (return/standard deviation) was 0.80% versus only 0.71% for the US index.[10]

As far as bonds are concerned, international diversification also seems to be effective. A study by Chollerton, Pieraerts and Solnik covering the period 1971–84 showed that internationally diversified bond portfolios had returns per unit of risk substantially higher than the

[7] B. Solnik, "Why not diversify internationally rather than domestically", *Financial Analysts Journal* (July–August 1974), p.p. 48–54.

[8] J.E. Hunter and T.D. Coggin, "An analysis of the diversification benefit from international equity investment", *Journal of Portfolio Management* (Fall 1990), p.p. 33–36.

[9] W. Bailey and R.M. Stultz, "Benefits of international diversification: The case of Pacific Basin stock markets", *Journal of Portfolio Management* (Summer 1990), p.p. 57–61.

[10] B. Solnik, *International Investments* (Addison-Wesley Publishing Co., Inc., 1996), p. 102.

portfolios of 100% US bonds.[11] L. Thomas found similar results for the period 1975–88.[12] Combining stocks and bonds in a mean-variance Markowitz optimization, Solnik and Noetzlin found that spreading investments over all major foreign markets reduces risk while increasing return and that including bonds with stocks results in substantially lower risk than pure stock or pure bond portfolios without reducing returns.[13]

In spite of the growing body of literature confirming the potential benefits to be realized through international diversification, some caution is in order. The results have been obtained using past data whereas the theory calls for using the distribution of future returns. In practice, it is difficult to know what the distribution of future returns will be. Jorion, for example, underlines this difficulty by demonstrating the relatively poor performance of optimized portfolios generated from historical data when they are tested outside the sample period.[14] When he "shrinks" the sample averages towards a common mean, he finds that the out-of-sample performance of the optimal portfolio is substantially increased. One of the implications of his study is that potential gains in average returns are overestimated by the studies using historical data. Nevertheless, he shows that the benefits from international diversification are still substantial but that they are more likely to accrue from a reduction in risk than from an increase in returns. Longin and Solnik (1994) confirm Jorion. They found that over the period 1960–90 international correlation is not constant and tends to increase during periods of high stock market volatility.[15]

International capital asset pricing

Market risk and currency risk

International investment returns are often measured in two steps: first in terms of the currency of the investment and, secondly, in terms of the investor's base currency. This procedure recognizes the fact that variations in the exchange rate can have a profound effect on the returns of foreign investments in the investor's base currency. Consider a sterling-based investor who pays GBP 1 million for JPY 225 million worth of Japanese government bonds sold at par and paying 5%. At the end of a year the investor collects interest of JPY 11.25 million and sells the bonds, the price of which is unchanged, for JPY 225 million. He now has JPY 236.25 million and his return in yen is 5% (11.25/225). However, over the year the value of the pound has fallen from JPY 225 for one pound to JPY 200. Hence, when he converts his yen into pounds he will have GBP 1,181,250, which represents a gain in sterling of over 18% (1,181,250/1,000,000 – 1).

Thus, when a sterling-based investor makes a foreign investment, his expected return will take two forms: the expected return on the investment in foreign currency and the expected percentage change in the exchange rate. We can see how these two components can be broken down into market risk and currency risk.

[11] K. Chollerton, P. Pieraerts and B. Solnik, "Why invest in foreign currency bonds?", *Journal of Portfolio Management* (Summer 1986).

[12] L.R. Thomas, "The performance of currency hedged foreign bonds", *Financial Analysts Journal* (May–June 1989).

[13] B. Solnik and B. Noetzlin, "Optimal international asset allocation", *Journal of Portfolio Management* (Fall 1982).

[14] P. Jorion, "International portfolio diversification with estimation risk", *Journal of Business*, Vol. 58, No. 3 (1985), p.p. 259–278.

[15] F. Longin and B. Solnik, "Is the international correlation of equity returns constant: 1960–1990?", *Journal of International Money and Finance* (February 1995).

Ignoring the bid–ask spread on foreign exchange transactions, suppose that the sterling-based investor wants to invest GBP 1 in the US stock market. He first purchases dollars at the spot rate which will leave him with

$$\frac{1}{S_0(\text{GBP/USD})}\ \text{USD}.$$

He then uses these dollars to make his investment. The expected dollar value of the investment at the end of the period will be equal to the initial dollar value of the investment increased by the expected dollar return on the investment over the period. This can be written as

$$\frac{1}{S_0(\text{GBP/USD})}\ \text{USD} \times (1 + \bar{R}_{\text{USD}})$$

where the bar over R denotes expectation and $\bar{R}_{\text{USD}}$ is the expected dollar rate of return on the investment. Assuming that the investor converts the entire amount into pounds at the end of the period, the expected value of the investment in sterling will be equal to the expected dollar value of the investment at the end of the period multiplied by the expected spot exchange rate at the end of the period:

$$(1 + \bar{R}_{\text{GBP}}) = \frac{\bar{S}_1(\text{GBP/USD})}{S_0(\text{GBP/USD})} \times (1 + \bar{R}_{\text{USD}}) \tag{11.10}$$

The expression

$$\frac{\bar{S}_1(\text{GBP/USD})}{S_0(\text{GBP/USD})}$$

can be written as $1 + \Delta\bar{S}$ where $\Delta\bar{S}$ represents the expected percentage change in the exchange rate. Thus, the expected value of the investment in sterling can be separated into two parts. The first part, $1 + \Delta\bar{S}$, depends on the expected evolution of the relative values of the two currencies, and the second part, $1 + \bar{R}_{\text{USD}}$, depends on the expected performance of the investment in dollars:

$$(1 + \bar{R}_{\text{GBP}}) = (1 + \Delta\bar{S}) \times (1 + \bar{R}_{\text{USD}}) \tag{11.11}$$

The expected return in the investor's base currency is often presented as the linear approximation of Equation 11.11, obtained by ignoring the cross product on the right-hand side ($\Delta\bar{S} \times \bar{R}_{\text{USD}}$) and subtracting 1 from both sides:

$$\bar{R}_{\text{GBP}} = \Delta\bar{S} + \bar{R}_{\text{USD}} \tag{11.12}$$

Expressed in this way, base currency returns are clearly divided into their currency and foreign market components. This makes it possible to separate the risk associated with base currency returns into currency risk and foreign market risk. The variance of base currency returns is

$$E(R_{\text{GBP}} - \bar{R}_{\text{GBP}})^2 = E[(\Delta S - \Delta\bar{S}) + (R_{\text{USD}} - \bar{R}_{\text{USD}})]^2$$

$$= \sigma^2_{\text{GBP}} = \sigma^2_{\Delta S} + \sigma^2_{R_{\text{USD}}} + 2\rho\sigma_{\Delta S}\sigma_{R_{\text{USD}}} \tag{11.13}$$

where ρ is the correlation coefficient between the exchange rate and the return on the dollar investment.

Equation 11.13 shows that the variance of sterling returns on a dollar investment can be divided into the variance of the sterling–dollar exchange rate, the variance of the return on the dollar investment, and the covariance between the exchange rate and the return on the dollar investment. Since ρ, the correlation coefficient, is less than 1, the standard deviation of the return in sterling will be less than the sum of the standard deviations of the exchange rate and the return on the dollar investment. To illustrate this, we can take an example using the following data:

$$\sigma_S = 0.1$$
$$\sigma_{USD} = 0.2$$
$$\rho = 0.5$$

Using Equation 11.13 we have

$$\sigma^2_{GBP} = (0.1)^2 + (0.2)^2 + 2(0.5)(0.1)(0.2) = 0.07$$

and

$$\sigma_{GBP} < \sigma_{\Delta S} + \sigma_{R_{USD}}$$

since

$$\sqrt{0.07} = 0.2646 < 0.1 + 0.2$$

For a portfolio of stocks from different countries, risk can be broken down in the same way:

$$\sigma^2_p = E[R_p - E(R_p)]^2$$

$$= E\left[\begin{array}{c} x_1(R_{1j} + \Delta S_{1j}) + x_2(R_{2j} + \Delta S_{2j}) + \ldots \\ + x_n(R_{nj} + \Delta S_{nj}) - x_1(\overline{R}_{1j} + \Delta \overline{S}_{1j}) - x_2(\overline{R}_{2j} + \Delta \overline{S}_{2j}) - \ldots - x_n(\overline{R}_{nj} + \Delta \overline{S}_{nj}) \end{array} \right]^2$$

$$= \sum_{i=1}^{n} x_i^2 \sigma^2_{R_i} + \sum_{i=1}^{n} x_i^2 \sigma^2_{S_i} + 2 \sum x_i^2 \sigma^2_{R_i S_i} + \sum_{\substack{i=1 \\ i \neq k}}^{n} \sum_{k=1}^{n} x_i x_k \sigma_{R_i R_k}$$

$$+ \sum_{\substack{i=1 \\ i \neq k}}^{n} \sum_{k=1}^{n} x_i x_k \sigma_{S_i S_k} + \sum_{\substack{i=1 \\ i \neq k}}^{n} \sum_{k=1}^{n} x_i x_k \sigma_{R_i S_k} \qquad (11.14)$$

The contribution of exchange rate variance to total portfolio variance is equal to the weighted sum of the individual exchange rate variances plus the sum of the weighted covariances between all the exchange rates. The contribution of market return variance to total portfolio variance is equal to the weighted sum of the variances of all the individual foreign investments plus the sum of the weighted covariances between all the individual investments. Finally, the contribution of the covariance between the exchange rate and the return on investment in foreign currency is equal to the weighted sum of the covariances between each exchange rate and each market return. Empirical studies indicate that currency risk represents a substantial proportion of the total risk associated with cross-border portfolio investment.[16]

International asset pricing

Efficient markets

The concept of efficient markets plays a major role in modern financial theory. In an efficient market security prices fully reflect all pertinent past information, and price adjustments to new information are fast enough so that investors cannot use such information to make excess profits. Thus, the announcement of an unexpected change in a company's profits would incite investors to buy or sell the company's stock until it reached a new level consistent with the news. Those investors who reacted first to the information might be able to realize a profit but, once the price of the stock started to move, even the early birds would have no way of knowing what the new equilibrium price level will be. Consequently, they have no guarantee that they are entering or leaving the market on the right side of the new price level. In an efficient market, then, an asset's current price reflects its "true investment value", which will change only in response to new unanticipated information. Efficiency itself can take on different meanings depending on which information is assumed to be available to investors. Weak form efficiency includes only historical prices or returns, semi-strong form efficiency includes all publicly known information, and strong form efficiency includes all information, both public and private.

Studies of some of the world's major stock markets indicate that individually they are efficient and, consequently, as in the CAPM, it would be difficult to consistently outperform the local market index for the same level of risk.[17] The question for international asset pricing is whether there is efficiency across the individual domestic markets or whether, because of inefficiency, it is possible to pursue a strategy of active asset allocation that would consistently outperform the world index. The issue of international market efficiency depends on the degree of market integration or segmentation. If international markets are integrated, they can be considered efficient in the sense that new information will be reflected in world prices through cross-market arbitrage. For example, a British portfolio manager who moves from British stocks to French government bonds in response to new information on the prospective performance of these two investments is engaging in cross-market arbitrage. He transmits the effects of the new information from one market to the other through the sale of British stocks and the purchase of French government bonds. Market integration, then, implies that investors are open to moving their assets from one market to another and that they also have the means to do so.

On the other hand, if markets are segmented, new information will not be transmitted in a timely fashion from one market to another and it will be possible for those investors able

---

[16] See, for example, B. Solnik, *International Investments* (Addison-Wesley Publishing Co., Inc., 1996) p.p. 102–103; B. Solnik and B. Noetzlin, "Optimal international asset allocation", *Journal of Portfolio Management*, (Fall 1982); C.S. Eun and B. Resnick, "Exchange rate uncertainty, forward contracts and international portfolio selection", *Journal of Finance* (March 1988), p.p. 197–215.

[17] For the Japanese stock market see K. Kato and J. Schallheim, "Seasonal and size anomalies in the Japanese stock market", *Journal of Financial and Quantitative Analysis*, (June 1985); J. Jaffee and R. Westerfield, "Patterns in Japanese common stock returns: Day of the week and turn of the year effects", *Journal of Financial and Quantitative Analysis* (June 1985). E.J. Elton and M.J. Gruber, *Modern Portfolio Theory and Investment Analysis*, 2nd edition (John Wiley & Sons, 1984) summarize the evidence on the US stock market. For some other markets see J. Ang and R.A. Pohlman, "A note on the price behaviour of Far Eastern stocks", *Journal of International Business Studies* (Spring 1978); R.R. Officer, "Seasonality in Australian capital markets", *Journal of Financial Economics* (March 1975).

to overcome the obstacles causing the segmentation to create a risk–return portfolio that will outperform the world market portfolio. Two of the major sources of market segmentation are legal restrictions and transaction costs.

Legal restrictions can take many forms from outright controls to discriminatory taxation. Some national markets regulate foreign investment by limiting the amounts that can be invested or repatriated or by restricting foreign investors to certain sectors or types of investment. Others tax foreign investment more heavily than domestic investment or use withholding taxes and double taxation to discourage foreign investment. Some types of legal restrictions are more insidious such as special authorizations or restrictions on how trades can be made or who they can be made with. In fact, the variety of potential legal restrictions is limited only by the ingenuity and imagination of the bureaucrats who dream them up and administer them.

Transaction costs are more straightforward, although the consequences of legal restrictions are often an increase in transaction costs. They represent indirect barriers to integrated markets. Besides the added cost of foreign exchange transactions associated with most cross-market investment, they include the cost of accessing sources of information throughout the world, management fees and custodial services. Their effect is to reduce the after-cost return on a cross-border investment, thereby reducing the incentive to invest.

Market segmentation can also arise when expected returns and risks differ according to where an investor lives. This can occur when the prices of what an investor consumes relative to the returns on his investments change differently in different countries. In this case the purchasing power of investment returns would depend on where the investor resides and implies that PPP does not hold. Remember in Chapter 3 that the PPP relation combined with the other international parity relations indicate that real returns across countries should be equal – that is, the interest rate differential is equal to the inflation differential:[18]

$$r_{GBP} - r_{USD} = \bar{i}_{GBP} - \bar{i}_{USD} \qquad (11.15)$$

where r is the nominal interest rate and $\bar{i}$ is the expected rate of inflation. This relation breaks down when PPP does not hold. In fact, for equilibrium pricing of international assets to follow the CAPM as presented above, it is necessary for PPP to hold exactly. It is also necessary that investors throughout the world have identical consumption baskets. In this scenario, all investors would hold the same portfolio of risky assets, the world portfolio, represented by W in Figure 11.4. The international capital asset pricing model would then only be an extension of the domestic CAPM where the world portfolio replaces the domestic market portfolio and all investors would combine this portfolio with borrowing and lending at the riskless rate to position themselves on the international capital market line, $R_F WZ$ in Figure 11.4.

International asset pricing model

Exact PPP and an identical world consumption basket are clearly unrealistic assumptions. We have already shown that deviations from PPP are a major source of exchange rate variation, at least in the short run. There is real exchange rate risk and real rates of return differ from country to country. Furthermore, consumption preferences also differ from country to country. In these conditions, international asset pricing is more complex than a simple reinterpretation of the domestic CAPM. Investors will want to hedge against real exchange risk

---

[18] Obtained by combining the efficient markets form of PPP (Equation 3.7′) with interest rate parity (Equation 3.12) and forward rate parity (Equation 3.20).

Figure 11.4 World portfolio and capital market line

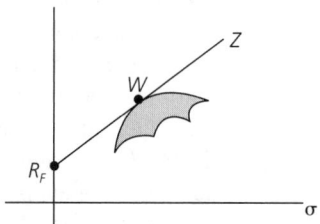

so that in equilibrium each investor's optimal investment strategy will be a combination of two portfolios, a risky portfolio common to all investors and a portfolio specific to each investor used to hedge the real exchange risk as he perceives it.[19] Furthermore, the common risky portfolio will not be the world market portfolio because the world market portfolio contains assets correlated with the investor's consumption basket. The problem is that insofar as a practical tool for international asset pricing goes, this kind of model does not look too promising. Even if it were possible to estimate the common risky portfolio, computing optimal hedge portfolios for millions of individual investors just does not seem reasonable. The analysis can be simplified, however, by assuming that there is no uncertainty about inflation rates in any country and that currency hedging is fully available. In these conditions the common risky portfolio reduces to the world market portfolio and the expected return on an asset hedged against currency risk is equal to the investor's riskless rate, such as his domestic Treasury bill rate, for instance, plus a risk premium proportional to the beta of the asset with the world market portfolio.

The practical relevance of this simplified international asset pricing model depends on international market efficiency as well as on how much the assumption of no uncertainty about inflation rates distorts reality. In fact, the variation of rates of inflation is far less pronounced than the variation of exchange rates or asset returns so that the relative distortion might be quite small. In this respect, then, the simplified model might be a good practical approximation when markets are efficient. International market efficiency, however, is an empirical question.

Empirical evidence on international market integration

Based on the argument that integration means that expected returns depend only on international factors, Jorion and Schwartz found evidence for some degree of market segmentation by showing that domestic factors are relevant for expected returns on Canadian securities.[20] Alexander, Eun and Janakiramanan hypothesized that if markets are segmented, the foreign listing of a security should increase demand for the security, thereby raising its price and reducing its expected rate of return. They found evidence of a lower expected return on non-Canadian stocks after they obtained a foreign listing, which also indicates some market segmentation.[21] Further evidence on market segmentation was presented by Agmon and

---

[19] For a comprehensive discussion of this problem see M. Adler and B. Dumas, "International portfolio choice and corporation finance: A synthesis", *Journal of Finance*, No. 3 (June 1983), p.p. 925–984.

[20] P. Jorion and E. Schwartz, "Integration versus segmentation in the Canadian stock market", *Journal of Finance* (July 1986), p.p. 603–616.

[21] G.J. Alexander, C.S. Eun and S. Janakiramanan, "International listings and stock returns: Some empirical evidence", *Journal of Financial and Quantitative Analysis* (June 1988), p.p. 135–151.

Lessard who found a weak indication that multinationals, through their ability to invest in countries that may be unavailable to the common US investor, offer some diversification benefits.[22] Their results, however, disagree with those of Jacquillat and Solnik who concluded that multinationals are poor tools for diversification.[23]

A more recent study by Cochran and Mansur examined the interrelationships between yields on the US and several foreign equity markets over the period 1980–89.[24] Tests of Granger causality are employed to investigate uni-directional causality, bi-directional causality and contemporaneous adjustment in the determination of market rates of return. Market integration is supported by the finding that contemporaneous adjustment is the most important factor in the determination of market returns. However, the existence of significant uni-directional and bi-directional causality suggests that international equity markets are not completely integrated. Furthermore, it seems that these causality effects alter in intensity from one period to another, thereby indicating that the level of market integration is somewhat unstable and varies over time.

So far the empirical evidence on international market efficiency is pretty thin. While legal restrictions, transaction costs and real exchange risk tend to reduce international capital flows and might create a certain amount of market segmentation, international market integration only requires enough cross-market arbitrage to transmit new market information quickly and efficiently. Thus, international market integration does not require that all investors have equal access to all markets. It only requires that some of them do. Today, most major corporations have multinational operations. They raise debt in the international markets and most of the major national markets. Their shares are listed on several stock exchanges and are held by residents of many different countries. The major banks have followed the corporations abroad and have activities in a wide range of currencies and capital markets. Many private and institutional investors are also extensively invested abroad. Taken together, all these players represent a substantial share of the financial activity that goes on worldwide. They have the knowledge, the experience and the means to take advantage of any relative mispricing. The magnitude of international investment has also increased substantially over the past two decades, enough so that fully segmented markets are surely a thing of the past – if they ever existed at all. While the degree of international market efficiency is an empirical question that has not yet been answered, the ongoing tendency seems to be one of increasing integration and efficiency.

Other costs and risks in international investment

Information costs of international financial analysis

One of the main problems in international financial analysis is obtaining timely information. In the US companies registered under the Securities Exchange Act of 1934 are obliged to file quarterly reports (Form 10-Q) which are available within a few weeks. In the United Kingdom half yearly reports must be prepared and published in accordance with the provisions concerning the annual report. However, many other countries only require

[22] T. Agmon and D.R. Lessard, "Investor recognition of corporate international diversification", *Journal of Finance* (September 1977), p.p. 1049–1056.

[23] B. Jacquillat and B. Solnik, "Multinationals are poor tools for diversification", *Journal of Portfolio Management* (Winter 1978), p.p. 8–12.

[24] S.J. Cochran and I. Mansur, "The interrelationships between US and foreign equity market yields: Tests of Granger causality", *Journal of International Business Studies* (Fourth Quarter, 1991), p.p. 723–736.

published reports once a year. Furthermore, the information is often far from timely. For example, the average lag between the end of the fiscal year and the publication of the annual report is 12 weeks in Japan, 14 in the United Kingdom, 16 in Germany, and 24 in France. To remedy this situation many large companies with wide foreign ownership have begun to publish more frequent and timely reports. Some German companies, for example, publish quarterly reports, the year-end report is often published in English as well as German, and, although the law only requires a balance sheet in which all German activities are consolidated, several large corporations also publish a balance sheet containing a consolidation of worldwide activities. Unfortunately, reporting of this type is not really widespread and the quality of reports varies from company to company.

The upshot of all this for the international financial analyst is that, generally speaking, the minimum data inputs for effective financial forecasting and analysis are not readily available. The proliferation of financial data services offering detailed financial information has made it possible to overcome this problem to some extent. Telerate and Reuters, for example, provide real-time news and prices on selected markets and securities while Interactive Data Corporation (IDC) and Data Resources Inc. feature databases and easy to use software to assist econometric modeling and financial research. The most comprehensive services are available from Datastream in the United Kingdom, Dun & Bradstreet in the United States, Daiwa and Nomura in Japan and Dafsa, Kompass and Hoppenstadt in continental Europe. The problem is that all these services are costly. Furthermore, even when timely information is available, it is often unsuited for comparative analysis. Different accounting practices, tax treatment and financial organization make cross-country comparisons of financial statements hazardous, at best.

Take, for instance, the ubiquitous price/earnings (P/E) ratio. This can differ substantially from country to country. Japanese P/E ratios, for example, are several times higher than those in the United States and Britain, mainly because generous tax treatment for depreciation and reserves tends to understate earnings in Japan. If earnings were calculated on a common basis such as generally accepted US accounting principles (GAAP), Japan's earnings would be considerably higher, thereby lowering their P/E ratios. Attempts are being made to overcome this problem. In the late 1980s, for instance, Randall-Helms, a New York financial consultancy teamed up with the Center for International Financial Analysis and Research based in Princeton, New Jersey, to develop a system for presenting a large number of financial accounts from major companies of different nationalities into a fully comparable format under a variety of accounting standard conventions.

Even when financial information is presented in a common format such as US GAAP, however, the financial ratios generated with this information are difficult to interpret due to the cultural and institutional environment that they reflect. For example, banks and industry have enjoyed a closer relationship in Japan and many west European countries such as France and Germany than they have in the United States and the United Kingdom. Consequently, leverage ratios tend to be somewhat higher in the former countries than in the latter. Whether or not the higher leverage reflects an increased financial risk or simply a different institutional relationship is far from clear, thereby making it difficult to rely on leverage ratios as a tool for comparative analysis.

Differences often go beyond the realm of interpretation. Basic analytical concepts themselves can also differ. For example, the French concept "need for working capital" (*besoin de fonds de roulement*), which can generally be defined as net working capital less the net cash position, is unfamiliar to the Anglo-Saxon analyst. Nevertheless, because of the relationship in France between company and bank, it is indispensable in the analysis of the financial position of a French firm. Difficulties such as these can only be overcome by engaging expert advice. Such advice is costly whether it is in-house or from outside consultants.

Administrative costs

Management costs

International management fees tend to be higher than fees charged by domestic management. They average around 85 basis points for equities and 50 basis points for bonds, which is typically 10 to 30 basis points higher than fees on similar domestic portfolios. The higher costs are justified by the more complex decision-making process, costly and time-consuming communication overheads such as international telephone, computer links and travel, and the more specialized staff requirements. International database subscriptions are also more costly than those for purely domestic databases. Because of the complex nature of the international system, research and analysis is more difficult and costly as well. All this adds up to higher management fees.

Management fees vary depending on whether the strategy adopted is active or passive. Passive portfolio management is based on the belief in international market efficiency and typically refers to constructing a portfolio that reproduces the performance of an international market index such as the EAFE. Active portfolio management is based on the belief that international markets are not completely efficient and that superior returns can be achieved through skill in active asset allocation and market timing. Active portfolio management is clearly more time-consuming than passive management because it requires constant monitoring. Consequently, it is more costly. Active management fees are generally about double those of passive management fees. For a USD 20 million portfolio, for example, fees will come to about 0.65% to 0.70% of the total portfolio compared to 0.30% for passively managed portfolios of the same size.

Global custody costs

The role of an international investment manager is to maximize the client's risk–return trade-off. Because of the diversity of the markets and instruments involved, he may be unaware of some of the basic problems in managing an internationally diversified portfolio or at least unable to monitor them on a regular basis. These problems stem from the varying standards applied by countries in their settlement procedures, the lack of automation, time zone differences, poor communications, etc. The role of the global custodian is to provide the investment manager with the necessary administrative expertise to overcome these problems.

The core operations of a custodial service involve settlement and reporting. They include:

- safekeeping of securities
- settlement of all stock exchange transactions
- collection of dividends and interest
- reporting detailed and comprehensive information relating to the investments and legislative requirements in each market
- advice on administration of new financial instruments.

The range of services offered by global custodians goes far beyond the core operations. Exhibit 11.1 gives an outline of the overall global custody product.

International custody costs tend to be higher than domestic custody costs because of the multilateral nature of international investment. This leads to a two-tiered custodial arrangement with an extra layer of costs where a money manager usually acquires a master custodian with a network of subcustodians in every country. A multi-currency system of accounting, reporting and cash flow collection also raises costs.

The average global custodian uses a hierarchical fee structure, charging by market or geographical band according to the value of assets, the number of holdings and the

Exhibit 11.1 The global custody product

1. **Security settlement**: The delivery and receipt of currency and securities on behalf of investors. It involves the provision of a clearing service and necessitates membership, either directly or via the subcustodian network, of all major clearing organizations.

2. **Reporting of corporate actions**: Advising on potential or real corporate actions such as capital increases, debt redemption and conversions.

3. **Trustee services**: Acting as the trustee for authorized unit trusts, pension funds, etc.

4. **Cash management**: The actual management of cash assets or providing the capability for clients to manage their cash movements electronically.

5. **Income collection**: The collection of dividend and income payments on behalf of investors.

6. **Security safekeeping**: The safekeeping of physical and book entry securities.

7. **Tax reclaims**: Reclaiming withholding taxes or arranging for tax exempt investors to be paid gross.

8. **Electronic banking**: Providing electronic banking facilities for a wide range of products.

9. **Real-time systems**: Real-time computer facilities for multi-currency reporting, security analysis and cash movement.

10. **Swift interfaces**: Providing client access to the SWIFT telecommunications system.

11. **Cash projections**: Forecasting cash flows on client accounts based on known unsettled trades, maturities, interest and dividend payments, etc.

12. **Online access to the custodian's computer system.**

13. **Market information services.**

14. **Electronic funds transfer**: The capability to transmit all major currencies electronically through CHAPS, CHIPS, etc.

15. **Automated links to depositories.**

16. **Portfolio evaluations**: A regular update on securities values and cash values.

17. **Stock lending**: Loaning client's stock to generate income and increase portfolio yield for the client.

18. **Consolidated reporting**: Generating consolidated reports for clients trading on behalf of several group companies.

number of transactions. Some custodians will also charge additionally for income collection, corporate action notification, subcustodian fees, telexes and other out of pocket expenses. Depending on the market, a rough estimate of the fees charged by the larger custodians is 4–17 basis points per year on the value of assets and USD 20–120 flat fee per transaction. Most custodians also take a 100–300 basis point margin on customer settlement account cash balances.

Market characteristics

Another source of risk in international portfolio investment comes from the wide diversity of stock market organizations across countries. These differences include:

1. Market size and turnover
2. The key market participants
3. Transaction, settlement and delivery procedures
4. The types of instruments available to investors
5. Brokerage fees, stamp duties and other costs for a foreign investor
6. Taxation and other regulations such as foreign exchange controls affecting the foreign investor.

Market size and turnover

Market size and turnover are good indicators of a market's depth and liquidity. Other things being equal, a larger market and higher turnover suggest less vulnerability to fluctuations caused by large orders or outright manipulation. In this context, the market's breadth is also important. Switzerland, Sweden and The Netherlands, for example, have relatively high levels of market capitalization and turnover. However, the breadth of these equity markets is somewhat limited. The six largest quoted companies account for over 40% of the Zürich Stock Exchange's market capitalization, the ten largest companies account for over 34% of the Stockholm exchange's market capitalization and just three companies account for over 44% of the Amsterdam market, with Royal Dutch alone accounting for 29.6%. This level of concentration exposes equity investments in these markets to the fortunes of a very small number of firms and makes them vulnerable to financial and political manipulation.

Key market participants

Share ownership across different categories of investors differs widely from country to country. In Korea, for example, private individuals hold the large majority of shares while in Australia they hold just a tiny percentage. Institutional investors dominate the US and Japanese markets and in The Netherlands close to 50% of equity is held by foreigners.

Different patterns of shareholdings lead to different political responses to changing market conditions. The early 1990s fall in the Korean market caused widespread protests by individual investors and sparked government attempts to prop up prices. It is said that complicity between the Japanese Ministry of Finance and the financial institutions that own 42% of Japanese equity buoyed stock prices in the massacre of October 1987. This sort of collusion would be impossible in the United States because commercial banks are prohibited by law from participating in their clients' equity. On the other hand, equity holdings by Japanese banks is a double-edged sword when prices continue to fall in spite of efforts to prop them up. In the early 1990s Japanese banks were finding it difficult to meet minimum BIS capital requirements in the face of a falling stock market, thereby causing them to restrain lending to their clients which further exacerbated falling stock prices.

At the least, these considerations can have a significant short-term effect on share prices and represent another source of risk that the foreign investor should consider before undertaking an investment. In fact, the structure of the stock market may make it more or less susceptible to political manipulation. Other things being equal, the public stock markets of France, Belgium, Spain, Italy, Greece and some Latin American countries are more highly regulated and susceptible to political control than the private stock exchanges found in the United States, Japan, Canada, Australia, South Africa and the United Kingdom, or the Germanic bankers' exchanges found in Germany, Austria, Switzerland, Scandinavia and The Netherlands. Although subject to some government regulation, the private exchanges are probably the most independent of the three types. Bankers' bourses have the disadvantages associated with the concentration of power in the hands of a narrow interest group.

Government regulation of derivative markets related to the stock markets is another important consideration. Many investment strategies incorporate trading in futures and options markets to hedge or enhance returns. For strategies of this type the performance of the derivative markets is as important as the performance of the cash market in the underlying securities.

Instruments and procedures

Another source of uncertainty for the international investor is the differences that exist across countries in financial instruments and trading procedures.

Bonds are a classic example of the diversity of the instruments that are available. They range from classic fixed interest through FRNs, zero coupons, convertibles and bonds with warrants attached to the more exotic with simultaneous call and put options or links to an index such as gold or a stock market. The possibilities are virtually limitless and new configurations appear regularly.

When comparing prices and returns between equity instruments in different countries, care must be taken to understand the rights and obligations associated with each instrument. Some instruments that seem cheap may contain subordination clauses and restricted rights. Others that seem expensive may contain preference clauses or other expanded rights. Canada, for example, has three types of equity traded on its stock exchanges – common shares, preferred shares and restricted shares. Common shares come with full voting rights. Preferred shares have genuine preference over the shares of another class of residual equity, typically the rights to priority in payment of dividends and in the repayment of capital on dissolution. Restricted shares include any fully participating shares that are not common shares such as those with non-voting or subordinated voting powers.

Besides common and preferred shares, France has investment certificates designed to provide finance for companies in the public sector that allow investors to participate in the profits but carry no voting rights. France also features participation bonds that entitle holders to both a fixed income and a variable return geared to the company's performance and profit.

Switzerland is the classic case of different classes of equity leading to wide price discrepancies. Until 1988, the Swiss equity market was divided into three categories: bearer shares, registered shares and participation certificates. Registered shares, which carried voting and certain other rights, were restricted to Swiss nationals and traded at a considerable discount to the bearer shares available to foreign investors. Following Nestlé's decision in November 1988 to make its registered shares available to foreigners, the distinction between registered and bearer shares has changed considerably and caused a sharp reduction in the price differential between the two types of security.

Trading procedures also vary from market to market. Some exchanges operate a continuous market where transactions take place throughout the day with market-makers ensuring liquidity. Other exchanges operate a call market where a given asset is traded through auction once or several times a day. These distinctions are important for investment strategies based on timing such as portfolio insurance and arbitrage operations. They are also meaningful in times of market crisis or euphoria.

Commissions and other transaction costs

Commissions and other transaction costs can significantly affect an investment's rate of return. Different investment strategies generate different levels of transaction costs. Strategies that require frequent trading, like market timing or portfolio insurance, also generate higher transaction costs. Consequently, the commissions and transaction costs associated with different exchanges have a major influence on which exchanges are suitable for different investment strategies.

Taxation

After the performance of the security itself, tax effects are probably the single most important factor in determining the investor's ultimate rate of return. In international investments tax effects are two dimensional as they arise in the country where the investment is made and in the investor's country of residence. They concern both dividends and capital gains for equities and vary according to whether or not the two countries have a tax treaty. On bonds they generally only concern coupon payments. A detailed analysis of the tax consequences of international portfolio investment is beyond the scope of this book. However, the principle on the international level is the same as that on the domestic level: governments appropriate a share of the investor's gains. Thus, the higher the rate of taxation, the lower the investor's rate of return.

Most countries have a withholding tax on dividends and many have a tax on interest and capital gains. Where tax treaties are involved, some or all of the taxes withheld can be credited against the tax liability in the investor's home country. Where no tax treaties exist, double taxation can make even the most lucrative investments unattractive.

Summary

1. The main argument for international portfolio investment is based on the principle of diversification. Diversification means spreading a portfolio over a wide range of assets in order to reduce risk for a given level of return or increase return for a given level of risk. The success of diversification depends on the extent that the various assets are correlated among themselves. The lower the correlation, the more to be gained from diversification.

2. For domestic investing, the conclusions of the capital asset pricing model (CAPM) suggest that in equilibrium all investors should hold the same portfolio of risky assets and that each individual asset or portfolio of assets will offer an expected rate of return equal to the risk-free interest rate plus a risk premium that is linearly related to the risk that the asset or portfolio of assets contributes to the market as a whole.

3. Value at risk (VaR) offers a mean-variance based methodology to measure and monitor the risk in a portfolio.

4. Arbitrage pricing theory, which is not necessarily incompatible with the CAPM, is based on arbitrage arguments and offers an alternative methodology for pricing assets. Its compatibility with the multi-factor models makes it especially adapted to international investments that need to account for individual risks associated with currency fluctuations, macroeconomic growth differentials and the like.

5. The evidence suggests and studies confirm that the potential benefits from international diversification are considerable. Actually realizing the potential benefits has proven more elusive.

6. International investment risk and return can be divided into currency and foreign market components. The currency component is due to changes in the exchange rate while the foreign market component is due to the performance of the foreign market in its domestic currency.

7. International asset pricing depends on whether there is efficiency across the individual domestic markets or whether, because of inefficiency, it is possible to pursue a strategy of active asset allocation that would consistently outperform the world index. The issue of international market efficiency is usually presented in terms of the degree of market integration or segmentation. If international markets are integrated, they can be

considered efficient in the sense that new information will be reflected in world prices through cross-market arbitrage.

8. For equilibrium pricing of international assets to follow the CAPM, it is necessary for PPP to hold exactly. It is also necessary that investors throughout the world have identical consumption baskets. Exact PPP and an identical world consumption basket are clearly unrealistic assumptions because deviations from PPP are a major source of exchange rate variation and consumption preferences also differ from country to country. In these conditions, international asset pricing is more complex than a simple reinterpretation of the domestic CAPM. Practically, it is difficult to apply.

9. The analysis can be simplified by assuming that there is no uncertainty about inflation rates in any country and that currency hedging is fully available. In these conditions the common risky portfolio reduces to the world market portfolio and the expected return on an asset hedged against currency risk is equal to the investor's riskless rate such as his domestic Treasury bill rate plus a risk premium proportional to the beta of the asset with the world market portfolio.

10. The practical relevance of this simplified international asset pricing model depends on international market efficiency as well as on how much the assumption of no uncertainty about inflation rates distorts reality. In fact, the variation of rates of inflation is far less pronounced than the variation of exchange rates or asset returns so that the relative distortion might be quite small. In this respect, then, the simplified model might be a good practical approximation when markets are efficient. The evidence on international market efficiency, however, is thin and inconclusive.

11. One of the main problems in international financial analysis is obtaining timely information. Even when timely information is available, interpreting it is difficult due to different accounting practices and institutional arrangements.

12. Administrative considerations concerning management and global custody raise the costs of international portfolio investment and increase its risk.

13. Another source of risk in international portfolio investment comes from the wide diversity of stock market organizations across countries. The differences include market size and turnover, who the key market participants are, transaction, settlement and delivery procedures, the types of instruments available to investors, brokerage fees, stamp duties and other costs for a foreign investor, and taxation and other regulations such as foreign exchange controls affecting the foreign investor. All of these elements can affect the performance of a foreign investment.

Questions

Solutions to the following questions are set out on the web site, details of which are included in the Preface.

1. Define covariance and explain the role it plays in determining the volatility (riskiness) of a portfolio of risky assets.

2. How does the CAPM help to simplify investment decisions?

3. Define beta, systematic risk and the security market line.

4. Explain why there are benefits to be derived from international diversification.

5. What is value at risk?

6. What is APT and how does it differ from mean-variance analysis?

7. Given:

$$S_0(DKK/USD) = 5.0000$$
$$S_1^*(DKK/USD) = 5.1000$$
$$R_{USD}^* = 10\%$$
$$\sigma_s = 0.3$$
$$\sigma_{RUSD} = 0.1$$
$$\rho_{RUSD,S} = 0.6$$

Calculate the expected return and standard deviation in Danish kroner for an investment in dollars by a krone-based investor.

6. Explain the concept of efficient markets. What might keep international markets from being efficient?

7. What are the problems with applying the CAPM on the international level?

8. What are the incremental costs associated with international investing?

9. How can differences in market characteristics add to the risk associated with international investing?

Advanced techniques for country and political risk assessment

12

Modern financial theory has made major strides in improving our understanding of economic and financial risk and how they can be measured and managed. These same methods have been applied to the problem of country-specific risk and have made it possible to give a much more accurate and precise picture of what is involved. This, in turn, has enhanced the importance of traditional political risk analysis, which enters the framework as a valuable input in the process of parameter estimation. In this chapter we discuss the shortcomings of traditional international risk analysis. We then develop a new analytical framework that makes it possible to apply the tools of modern financial theory to the assessment of country-specific risk. Finally, we show how the new framework can be applied to assess the economic and financial health of a national economy.

Conventional cross-border economic and financial risk analysis suffers from a number of shortcomings in the analytical framework that make systematic comparisons across countries conceptually inappropriate.[1] First of all, the data is not well adapted to the task at hand. Looking back at the variables and ratios of Chapter 10, you will notice that most of the relevant economic data comes from the national accounts, such as GDP, GNP, exports, imports, savings and investment. Flow data gross of costs, such as GDP and its derivatives, are incomplete as measures of economic performance because they give no information on the economy's overall outstanding assets and liabilities or the contribution of the flow data to the evolution of assets and liabilities. Basing an analysis on such limited information is roughly equivalent to assessing the economic and financial health of a firm based only on the firm's turnover without regard to operating costs or how the turnover is financed. A balance sheet linking the macroeconomic flows net of costs over time is necessary to complete the analysis. This implies a system of accounting discipline where consequences on the various categories of assets and liabilities are explicit. It also implies that concepts such as profits and costs be defined appropriately. Profits reported in the national accounts are generally useless where cross-border risk is concerned because they only reflect the criteria for income distribution as defined within the geographic area of the country itself. The criteria for income distribution elsewhere in the world may be quite different. Relative price discrepancies between countries can further mask international economic reality.

The difficulty stems from the fact that the national accounts are prepared and presented in the context of traditional macroeconomic analysis where the perspective is the national

---

[1] For a discussion of this problem and the theoretical background for the new techniques of cross-border risk assessment, see E.A. Clark, *Cross-border Investment Risk: Applications of Modern Portfolio Theory* (Euromoney Publications, 1991).

authority seeking to maximize internal levels of output, employment and consumption. The international investor, however, has a different perspective. He can buy and sell, borrow and lend elsewhere than the particular country in question. His interest in internal levels of output, employment and consumption concern the extent to which they affect the risk and return on his investment in terms of his base currency. His main concern is the economy's ability to generate the net foreign exchange value necessary to meet current and future foreign interest, dividend and principal obligations. This subtle change of perspective radically alters the context surrounding macroeconomic analysis and the discussion of cross-border risk. It implies that the analysis should be based on international criteria for income distribution, that it should be effected in foreign exchange value and international relative prices, and that it should include the concepts of profits and a balance sheet.

New analytical framework

The analytical framework developed in this section[2] uses the discounted cash flow model to establish the relationship between macroeconomic cash flows from period to period and the macroeconomic balance sheet. Cash flows are measured in foreign exchange (US dollars in our examples) and defined so that they reflect the perspective of the international investor whose concern is the economy's ability to generate the net foreign exchange value necessary to meet foreign interest, dividend, principal and depreciation payments.

Presentation of the model

When macroeconomic performance is measured in foreign currency, accounting discipline is imposed through the transactions involving the external sector. The reason is straightforward. While the economic and financial authorities of a sovereign nation are potentially free from accounting discipline in their own currency through unlimited access to central bank credit, the same cannot be said for their position in foreign currency. Foreign currency must either be earned with exports or borrowed. This is known as balance of payments discipline or the foreign exchange constraint, which we presented in Equation 1.2. In this chapter, we want to concentrate on the role of interest and dividend payments abroad. Therefore, we simplify the notation by including BP in F. Thus, Equation 1.2 becomes:

$$X_t - M_t + FS_t + F_t = 0 \qquad (12.1)$$

where

X = merchandise exports plus exports of all services except investment income plus unrequited transfers and other income (credit)

M = merchandise imports plus imports of all services except investment income plus unrequited transfers and other income (debit)

FS = net investment income (investment income (credit) minus investment income (debit))

F = net inflow (outflow) of foreign capital including operations by the monetary authority.

[2] This analytical framework was first developed in E.A. Clark, *Cross-border Investment Risk: Applications of Modern Portfolio Theory* (Euromoney Publications, 1991). It was restated and applied in E. Clark and B. Marois, *Managing Risk in International Business* (Thomson Learning, 1996) and E. Clark, "A general international market index", *International Journal of Finance*, Vol. 7, No. 3 (1995), p.p. 1288–1312.

The next step is to determine the macroeconomic cash flows relevant to the international investor. Let b_t represent the foreign exchange value of income from the sale of the economy's output of final goods and services for period t and a_t the foreign exchange value of the economy's expenditure on final goods and services for period t. From the standpoint of the international economic agent, exports, whether raw materials or investment goods, represent final output because they leave the domestic economy. Thus, the b_ts are equal to the foreign exchange value of exports plus the foreign exchange value of internal sales of domestically produced final goods and services. The foreign exchange value of domestically produced final goods and services is equal to total consumption less imports of consumption goods. This can be written:

$$b_t = X_t + (C_t - M_{ct}) \qquad (12.2)$$

where C is domestic consumption and M_c represents imports of consumption goods.

The a_ts comprise the foreign exchange value of the economy's expenditure on final goods and services and as such represent the cost of production of the economy's gross output, including consumption and investment goods. Thus, the a_ts are composed of the foreign exchange value of the final goods and services consumed by the sector producing consumption goods (the cost of production of consumption goods), the foreign exchange value of the final goods and services consumed by the sector producing replacement investment goods (cost of production of replacing worn out investment goods), and the foreign exchange value of the final goods and services consumed by the sector producing new net investment (cost of production of net investment). Imports, regardless of their nature, come from outside the economy and therefore represent a final expenditure for the economy. The a_ts, then, include the foreign exchange value of imports plus the foreign exchange value of internal expenditure for domestically produced final goods and services:

$$a_t = M_t + (C_t - M_{ct}) \qquad (12.3)$$

Because the foreign exchange value of internal expenditure for domestically produced final goods and services is exactly equal to the foreign exchange value of internal sales of domestically produced final goods and services, $(b_t - a_t)$ will always be equal to $(X_t - M_t)$. From Equation 12.1 we can see that this is an expression of balance of payments accounting discipline. It is clear from the balance of payments identity that net exports determine the ability of an economy to meet interest, dividend, principal and depreciation payments on its foreign borrowing. In the absence of foreign capital inflows, interest, dividend, principal and depreciation payments abroad are limited by the level of net exports. Foreign capital inflows will be forthcoming only if expected levels of net exports are deemed sufficient to meet the expected payments associated with foreign liabilities. Take a bank loan, for example. In the absence of new borrowing over the life of the loan, the economy's ability to meet interest and principal payments depends on its outstanding financial obligations and the level of net exports. If the level of net exports is deemed inadequate, the loan will only be granted if it is decided that foreign capital will be available to make up the shortfall. When that time comes, the same type of analysis will determine whether or not the required capital is forthcoming. Thus, at any point in time, F, the net supply of foreign capital, depends on the expected future flows of net exports. Consequently, the supply and demand for foreign exchange is determined by current effects of past borrowing represented by financial service payments, the current flow of net exports and expected future flows of net exports. Any disequilibrium will be reflected in the exchange rate.

With this in mind we can use the cash flows of income and expenditure to measure the foreign exchange value of the economy at time T. Suppose that all transactions take place on the first day of each period and that the capital markets are in equilibrium so that the economy's cost of capital is equal to its internal rate of return, r. The foreign exchange value of the economy at time T is:

$$V_T = E\left[(b_T - a_T) + (b_{T+1} - a_{T+1})\,R^{-1} + \ldots + (b_n - a_n)R^{-(n-T)}\right] \qquad (12.4)$$

where V_T represents the capital value of the economy at the beginning of period T, $R = 1 + r$, and E is the expectations operator.

It is important to see the relationship between Equation 12.4 and the traditional national accounting equation. Taking the formula for V_{T+1} gives:

$$V_{T+1} = E\left[(b_{T+1} - a_{T+1}) + (b_{T+2} - a_{T+2})\,R^{-1} + \ldots + (b_n - a_n)R^{-(n-(T+1))}\right] \qquad (12.5)$$

Substituting 12.5 into 12.4, multiplying by $1 + r$ to obtain the value of the economy at the end of period T, rearranging, and remembering that b_T and a_T are known because they take place on the first day of the period, yields the national accounting equation for period T:

$$r(V_T + a_T - b_T) + a_T = b_T + (V_{T+1} - V_T) \qquad (12.6)$$

where $r(V_T + a_T - b_T)$ represents profits before interest and dividends paid abroad, a_T represents cost, b_T represents income and $(V_{T+1} - V_T)$ represents net investment. It can be more easily recognized if we substitute Equations 12.2 and 12.3 into 12.6 and rearrange:

$$r(V_T + M_T - X_T) + C_T = X_T - M_T + C_T + (V_{T+1} - V_T) \qquad (12.7)$$

The right-hand side of Equation 12.7 is immediately recognized as a derivative presentation of net domestic product. The difference between this presentation and the traditional format is that unrequited transfers and other non-financial income are included in exports and imports. The left-hand side of the equation shows the economy's earnings before interest and dividends paid abroad plus consumption. Consumption, then, appears directly as a cost. However, it does not represent the total cost. Total cost would include expenditure on imports of investment goods.

This presentation of the national accounts has several practical advantages. On the one hand, net national product is well known to economists and macroeconomic data is usually presented in this format. On the other hand, the left-hand side of the equation presents net national product in a new format that is pertinent to the international investor and more useful for financial analysis: earnings and consumption are broken down to reflect international criteria for income distribution.

Applying the model

Generating the foreign currency values

The individual Vs in the foregoing accounting format cannot be observed directly for two reasons. First of all, we are dealing with expected future flows and, secondly, a country's national accounts are presented in domestic currency rather than foreign currency. The market information does, however, exist so that they can be estimated. The estimation procedure involves using the exchange rate to link the V_ts to the domestic currency statistics presented in the national accounts.

The domestic currency equivalent of Equation 12.4 is:

$$V'_T = E[(b'_T - a'_T) + (b'_{T+1} - a'_{T+1})R'^{-1} + \ldots + (b'_n - a'_n)R'^{-(n-T)}] \qquad (12.8)$$

where the primes denote domestic currency values and $R' = 1+r'$. r' is the economy's internal rate of return in domestic currency. Since $b - a$ equals $X - M$, Equation 12.8 can be rewritten using the exchange rate. Let

$$X'_t = S_t X_t$$

and

$$M'_t = S_t M_t$$

where S_t is the spot exchange rate at time t expressed as the number of units of domestic currency for one unit of foreign currency. Then

$$V'_T = E[S_T(X_T - M_T) + S_{T+1}(X_{T+1} - M_{T+1})R'^{-1} + \ldots + S_n(X_n - M_n)R'^{-(n-T)}] \qquad (12.9)$$

Using the forward rate parity and interest rate parity hypotheses, in Appendix 12.1 at the end of the chapter we show that:

$$V'_T = S_T V_T \qquad (12.10)$$

so that:

$$V_T = \frac{V'_T}{S_T} \qquad (12.11)$$

and at the end of the period

$$V_{T+1} = \frac{V'_{T+1}}{S_{T+1}} \qquad (12.12)$$

V' can be estimated directly from readily available statistical data. The domestic currency value of net investment at market prices is a component of the traditional presentation of the national accounts or it can be estimated from gross fixed capital formation, which is also presented therein. The domestic currency value of what has been invested in the economy from time 0 to the end of $T - 1$ is:

$$V'_T = \sum_{t=0}^{T-1} (V'_{t+1} - V'_t) \qquad (12.13)$$

and

$$V'_{T+1} = \sum_{t=0}^{T} (V'_{t+1} - V'_t) \qquad (12.14)$$

Thus, the right-hand side of Equation 12.7 can be obtained by applying the spot exchange rate to X', M' and C' and using Equations 12.11–12.14 to estimate V_T and V_{T+1}.

New accounting information and analytical ratios

Macroeconomic profits

The first type of information that can be generated with this framework is purely accounting in nature. Nevertheless, it affords some interesting insights into the economic and financial situation of a national economy. Starting from Equation 12.7, subtract C from both sides to yield:[3]

$$rV_t = X_t - M_t + (V_{t+1} - V_t)$$ (12.15)

Profits before interest and dividends paid abroad are equal to net exports plus net investment. Starting from this equation, the information necessary for the new techniques in cross-border risk assessment can be developed. An example demonstrates how this is done. Table 12.1 shows the relevant information taken from the national accounts and the balance of payments for The Philippines for 1987.[4]

All the data in this table is generally available in the publications listed as sources or can be calculated directly from this data.[5] The US dollar data for the national accounts, for instance, was calculated by dividing the peso value by the exchange rate. Since we are dealing with flows we used the average exchange rate over the period. Thus, the dollar value of GDP was given by

PHP 708.37 billion ÷ 20.568 (PHP/USD) = USD 34.44 billion.

The calculations for gross fixed capital formation, increase in stocks, and depreciation followed the same procedure.

We can use the Table 12.1 information in Equation 12.15 to calculate the dollar value of the accounting profits generated by the Philippine economy during 1987. $X - M$ is equal to the current account balance before subtracting interest and dividends and is found by adding interest and dividends back into the current account balance:

$$X_{1987} - M_{1987} = -USD\ 0.543\ billion + USD\ 2.066\ billion = USD\ 1.523\ billion.$$

Net investment for 1987 $(V_t+1 - V_t)$ is equal to gross fixed capital formation plus the increase in stocks minus depreciation. Depreciation is the difference between gross national expenditure and national income at market prices:

$$V_{1988} - V_{1987} = USD\ 4.793\ billion + USD\ 0.575\ billion - USD\ 3.773\ billion = USD\ 1.595\ billion.$$

[3] To simplify the equation we assume that interest on net exports $[r(M_t - X_t)]$ is negligible so that this term disappears from the left-hand side of the equation. In fact, in continuous time this term does disappear. See Clark (1991), p.p. 43–44.

[4] This analysis was part of a study of 60 countries, the results of which were published in E. Clark, "An alternative ranking", *Euromoney* (September 1988), p. 234. We use the study as an example throughout the chapter because it was published as a forecast, which makes it possible to compare what was forecast with the actual results. The 60 countries comprise: Argentina, Australia, Austria, Belgium, Bolivia, Brazil, Canada, Chile, Colombia, Costa Rica, Denmark, Dominican Republic, Ecuador, Egypt, El Salvador, Finland, France, Germany, Greece, Guatemala, Honduras, Iceland, India, Indonesia, Ireland, Israel, Italy, Japan, Jordan, Kenya, Morocco, Malaysia, Mexico, Netherlands, New Zealand, Nigeria, Norway, Pakistan, Panama, Paraguay, Peru, Philippines, Portugal, Singapore, South Africa, South Korea, Spain, Sri Lanka, Sweden, Switzerland, Taiwan, Thailand, Tunisia, Turkey, United Kingdom, United States, Uruguay, Venezuela, Zambia and Zimbabwe.

[5] Information on the International Monetary Fund (IMF) can be found at www.imf.org.

Table 12.1 Selected statistics for The Philippines in pesos and US dollars for 1987 (exchange rate = PHP 20.568 pesos/USD 1

	Pesos (bn)	*Dollars (bn)*
GDP	708.37	34.440
Gross fixed capital formation	98.59	4.793
Change in inventories	11.82	0.575
Depreciation	77.61	3.773
Current account balance		–0.543
Net financial services		–2.066

Sources: IMF, *International Financial Statistics*, **LXII** (No. 11; November 1989), 428–431; IMF, *Balance of Payments Statistics* (Yearbook), Vol. 39, Part 1, pp. 553–557.

The Philippine economy's total profits for 1987 (*rV*) are thus equal to:

$$rV_{1987} = (X_{1987} - M_{1987}) + (V_{1988} - V_{1987})$$

which gives macroeconomic profits = USD 1.523 billion + USD 1.595 billion = USD 3.118 billion.

Foreign interest coverage ratio

By comparing profits to foreign interest payments, we have a good measure of how easily each economy can meet these obligations. In the World Bank's *World Debt Tables 1988–89* we can see that The Philippines had interest obligations of USD 1.882 billion. By dividing profits by interest obligations we have the foreign interest coverage ratio:

$$\text{Foreign interest coverage ratio} = \frac{rV}{INT} \qquad (12.16)$$

Foreign interest coverage for The Philippines in 1987 = USD 3.118/USD 1.882 = 1.66. Thus, the Philippines' macroeconomic profits covered its interest obligations by 1.66 times.

Cash flow coverage ratio

Cash flow coverage gives another perspective on how easily a country can meet its foreign cash flow obligations. Cash flow coverage is calculated by dividing total cash flows, which are equal to profits before interest and dividends paid abroad plus depreciation, by total foreign cash obligations, which are equal to foreign interest and dividends plus foreign debt service:

$$\text{Cash flow coverage ratio} = \frac{rV + \text{Depreciation}}{FS + \text{Principal repayment}} \qquad (12.17)$$

From Table 12.1, The Philippines' profits were USD 3.118 billion, depreciation was USD 3.773 billion, and foreign interest and dividend payments were USD 2.066 billion. From *World Debt Tables 1988–89*, foreign debt repayment was USD 0.778 billion. Thus

$$\text{The Philippines cash flow coverage ratio} = \frac{(\text{USD } 3.118 + \text{USD } 3.773)}{(\text{USD } 2.066 + \text{USD } 0.778)} = 2.42.$$

Interpreting the coverage ratios

Care must be taken in the interpretation of the interest coverage and cash flow coverage ratios because the numerator is composed only partially of foreign exchange inflows represented by $X - M$. The other components of the numerator refer to foreign exchange "value" and not to foreign exchange, while the denominator refers specifically and totally to foreign exchange expenditure. Consequently, these ratios do not indicate the foreign exchange available to cover current foreign expenditure. Traditional ratios such as INT/X or TDS/X are entirely in terms of foreign exchange and would therefore seem to be a better indicator of the economy's ability to meet foreign exchange obligations. However, these ratios present only one side of the coin, the export side. The ability to meet foreign obligations depends on net exports – that is, exports minus imports. As we have seen in Chapters 1 and 2, the levels of exports and imports are intimately related to domestic economic activity. Taking exports out of context gives no indication of what net exports will be nor of the hardship that will be caused if meeting foreign obligations necessitates a fall in domestic consumption through a reduction of imports or an increase in exports achieved through a reduction in the domestic supply of exportable products (see Chapters 1 and 2 for a discussion of the relationship between balance of payments accounting discipline and economic activity).

The interest and cash flow coverage ratios do not have these shortcomings because they explicitly include both net exports and the surplus generated by the economy. Combined with complementary analysis, they thus offer some interesting insights on the riskiness of outstanding external obligations.

In The Philippines, for example, total cash flow was USD 6.891 billion. Foreign interest, dividends and debt repayment totalled USD 2.844 billion. The country's capacity for self-financed investment is equal to total cash flow less interest, dividends and principal paid abroad. Thus, without foreign resources gross investment would only have been

$$USD\ 6.891 - USD\ 2.844 = USD\ 4.047\ billion$$

instead of USD 5.368 billion and net investment

$$USD\ 4.047 - USD\ 3.773 = USD\ 0.274\ billion$$

instead of USD 1.595 billion. This represents a fall of 25% in gross investment and 83% in net investment.

We can appreciate what a reduction of this magnitude means in terms of risk by estimating the effect that the loss of foreign resources would have on economic activity. This can be achieved through standard macroeconomic analysis by calculating the economy's investment income multiplier and applying it to the reduction in gross investment caused by the absence of foreign resources. From Chapter 2, footnotes 4 and 9, we know that the investment income multiplier is equal to

$$\frac{dGNP}{dI_g} = \frac{1}{dS/dGNP + dM/dGNP} \tag{12.18}$$

where $dS/dGNP$ is the marginal propensity to save and $dM/dGNP$ is the marginal propensity to import. Suppose that for The Philippines the marginal propensities to save and to import are the same as the average propensities. The investment income multiplier would then be

$$1 / (0.2 + 0.27) = 2.13.$$

The reduction in gross investment would be

$$\text{USD } 4.793 + \text{USD } 0.575 - \text{USD } 4.047 = \text{USD } 1.321 \text{ billion}$$

and the reduction in economic activity would be

$$2.13 \times \text{USD } 1.321 \text{ billion} = \text{USD } 2.81 \text{ billion}.$$

This represents a reduction of 8.2% of GDP. A reduction of this magnitude would not be impossible but it would be politically and socially difficult enough to suppose that the authorities would rather sacrifice foreign interest, dividend and principal repayments than face the alternative.

Interest coverage is another story. If no new foreign capital were available but existing loans could be rolled over, meeting foreign interest payments of USD 1.883 billion would reduce gross investment to

$$\text{USD } 6.891 - \text{USD } 1.883 = \text{USD } 5.008 \text{ billion},$$

instead of USD 5.368 billion, a loss of USD 0.36 billion. With the investment income multiplier of 2.13, GDP would fall by USD 0.767 billion or 2.2%. A one-time reduction of this magnitude might be tolerable, which means that interest payments are less at risk than principal payments. Nevertheless, both ratios are low enough and the economic costs of honoring outstanding foreign obligations high enough to suggest that by the end of 1987 The Philippines had surpassed or was close to surpassing its maximum debt level.

This example suggests how information generated by the new framework can be exploited by the risk analyst. It can be extended by comparing ratios across countries and charting their evolution over time. Just as with any type of ratio analysis, interpreting the interest coverage and cash flow coverage ratios requires knowledge and skill. Nevertheless, these ratios are far more informative than the corresponding ratios traditionally employed in cross-border risk analysis.

The degree of financial leverage

The concept of the degree of financial leverage complements the two preceding ratios. The degree of financial leverage is defined as the percentage change in macroeconomic profits accruing to domestic residents per each percentage change in total macroeconomic profits. It can be written as[6]

$$\text{Degree of financial leverage} = \frac{rV}{rV - FS} \qquad (12.19)$$

where rV are the economy's total profits and $rV - FS$ are the macroeconomic profits accruing to domestic residents.

---

[6] The formula is derived as follows:

$$\text{Degree of financial leverage} = \frac{\Delta(rV - FS)}{(rV - FS)} \div \frac{\Delta rV}{rV}$$

Since interest charges are constant, $\Delta(rV - FS) = \Delta rV$, and therefore

$$\frac{\Delta rV}{(rV - FS)} \div \frac{\Delta rV}{rV} = \frac{rV}{rV - FS}.$$

Whereas the interest and cash flow coverage ratios indicate the economy's ability to meet external obligations in the absence of supplementary foreign resources, the degree of financial leverage indicates the vulnerability of this ability due to fluctuations in expected profits. For The Philippines the degree of financial leverage is

$$\frac{USD\ 3.118}{USD\ 3.118 - USD\ 2.066} = 2.96.$$

This means that a *ceteris paribus* 1% change in gross profits would cause a reduction of 2.96% in the economy's net profits after interest and dividends paid abroad. For a country exporting a high percentage of commodities with volatile prices such as sugar, copra, coconut oil, wood and copper, and importing large quantities of products with equally volatile prices such as petroleum, this is a high degree of leverage. Suppose, for example, that adverse price movements cause the foreign exchange value of net exports to fall by USD 0.156 billion.[7] Total macroeconomic profits fall by 5% to USD 2.962 billion (USD 3.118 – USD 0.156 = USD 2.962) while profits after interest and dividends paid abroad falls 2.96 × 5% = 14.8% to USD 0.896 billion (USD 2.962 – USD 2.066 = USD 0.896).

Profits after interest and dividends paid abroad represent the economy's capacity for self-financed growth. Before the fall in net exports, 33.7% of total profits were available for self-financed growth. After the fall, only 30.2% are available. If the economy's internal rate of return is 10%, this implies that the rate of growth that can be self-financed by the domestic economy falls by over 10% from 3.37% to 3.02%. Both figures are lower than the rate of growth of the population since 1950, the geometric mean of which is over 3.9%. In fact, reality is even worse because the Philippine economy's internal rate of return through 1987 was only 6.2%, indicating a self-financed rate of growth of only 2.1%. We will come back to the concept of the economy's rate of return at the end of this chapter. Before doing that, however, we can derive a good indication of how per capita economic growth will evolve by taking a look at net profits per resident.

Net profits per resident

Net profits after payment of interest and dividends abroad per inhabitant give a good idea of prospective economic well-being. This is a concept similar to earnings per share, which, in the case of a national economy, gives an accounting estimate of equity investment per resident. For the foreign investor, this ratio gives a far more accurate picture of economic reality than the conventional per capita GDP. First of all, it considers the external sector directly in international prices, which reduces its vulnerability to domestically induced price distortions. Secondly, and most importantly, it treats consumption directly as a cost, thereby eliminating a major conceptual contradiction associated with per capita GDP as a measure of economic performance or well-being. Thirdly, rather than focusing on gross output that may or may not be pumped up by price distortions and foreign capital used for current consumption, per capita investment gives a relatively unbiased picture of how productivity and living standards are likely to evolve in the future. Other things being equal, more investment per head means more growth per head.

---

[7] A.J. Ergueta and R. Shrieve suggest an interesting approach to forecasting exports. They treat exports as a portfolio of the individual products actually exported and assume that world prices are the main source of variability of export revenues. Correlation coefficients are estimated from the price series and a Monte Carlo simulation is used to estimate the mean growth rate of exports and its standard deviation. See A.J. Ergueta and R. Shrieve, "Assessing the debt servicing capacity of Peru", in G. Feiger and B. Jacquillat (Eds.), *International Finance: Text and Cases* (Boston: Allyn and Bacon, 1982), p.p. 415–437.

For The Philippines in 1987 net per capita profits were only USD 18.18. This is exceptionally low. In Thailand, for example, a country in the same region with a similar mix of exports and imports, per capita profits were USD 130.60. The per capita net profit picture is very different from that given by per capita GDP, which was USD 595.22 in The Philippines and USD 887.13 in Thailand. The per capita net profits picture is closer to reality as can be seen in Table 12.2, which compares the relevant data for the two countries. The Philippines is significantly worse off in all categories.

The Philippines/Thailand 1988–95: Comparing outcomes

As an example of the power of the foregoing analytical approach, we can compare the outcomes of The Philippines and Thailand in the years immediately after the analysis of the two countries was undertaken in 1987.[8] The outcomes are as forecast by the analysis. Thailand had no debt rescheduled between 1988 and 1994 while The Philippines rescheduled its debt every year from 1988 to 1993 involving a total of USD 10.756 billion. Furthermore, real per capita growth of GDP averaged 8.356% in Thailand from 1987 to 1994 while in The Philippines it averaged only 0.879%.

The macroeconomic balance sheet

An economy's capital structure is an important consideration for risk assessment. For the international investor, capital structure refers generally to the proportion of the economy's assets financed by non-residents and particularly to a breakdown by type. Debt is especially important because it concerns rigid payment schedules. In corporate finance, one way of determining a company's capital structure is to analyze the balance sheet. Although no formal balance sheet exists for a national economy, one can be constructed from the preceding information.

Economic activity can be presented in the form of sources and uses as a first step in constructing a macroeconomic balance sheet. Let s represent the percent of profits before interest and dividends paid to non-residents that is reinvested in the economy. Then $(1-s)$ represents the percent of profits paid out to foreign investors. Thus, we can write

$$\text{Interest and dividends paid abroad} = FS = (1-s)rV.$$

Table 12.2 Comparative data for The Philippines and Thailand, 1987

	Philippines	*Thailand*
GDP	USD 34.44 billion	USD 47.55 billion
Profits	USD 3.118 billion	USD 8.612 billion
Interest coverage ratio	1.66	6.43
Cash flow coverage ratio	2.42	3.18
Degree of financial leverage	2.96	1.18
Saving out of profits	34%	81%
Net profit per inhabitant	USD 18.18	USD 130.60
Per capital GDP	USD 595.22	USD 887.13

[8] This analysis is part of the study mentioned earlier of 60 countries, the results of which were published in E. Clark, "An alternative ranking", *Euromoney* (September 1988), p. 234.

Subtracting this from both sides of Equation 12.15 gives

$$srV_t = X_t - M_t - (1 - s)rV_t + (V_{t+1} - V_t) \qquad (12.20)$$

This is the expression for net profits.

When net financial services are known to be negative, the balance of payments accounting identity, Equation 1.2 in Chapter 1, can be written

$$BP_t - F_t = X_t - M_t - (1 - s)rV_t \qquad (12.21)$$

If we substitute Equation 12.21 into 12.20 and rearrange, we have the macroeconomic sources and uses for the period:

$$srV_t + F_t = BP_t + (V_{t+1} - V_t) \qquad (12.22)$$

where the sources are on the left-hand side of the equation and represent profits accruing to domestic residents plus net inflows of foreign capital and the uses on the right-hand side represent the net gain (loss) of foreign reserves plus net investment.

The balance sheet can be determined by summing across all past years up to the present.[9] Exhibit 12.1 shows the result.

Other new ratios

A macroeconomic balance sheet makes it possible to generate other previously unavailable information that is quite useful for an assessment of the economic and financial health of the economy. For instance, the foreign debt to total assets ratio complements the other financial ratios we have mentioned. We can also generate activity ratios and profitability ratios.[10] GDP to total assets is an important activity ratio corresponding to the sales/total assets ratio in corporate finance. Net profits to GDP corresponds to the profit margin on sales ratio and net profits to the sum of srV from 0 to t corresponds to return on net worth.

Exhibit 12.1 Macroeconomic balance sheet

Assets	Liabilities
Total reserves outstanding at the end of t	Net short-term foreign liabilities outstanding at the end of t
Sum of gross fixed investment from 0 to the end of t	Net medium and long-term foreign debt outstanding at the end of t
Less: Sum of depreciation from 0 to the end of t	Net portfolio investment outstanding at the end of t
Sum of change in stocks from 0 to the end of t	Net direct investment outstanding at the end of t
	Sum of srV from 0 to the end of t

[9] In this exercise domestic data should be converted at the average exchange rate for each period. Furthermore, since it would be impractical to go back infinitely in time, a regression can be used to determine, the capital stock incorporated in a national economy up to a given time in the past. For this technique, see E.A. Clark, op. cit. (1991), p.p. 79–80.

[10] Most standard textbooks in managerial finance discuss the types and uses of financial ratios.

Once the balance sheet items have been estimated, the other information necessary for generating these ratios is available for most countries. Other ratios can also be generated, depending on the statistical sophistication of the country in question.

As useful as ratios are, they should be treated with caution because they are constructed with accounting data that can be manipulated by the authorities. For example, two countries may use different methods for treating depreciation and inventory valuation. Differences may also be found in the way pension plan costs and bad debt reserves are treated. When a country has a major seasonal or cyclical product, this can also affect ratios.

Ratio interpretation can be aided by trend analysis and comparison with ratios of other countries. Trend analysis is useful because ratios only capture one period. By examining several periods, it is often possible to determine a tendency towards a stronger or weaker position. Comparing ratios across countries in similar economic conditions makes it possible to develop a basis against which ratios can be judged. Even when ratios diverge from those of the other countries, however, it does not necessarily mean that something is wrong. It could actually mean that the country is doing something better than the others. The analyst must develop in-depth knowledge of the country, its customs and its government in order to interpret what the ratios really mean.

In conclusion, ratios can be extremely useful but they must be used with caution and good judgement.

New market information and analytical techniques

While the accounting relations developed above add important new insights concerning the riskiness of national economies, the risk parameters relevant to modern financial theory are those derived from the market. Market-based risk parameters can be derived for a national economy by applying the principle of capital gains and losses.

Consider a country with no growth prospects, $X - M$ equal to USD 1 billion, and an internal rate of return of 12%, which, because the capital markets are in equilibrium, is just equal to its cost of capital. Because there is no growth, there is no net investment and V_{t+1} is equal to V_t. In these conditions, from Equation 12.15, V_t, the economy's market value, is equal to[11]

$$\frac{1}{0.12} \times \text{USD 1 billion} = \text{USD 8.33 billion.}$$

As long as things stay this way accounting profits and market profits are both equal to USD 1 billion. Suppose, however, that at the end of year t a fall in the price of the country's main export makes the forecast for all future net exports fall to USD 750 million. There has been no net investment and year t is over so accounting profits, $X_t - M_t$, are unchanged at USD 1 billion. However, V_{t+1}, the discounted value of all future net cash flows, falls to

$$\frac{1}{0.12} \times \text{USD 750 million} = \text{USD 6.25 billion.}$$

The decline in the economy's capacity to generate net foreign exchange value translates into a fall of 25% in the economy's value from USD 8.33 to USD 6.25 billion. Thus, from Equation 12.15, the economic profits based on market value are:

USD 1 billion + USD 6.25 billion − USD 8.33 billion = −USD 1.08 billion.

---

[11] Remember that Equation 12.15 ignores the interest on net exports.

Instead of a USD 1 billion gain, the economy made a net loss of USD 1.08 billion. The loss reflects the economy's real economic performance insofar as its capacity to generate net foreign exchange value is concerned. Effective cross-border risk analysis should take this information into consideration. One way to do this is to use historical data to estimate expected rates of return, variance and covariance, which can then be applied in the financial models such as the CAPM or the options pricing model. In the following sections we show how the data can be used along with options pricing theory to estimate financial risk premiums and maximum debt levels for international bank loans.

Assessing country creditworthiness: advanced techniques

A country's ability to service foreign debt obligations depends to a large extent on its financial health. The methods and financial ratios developed in Chapter 10 give a good indication of a country's financial health but fall far short of the more precise formulations prevalent in more advanced areas of financial theory and practice. As we saw in Chapters 8 and 9, one of the most important recent developments in the field of finance has been in options pricing theory and its application to all sorts of financial contracts. It is regularly applied to analyze investments in stocks, bonds, currencies, commodities and real estate. In this chapter we will show how options pricing theory can be applied to the problem of assessing a country's financial health and international creditworthiness.[12] First, we show how options pricing theory can be used to value corporate equity and debt. Particular emphasis is placed on two problems especially important in country-specific financial risk analysis: subordination of outstanding claims and agency conflict. We then go on to show how options pricing techniques can be applied to assessing country-specific financial risk. Procedures for generating all the relevant information and applying the model are presented in detail and special attention is paid to estimating the financial risk premium and using it to distinguish between short-term liquidity problems and full-blown solvency crises. In this context we highlight the role of political risk analysts and show how their knowledge and skills can be effectively applied in the options pricing approach to generate estimates of maximum debt levels and future volatility. We conclude the chapter with some empirical evidence of the option pricing approach's actual performance.

Using options to value securities

Using options pricing theory for debt valuation

Options pricing theory has become a standard tool in modern financial analysis and is employed extensively by both academics and practitioners to estimate the equilibrium market value of a wide range of corporate securities including stocks, bonds, warrants and other types of debt instruments. It has recently been extended to the realm of project evaluation, a subject we will deal with in Chapter 21.[13] In this chapter we will show how it can be employed to estimate country-specific financial risk. We start with an example of how

---

[12] This methodology was first presented in E. Clark, *Cross-border Investment Risk* (London: Euromoney Books, 1991), p.p. 85–110; "Briefing", *Euromoney* (February 1991), p.p. 73–76; "Briefing", *Euromoney* (April 1991), p.p. 79–82.

[13] See A.K. Dixit and R.S. Pindyck, *Investment Under Uncertainty* (Princeton, N.J.: Princeton University Press, 1994); L. Trigeorgis (1996), *Real Options* (Cambridge, MA: The MIT Press); M. Amram and N. Kulatilaka (1999), *Real Options: Managing Strategic Investment in an Uncertain World*, Boston, MA: Harvard Business School Press.

options pricing theory can be used to evaluate corporate equity and debt. Basic information on options and the Black-Scholes pricing formula are given in Chapter 8 and reproduced here for convenience.

$$C = V_t N(d_1) - Xe^{-r(T-t)} N(d_2) \qquad (12.23)$$

where V is the underlying asset, X is the exercise price, σ is the standard deviation of the percentage change in V, T is the expiry date and $N(d)$ = the value of the cumulative normal distribution evaluated at d:

$$d_1 = \frac{\ln(V_t / X) + (r + \sigma^2 / 2)(T - t)}{\sigma\sqrt{T - t}} \qquad (12.24)$$

$$d_2 = \frac{\ln(V_t / X) + (r - \sigma^2 / 2)(T - t)}{\sigma\sqrt{T - t}} \qquad (12.25)$$

In their original article Black and Scholes showed how options pricing theory can be applied to the equilibrium market pricing of corporate equity and debt. Corporate debt can be considered as a sale of the company's assets to creditors with shareholders owning an option to buy the assets back. On the exercise date, if the value of the assets is higher than the nominal value of the debt, the shareholders will exercise their option and buy back the assets by paying off the debt. In the opposite case, the company defaults and the creditors take possession of the assets. An example will make this clear.

Take company A that has all its assets invested in company B.[14] Company A owns 1000 shares of company B with a total value of USD 150,000 (USD 150 per share). Thus, since all company A's assets are invested in company B, the total value of company A is USD 150,000. Company A has two classes of securities outstanding: 1000 shares of its own common stock and 140 **zero coupon bonds**, each of which will pay USD 1000 at maturity in 365 days. A zero coupon bond is a bond that pays no interest premiums but which is issued at a discount to its face value. Thus, at maturity the total amount due on the bonds will be USD 140,000. Company B pays no dividends and, consequently, company A will make or receive no cash payments until the maturity date.

On the maturity date, company A plans to pay off the old debt with a new debt issue. However, if company B is worth less than USD 140 per share on the maturity date, it will be unable to do so because no one will pay USD 140,000 for a partial claim on assets worth less than USD 140,000. In this case, ownership of the stock of company B will pass into the hands of the bondholders. In other words, company A's shareholders have an option on the company's assets with an exercise price of USD 140,000 and a maturity of one year.

What we want to know is the present market value and financial risk premium on company A's debt. Suppose that research shows that the value of company B's stock follows a continuous process with a constant standard deviation of 0.4 and that the rate on a one-year Treasury bill, the riskless rate, is 10%. With this information the options pricing formula can be applied to determine the correct current value and risk premium on the bonds issued by company A. Three steps are involved.

---

[14] Similar examples were developed by R. Merton, "On the pricing of corporate debt", *Journal of Finance*, Vol. 29 (May 1974), p.p. 449–470 and Cox and Rubenstein, 1985, op. cit., p.p. 375–384 and E. Clark, 1991, op. cit., p.p. 86–88.

- First, the market value of company A's common stock is estimated in the options pricing formula.
- Secondly, the market value of the debt is determined by subtracting the market value of the common stock from the total value of company A.[15]
- Thirdly, by comparing the value of the debt given by this formula with the value it would have if there were no default risk, the financial risk premium is determined.

Applying this information on companies A and B in equations 12.24 and 12.25, we have

$$d_1 = [\ln(150,000/140,000) + (0.1 + 0.16/2)] / 0.4 = 0.6225$$

$$d_2 = d_1 - 0.4 = 0.2225$$

By looking up these values in the cumulative normal curve tables, we find:

$$N(d_1) = 0.7332$$

$$N(d_2) = 0.5881$$

and substituting this information into Equation 12.23 gives

$$C_0 = \text{USD } 150,000 \times 0.7332 - \text{USD } 140,000 \times 0.5881 \times e^{-0.1} = \text{USD } 35,481$$

Hence, the value of company A's equity is equal to USD 35,481. Since the total value of the company is equal to USD 150,000, the value of the zero coupon bonds can be found by subtracting the equity value from the total value of the company. The market value of the bonds is thus equal to

$$\text{USD } 150,000 - \text{USD } 35,481 = \text{USD } 114,519.$$

The risk-adjusted interest rate can be found by taking the natural logarithm of the face value of the bonds divided by their current market value:

$$\ln(\text{USD } 140,000/\text{USD } 114,519) = 0.2009 = 20.09\%.$$

The financial risk premium is equal to the risk-adjusted interest rate less the riskless interest rate:

$$0.2009 - 0.1 = 0.1009 \text{ or } 10.09\%.$$

Hence, the financial risk premium depends on three parameters:

1. the company's capital structure represented by the reciprocal of the debt/total assets ratio (V/X),

---

[15] The market value of the bond could be calculated directly by remembering that B, the market value of the bonds, is equal to $V_0 - C_0$ and substituting this into Equation 12.23 so that:

$$B_0 = V_0 N(-d_1) - Ee^{-(r)} N(d_2)$$

where $N(-d_1) = 1 - N(d_1)$ because of the symmetry of the normal distribution.

2. the firm's operating risk represented by the standard deviation (σ) or variance of the percentage change in firm's total market value and

3. the maturity of the debt (t).

It is important to note that the firm's financial risk always increases as its operating risk and debt/market value ratio increase. As we will see below, this fact gives rise to agency problems between the different categories of securities holders. However, the maturity of the debt has no such straightforward effect. For low and medium debt ratios an increase in the debt's maturity will increase the financial risk premium, while for high debt ratios it will decrease the financial risk premium. It is said that this is because the probability of default increases with time for low debt ratios while it decreases with time for high debt ratios.

Pricing subordinated debt

The possibility of subordinating one class of debt to other types of claims is a major consideration for country-specific financial risk assessment. This is because of the relative autonomy that national governments have in determining when, how and if foreign creditors will be paid. The link between subordination and risk can be illustrated by an example.

Suppose that company A, in addition to its 140 zero coupon bonds, has also issued 30 subordinated zero coupon bonds, each of which promises to pay USD 1000 in 365 days.[16] These subordinated bonds will be paid off only after the 140 senior bonds have been paid in full. If company A is worth less than USD 140,000 on the maturity date, all the assets will go to the senior bondholders. If company A is worth between USD 140,000 and USD 170,000, the senior bondholders will be paid in full and the subordinated bondholders will receive the difference. If the company is worth more than USD 170,000, all the bondholders will be paid in full and the shareholders will receive the difference.

The senior bondholders' situation has not changed from the previous example but the shareholders' situation has. Each share of stock now represents a call option on the company's assets with a strike price of USD 170 instead of USD 140. The subordinated bondholders are in the position of someone who owns a call option with a strike price of USD 140 and who has sold another call option with the same maturity date and a strike price of USD 170. The value of the subordinated bonds can be found by evaluating both types of options and subtracting the value of the option with the strike price of USD 170 from the value of the option with the strike price of USD 140 and multiplying by 1000, the number of shares.

Using the options pricing formula we find:

- Value of the option (USD 140 strike price) = USD 35.481
- Value of the option (USD 170 strike price) = USD 22.217
- Value of subordinated debt = (USD 35.481 – USD 22.217) × 1000 = USD 13,264.

The yield to maturity is:

$$\ln(\text{USD } 30,000/\text{USD } 13,264) = 0.8161 = 81.61\%$$

and the risk premium is:

$$81.61\% - 10\% = 71.61\%.$$

---

[16] This type of example, presented by Cox and Rubenstein, 1985, p.p. 384–387, was first developed by Black and Cox in "Valuing corporate securities: Some effects of bond indenture provisions", *Journal of Finance*, Vol. 31 (May 1976), p.p. 351–368.

The agency problem

An agency problem exists when principals and agents have a conflict of interest. In the absence of protective covenants, for example, the owners of company A could benefit at the expense of both types of bondholders by taking actions that change the firm's volatility or its debt/asset ratio. Suppose that the owners sell the shares of company B, which has volatility of 0.4, and purchase USD 150,000 of a firm with volatility of 0.6. Table 12.3 compares the outcomes for the different classes of security holders with the outcomes of the preceding case. Owners gain USD 11,727 at the expense of senior bondholders who lose USD 10,048 and junior bond-holders who lose USD 1679. Owners clearly have an interest in increasing the firm's volatility whereas the bondholders clearly have an interest in preventing them from doing so.

To see the effect of increased financial leverage on the bondholders' position, we can go back to the original scenario where company A owns USD 150,000 worth of company B and has only two classes of securities outstanding: 1000 shares of its own common stock and 140 zero coupon bonds. Suppose that the firm issues zero coupon senior debt with a face value of USD 5000, the proceeds of which it will distribute to shareholders as a dividend. Total face value of outstanding debt goes up to USD 145,000, which means that the new exercise price of the shareholders' option goes up to USD 145,000 as well. The new bondholders will pay what the bonds are worth under the new debt/assets structure. The market value of the total USD 145,000 of debt is USD 117,095 and their share is 5/145. Thus, they pay USD 4038, which is distributed to the shareholders as a dividend. Table 12.4 summarizes the outcome. The new bondholders pay the fair market price for their investment. The shareholders lose USD 2576 in equity value but receive the dividend worth USD 4038. Their net gain is USD 1462 which comes at the expense of the original bond-holders whose claims fall from a value of USD 114,519 to USD 113,057.

Agency conflicts and the effects of subordination are particularly pertinent for cross-border lending. Through legislation and other incentives and controls, national governments have the power to influence domestic resource allocation and control investment policy. As major international borrowers they can influence the country's capital structure. Under the guise of national sovereignty, they also have wide scope for issuing unilateral decrees that have the effect of creating subordinating clauses where formerly there were none. Macroeconomic policy influences resource allocation, economic performance and its volatility. Capital flight financed with foreign loans is the equivalent of a debt-financed stock buy-back. Debt moratoriums or decrees to the effect that external obligations will be honored only up to a certain percentage of export income have the effect of subordinating foreign claims to the claims of residents. Judicious country-specific financial risk assessment requires awareness of these realities as well as the means of measuring their consequences.

Table 12.3 Volatility-induced wealth transfers (in US dollars) according to type of claimholder

	Former case: Volatility of underlying assets = 0.4	Case 2: Volatility of underlying assets = 0.6	Difference
Senior bondholders	114,519	104,471	−10,048
Junior bondholders	13,264	11,585	−1,679
Owners	22,217	33,944	+11,727

Source: E. Clark and B. Marois, *Managing Risk in International Business* (London: Thomson Learning, 1996).

Table 12.4 Leverage-induced wealth transfers (in US dollars) according to type of claimholder

	Original position	*Position after issue of USD 5000 in debt and dividend distribution*	*Difference*
Bond value	114,519	117,095	+2,576
Equity value	35,481	32,905	−2,576
Dividend	0	4,038	+4,038
Value of original bondholder claims	114,519	113,057	−1,462

Source: E. Clark and B. Marois, *Managing Risk in International Business* (London: Thomson Learning, 1996).

Estimating the maturity of non-zero coupon debt

Before moving on to practical applications of options pricing theory to the assessment of country-specific financial risk, one last problem must be addressed. In the preceding example, company A's debt was composed entirely of one-year zero coupon bonds. Therefore, it was equal to the bond's maturity. In reality, a company's or a country's debt is more likely to be composed of many different maturities and cash flow profiles. One possible solution to this problem is to evaluate each cash flow separately. However, the practical obstacles to such a procedure are prodigious. Another more promising route involves estimating the debt's average maturity (t).

Consider a bond with a nominal value of USD 100,000 that will be repaid in full at the end of five years and that makes annual interest payments of USD 20,000. To calculate the average time to maturity we can consider each payment as a zero coupon bond, the first payment with a maturity of one year, the second with a maturity of two years and so on. The last payment of USD 120,000 (USD 20,000 of interest and USD 100,000 of principal) will have a maturity of five years. The overall bond issue will then be a portfolio of zero coupon bonds with the following payment profile:

- USD 20,000 one-year maturity
- USD 20,000 two-year maturity
- USD 20,000 three-year maturity
- USD 20,000 four-year maturity
- USD 120,000 five-year maturity.

What we need to know in Equation 12.23 is the present value of the nominal debt discounted at the riskless rate (Xe^{-rt}). The nominal debt, X, is equal to the total liabilities arising from the loan, that is, the sum of the five US dollar payments: USD 20,000 + USD 20,000 + USD 20,000 + USD 20,000 + USD 120,000 = USD 200,000. Suppose that the riskless rate is 10%. We can find t by setting Xe^{-rt} equal to the sum of the present values of the individual payments (CF) and solving for T:

$$Xe^{-rT} = \sum_{t=1}^{5} CF_t e^{-rt} \tag{12.26}$$

USD $200,000e^{-0.1T}$ = USD $20,000e^{-0.1}$ + USD $20,000e^{-0.2}$ + USD $20,000e^{-0.3}$ + USD $20,000e^{-0.4}$ + USD $120,000e^{-0.5}$

$$T = \frac{\ln\left[\dfrac{USD\ 200{,}000}{USD\ 135{,}478}\right]}{0.1} = 3.895 \text{ years.}$$

It is important to note that although the nominal value of the bond is USD 100,000, the total amount of debt outstanding is USD 200,000 because the interest payments for each year also constitute a claim on the company and must be included.

Using options pricing theory in country-specific financial risk assessment: The case of Brazil

Before going on to discuss how the Black-Scholes options pricing formula can be applied to country-specific financial risk assessment, we should say something about some of the potential problems. The Black-Scholes options pricing formula depends on at least ten unrealistic assumptions:

1. The stock's volatility is known and does not change over the life of the option.
2. The stock price changes smoothly insofar as it never makes large changes in a short period of time.
3. The riskless rate never changes.
4. Anyone can borrow or lend as much as he wants at a single rate.
5. A short seller will have the use of all the proceeds of the sale and receive all returns from investing these proceeds.
6. There are no trading costs for either the stock or the option.
7. There are no tax consequences.
8. The stock pays no dividends.
9. Exercise of the option can occur only at expiration.
10 There are no takeovers or other events that can end the option's life early.

Although these assumptions are false and, consequently, the formula is wrong, no other formula has been developed that gives better results in a wide range of circumstances. In fact, after more than 25 years, the formula has proved its reliability and is more popular than ever with practitioners. When pricing longer-term securities, however, such as corporate bonds and cross-border debt, the assumptions concerning constant volatility and interest rates are particularly unrealistic. Black (1989) and Cox and Rubenstein (1985), discuss the loss of precision that these shortcomings entail as well as ways of deriving the parameters so as to minimize the problem.[17] Other formulas have been derived to specifically overcome them.[18] In the following discussion, then, we are aware that the level of precision probably falls short of what can be achieved with traditional short-term European options pricing. Nevertheless, we present strong evidence that, compared with

[17] F. Black, "How to use holes in the Black-Scholes", *Journal of Applied Corporate Finance*, Vol. 1 (winter 1989); J.C. Cox and M. Rubenstein, *Options Markets* (Englewood Cliffs, N.J.: Prentice Hall Inc., 1985).

[18] See, for example, J.C. Cox and S.A. Ross, "The valuation of options for alternative stochastic processes", *Journal of Financial Economics*, Vol. 3 (January–March, 1976), p.p. 145–166.

the results of traditional techniques (logit and discriminant analysis, for example), the level of precision is surprisingly high.

Estimating the parameters

To evaluate the financial situation of a national economy the procedure is the same as for a corporation. However, where corporate market values, rates of return and volatility can normally be determined directly from published sources, the framework developed at the beginning of this chapter must be applied to generate the relevant data for the economy of a sovereign nation. Once the economy's market value, rate of return and standard deviation have been calculated, the remaining information concerning riskless interest rates and the nominal value of outstanding debt is available in numerous publications.[19] This is all the necessary data for using the options pricing formula to assess macroeconomic financial risk. It is worthwhile to work through an example to see how this can be done.

Going through the steps outlined above for Brazil from 1970 to 1987, we find the following information at the end of 1987:

V = the market value of Brazil's economy = USD 45.85 billion
σ = the standard deviation of $\ln(V_T/V_{T-1})$ = 0.3775.

To apply the Black-Scholes options pricing formula to Brazil's financial situation at the end of 1987, we need to know the amount of debt outstanding (X), its duration (T), and the riskless rate of interest (r). We proceed by estimating each of these parameters one by one.

Estimating X, the amount of debt outstanding

Brazil's debt is not composed of single-maturity, zero coupon securities as in the foregoing examples. On the contrary, it is composed of a wide range of securities with differing maturities, interest rates and amortization schedules. As we saw, however, this problem can be overcome by considering the individual dated cash flows as distinct zero coupon bonds. Then X, face value or nominal debt as defined above, is the sum of all the contractual cash flows coming due in the future, including interest and principal.

In the *World Debt Tables* published by the World Bank, Brazil had outstanding long-term debt of USD 106.06 billion at the end of 1987. This is the face value of the outstanding principal. Thus, X is equal to USD 106.06 billion plus all projected interest payments. Column 1 of Table 12.5 shows the year-by-year estimates of interest payments including interest on short-term debt. Estimates of interest payments on long and short-term debt are based on projections by the World Bank published in the *World Debt Tables* and personal calculations. Column 2 shows the schedule for principal repayments including the USD 106.6 billion of long-term debt and USD 17.84 billion of short-term debt based on World Bank projections and personal estimates. Column 3 is the sum of columns 1 and 2. Thus, Brazil's total debt outstanding at the end of 1987 is the sum of column 3, USD 167.06 billion.

[19] Some of the best information comes from international organizations such as the World Bank, *Global Development Finance* (formerly the *World Debt Tables*); the International Monetary Fund, *International Financial Statistics*; the Bank for International Settlements, *Annual Report, Evolution de l'Activité Bancaire et Financière Internationale, Ventilation par Echéance et par Secteur des Prêts Bancaires Internationaux, Statistiques sur l'Endettement Extérieur* (with the OECD); OECD, *Financial Market Trends*. See the publication lists of these organizations for complete details of what is available.

Table 12.5 The present value of Brazil's projected debt service at the end of 1987 (US dollars bn)

Year	Interest 1	Principal 2	Total 1 + 2 3	Discount factor (8.05%) 4	Present value 3 × 4 5
Short-term	1.30	17.84	19.14	0.96	18.39
1988	8.13	15.87	24.00	0.92	22.15
1989	7.14	12.91	20.05	0.85	17.06
1990	6.58	12.73	19.31	0.79	15.16
1991	5.49	12.76	18.25	0.72	13.23
1992	4.28	14.80	19.08	0.67	12.73
1993	3.03	11.79	14.82	0.62	9.14
1994	2.13	7.70	9.83	0.57	5.59
1995	1.67	3.93	5.60	0.53	2.94
1996	1.37	3.15	4.52	0.48	2.19
1997	1.11	2.91	4.02	0.45	1.80
1998	0.60	3.77	4.37	0.41	1.80
1999	0.30	3.77	4.07	0.38	1.55
Totals	43.13	123.93	167.06		123.75

Source: E. Clark and B. Marois, *Managing Risk in International Business* (London: Thomson Learning, 1996).

Estimating duration (*T*) and the riskless rate (*r*)

Since Brazil's debt is not the single-maturity, zero coupon liabilities assumed by options pricing theory, we have to estimate the duration of all the projected cash flows to get an estimate of T. This requires knowledge of the discount factor for each cash flow as well as the riskless rate. If the yield curve is not flat, each cash flow should be discounted at the spot rate corresponding to its maturity. Spot rates are interest rates on riskless zero coupon bonds. Since the dollar is our base currency, the riskless rates must be associated with a US government security. Unfortunately, US government instruments of this type are only available for a limited number of maturities. Ideally, the term structure of interest rates would be constructed and applied to the corresponding cash flows.[20] However, these procedures are complicated, time-consuming and have several practical shortcomings. Where construction of the term structure is impractical, a simplifying assumption can be made to determine the riskless rate.

The most common practice is to assume that the yield curve is flat. Most estimations of duration make this assumption. In this case, we could use the rate on US Treasury bills to represent the riskless rate. Under the flat yield curve assumption, one estimate of the riskless rate would be the bond equivalent of the Treasury bill rate, line 60cs in the International Monetary Fund's *International Financial Statistics*. This refers to the simple arithmetic average of daily yields on a coupon equivalent basis on three-month bills.

[20] Several methods for estimating the term structure of interest rates have been discussed in the literature. See W.T. Carelton and I.A. Cooper, "Estimation and uses of the term structure of interest rates", *Journal of Finance*, Vol. 31 (September 1976), p.p. 1067–1083; J.H. McCulloch, "An estimate of the liquidity premium", *Journal of Political Economy*, Vol. 83 (February 1975), p.p. 95–119; S.M. Schaefer, "Measuring a tax-specific term structure of interest rates in the market for British government securities", *Economic Journal*, Vol. 91 (June 1981), p.p. 415–438.

The problem with this method is that the yield curve is usually not flat and the Treasury bill bond equivalent rate is likely to change over the multi-year life of the debt. Thus, a more appropriate estimate of the riskless rate would be the yield to maturity on a government bond that has a cash flow profile which approximates that of the country's debt service (i.e. the percent of total payments period-by-period is the same for both). In this case the value of T for the country's debt would be the same as the government bond's duration, a convenient outcome for problems associated with the unrealistic assumption of a constant interest rate over the life of the option. Robert Merton has shown that the problems associated with this assumption can be overcome by using the zero coupon bond yield corresponding to the maturity of the option.[21] With perfectly matched cash flow profiles, this condition would be met.

As a practical matter, we have found that the annual average yield to maturity on a US government ten-year constant maturity published in line 61 of *International Financial Statistics* is a reliable proxy. Although the cash flow profile of this security generally differs from that of individual country debt, it is still composed of a series of cash flows distributed over the life of the security and its yield to maturity reflects the term structure over its life. The average yield to maturity on the long-term government bond for 1987 was 8.38%. The appropriate rate for the options pricing formula is the continuously compounded rate, calculated as:

$$\ln(1.0838) = 0.0805 = 8.05\%.$$

Assuming that the yield to maturity on long-term US government bonds is the appropriate riskless rate, the discount factors in column 4 were calculated at the continuous compound rate of 8.05%.

Column 5 is the present value of each year's cash flow ($CF_t e^{-r(t-1987)}$), calculated by multiplying column 3 by column 4. At the end of 1987, the present value of the projected cash flows of Brazil's debt service was USD 123.75 billion, calculated by

$$\sum_{t=1987.5}^{1999} CF_t e^{-r(t-1987)}.$$

The nominal value (X) was USD 167.06 billion. The average maturity or duration of Brazil's foreign debt obligations can be calculated by remembering that in the Black-Scholes pricing formula Xe^{-rT} represents the present value of the exercise price or, in the case of country debt analysis, the present value of outstanding debt obligations including interest payments:

$$Xe^{-rT} = \sum_{t=1988}^{1999} CF_t e^{-r(t-1987)}$$

and solving for T:

$$T = \ln(\text{USD } 167.06/\text{USD } 123.75)/0.0805 = 3.73 \text{ years}.$$

---

[21] See R. Merton, "Theory of rational option pricing", *Bell Journal of Economics and Management Science*, Vol. 4 (spring 1973), p.p. 141–183.

Estimating the financial risk premium

We now have all the necessary information for the options pricing formula, which we show here as an explanatory aid. In practice, these tedious calculations are unnecessary. There are many calculators and computer programs containing the Black-Scholes algorithm that are fast, cheap and easy to use.

$$d_1 = \frac{\ln(USD\ 45.85\ /\ USD\ 167.06) + (0.0805 + 0.1425\ /\ 2)3.73}{0.3775\sqrt{3.73}} = -0.9971$$

$$d_2 = \frac{\ln(USD\ 45.85\ /\ USD\ 167.06) + (0.0805 - 0.1425\ /\ 2)3.73}{0.3775\sqrt{3.73}} = -1.7262$$

$N(d_1) = 0.1594$
$N(d_2) = 0.0422$

$$C_0 = USD\ 45.85(0.1594) - USD\ 167.06e^{-(0.0805)3.73}\ (0.0422) = 2.087$$

We can interpret this result as: the value of Brazilian residents' equity in the total value of the economy at the end of 1987 was USD 2.087 billion. Proceeding as we did in the example at the beginning of the chapter, the market value of Brazilian debt is equal to the difference between the total value of the economy and the value of Brazilian resident equity:

Market value of Brazilian debt = USD 45.85 – USD 2.087 = USD 43.76 billion.

The risk-adjusted rate of interest on Brazilian debt is equal to the log of the nominal value of outstanding obligations divided by the average maturity:

Risk-adjusted cost of debt = ln(USD 167.06/USD 43.76)/3.73 = 0.359 = 35.9%

and the financial risk premium is equal to the difference between the risk-adjusted cost of debt and the riskless rate:

Financial risk premium for Brazil at the end of 1987 = 35.9% – 8.05% = 27.85%.

The zero rate solvency test

The financial risk premium is sensitive to the riskless rate employed in the options pricing formula. As we mentioned above, assuming that the riskless rate remains constant over the life of the option is unrealistic and can be a source of error in the pricing exercise. Although the problem can theoretically be overcome by using the riskless rate appropriate to the maturity of the option, in practice this solution is often unworkable. Where multiple cash flow country debt is concerned, it is virtually always unworkable. Thus, the chosen riskless rate will always be off the mark to a certain extent. One way to partially compensate for this bias is to estimate the risk premium with the riskless rate set at zero. Then, the risk premium will depend only on the economy's volatility (σ), the reciprocal of the leverage ratio (V/E) and the debt's duration (t). We say that the compensation will only be partial because, as we have seen, in most cases the debt's duration itself depends on the riskless rate that has been chosen.

Using the zero rate solvency test to distinguish between liquidity problems and solvency crises

In cross-border risk analysis the distinction must be drawn between liquidity and solvency. As we have seen, measures of liquidity tend to dominate financial risk analysis. This, of course, reflects the lender's primary concern that a country will be able to meet its debt service payments in the near term. In the long term, however, the lender wants to be assured that the country is "solvent" and that principal will be repaid in full, in spite of short-term liquidity problems. It is an accepted fact that solvency ultimately depends on how productively the economy employs its resources. A country is insolvent when its long-term net cash flows of foreign currency are inadequate to cover foreign debt servicing obligations. This is the case if the amount of debt is excessive. It is also the case if the rate of return on the country's assets is lower than the cost of borrowing.

The simple solvency test of traditional country risk analysis says that the rate of growth of exports must exceed the nominal rate of interest on debt. Otherwise, the debt/exports ratio will grow without limit. While helpful, this test is not reliable. As we mentioned in Chapter 10, the debt/exports ratio presents only one side of the coin, the export side. The ability to meet foreign obligations depends on net exports, that is, exports minus imports. The same goes for solvency. It is the rate of growth of net exports, not the rate of growth of exports that determine solvency. At the beginning of this chapter we proposed several ratios based on net exports for assessing a country's financial position. The zero rate solvency test complements these ratios by combining macroeconomic volatility and leverage with the payment profile of outstanding obligations to measure the financial risk in terms of interest rate basis points.

In 1987 the average interest rate on new debt commitments to Brazil was 8.3%. Between 1970 and 1987 the average rate was well above 10%. Over the same period exports had a geometric growth rate of over 14%, which means that Brazil was passing the simple solvency test. Other ratios such as interest/exports also looked pretty good, although the total debt/exports ratio was above 400%. In any case, since interest rates were relatively high in 1987, it might be argued that Brazil's problem, including the high risk premium estimated above, was only one of liquidity and that a more reasonable riskless rate would bring the risk-adjusted borrowing rate into line with the economy's rate of return, which we estimated as 12%. We can test this proposition by estimating the risk premium with the riskless rate equal to zero. If the risk premium is unreasonable (above 3% or 4%), we conclude that the country is insolvent. If the risk premium is reasonable, we then compare the risk premium with the economy's rate of return. If the rate of return is higher than the risk premium, we might conclude that the problem is only one of liquidity. If, however, the risk premium is close to or greater than the economy's rate of return, we can conclude that there is a solvency crisis.

We applied this "zero rate" solvency test to Brazil at the end of 1987 and found the financial risk premium to be 35.2% This is clearly far too high, thereby confirming Brazil's situation of bankruptcy.[22] This outcome was pretty obvious, given the extreme nature of Brazil's financial predicament. Nevertheless, the zero rate solvency test can be very helpful when interest rates are high and the financial situation of the borrowing country is more reasonable. Combined with further analysis, it can be an important element in determining a country's creditworthiness as we show in a later section of this chapter.

The role of political risk analysis

Political risk analysis has an important role to play in the options pricing approach to macroeconomic financial risk analysis. Although similar in many ways, countries are not

[22] It is interesting to note that in 1988 Brazil rescheduled the enormous sum of USD 53.9 billion.

companies. We have made this clear in the chapters dealing with political risk. Countries have considerably more autonomy than a private firm. In the most drastic cases, they can declare debt moratoriums or issue decrees that external obligations will be honored only up to a certain point, such as a given percentage of exports. This has the effect of subordinating foreign claims to the claims of domestic residents. They can act in more subtle ways as well. For instance, they can finance capital flight with foreign loans, which is equivalent to increasing the debt/equity ratio as in a debt financed stock buy-back, or they can use economic and monetary policy to influence economic activity and resource allocation with consequences on the economy's volatility. All of these things will impact on the economy's financial situation.[23] Their impact can be measured in the options pricing approach. If and when they occur, however, and with what probability and magnitude, pertain to the domain of political risk analysis. Thus, the options pricing approach is a powerful tool for exploiting the insights and analysis of the political risk analyst.

Political risk and subordination

Remember that the application of the options pricing formula to the assessment of country-specific financial risk assumes that the assets are "sold" to the creditors who retain ownership in the case of default. This device makes it possible to value the debt and estimate the risk premium. However, the assumption must be handled carefully if the seizure of foreign assets is considered as a practical possibility in the case of default. Most countries have strict controls on foreign ownership of domestic resources. Through legislation and decrees, governments also have the ability to take unilateral decisions against their foreign creditors. Consequently, it cannot be realistically assumed that the full value of the economy could effectively become the property of foreign creditors. The actual figure is probably much lower and must be determined on a country-by-country basis in relation to each country's legal, political, economic, social and cultural conditions. The effect of this unilateral action factor, when it is exercised, is to subordinate foreign claims to those of nationals. The ultimate degree of subordination depends on the extent of the economy's vulnerability to foreign retaliatory actions. For example, even if no assets could be seized directly by foreign creditors in the aftermath of a unilateral government decision to default on interest or principal payments, a shut down of credit lines and trade financing might cost the economy 10% to 20% of its output.[24] The degree of subordination would thus be limited by this fact. In any case, as we have seen, the principle of subordination has a drastic impact on financial risk premiums and permissible debt levels.

One way of looking at the degree of subordination attached to foreign debt is to establish **collateralization** levels. Collateralization is the flip side of subordination and refers to the percent of the economy's total value that is realistically vulnerable to actions undertaken by foreign creditors in the case of default. Thus, collateralization represents the upper limit on a government's capacity to subordinate. Recent experience has shown that although foreign takeovers of domestic resources are severely limited in scope and difficult and costly to implement., other actions can be undertaken by creditors that set limits on the abilities of government to unilaterally modify or repudiate their bona fide international obligations. One promising avenue for exploiting political risk analysis lies

[23] As we showed above, an increase in volatility increases the value of the call option. A *ceteris paribus* increase in the debt/assets ratio improves the shareholders' position at the expense of the bondholders. Subordination weakens the position of bondholders.

[24] E. Clark and A. Zenaidi (1999) "Sovereign debt discounts and the unwillingness to pay", *Finance*, Vol. 20, No. 2, p.p. 185–199 model this trade-off, which they call the "willingness to pay", as the value of the government's option to default.

in expressing its conclusions in terms of a collateralization level for individual countries. An example will make this clear.

Suppose that instead of the Brazilian economy's total value of USD 45.85 billion, in-depth analysis of the country's legal, political, social, cultural and economic conditions concludes that only 20% or USD 9.17 billion is vulnerable to foreign creditor influence in the case of default. Substituting this figure for V in the options pricing formula (Equation 12.23) and proceeding as we did above yields a risk-adjusted interest rate of 77.8% and a financial risk premium of 69.8%, a figure 2.5 times higher than with 100% collateralization.

Collateralization has this effect because it raises the leverage ratio (lowers the market value/debt (V/X) ratio). Most countries have restrictions on foreign ownership of domestic assets or the ability to make them off limits to foreigners. Furthermore, these restrictions often concern state-owned sectors that are the heaviest foreign borrowers or the very sectors, such as natural resources, transport and communications, that would be of interest to foreign investors. Where restrictions on foreign ownership exist, they have the effect of subordinating foreign claims, thereby making them more risky. The collateralization analysis means determining to what extent outstanding debt is subordinate. Once this is done, pricing the subordinated debt through the options pricing formula is straightforward.[25]

Maximum debt levels

The financial risk premium is especially valuable in determining the creditworthiness of a national economy. The absolute level of the premium indicates the economy's overall financial health vis-à-vis the rest of the world. The higher the risk premium, the higher the chances of a debt service problem. The zero rate risk premium can also be compared with the economy's rate of return to aid in distinguishing between a simple liquidity crisis and a more serious solvency crisis. Remember that a solvency crisis is implied when the zero rate risk premium is absolutely too high or relatively too high compared to the economy's rate of return. When the zero rate risk premium is low enough and payments problems arise, illiquidity is implied. However, as the debt/assets ratio increases and the zero rate risk premium rises, the economy passes from illiquidity to insolvency. This suggests a theoretical maximum debt level. One definition of the maximum debt level is the point where the marginal cost of debt is just equal to the economy's rate of return. Another could be the point that yields a given zero rate risk premium. Others, of course, are possible but it is these two that we feel are the most pertinent.

In determining maximum debt levels, three steps are involved:

1. Determine which criteria will be used to define the maximum debt level (the country's rate of return or a given risk premium).
2. Determine a collateralization level.
3. Substitute the information in the options pricing formula and proceed by trial and error to the level of debt that yields the required criteria (the country's rate of return or the given risk premium).

Suppose, for example, that the maximum level criteria is the country's rate of return. The expected rate of return for the Brazilian economy between 1970 and 1987 was 12%. Supposing 100% collateralization, we can see in Table 12.6 that Brazil's risk-adjusted interest rate approaches 12% at a debt level of just over USD 38 billion (including interest

---

[25] It should be remembered that we are referring to macroeconomic financial risk or the risk that is associated with the overall economy. For individual loans to individual borrowers, their creditworthiness would also have to be evaluated.

and principal obligations). Thus, in the conditions prevailing at the end of 1987, Brazil's maximum debt level was about USD 38 billion, far lower that the USD 167.06 billion that was actually outstanding. A lower collateralization level will, of course, lower the maximum debt level. If astute political analysis had determined that a more reasonable collateralization level was USD 9.17 billion, the maximum debt level would fall to about USD 7.6 billion.

Using the zero rate risk premium as the maximum level criteria, the maximum debt level was even lower. Based on a zero rate risk premium of 3% and a collateralization rate of 100%, the maximum debt level was USD 25 billion. At a collateralization rate of 20% it was only USD 5 billion.

Volatility analysis

Political risk and volatility estimates

As we have seen, volatility or operational risk, defined as the standard deviation of the economy's rate of return, plays an important role in determining the macroeconomic financial risk premium. The accuracy of the estimate of the macroeconomic financial risk premium depends on the accuracy of the estimate of the economy's volatility. Up to now, we have used historical volatility. We believe that the use of historical volatility is justified insofar as most factors that determine macroeconomic volatility evolve relatively slowly. Outside of a chance discovery of gold or oil, a country's geography and dotation in natural resources are pretty much given over the medium term. So are its neighbors and the relations it enjoys with them. The evolution of its cultural fabric represented by its social and political organization has also shown itself to be a relatively slow process, no matter what name is given to the dominant regime of the moment. Because all of these factors, whatever they are called – geo-strategic, politico-economic, socio-cultural, etc. – are reflected in a country's past economic performance, and because they seem to evolve relatively slowly, in most cases the fairly recent past should be a good estimator of the not too distant future.

Nevertheless, exceptional situations crop up more or less regularly. Eastern Europe's current transition comes immediately to mind. Time will tell how much has actually changed but the fact of the matter is that uncertainty has increased. The Philippines is another case where social and political transition from Marcos to democracy increased uncertainty. Other less obvious situations also exist, and once analysts have identified them, they should be able to apply their expertise in a systematic fashion.

The nice thing about historical volatility is that it gives a reliable starting point so that when the analyst says that a country's situation is more risky it will be clear what the new risk level will be and what effect it will have on the country's financial risk. If, for example, an in-depth analysis of Brazil's political, social, strategic and economic conditions suggests that the situation is 50% more risky now than in the past, this conclusion can be translated

Table 12.6 Maximum debt levels for Brazil under different criteria at the end of 1987

	Criteria: Zero rate risk premium = 3%	Criteria: Risk-adjusted cost of borrowing = the country's rate of return (12%)
100% collateralization	USD 25 billion	USD 38 billion
20% collateralization	USD 5 billion	USD 7.6 billion

Source: E. Clark and B. Marois, *Managing Risk in International Business* (London: Thomson Learning, 1996).

into a volatility estimate of 56.625%, which is the historical volatility of 37.75% multiplied by 1.5. This figure can, in turn, be applied in the options pricing formula to determine exactly what effect it will have on the economy's financial health.

Using market information to determine volatility

Because operating risk may be changing over time, individual volatility estimates can be checked against the volatility implied by the overall market. Up to now we have been using the options pricing formula to determine the value of the country's call option on the assets "sold" to foreign creditors. Because we know the total value of the assets, we can derive the value of the foreign claims by subtracting the value of the call from the value of the total assets. However, if we know the value of the call we can leave the volatility as the unknown and solve the options pricing formula for this variable.

A secondary market for cross-border debt has developed and bid–ask prices for claims on many of the crisis countries are quoted regularly. This information makes it possible to determine the value of the call option and, subsequently, the volatility that this value implies.[26]

Suppose, for example, that Salomon Brothers' bid price for Brazilian debt was 30 at the end of 1987, meaning that it was selling for 30% of its face value.[27] From the *World Debt Tables* we know that the face value of outstanding Brazilian debt at the end of 1987 was USD 123.865 billion. The market value of the debt was thus 30% of USD 123.865 billion = USD 37.16 billion. It is important to note that here we have to use the face value of outstanding debt and not the total amount of foreign obligations that includes anticipated interest payments. This is because the market value of the debt quoted as a percentage of the face value already represents the present value of all future cash flows. When we apply the options pricing formula, however, E must still include interest payments.

Assuming 100% collateralization, the value of the call was equal to the difference between the economy's market value and the market value of the foreign debt:

$$USD\ 45.85 - USD\ 37.16 = USD\ 8.69\ billion.$$

Substituting this value for C in the options pricing formula and solving for volatility gives:

$$\sigma = 60.35\%.$$

In these conditions the volatility implied by the market is considerably higher than the historical volatility of 37.75%.

Although the methodology outlined above has strong theoretical foundations and a wide range of potent practical applications, the ultimate test of its eventual usefulness is whether or not it works. In Appendix 12.2 we show some strong evidence that it does.

Estimating systematic country risk

In the foregoing case studies, the standard deviation of profits and rate of return was used to measure the country's riskiness. This measure of risk is appropriate for a decision on

---

[26] M. Bouchet, E. Clark and B. Groslambert, "Revisiting the Asian financial crisis: Were capital markets caught by surprise?", *International Journal of Finance* (forthcoming) measure implied volatility for Indonesia, Korea, Malaysia, The Philippines and Thailand for the period leading up to the Asian crisis of 1997 (1993–96) to show that markets were aware of these countries' high riskiness (and took measures to hedge it) long before the crisis occurred.

[27] For information on country market prices for country debt, see www.bradynet.com.

whether or not a country is creditworthy. It is not appropriate, however, for a decision on whether or not, or to what extent, a creditworthy country should be included in an investment portfolio. We know from Chapter 11 that systematic or undiversifiable risk, which depends on the covariance structure of asset returns, is the appropriate parameter for this type of question. We also know that beta in the CAPM is a widely used measure of systematic risk by both practitioners and academics. The framework developed at the beginning of the chapter can be applied to obtain estimates of country betas in order to estimate systematic country economic risk. In this section, we will first show how the country betas can be estimated. We will then discuss whether or not the techniques outlined in this section have any practical value.

Estimating country betas

Problems with the CAPM

The practical value of the capital asset pricing model as an effective tool for portfolio management suffers from the necessity to use proxy portfolios to represent the true market portfolio. Roll, for example, pointed out that the theory is untestable unless the exact composition of the true market portfolio, which must include all risky assets – stocks, bonds, commodities, real estate and even human capital – is known and used in the tests.[28] In fact, most proxy portfolios contain only a sample of common stocks. The implication of his paper is that the choice of the proxy portfolio determines the empirical content of the model. The point is important because, more recently, Fama and French have reported such a weak relation between beta and average returns that they call into question the CAPM itself.[29] Roll and Ross, however, show that the cross-sectional relation is very sensitive to the choice of a proxy index and that if the proxy index is not on the mean-variance efficient frontier the Fama-French results can occur even when the CAPM holds.[30]

On the international level the problem is even more complicated. For equilibrium pricing of international assets to follow the CAPM it is necessary for investors throughout the world to have identical consumption baskets and for purchasing power parity (PPP) to hold exactly. In fact, deviations from PPP are a major source of exchange rate variation and consumption preferences also differ from country to country. In these conditions, investors will want to hedge against real exchange rate risk so that in equilibrium each investor's optimal investment strategy will be a combination of two portfolios, a risky portfolio common to all investors and a portfolio specific to each investor used to hedge the real exchange risk as he perceives it. Furthermore, the common risky portfolio will not be the world market portfolio because the world market portfolio contains assets correlated with the investor's consumption basket. Adler and Dumas showed that when there is no uncertainty about inflation rates in any country and when currency hedging is fully available, the common risky portfolio reduces to the world market portfolio.[31] Finding an adequate proxy for the world market portfolio is even more difficult than finding an adequate proxy for a national market portfolio.

[28] R. Roll, "A critique of the asset pricing theory's tests", *Journal of Financial Economics* (March, 1977), p.p. 349–357.

[29] E.F. Fama and K.R. French, "The cross-section of expected stock returns", *Journal of Finance*, Vol. XLVII, No. 2 (June 1992), p.p. 427–465.

[30] R. Roll and S.A. Ross, *On the Cross-sectional Relation between Expected returns and betas*, paper presented at the French Finance Association's International Conference in Finance (29 June, 1992).

[31] M. Adler and B. Dumas, "International portfolio choice and corporation finance: A synthesis", *Journal of Finance*, No. 3 (June 1983), p.p. 925–984.

The usual procedure is to adopt an index calculated in a base currency such as the US dollar with a representative mix of the major stocks from the world's stock markets. Bonds are sometimes included as well. However, Solnik points out that, judging from historical data, international market portfolios seem far from efficient, implying that there is much room for improvement.[32] Clark (1995) argues that a general international market index, which does in fact include all risky assets, can be generated by applying the model developed at the beginning of this chapter.[33]

Generating the index for calculating country betas

Equation 12.4 gives the capital value of an economy at the beginning of period t. As we have shown, it can be estimated by applying Equation 12.11. Thus, the world index at time t is simply the sum of the capital values in dollars of all the individual national economies from 1 to m:

$$I_t = \sum_{i=1}^{m} V_{it} \qquad (12.26)$$

where I is the world index.

Let R_{wt} represent the return on the world index for period t. Since, at the world level, total exports equal total imports, the return on the world index is:

$$R_{wt} = \frac{I_t}{I_{t-1}} - 1 \qquad (12.27)$$

The return on the world index corresponds to R_M in Equation 11.6 in Chapter 11.[34]

Estimating the country beta

To estimate the individual country betas we proceed with an ordinary least squares regression of the form:

$$(R_{it} - R_{Ft}) = c + B_i (R_{wt} - R_{Ft}) \qquad (12.28)$$

where R_{it} is the return on country i for year t, and c and B are estimated coefficients. B represents the beta coefficient in the CAPM and in equilibrium c should be equal to zero. R_{Ft} represents the riskless rate of return in the CAPM and for dollar-denominated assets is often represented by the rate of return on US Treasury bills.

The case of Korea

Suppose we want to estimate Korea's beta as it stood at the end of 1987. Looking at Equation 12.28 we can see that we need to know R_w, R_F, and R_i for each year of the estimation period 1970–87. To calculate R_w we use Equation 12.27 and to calculate R_i we use the formula $profits_t / V_{t-1}$. For R_F, we use the average rate of return of the US Treasury bill for

---

[32] B. Solnik, *International Investments* (Addison-Wesley Publishing Co. Inc., 1996).

[33] To see that this is true, go back to the beginning of the chapter and see how the cash flows, the *a*s and the *b*s, were defined. They include all income and expenditure on final goods and services.

[34] For the reader's convenience, Equation 11.6 is given as follows:

$$E(R_i) = R_F + \beta_i [E(R_M) - R_F]$$

each year. This information is then used in the least squares regression on Equation 12.28 where we find $B = 0.56$.

Thus, Korea's beta at the end of 1987 was 0.56. This is relatively low and indicates that Korea has relatively low systematic risk. By applying the CAPM, we can translate the systematic risk into interest rate basis points. Consider the following information: $E(R_w) = 9.72\%$ and $R_F = 8.38\%$. Applying this information in Equation 11.6 (the security market line), gives:

$$E(R_i) = 0.0838 + 0.56\,(0.0972 - 0.0838) = 0.0913$$

where the risk premium is:

$$0.56(0.0972 - 0.0838) = 0.0075$$

In other words the risk premium associated with Korea's macroeconomic risk was equal to 75 basis points at the end of 1987.

Does the index work? Some proof from portfolio investment

The usefulness of the index developed above for estimating a country's systematic risk depends ultimately on how well it works. Some strong proof exists that it does.

Clark (1995) constructed an index comprising 60 countries.[35] He then tested the index's ability to forecast the risk–return relationship over a ten-year period (1982–91) across a wide range of countries in three separate asset classes: money market instruments, long-term government bonds and equity indices. The procedure involves using the index to estimate the betas for each country in each asset class. He then used the estimated betas and historical expected rates of return, variance and standard deviation as forecasts to generate forward-looking portfolios for each year from 1982 to 1991 using the Elton-Gruber-Padberg procedure to maximize the Sharpe index.[36] Forward-looking means that the portfolio for 1982 was generated with data available at the end of 1981, the portfolio for 1983 with data available at the end of 1982, and so on to the end of the period under consideration. Rather than the full covariance matrix, the Elton-Gruber-Padberg procedure uses betas in the optimization procedure.[37] Thus, if the betas estimated against the index capture the covariance structure of country returns, this should be reflected in the performance of the optimized portfolios.

The test consists in comparing the *ex post* performances of the individual optimized portfolios with the performances of portfolios generated by "naive" diversification strategies.

---

[35] E. Clark, "A general international market index", *International Journal of Finance,* Vol. 3 (1995). The 60 countries are listed in footnote four.

[36] The Sharpe index is:

$$\text{Sharpe index} = \frac{E(R_p) - R_f}{\sigma_p}$$

where $E(R_p)$ is the expected return on the portfolio, and σ_p is the portfolio's standard deviation.

[37] For details on the optimization process see E.J. Elton, M.J. Gruber and M.F. Padberg, "Simple criteria for optimal portfolio selection", *Journal of Finance,* Vol. 11, No. 5 (December 1976), p.p. 1341–1357; E.J. Elton, M.J. Gruber and M.F. Padberg, "Simple rules for optimal portfolio selection: The multi-group case", *Journal of Financial and Quantitative Analysis,* Vol. 12, No. 3 (September 1977), p.p. 329–345; E.J. Elton, M.J. Gruber and M.F. Padberg, "Simple criteria for optimal portfolio selection: Tracing out the efficient frontier", *Journal of Finance,* Vol. 13, No. 1 (March 1978), p.p. 296–302; E.J. Elton, M.J. Gruber and M.F. Padberg, "Optimal portfolios from simple ranking devices", *Journal of Portfolio Management,* Vol. 4, No. 3 (spring 1978), p.p. 15–19.

The "naive" diversification strategies include portfolios of equal weights for all countries in the potential investment universe, weights based on relative gross domestic products (GDP), and an equally weighted portfolio comprised of Germany, Japan and Switzerland (suggested by a portfolio manager in the *Financial Analysts Journal*). The results are unambiguous. Clark found that in every case the optimized portfolio outperformed all the others in terms of the arithmetic mean, the geometric mean, return per unit of risk, and excess return per unit of risk for all periods and sub-periods. Table 12.7 shows the results for the Sharpe index over the whole ten-year period. It is clear that the optimized portfolio outperforms the naive portfolios by substantial amounts in all three markets. Appendix 12.2 gives an example of the Clark methodology's ability to forecast debt defaults and reschedulings.

Summary

1. The new analytical framework uses the discounted cash flow model to establish the relationship between macroeconomic cash flows from period to period and the macroeconomic balance sheet. Cash flows are measured in foreign exchange (US dollars, in our examples) and defined so that they reflect the perspective of the international investor whose concern is the economy's ability to generate the net foreign exchange value necessary to meet foreign interest, dividend, principal and depreciation payments. This framework can be used to generate analytical ratios such as macroeconomic profits and rate of return, foreign interest coverage ratio, cash flow coverage ratio, the degree of financial leverage and net profits per resident.

2. It can also be used as the underlying security to estimate financial risk using the options pricing techniques. These techniques make it possible to distinguish between solvency and insolvency, determine maximum debt levels and calculate implied volatility.

3. The framework can also be used to generate an international market index that makes it possible to estimate a country's systematic risk in the CAPM.

Appendix 12.1: Derivation of an economy's net export value (macroeconomic market value) in foreign currency

Remembering that $b_t - a_t = X_t - M_t$, we can rewrite Equation 12.4 as:

$$V_T = E[(X_T - M_T) + (X_{T+1} - M_{T+1})R^{-1} + \ldots + (X_n - M_n)R^{-(n-T)}] \qquad \text{(A12.1.1)}$$

Table 12.7 Excess return to standard deviation (Sharpe index) for selected portfolios over the period 1982–91

	Optimized	Equal weights	Japan–Germany–Switzerland
Money market	0.700	0.331	0.210
Long-term government bond	0.567	0.364	0.261
Equity index	0.484	0.409	0.375

Source E. Clark (1995) "A general international market index", *International Journal of Finance*, Vol. 3, 1288–1312.

The corresponding expression for Equation 12.5 is:

$$V_{T+1} = E[(X_{T+1} - M_{T+1}) + (X_{T+2} - M_{T+2})R^{-1} + \ldots + (X_n - M_n)R^{-(n-(T+1))}] \quad \text{(A12.1.2)}$$

Remembering that $X'_t = S_t X_t$ and $M'_t = S_t M_t$ gives Equation 12.9 in the text:

$$V'_T = E[S_T(X_T - M_T) + S_{T+1}(X_{T+1} - M_{T+1})R'^{-1} + \ldots + S_n(X_n - M_n)R'^{-(n-T)}] \quad \text{(A12.1.3)}$$

Forward rate parity can be expressed as:

$$E[S_t] = F_t \quad \text{(A12.1.4)}$$

Substituting A12.1.4 into A12.1.3 gives:

$$V'_T = S_T E(X_T - M_T) + F_{T+1}E(X_{T+1} - M_{T+1})R'^{-1} + F_{T+2}E(X_{T+2} - M_{T+2})R'^{-2}$$
$$+ \ldots + F_n E(X_n - M_n)R'^{-(n-T)}] \quad \text{(A12.1.5)}$$

Interest rate parity can be expressed as:

$$F_{T+1} = S_T \frac{R'^t}{R^t} \quad \text{(A12.1.6)}$$

Substituting A12.1.6 into A12.1.5 and simplifying gives:

$$V'_T = S_T E[(X_T - M_T) + (X_{T+1} - M_{T+1})R^{-1} + \ldots + (X_n - M_n)R^{-(n-T)}] \quad \text{(A12.1.7)}$$

Substituting A12.1.1 into A12.1.7 gives Equation 12.11 in the text. Equation 12.12 can be derived in the same way.

Appendix 12.2: The performance of the options pricing approach: Results of a 60-country study

In 1987 the options pricing approach to assessing international creditworthiness was applied to 60 countries in a study undertaken for a major financial institution. The general results were published in an article by Ephraim Clark in the September 1988 issue of *Euromoney*.[38] We can compare the results forecast by the study back in 1988 with the actual outcomes for the 60 countries in the succeeding four years, 1989–92.

The ranking process involved three steps (quoting from the *Euromoney* article, p. 234):

> First, the countries were ranked by the financial risk premium and grouped in categories of 0%–1%, 1%–2%, etc. Second, countries with the expected rates of return lower than their corresponding risk-adjusted interest rate were removed, grouped together in a lower bracket, and re-ranked according to their financial risk premiums. This was necessary to reflect the inherent financial risk of an economy whose marginal cost of foreign funds is higher than the marginal rate of return that

---

[38] See E. Clark (1988). The 60 countries are listed in footnote four to this chapter.

can be earned by employing these funds. Finally, countries within each risk category were ranked according to their economic risk premiums and expected rates of return.

The conclusion of the analysis was as follows:

> Rank alone does not tell the whole story: countries 1 to 11 represent little or no financial risk and they are far from a level of external debt which would compromise this situation; countries 12 to 19 represent little or no financial risk but their debt is at a level where increases will begin to affect the financial risk premium; countries 20 to 25 are in the same position but closer to what financial prudence would dictate as maximum external debt levels; countries 26 to 33 have reached or slightly surpassed their maximum external debt levels; and countries 34 to 60 are far past the point where loans could be justified on economic and financial criteria.

Before we compare the forecast with the actual results, it might be a good idea to put the exercise in perspective by reporting the conventional wisdom of the time reflected in what *Euromoney* had to say about the ranking system in the preface to the article:

> This may be the strangest list ever printed in *Euromoney*. How could Taiwan be higher than the United States in a country risk rating? How, for that matter, could El Salvador be a better risk than Australia, Sweden and Denmark?

In fact, *Euromoney* was right about El Salvador, which rescheduled USD 152 million between 1989 and 1992. But that is as far as it goes. Of the 33 countries that were deemed creditworthy, one other country, Panama, rescheduled to the tune of USD 202 million. Together, the sum of their reschedulings amounted to 0.27% of the total USD 130,258 million rescheduled by the 60 countries over the period. This is almost a perfect score that can be compared with *Euromoney*'s own country ranking that appeared in the same issue on the page preceding the Clark ranking.

Euromoney's ranking system, which was described in some detail in Chapter 10, contained 117 countries at the time of the article. In order to compare the two forecasts, we eliminated the countries not included in the Clark ranking so that both systems would include the same 60 countries and have the same total amount of rescheduled debt between 1989 and 1992 (USD 130.258 billion). Table 12.8 compares the results for the two rankings. It shows the cumulative amount of rescheduled debt for each system at each rank starting with rank 33, the cut-off point for solvency in the Clark ranking. Less debt rescheduled at the higher rankings indicates more accuracy in the rankings. When two or more countries had the same rank in the *Euromoney* system, we placed them in ascending order beginning with the smallest amount of rescheduled debt. Hence, the *Euromoney* ranking is presented in the most favorable way possible.

The results are striking. The Clark system is clearly superior by a wide margin. The *Euromoney* system has more cumulative rescheduled debt at every step of the process until rank 58. In fact, by rank 40 the *Euromoney* ranking has already reached cumulative rescheduled debt of over USD 68 billion whereas at rank 55, the Clark ranking is still only at slightly over USD 66 billion. Figure 12.1 underlines the superior performance of the Clark ranking by presenting the information in a dominance graph representing the percent of total rescheduled debt outstanding at each rank.

Table 12.8 Comparison of the 1988 *Euromoney* and Clark country rankings: Cumulative rescheduled debt at each rank over the period 1989–92

	Cumulative rescheduled debt (millions of US dollars)		
	Euromoney's ranking system	*Clark's ranking system*	*Difference*
Ranks 1 to 33	4,329	354	3,975
34	4,329	988	3,341
35	4,329	988	3,341
36	5,620	988	4,632
37	23,279	988	22,291
38	29,629	18,647	10,982
39	29,629	19,083	10,546
40	68,762	19,810	48,952
41	68,762	19,878	48,884
42	68,762	24,958	43,804
43	84,193	24,958	59,235
44	84,978	31,308	53,670
45	90,058	31,308	58,750
46	90,494	32,599	57,895
47	98,939	49,062	49,877
48	98,939	50,163	48,776
49	99,141	50,163	48,978
50	102,028	58,608	43,420
51	103,365	59,120	44,425
52	119,828	60,457	59,371
53	120,929	64,786	56,143
54	120,997	66,184	54,813
55	121,724	66,184	55,540
56	122,358	105,317	17,041
57	122,870	111,155	11,715
58	124,268	126,586	–2,318
59	124,420	129,473	–5,053
60	130,258	130,258	0

Source: World Bank (1993–1994), *World Bank Debt Tables*. Vol. II.

Figure 12.1 Percent of unrescheduled debt at each rank

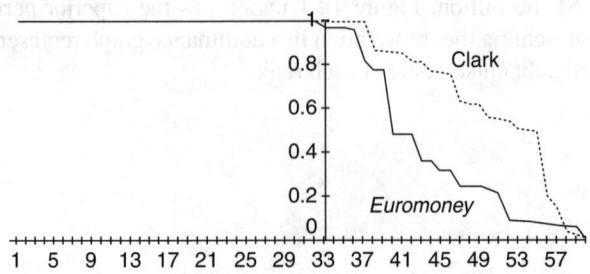

FOREIGN EXCHANGE RISK MANAGEMENT

Current operations and foreign exchange exposure

13

In this chapter we examine the main issues involved in exchange rate exposure and international cash management. We start with the choice of currencies for invoicing cross-border transactions and the terms of payment. These decisions are of primary importance because, by their nature, they influence the company's exposure to credit and foreign exchange risk. Ensuring that claims generated can be recovered in a satisfactory manner is an important element in the decision-making process. The second part of the chapter deals with the major techniques associated with the particular problems of managing cash flows in a number of currencies. We conclude the chapter with an analysis of the company's overall foreign exchange exposure.

Payment terms in international trade

Every commercial transaction specifies the price of the merchandise and how and when it will be paid for. Pricing merchandise in an international transaction is more complicated than in a purely domestic setting because more than one currency is involved. Determining the precise method that will be used to make the payment is also more difficult because traditional methods like checks and drafts pose legal and technical problems in processing, clearing and enforcement. As a result, the financing terms of an international transaction are often restricted.

Currency choice in invoicing

One of the most important elements in an international commercial transaction is the currency used for invoicing. In some transactions no choice exists. This is the case when convention has it that all deals are done in a certain currency. Crude oil trading, for example, takes place exclusively in US dollars. It can also be the case when a firm refuses any currency other than its own home currency. Many small or medium-sized firms lacking international experience have such a policy because they fear the unknown in general, because they fear foreign exchange risk in particular, or because they fear neither but cannot afford to work out new price lists and manage the resulting exchange risk. However, for firms willing and able to make the effort, currency flexibility in invoicing can be commercially advantageous and financially profitable.

Choosing an invoicing currency involves comparing the amount of the invoice billed directly in domestic currency with the domestic currency equivalent of the amount of the invoice if billed in foreign currency. Making the comparison is not a straightforward operation. Because payment will be made sometime in the future, the spot rate cannot be used in making the comparison because the spot rate can, and probably will, change in the meantime. The forward rate is the obvious solution. In practice, however, the forward rate is not always directly applicable. Take the case where deliveries and invoices will occur several times over the year. Applying the appropriate forward rate to each separate invoice implies a different price for each delivery. In this case, an average forward price would probably be better.

The problem is the same for both buyer and seller. If the buyer agrees to be billed in foreign currency, the amount he owes will be exposed to foreign exchange risk. If the seller agrees to bill in foreign currency, the amount he receives will be exposed to foreign exchange risk. One or the other is going to have to cover his foreign exchange risk and they will both have recourse to the same financial intermediaries offering the same products. If markets were perfectly efficient, it seems then that the choice of the invoicing currency would be completely neutral. In fact, it is not neutral at all. In the first place, not all companies have access to the same financial products at the same prices. Smaller companies are limited in the products they can use and often pay higher prices for the ones that are available to them. Furthermore, rules and regulations imposed by the monetary and tax authorities can create barriers and supplementary costs. Finally, all companies are not equally endowed with the knowledge and expertise to deal with problems associated with foreign exchange transactions. Thus, companies with the required know-how can offer the financial service of billing in their clients' domestic currency along with the merchandise they are selling and make a profit on both ends.

There can also be a speculative element involved in pricing and billing in foreign currency. A professional that follows the foreign exchange market closely is going to form opinions on how the values of different currencies will develop. He may feel that some currencies are strong and likely to appreciate. Others, he may feel, are weak and likely to depreciate. If he has any confidence in his opinions, he will try to take advantage of them by selling in strong currencies and purchasing in weak ones. A word of caution is in order. Most corporate treasurers agree that multi-currency invoicing should exclude exotic currencies with narrow markets where financial services are costly or non-existent.

Methods of making payments

For international payments, the traditional means of settling debts in a domestic economy such as cash, credit cards and traveler's checks, are only relevant for tourism. Bank transfers are probably the fastest and most efficient means of settling international debts. In a bank transfer, the importer instructs his bank to debit his account and credit the exporter's account at the exporter's bank. The transfer is made by telex or SWIFT, which guarantees its speedy execution. The disadvantage of a bank transfer is that it is generated at the initiative of the importer and the exporter has no guarantee in the case of non-payment. Consequently, except for cash payments in advance, bank transfers are appropriate only for the most trustworthy relationships.

Checks are another instrument generated at the initiative of the importer. Unlike the bank transfer, however, they are not rapid. First of all, they have to be sent, which takes time, and they could get lost in the mail. Furthermore, banks credit foreign checks only after a long delay due to difficulties in processing and clearing them.

A **promissory note** is a written promise by the importer to pay a given sum on a given date in the future. They play a small role in international trade but are often used as a support to financing operations as in bridge loans, for example.

A **draft** or **bill of exchange** (see Figure 13.1) is the most common means of payment in international trade. A draft is an unconditional order in writing, initiated and signed by the exporter, ordering the importer to pay on demand or at a given future date a given sum of money. A draft is usually addressed to the importer or the importer's agent. It can be payable to a particular beneficiary or to bearer. Bearer drafts are negotiable. When it is payable on demand it is called a sight draft. When it is payable at a future date it is called a time draft.

In most cases three parties are involved in the draft. The "drawer" is the party that draws up the draft, signs it and sends it to the second party, called the "drawee". The drawer is usually the exporter and the drawee is the importer or the importer's agent. The beneficiary of the draft is called the "payee". Normally, the drawer and the payee are the same. When the drawee receives the draft, he writes "accepted" on its face, followed by the date and his signature. When this has been done, the draft becomes an "acceptance" and the party that does the accepting has the obligation to pay at maturity. If the accepting party is a commercial enterprise, it is known as a trade acceptance. If a bank accepts the draft, it is known as a bankers' acceptance.

Documentary methods of payment

Documentary draft

The simplest method of documentary payment is a draft accompanied by certain documents, called a documentary draft. In this scenario, the exporter, after having shipped the merchandise, forwards the draft along with the required documents to his bank. The required documents include a commercial invoice and sometimes a consular invoice as well, an insurance certificate, a certificate of origin, and a **bill of lading** in negotiable form. The bill of lading is a contract between the shipper (exporter) and a transportation company in which the latter agrees to transport the goods under specified conditions that limit its liability. It is the shipper's receipt for the goods as well as proof that the goods have been or will be shipped. An order bill of lading consigns the goods to the order of a named party (usually the exporter) and is negotiable. Ownership can be transferred by endorsing the bill on the reverse side. Therefore, it can serve as collateral for loans. When goods are sent by air, the equivalent of the bill of lading is called an air waybill.

The negotiable bill of lading is the most important document for a documentary draft because it gives its holder title to the merchandise in question. Having received the required documents, the bank notifies the importer who then accepts the draft and receives the bill of

Figure 13.1 Specimen of a bill of exchange

| LILLE, FRANCE | AUG 8 | , 20 XX No 430 |

AT NINETY DAYS SIGHT OF THIS **ORIGINAL** OF EXCHANGE (DUPLICATE UNPAID)

PAY TO THE ORDER OF BANK OF LILLE U.S. $ 92,000.00

THE SUM OF NINETY TWO THOUSAND AND NO/100 ★ ★ ★ ★ ★ ★ ★ ★ ★ ★ ★ ★ ★ ★ ★ ★ ★ ★ ★ U.S. Dollars

DRAWN UNDER LETTER OF CREDIT NO.	DATED	ISSUED BY
RBD 69 69	JUL 19, 20XX	BANK OF CHARLESTON

To BANK OF CHARLESTON

13 EDGEWATER DRIVE *SPECIMEN*

SOUTH CAROLINA, 29047 PHI EXPORT INC.

18-178 (REV 18-91)

lading in return. In this way, the exporter is sure that the importer will not get title to the goods until he has accepted the draft.

Documentary drafts are not foolproof because drafts are not always accepted and paid. If the draft is refused by the importer, the exporter still has the problem of either repatriating the goods or selling them somewhere else, probably at a loss. If the draft is not paid the exporter is left with a bad debt.

Letter of credit

The **letter of credit** offers the exporter a high degree of safety. A letter of credit is a document addressed to the exporter that is written and signed by a bank on behalf of the importer. In the document, the bank undertakes to guarantee for a certain time span the payment for the specified merchandise, either by paying directly or by accepting drafts, if the exporter conforms to the conditions of the letter of credit by presenting the required documents. The letter of credit is thus a financial contract between the issuing bank and the exporter that is separate from the commercial transaction.

Letters of credit can be revocable or irrevocable. Revocable letters of credit can be canceled at any time by the bank and consequently are rarely used except for transactions between subsidiaries of the same company. An irrevocable letter of credit can be modified or canceled only with the agreement of both parties. If a bank in the exporter's country adds its guarantee to the letter of credit issued by the importer's bank, it is called a confirmed letter of credit. This means that if the importer's bank does not honor its promise to pay for one reason or another, the exporter's bank will make good on the promise.

Letters of credit give rise to three types of settlement: by payment, by acceptance and by negotiation. Figure 13.2 outlines the various stages involved in operations using a letter of credit. These are as follows:

1. The importer and exporter make a commercial deal.
2. The importer asks his bank to issue a letter of credit in favor of the exporter. At this stage the terms of the deal are clearly spelled out in the letter of credit, including the characteristics of

Figure 13.2 Application of a letter of credit

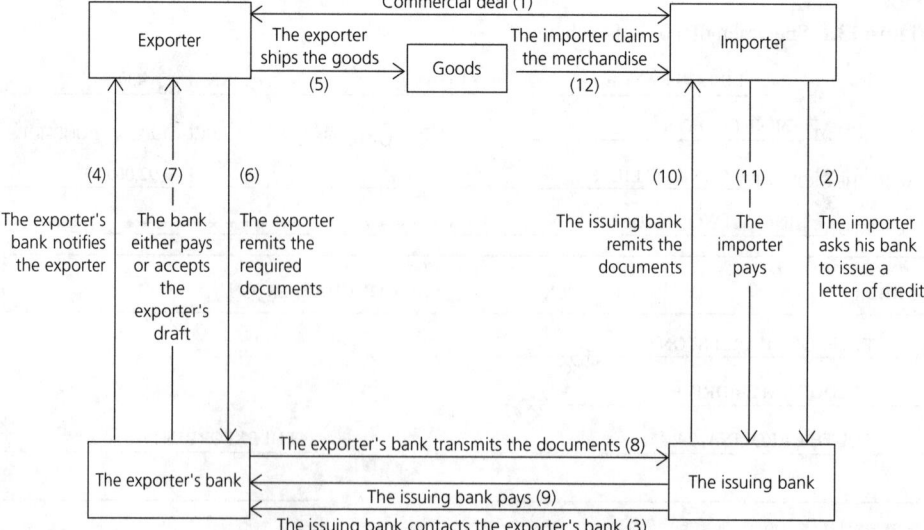

the merchandise, the amount to be paid, the time period, the required documents and the means of settlement.

3. The issuing bank contacts the exporter's bank and asks it to advise the exporter that a letter of credit has been opened on his behalf.

4. The exporter's bank notifies the exporter and confirms the letter of credit if necessary.

5. The exporter ships the goods and prepares the required documents.

6. The exporter remits the required documents to its bank.

7. The bank either pays the exporter or accepts the exporter's draft and delivers it to him. The exporter can then discount the draft if need be. If settlement is by negotiation, the bank pays the exporter after deducting all charges and conserves the draft.

8. The exporter's bank transmits the documents to the issuing bank.

9. The issuing bank pays the exporter's bank.

10. The issuing bank remits the documents to the importer.

11. The importer pays the issuing bank.

12. The importer presents the documents and claims the merchandise.

A letter of credit (see Figure 13.3) is one of the most reliable means of settling foreign accounts receivable. The exporter knows all the requirements for payment because they are spelled out in the letter of credit. The institution guaranteeing payment is a bank, and procedures are standardized and well known to the banking community. Furthermore, it facilitates financing because a bankers' acceptance can easily be discounted. It also has the advantage of guaranteeing against order cancelation during the manufacturing stage. The disadvantage is that it is costly and cumbersome to set up. Furthermore, it does not guarantee against all possible risks. Technical errors in the documents can cause non-payment. Worse again, in many third world countries, importers can sometimes gain access to goods before paying for them. Complaints by the importer about the quality of supposedly protected merchandise are often received at the same time that the issuing bank is refusing payment because of errors in one or more documents. Unconfirmed letters of credit are also subject to government inspired measures that forbid, reduce or delay payment. In all this, exporters should always deal directly with a trusted bank and resist pressure by the importer to name the receiving bank in the exporter's country. He will thus at least be assured that in the case of a problem his interests will be protected.

Other payment terms

Cash in advance

Cash in advance is the safest way for an exporter to sell because he receives payment for the goods before they are shipped. For made-to-order goods, cash in advance is the rule. For other types of merchandise, it is less widespread except in particularly unstable countries or for importers with doubtful credit. Cash against documents, however, is still a popular way to do business.

Open account

Selling goods on open account enables an importer to avoid the cost of opening a letter of credit and provides him with financing. It is the way much business is done domestically. It involves shipping the goods to the importer, invoicing him and trusting him to pay within the prescribed limits. Payment may be made by draft, by check or by bank transfer. Selling on open account should only be considered for the most trustworthy clients.

Figure 13.3 Specimen of a letter of credit

IRREVOCABLE
COMMERCIAL
LETTER OF
CREDIT

BANK OF CHARLESTON
13, EDGEWATER DRIVE, CHARLESTON,
SOUTH CAROLINA, 29047

INTERNATIONAL DIVISION **COMMERCIAL L/C DEPARTMENT** CABLE ADDRESS CHARLESTON

OUR LETTER
OF CREDIT NO. RBD 6969   AMOUNT US$92,000   DATE JUL 19, 20XX

THIS NUMBER MUST BE MENTIONED
ON ALL DRAFTS AND CORRESPONDENCE

- PHI EXPORT INC.   • PHI EXPORT INC.
- LILLE FRANCE   • LILLE FRANCE
-
-

GENTLEMEN:

BY ORDER OF U.S.A. IMPORTERS INC.

AND FOR ACCOUNT OF SAMF

WE HEREBY AUTHORIZE YOU TO DRAW ON OURSELVES

UP TO AN AGGREGATE AMOUNT OF NINETY TWO THOUSAND AND NO/100 U.S. DOLLARS

AVAILABLE BY YOUR DRAFTS AT ON OURSELVES, IN DUPLICATE, AT 90 DAYS SIGHT
ACCOMPANIED BY

SIGNED INVOICE IN TRIPLICATE
PACKING LIST IN DUPLICATE
FULL SET OF CLEAN OCEAN BILLS OF LADING, MADE OUT TO ORDER OF SHIPPER, BLANK ENDORSED,
    MARKED FREIGHT PREPAID AND NOTIFY: U.S.A. IMPORTERS, INC., CHARLESTON, SOUTH CAROLINA,
    DATED ON BOARD NOT LATER THAN AUG 31, 20XX.
INSURANCE POLICY/CERTIFICATE IN DUPLICATE FOR 110% OF INVOICE VALUE, COVERING ALL RISKS.

COVERING: SHIPMENT OF AUTOMOBILE SPARE PARTS, AS PER BUYER'S ORDER NO. 900 DATED MARCH 6,
    20XX FROM ANY FRENCH PORT C.I.F.
    CHARLESTON, SOUTH CAROLINA
PARTIAL SHIPMENTS ARE PERMITTED.
TRANSHIPMENT IS NOT PERMITTED.
DOCUMENTS MUST BE PRESENTED WITHIN 7 DAYS AFTER THE BOARD DATE OF THE BILLS OF LADING,
    BUT IN ANY EVENT NOT LATER THAN SEPT 6, 20XX

DRAFTS MUST BE DRAWN AND NEGOTIATED NOT LATER THAN SEPT 6, 20XX   **SPECIMEN**
ALL DRAFTS DRAWN UNDER THIS CREDIT MUST BEAR ITS DATE AND NUMBER AND THE AMOUNTS MUST BE ENDORSED ON THE REVERSE
SIDE OF THIS LETTER OF CREDIT BY THE NEGOTIATING BANK. WE HEREBY AGREE WITH THE DRAWERS, ENDORSERS, AND BONA FIDE
HOLDERS OF ALL DRAFTS DRAWN UNDER AND IN COMPLIANCE WITH THE TERMS OF THIS CREDIT, THAT SUCH DRAFTS WILL BE DULY
HONORED UPON PRESENTATION TO THE DRAWEE.
THIS CREDIT IS SUBJECT TO THE UNIFORM CUSTOMS AND PRACTICE FOR DOCUMENTARY CREDITS (1974 REVISION). INTERNATIONAL
CHAMBER OF COMMERCE PUBLICATION NO. 290.

SPECIMEN

AUTHORIZED SIGNATURE

Selling on open account can be combined with **factoring** as a means of managing accounts receivable and providing short-term financing. A factor purchases a company's receivables at a discount. This can be done on a recourse or a non-recourse basis. Recourse means that the exporter accepts all credit and cross-border risks. Non-recourse means that the factor accepts all credit and cross-border risk except those involving disputes between exporter and importer. Most factoring is carried out on a non-recourse basis.

In a typical factoring transaction, the exporter submits new orders directly to the factor. The factor evaluates the creditworthiness of the potential client and makes a recourse/non-recourse decision as quickly as possible (sometimes as quickly as several days, sometimes as long as several weeks, depending on the availability of information). When the decision is made, the exporter sells its claim to the factor and receives payment.

Factoring is expensive, costing around 2% of sales plus interest. Smaller claims are more expensive due to the fixed costs associated with information gathering. Nevertheless, it can be worthwhile to many firms, such as the occasional exporter or the exporter with a geographically diverse portfolio of clients for whom it would be organizationally complicated and expensive to internalize the collection process of accounts receivable.

Consignment

Selling on consignment involves shipping goods to the importer but maintaining title to them until they have been sold to a third party. In this kind of arrangement payment is not made by the importer until after he has sold the goods. If they remain unsold, the exporter is left holding the proverbial bag. He either has to take them back or find another purchaser.

International cash management

Basic requirements

To be able to manage exchange rate risk, the treasurer has to know what these risks are for the company. This involves setting up a computerized system fulfilling at least five requirements:

1. The first requirement is to set up a currency by currency forecast of income and expenditure for each day. The necessary information can be found in the budget, orders outstanding, accounts receivable and accounts payable.

2. Once the day-by-day forecast of income and expenditure for each currency has been established, the second requirement is to measure the exchange exposure in each currency generated by the company's operations.

3. The third requirement is to account for all foreign exchange transactions, both spot and forward. This is probably the most difficult task because, as we will see in Chapters 14–16, hedging instruments have become increasingly complex. They include forwards, futures, swaps, options, borrowing and lending. Positions can be closed out and rolled over. Only by recording and measuring their impact can the company's true foreign exchange position be accounted for.

4. The fourth requirement is to translate all the foregoing information into a value date forecast of all the company's bank accounts in foreign exchange. This must be done day-by-day, account-by-account, currency-by-currency. Any sizeable international company will have numerous foreign currency accounts with a number of banks, so the task is complicated. Many types of transaction, such as spot trades, forward trades and options premiums, pose no problem because the transaction date and both sides of the operation in domestic and foreign currency are known in advance. Commercial transactions are another story, however. Exact dates are often not known in advance. Sometimes, even the amounts are uncertain, depending on whether or not the client takes advantage of a discount. The forecast must be updated regularly to account for transactions that have actually taken place.

    The reason for laying out all the foreign currency cash flows on a day-by-day, value date basis is the same as for domestic cash management, that is, to minimize financial charges and maximize financial income by reducing non-interest paying balances to zero on a value date basis. This involves transferring funds from surplus accounts to deficit accounts and lending anything that is left over. Borrowing and lending decisions should take into consideration the company's policy on its foreign exchange position.

5. The fifth requirement corresponds to the needs of internal control. Where foreign exchange is concerned, these needs are quite elaborate. The treasurer must verify that the bank's conditions regarding value dates, commissions, interest rates, day count factors, etc., have been assiduously respected. The same goes for sophisticated hedging instruments, which require a high quality "back office". Furthermore, discrepancies between forecast and realized figures must be available for commercial as well as for financial transactions.

In-house hedging

Hedging exchange risk operation-by-operation can prove extremely costly because of the large number of transactions and the commissions, fees and spreads they imply. Many operations could be avoided if a company's successive claims and debts in a given currency are brought together. Suppose that a Dutch company has made the following forecast:

15 November: collect GBP 30,000
3 December: pay out GBP 20,000
20 December: pay out GBP 25,000
30 December: collect GBP 20,000.

Taken separately, each flow would generate a forward transaction. Taken together, there is only a difference of GBP 5000 that would have to be covered. Ignoring interest, this could be achieved by lending GBP 20,000 from 15 November to 3 December and GBP 10,000 from 15 November to 20 December. On 3 December the proceeds from the first loan go to make the payout. On 20 December the proceeds from the second loan go towards the GBP 25,000 payout and GBP 15,000 is borrowed until 30 December to make up the difference. On 30 December, the proceeds from the collection go to pay off the loan and GBP 5000 is left over.

Globalized accounts

This technique is appropriate for a company with small amounts of income and/or expenditure on a frequent and regular basis in a given currency. Administratively and transactionally it would be too costly to cover each transaction. To avoid the cost the company sets up a central or global account through which all transactions in the foreign currency will be handled. Periodically – every month, for example – it converts the balance. If it is positive, it purchases domestic currency. If it is negative, the company purchases foreign currency to make up the difference. Over the course of the month it monitors the account: as it becomes positive it invests the balance and earns interest and if the account is negative it pays interest.

The exchange risk can be managed on the basis of the periodic balances. Suppose, for example, that the treasurer forecasts income of GBP 1,000,000 over the period in question and no expenditure. His foreign exchange exposure is thus GBP 1,000,000 because it is at the end of the period that he will convert into domestic currency. As we have seen in Chapters 7, 8 and 9, he can cover his position by making a forward sale of foreign exchange or by purchasing an option. An example will clarify how this strategy works.

After having forecast GBP 1,000,000 in total income over the period, the treasurer decides to sell GBP 1,000,000 forward at the rate of EUR 1.6 = GBP 1 in order to cover his foreign exchange risk. At the end of the period he finds that he has actually collected GBP 1,017,900. He delivers GBP 1,000,000 and receives EUR 1,600,000 from the forward contract and his foreign currency account drops to GBP 17,900.

Netting

Many multinational corporations have their production organized on a worldwide basis where raw materials, spare parts, sub-assemblies and finished products are exchanged among the subsidiaries of the group. These physical flows of goods and services generate financial flows and cross-border fund transfers. As we have seen, foreign exchange transactions are costly in terms of the bid–ask spread. There are also bank charges for transferring funds and opportunity costs of lost interest while the funds are being transferred (value dates applied by the banks).

The **netting** procedure seeks to reduce the cost of foreign exchange management within groups where many currencies and many transactions are involved. A multinational, for example, may have subsidiaries in London, Toronto, Mexico City and Tokyo, with each one dealing regularly with each other in pounds, Canadian dollars, pesos and yen. The relationships are too complex to be handled by a system of globalized accounts and a more sophisticated system is necessary. Netting is a system of intra-group compensation. It involves setting up a control point called the "netting center" that handles all the financial transactions. Very often a subsidiary created especially for this purpose is set up in a location where there is a minimum of foreign exchange controls.

In order to set up a netting system, the company has to establish the periodic basis on which it will operate – the day, the week or the month. It then has to identify the characteristic payment flows between the group's subsidiaries for the period in question. This involves setting up a clearing matrix. An example will illustrate the major issues.

Agreement Inc. is composed of four subsidiaries: JA is the German subsidiary, YES is the UK subsidiary, NA is the Chinese subsidiary and OK is the US subsidiary. Agreement has decided that the US dollar will serve as its base currency. The following intra-group payment flows have been established:

- JA owes EUR 492,000 to YES; owes CNY 1,000,000 to NA
- YES owes GBP 300,000 to NA; owes GBP 105,000 to OK
- NA owes USD 600,000 to OK
- OK owes USD 720,000 to JA.

The reference exchange rates are as follows: GBP 1 = USD 1.5000; CNY 1 = USD 0.1250; and EUR 1 = USD 0.9000. Converting the debts between the different subsidiaries at the reference exchange rates gives the matrix set out in Table 13.1, where columns represent claims and rows represent liabilities. Thus, for example, JA has a USD 648,000 claim on OK. It has liabilities of USD 738,000 to YES and USD 125,000 to NA. Its total liabilities are USD 863,000. Before compensation, bilateral payments between group members amount to USD 2,486,000.

Table 13.1 Intra-group claims and liabilities (in thousands of US dollars) for Agreement Inc.

	JA claim	YES claim	NA claim	OK claim	Total
JA liability		738	125		863
YES liability			270	105	375
NA liability				600	600
OK liability	648				648
Total	648	738	395	705	2486

Table 13.2 Net positions of subsidiaries of Agreement Inc. in local currency (thousands)

	Claims	Liabilities	Net position in US dollars	Compensation in local currency
JA	648	863	−215	−EUR 238.89
YES	738	375	+363	+ GBP 242.00
NA	395	600	−205	−CNY 1,640.00
OK	705	648	+57	+USD 57.00
Total	3612	3612	0	

Using the information from Table 13.1 makes it possible to determine the net position of each subsidiary as presented in Table 13.2. Instead of making all the bilateral payments implied in Table 13.1, each subsidiary will be credited or debited for its net position in its domestic currency. Hence, JA and NA are debited for EUR 238,889 and CNY 1,640,000 respectively. On the other hand, YES is credited for GBP 242,000 and OK for USD 57,000. These transfers are effected on a given date such as the last business day of the month. By netting, total fund transfers fall from USD 2,486,000 before compensation to USD 840,000 after compensation.

There are many advantages to the netting procedure. First of all, commissions on foreign exchange transactions and fund transfers are drastically reduced. Secondly, by reducing the size and number of transfers, thereby reducing the number of days lost in transferring funds and the amounts, the opportunity cost of float is reduced. Furthermore, the individual subsidiaries have reduced foreign exchange risk because payments are made in their domestic currency.

An effective netting system requires a solid administrative organization, good bankers and advantageous banking terms concerning value dates, spreads, commissions and fees. When these are present, profits can be substantial. It should not be forgotten, however, that some countries impose restrictions on netting operations. Thus, it is also necessary to have a thorough knowledge of exchange controls in the countries where operations take place.

Reinvoicing centers

Netting is a solution to intra-group currency flows. It does not solve the problem of currency flows between subsidiaries and outside institutions. Each subsidiary has its own set of suppliers and clients that generate flows of funds in different currencies. There are two solutions to this problem. One solution is to let each individual subsidiary manage its own foreign currency situation. The other solution is to set up a centralized operation that handles all foreign exchange transactions for the whole group, which is called a **reinvoicing center**.

The reinvoicing center does not get involved with the flow of goods to and from the subsidiaries. Commercial practices and customs formalities remain unchanged. The role of the reinvoicing center is strictly financial. By concentrating all currency transactions in one center, it should be able to negotiate better bank terms and reduce opportunity costs in the same way as a netting center. It also eliminates the problem of export financing for the individual subsidiaries. In this way it is more than a simple centralized foreign exchange trader. It is a fully fledged financial service center responsible for financing current operations and managing the collection of accounts receivable.

This brings up the question of assigning costs throughout the group for the financial services of the reinvoicing center. The most typical solution is to have the reinvoicing center operate as an autonomous profit center in a low tax country with commissions and fees for each type of service rendered. The group's subsidiaries then pay according to the transactions performed on their behalf by the reinvoicing center. An example will illustrate the idea. Consider a French multinational with subsidiaries in the United Kingdom and Switzerland. The French company imports goods billed in US dollars. It also exports goods to its UK subsidiary billed in pounds sterling. The Swiss subsidiary exports and bills in euros. Figure 13.4 summarizes these transactions.

Reinvoicing operations can be done on a continuous basis or a weekly, bimonthly or monthly basis. Invoices in the different currencies are transmitted to the center and the subsidiaries are credited and debited in their own domestic currency. The exchange rate used is based on the forward rate plus a commission corresponding to the payment date of each invoice. Thus, the French company is debited for the euro value of its liability in US dollars. It is credited for the euro equivalent of its claim in pounds sterling. Interest will be charged and credited according to when the funds are actually transferred. It has no exchange risk. The exchange risk has been taken on by the reinvoicing center, which has the responsibility of collecting from the UK subsidiary and paying the exporters.

Leads and lags

Leading means accelerating payments. Lagging means delaying payments. Before the development of financial products, leading and lagging was a means of speculating on currency movements. Payments were accelerated on debts in currencies that were expected to appreciate and delayed on payments in currencies that were expected to depreciate. Needless to say, a wrong guess could be costly. Today, leading and lagging for currency speculation is obsolete because of the wide range of financial products that can do the job

Figure 13.4 A reinvoicing center

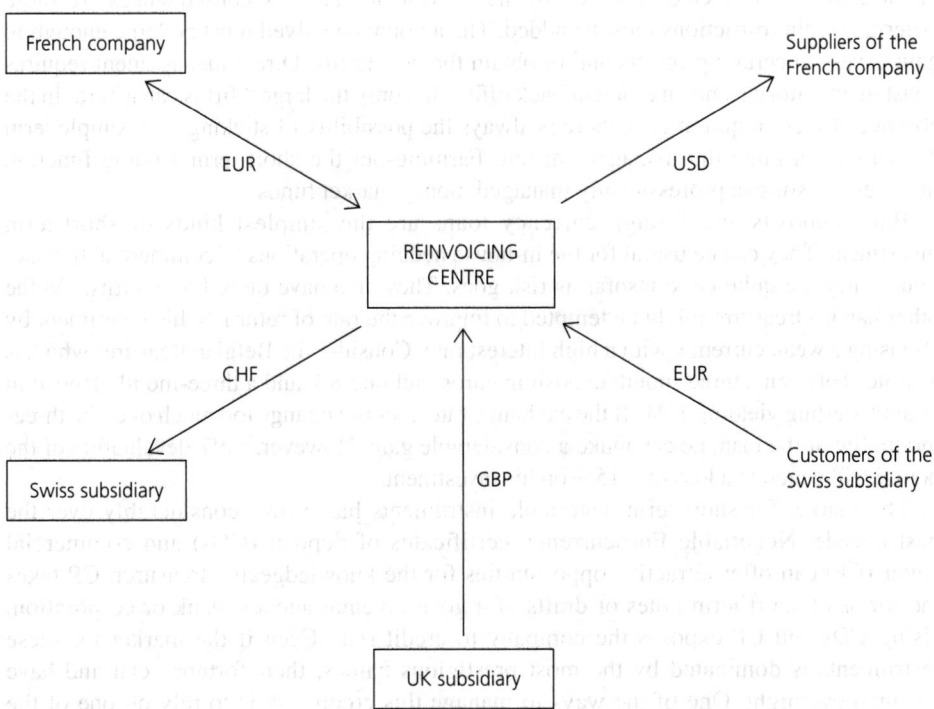

more efficiently. Leading and lagging does exist to a certain extent within groups, however, as a means of shifting liquidity between subsidiaries to avoid bid–ask spreads and take advantage of interest rate differentials. An example will illustrate the point.

Consider the following information: Subsidiary USA has a three-month financing need of USD 2 million and owes the German subsidiary DMB USD 2 million payable now. Subsidiary DMB has a cash surplus of USD 2 million that will last for three months. US interest rates are 9–10% and euro interest rates are 5–6%. If USA borrows to pay off DMB its cost will be

$$\text{USD } 2,000,000 \times 0.10 \times \frac{3}{12} = \text{USD } 50,000.$$

If DMB loans its USD 2 million in the United States it will earn:

$$\text{USD } 2,000,000 \times 0.09 \times \frac{3}{12} = \text{USD } 45,000.$$

There is a loss on the interest rate spread of USD 5000 that the group could save if DMB allowed USA to lag its payment by three months. The gain would be even larger if borrowing rates in dollars are compared with lending rates in euros. This implies speculation on how the exchange rate between the dollar and the euro is going to move because we know from interest rate parity and the forward rate hypothesis presented in Chapter 3 that the expected future spot rate is already incorporated in the interest rate differential.

Short-term lending in foreign currency

Short-term lending in foreign currency poses the same problems as short-term lending in domestic currency. Selection criteria are the same: the quality of the borrower, the liquidity of the asset, the expected evolution of the interest rate and tax consequences. To these criteria, certain restrictions must be added. The amounts involved must be large enough to gain access to certain products and to obtain the best terms. Direct management requires constant monitoring and an efficient back office that only the largest firms can afford. In the absence of these requirements, there is always the possibility of sticking with simple term deposits or farming the management out. Farming-out the short-term lending function involves investing in professionally managed money market funds.

Bank deposits and foreign currency loans are the simplest kinds of short-term investment. They can be useful for the in-house hedging operations of commercial transactions. They are quite tame insofar as risk goes. They also have quite low returns. On the other hand, a treasurer might be tempted to improve the rate of return on his investment by choosing a weak currency with a high interest rate. Consider the Belgian treasurer who has a choice between a three-month deposit in euros yielding 8% and a three-month deposit in pounds sterling yielding 12%. If the exchange rate does not change too much over the three-month life of the loan, he can make a considerable gain. However, a 5% devaluation of the pound will generate a loss of 2.15% on his investment.

The market for short-term negotiable instruments has grown considerably over the past decade. Negotiable Eurocurrency certificates of deposit (CDs) and commercial paper (CP) can offer attractive opportunities for the knowledgeable treasurer. CP takes the forms of short-term notes or drafts of a governmental agency, bank or corporation. Using CDs and CP exposes the company to credit risk. Even if the market for these instruments is dominated by the most prestigious names, their fortunes can and have changed overnight. One of the ways to manage this credit risk is to rely on one of the rating agencies. Standard & Poor's and Moody's worldwide, Duff and Phelps in the United States, Australian Ratings in Australia and Fitch IBCA in Europe all supply regular ratings on the paper of the major issuers (see Table 13.3).

Corporate treasurers should not hesitate to imitate bankers by fixing lending limits for each borrower in order to control default risk. Finally, the company treasurer must have a solid internal organization that enables him to verify that credit limits are respected and to ensure that the back office follows up on all the decisions that have been made.

Short-term financing in foreign currency

Medium-sized companies as well as the large multinationals have access to the Eurocurrency market. Maturities are standardized:

- one day overnight (funds are credited on the same day)
- one day Tom next (funds are credited d+1)
- one day spot next (funds are credited d+2)
- seven days
- one, two, three, six and nine months.

Interest is calculated *ex post* usually on the basis of the actual number of days in a 360-day year (some countries like the United Kingdom use a 365-day year). The usual reference rate is Libor.

The Eurocurrency markets can be used as a financing instrument as well as a means of covering foreign exchange risk. If a French company has made a sale for USD 1,000,000 due in three months, it can do the following:

- borrow USD 1,000,000/(1+r) dollars
- sell dollars spot for euros
- use the euros to finance ongoing operations
- receive the USD 1,000,000 and use it to pay off the loan.

Table 13.3 Notation for rating short-term debt

Euro Ratings	Fitch Investors Service	Moody's Investors Service	Standard & Poor's	Duff & Phelps	Japan Credit Ratings Agency
E–1+	F–1+	P–1	A–1+	1+	A1
E–1	F–1		A–1	1	
				1–	
E–2+	F–2+	P–2	A–2	2	A2
E–2	F–2				
E–3+	F–3+	P–3	A–3	3	A3+
E–3	F–3				A3
					A3–
E–4	F–4		B		B+,B,B–
			C		C
			D		D

USD 1 million worth of financing was achieved and there was no foreign exchange risk because the foreign exchange transaction took place at the beginning of the operation.

The financing needs of a firm dealing in many different currencies can vary according to the evolution of its operations as well as in relation to market conditions in the individual currencies. In response to this, the banks developed a product called the **multi-option financing facility (MOFF)** that was popular in the 1980s but has since fallen from favor. A MOFF is a syndicated confirmed credit line with attached options. The confirmed credit line gives the firm the right to borrow in different currencies at terms that are fixed when the credit line is granted. For this right the firm pays a commission whether the credit facility is drawn on or not. When the firm requires financing in one currency or another, it solicits bids from banks. If the conditions that the banks are offering are more favorable than the conditions of the MOFF, the firm borrows at the more favorable conditions and does not draw on the MOFF. If the conditions of the MOFF are more favorable, the firm draws on the MOFF.

Many countries offer export credit facilities. In France, for example, credits are available for financing the production cycle of an export project. Other facilities are also available whereby the exporter can discount bona fide commercial claims resulting from export operations. Most countries have facilities of this sort.

Evaluating foreign currency exposure

A firm is said to have an open foreign exchange position when the variation of the exchange rate of one or more currencies will affect the level of its income or expenditure in domestic currency. An open foreign exchange position implies foreign exchange risk. Thus, an export billed in foreign currency exposes the firm to a loss of income in domestic currency if the value of the foreign currency depreciates. When a firm owns an uncovered claim in foreign currency it is said to be "long". An import billed in foreign currency exposes the firm to increased expenditure in domestic currency if the value of the foreign currency appreciates. When a firm has an uncovered liability in foreign currency, it is said to be "short".

There are several ways of measuring the foreign currency exposure of a firm. One measure limits the analysis to commercial transactions and financial flows. Other measures look at the overall balance sheet, including foreign investments and liabilities. These types of exposure will be considered in Chapter 22. For the moment, we will consider the foreign exchange exposure resulting from commercial transactions and financial flows.

The departure point for evaluating the financial consequences of exchange rate variations on the firm's domestic currency cash flows is the information in the company's accounts. Accounts receivable and short-term financial claims grouped by currency indicate the firm's long position. Accounts payable and short-term financial liabilities grouped by currency indicate the firm's short position. The accounting information must be complemented by expected cash flows resulting from decisions that have already been made or that are likely to be made. Outstanding orders by foreign clients and suppliers will affect the firm's foreign exchange position. Bids on potential export projects will also affect it if they are accepted. Even domestic orders and bids can affect the firm's foreign exchange position insofar as the production process requires foreign inputs. These effects must be taken into consideration.

Cash flows resulting from non-commercial transactions must also be considered. Expected dividends from foreign subsidiaries will increase the firm's long position, while interest and principal payments on the firm's long-term foreign currency debt will increase the short position. In fact, judicious assessment of the firm's foreign exchange position requires mastery of all the firm's decision-making circuits. The treasurer has to be aware of purchasing policy, sales policy, investment policy and financing policy in order to project future cash flows. From this perspective, the foreign exchange position is more than a simple accounting exercise. It reflects the firm's economic position in foreign exchange. We will come back to this point in Chapter 22.

Summary

1. One of the most important elements in an international commercial transaction is the currency used for invoicing. For firms willing and able to make the effort, currency flexibility in invoicing can be commercially advantageous and financially profitable. Choosing an invoicing currency involves comparing the amount of the invoice billed directly in domestic currency with the domestic currency equivalent of the amount of the invoice if billed in foreign currency.

2. For international payments, the traditional means of settling debts in a domestic economy such as cash, credit cards and traveler's checks, are only relevant for tourism. Bank transfers are probably the fastest and most efficient means of settling international debts. Checks can also be used but, unlike the bank transfer, they are not rapid. A draft or bill of exchange is the most common means of payment in international trade. A draft is an unconditional order in writing, initiated and signed by the exporter, ordering the importer to pay on demand or at a given future date a given sum of money.

3. The simplest method of documentary payment is a draft accompanied by certain documents, called a **documentary draft**. In this scenario, the exporter, after having shipped the merchandise, forwards the draft along with the required documents to his bank. The required documents include a commercial invoice and sometimes a consular invoice as well, an insurance certificate, a certificate of origin and a bill of lading in negotiable form.

4. The letter of credit facilitates cross-border trade by offering the exporter a high degree of safety. A letter of credit is a document addressed to the exporter that is written and signed by a bank on behalf of the importer. In the document, the bank undertakes to guarantee for a certain time span the payment for the specified merchandise, either by paying directly or by accepting drafts, if the exporter conforms to the conditions of the letter of credit by presenting the required documents.

5. Other export payment terms are cash in advance, open account and consignment.

6. Managing exchange rate risk involves setting up a computerized system that provides a currency-by-currency forecast of income and expenditure for each day, measurement of the exchange exposure in each currency generated by the company's operations, accounting for all foreign exchange transactions both spot and forward, translation of all the foregoing information into a value date forecast of all the company's bank accounts in foreign exchange, and verification that the bank's conditions regarding value dates, commissions, interest rates, day count factors, etc., have been assiduously respected.

7. Companies can undertake in-house hedging by looking at the overall cash flows in a given currency rather than transaction-by-transaction.

8. Organizing foreign income and expenditure into accounts by currency and administering each one on a periodic basis can facilitate foreign currency cash management.

9. Netting is another means of rationalizing foreign currency management. It is a system of intra-group compensation that involves setting up a control point called the netting center that handles all intra-group financial transactions.

10. A reinvoicing center is a centralized operation that handles all foreign exchange transactions that occur between group members and their clients and suppliers.

11. Leading and lagging involves accelerating and delaying payments. Today, leading and lagging for currency speculation is obsolete because of the wide range of financial products that can do the job more efficiently. Leading and lagging does exist to a certain extent within groups, however, as a means of shifting liquidity between subsidiaries to avoid bid–ask spreads and take advantage of interest rate differentials.

12. Short-term lending in foreign currency poses the same problems as short-term lending in domestic currency. Selection criteria are the same: the quality of the borrower, the liquidity of the asset, the expected evolution of the interest rate and tax consequences.

13. Evaluating a firm's foreign currency exposure involves estimating outstanding assets and liabilities in foreign currency as well as future foreign currency income and expenditure.

Questions

Solutions to the following questions are set out on the web site, details of which are included in the Preface.

1. One of your suppliers from Valonia offers to bill you in his currency or yours. He quotes you prices that he converts from one currency to the other at the current spot exchange rate. The prices that he quotes will hold for one year. Knowing that interest rates in Valonia are higher than they are in your country, which currency will you choose to be billed in?

2. Explain the roles of the drawer, the drawee and the payee when paying for goods by draft.

3. Put the following operations in the correct order when paying by letter of credit:
   a. The importer and exporter make a deal.
   b. The exporter ships the goods and prepares the required documents.
   c. The importer asks his bank to issue a letter of credit in favor of the exporter.
   d. The importer pays the issuing bank.
   e. The issuing bank pays the exporter's bank.

4. What is the role of a factor?

5. A multinational company has three large subsidiaries, one in Switzerland, one in the United States and one in Japan. The spot exchange rates are: USD 0.80 = JPY 100; USD 0.70 = CHF 1. The Swiss subsidiary owes CHF 500,000 to the Japanese subsidiary and USD 300,000 to the US subsidiary. The US subsidiary owes JPY 40,000,000 to the Japanese subsidiary. Show how these positions can be netted out and explain how netting can benefit the multinational.

6. True or false:
   a. A reinvoicing center centralizes all purchases within a group.
   b. Euro-commercial paper is commercial paper issued by a European company on the US market.
   c. Leading and lagging can make it possible to reduce financing costs.
   d. Short-term financing in a foreign currency can sometimes be used to hedge foreign exchange risk.

Managing foreign exchange risk

As we saw in Chapters 3, 6 and 11, currency risk or (as it is often called) foreign exchange risk refers to fluctuations in the domestic currency value of assets, liabilities, income or expenditure due to unanticipated changes in exchange rates. Many techniques are available to cover or hedge exposure to risk of this kind. The simplest and most common technique involves using a forward contract. Remember from Chapters 3 and 6 that the forward market is where currencies are traded for future delivery and that the forward exchange rate is the current price of one currency for another for delivery at a specified date in the future. In the first part of this chapter we will see how a forward contract can be employed to hedge foreign exchange risk. We will then apply these principles to currency futures. Finally, we will look at some of the most common hedging instruments available to the corporate treasurer. They include the over-the-counter forward market, the Eurocurrency market and swaps. In the next chapter we will show how currency options can be used in managing foreign exchange risk.

Hedging with forward contracts

The exposure to be hedged can arise from a commercial transaction, a foreign investment or a liability in foreign currency. It can also be long or short. A position is said to be long when foreign currency or a claim in foreign currency is owned. It is short when there is a liability in foreign currency. For example, an export billed in foreign currency creates a long position for the exporting firm in the form of a claim in foreign currency for the value of the merchandise. On the other hand, an import billed in foreign currency creates a short position for the importing company in the form of a liability for the amount of the purchase.

Hedging a long position

Consider a French cheese company that has just signed a contract for USD 1 million worth of Camembert cheese to be shipped to the United States and paid for in three months time. The spot exchange rate in Paris is:

$$S_0(\text{EUR/USD})\text{bid} = 1.1000.$$

The treasurer of the company fears a fall in the value of the dollar, which would reduce the company's income when the cheese is finally delivered and the dollar proceeds are converted into euros. In order to cover this risk his banker suggests that he sell USD 1 million three months forward. The forward rate is:

$$F_{0,1/4}(\text{EUR/USD})\text{bid} = 1.1000.$$

As we saw in Chapter 6, this means that no matter what the spot exchange rate is in three months time the company will deliver USD 1 million to the bank and the bank will credit the company's account for EUR 1.1 million. By selling its dollars forward, the company can guarantee what its income will be in euros.

Figure 14.1 illustrates the change in the company's risk exposure resulting from the forward transaction. The solid line represents the company's income in euros before making the forward transaction. It depends on the level of the exchange rate. At higher values of the dollar, euro income is higher. At lower dollar values it is lower. The broken line represents the company's income after the forward transaction. Income in euros is insensitive to the level of the exchange rate. No matter what the value of the dollar, euro income is the same. The forward transaction has effectively eliminated the foreign exchange risk.

Eliminating foreign exchange risk has disadvantages as well as advantages. The main advantage is that if the value of the dollar falls, the company has no loss of income, which is guaranteed at EUR 1.1 million. The disadvantage is that if the value of the dollar goes up, the company will not benefit from the appreciation. Furthermore, hedging the foreign exchange risk exposes the company to another kind of risk. Suppose that the exporter is not paid on time or that some of his merchandise is refused. The exporter will not have enough dollars to honor his forward contract. In order to make up the difference he will either have to roll over the forward contract at a new rate or buy dollars at the going spot rate. Either rate might be different from the 1.1000 exchange rate of the forward contract. If the rollover rate is lower or the spot ask rate is higher, the company will make an unanticipated loss. Hedging in the forward market is a two-edged sword.

As a general rule of thumb, then, we can say that if the treasurer feels that there is a strong chance that the value of the dollar will fall and a weak chance that it will rise, the treasurer should hedge with a forward contract. In the opposite case where there is a strong chance that the dollar will appreciate and a weak chance that it will depreciate, he should not hedge.

Figure 14.1 Hedging a long position

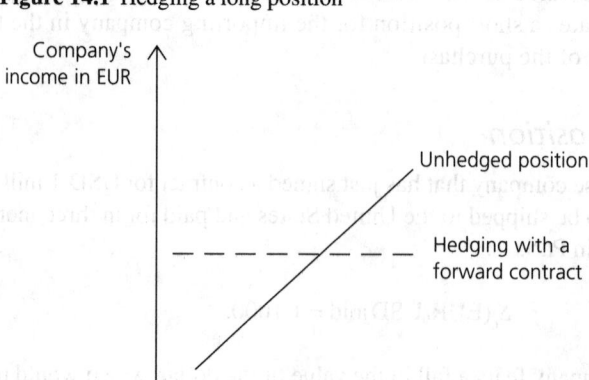

Hedging a short position

Hedging a short position involves buying foreign exchange forward. Consider a French mail order company that has just signed a contract to buy USD 1 million of men's clothing in three months time from its Hong Kong supplier. The current spot exchange rate in Paris is:

$$S_0(\text{EUR/USD})\text{ask} = 1.1000.$$

The treasurer of the French company fears that the dollar will appreciate and thus raise the cost of the merchandise in euros when the time comes to pay for them. In order to avoid this undesirable eventuality, the treasurer goes to the company's banker and buys USD 1 million three months forward. The forward rate is:

$$F_{0,1/4}(\text{EUR/USD})\text{ask} = 1.1000.$$

In three months the French company will deliver EUR 1.1 million and receive USD 1 million, no matter what the exchange rate is. Figure 14.2 illustrates the change in the company's risk exposure resulting from the forward transaction. The solid line represents the company's expenditure in euros before making the forward transaction. It depends on the level of the exchange rate. At higher values of the dollar, euro expenditure is higher. At lower dollar values it is lower. The broken line represents the company's expenditure after the forward transaction. Expenditure in euros is insensitive to the level of the exchange rate. No matter what the value of the dollar, euro expenditure is the same. The forward transaction has effectively eliminated the foreign exchange risk.

Here again, eliminating foreign exchange risk has disadvantages as well as advantages. The key advantage is that if the value of the dollar rises, the company has no increase in expenditure, which is guaranteed at EUR 1.1 million. The disadvantage is that if the value of the dollar goes down, the company will not benefit from the depreciation. Furthermore, as we saw in the preceding example, hedging the foreign exchange risk exposes the company to another kind of risk. Suppose that delivery dates from the Hong Kong company are not respected or that some of the merchandise is not up to standards and must be refused. Expenditure for the merchandise will be lower than expected, which will leave the company with dollar balances once the forward contract is consummated. When the dollar balances are converted back into euros, the spot exchange rate might be higher or lower

Figure 14.2 Hedging a short position

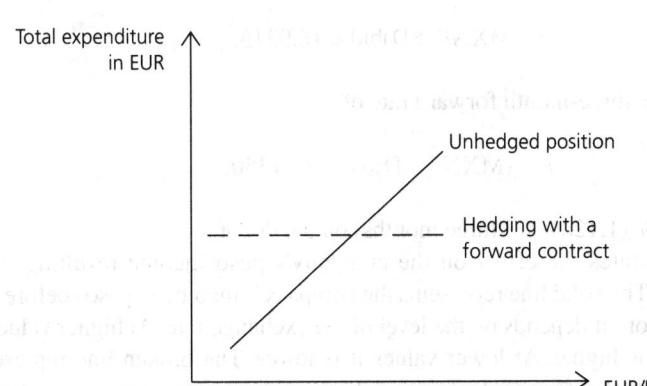

than the 1.1000 exchange rate of the forward contract. If it is higher the company will make an unanticipated gain. If it is lower it will make an unanticipated loss. This kind of risk would not be present in the absence of the forward contract.

Forward discounts and premiums: Long positions

In the foregoing examples we have assumed that the forward rate is the same as the current spot rate. While this is possible, we know from Chapter 6 that it is more likely that the forward rate will be higher or lower than the spot rate due to the interest rate differential. The existence of a forward premium or discount affects the economics of a hedging transaction.

Take the case of an US producer of machine tools that sells to a Swiss importer for delivery and payment in six months and bills the merchandise in Swiss francs. The spot exchange rate in New York is:

$$S_0(\text{USD/CHF})\text{bid} = 0.6100$$

but, because Swiss interest rates are higher than US interest rates, the six-month forward rate is:

$$F_{0,1/2}(\text{USD/CHF})\text{bid} = 0.6000,$$

a discount of 3.28% on the franc. This means that if the US company hedges its position by selling its franc income forward, its dollar income will be 1.64% lower than it would be at the current spot rate. (Premiums and discounts are quoted in yearly percentages. The yearly discount is 3.28% or 1.64% for six months.) If the US company intends to hedge, the loss of income should be taken into consideration when establishing its price in francs.

Figure 14.3 illustrates the change in the company's dollar income resulting from the forward transaction. The solid line represents the company's income in dollars before making the forward transaction. It depends on the level of the exchange rate. At higher values of the dollar, dollar income is lower. At lower dollar values it is higher. The broken line represents the company's income after the forward transaction. Dollar income is insensitive to the level of the exchange rate. No matter what the value of the dollar, dollar income is the same. However, the dollar income that is locked in is lower by $B - A$ than it would be at the current spot rate.

The situation is different when the foreign currency to be received is at a premium. Consider a Mexican exporter of olive oil that makes a sale in the United States for delivery and payment in three months. Commercial expediency dictates that he bill in US dollars. The spot exchange rate in Mexico is:

$$S_0(\text{MXN/USD})\text{bid} = 18.9215.$$

His bank offers him a three-month forward rate of

$$F_{0,1/4}(\text{MXN/USD})\text{bid} = 19.1350,$$

a premium of 4.513% (1.128% for three months) on the dollar.

Figure 14.4 illustrates the effect on the company's peso income resulting from the forward transaction. The solid line represents the company's income in pesos before making the forward transaction. It depends on the level of the exchange rate. At higher values of the dollar, peso income is higher. At lower values it is lower. The broken line represents the company's income after the forward transaction. Income in pesos is insensitive to the level of

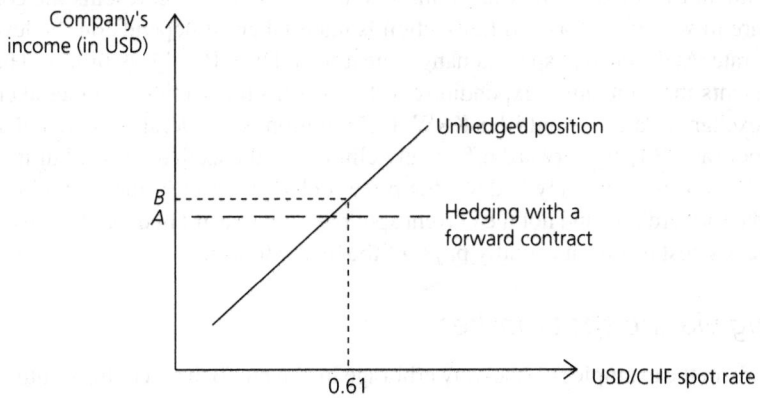

Figure 14.3 Hedging a long position with a forward discount

the exchange rate. No matter what the value of the dollar, peso income is the same. However, the premium on the forward dollar makes the peso income that is locked in higher by $B - A$ than what it would be at the current spot rate. The gain resulting from the premium on the dollar should be considered when pricing the merchandise because this is the effective peso income generated by the transaction.

Forward discounts and premiums: Short positions

Forward discounts and premiums also influence the economics of short positions. In the case of short positions, a discount is favorable to the hedger because it enables him to obtain foreign exchange at a rate lower than the current spot rate. On the other hand, a premium is unfavorable because it makes forward foreign currency more costly.

Take, for example, the case of a Korean importer of petroleum products who must pay USD 10 million in three months. He is faced with the following situation:

$$S_0(\text{KRW/USD})\text{ask} = 1129$$

$$F_{0,1/4}(\text{KRW/USD})\text{ask} = 1151.$$

Figure 14.4 Hedging a long position with a forward premium

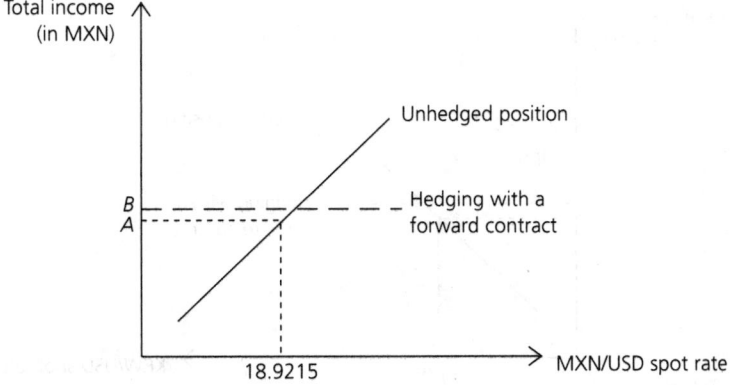

The dollar is at a premium. Figure 14.5 illustrates the change in the company's expenditure in won with and without the forward transaction. The solid line represents the company's expenditure in won if no forward transaction is undertaken. It depends on the level of the exchange rate. At the current spot exchange rate it would be KRW 11.29 billion. The broken line represents the company's expenditure if the forward transaction is undertaken. At the forward exchange rate it would be KRW 11.51 billion, considerably higher than at the current spot rate. Buying forward effectively eliminates the exchange risk but it increases the cost. Thus, if the company hedges, the price it charges its customers should be calculated on the forward rate and not the current spot rate. If it doesn't hedge, of course, it won't know what its cost is until it actually pays for the merchandise.

Hedging via the spot market

We know from the examples of one-way arbitrage in Chapter 6 that hedging a future income or expenditure in foreign currency can be achieved without using the forward market. It involves borrowing or lending and then using the spot market. Going back to the Korean importer of petroleum products, for example, we know he could have eliminated his foreign exchange risk by using won to buy spot dollars and then lending his dollars until payment was due when he would use the dollars from the loan to pay off the merchandise. However, since the Korean importer's business is petroleum products and not financial arbitrage, he probably would not want to tie his money up in this way. Insofar as arbitrage ensures that both routes are equivalent, he would let the bank do the work and use the forward market.

When the bank makes a forward contract, it exposes itself to foreign exchange risk just like any other enterprise. Suppose that the interbank exchange rate and interest rates are (see Chapters 5 and 6 for conventions on foreign exchange and interest rate quotes):

Spot KRW/USD = 1126–1128
Three-month dollars: $4-4\frac{1}{8}$
Three-month won: $11\frac{5}{8}-11\frac{3}{4}$

In order to hedge its position with the Korean exporter, the bank will buy dollars spot at KRW 1128 per dollar and lend the dollars for three months at 4% per year. The bank needs to deliver USD 10 million to the Korean importer in three months. Thus, it will buy

$$\frac{USD\ 10,000,000}{1+(0.04 \times {}^3/_{12})} = USD\ 9,900,990.1$$

Figure 14.5 Hedging a short position with a forward premium

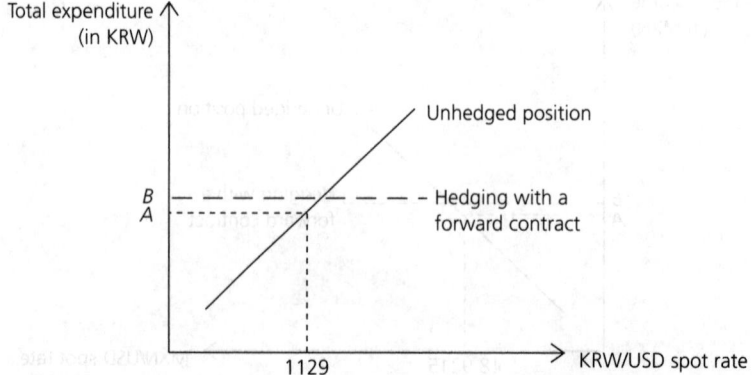

and pay

$$USD\ 9,900,990.1 \times 1128\ KRW/USD\ 1 = KRW\ 11,168,000,000.$$

It can finance the dollar purchase by borrowing KRW 11.168 billion at 11.75% for three months. At the end of three months it will pay

$$KRW\ 11,168,000,000 \times [1 + (0.1175 \times \tfrac{3}{12})] = KRW\ 11,496,060,000.$$

Thus, the bank would be fully hedged if it charged a forward rate of KRW 1149.61 (KRW 11.49606 billion USD 10 million). At the rate of 1151, its profit will be the difference between the KRW 11.51 billion it will receive from the forward transaction and the KRW 11.49606 billion to pay off the loan.

Hedging positions longer than one year

The transactions undertaken by the bank in the foregoing example can be recognized as the arbitrage described in Chapter 6 and summarized in Equation 6.4. Equation 6.4 relates the spot and forward ask rates to the bid–ask interest rates in the two currencies. Equation 6.5, reproduced here as Equation 14.1 for the reader's convenience, relates the spot and forward bid rates to the bid–ask interest rates in the two currencies.

$$F_{0,1}(USD/CHF)_{bid} = S_0(USD/CHF)_{bid} \frac{(1 + r_{USD,bid})}{(1 + r_{CHF,ask})} \tag{14.1}$$

We can generalize these arbitrage relations for periods longer than one year. Suppose, for example, that the period to be covered is n years. Equation 14.1 becomes

$$F_{0,n}(USD/CHF)_{bid} = S_0(USD/CHF)_{bid} \frac{(1 + r_{USD,bid})^n}{(1 + r_{CHF,ask})^n} \tag{14.2}$$

where r_{USD} and r_{CHF} represent the interest rates on two-year zero coupon US dollar and Swiss franc loans.

Consider the following information:

Spot USD/CHF exchange rate = 0.6005–0.6015
Interest rate on two-year zero coupon dollar loans = $4\frac{1}{2}$–$4\frac{3}{4}$
Interest rate on two-year zero coupon franc loans = $9\frac{3}{4}$–10.

According to Equation 14.2 the bank could hedge a two-year forward contract to sell francs by borrowing francs for two years, selling the francs spot for dollars and lending the dollars for two years. The forward rate that the bank would have to charge its customer would be somewhere below

$$F_{0,2}(USD/CHF)_{bid} = 0.6005\ \frac{(1.045)^2}{(1.10)^2} = 0.5420.$$

In practice there are not many zero coupon loans available. Consequently, an exact hedge calculation must take into consideration the cash flows resulting from interest payments at the end of the year. In Appendix 14.1 we show how to take interest payments into consideration.

Rolling over and closing out forward contracts

As mentioned above, expected inflows or outflows of foreign currency are not always realized. When this happens, the company can ask its bank to roll the forward contract over or to make a partial settlement and roll over the difference. The procedure is straightforward and is equivalent to closing out the old forward contract and making a new one.

Take the case of an Israeli company that bought USD 1 million three months forward at the end of June at ILS 5.0860 (shekels) for one USD. At the end of September, the merchandise that it ordered still has not been shipped, so the treasurer calls his bank and asks to roll the forward contract over for two months. On the day he calls, the spot ask rate is 5.1500 and the two-month forward premium on the dollar is 765 (see Chapter 6 for foreign exchange quotations). The new forward rate is thus 5.1500 + 0.0765 = 5.2265. However, the company has made a profit on the difference between the current spot rate and the old forward rate equal to

$$5.1500 - 5.0860 = 0.064.$$

The effective rate that the company will pay for the dollars after the forward contract is rolled over is equal to the new forward rate less the profit on the old forward contract:

$$5.2265 - 0.064 = 5.1625.$$

It is higher than the 5.0860 that it would have paid had the merchandise been shipped on time but it is lower than the 5.2265 that it would have had to pay if there had been no forward cover at all.

In accounting for rollover transactions, banks have several possibilities. They can debit the company's account for ILS 5,086,000 from the forward transaction and simultaneously credit the account for ILS 5,150,000 as a resale of the currency. Then two months later they debit the account for ILS 5,226,500 and credit it for USD 1,000,000 for a net cost of ILS 5,162,500. An alternative is to make no entries at the time of the rollover and at maturity to debit the company's account at a rate equal to the rate on the old forward contract plus the new premium (or discount):

$$5.0860 + 0.0765 = 5.1625.$$

Whatever method is chosen, the cost to the company will be the same.

A company can also terminate a forward contract before maturity. Suppose that for some reason foreign currency that was expected in three months is actually paid at the end of two months. The company can terminate the forward contract by buying foreign currency one month forward to offset the ongoing forward three-month contract. It then sells the currency it has received on the spot market.

Consider the following information:

An ongoing forward contract that matures in one month to sell USD 1 million at ILS 5.0100 per dollar
Spot exchange rate = 4.9950–5.0050
One-month forward rate = 5.0100–5.0231.

The company can terminate the ongoing forward contract by buying USD 1 million one month forward at the ask rate of 5.0231. It loses the difference between what it receives for the dollars it sells in the ongoing contract and what it pays for the dollars in the new one-month forward contract:

$$(5.0100 - 5.0231) \times USD\ 1,000,000 = -ILS\ 13,100.$$

It then sells its dollars at the spot bid rate and receives

$$4.9950 \times USD\ 1,000,000 = ILS\ 4,995,000.$$

Thus, ignoring discounting on the ILS 13,100 it loses on the difference between the two forward contracts, it nets only 4,981,900 or ILS 4.9819 per dollar. Part of the difference is that the dollar is selling at a premium and part is due to the bid–ask spreads on the supplementary forward and spot transactions. If the dollar were at a discount, there would be a gain if the ongoing forward contract were terminated prematurely. However, part of the gain on the offsetting forward transaction would be neutralized by the cost implicit in the bid–ask spreads.

Hedging with futures contracts on organized markets

On 16 June, 1972 the Chicago Mercantile Exchange (CME) opened the market for futures contracts on the pound sterling, the Canadian dollar, the German mark, the yen, the Mexican peso, the Swiss franc and the Italian lira. The popularity of these and later contracts caused other exchanges to introduce their own contracts and by 1992 currency futures were traded on exchanges all over the world. Table 14.1 summarizes some of the currency futures available on the CME as of October 2000.

As we saw in Chapter 7, the organized futures markets have four important features: the contracts are standardized; trading takes place in one location; contracts are settled through the exchange's clearing house; and contracts are **marked to market** each day, which means that they are revalued according to their market value.

Contrary to the workings of the interbank market , CME trading conforms strictly to the exchange's internal rules and the currencies that are traded are limited. Maturities are based on a quarterly cycle of March, June, September and December and each contract has a precise delivery date. Each contract also corresponds to a given amount of foreign

Table 14.1 Examples of CME currency futures contracts

Contract	Size
Japanese yen	JPY 12.5 million
Deutschmark	DEM 125,000
Canadian dollar	CAD 100,000
British pound	GBP 62,500
Swiss franc	CHF 125,000
Australian dollar	AUD 100,000
Mexican peso	MXN 500,000
Euro FX	EUR 125,000

Source; Wall Street Journal Europe 6 October 2000.

exchange. For example, the yen contract is for JPY 12,500,000 and the sterling contract for GBP 62,500. Contrast this with the interbank over-the-counter market. On the interbank market there is no unique trading area and transactions are carried out by phone between traders and brokers. On the organized futures markets only those owning or renting a seat on the exchange are allowed to trade. The system of continuous trading is transparent and competitive and ensures that the buy price is the same as the sell price. There is no bid–ask spread as there is in the interbank market. The broker makes his money by charging the client a commission and in practice these are quite small. A "round trip", meaning one buy and one sell, can be as low as 0.05% of the value of the contract.

Hedging with futures is similar to hedging with forwards. Furthermore, the futures markets are easy to use. To cover a short position in foreign currency, a futures contract can be bought with a maturity closest to the maturity of the short position. To cover a long position in foreign currency, a futures contract with a maturity closest to the maturity of the long position can be sold. Because the contracts are standardized and guaranteed by the clearing house, they are liquid and positions can be closed out easily. A short position in futures can be closed out by a purchase of the same contract. A long position in futures can be closed out by a sale of the same contract. The facility of opening and closing out positions makes it possible to manage relatively small levels of foreign exchange exposure on a continuous basis. This is especially attractive to commercial customers who have a fairly regular stream of payments and receipts.

Let's examine the following example. In October a US exporter makes a sale for EUR 3 million to be paid in three equal installments on 15 December, 15 March and 15 June. To avoid a drop in the value of the euro, he sells eight December euro contracts selling for 0.8978, eight March euro contracts selling for 0.8956 and eight June euro contracts selling for 0.8935. (Notice that the euro is selling at a discount, which implies that euro interest rates are higher than dollar interest rates.) Each contract is for EUR 125,000. In December he receives the euros from his client and takes delivery on the futures contracts. He receives

$$8 \times 125,000 \times 0.8978 = \text{USD } 897,800.$$

In March and June he repeats the same operation and receives respectively

$$8 \times 125,000 \times 0.8956 = \text{USD } 895,600$$

and

$$8 \times 125,000 \times 0.8935 = \text{USD } 893,500.$$

We saw in Chapter 7 that when contract maturities do not correspond exactly to the cash flows being hedged or when there is no contract on the currency in question, unexpected variations in the basis subject the hedger to basis risk. Expected variations in the basis are associated with the passage of time and the convergence of the futures and spot prices. Unexpected variations are associated with unexpected changes in the interest rate differential. With this in mind, a perfect hedge using futures contracts can only be achieved if the hedging instrument is the same as the currency being hedged and if the hedge date corresponds perfectly with the futures maturity date. Investors should be aware of this risk and realize that the basis increases with a contract's time to maturity. In practice, investors with imperfect hedges tend to use contracts closer to maturity in spite of the cost of rolling them over.

Also in Chapter 7 we showed how to construct a minimum-variance delta hedge when there is a maturity mismatch and a minimum-variance cross hedge when the contract differs from the currency being hedged. The minimum-variance delta cross hedge is used when there is a maturity mismatch and when the instruments differ.

Other hedging instruments

Hedging with foreign currency loans

Besides the foreign exchange risk, a company that has accounts receivable in foreign currency also has to worry about financing its claim. As we have seen, using forward contracts solves the problem of foreign exchange risk but it does not solve the financing problem. Financing in foreign currency solves both problems simultaneously. Furthermore, the technique is simple, easy to set up and is accessible to medium-sized companies.

Take the example of a French wine exporter who has just signed a contract with an US importer for USD 100,000 worth of wine to be paid for in three months. A Parisian bank has offered the exporter the opportunity of borrowing dollars at the rate of Pibor plus 0.25%. The spot bid rate for dollars is 0.9000 and three-month dollar Pibor is 4%. The company's borrowing cost is thus 4.25% per year. It will use the USD 100,000 income from the wine sale to pay off the loan, so it should borrow

$$\frac{USD\ 100,000}{(1 + \dfrac{0.0425}{4})} = USD\ 98,949.$$

At the end of three months it will owe USD 100,000, comprising USD 98,949 in principal and USD 1051 in interest. There is no exchange risk because it can use the dollar income from its sale to the American importer to pay off the USD 100,000. Meanwhile it has USD 98,949 that it can convert into euros and use to finance its activity.

This type of operation is especially attractive to professionals when interest rates in foreign currency are low. Nevertheless, it should not be forgotten that the premium on the forward dollar offsets the interest rate advantage. Still, borrowing in foreign currency can be advantageous insofar as it reduces the number of transactions (the forward transaction is eliminated) and the Eurocurrency market is generally more competitive than domestic financial markets and spreads are lower.

For companies with a foreign exchange liability, the Eurocurrency markets can also be used to cover, as we have already mentioned. In this case, the company buys foreign currency on the spot market and then sets up a foreign currency loan to coincide with the future foreign currency payment. This type of transaction has the disadvantage of tying up the company's money for the duration of the loan. Only companies with excess liquidity would find it advantageous and then only if the conditions in foreign currency are better than those available in the national market.

Another instrument for managing currency risk and financing problems that was popular in the 1980s is the multi-option financing facility (MOFF). A MOFF allows for the issuance of Euronotes and short-term bank advances by competitive bidding against a variety of funding bases and currencies. If notes/advances cannot be issued at an acceptable rate, the issuer typically draws on a backstop revolving credit facility. MOFFs have the advantage of leaving companies with a wide latitude concerning the choice about when to finance and in what currency.

Swap markets

As we saw in Chapter 9, a **swap** is an exchange of streams of payments between two counterparties, either directly or through an intermediary. They are useful for cash management in a multi-currency environment.

Foreign exchange swap

Foreign exchange swaps, as discussed in Chapter 6, involve a spot buy (sale) of foreign exchange and a simultaneous offsetting forward sale (buy). They are useful when a treasurer is confronted with a temporary excess in one currency and a shortage in another.

Suppose, for example, that a treasurer of a multinational company has GBP 100,000 that he will not need for 30 days and a current shortage of marks. Rather than lending the pounds and borrowing the marks, he can make a swap with his banker. He sells the GBP 100,000 for Swiss francs at the spot rate. At the same time he makes a 30-day forward contract to sell the francs and buy the pounds back. Figure 14.6 shows how the flows look.

Fixed rate currency swaps

In the case of a fixed rate currency swap a company seeks to exchange a loan in one currency for a loan in another. Three stages are involved. First, the principal is exchanged at the spot rate. Secondly, on each coupon date interest payments are exchanged. Finally, at the swap's maturity the principal is re-exchanged, usually at the original exchange rate.

Suppose, for example, that a Swiss company wants to invest in Korea. It needs won but is not known by Korean banks and cannot borrow on favorable terms. It decides to borrow CHF 1,000,000 at 9% for five years with the principal to be repaid at maturity. It wants to exchange its franc debt for debt in won because the cash flows to pay off the loan will be generated in won. It goes to its bank and arranges a swap with the following terms:

8.75% on the franc loan
16% on the won loan
63.63 KRW/CHF.

The outcome of the operation is summarized in Figure 14.7. On day one the company gives the bank CHF 1,000,000 and receives KRW 63,000,000. Each year on the coupon date the bank gives the company CHF 87,500 and receives KRW 10,180,800 from the company. On the maturity date the bank gives the company CHF 1,000,000 and the company gives the bank KRW 63,000,000.

The swap permitted the company access to credit in won. By exchanging its franc loan it was able to use KRW 63,000,000 for five years. There was no exchange risk on the principal because it was exchanged at the same fixed rate. There was a little exchange risk on the interest payments because the CHF 87,500 paid by the bank only covered part of the CHF 90,000 marks that the company was obliged to pay on its loan. Swaps can be arranged to cover the entire interest payment and, in cases where it is not entirely covered, the exposure can be hedged in the forward market.

Figure 14.6 Foreign exchange swap

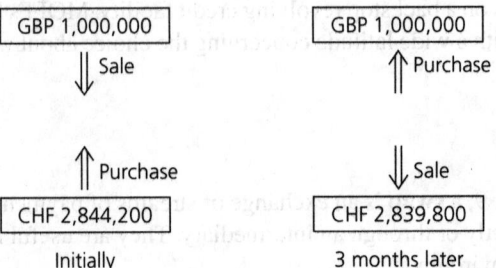

Figure 14.7 Fixed rate currency swap

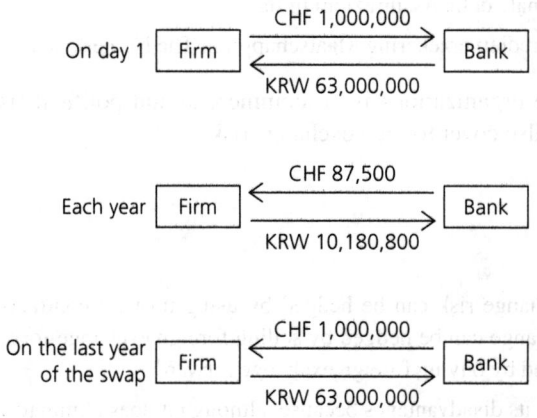

A currency swap, then, is like a series of forward foreign exchange contracts. The forward rate for each year that only involves interest payments is the ratio of the two cash flows:

$$\frac{\text{KRW } 10,180,800}{\text{CHF } 87,500} = 116.352.$$

On the last year of the swap, both interest and principal are exchanged. The cash flow in won is

$$63,000,000 + 10,180,800 = 73,180,800.$$

The cash flow in francs is

$$1,000,000 + 87,500 = 1,087,500.$$

The forward rate for this year is the ratio of these two cash flows:

$$\frac{73,180,800}{1,087,500} = 67.29.$$

It is also interesting to note that the foreign exchange swap that we considered earlier is similar to a zero coupon currency swap. The principal is exchanged at the beginning and there are no intermediate interest payments. The interest rate differential is accounted for at maturity insofar as the forward rate is different from the original spot rate. It is not strictly equivalent, however, because the principal is not adjusted at maturity.

Hedging with insurance

Many countries have insurance organizations that provide protection against foreign exchange risk. Most of the industrialized countries have organizations of this type that are linked directly or indirectly to the government. Examples include:

- L'Office National du Croire in Belgium
- Coface in France
- the Export Credit Guarantee Department in Great Britain

- Hermes in Germany
- L'Instituto Nazionale delle Assiurazioni in Italy
- Nederlandsche Credietverzekering Maatschappij in The Netherlands.

The focus of these organizations is on commercial and political risk but many of the policies they offer also cover foreign exchange risk.

Summary

1. Foreign exchange risk can be hedged by using forward contracts. A long position in foreign exchange can be hedged by selling foreign exchange forward. A short position can be hedged by buying foreign exchange forward.

2. Hedging has its disadvantages because, although it does eliminate adverse moves in the exchange rate, it also eliminates the possibility of benefiting from favorable moves.

3. Forward discounts and premiums make domestic currency cash flows differ from what they would be at the spot rate, and the bid–ask spread accentuates the difference.

4. Hedging operations can also be accomplished by combining borrowing and lending with a purchase or sale of foreign currency in the spot market.

5. Forward rates can be determined for periods exceeding one year but hedging transactions are complicated by the necessity of covering the cash flows from interest payments over the life of the contract.

6. Forward contracts can be rolled over or closed out prematurely when the timing of cash flows they were meant to cover does not conform to expectations.

7. Foreign currency loans can be used as a medium to simultaneously cover foreign exchange risk and solve financing problems. It is often a cheaper solution to the problems insofar as the number of transactions are reduced and the Eurocurrency markets often have lower spreads than domestic markets.

8. Foreign exchange swaps can be used to eliminate the foreign exchange risk inherent in a temporary long or short position in foreign currency.

9. Currency swaps solve the problem of foreign exchange risk when financing cannot be obtained in the currency in which the cash flows are generated.

10. Futures contracts are similar to forward contracts. The smaller size of the contract and the possibility of liquidating a position quickly and cheaply in an organized market are advantageous to small users as well as those with steady streams of income and expenditure. The disadvantages are the limited number of traded contracts and delivery dates.

11. Many countries have government-sponsored insurance organizations that offer guarantees against exchange risk.

Questions

Solutions to the following questions are set out on the web site, details of which are included in the Preface.

1. A Belgian company importing motorcycles from Japan is billed in yen. What should it do to hedge its foreign exchange risk?

   a. Buy US dollars forward with euros.

   b. Sell yen forward for euros.

   c. Buy yen forward with euros.

2. The one-year interest rate is 8% in Germany and 5% in the United States. Is the one-year forward dollar selling at a discount or a premium against the euro? By how many percent?

3. A UK company intends to import a large quantity of high quality US California wine. It decides to purchase dollars forward with pounds. The spot exchange rate is USD 10 = GBP 1. The six-month interest rates are UK = 15–15.25% and US = 9.75–10%.

   Three months later the UK company decides to pay for the wine in advance. The spot exchange rate has gone to USD 8 = GBP 1 and the three-month interest rates are UK = 10.5–10.75% and US = 10–10.25%.

   In order to make the payment the company has to purchase dollars spot. It also has to make another forward transaction to undo its outstanding position. After calculating the initial bid–ask forward exchange rate and the bid–ask forward exchange rate three months later, calculate how much the US dollars actually cost the company. How effective was the forward hedge?

4. What are fixed rate currency swaps and how can they be used?

5. True or false:

   a. Futures contracts are forward purchases or sales of several currencies by a central bank.

   b. Purchases and sales of futures contracts do not use bid–ask prices.

   c. Deposits are required when selling or purchasing a futures contract?

Appendix 14.1: Hedging long-term foreign exchange risk with non-zero coupon loans

Suppose that the bank borrows CHF 0.826446 $[(1/1.1)^2]$, changes them for USD 0.496281 at the spot rate (0.6005) and invests them at 4.5% for two years. According to Equation 14.2, it would be completely hedged and end up with USD 0.5420. The situation is different, however, if the loans are not zero coupon. If interest payments are made annually, for example, it would pay CHF 0.082645 and receive USD 0.0223333 at the end of the first year. Since the rate at which the dollar income could be converted into francs to pay the interest liability is unknown, it would be exposed to foreign exchange risk.

   In order to avoid this exposure, the hedging operations are more complicated. Rather than borrowing in one currency and lending in the other, both borrowing and lending operations will have to be undertaken in each of the currencies. In francs more will have to be borrowed for two years, some of which will be re-lent for one year to meet the interest payment at the end of the first year.

   In the forward contract the bank buys CHF 1, which it will use to pay off the loan. Hence the amount owed at the end of year two including interest and principal must be equal to one. Since interest is paid yearly, the outstanding principal at the beginning of year two will be the same as the amount borrowed at the beginning of year one. At an interest rate of 10% that amount will be

$$\frac{1}{1.10} = CHF\ 0.909091.$$

Suppose that the bid rate on one-year francs is 9.75%. Then the amount that must be lent for one year to meet the interest payment is

$$\frac{0.1(0.909091)}{1.0975} = \text{CHF } 0.082833.$$

The amount of the two-year loan available to buy dollars spot will be equal to the proceeds from the two-year borrowing less the amount loaned for one year:

$$0.909091 - 0.082833 = 0.826258.$$

At the spot rate of 0.6005 this will yield USD 0.496168 (calculated as 0.826258 × 0.6005).

Now we have to find the amount of dollars that must be borrowed for one year that will be paid off with the interest received at the end of the first year from the two-year loan. Suppose that the ask rate on one-year dollars is 4.75%. Some dollars will have to be borrowed for one year and reinvested for two years along with the USD 0.496168 obtained in the spot transaction. Let X represent the amount to be borrowed. Then

$$\frac{0.045 (X + \text{USD } 0.496168)}{1.0475} = X$$

and solving for X:

$$X = \text{USD } 0.022272.$$

The amount to be lent for two years is USD 0.51844, the proceeds from the spot transaction (USD 0.496168) plus the amount borrowed for one year (USD 0.022272). At the end of year one the bank will owe USD 0.02333 for interest and principal on its one-year borrowing and will receive USD 0.02333 in interest on its two-year loan. It uses the one to pay the other. At the end of year two, the bank will receive

$$\text{USD } 0.51844 \times 1.045 = \text{USD } 0.5418$$

in interest and principal on its two-year loan.

All the cash flows for interest and principal are perfectly matched and the bank ends up owning USD 0.5418 and owing CHF 1. Thus, the bank can offer a two-year forward USD/CHF bid rate of 0.5418 and be fully covered. This is lower than the 0.5420 obtained from Equation 14.2 due to the difference between the one and two-year interest rates and the increased amounts that are borrowed. It is interesting to note, then, that when interest payments occur during the life of the forward contract, the forward rate cannot be determined by the interest rate differential alone. Differences in the term structure of interest rates are also explicitly involved.

Economic and financial analysis of currency option uses

International cash management is an exercise in controlling risk in a multi-currency environment while minimizing costs and maximizing returns. Besides a solid grasp of the basic economic and financial relationships underlying the international system, it requires the technical expertise to obtain an adequate mix of risk and return. As we saw in Chapter 8, the options markets make it possible to eliminate much of the risk that treasurers deem excessive. They are effective at ensuring wealth protection while avoiding many costly and useless transactions. They are also a vehicle for limiting liabilities while testing new strategies or financial instruments. Although options markets are essentially different from the traditional futures and forwards markets, they are, at least, auxiliary to them.

While options markets are useful for traditional risk hedging, they also attract traders seeking innovative products with more precise applications. These include the "aggressive" managers of modern financial theory who feel able to anticipate short-term currency movements better than the average. At each judgement level they seek a corresponding optimal strategy. All shades and grades are possible. Whether they feel that rates will remain stable, advance moderately, dramatically, fall or reverse course, there exists a strategy for transforming professional judgement into exceptional performance, if they are right.

In this sense, the options markets attract speculators whose profits and risks can be considerable. Nevertheless, hedging should not be confused with speculation, although they are both often present in a single transaction. In what follows we will present the different intervention strategies of hedging and speculation, conscious of the fact that for a given level of risk, some strategies will interest hedgers and others speculators, but that in any single transaction they both can come together. In this chapter we will limit the presentation to basic strategies and reserve the discussion of the more sophisticated products, such as hybrids and second generation options, to Chapter 16.

Speculative uses

An investor can have three types of expectation about the evolution of a price: it can rise, it can fall or it can remain unchanged. On the spot markets profits can be made when the price rises if one buys before the rise. If a fall is anticipated and a sale is made before the fall, nothing is lost but nothing is gained either. With futures markets the game is more interesting. Profits can be made with a rise or a fall. Selling forward before a fall and buying back after it yields a profit. If the price doesn't move, however, profits cannot be made even on the futures markets. With options markets the possibilities are even broader. Profits can be made if the price rises, if it falls and even if it remains unchanged.

Speculating on a price rise: Buying calls

Purchasing a currency call can be extremely profitable if the underlying exchange rate undergoes a sharp rise before the expiration date. More often than not, however, the option expires worthless and the full amount of the premium is lost.

Figure 15.1 illustrates what happens on a call's expiration date. If the spot exchange rate is higher than the strike price plus the premium paid for the call, there is a profit for the buyer. If the exchange rate is equal to or lower than the strike price, the buyer loses the full value of the premium. If it is between the strike price plus the premium, he loses part of the premium. Calls, then, have a very risky side to them. Take the case of the most popular calls: those that are close-to-the-money. If the exchange rate stays stable over the life of the option, the outcome for those having an uncovered position in foreign exchange is neutral. They neither gain nor lose. For the option holder the result is different. He loses the entire amount of the premium if the exchange rate stays stable over the life of the option even if it soars in the days following the expiration date. The call option is risky, then, for two reasons: first, because it is a bet on the evolution of the exchange rate, and, secondly, because the expected evolution must take place in a limited period of time. Options are mortal. They age and die.

Take an out-of-the-money three-month call on US dollars with a strike price of ILS 5.29 quoted at 2.01% and a spot rate of 5.19 on the purchase date. In Israeli shekels the premium is worth $5.19 \times 2.01\% = $ ILS 0.1043. On the expiration date, if the spot rate has moved to 5.29, the call buyer will have lost the whole premium whereas someone who had been long in dollars would have made nearly 2% (calculated as $5.29/5.19 - 1$). If the rate has moved to 5.3943, the option buyer still would not make a profit while the long position in foreign exchange would show a return of nearly 4%. Above the rate of 5.3943, the option buyer begins to make a profit where small increases yield high returns. At a rate of only 5.4000 he would have a return of almost 5.5% [calculated as $(5.4000 - 5.3943)/0.1043$]. The long position would only yield slightly more than 4%. If the rate goes to 6.00, the long position will yield about 16% while the call buyer's return will be over 580%. Calls have a very high degree of leverage.

To summarize, we can say that the call has four major characteristics:

1. The time frame is limited to the life of the call.

2. In the case of sharp rises within the time span, the leverage is considerable.

Figure 15.1 Speculating on a price rise: buying calls

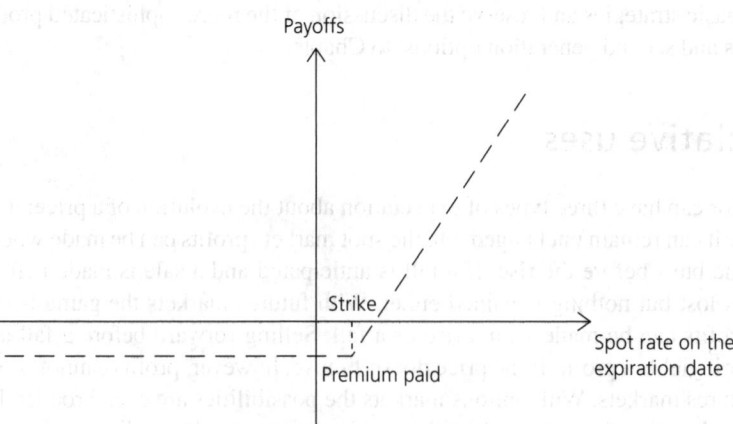

3. In the case of sharp falls, losses are limited to the amount of the premium paid.

4. In the case of relative stability, profits only appear once the level of the strike price plus the premium has been passed.

Buying a currency call means betting on a relatively sharp move in the exchange rate in a limited period of time.

For professional investors and money managers, the organized futures exchanges represent marked progress. Because of their liquidity, they make it possible to open and close positions cheaply and quickly in response to new information. In fact, most exchange-traded options are closed out before their expiration date. Figure 15.2 shows the evolution of the outcome of holding a call for a period less than the time to expiration when volatility is constant. The origin represents the spot rate on the date of the purchase and the broken curve represents the difference between the sales price and the purchase price. The curve is convex and increasing. The call's delta and gamma are positive. The call is only profitable if the spot rate rises enough to compensate for the call's loss of time value. This position below this point is sometimes referred to as the "bottom", meaning that it is the point that must be passed in order to make a profit. The bottom will be lower the longer the option is held. This is because theta, the change in the price of the call with respect to time, is usually negative.[1] The bottom can also swell downward and outward as a result of a fall in volatility, thereby raising the minimum profit level of the exchange rate. This is because vega is positive. We can see that a straightforward application of the parameters developed in Chapter 8 give investors a clear picture of the advantages and risks associated with their position.

For a given currency, an investor has several different calls to choose from. The performance of the individual calls can be quite different, depending on their strike price and expiration date and he should be careful to choose the one best adapted to his risk objectives and cost constraints.

Figure 15.3 shows the payoff profile for naked calls with different strike prices. We can see that a call with a low strike price (in-the-money) resembles a foreign currency

Figure 15.2 Holding a call for a period less than the time to expiration when volatility is constant

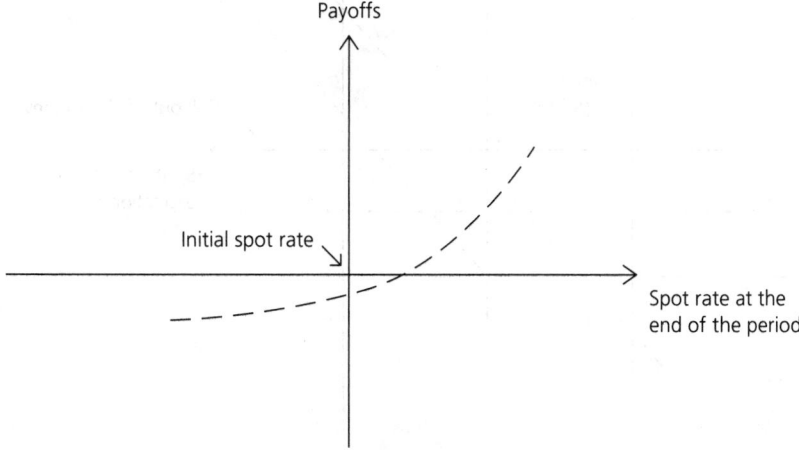

---

[1] It can be positive when early exercise is advantageous (see Chapter 8).

purchase at a fixed rate. In the zone of highest probability for values of the exchange rate, the investor gains if the rate rises and loses if it falls. The payoff profile is the same as that for a forward purchase.

An investor who buys a call with a very high strike price (out-of-the-money) is buying a lottery ticket. He will probably lose what he paid but there is always a small possibility of making a big profit.

To really make the most of the characteristics of an option, however, the investor should choose one with a strike price near the actual spot rate (at-the-money). Here he has a reasonable probability of making a considerable gain and his losses are limited no matter how badly the exchange rate fares. Out-of-the-money calls and in-the-money calls have low gammas. At-the-money calls have the highest gammas and these are the ones that offer unique properties compared to other types of financial instruments. In practice, it is at this level that transaction volume is highest and the market is most liquid.

When the expiration date is far in the future, holding a call is relatively less risky. The expected movement in the exchange rate has a better chance of being realized over six months than it does over two months. On the other hand, premiums are higher and the probability of extreme outcomes is lower. In practice, it has been observed that options with the nearest expiration date are the most frequently traded. Without a doubt, investors' forecasting horizon is short term and options are the most sensitive instruments. Unfortunately, short-term options also have the lowest thetas (the highest in absolute value, meaning that the price degenerates faster) and, consequently, they are the costliest to hold. In the options market, everything has a price.

Figure 15.3 Payoffs for naked calls with different strike prices

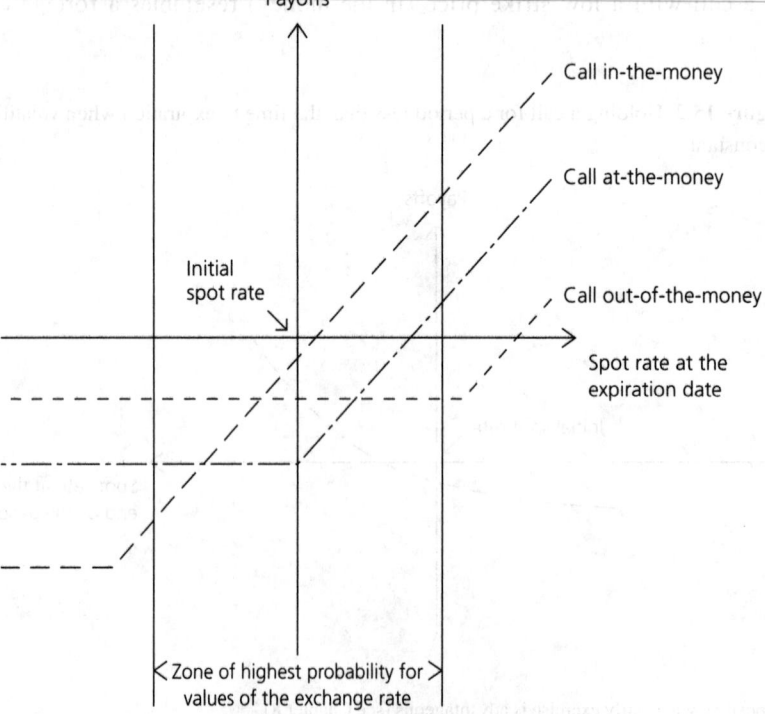

Speculating on a price fall: buying puts

The purchase of a put is especially recommended if a fall in the exchange rate is anticipated. Although the principle of a put is similar to that of a call, a put is not perfectly symmetrical with a call. It would be a costly error, for example, to think that the simultaneous purchase of a call and a put constitutes a position with no risk.

Figure 15.4 illustrates the profit and loss implications of a long position in puts on the expiration date. If the spot exchange rate is lower than the strike price minus the premium paid for the put (the breakeven point), the transaction will be profitable. If the exchange rate is equal to or greater than the strike price, the whole amount of the premium will be lost. As with a call, a put is a bet on future movements in the exchange rate within a fixed time period, but a call purchase is a bet on a rise while a put purchase is a bet on a fall. Purchasing a put is different from selling a futures contract. To be profitable, puts require relatively large moves in the exchange rate whereas the seller of a futures contract makes a profit if the rate falls by only a small amount. On the other hand, a put, like a call, represents an exceptionally high degree of financial leverage. Beyond the breakeven point, it amplifies the returns to be gained from a fall in the exchange rate.

The organized exchanges with low costs and high liquidity make dynamic management of put positions possible. Investors can close out their positions before the expiration date. Figure 15.5 shows the outcome profile (sales price minus purchase price) to be obtained from holding a put for a period shorter than its time to expiration when volatility is constant.

The outcome curve is decreasing and convex. A put purchase produces a negative delta and a positive gamma. It is only profitable in the case of a fall in the exchange rate and then only if the fall is pronounced enough to overcome the loss in the put's time value. This position is also called the "bottom". It is necessary to get off the bottom to make money. As with calls, the bottom will be lower the longer the put is to be held. Remember again that theta is usually negative and, when it is not, early exercise occurs. Because vega is positive, the bottom will also be lower if volatility increases after the put is purchased.

Puts on the same currency but with different characteristics are also available (see Figure 15.6). A put with a high strike price (in-the-money) resembles a futures contract in the zone with the most likely outcomes for the exchange rate. A put with a very low strike price (out-of-the-money) resembles a lottery ticket. Once again, it is at-the-money puts that have the highest gammas and represent unique properties compared with other types of financial instruments. It is also at this level that transaction volume is highest and the market is most liquid.

Figure 15.4 Buying puts

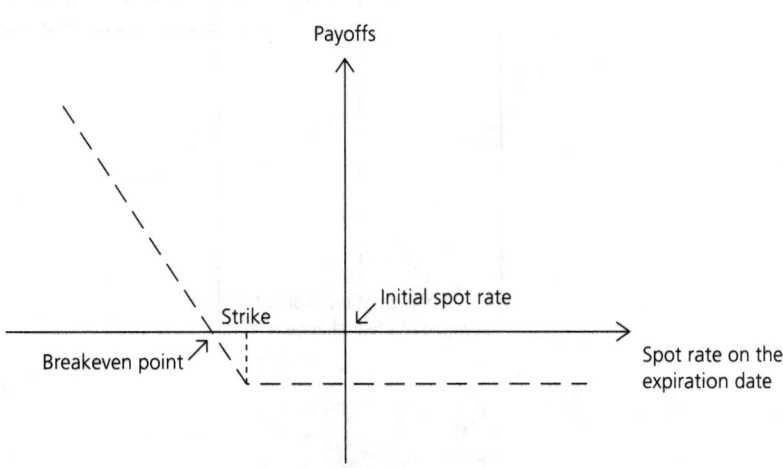

Figure 15.5 Holding a put for a period less than the time to expiration when volatility is constant

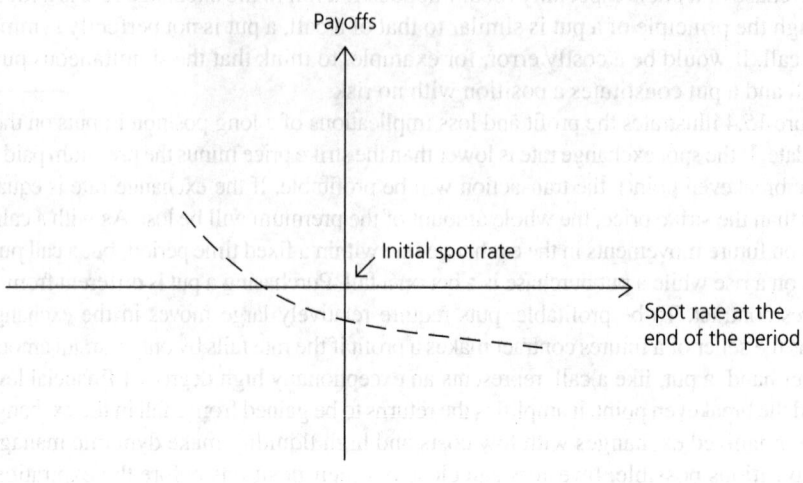

Figure 15.6 Payoffs for naked puts with different strike prices

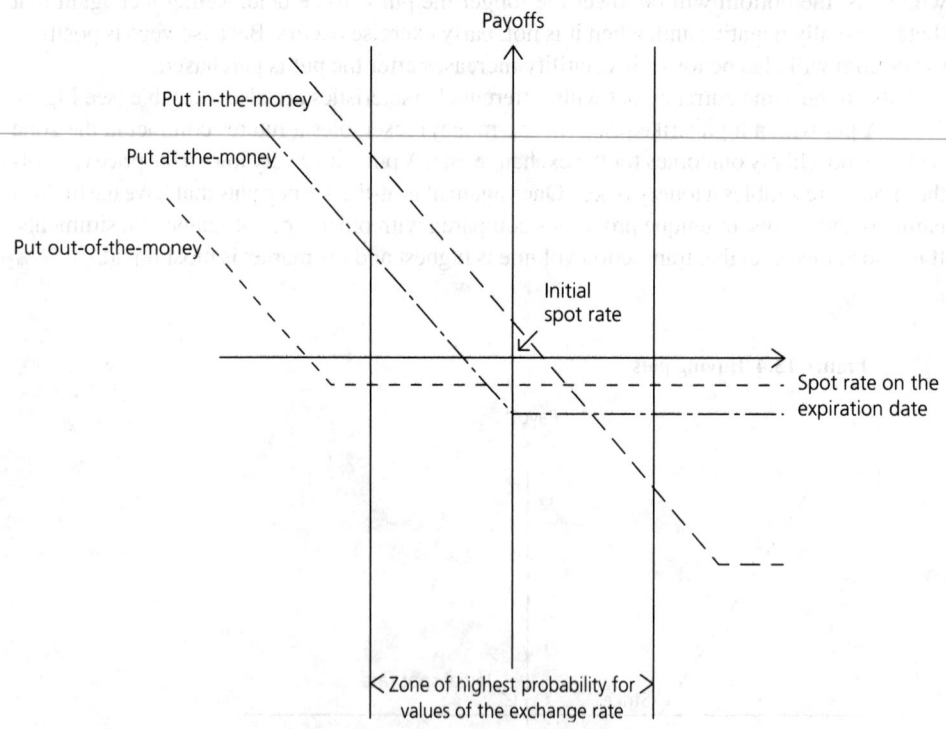

When the expiration date is far in the future, holding a put is relatively less risky because a fall in the exchange rate is more likely. Consequently, premiums are higher. Although options with the nearest expiration date are the most frequently traded, they also have the lowest thetas (or the highest in absolute value, meaning that the price degenerates faster) and, consequently, they are the costliest to hold.

Speculating on price stability: Selling puts and calls

Selling a naked call or put involves writing an option without taking an offsetting position on the spot or forward market. This is a very risky strategy and it has given the options markets a bad name. However, if it is well understood and correctly employed, it can offer solid opportunities for profit making when the exchange rate is stable.

Writing a naked call in the over-the-counter market is always considered highly speculative. In exchange for a small and limited profit (the premium) the writer accepts a risk that is theoretically unlimited. Figure 15.7 shows that no matter what the exchange rate does, the writer's only gain is the premium. On the other hand, if the exchange rate rises sharply, he is obliged to buy the foreign currency at the high price and sell it to the call holder at the lower strike price.

On the organized exchanges it is always possible for the speculator to close out his position before the expiration date. This contract liquidity enables speculators to limit their losses. In this sense, writing a naked call does not expose its author to unlimited risk, although it is always a speculative operation. Figure 15.8 illustrates the profit and loss profile of a position in naked calls closed out before the expiration date. In the absence of sharp moves in the exchange rate and variations in volatility, writing a naked call is profitable. The simple passage of time guarantees a profit. This strategy is only optimal when the exchange rate is stable. For example, if the exchange rate falls sharply, the speculator would have done better to buy a put. If it rises sharply, he loses heavily. The delta of writing a naked call is negative (since the call is sold). The gamma is also negative. The theta is positive and reflects the favorable effect of the passage of time. The professionals call this position the "top".

Writing a naked put completes the picture. It also is a risky strategy. In exchange for a small, limited profit (the premium) the speculator exposes himself to considerable risk. The risk is not unlimited because the exchange rate cannot be negative. As in the case of the naked call, the existence of organized exchanges makes it possible to limit the risks and makes the strategy accessible to competent speculators.

Figure 5.7 Writing a naked cell

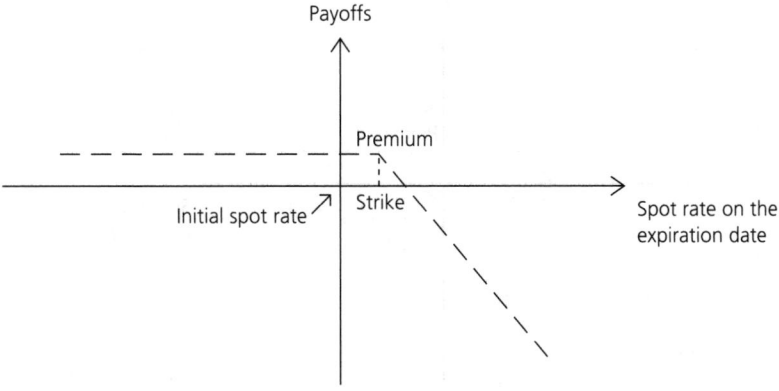

Figure 15.8 Writing a naked call: payoffs of a position closed out before the expiration date

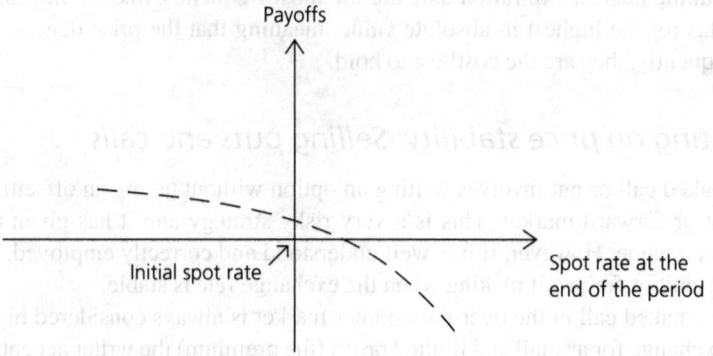

The writer of a naked put counts on the exchange rate not weakening over the life of the option. If that in fact is what happens, Figure 15.9 shows that he makes a profit equal to the amount of the premium. If it does weaken, his losses grow as the exchange rate falls.

Figure 15.10 shows the profit profile of a naked put position that is closed out before the expiration date. It is increasing and concave. It indicates that its delta is positive (put sold) and its gamma is negative. The risk is associated with downward moves in the exchange rate and the profit of this position at the "top" is assured if the exchange rate does not move too much. The theta is positive and indicates that time is a precious ally of a speculator in this position. The key to the success of this strategy is the stability of the exchange rate. A big downward move would cost the speculator money while a large upward move would make him regret that he did not buy a call.

Hedging with options

The positions to be hedged can come from many sources, such as commercial transactions, foreign investments or from loans raised in other currencies. The positions can be long or short and the options to hedge them can be traded on either the domestic market or a foreign market. Finally, the hedge can be constructed by buying an option, by selling an option or

Figure 15.9 Writing a naked put

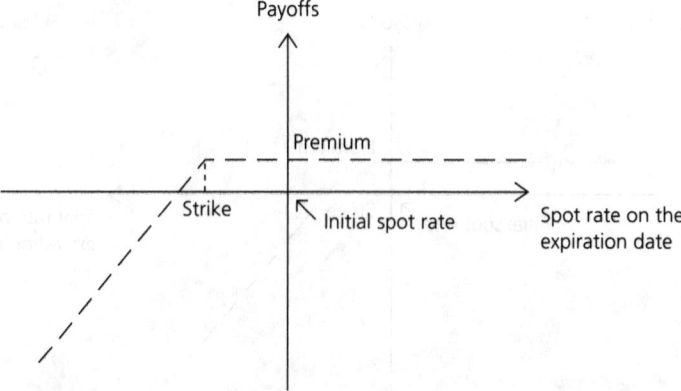

Figure 15.10 Writing a naked put: payoffs of a position closed out before the expiration date

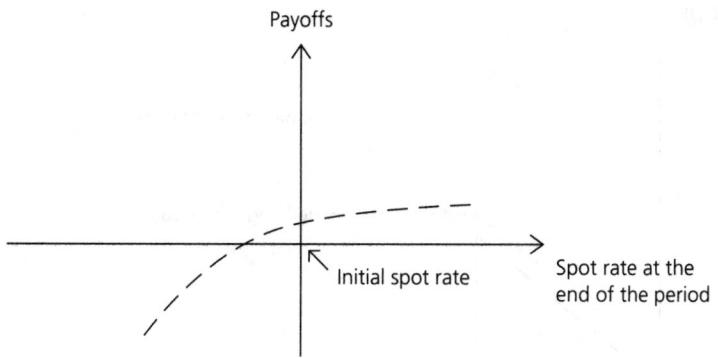

by a combination of both. In this section we will consider only the basic strategies. The more sophisticated strategies will be examined in the next chapter.

Hedging with an option purchase

The position to be covered can be short if, for example, it is used to finance imports, or it can be long if the exposure comes from a future receipt from the sale of exports. The appropriate hedging strategies should therefore be symmetrical. In the first case, when the exchange rate is quoted as the number of units of domestic currency to buy one unit of foreign currency [S(domestic/foreign)], calls should be bought, or, looked at another way, the delta should be positive. In the second case from the same perspective, puts should be bought (the delta should be negative). It is important to remember how the exchange rate is quoted because if it were quoted the other way [S(foreign/domestic)] the operations would be reversed.

Hedging an import in the United States

Suppose that a US importer has to pay a bill for JPY 25 million in two months time. The spot rate in New York, S(USD/JPY), is USD 0.7764 per JPY 100. He fears that the rate will rise (the yen will appreciate) but he is not too sure that this, in fact, will actually happen. The markets are volatile and a fall in the exchange rate (the yen depreciates) cannot be excluded. If the yen does fall, the other importers will pay fewer dollars for their imports and thus be able to lower their prices. Competition is tough and our importer cannot afford to be wrong either way.

The key to the importer's problem is the number of dollars that he will have to pay for the JPY 25 million. He needs an instrument that will allow him to hedge against a rise in the value of the yen without eliminating the gains that he can realize if the value of the yen falls. The objective is met by a call option on yen that is traded on the Philadelphia Stock Exchange. The call contract is for JPY 6,250,000 with a strike price of 78 and expiration time of two months selling at 1.18. In other words, he can buy the right to buy JPY 6.25 million in two months for USD 0.78 per JPY 100 for 1.18 cents per JPY 100. To cover the JPY 25 million that he owes, he will have to buy four contracts. Figure 15.11 illustrates the possible outcomes to be obtained in two months according to how the exchange rate behaves.

If in two months the exchange rate is a higher than USD 0.78, the calls will be exercised and he will pay USD 195,000 for the JPY 25 million. The total cost of the operation will be

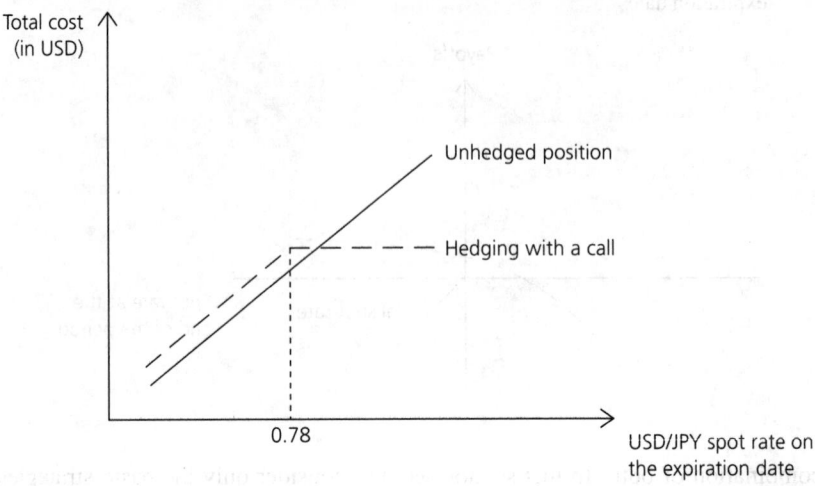

Figure 15.11 Hedging an import in the United States

USD 197,950 (USD 195,000 for the yen plus USD 2950 for the premium) and the effective exchange rate will be USD 0.7918 [calculated as 197,950/(25,000,000/100)]. If the exchange rate is lower than USD 0.78 the calls will expire worthless.

Suppose that the exchange rate falls to USD 0.7143. The importer will pay USD 178,575 for the yen and his total cost will be USD 181,525 (USD 178,575 for the yen and USD 2950 for the premium). The effective exchange rate would be USD 0.7261. Although he would pay more for the yen than the current exchange rate because of the premium, he still would benefit considerably from the yen's fall.

Besides the obvious advantages of hedging with a call option, there are also disadvantages. One of the main disadvantages cited by professional investors is the cost. When the maximum cost of foreign currency hedged with a call option (the strike price plus the premium) is compared with the cost of a forward contract, option hedging is always more costly. Figure 15.12 compares the costs of the two strategies.

Figure 15.12 Hedging an import in the United States: comparison between two strategies

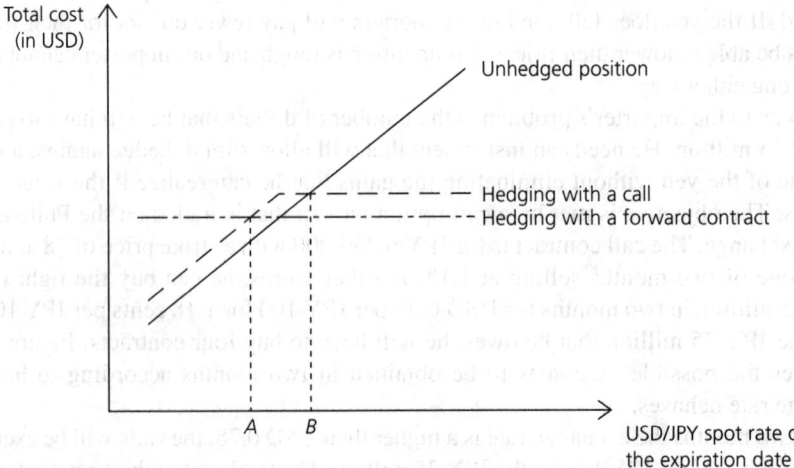

With this in mind the question is when should a call be used to hedge foreign exchange risk. To answer the question we must distinguish between three situations:

1. When a rise in the exchange rate is expected and the probability of this outcome is very high.
2. When a fall in the exchange rate is expected and the probability of this outcome is very high.
3. When there is an expected movement one way or the other but there is also a strong possibility of a move in the opposite direction.

In the first case, when a rise in the exchange rate is very probable, a classic forward hedge is the best strategy because it is the least costly. In the second case, when a fall in the exchange rate is very probable, the best strategy is not to cover and avoid all costs while benefiting fully from the lower rate. In the third case of considerable uncertainty, the option might be the best strategy. If there is a sharp rise in the exchange rate, total costs are limited. If there is a sharp fall, some of the benefits are captured. Only in the zone of relative stability, between A and B in Figure 15.12, is an option hedge clearly the inferior strategy. This is because it is the costliest strategy and no benefits accrue to the option holder if the exchange rate does not move outside the range AB. In conclusion, we can say that hedging with options is the most advantageous when uncertainty is the greatest and big moves in both directions are a strong possibility. Remember that the purchase of an option gives the holder the rights to gains from a positive gamma. This right has a cost that can only be recovered through a strong price movement.

Hedging a European import on the US futures market

Purchasing a currency call does not always constitute an appropriate hedge. It should not be forgotten that the US exchanges offer written contracts on exchange rates in terms of US dollars. From the point of view of a non-US importer, however, the problem is in reverse. He wants to protect himself against an appreciation of the dollar in his domestic currency or, put another way, against a depreciation of his domestic currency against the dollar. Consequently, when hedging on a US exchange, it is a put that he must purchase and not a call.

Suppose that in Zürich, the dollar is quoted at CHF 1.3949. We know that this implies a Swiss franc rate of USD 0.7169 in New York. On the same day a put with a time to expiration of two months and a strike price of 73 is trading on the Philadelphia Stock Exchange for USD 0.0096. Each contract is for CHF 62,500. A Swiss importer has a bill of USD 90,000 to pay in two months. Two puts will just about cover his exposure (one contract is worth $0.7169 \times 62,500 = $ USD 44,806.25 at the current exchange rate). If in two months time the value of the Swiss franc falls below USD 0.73, he will exercise his contract and obtain USD 91,250 for CHF 125,000. Including the premium, which cost USD 1200 (calculated as $0.0096 \times 62,500 \times 2$), he will net USD 90,050 for an effective exchange rate of 1.3882. If the dollar goes to CHF 1.30, a rate of USD 0.7692 in New York, the put will expire worthless. The Swiss importer will be able to obtain USD 90,000 at the spot rate for CHF 117,000. Including the premium of USD 1200 or CHF 1674, he will have paid CHF 118,674 for USD 90,000 or an effective exchange rate of 1.3186.

In conclusion, then, two things should be mentioned. First, we can see in Figure 15.13 that the option hedge is preferable to a classic forward hedge or no hedge at all only in the case of considerable uncertainty when the exchange rate has a strong possibility of moving outside the range of AB. It is never the best strategy – a forward purchase of dollars is less costly if the exchange rate falls sharply whereas no cover is better if it rises sharply – but, since it covers both eventualities, it might be the best overall strategy. Secondly, it is obvious that the Swiss importer could have hedged in Switzerland by buying calls on the US dollar in Swiss francs. Thus, a particularity of currency options is that call on currency f in currency d is equivalent to a put on currency d in currency f.

Figure 15.13 Hedging a European import on the US market

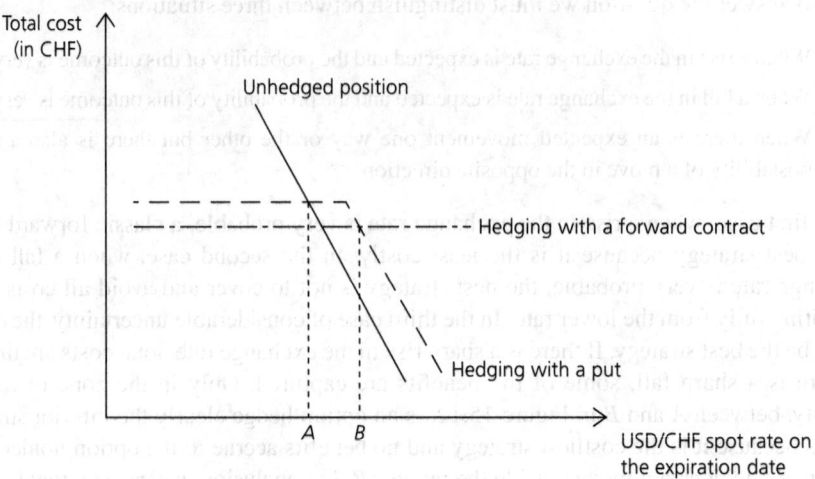

Covering an export from Europe on a European OTC market

A large French cheese company has just signed a contract for USD 1 million worth of Camembert cheese that will be paid for in three months. The spot rate in Paris is EUR 1.1. The company treasurer fears that the dollar might depreciate and reduce his income in euros. On the other hand, there is also a strong chance that the dollar will appreciate and, if this happens, he does not want to miss out on the increase in income that it will bring. His banker offers to sell him a dollar put with a strike price of 1.10 and an expiration date that coincides with his expected dollar income in three months. The premium is 2% that is to be paid on the expiration date. This put on USD 1 million will cover him if the dollar falls sharply. If, for example, it falls to 1.0100, the treasurer will exercise the put and receive an effective rate of 1.0780 (calculated as $1.10 - 0.02 \times 1.10$). If the dollar rises above 1.10, the put will expire worthless and the treasurer will sell his dollars at the spot rate. His effective rate will be equal to the spot rate less the premium of 0.022. Figure 15.14 compares the option hedge with a forward hedge and the unhedged position.

Note that here again an option hedge is only advantageous if the exchange rate has a good chance of making a wide swing in either direction. We should also point out that the option hedge has another advantage when the commercial cash flow is not entirely certain. The order could be canceled, for example. With a classic hedge of dollars sold forward, the exporter would find himself in a purely speculative position. On the maturity date he would have to come up with the dollars. If the value of the dollar has fallen he would make money but if it has risen he will lose money. The potential loss is theoretically unlimited. As we saw in Chapter 14, it is always possible to close out the position but that generates another transaction cost and the treasurer would still have to pay the difference in the two forward prices if the rate has moved against him. In the case of a put, he is still in a speculative position but his exposure is limited to the amount of the premium. In a case like this of a potential unwanted speculative position generated by foreign currency hedging, the option hedge is clearly preferable.

Covering a European export on the US futures market

As we mentioned, the Chicago Mercantile Exchange trades puts and calls on currency futures rather than on the currency itself. The buyer of a call on a futures contract buys the right to buy a futures contract on the underlying currency on a given expiration date. The

Figure 15.14 Hedging a European export on a European over-the-counter market

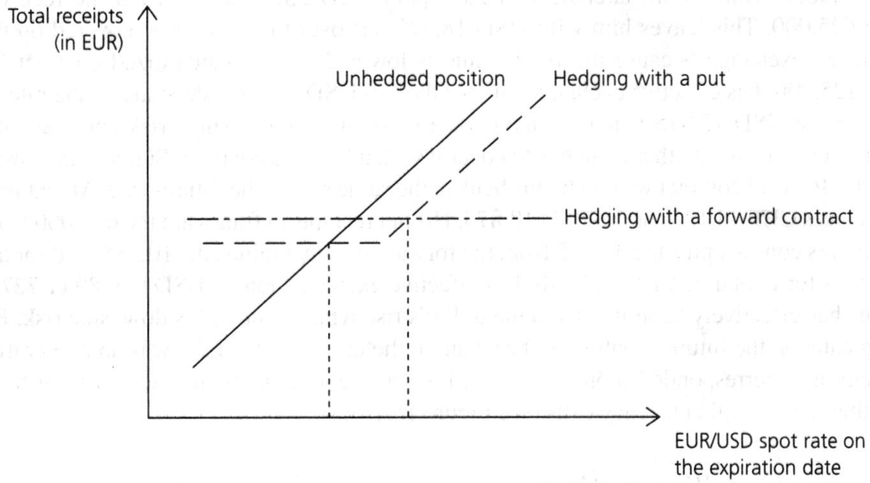

futures position is recorded in the framework of the futures traded on the CME. The use of these options is very close to the use of straightforward currency options as illustrated in the following example.

Suppose that a Swiss exporter expects a payment of USD 375,000 four months in the future from a South American client. The exchange rate in Zürich is CHF 1.6955 for USD 1. A potential monetary crisis is on the horizon and the exporter wants to be covered on the downside but he would also like to profit if the dollar moves up. Consequently, he decides to use the CME's futures options. An American broker quotes him a price of 0.98 for a call on a Swiss franc futures contract with a strike price of 60 and expiration time of three months. This means that by paying USD 0.0098 per franc he has the right in three months time to buy a futures contract worth CHF 125,000 for a price of USD 0.60 per franc. When the three months are up he will have to decide whether or not to exercise his option to buy a futures contract on francs. If he exercises, he will own a futures contract on francs but not the francs themselves. The option, in this case, will be transformed into a firm futures position. The important point to remember is that the exchange rate pertinent to the option contract is the future rate and not the spot rate.

Because he is expecting USD 375,000, he will need about CHF 625,000 or five calls. If in three months the one-month forward rate on francs is higher than USD 0.60 (1.6667 CHF/USD), he will exercise his call. If it is lower, he will let it expire.

Suppose that the futures rate goes to USD 0.6452 (1.55 CHF/USD). The Swiss exporter will exercise his option and acquire five one-month futures contracts for a total amount of CHF 625,000. Abstracting from the intricacies of the marking to market operations on futures contracts (see Chapter 7), he will end up paying USD 375,000 (0.60 × 625,000) for CHF 625,000. The calls cost him USD 6125 (calculated as 0.0098 × 625,000) or 10,385 converted at the spot rate of 1.6955 when he bought the calls. His net income in francs, then, was 614,615 (calculated as 625,000 − 10,385) and he paid USD 375,000 for an effective exchange rate of 1.6390, better than the futures rate of 1.55 on the calls' expiration date.

In the case that the dollar does not appreciate, it is obvious that the Swiss exporter will not exercise the calls. Suppose that on the expiration date the futures exchange rate is USD 0.5698 (CHF 1.7550). They will not be exercised because it is lower than the strike price of USD 0.60. This brings up another problem. Because the exporter will not receive his dollars for another month, he has to decide whether or not to hedge his exposure for the remaining month. Suppose that he decides to cover and buys five futures contracts at USD 0.5698. One month later he will have paid USD 356,125 for which he receives CHF 625,000. This leaves him with USD 18,875 left over that cannot be covered on the organized exchange because the franc value is lower than the standardized contract for CHF 125,000. His effective exchange rate for the full USD 375,000 depends on the rate he gets for the USD 18,875 balance. One choice is to take the exchange risk and leave the balance unhedged. Another choice is to cover it with a forward contract. Suppose he covers it with a forward contract written by his bank at the same rate as the futures rate. At maturity he receives CHF 33,125 for the USD 18,875. His net receipts in francs are the 625,000 from the futures contract plus the 33,125 from the forward contract minus the 10,385 paid for the five calls for a total of CHF 647,740. His effective exchange rate is USD 0.5789 (1.7273) and he has effectively benefited from the dollar's rise while limiting his downside risk. By using calls on the futures contract rather than on the currency itself, he was able to craft a strategy that corresponded more closely to his time requirements than would have been possible with straight currency calls (see Figure 15.15).

Hedging by selling options

The main criticism by company treasurers of using options to hedge foreign exchange risk is the cost – that is, the premium – that they must pay. As we have seen, an option purchase is only advantageous if wide swings of the exchange rate in both directions are probable (high volatility). If the forecast is for relative stability (low volatility), it might be better to sell options. In this section we will consider two examples: covering imports by selling puts and covering exports by selling calls.

Covering imports by selling puts

An importer billed in foreign exchange is exposed to the risk that the foreign exchange will become more costly before the bill is due. To reduce or eliminate this risk he can buy calls on the foreign currency if he uses his domestic market or buy puts on the domestic currency if he uses a foreign market. We characterized this position as having a positive delta, meaning that if the foreign currency gains in value our position also gains in value. Another

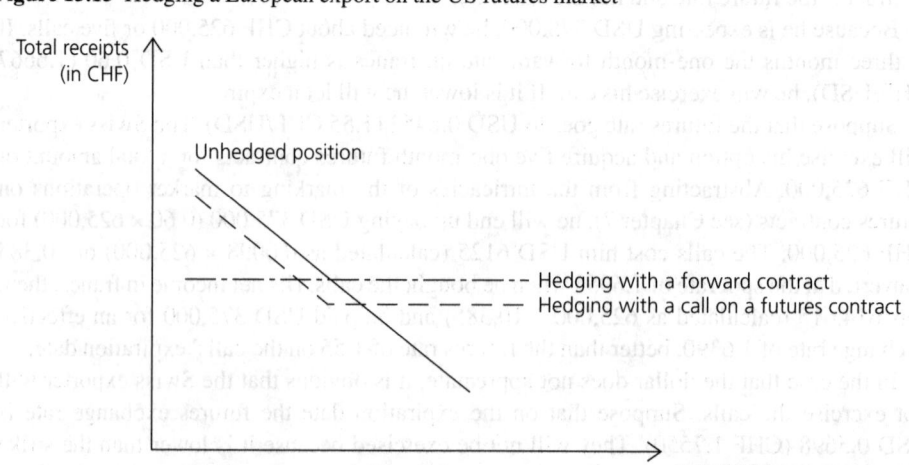

Figure 15.15 Hedging a European export on the US futures market

way of generating a positive delta is to sell a put on the foreign currency because a put's delta is negative. Shorting a negative delta generates a positive delta. As usual, the best way to illustrate this point is with an example.

Imagine the case of a Korean importer of petroleum products who has a bill of USD 10 million to pay in three months time. The current spot exchange rate in Seoul is KRW 1129 per dollar and the three-month forward rate is 1151. A three-month dollar put with a strike price of 1129 is selling over the counter at 3.4%, or about KRW 38 per dollar. If the dollar appreciates to KRW 1160 in three months, the put will expire worthless and the importer will keep the premium. The cost of his dollars will then be KRW 1160 paid spot less the KRW 38 won received for the premium for a total of KRW 1122 per dollar. This rate is far better than the spot rate of 1160 or the 1151 he could have paid to cover himself with a forward contract. If the value of the dollar falls to 1110, the put will be exercised and the importer will pay 1129 for the dollars. His all-in cost will be the 1129 paid less the 38 received for the premium for a total of 1091, a much better price than the market rate of 1110 or the forward rate of 1151.

The situation looks almost too good to be true. In fact, it is. If the dollar falls to 1000, for example, the put will be exercised and the cost to the importer will still be 1091, far higher than the spot rate. By the same token, if the dollar rises to 1300, the put will expire and the cost of the dollars will be 1262, the spot rate less the premium. This rate is higher than the 1151 that could have been obtained with a forward contract and, thus, the hedge was inadequate.

Figure 15.16 summarizes these results. Hedging by selling puts is the best strategy as long as the exchange rate stays between 1091 (1129 – 38) and 1189 (1151 + 38). One of the reasons that the band is so wide is that the forward dollar is at a premium. If it had been at a discount the band would have been narrower. In any case, selling puts can be a profitable hedging strategy if the exchange rate is expected to remain relatively stable.

Covering exports by selling calls

An exporter who bills in foreign currency fears a fall in the value of that currency before he is paid. To reduce or eliminate this risk he can buy puts on the foreign currency if he uses his domestic market or buy calls on the domestic currency if he uses a foreign

Figure 15.16 Hedging imports by selling puts

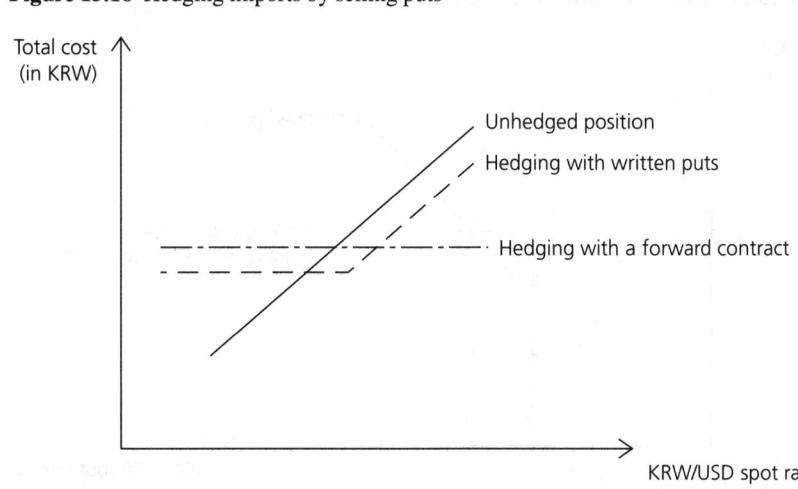

Total cost (in KRW)

Unhedged position

Hedging with written puts

Hedging with a forward contract

KRW/USD spot rate on the expiration date

market. We characterized this position as having a negative delta, meaning that if the foreign currency loses value, our position gains in value. Another way of generating a negative delta is to sell a call on the foreign currency because a call's delta is positive. Shorting a positive delta generates a negative delta. The best way to illustrate this point is with an example.

Imagine a Mexican exporter that sells textiles in the United Kingdom. He bills his clients in pounds and wants to protect himself against a fall in its value. The spot exchange rate is MXN 18.9215 and 19.1350 three months forward. He sells a three-month call on Mexican pesos with a strike price of 19 to his bank for 2.7% or MXN 0.51 for each pound. If the value of the pound falls below 19 to 18.70, for example, the call will not be exercised. He will sell his pounds for the spot rate of 18.70 and pocket the premium of 0.51 on the call. His effective exchange rate will be 19.21, better than the spot rate or the forward rate of 19.135 he could have contracted for.

Suppose that the pound appreciates to 19.40. The call will be exercised and he will receive MXN 19 for each pound. His effective rate will be the MXN 19 strike price plus the MXN 0.51 premium for a total of 19.51, a rate better than the spot rate of 19.40 and the forward rate of 19.135.

The risk from selling the call comes if the pound falls sharply in value, to 18 for example. The call is not exercised and the exporter receives the spot rate plus the premium for each pound, a rate of 18.51, far lower than the forward rate.

Figure 15.17 summarizes these results. Hedging by selling calls is the best strategy as long as the exchange rate stays in the band between 18.625 (19.135 – 0.51) and 19.51 (19 + 0.51). Selling calls can be a profitable hedging strategy if the exchange rate is expected to remain relatively stable.

Tunnels: Hedging with sales and purchases of options

Hedging by purchasing options is costly because of the premium and effective only in times of high volatility. Hedging by selling options can be advantageous in times of low volatility. The two strategies are complementary leading professionals to devise strategies combining both of them.

Figure 15.17 Hedging exports by selling calls

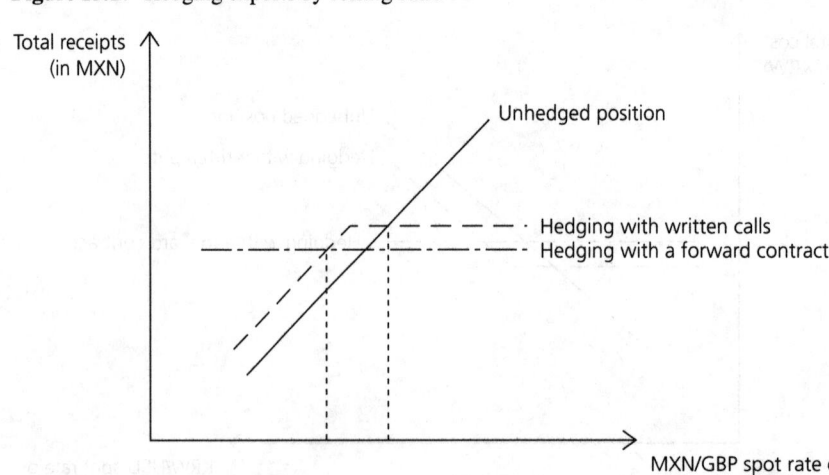

The tunnel for imports

Covering exchange risk on an import transaction can be achieved on the domestic market by buying calls or by selling puts. To reduce the cost of an option hedge, the treasurer may want to combine both of them. Selling the put enables him to choose an out-of-the-money call that is less expensive. The cost reduction is complete if the premium on the sale of the put covers the premium on the call purchase.

Take the case of a Swiss importer who has a bill in dollars to pay in three months. The spot exchange rate is 1.54 CHF/USD and the three month forward rate is 1.559. He can buy a three-month out-of-the-money call with a strike price of 1.64 for 0.4%. The call is not expensive because the strike price is high. He can also sell a three-month put with a strike price of 1.49 for 0.4%. The two premiums offset each other and the cost is zero.

Figure 15.18 illustrates the outcome profile of this strategy. If the dollar appreciates sharply, the importer will exercise his call at 1.64 and pay CHF 1.64 per dollar. On the other hand, if the dollar depreciates sharply, the put will be exercised and he will pay CHF 1.49 per dollar. The band between these two limit rates is called the tunnel. Inside the tunnel the importer will receive whatever the spot rate happens to be, but he can never pay more than 1.64 and never less than 1.49. The cost of this position resides in the fact that if the rate goes below 1.49 he will not benefit from the lower rate. Treasurers like this kind of position because their risk is limited, they can benefit from favorable moves in the exchange rate and costs are low.

The tunnel for exports

The export tunnel is symmetrical to the import tunnel. The treasurer simultaneously buys a put and sells a call. Both instruments are chosen out-of-the-money. Thus, if the value of the foreign currency falls sharply, the put guarantees a minimum price. If it rises sharply, the call will be exercised but will have benefited from the rise up to the strike price. Costs are reduced because the premium he receives from the sale of the call goes to offset the purchase of the put. The two premiums might not be equal so the final result must include the difference between the two. Figure 15.19 shows the outcome profile when the tunnel is generated on the domestic market. If it were generated on a foreign market, a call would be bought instead of a put and a put would be sold instead of a call.

Figure 15.18 The tunnel for imports

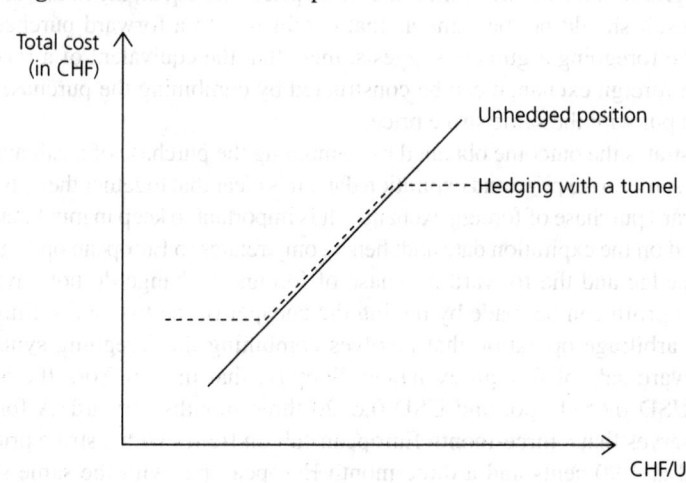

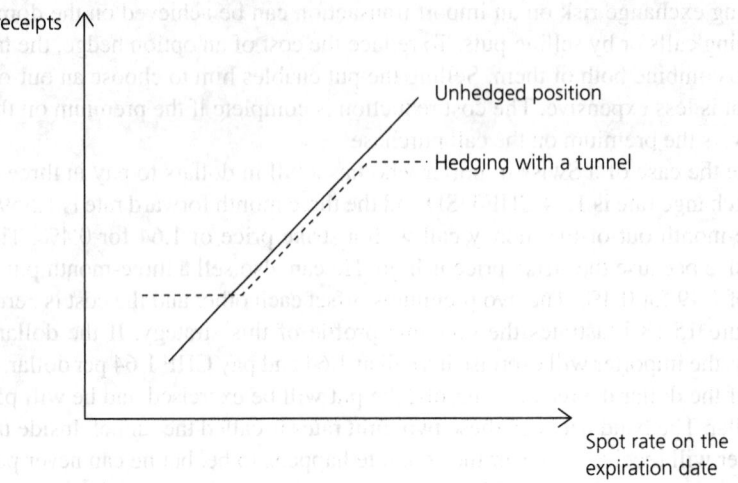

Figure 15.19 The tunnel for exports

An example of arbitrage: Put–call parity

On the futures and options markets a distinction is usually made between hedging, speculation and arbitrage. Arbitrage operations are undertaken by professionals and involve establishing a riskless position that generates a net profit. Positions like this are hard to come by insofar as the markets are very competitive. They require low transaction costs and constant vigilance on the part of the arbitragers in the markets. The **put–call parity** relation presented in Chapter 8 is a well known example. It is interesting to study because it illustrates the relationships between calls and puts and all the other positions that incorporate calls and puts.

The starting point of the analysis is the tunnel that we presented in the preceding section. In the case of an import hedge, the importer had the choice between a forward purchase of foreign currency or a purchase of calls financed by a sale of puts. The position is not entirely riskless because inside the tunnel the exchange rate can fluctuate. Notice, however, that the tunnel limits are the strike prices for the calls and puts. As the strike prices come closer together, the tunnel gets smaller. At the limit, if the strike prices are equal, the tunnel should be closed and the result should be the same as that obtained with a forward purchase of foreign currency. The foregoing argument suggests, then, that the equivalent of a forward contract to purchase foreign exchange can be constructed by combining the purchase of a call and the sale of a put with the same strike price.

Figure 15.20 illustrates the outcome obtained by combining the purchase of a call and the sale of a put with the same strike price and expiration date. It is clear that together they give the same result as a forward purchase of foreign exchange. It is important to keep in mind that this result is only obtained on the expiration date and, hence, only relates to European options.

If the synthetic hedge and the forward purchase of foreign exchange do not have the same cost, a riskless profit can be made by buying the cheaper of the two and selling the other. Consider the arbitrage operation that involves combining the foregoing synthetic position with a forward sale of foreign exchange. Suppose that in New York the Swiss franc is quoted at USD 0.6511 spot and USD 0.6420 three months forward. A foreign exchange trader observes that a three-month European call on francs with a strike price of USD 0.63 is quoted at 1.90 cents and a three-month European put with the same strike price is quoted at 0.75 cents. He thinks it will be advantageous to buy a call, sell a put and

Figure 15.20 Put–call parity: the purchase of a call and the sale of a put

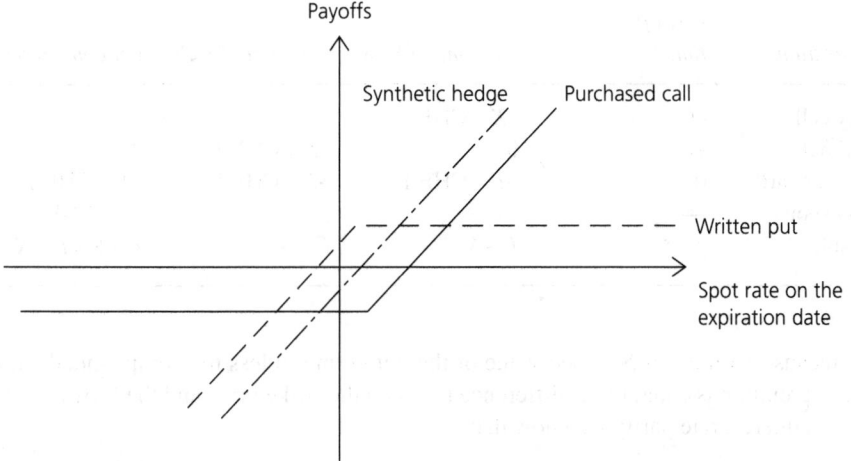

cover himself by selling francs forward. This he does. On the expiration date, if the exchange rate has gone above USD 0.63 the put expires and he exercises his call. His total cost for each franc he receives is USD 0.6415, the USD 0.63 strike price plus the difference between the USD 0.019 he paid for the call and the USD 0.0075 he received for his put. He then delivers the francs on his forward contract and receives USD 0.6420, a gain of USD 0.0005 per franc.

If the exchange rate has gone below USD 0.63, the call expires and the put is exercised. His cost as before is USD 0.6415, the strike price plus the difference between the two premiums. He delivers the francs for the forward contract and receives USD 0.6420, a gain of USD 0.0005 per franc. If the exchange rate stays at USD 0.63, he buys francs spot and has the same cost and profit.

Based on this type of arbitrage and incorporating the compounding that goes on over the life of the option, we can make the relationship between puts, calls, and the forward and the spot exchange rates explicit.

C = the price of the call
p = the price of the put
S = the spot exchange rate
F = the forward exchange rate
X = the strike price
r = the domestic interest rate
r^* = the foreign interest rate.

The arbitrage can be summarized as set out in Table 15.1.

We can see that the outcome is the same for all possible outcomes. Because the outcome is certain, the investment should earn the riskless rate in domestic currency. Thus, when t is the time to expiration:

$$(p - C)e^{rt} + F - X = 0$$

or

$$pe^{rt} - Ce^{rt} = -F + X \tag{15.1}$$

Table 15.1 Arbitrage summary

Operation	Cash flow at time 0	Outcome if S>X	Outcome if S<X	Outcome if S=X
Buy call	$-C$	$-X + \text{CHF } 1$	0	0
Sell put	$+p$	0	$-X + \text{CHF } 1$	0
Sell forward	0	$+F - \text{CHF } 1$	$+F - \text{CHF } 1$	$+F - \text{CHF } 1$
Buy spot	—	—	—	$-S + \text{CHF } 1$
Result	$p - C$	$F - X$	$F - X$	$F - S = F - X$

This means that the compounded value of the put premium less the compounded value of the call premium is equal to the difference between the strike price and the forward rate.[2]

From interest rate parity we know that:

$$F_{0,t} = S_0 \frac{e^{rt}}{e^{r^*t}}$$

Substituting this value for F in Equation 15.1 and dividing by e^{rt}, gives the put–call parity equation mentioned in Chapter 8:[3]

$$p - C = -Se^{-r^*t} + Xe^{-rt} \qquad (15.2)$$

Summary

1. Options markets offer special opportunities for hedging and speculation. They are especially suited to situations where wide swings in the exchange rate are expected. Speculation on a sharp price rise involves buying calls while speculation on a sharp fall involves selling puts. Speculation on price stability involves selling calls or puts.

2. A short position in foreign exchange can be hedged in the domestic market by buying a call on foreign exchange and a long position can be hedged by buying a put on foreign

---

[2] By changing the signs of Equation 15.1 we would have

$$Ce^{rt} - pe^{rt} = F - X \qquad (15.3)$$

In other words, the compounded value of the call premium less the compounded value of the put premium is equal to the difference between the forward rate and the strike price.

[3] The situation is more complicated for American options because of the possibility of early exercise. If the forward exchange rate is at a premium, we have seen that an American put is worth more than a European call. Thus, Equation 15.1 becomes an inequality:

$$pe^{rt} - Ce^{rt} > -F + X$$

If the forward exchange rate is at a discount, then it is the American call that is worth more than the European call and Equation 15.3 also becomes an inequality:

$$Ce^{rt} - pe^{rt} > F - X$$

Consequently, it is not possible to find an exact relation between American calls and puts. However, the difference between the premiums is limited by the interest rate differential.

exchange. When the hedge is undertaken in another country, the operations are reversed because the options are quoted in reverse. The short position is hedged by buying a put and the long position is hedged by buying a call.

3. It is possible to hedge foreign currency exposure by selling options. A short position in foreign exchange can be hedged by selling a put. A long position can be hedged by selling a call. A hedge achieved through the sale of an option is a bet on the relative stability of the exchange rate. If the exchange rate moves outside the limits of the hedge, the operation could be costly.

4. Because of their nature, options are relatively expensive. One way of reducing hedging costs is to create a tunnel. A tunnel is the purchase of one type of option and the simultaneous sale of the other type. Hedging a short position in foreign exchange with a tunnel involves buying a call at one strike price and selling a put at another strike price. Minimum and maximum prices for the purchase of the foreign exchange are thus established by the strike prices and the cost of the call is offset to some extent by the premium on the put. Hedging a long position in foreign exchange with a tunnel involves buying a put and selling a call. Again, the strike prices establish the maximum and minimum sales prices for the foreign currency and the premium on the call helps offset the cost of the call.

5. The concept of the tunnel makes it possible to work out some of the basic relationships between puts, calls, and the forward and spot exchange rates. As the strike prices come closer together, the tunnel gets smaller. At the limit, if the strike prices are equal, the tunnel should be closed and the result should be the same as that obtained with a forward purchase of foreign currency. One relation is that the compounded value of the put premium less the compounded value of the call premium is equal to the difference between the strike price and the forward rate. Put another way we can say that the compounded value of the call premium less the compounded value of the put premium is equal to the difference between the forward rate and the strike price. Put–call parity suggests that the difference between the put premium and the call premium is equal to the difference of the present value of the strike price discounted at the domestic interest rate minus the present value of the spot rate discounted at the foreign interest rate. Because of interest rate parity, the forward rate discounted at the domestic interest rate is another way of looking at the present value of the spot rate discounted at the foreign interest rate. Thus, we can say that put–call parity also suggests that the difference between the put premium and the call premium is equal to the difference of the present value of the strike price discounted at the domestic interest rate minus the present value of the forward rate discounted at the domestic interest rate.

Questions

Solutions to the following questions are set out on the web site, details of which are included in the Preface.

1. Choose the correct response. An investor buys a call on the US dollar with a strike price of DKK 5.50 for a premium of DKK 0.36. On the expiration date, he should exercise the call (a) if the spot rate is higher than DKK 5.50; (b) only if the spot rate is higher than DKK 5.86.

2. Calculate the time value and the intrinsic value of the following American options:

Spot rate = USD/CHF = 66.86

Strike	Call premium	Put premium
66	1.36	0.88
67	0.85	1.34

3. Choose the correct response. An increase in the expected volatility will cause

   a. A rise in the call premium and a fall in the put premium.

   b. A fall in the call premium and a rise in the put premium.

   c. A rise in both the call and the put premiums.

4. Suppose that the spot rate on the CHF is 66 cents and that in the next period it will go to either 66.5 or 65.5 with an equal probability. The interest rate on the USD is 1%. The interest rate on the CHF is 2%. Using calls with a strike price of 66, set up an arbitrage position and calculate the theoretical value of the call if the premium is paid when the call is purchased.

5. Using Garman and Kohlhagen's formula (Chapter 8), calculate the value of a European call on USD 100,000 when

   S(DKK/USD) = 5.50

   Three-month interest rate on DKK = 10%

   Three-month interest rate on USD = 4%

   Expected volatility = 9%

   Option expiration date = three months

   Strike price = 5.50.

6. Choose the correct response (responses). Implicit volatility is

   a. Equal to the standard deviation of the spot rate measured over the last 90 days.

   b. Equal to the moving average of the difference between the spot rate and the forward rate over the last 15 days.

   c. Equal to the standard deviation expected by the market for the market forecast of future spot rates.

7. On 6 July the Australian dollar is worth USD 0.7421. An August 74 call on the Australian dollar is quoted at USD 0.081. By 20 July, the spot rate on the Australian dollar was USD 0.7446 and the August 74 call was quoted at USD 0.062. Explain why using the purchase of a call to speculate on a rise in the spot rate would produce a loss.

8. Estimate the percentage loss or gain for a buyer of a CHF call August 69 at USD 0.02 on 6 July that is sold for USD 0.062 on 20 July, knowing that the spot exchange rate has gone from 66.22 to 68.53 over the same period. Comment on the leverage effect.

9. A September 187.5 put on the pound sells for 2.87 US cents on 6 July. It falls to 2.08 cents by 20 July. Over the same period the spot exchange rate goes from 192.08 to 195.03. Comment on the position of a seller of a put.

10. A UK exporter of Christmas pudding to the United States decides to cover his foreign exchange position with the purchase of options. The spot exchange rate is USD 1.9208 = GBP 1. The information on options is: Call GBP December 190 = 4.15; Put GBP December 190 = 7.60. What strategies could be followed?

11. Construct a tunnel for an American importer from Switzerland given the following information:

	Put	Call
Sep 63	0.21	4.65
Sep 64	0.22	—
Sep 65	0.38	2.93
Sep 66	0.58	—
Sep 67	0.92	1.89
Sep 68	1.41	1.28
Sep 69	—	0.86

12. Using the information from the previous question, construct a synthetic forward contract. Graph the outcomes.

13. Explain why the price of a European call and an American call can be different.

14. Explain what is meant by negative delta and negative gamma.

Sophisticated hedging techniques

O ver the past 20 years, financial intermediaries have developed an ever more sophisticated array of financial instruments designed for hedging risk. In Chapters 7–9 we
presented the most popular instruments and developed the methodology for pricing them.
In this chapter we will show how they can be applied to manage exchange rate risk.
Applications to interest rates and commodities will be addressed in Chapters 18 and 19.

The products examined in this chapter can be divided into two categories: those that are
more or less elaborate combinations of simple options and those that comprise what have
come to be called "exotic options".

Combinations of simple options

Calls and puts offer investors the possibility of adjusting risk exposure to desired levels.
New opportunities can be created by combining one or more simple options. The tunnel,
discussed in Chapter 15, is an example. The operations often seem complex and the
language that describes them is colorful. We can distinguish between two types of combinations. The first type, called **spreads**, combines options of different series but of the same
class, where some are bought and others are written. The second type, like **straddles** and
strangles, combines different types (calls and puts) of options.

Strategies based on call combinations

The simplest strategies combine the purchase and sale of calls with the same expiration date
but with different strike prices or with the same strike price but different expiration dates.
When the expiration date is the same and the strike price is different, they are called vertical
spreads. When the expiration date is different and the strike price is the same, they are called
horizontal spreads.

Purchased vertical spreads

Table 16.1 shows the quotes on the Philadelphia Stock Exchange for premiums on Swiss
franc calls at various strike prices and expiration dates.

Consider the two contracts July CHF 65½ and July CHF 66. Buying a July CHF 65½
and selling a July CHF 66, constitutes a purchased spread. It is called a purchased spread
because it requires an initial cash outlay – the premium paid is higher than the premium
received. It is also called a bullish spread because upward moves in the exchange rate will
make it profitable. On the other hand, if CHF 65½ had been sold and CHF 66 had been

Table 16.1 Quotes on Swiss franc calls on the Philadelphia Stock Exchange

Currency	Strike	July	August	September
CHF	63½	1.61	1.66	—
CHF	64	1.12	1.26	1.42
CHF	64½	0.75	1.14	—
CHF	65	0.54	0.85	1.08
CHF	65½	0.35	0.63	—
CHF	66	0.18	0.45	—

bought, we would have a bearish or written spread because it generates a cash inflow and downward moves in the exchange rate make it profitable.

Three types of purchased vertical spreads can be distinguished: "out-of-the-money", "at-the-money", and "in-the-money".

Out-of-the-money purchased (bullish) vertical spreads

An out-of-the-money purchased vertical spread involves buying a call with a strike price above the spot exchange rate and selling a call with the same expiration date and an even higher strike price. Both calls are out-of-the-money.

Consider the former purchased spread where CHF 65½ is purchased and CHF 66 is sold. If the spot exchange rate is 65.11 (USD 0.6511), this spread is out-of-the-money. Table 16.2 gives the outcomes of this position for different values of the exchange rate on the expiration date.

We can see that the cash outlay is 0.17 and the maximum that can be earned on the spread is 0.50. When he buys the July 65½ call the investor expects a rise in the exchange rate from 65.11 above 65.50. By selling the July 66 call he reduces his investment by more than half from 0.35 to 0.17. If the exchange rate stays below 65.50, both calls expire worthless and the investor loses 0.17. If it goes to 66, the spread is worth 0.50 and he makes a profit of 0.33 (0.50 − 0.17). If it goes above 66, however, his profit is limited to 0.33 because the call he sold at 66 will be exercised.

Figure 16.1 shows the payoff profile for the spread. It is only profitable if the exchange rate rises. It gives a better return than the simple purchase of a July 65½ call when the exchange rate stays below 66.529. Above this level, the simple call purchase yields a higher return. This can be verified by comparing the return on the spread [(0.5/0.17 − 1) = 194%] with the return on the simple call purchase at an exchange rate of 66.529: [(66.529 − 65.5)/0.35 − 1] = 194%.

Table 16.2 Sample outcomes of an out-of-the-money purchased vertical spread

Dates	Spot exchange rate	Call July 65½	Call July 66	Value of the spread
Transaction date	65.11	0.35	0.18	−0.17
Expiration date	65.11	0	0	0
Expiration date	65.50	0	0	0
Expiration date	66.00	0.50	0	0.50
Expiration date	66.50	1.00	0.50	0.50

Figure 16.1 Out-of-the-money purchased vertical spread

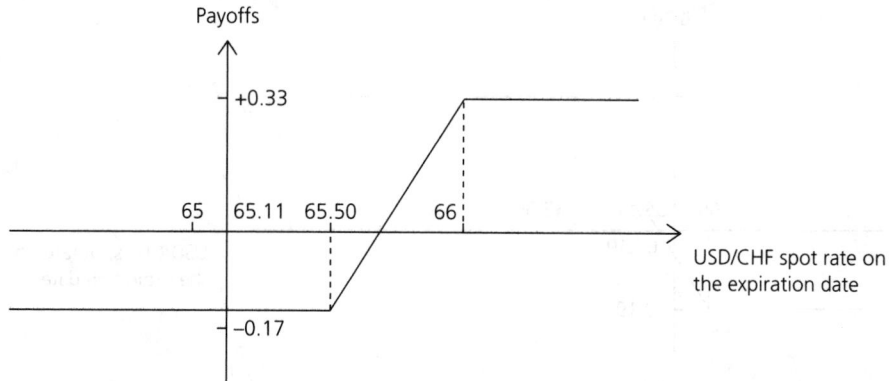

The strategy is advantageous insofar as the sale of the call reduces the cash outlay. The disadvantage is that profit is strictly limited to the difference between the strike prices.

At-the-money purchased vertical spreads

At-the-money purchased vertical spreads involve the purchase of an in-the-money call and the sale of an out-of-the-money call with the same expiration date. Suppose that the call July 65 in Table 16.1 is purchased and the call July 65½ is sold. Table 16.3 shows the outcomes for different exchange rates on the expiration date.

The maximum income from the spread is still 0.50, the difference in the strike prices, so the maximum profit is limited to 0.31, the difference between the maximum income and the cost of the spread. The maximum loss is also limited to the difference in the premiums. The difference between this strategy and the preceding out-of-the-money spread is that in order to be profitable the exchange rate does not have to appreciate as much. At 65.19 the breakeven point is reached. Any further increases up to 65.50 are pure profit. The advantage of this position is that the downside risk is limited to the net premium (0.19). The disadvantage is that income is capped at 0.50. Figure 16.2 shows the payoff profile of this at-the-money purchased vertical spread.

As a hedging strategy, this technique can be used for currencies where fluctuations are limited (by regulations for example). Figure 16.3 shows the profile of net cash flows in domestic currency (income minus expenditure) using the at-the-money purchased vertical spread as a hedge for an import transaction. Net income varies as expenditure goes up or

Table 16.3 Sample outcomes of an at-the-money purchased vertical spread

Dates	Spot exchange rate	Call July 65	Call July 65½	Value of the spread
Transaction date	65.11	0.54	0.35	−0.19
Expiration date	64.50	0	0	0
Expiration date	65.00	0	0	0
Expiration date	65.11	0.11	0	0.11
Expiration date	65.50	0.50	0	0.50
Expiration date	66.00	1.00	0.50	0.50

Figure 16.2 At-the-money purchased vertical spread

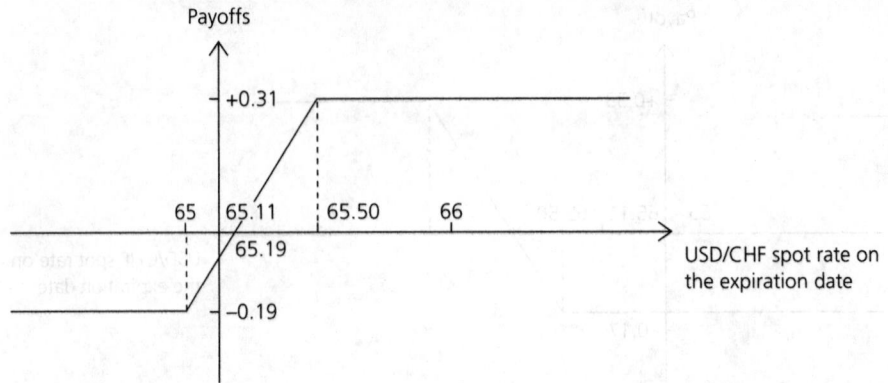

down with different levels of the exchange rate. In the zone between the strike prices the hedge is effective. At exchange rates below the lower strike price, the importer benefits from the depreciation because neither call is exercised. At exchange rates above the higher strike price, the importer is exposed to currency risk because both calls will be exercised, the one offsetting the other and thereby making it necessary to obtain the foreign exchange to pay for the merchandise at the spot rate.

In-the-money purchased vertical spreads

In-the-money purchased vertical spreads involve the purchase of an in-the-money call and the sale of another in-the-money call but with a strike price higher than the call that is purchased. An investor in this position is not hoping for a rise in the exchange rate. He is hoping that the exchange rate stays at its current level or at least that it does not go below the strike price of the written call.

Table 16.4 shows the outcomes at different exchange rates for an in-the-money purchased vertical spread composed of a purchased July CHF 64 and a written July CHF 64½. The cost of the spread is 0.37 and this is the most that can be lost if the exchange rate falls below the strike price of the purchased call. The most that can be earned from the spread is 0.50 for a profit of 0.13, if the exchange rate stays above the strike price of the written call. Thus, it is not an increase in the exchange rate that generates the profit. It is the

Figure 16.3 A hedging strategy using an at-the-money purchased vertical spread

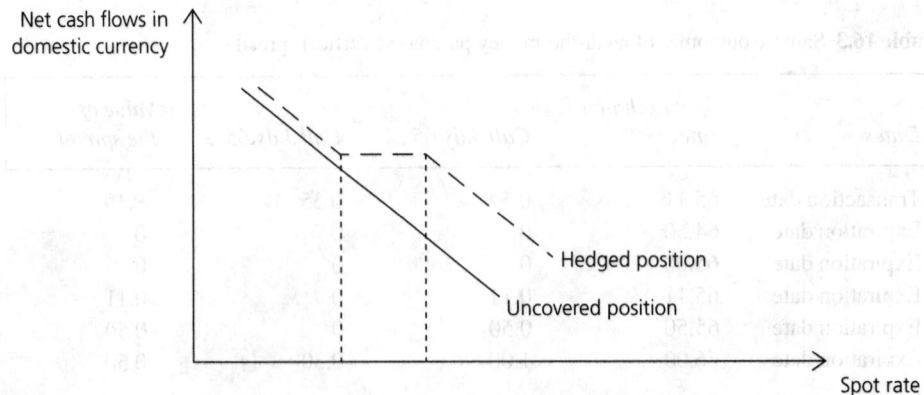

Table 16.4 Sample outcomes of an in-the-money purchased vertical spread

Dates	Spot exchange rate	Call July 64	Call July 64½	Value of the spread
Transaction date	65.11	1.12	0.75	−0.37
Expiration date	63.50	0	0	0
Expiration date	64.00	0	0	0
Expiration date	64.50	0.50	0	0.50
Expiration date	65.00	1.00	0.50	0.50
Expiration date	65.11	1.11	0.61	0.50

time value factor. The written option has a higher time value than the purchased option. Remember that the time value is the difference between the premium and the intrinsic value. The intrinsic value is the difference between the exchange rate and the strike price. The intrinsic value of the purchased call is $65.11 - 64 = 1.11$ and the time value is $1.12 - 1.11 = 0.01$. The intrinsic value of the written call is $65.11 - 64.50 = 0.61$ and the time value is $0.75 - 0.61 = 0.14$. The difference in the time values is $0.14 - 0.01 = 0.13$, the maximum profit that can be earned on the spread.

An in-the-money purchased vertical spread will be most profitable when the difference in the time values is the most pronounced. In Chapter 8 we saw that this is the case in periods of high implied volatility. Consequently, an in-the-money purchased vertical spread reflects a contrary point of view. Whereas the market anticipates a certain level of volatility, the holder of this kind of spread is signaling a belief in stability.

If he is wrong, what happens? Figure 16.4 shows the payoff profile for this position. If the exchange rate goes up, he realizes the maximum profit but he loses the benefit of the increase. He would have been better off with an out-of-the-money spread. If the market goes down he can lose all of his outlay. His loss will be partial if the exchange rate stays between the two strike prices. Therefore, this is not one of the riskiest strategies. It suits investors that want to play on volatility and it can generate respectable returns for a financial profit center.

One note of caution is in order. Where American calls are concerned, an in-the-money bullish vertical spread has the added risk of early exercise because the written call is in-the-money. If that happens, the spread is undone.

Figure 16.4 In-the-money purchased vertical spread

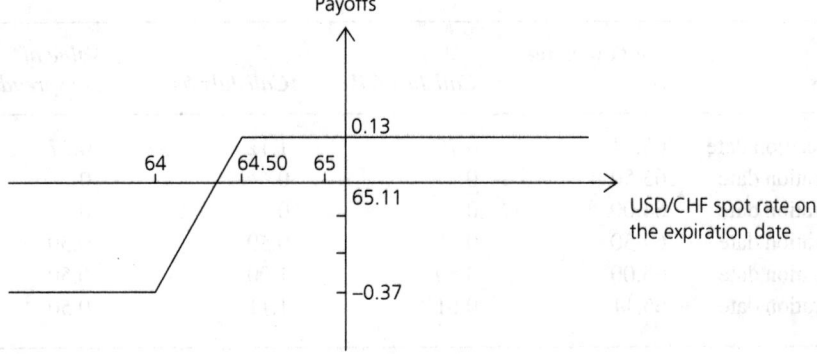

To summarize, then, we can say that the three foregoing strategies are rich in opportunities. Although they are similar in appearance, in fact they have distinct risk–return profiles that are suited to different investment goals and market conditions.

Written vertical spreads

Written vertical spreads generate a net cash inflow at the outset. They are also called bearish spreads because a favorable outcome depends on a fall in the exchange rate. As with the purchased vertical spreads, written vertical spreads can be grouped into three categories: out-of-the-money, at-the-money, and in-the-money.

Out-of-the-money written vertical spreads.

An out-of-the-money written vertical spread consists of the purchase of a call with a strike price below the spot exchange rate and a sale of another call with the same expiration date and a lower strike price. In fact, each individual call is in-the-money because the strike prices are below the current exchange rate. The spread, however, is out-of-the-money because the exchange rate must fall for the investor to make a profit.

Table 16.5 shows the outcomes of a spread composed of the sale of a July 64 and the purchase of a July 64½ for different levels of the exchange rate. The simultaneous sale and purchase gives the investor a net inflow of 0.37 at the outset. On the expiration date the most he can pay out is 0.50, the difference between the strike prices. Thus, his maximum loss is 0.13. If the exchange rate falls below 64, neither option will be exercised and his maximum profit is 0.37, the difference between the two premiums.

Figure 16.5 shows the payoff profile for this position. Notice that it is symmetrical to the in-the-money purchased vertical spread. At levels of the exchange rate above 64.50, the investor loses 0.13. As it drops below 64.50, the position improves until it reaches 64. At 64 it realizes its maximum profit of 0.37. Although this position is out-of-the-money, both calls are in-the-money and the one that is sold could be the object of an early exercise if it is an American option.

At-the-money and in-the-money written vertical spreads

We do not have to go through each one of these spreads because they are symmetrical with the at-the-money and out-of-the-money purchased vertical spreads. An at-the-money written vertical spread is similar to a forward contract with upper and lower limits, whereas an in-the-money written vertical spread is speculation on the stability of the exchange rate.

Figure 16.6 shows the outcome profile of an at-the-money and an in-the-money written vertical spread. For the at-the-money spread a small fall in the exchange rate makes the position

Table 16.5 Sample outcomes of an out-of-the-money written vertical spread

Dates	Spot exchange rate	Call July 64½	Call July 64	Value of the spread
Transaction date	65.11	0.75	1.12	0.37
Expiration date	63.50	0	0	0
Expiration date	64.00	0	0	0
Expiration date	64.50	0	0.50	–0.50
Expiration date	65.00	0.50	1.00	–0.50
Expiration date	65.11	0.61	1.11	–0.50

Figure 16.5 Out-of-the-money written vertical spread

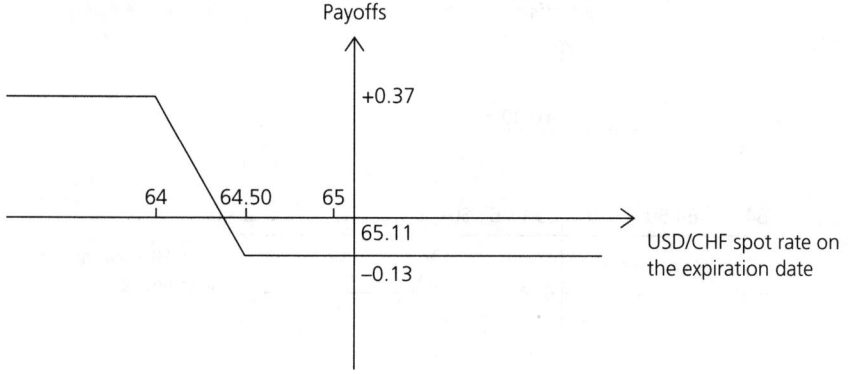

Figure 16.6 At-the-money and in-the-money written vertical spreads

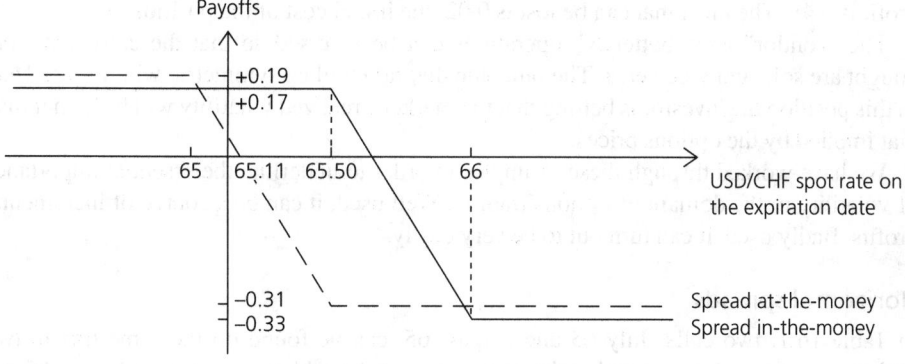

profitable. If the rate rises, losses are limited to the difference in the strike prices less the income from the difference in the premiums. The in-the-money spread is a bet against a big rise in the exchange rate, which is profitable as long as the increase in the exchange rate is small.

Combinations of purchased and written vertical spreads.

Both the written and purchased in-the-money vertical spreads are bets against large moves in the exchange rate, contrary to the market's anticipations reflected in the implied volatility. The spreads, then, have the same goal and can be used together. In this case, the investor should buy a call well in-the-money, the July 64 for example, and sell a call a little less in-the-money, the July 64½. This position corresponds to the purchased in-the-money vertical spread. He should also sell a call out-of-the-money, the July 65½, and buy a call well out-of-the-money. This position corresponds to the written in-the-money vertical spread. The whole operation is called a "condor". Figure 16.7 shows the payoff profile. The position is profitable within the narrow band of stability and unprofitable everywhere else. One advantage of this operation is that it has a low cost insofar as the income from the written position helps to offset the outlay for the purchased position. Because of the multiple transactions, operations like this can only be realized when costs for each transaction are low.

A well known variation of the condor is called the "butterfly spread". In this scenario, the two calls that are sold have the same strike price. For example, buy July 64½, sell two calls July 65, and buy one July 65½. From Table 16.1 we can see that this generates a cost of $0.75 - (2 \times 0.54) + 0.35 = 0.02$. Figure 16.8 shows the payoff profile. The maximum

Figure 16.7 A "condor" based on calls

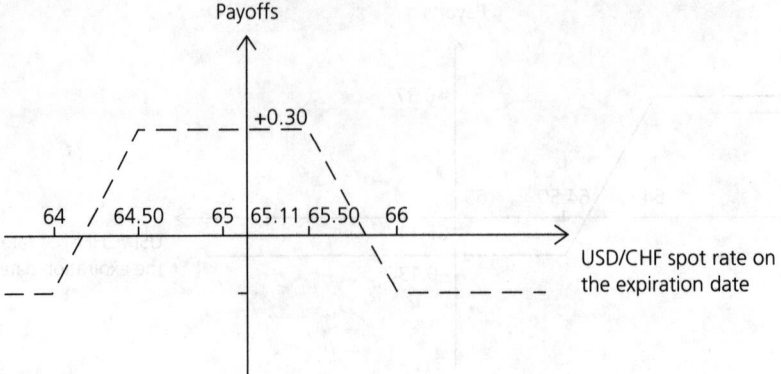

profit will be realized if the spot exchange rate is at 65. At this point income is 0.50 and profit is 0.48. The most that can be lost is 0.02, the initial cost of the position.

The "condor" and "butterfly" operations can be reversed so that the calls that were bought are sold and vice versa. The outcome diagram will be symmetric with Figure 16.8. In this position the investor is betting that the market's realized volatility will be higher than that implied by the options prices.

We have worked through these examples in order to underline the essential importance of volatility in the domain of options trading. Well used, it can be a source of incremental profits. Badly used, it can turn out to be very costly.

Horizontal spreads

In Table 16.1, two calls, July 65 and August 65, can be found on the same line in two different columns. A purchased horizontal spread can be achieved by buying August 65 and

Figure 16.8 A "butterfly" spread

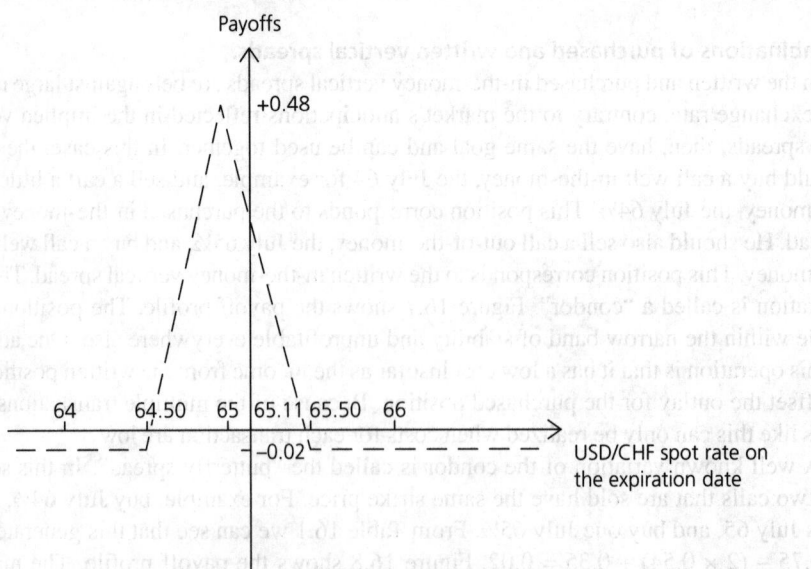

selling July 65. The difference in price is 0.85 – 0.54 = 0.31. The investor in this position is hoping that the price differential will widen either because of a more rapid depreciation in the price of the call that was sold or a more rapid appreciation in the price of the call that was purchased. Because both calls will be affected simultaneously by variations in the exchange rate, the effect of the passage of time is the key to the investor's position.

As in the case of vertical spreads, three types of purchased horizontal spreads are available: in-the-money, at-the-money, and out-of-the-money.

An in-the-money purchased horizontal spread involves buying and selling calls that are in-the-money; an at-the-money purchased horizontal spread involves calls that are at-the-money; and an out-of-the-money purchased horizontal spread involves calls that are out-of-the-money. In the following paragraphs we will limit the discussion to at-the-money horizontal spreads because on the organized exchanges these are the only instruments with enough liquidity to make them feasible.

The analysis of a horizontal spread is more delicate than that of a vertical spread. Take the July–August 65 horizontal spread above. On the July expiration date the July call will either have a value of zero or a value equal to the difference between the exchange rate and the strike price. The August call, however, will still have a month to live. Its value will depend on the level of the exchange rate as well as on volatility and the interest rate differential. In order to simplify the analysis, suppose that between the end of June and the July expiration date nothing changes. The July call is exercised for a gain of 0.11 and the August call is worth what the July call was worth at the end of June: 0.54. The spread is worth 0.54 – 0.11 = 0.43. Since the cost of the spread was 0.31 (0.85 – 0.54), there is a profit of 0.12.

The profit appears because the call that was sold depreciated faster than the purchased call. The reason is because the loss of time value was higher for the July call than for the August call. This result has nothing to do with the particular data in the example. Shorter-term options always lose time value faster than longer-term options. In other words, shorter-term options have higher absolute values of theta. The profit is derived from exploiting this phenomenon. As we will see, the profit is maximum when the exchange rate remains stable. A horizontal spread is speculation on the passage of time.

The result will be quite different if the exchange rate undergoes a sharp rise or fall. A sharp fall in the exchange rate at the end of July will cause the July call to expire worthless. The value of the August call will not be worth much either because it has become a long way out-of-the-money. The horizontal spread that cost 0.31 is now worth very little. The larger the fall in the exchange rate, the closer the value of the spread comes to zero.

A sharp rise in the exchange rate will put the calls well in-the-money. On the expiration date, then, the July call will be worth its intrinsic value and the August call will not be worth much more than its intrinsic value. Remember from Chapter 8 that the time value of an option is highest when the option is at-the-money. As the value of the exchange rate gets farther from the strike price, the option's time value decreases. Take a look back at Table 16.1. The July 64 is worth 1.12. The intrinsic value is 1.11, which means that the time value is only 0.01. Suppose that the exchange rate goes to 67. The July call will be worth 2 and the August call might be worth around 2.01. The value of the spread is worth only 0.01. Most of the initial outlay has been lost. Figure 16.9 shows the payoff profile for the spread.

Thus, the at-the-money purchased horizontal spread is a bet on the stability of the exchange rate. Reversing the spread by buying the shortest maturity and selling the longest would be the strategy to follow if the investor feels that volatility will be higher than that which is implicit in the premiums for the calls.

Other combinations of calls

It is clear by now that the possible permutations of call combinations are almost limitless. Most of them are not practical because of insufficient liquidity, high transaction costs or

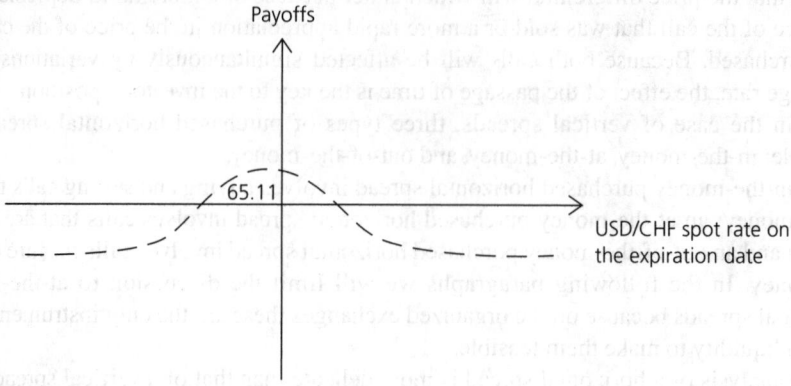

Figure 16.9 A horizontal purchased spread at-the-money

inadequate returns. There are two that we should mention, though, because they can be useful for international risk management: the diagonal spread and the ratio spread.

Diagonal spread

In a diagonal spread, one call is bought and another sold but with different strike prices and different expiration dates. In reality, a diagonal spread is a combination of a vertical spread and a horizontal spread. The investor buys a call with a relatively long time to expiration and sells another call with a shorter time to expiration and a higher strike price. The diagonal spread can be analyzed like a vertical spread with the advantage of a horizontal spread to back it up. Normally, the premium on the purchased call depreciates more slowly than the premium on the written call because, other things being equal, the absolute value of at-the-money thetas are higher for shorter-term options. The longer-term call costs more but its resale value is higher.

A diagonal spread can also be analyzed like a horizontal spread with the advantage of a vertical spread. Since the strike price of the written call is higher, possible gains from an appreciation of the exchange rate are also higher. The disadvantage of the diagonal spread is that it is more costly. In fact, its cost is equal to the sum of the cost of a vertical spread and a horizontal spread.

The purchase of an August 65½ call and the sale of a July 66 call are an example of a diagonal spread. It can be analyzed as the sum of a horizontal spread [August 65½ purchased, July 65½ sold] and a vertical spread [July 65½ purchased, July 66 sold].

Ratio spread

A ratio spread involves taking any spread already encountered and augmenting it with the purchase or sale of one or more calls. Possible combinations are limited only by the imagination of the investor. Understanding how they work, however, is simple. One of the sides of the spread is doubled or tripled. For example, a purchased out-of-the-money vertical ratio spread could be composed of two July 65½ purchased and one July 66 sold. Table 16.6 and Figure 16.10 summarize the characteristics and possible outcomes of this spread.

Because two calls are purchased, the cost is higher. The ratio is 2/1, or two purchased against one sold. Thus the payoff is doubled compared to a simple spread.

Either side of the spread could have been multiplied. For example, two July 66 could have been sold and one July 65½ bought. Indeed, this 1/2 ratio is less bullish than the 2/1 ratio spread or the simple vertical spread. Its payoff profile is illustrated in Figure 16.11.

Table 16.6 Sample outcomes of an out-of-the-money purchased vertical ratio spread

Dates	Spot exchange rate	Call July 65½	Call July 66	Value of the spread
Transaction date	65.11	0.35	0.18	−0.52
Expiration date	65.11	0	0	0
Expiration date	65.50	0	0	0
Expiration date	66.00	0.50	0	1.00
Expiration date	66.50	1.00	0.50	1.50
Expiration date	67.00	1.50	1.00	2.00

Figure 16.10 An out-of-the-money purchased vertical ratio spread (2/1)

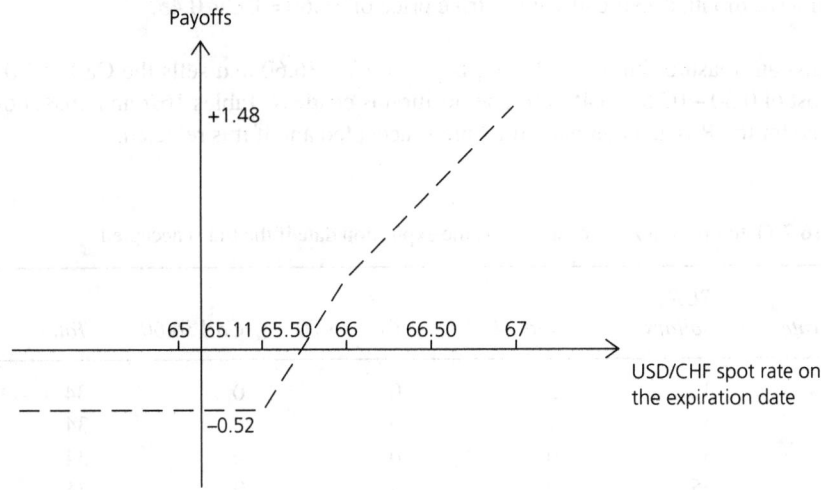

Figure 16.11 A purchased vertical ratio spread (1/2)

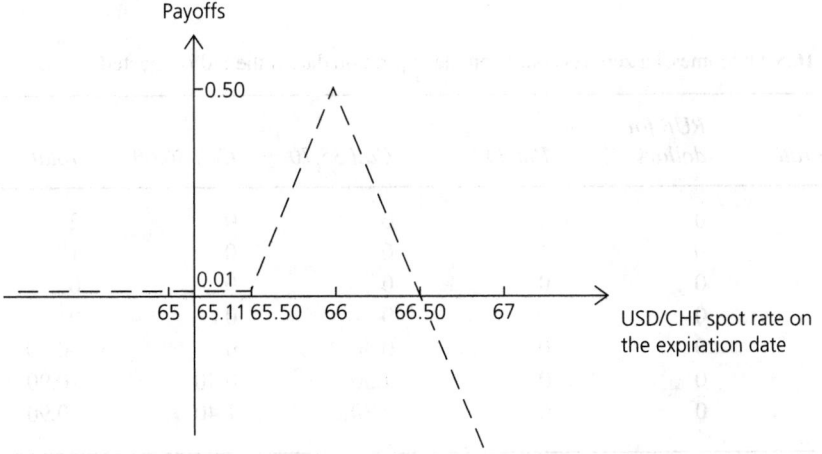

Zero premium reversibles

Vertical spreads can be combined with a simple option hedge to create what are called reversible positions. They are useful when conditions are such that the simple option hedge might prove to be unnecessary. This is possible, for example, when making a competitive bid on a contract.

Take the case of a Russian company tendering a bid for a project in US dollars. To cover the bid price, the company could buy dollar puts for Russian rubles. If their bid is accepted, their income in Russian rubles will be assured. If it is rejected, the worst they can do is lose the premium. In order to reduce the cost of the hedge it is decided to buy out-of-the-money puts. The puts cannot be too far out-of-the-money, though. Otherwise the coverage will be insufficient. By combining the required put coverage with a written vertical hedge, the Russian company can improve its position.

Suppose that the company treasurer is faced with the following conditions:

S(RUR/USD) = 35.35
Cost of a six-month dollar put with a strike price of 34 = RUR 0.30 per USD
Cost of a six-month dollar call with a strike price of 35.70 = RUR 0.75
Cost of a six-month dollar call with a strike price of 36.60 = RUR 0.45.

The Russian treasurer buys the Put 34, buys the Call 36.60 and sells the Call 35.70 for a total cost of 0.30 − 0.75 + 0.45 = 0. The position is costless. Tables 16.7 and 16.8 show the outcome for the Russian company if its bid is accepted and if it is rejected.

Table 16.7 Outcome of a zero reversible on the expiration date if the bid is accepted

Spot rate	RUR for dollars	Put 34	Call 35.70	Call 36.60	Total
32	32	2	0	0	34
33	33	1	0	0	34
34	34	0	0	0	34
35	35	0	0	0	35
36	36	0	0.30	0	35.70
37	37	0	1.30	0.40	36.10
38	38	0	2.30	1.40	37.10

Table 16.8 Outcome of a zero reversible on the expiration date if the bid is rejected

Spot rate	RUR for dollars	Put 34	Call 35.70	Call 36.60	Total
32	0	2	0	0	2
33	0	1	0	0	1
34	0	0	0	0	0
35	0	0	0	0	0
36	0	0	0.30	0	−0.30
37	0	0	1.30	0.40	−0.90
38	0	0	2.30	1.40	−0.90

In Table 16.7 we can see that if the bid is accepted, the company locks in a floor price of RUR 34 for no additional cost. If the dollar appreciates, it will benefit from the appreciation for a cost of RUR 0.90, the difference between the strike prices of the two calls. The risks are limited and the hedge is still conditional on the outcome of the bid. Figure 16.12 illustrates the outcome profile of the position in the case of a successful bid.

Table 16.8 shows the company's position if the bid is rejected. It still benefits if the dollar falls below 34. Between 34 and 35.70 there is no loss and no gain. At dollar levels above 35.70 the maximum cost to the company is 0.90. By combining the vertical spread with the put, the cost of the put has been transformed into a potential cost that will only be due if the exchange rate rises significantly.

Strategies based on put combinations

All the foregoing combinations using calls can be applied to puts where we find the four major spread categories: purchased vertical spreads, written vertical spreads, and purchased and written horizontal spreads. We will not go back through the detailed list as applied to puts, but will limit ourselves to three basic examples and then tie everything together with a discussion of the links that exist between call and put-based spreads.

The logic of put-based spreads

Put-based spreads can be out-of-the-money, at-the-money and in-the-money.

Purchased vertical spreads

In a purchased vertical spread the investor buys one put and simultaneously sells another with the same expiration date but a lower strike price. The spreads are in-the-money if both strike prices are higher than the spot exchange rate. They are at-the-money if the strike price of the purchased put is above the spot rate and the written put is below it. They are out-of-the-money if both strike prices are below the spot exchange rate. Whereas the out-of-the-money purchased vertical spread composed of calls was a bet on a rise in the exchange rate, the out-of-the-money purchased vertical spread composed of puts is a bet on a fall in the exchange rate. The maximum return is achieved when the exchange rate falls to the level of the lower strike price. Figure 16.13 shows the payoff profile of this type of spread for the CHF/USD exchange rate when a put with a strike price of 64.5 is purchased and one with a strike price of 64 is sold. The net cost is 0.13,

Figure 16.12 Hedging with a zero reversible

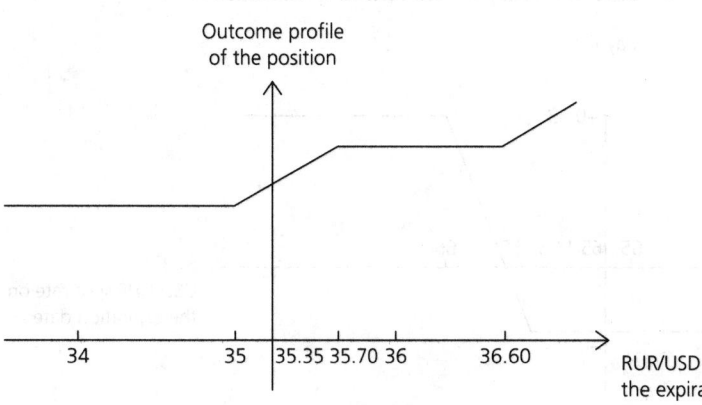

Outcome profile
of the position

34   35   35.35 35.70 36   36.60   RUR/USD spot rate on
the expiration date

Figure 16.13 A purchased vertical spread based on puts

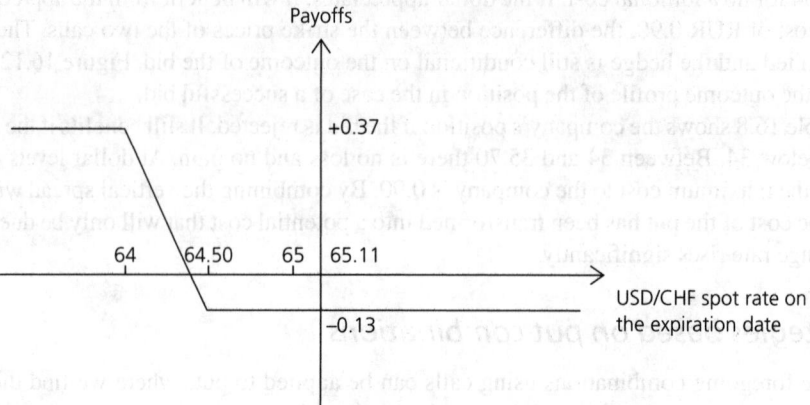

which is lost if the exchange rate stays above 64.50. The maximum gain is 0.37 if the exchange rate falls below 64.

Written vertical spreads

In a written vertical spread the investor buys one put and sells another with the same expiration date but a higher strike price. The spreads can be in-the-money, at-the-money or out-of-the-money. Whereas the written vertical spread composed of calls was a bet on a fall in the exchange rate, a written vertical spread composed of puts is a bet on a rise in the exchange rate. The maximum return is achieved when the exchange rate rises to the level of the higher strike price. Figure 16.14 illustrates the payoff profile.

Horizontal spreads

In a horizontal spread the investor buys a put with a relatively long time to maturity and simultaneously sells another with the same strike price but a shorter time to expiration. The spreads can be in-the-money, at-the-money or out-of-the-money. Horizontal spreads with puts work like horizontal spreads with calls. They are a bet on the evolution of the time value of the two puts with a maximum return achieved when the exchange rate is equal to the strike price on the expiration date of the shortest-term put.

Figure 16.14 An out-of-the-money written vertical spread based on puts

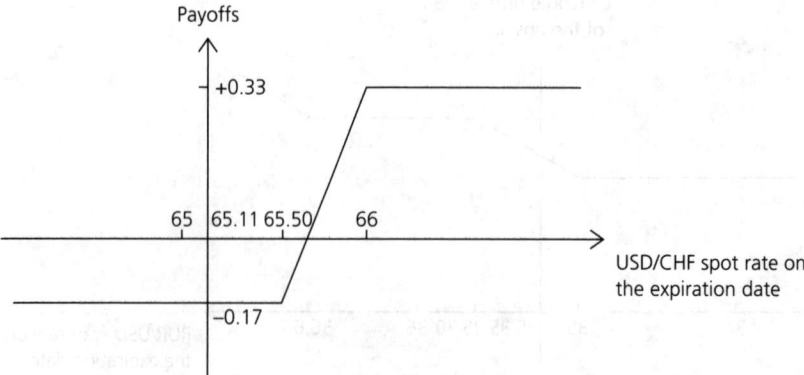

Links between call-based spreads and put-based spreads

The three preceding examples underline the similarities between certain spreads composed of puts and spreads composed of calls. The similarities are not surprising if we remember from Chapter 8 that a European put is the equivalent of a European call combined with a forward contract. Although the relationship is not exact for American options, it is close enough to justify the similarities between spreads.

For example, using put–call parity, we can say that a purchased vertical spread composed of a purchased put at 65½ and a written put at 65 is equivalent to a forward sale at 65½, the purchase of a call with a strike price of 65½, a forward purchase at 65 and the sale of a call with a strike price of 65. The purchase of a call at 65½ and the sale of a call at 65 is a written vertical spread and the relationship is explicit. The forward purchase at 65½ combined with a forward sale at 65 generates a cost of ½ that can be considered as a deposit necessary to cover the risks from the written spread. This equivalency relationship applies to all spreads composed of calls and all spreads composed of puts.

Relative advantages and disadvantages of call and put spreads

Although call spreads have their put spread equivalents, the two strategies are not always financially equivalent. The relationships that have been developed up to now have abstracted from the cost of undertaking transactions and the possibility of early exercise. In practice, equivalent strategies can generate different transaction costs or be more or less susceptible to early exercise. An in-the-money purchased vertical call spread, for example, has a high probability of early exercise if the underlying currency is at a forward discount. Furthermore, it is probable that in order to realize his profit (loss) on the expiration date, the investor will be forced to repurchase the written option and sell the purchased one, thereby incurring incremental transaction costs. On the other hand, the equivalent put spread has little chance of being exercised early. Furthermore, if the operation succeeds, the puts will have a value of zero and will not have to be exercised on the expiration date for the investor to realize his profit, thereby eliminating the transaction costs associated with closing out his position. The saving in transaction costs and the low risk of early exercise make the put spread preferable to the call spread. Considerations such as this make it important for investors to have a clear theoretical and practical understanding of the ins and outs of the strategies that they intend to implement.

Table 16.9 Correspondence between call spreads and put spreads

Call spreads	Put spreads
Out-of-the-money purchased vertical	Out-of-the-money written vertical
At-the-money purchased vertical	At-the-money written vertical
In-the-money purchased vertical	In-the-money written vertical
Out-of-the-money written vertical	Out-of-the-money purchased vertical
At-the-money written vertical	At-the-money purchased vertical
In-the-money written vertical	In-the-money purchased vertical
Out-of-the-money horizontal	In-the-money horizontal
At-the-money horizontal	At-the-money horizontal
In-the-money horizontal	Out-of-the-money horizontal

Other combinations of puts

All the more complex combinations of calls that we examined can be reproduced with puts. This rewarding exercise we will leave to the reader, although Table 16.9 will be a valuable aid. This having been said, it should not be forgotten that complex strategies suffer in practice from the existence of transaction costs, early exercise and the technical difficulties involved in synchronizing the execution of such complicated orders, even in efficient markets.

Straddles and strangles

When the purchase of a call is combined with the purchase of a put, the result is either a **straddle** or a **strangle**. A straddle is when the two options have the same strike price and expiration date. In the other cases a strangle results.

Straddles

An investor buys a straddle when he expects a sudden large rise or fall in the underlying exchange rate.

Risk and return

When a sharp rise occurs, the call generates a profit while the put becomes worthless. When a sharp fall occurs, the put generates a profit while the call becomes worthless. The rise or fall must be sharp enough to offset the cost of buying the options. If the rise is not sharp enough, the straddle will generate a loss. The loss is maximum when the exchange rate ends up at the strike price on the expiration date. To summarize, then, we can say that a straddle strategy will end in a loss if the exchange rate stays stable or moves only moderately.

Table 16.10 shows some possible outcomes of a straddle with a strike price of 65 and a July expiration date. The straddle costs 1.12, the sum of the two premiums. Its breakeven points are attained when the gain on one of the two options is high enough to offset the cost. This occurs at an exchange rate of 66.12 or 63.88. The possibility of a total loss is quite small. For this to happen, the exchange rate would have to end up at exactly 65. More often than not, losses that do occur are only partial. In this sense, a straddle is less risky than the purchase of a simple put or call. On the other hand, possible returns are also more limited. For example, when the exchange rate is at 64, the holder of a simple put will have a profit of 0.42 for a return of 78% on his investment (0.42/0.58). A straddle holder will have a loss of 0.12 for a return of –11% on his

Table 16.10 An example of a straddle

Dates	Spot exchange rate	Call July 65	Put July 65	Value of the straddle
Transaction date	65.11	0.54	0.58	–1.12
Expiration date	63.00	0	2.00	2.00
Expiration date	64.00	0	1.00	1.00
Expiration date	65.00	0	0	0
Expiration date	66.00	1.00	0	1.00
Expiration date	67.00	2.00	0	2.00

investment (–0.12/1.12) . A call holder would have lost his entire investment of 0.54 for a return of –100%. Figure 16.15 depicts the outcome profile of the foregoing straddle. Straddles are useful when a wide swing in the exchange rate is expected but the direction of the swing is unknown.

Managing a straddle

The above example situated the straddle at-the-money because this corresponds to a straddle's internal logic. However, there is no reason why a straddle in-the-money or out-of-the-money could not be constructed. A straddle can also be constructed with options having relatively long expiration times. A longer-term straddle would cost more of course but there is also a greater chance of a sharp move in the exchange rate. Exactly how the straddle is to be set up depends on the investor's anticipations concerning the evolution of the exchange rate.

Managing a straddle also requires knowing when to close it out. Closing out the straddle before its expiration would be justified if a sharp upward or downward move takes place and one of the two options acquires a significant intrinsic value. Early closure would also be justified if a sharp increase in volatility causes an important rise in the time value of the two options. In this case it would be better to take advantage of the gains before the passage of time wears them away.

Closing out the whole position, of course, is not always necessary. In the case where one of the two options acquires significant intrinsic value, it might be better to close out this side only, because most of the profit is here. The other option will be far out-of-the-money with little time value and holding onto it will save transaction costs. Furthermore, something might be gained if the exchange rate starts to move the other way.

Strangles

Buying a strangle corresponds to the same type of logic as a straddle: an expected sharp move in the exchange rate one way or the other. When an investor buys a call and simultaneously buys a put with the same expiration date but with a different strike price, he has purchased a strangle. Figure 16.16 shows the payoff profile of this kind of position. The loss is total if the exchange rate stays between the two strike prices. The breakeven points are therefore farther apart than in the case of a straddle. The advantage of a strangle resides in the lower premiums due to the fact that the two options are out-of-the-money.

Figure 16.15 An example of a straddle

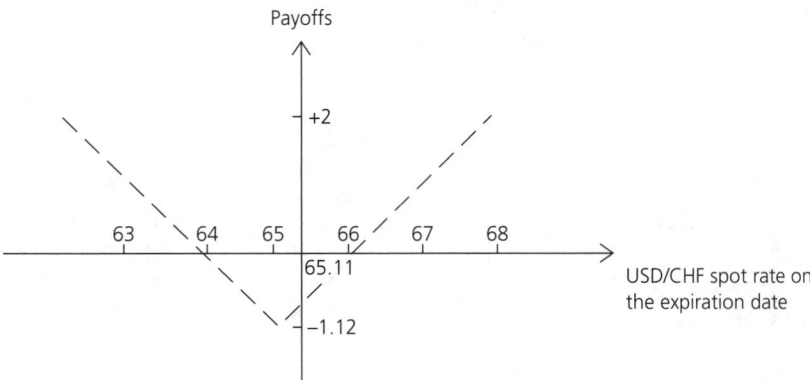

Figure 16.16 An example of a strangle

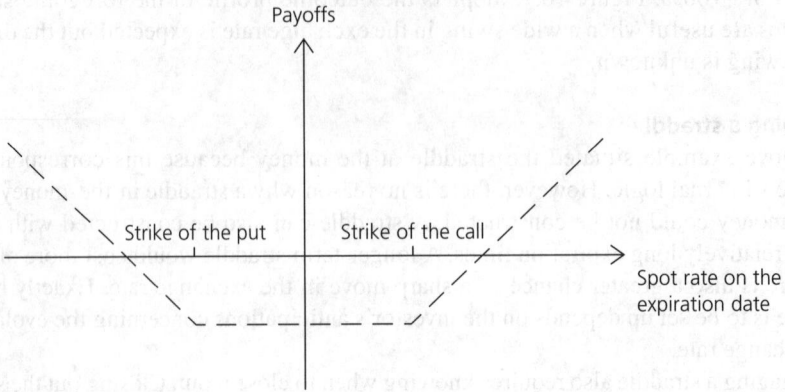

Selling straddles and strangles

If straddles and strangles can be bought, they can also be sold. A written straddle or strangle consists of the sale of a call and a put. Consequently, the risks are high. Since the risks are high, written straddles and strangles should only be entered into by knowledgeable investors.

Figure 16.17 illustrates the payoff profile of straddles and strangles. At first glance a written straddle or strangle seems unreasonable. Upside and downside risk is virtually unlimited while potential profits are strictly limited and relatively small. The strategy can be appropriate, however, when the exchange rate is expected to remain stable or when volatility is expected to drop. Because of the inherent risk associated with written straddles and strangles, they should only be undertaken on organized exchanges where the position can be easily closed out in the case of adverse moves in the exchange rate.

Exotic options

The over-the-counter options markets have outgrown their development stage and become mature markets, at least for products involving exchange rates and interest rates. Consequently, the margins that banks can charge for these products has fallen sharply.

Figure 16.17 Examples of a written strangle and straddle

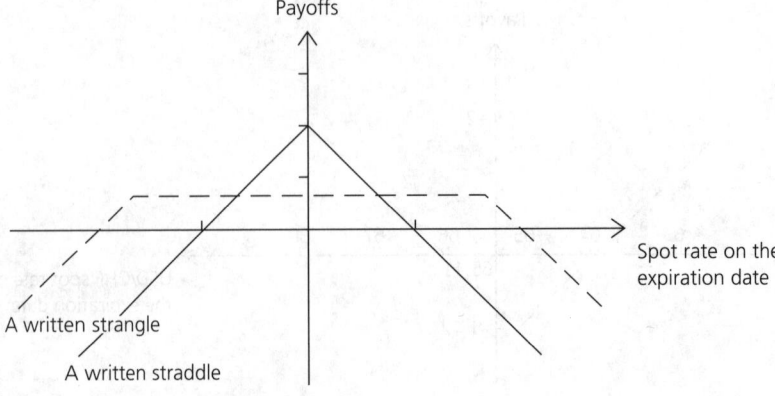

Furthermore, as investors have learned to use options, they have also become aware of their limits and disadvantages, including high initial costs and the necessity of constant monitoring. Based on this, the banks have sought innovative new products as a means of developing new markets. The fruits of their effort gave birth to what are called exotic options that we introduced in Chapter 9. Some of these exotic options have proven to be popular and useful for managing foreign exchange risk. In this section we will present several examples that underline how they can be used.

Lookback currency options

From Chapter 9 we know that a **lookback option** gives its holder the right to purchase or sell foreign exchange at the most favorable exchange rate realized over the life of the option. The buyer of a lookback call, for example, has the right to purchase a certain amount of foreign exchange at the lowest exchange rate realized between the creation of the call and its expiration date. The buyer of a lookback put has the right to sell foreign exchange at the highest exchange rate realized between its creation and its expiration date. In other words, the strike price of a lookback option is not known until the expiration date. This is the fundamental difference between a traditional option and a lookback. Since the new twist is favorable to the owner, the premium on a lookback is higher than the premium on a traditional option. Historically the premium has been approximately twice as high.

The major features of a lookback option can be summarized in three examples:

1. Suppose that the exchange rate follows a path of regular growth over the life of the option, as in Figure 16.18. In this case, the strike for a lookback call will be the first exchange rate. A traditional at-the-money call written at the same time as the lookback would have the same strike price. It would, therefore, give the same result. Because the cost would be much lower, the traditional call would give a better result than the lookback. Lookbacks are not appropriate instruments for situations when the exchange rate is in a period of expected regular appreciation.

2. Suppose now that the exchange rate depreciates regularly over the period, as in Figure 16.19. The strike price for the lookback will be the last exchange rate. Here again, the lookback is less attractive than a traditional at-the-money call. The traditional at-the-money call would cost much less than the lookback. On the expiration date, it would be out-of-the-money and would expire worthless. However, the investor could obtain the foreign exchange at the spot rate, the same rate as the strike price for the lookback.

Figure 16.18 A lookback call when the exchange rate follows a path of regular growth

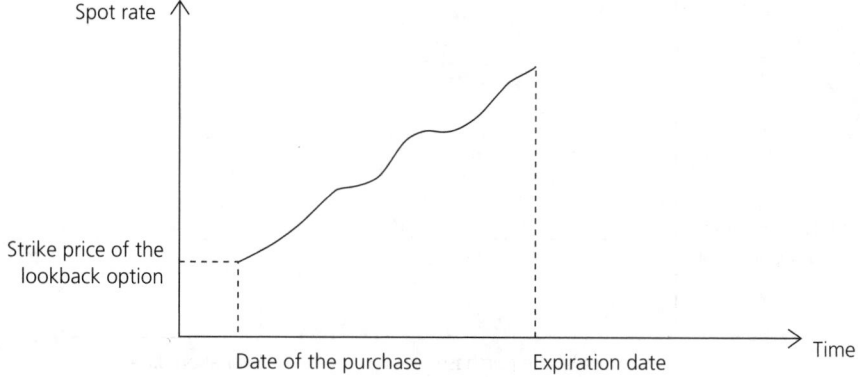

Figure 16.19 A lookback call when the exchange rate follows a path of regular depreciation

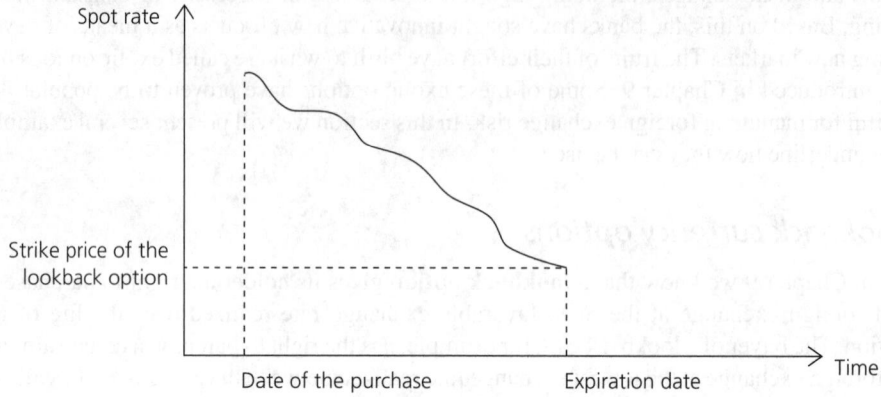

Because the premium for the traditional call is lower than for the lookback, the overall cost of the foreign exchange would be lower for the traditional call holder. Lookbacks are not appropriate instruments for situations when the exchange rate is in a period of expected regular depreciation.

3. Suppose, as in Figure 16.20, that the exchange rate is in a period of high volatility. The lookback strike price would be below the exchange rate registered on the first and last days of the option's life. Thus, it would be lower than the strike price of the traditional call option. For the lookback to be preferred to the traditional call option, the difference between the minimum rate over the life of the option and the beginning rate must be larger than the difference between the premium of the lookback and the traditional at-the-money call.

The analysis of lookback puts is symmetrical to that of lookback calls. In general, lookback options are especially attractive during periods of relatively high volatility for firms unable or unwilling to pay a higher price than their competitors for their foreign currency. This would be the case, for example, for a company with a payment to be made at the beginning of a period when the exchange rate is expected to experience a temporary decline. A lookback would make it possible to take advantage of the decline even after the payment has been made.

Figure 16.20 A lookback call in a period of high volatility

Average rate options

An average rate option gives its owner the right to the nominal amount of the difference between the strike price and the arithmetic average of the daily spot exchange rates realized over the life of the option. This type of option makes it possible to hedge a series of daily cash inflows over a given period in one single contract.

In practice, it operates like this. The company treasurer changes his foreign currency income day by day at the exchange rate of the moment. On the expiration date of his average rate option, if the average rate is lower than the strike price, he receives the difference between the two. A lower average rate means that over the life of the option he has been changing his foreign currency income at a relatively unfavorable rate. The payoff from the option enables him to make up the difference so that he effectively has changed all his foreign income at the strike price less the value of the premium. If the average rate is higher than the strike price, the option expires worthless. A higher average rate means that over the life of the option he has been changing his foreign currency income at a favorable rate. His effective exchange rate is the average rate diminished by the value of the premium.

It is important to note that an average rate option is not the same thing as the purchase of a series of options with the same strike price, each one expiring on a different day over the period to be covered. In this case some options would be exercised while others would expire worthless. Consequently, the average effective rate would be higher than the strike price. Because the outcome for this strategy is higher than the outcome for the average rate option, its premium should be higher.

We can look at this in another way. The underlying support for a normal option is the spot exchange rate. The underlying support for an average rate option is the average rate. An average is less volatile than the rate itself and thus lowers the premium relative to the premium of a normal option. Remember from Chapter 8 that vega, the sensitivity of the price of the option to a change in volatility, is positive.

The advantages of an average rate option for a company with regular daily foreign currency cash flows is obvious. If the flows are not regular, the average rate is not an accurate reference for hedging them. However, it might be a pretty good approximation. Furthermore, it would be difficult and costly to set up a series of options designed to expire on a daily basis. Just trying to manage such a system would be complicated and costly. Hence, an average rate option might be an imperfect substitute that gives adequate coverage, is relatively inexpensive and is easy to monitor and manage.

Basket options

Some companies are confronted by foreign exchange exposure in a number of currencies. In this case there might be an advantage to grouping exposure and negotiating a **basket option** with a bank. A basket option does not have one single underlying currency. It has several. For example, a basket option might be used to cover a long position of USD 30 million worth of yen, USD 30 million worth of Swiss francs, USD 15 million worth of pounds, USD 15 million worth of Australian dollars and USD 10 million worth of Korean won. The premium will be based on a contract for USD 100 million. Suppose the strike price is USD 98 million. If the weighted average exchange rate yields less than USD 98 million the option is exercised. If it yields more the option expires.

Instead of the basket put, the company could have purchased five different puts for the different amounts in question in each separate currency at a strike price 2% below the exchange rate being covered. Neither the results nor the costs, however, would be the same. The puts do not have to be exercised or abandoned *en masse*. Some can be exercised while others can be abandoned. Thus, the strategy of individual puts has a good chance of securing a better outcome than the basket option, which only guarantees the average rate. The average of the exchange rates has less volatility than each individual currency. Thus its cost should be lower than the cost of the strategy composed of individual puts.

Compound options

A **compound option** is an option on an option. This kind of instrument is useful for managing risks associated with conditional cash flows. The classic example is that of a company preparing to tender a bid for a contract. The deadline for the bid is three months in the future and the results will be known six months after that – a total of nine months in the future. The currency risk takes effect only when the bid has been submitted, that is, in three months time. Once the bids are submitted the company is sure to want to hedge its exposure with the purchase of an option. However, it might want to know right now how much that coverage will cost. A three-month compound option on the cost of the six-month option that it might want to buy if it wins the contract would suffice.

Shared currency option under tender (scout)

As with the compound option, a scout is designed to help companies in the context of tendering a bid for a contract. The procedure is straightforward. The bank that is offering the scout persuades its client to purchase an option and to share its cost with the other companies that are bidding on the contract. When the outcome of the bidding is announced, the company that has won becomes the owner of the option and its bid is covered for a fraction of the cost. The losing bidders, however, lose the part of the premium they have paid but they would have lost the premium anyway had they elected to take out individual coverage. This technique reduces the cost of the hedge considerably for all the participating companies in all circumstances. The problem is getting the competing companies to collaborate in the collective coverage.

Hybrids

Hybrid contracts, like participating forwards, employ a mixed formula with one element of fixed forward cover and one element of option coverage. They can also belong to the category of zero premium coverage. Zero premium, of course, does not mean zero cost. The contracts that are proposed revolve around import and export coverage and can generally be classed as export participating forwards and import participating forwards.

In the case of an export participating forward, the bank guarantees its client a minimum exchange rate for a given amount of foreign currency plus the possibility of a higher rate if the exchange rate appreciates. An example will make this clear.

Assume the following market conditions:

$$S(\text{DKK/USD})_{\text{bid}} = 5.0000$$
$$F_{1/4}(\text{DKK/USD})_{\text{bid}} = 5.0700$$

The bank offers to guarantee an exchange rate of 5.00 plus 50% of anything over 5.00. Thus, if the dollar is quoted at 4.80 on the maturity date, the company receives DKK 5.00 per dollar. If the dollar goes to 5.50, the company will receive DKK 5.25 per dollar (the DKK 5 minimum rate plus 50% of the DKK 0.50 above 5.00. Figure 16.21 compares the payoff profiles of the participating forward with a classic forward contract, a simple put and no coverage at all.

Figure 16.21 An example of an export participating forward

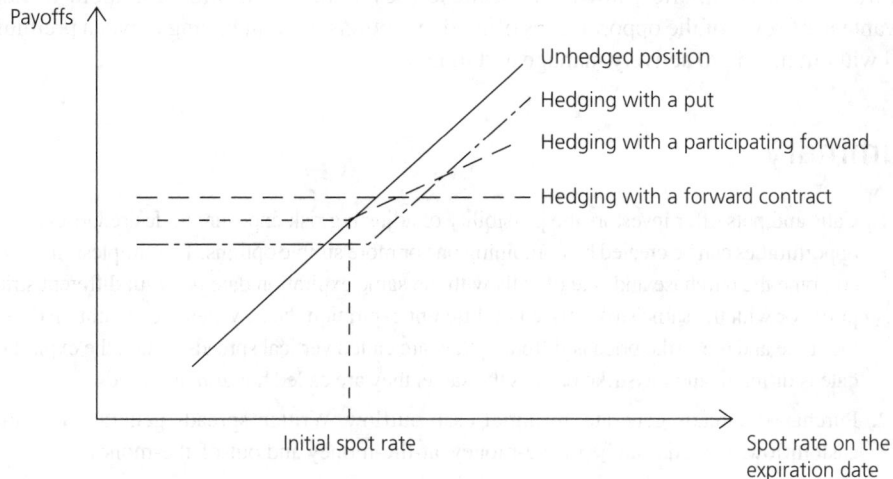

If the exchange rate falls or appreciates a little bit, forward coverage is the optimal strategy. If the exchange rate appreciates sharply, a simple option is the best hedging strategy but the participating forward is better than the classic forward coverage. The export participating forward is a mixture of forward coverage and option coverage. Its premium will be lower than simple option coverage because the percentage of gains is only 50% and because the guaranteed exchange rate is lower than the forward rate. The guaranteed rate and the percentage of gains can be calculated so that the company has no premium to pay.

Import participating forwards are symmetrical to export participating forwards as we can see in Figure 16.22. In this case the bank guarantees a maximum exchange rate and the possibility of sharing the gains if the exchange rate falls below the guaranteed rate. Thus, it is a mixture of a forward contract and a simple call option. If it is to be zero premium, the guaranteed rate will be higher than the current forward rate to offset the cost of the call.

Figure 16.22 An example of an import participating forward

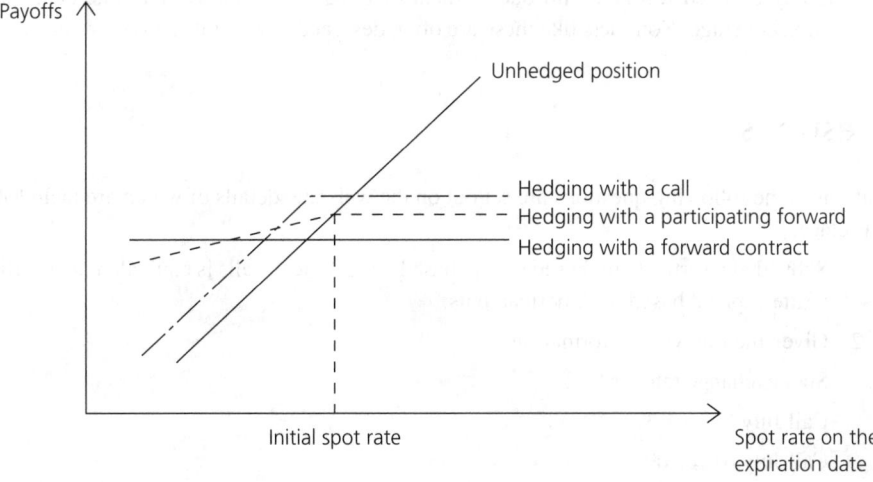

Hybrid contracts like these are relatively costly. They can be interesting to small and medium-sized companies, however, because they make it possible for them to take advantage of some of the opportunities offered by options without having to pay a premium and without having to actively manage and monitor them.

Summary

1. Calls and puts offer investors the possibility of adjusting risk exposure to desired levels. New opportunities can be created by combining one or more simple options. The simplest strategies combine the purchase and sale of calls with the same expiration date but with different strike prices or with the same strike price but different expiration dates. When the expiration date is the same and the strike price is different, they are called vertical spreads. When the expiration date is different and the strike price is the same, they are called horizontal spreads.

2. Purchased spreads generate an initial cash outflow. Written spreads generate an initial cash inflow. Spreads can be in-the-money, at-the-money and out-of-the-money.

3. Because spreads put limits on what can be earned and what can be lost, they are useful for strategies that expect exchange rate stability or only limited moves in the exchange rate.

4. Spreads can be combined with simple options or other spreads as a means of tailoring payoffs, premiums and costs to the specific needs and expectations of the investor. In practice, care must be taken when proceeding with different combinations of puts, calls and spreads. Complex strategies suffer in practice from the existence of transaction costs, early exercise and the technical difficulties involved in synchronizing the execution of such complicated orders, even in efficient markets.

5. The over-the-counter options markets have outgrown their development stage and become mature markets, at least for products involving exchange rates and interest rates. Consequently, the margins that banks can charge for these products has fallen sharply. Furthermore, as investors have learned to use options, they have also become aware of their limits and disadvantages, including high initial costs and the necessity of constant monitoring. Based on this, the banks have sought innovative new products as a means of developing new markets. The fruits of their effort gave birth to what are called exotic options, the more successful of which include lookback options, average rate options, basket options and compound options.

6. Banks have also developed hybrid contracts, such as participating forwards, which employ a mixed formula with one element of fixed forward cover and one element of option coverage. Contracts like these are often designed to generate zero premiums.

Questions

Solutions to the following questions are set out on the web site, details of which are included in the Preface.

1. Show that a vertical purchased spread based on American calls is equivalent to a vertical written spread based on American puts.

2. Given the following information:

   Spot exchange rate = 61.52

   Call July $60\frac{1}{2}$ = 1.37

   Call July 61 = 1.09

a. Calculate the time value for both calls.

b. Calculate the value of a vertical purchased spread.

c. Calculate the outcome on the expiration date if the spot rate does not change.

d. Show how the time value of the two options will evolve if the spot rate does not change and explain why this is so.

3. Why does an at-the-money purchased horizontal spread give a positive outcome when the spot rate remains unchanged?

4. Why is it that a zero premium reversible requires no initial outlay for premiums? How can the company treasurer bring out the cost that is implicit in an instrument like this?

5. Choose the correct response. A straddle generates a profit

a. when the spot rate makes a sharp move shortly after the expiration date

b. when volatility increases sharply before the expiration date

c. when the market incorrectly anticipates violent movements in the exchange rate due to the international monetary situation.

6. Choose the correct response. A lookback option

a. is an option whose exercise price is indexed to a basket of currencies

b. is an option that can be exercised after the expiration date

c. is an option whose strike price depends on the extreme values of the spot rate over the life of the option.

7. Show that an average rate option can be useful for a treasurer who has to manage regular purchases in one particular foreign currency.

8. Discuss the advantages and disadvantages of foreign exchange coverage when bidding on a foreign contract

a. using simple options

b. using a forward contract

c. using scouts.

9. What are the costs involved in participating forwards? Compare this type of coverage with simple option coverage.

10. Compare the purchase of a call-based butterfly spread with the sale of a call-based straddle.

BORROWING AND LENDING INTERNATIONALLY

International debt markets

The world market capitalization of bonds is larger than that of equity. The international market for bonds comprises three major categories: domestic bonds, foreign bonds and Eurobonds.

- Domestic bonds are issued by a domestic borrower in the domestic market, usually in domestic currency.

- Foreign bonds are issued on the domestic market by a foreign borrower, usually in domestic currency. The rules and regulations governing issuing and trading procedures are under the control of the domestic authorities.

- Eurobonds are issued in countries other than the one in whose currency they are denominated. They are not traded on a particular national bond market and, therefore, are not regulated by any domestic authority.

Financing and investing in the international bond markets is both technical and difficult. This stems from the vast diversity in regulation, instruments, terminology and techniques. For example, withholding taxes vary from market to market and some have none at all. Instruments range from straight, single currency bonds and floating rate notes to multi-currency issues with complex option clauses. Some markets pay interest on a semi-annual basis, others on an annual basis; some calculate interest on a 360-day year, others on a 365-day year. Differences such as these have important consequences for risk, returns and the cost of doing business.

We begin this chapter with a description of the major domestic bond markets. We then go on to look at the Eurobond market. Finally, we examine the market for syndicated Eurocredits and Brady bonds.

The major domestic bond markets

The globalization of the world's capital markets has introduced an element of competition among the different markets and has enabled borrowers to diversify their financing sources. For example, a German firm with an outstanding reputation in France might find that it can raise funds more cheaply on the French bond market than it can in Germany. By the same token, it might be advantageous for a large loan to be broken up into different tranches and floated in different markets so that each tranche benefits from the best conditions in each market. The World Bank's "global bonds" issued simultaneously in September 1989 on the Eurobond market and the US domestic market are a good example.

Investors also benefit from globalization. The different domestic bond markets can offer attractive diversification opportunities. They are also a source of products with unique characteristics arising from the different legal, fiscal and economic systems of the countries where they are issued.

For a firm raising funds in the international capital markets or for an investor managing an international bond portfolio, thorough technical knowledge of each domestic market is a fundamental requirement. This is an especially difficult proposition because there is a wide variety of instruments available. They range from classic fixed interest bonds, through FRNs, zero coupons, convertibles and bonds with warrants attached to the more exotic varieties with simultaneous call and put options or links to an index such as a stock market or gold. The possibilities are virtually limitless as new configurations appear regularly. Furthermore, trading and quotation practices concerning the various instruments can vary from market to market. In Europe, dealing and quotations are usually handled by brokers on the exchanges, although Germany, The Netherlands, Switzerland and the United Kingdom do some over-the-counter trading of non-government issues. In the United States most trading in domestic bonds is handled over the counter, while in Japan bond trading takes place over the counter and on the exchanges. When trading is handled over the counter, it is difficult to estimate costs which are hidden in the bid–ask spread. Even when commissions are charged by brokers on the organized exchanges, the fact that they are negotiable makes it hard to come up with an average figure.

Other costs must also be considered. Reclaiming withholding tax, for example, is a lengthy and costly process. Other regulations, such as exchange controls and surtaxes can generate substantial costs as well.

Price and yield quotations also differ from market to market and it is important to know and understand these differences when comparing the relative merits of different domestic bonds. Most bond prices are quoted as a percentage of the bond's nominal value with the accrued interest from the last coupon date not included in the price. The investor must pay the price of the bond as well as the accrued interest, but pricing the bond separately makes it possible to effect relevant comparisons among the different types of bonds. Not all bonds are quoted in this way, however. Convertible bonds, index-linked bonds and FRNs are usually quoted with the coupon attached. The calculation of accrued interest also differs from country to country. Countries such as Canada, Japan, Australia and the United Kingdom use a day count based on 365 days a year, while countries such as the United States, Switzerland, and Germany use a 30-day month based on a 360-day year.

Calculations of yield to maturity can also vary from country to country. Most European countries use the annual actuarial yield to maturity, which is the true yield. The United States uses the annualized six month yield to maturity, which underestimates the true actuarial yield because it ignores the compounding effect within the year. The Japanese use a simple interest yield to maturity which understates the true actuarial yield for bonds priced over par and overstates it for bonds priced under par.

Differences such as these can have a substantial effect on the pricing of an issue or the return on a portfolio and international financial agents should be aware of the differences. This requires an in-depth knowledge of the individual markets and instruments. In the next three sections we will look at the characteristics of the three major world bond markets – those of the United States, Japan and the United Kingdom – and their most frequently traded instruments.

The US bond market

The US bond market is the largest and most active in the world. It is also the one that offers the largest variety of issuers and terms. As in most countries, a large chunk of the market is devoted to government issues. Government issues are not the whole market, however. There are also substantial components of municipal bonds and mortgage bonds as well as a large and growing sector for corporate issues.

Government issues

US government bonds are the basic element in many, if not most, international portfolios. About two-thirds of this debt is composed of negotiable instruments with maturities of several days up to 30 years.

Treasury bills

Treasury bills have maturities of up to one year. They are issued in four main forms: three-month, six-month, one-year and cash management bills with variable maturities. They represent about one-third of the government's outstanding negotiable debt. The timetable is straightforward. Treasury bills with maturities of 13 weeks (91 days) and 26 weeks (182 days) are auctioned on a weekly basis. They are auctioned on a Monday and payment is due the following Thursday, the same day that earlier tranches of three-month paper matures. This enables investors to roll over their positions should they want to. The size of the intended issue is usually announced on the Tuesday preceding the auction.

The 52-week Treasury bills are auctioned once every four weeks on a Thursday. Payment is due one week later to coincide with the maturing of the previous 52-week issue. The size of the issue is usually announced on the Friday preceding the auction.

Cash management bills can have maturities of between a couple of days and nine months. They are issued on an irregular basis, depending on the Treasury's financing needs. Typically, the maturity of cash management bills is announced on a Thursday and set to match the maturity of outstanding bills as a means of enhancing market liquidity for trading purposes.

Treasury notes

Treasury notes have maturities from two to ten years. They represent more than half of the negotiable debt issued by the government. The auction of two-year notes takes place a week before the end of every month, usually on a Tuesday. The size of the intended issue is announced on the preceding Wednesday. Three-year notes comprise part of the Treasury's mid-quarterly refunding, which takes place about the 15th of the second month of every quarter (February, May, August and November). The terms of the issue are usually announced on the first Wednesday of the issue month.

Four-year notes are issued in the final month of each quarter (March, June, September and December), usually on a Wednesday. They mature at the end of the relevant month. Five-year notes are offered quarterly on the Thursday after the two-year issue. Seven-year notes are sold in the first month of every quarter (January, April, July and October). Ten-year notes are issued in the middle month of each quarter along with the three-year notes.

Treasury bonds

Treasury bonds are issued with maturities of 15, 20 and 30 years. The maturities are chosen depending on the Treasury's perceived financing needs. The 30-year bonds issued before November 1984 typically contained a call option five years before maturity. Since then the practice has been discontinued because it made "stripping" the bonds more difficult to achieve. Stripping involves separating interest and principal payments and trading them as individual securities. Thus, each individual payment effectively becomes an individual zero coupon bond.[1] Thirty-year bonds are sold as part of the quarterly refunding on about the 15th of the month.

Market structure

We have seen that most US Treasury debt is issued by auction on a regular calendar timetable. The auctions are conducted on a competitive basis. There are about 40 primary dealers, including some foreign-owned institutions, that dominate the auction process. No single dealer may bid for or be awarded more than 35% of the total offering. Official foreign entities that are not primary dealers, foreign monetary authorities, for instance, can also submit bids. These bids are allotted at the average auction price but the amounts are additional to the normal tendered debt and are called "foreign add-ons". Trading in new securities can also take place before the actual auction up to the settlement date and is called "when-issued trading".

The amounts of an issue typically range between USD 8–10 billion, although some older issues that are reopened can go as high as USD 20 billion. Minimum denominations range from USD 1000 for longer maturities to USD 5000 for two and three-year notes. Treasury bills have a discount structure while all other securities have fixed coupon payments and a bullet (in fine) principal payment.

Secondary market trading

The US Treasury market is the largest and most liquid fixed income market in the world. Most trading takes place on the over-the counter markets through a group of banks and dealer firms, although all bonds are listed on the New York Stock Exchange for the benefit of foreign institutional investors whose charters only allow the purchase of listed securities. Very little trading takes place on the exchange, however.

Primary dealers are chosen by the Federal Reserve and act as wholesale dealers between the Treasury and other investors and unapproved dealers. Specialized brokers enhance market liquidity by matching up bids and offers but without taking a position themselves. These brokers and an efficient screen price service ensure price transparency.

The official trading hours in the United States are from 9.00 a.m. to 4.00 p.m. New York time. In fact, the market is effectively open 24 hours a day, since active trading takes place in the London and Tokyo time zones. Treasury bills are quoted on a discount Actual/360 basis. For example, the price of a Treasury bill due in 275 days when the prevailing interest rate is 8% is:

$$\text{Price} = 100 - \left(\frac{275}{360} \times 8\% \right) = 93.889.$$

---

[1] Separately traded registered interest and principal security (STRIPS) is the generic term for US Treasury bonds and registered interest and securities from which the coupons have been detached. In 1985 the Treasury allowed all notes and bonds with ten years or more of maturity to be stripped into their component elements through the Fedwire system. This created a single, homogeneous Treasury strip instrument that could be traded and cleared in the same manner as other Treasury securities. A strip also refers to the coupon itself. Coupon strips are available in physical or certificate form and are traded as individual securities. The remaining corpus (principal payment) can be either callable or non-callable and is traded as an individual security with its own denominations and trading characteristics. A corpus Treasury receipt (corpus TR) is a zero coupon certificate issued in respect of principal payments on specific US Treasury securities. Holders of corpus TRs receive principal payments at maturity of the underlying Treasury security but no coupon payments prior to that time. A coupon Treasury receipt is a zero coupon certificate issued in respect of an interest payment on a US Treasury security.

Other treasury securities are quoted on a clean price basis as a percentage of the bond's nominal value with the accrued interest from the last coupon date not included in the price. The normal tick size is $\frac{1}{32}$ but can be as fine as $\frac{1}{256}$ on particularly liquid issues. Thus, an 8% bond quoted 91.3 bid–91.7 ask means that a dealer will pay $91\frac{3}{32}$ per USD 100 of par value to purchase the bond and charge $91\frac{7}{32}$ per USD 100 of par value to sell it. The quoted price is net of accrued interest and interest payments are made semi-annually. The next interest payment will be USD 4 per USD 100 of par value (0.5 × 8% × USD 100). If three months have elapsed since the last interest payment, accrued interest is equal to

$$\frac{3}{6} \times USD\ 4 = USD\ 2$$

and must be added to the bid–ask prices to determine the total amount to be paid on the transaction. Yield to maturity is quoted on a proportional six-month basis that ignores compounding over the year. The true yield to maturity can be found by the following formula:

$$True\ yield = \left(1 + \frac{Proportional\ yield}{2}\right)^2 - 1$$

Thus, if the yield to maturity is given as 10%, the true yield to maturity will be:

$$\left(1 + \frac{0.10}{2}\right)^2 - 1 = 10.25\%$$

There is no withholding tax for most US government securities.

Dealers make their money on the bid–ask spread and brokers charge dealers USD 40 for every million of par value bought or sold. The spread itself varies depending on the volatility, maturity and especially the liquidity of the issue concerned. On some short-term issues it can be as low as USD 50 per par amount while on longer maturities it can rise to $\frac{4}{32}$ or $\frac{5}{32}$. A full lot, or normal unit of trading, starts at 100 bonds or USD 100,000 of par value, although most transactions range between USD 1 million and USD 100 million.

The normal settlement date is the next business day following the trade. Other forms of settlement can be agreed upon, however. These include same-day settlement, called a cash trade, "skip day" payments which are settled two days later, and corporate trades, settled five days later. Almost all clearing is conducted through the Federal Reserve wire system or the book-entry system run by the Federal Reserve Bank of New York. Non-resident investors need a custodian who has access to the Fedwire system.

Non-government securities

Mortgage-backed securities

A mortgage-backed security is supported by an undivided interest in a pool of mortgages or trust deeds held by private lenders or government agencies. The market for mortgage-backed securities issued by the governmental agencies is right behind the market for Treasury securities insofar as liquidity and risk are concerned. Consequently, price differentials between the two for the same maturities is quite small. The market itself is concentrated around securities issued by three Government agencies:

- The Federal National Mortgage Association (called Fannie Mae)
- The Federal Home Loan Mortgage Association (Freddie Mac)
- The Government National Mortgage Association (Ginnie Mae).

International investors have been attracted to this market because of the high returns and relative safety.

Municipal bonds

Municipal bonds can be divided into two categories: the longer-term general obligations (GO bonds) and the shorter-term revenue notes issued in anticipation of tax receipts or other income. These securities are issued by municipalities, such as state and local governments, to finance schools, roads and other public works.

Corporate bonds

Issues of corporate bonds are often more complex than Treasury bond issues. They some-times include call options, sinking funds, warrants and indexing terms that complicate esti-mations of their relative riskiness and worth.

Some issues are backed by guarantees but most are not and defaults are not infrequent. Because of the associated risk, a number of rating systems have been developed to aid investors. The two most popular systems are managed by Moody's Investor Service and Standard & Poor's. Moody's Investor Service was founded in 1909 by John Moody, who developed the first rating system for fixed income securities that he applied to 1500 railroad companies. The company has been a subsidiary of Dun & Bradstreet since 1962. Standard & Poor's has been rating bonds since 1923 and has been a subsidiary of McGraw-Hill since 1966.

Table 17.1 shows an outline of the various categories included in the two rating systems. Any rank above BBB in Standard & Poor's system and Baa in Moody's is considered as "investment grade". Investment grade means that it is considered eligible for bank investment under US commercial bank regulations. Any ranking below investment grade qualifies the bond as **junk**. Junk bonds are high risk bonds that have low credit ratings or are in default.

A bond's rating is important because it helps issuers determine the spread in basis points that will be necessary relative to Treasury issues. It also helps to determine who the potential investors will be. Certain investors such as banks, savings institutions and pension funds are prohibited by charter or by law from investing in securities with an inadequate rating. The major investors in corporate bonds are life insurance companies, pension funds and foreign institutions.

Domestic corporate bond issues are usually underwritten by a syndicate of domestic banks. Commissions are relatively small compared to most financial markets. They depend on the quality of the issuer and the maturity of the loan. In most cases they range between 0.5% for the shorter maturities to 1% for the longer ones. Nevertheless, they are higher than the commissions found in the Eurobond market, although this market is inaccessible to most American corporations.

Foreign bonds

Foreign bonds are issued by foreign borrowers and called Yankee bonds. Most operations of this type are generated by Canadian utility companies or foreign governments.

Market regulation

Regulatory legislation remains based on the laws passed after the crash of 1929 and the ensuing depression. The Security Act of 1933 requires official registration with the SEC (Securities Exchange Commission) of any security offered to the public. The Security Exchange Act of 1934 requires issuers to provide the public with regular information. The registration procedure is long, often taking several months and thereby making it difficult for issuers to take advantage of market conditions.

Table 17.1 Rating systems for corporate bonds

Standard & Poor's	Moody's	Definitions
AAA	Aaa	Capacity to pay interest and principal is extremely strong.
AA+, AA, AA–	Aa1, Aa2, Aa3	Very strong capacity to pay interest and principal. Only a small difference with highest rated category.
A+, A, A–	A1, A2, A3	Strong capacity to pay interest and principal but is more susceptible to changes in circumstances and economic conditions than the debt in higher rated categories.
BBB+, BBB, BBB–	Baa1, Baa2, Baa3	Adequate capacity to pay interest and principal but more susceptible to changing circumstances and economic conditions than debt in the higher categories.
BB+, BB, BB–	Ba1, Ba2, Ba3	Speculative.
B+, B, B–	B1, B2, B3	Very speculative.
CCC+, CCC, CCC–	Caa	Debt in poor standing with probable default.
CC	Ca	Extremely speculative. Such issues are often in default or have other shortcomings.

Since 1982, Amendment 415 to the Securities Act has made it possible to speed up the registration procedure without sacrificing investor protection. In effect, it enables issuers to proceed with advance registration on future issues. The exact terms of an issue can be specified within two days after the issue has been realized. This piece of deregulation allowing "shelf registration" lay behind the expansion of the medium-term note (MTN) market. MTNs are debt instruments with maturities ranging generally from one to 15 years, offered under a program agreement through one or more dealers. The instrument has a fixed coupon and maturity dates can be targeted exactly to those required by investors. They can be issued at any time as long as they stay within the limits fixed at the initial registration.

Private placements make it possible for issuers to avoid the registration process. A privately placed security cannot be sold to the general public. Consequently, investors in private placements must hold the securities until their maturity. Private placements have the advantages of confidentiality and flexibility. For this reason they were a favorite instrument in the financial engineering of leveraged buyouts (LBOs). Ratings for private placements are usually quite low and insurance companies are the major investors.

Amendment 144A adopted by the SEC in 1990 led to the creation of a secondary market for private placements. In fact, a limited category of investors called qualified institutional buyers (QIBs) are allowed to deal on the secondary market. QIBs are defined as institutions that manage a minimum of USD 100 million worth of assets. An issue of USD 100 million by Enterprise Oil kicked off this market and made it possible for the company to reduce its costs by between 10 and 20 basis points compared to a traditional private placement.

The secondary market

Some non-Treasury securities are traded on organized exchanges. However, most of the trading volume is done in the over-the-counter markets. Liquidity and spreads are variable and depend on the size of the issue, larger issues usually having more liquidity and lower spreads. Institutional investors that acquire corporate bonds on the primary market attach considerable importance to the potential liquidity of the secondary market. Consequently, they are attracted to the larger issues.

The Japanese bond market

Until the 1970s the Japanese bond market was almost non-existent because of strict regulations designed to maintain an undervalued exchange rate and to insulate it from speculative international capital movements. Now the Japanese government bond (JGB) market is the second largest in the world behind the US Treasury market. This result is due to the program of liberalization organized by the Ministry of Finance, as the first oil shock in the early 1970s and the growing government budget deficits in the late 1980s made it clear that only a modernized JGB market would provide the government with the increased funding it needed.

Besides foreign investors who play an important role in market activity, the other major participants are long-term credit banks, trust banks, insurance companies, investment trusts and retail investors. The central instrument of the JGB market is the ten-year bond, accounting for over half of public government debt and 90% of daily market turnover. Understandably, foreign interest is concentrated on this segment of the market. However, there are some severe distortions involved here that all foreign investors should be aware of.

The major distortion is caused by the benchmark issue. In most government bond markets the benchmark issue is the most recently issued. In Japan the benchmark issue is decided upon in a process of negotiation that involves the large dealers that dominate the market. The importance of the benchmark issue stems from the fact that demand is concentrated on this single issue. Some benchmark issues have turned their volume over as much as five times in a single day. The concentration of demand makes the benchmark issue trade at a premium to the rest of the market, sometimes by as much as 70 basis points.

Besides the benchmark issue, other traded issues include "side issues", which are ten-year bonds that trade on either side of the benchmark. There is also a super long bond as well as short-term notes and bills. Non-government debt includes bank debentures, agency and municipal bonds, corporate bonds, Euroyen bonds, and Samurai and Daimyo bonds.

Government issues

As we mentioned, most activity is concentrated at the long-term end of the market. The short term end of the market is less liquid than the long-term sector and most foreigners are barred from it. Foreign participation is generally restricted to central banks and supranational institutions.

Financing bills

Financing bills are used mainly as instruments for open market operations in pursuit of monetary policy. They are sold mainly to the Bank of Japan and, therefore, hold little interest for foreign investors.

Treasury bills

Japanese Treasury bills resemble US T-bills. They have maturities of three and six months and are issued twice a month at public auction. Although they are discount securities rather than coupon securities, they are traded in terms of an effective money market yield.

Medium-term notes

Once every two months two-year bonds are issued by means of an auction. The size of an issue is typically JPY 200–400 billion. They pay a semi-annual coupon and are traded in the over-the-counter market. Trading is light because notes are targeted towards investors who are likely to hold them to maturity.

Zero coupon bonds

Five-year zero coupon bonds are issued by means of a syndicate once every two months. The average issue size is JPY 200–300 billion and is targeted towards retail investors, which explains why the syndication process rather than an auction is used to launch the issue.

Long-term bonds

Long-term bonds are issued once a month in a process that combines an auction with syndicated underwriting. The auction accounts for 60% of the issue and the syndication for 40%. The syndicate, which includes 840 institutions made up of banks, securities firms, life insurance companies and about 50 foreign institutions, wields considerable control over the issue process. It determines the yield at which bonds will be issued and controls the allocation of bonds among syndicate members.

In spite of the large number of syndicate members, the key players are a small number of leading securities houses and city banks. In fact, the Ministry of Finance has begun to formalize the role of the key syndicate members by setting up a system of primary dealers similar to that found in the United States.

The issue process begins just before the last week of the month when the syndicate members discuss the price among themselves and then make a recommendation to the Ministry of Finance. If the Ministry agrees, the announcement of the coupon and the size of the issue is made in the last week of the month. One day later the auction takes place. Each syndicate member is restricted to bidding for no more than 18% of the issue and investors can only bid through dealers. If an issue has the same coupon and maturity as outstanding bonds, then these tranches are assimilated under the old series number in order to generate a larger and more liquid bond. This is possible because JGBs pay coupons on a strict quarterly schedule (March, June, September and December) no matter in what month they were issued.

Once the auction has been completed, the remaining 40% of the issue is allocated to the syndicate members at the average auction price, called the issue price. Settlement occurs on the 20th of the month or the next business day.

Super long-term bonds

Before 1987 no modern super long-term bonds existed. The 15 and 20-year bonds that the Ministry of Finance had issued were all privately placed and did not trade. The modern super long-term bonds have 20-year maturities. They are auctioned every three months and are listed on the Tokyo Stock Exchange. The issue size is around JPY 500 billion.

Market structure

Over 80% of JGBs are issued in registered form and the rest in bearer form. Bonds can be converted from registered to bearer or vice versa within two market days. In the secondary market registered bonds are often quoted at a slightly higher price than bearer bonds because they are more liquid. JGBs are identified by trading numbers such as #140. When an issue is reopened the tranches are identified by month: March #140, June #140, etc. If the tranches are combined, the month designation disappears. Denominations vary but the most common denomination is JPY 100,000.

The 10 and 20-year JGBs are listed on the Tokyo Stock Exchange. However, most trading takes place on the over-the-counter market. JGBs cannot be delivered outside Japan and foreign investors wishing to purchase them must deal through a custodian bank that can effect transfers through the book-entry system.

The secondary markets

Trading hours are weekdays from 8.40 to 11.15 a.m. and 12.45 to 5.00 p.m. on the broker to broker (BB) screens. Dealers include securities houses, city banks, trust banks and regional banks as well as a number of foreign firms. Most trades take place over the counter on a bid–ask basis. The bid–ask spread varies with the liquidity of the issue, being as low as $\frac{1}{2}$ of a basis point for the most liquid benchmark bond and as high as 10 basis points for other less liquid bonds. The seller also pays a transfer tax of 0.03%, except on deals between non-residents.

As we mentioned in the introduction, JGB's are traded on a simple yield basis that ignores compounding. The following formula shows how this is done:

$$\text{Yield} = \left(\text{Coupon rate} + \frac{100 - \text{Current price}}{\text{Years to maturity}} \right) \frac{100}{\text{Current price}}$$

Foreign investors beware! The simple yield understates the true yield to maturity for bonds priced over par and overstates it for bonds priced below par. Foreign investors should be careful to convert simple yield to true yield to maturity in order to make adequate comparisons. Coupons are semi-annual, paid on the 20th of a month, and interest is accrued from the previous coupon date to the settlement date, calculated on an Actual/365 basis.

The settlement procedure for JGBs differs somewhat from other major bond markets and should be understood by the foreign investor. Trades on the Tokyo Stock Exchange settle four market days after the trade. Over-the-counter trades, however, settle according to the following schedule: 5th, 10th, 15th, 20th, 25th and the last day of each month. If any of these days are non-market days, the next market day is used – unless it falls in the next month, in which case settlement occurs on the previous market day. Each of the settlement days is related to a trading period, which can be determined by the following guidelines:

- trades cannot settle earlier than seven days after the trade date
- if two possible settlement days occur within ten market days of the trade, then the later date is the applicable one
- if another settlement date falls within two calendar days of the first settlement date, then the later one must be used
- no settlement can take place within 14 days of a coupon date, thereby postponing it to the next settlement date after the coupon.

As a result of all this, trades tend to settle between nine and 15 days after the trade.

Since all deliveries must be made inside Japan, foreign investors must deal through a custodian. If they want to hold own-name registered bonds they must set up an account with the Bank of Japan. Such bonds settle through the Net system, which is a wire transfer system, a letter of transfer system or a book-entry system operated by the Bank of Japan.

Non-government issues

Municipal bonds

Most municipal bonds have a maturity of ten years with semi-annual coupon payments. Different governmental agencies can also issue bonds that may or may not be guaranteed by the government. They have the same characteristics as municipal bonds with a maturity of ten years and a semi-annual coupon payment.

Corporate bonds

The principal corporate issuers on the Japanese market are the nine electricity companies and Nippon Telephone and Telegraph. Most other Japanese companies prefer issuing bonds directly on the Eurobond market even though the ultimate bondholders are usually Japanese residents. It is also interesting to note that a high proportion of Japanese corporate bonds are either convertible issues or have warrants attached.

Other types of bond issues

The Japanese equivalent of Yankee bonds in the United States is called a Samurai bond. A Samurai is a bond issued by non-Japanese residents in Japan. Shogun bonds are non-yen denominated issues by non-Japanese residents on the Japanese domestic market. This sector of the market has ceased being very active.

The UK bond market

UK government debt, called gilts, constitutes the most important sector of the sterling-denominated debt market. Of the four classes of gilts issued by the Treasury, only two – conventional and index-linked – currently have any relevance.

Gilt-edged securities

Conventional gilts

Conventional gilts, referred to as conventional stocks in the United Kingdom, represent 85% of the total market. They have a fixed coupon, ranging from 3% to 15.5%, and a fixed maturity. Some issues have an embedded call option. Issues with a call option can be recognized by the two dates given for their maturity.

Index-linked gilts

Index-linked stocks represent 15% of the gilt market. They were first issued in 1981 and have a fixed maturity with semi-annual interest payments linked to the Retail Price Index. The redemption value of the bond is also linked to the RPI to protect the investor against inflation.

Issuing procedures

There are four basic procedures for issuing gilts comprising auctions, taps, tenders and additions to existing issues. When the terms of a new issue are announced, the Bank of England publishes a prospectus and a press notice.

1. *The Tender.* The tender has been the traditional means for issuing government debt. In a tender, the Bank of England invites tenders for a new or existing issue and, where conventional gilts are concerned, specifies a minimum price, usually around the prevailing market level. If the issue is undersubscribed, any surplus is allotted to the Issue Department of the Bank as a "tap stock" and tenders are accepted at the minimum price. If the issue is oversubscribed, all allotments are granted at the lowest price for any tender that is accepted.

2. *Tap stock.* Issuing by **tap** refers to the Bank of England selling gilts to market-makers on the secondary market. The debt can be issued directly to the Bank for sale or it can come from unsubscribed portions of an issue allotted to the Issue Department of the Bank.

3. *Auction.* Issue by auction began in May 1987 and has since become as important as tenders and taps. Bidding can be competitive and non-competitive. Competitive bids are open to all, market-makers or not. Market-makers may submit bids by telephone up to 10.00 a.m. on the day of the auction. Other bids must be submitted in writing to the Gilts Office in London or the Registrar's Department in Gloucester by 10.00 a.m. on the morning of the auction or by 3.30 p.m. of the preceding day at branches and agencies of the Bank of England. Once the bids are in, the Bank sets the minimum price and all bids above this price are granted in full except that no single investor can be granted more than 25% of the total issue. In non-competitive bids, investors can make one bid for up to GBP 500,000 of par value. Bids are then settled at the weighted average price for successful bids. In order to ensure that market demand can only be met by bidding in the auction, the sale of any additional debt of similar maturity is prohibited for 28 days following the auction. This is known as the "fallow period".

The secondary market

London Stock Exchange dealings are carried out by telephone by gilt-edged market-makers. The exchange is open from 9.00 a.m. to 5.00 p.m. but trading takes place on a limited scale outside these hours. Prices are quoted on a bid–ask spread basis with a tick equal to $\frac{1}{32}$. A normal spread ranges from $\frac{2}{32}$ for a liquid issue of up to seven years maturity to $\frac{4}{32}$ or $\frac{5}{32}$ for longer less liquid issues. These thin margins have contributed to a reduction in the number of market-makers since 1987. Trades are normally settled on the next market day, but delayed payment can also be arranged up to a maximum of 14 days. Settlement can be made through the Bank of England's Central Gilts Office book-entry system if the dealer is a member. Non-CGO members settle by physical delivery through a member acting as proxy. Care should be taken that adequate delivery procedures are in place because failure to deliver is costly.

Some gilts are issued in bearer form but most are registered. Interest is paid semi-annually and accrued interest is calculated on an Actual/365 basis. Gilts go ex-coupon 37 days before interest payment except for coupon dates between the 5th and the 8th of the months of January, April, July and October, which go ex on the 1st of the preceding month.

The international bond market

Organization of the Eurobond market

Eurobonds are different from foreign bonds. Foreign bonds are issued by a borrower in a domestic capital market other than its own and usually denominated in the currency of that market. Eurobonds are issued in Eurocurrencies by an international syndicate of banks in several international financial markets. Because Eurobonds are issued and traded on international financial markets, they are not subject to the rules and regulations that are common to most domestic bond markets, although there are interprofessional rules and regulations issued by ISMA. Issuers are also subject to the rules and regulations of the monetary authorities in their country of residence. In any case, the development of the Eurobond market is synonymous with the absence of withholding tax. In fact, Eurobond contracts stipulate that if any withholding tax is imposed, the borrower is responsible for paying it.

The first Eurobond borrowing dates back to 1963 when the interest equalization tax (IET) imposed by the United States stopped the development of the Yankee bond market dead in its tracks. A Yankee bond is a foreign bond issued in the US market, payable in dollars and registered with the SEC. The IET was a tax on the interest income paid on securities issued by certain foreign borrowers in the United States. It discouraged the purchase of these securities and caused the issuers to move their borrowing activity offshore to markets where they would not be subject to the dictates of the US monetary authorities.

The real development of the Eurobond market came after 1982 when the debt crisis shut down the growth of the syndicated Euroloan. In 1982 syndicated Eurocurrency credit facilities amounted to close to USD 100 billion while Eurobond issues totaled less than half that amount at USD 46.44 billion. By 1991 Eurobond issues stood at USD 234.87 billion and Eurocurrency credit facilities were only USD 136.4 billion. Table 17.2 shows the development of the Eurobond market since 1982.

Eurobond issues characteristically have shorter maturities than those found on domestic markets. The large majority of Eurobond issues have maturities less than or equal to five years. The development of the Euronote facility and Euro MTNs in the 1980s reinforced this tendency. Euronotes are short-term, fully negotiable, bearer promissory notes, issued at a discount to face value and typically of one, three or six-month maturity. Euro MTNs are medium-term bearer notes of small denomination with maturities ranging from one to five years.

Issuing procedures

Issuing procedures have evolved since the Eurobond market's inception. At the beginning, the traditional issuing procedure, called "European", was cumbersome and could take several weeks. Syndicates often contained as many as several hundred members for the jumbo loans of USD 1 billion or more. Final investors were institutions like pension funds, investment funds and insurance companies, as well as private individuals attracted by the absence of withholding tax and the anonymity of bearer certificates. The French characterize this type of individual as "the Belgian dentist", a high income professional seeking to preserve his wealth from the prying eyes of the greedy tax authorities by investing in bearer Eurobonds held at a secret-respecting Luxembourg bank.

Table 17.2 Evolution of the Eurobond market, 1991–99

Years	Eurobond issues (USD bn)
1991	1579
1992	1739
1993	1946
1994	2123
1995	2296
1996	2615
1997	3142
1998	3406
1999	4095

Source: ISMA.

In the 1980s, market uncertainty pushed syndicating banks to speed up the issuing procedure in order to enable them and borrowers to take advantage of the ever-changing market conditions. The accelerated issuing procedure, called a bought deal, resembles the banking sector's club deal in the Euroloan market. It tended to reduce the size of the organizing syndicates and to concentrate offers to institutional investors. It also increased competition between potential organizers and participants and gave rise to new safety techniques such as the pre-offered price.

"European" issue procedure

The European issue procedure starts with a lead manager who has a mandate from the borrower to organize the operation. As in the Euroloan syndication, the lead manager is responsible for negotiating the overall conditions of the issue concerning the coupon, price, maturity, etc. He is also responsible for organizing the syndicate by finding other banks that want to participate. The borrower, of course, can require the participation of certain institutions and most syndicates will include one or more institutions with the same nationality as the borrower. For his efforts the lead manager will be paid a fee, usually about $\frac{1}{8}$%, called the praecipium.

There are three major dates in the issue procedure. The first is the launch date when a new issue's invitation telexes are officially sent out to the syndicate. The second is the pricing date, when the final terms of the issue are completed. The third is the closing date, when a new issue's proceeds are paid to the borrower by the lead manager and the securities, in temporary or definitive form, are delivered to the lead manager by the borrower. This usually occurs 10 to 15 days after the signing of the issue's subscription agreement.

The first phase of the operation occurs between the launch date and the pricing date and is when the syndicate is formed. Syndicates are traditionally three-tiered with a management group, an underwriting group, and a selling group.

The management group comprises 5–20 financial institutions that include the lead manager and the co-managers. The co-managers play an active role in the issuer's strategy and are chosen according to geographical diversification, the ability to effectively place securities and past relations with the borrower. Co-managers are always internationally recognized financial institutions. Members of the management group usually receive a fee of $\frac{3}{8}$% on operations with a maturity of less than ten years up to $\frac{1}{2}$% for longer maturities.

The underwriting group is much larger than the management group and can contain more than 100 institutions. Its role is to guarantee the placement of the securities. If demand from final investors is too low to enable the placement of the whole issue, the underwriting group has responsibility for holding the securities until they can be placed or, in certain conditions, for selling the securities at a discount to the issue price. The underwriting fee is usually about $\frac{3}{8}$% and the amounts that are underwritten by each institution usually represent only a small proportion of the total issue. "Major underwriters" take close to 1% while "minor underwriters" take close to 0.5%.

Traditional underwriting agreements usually contained a clause whereby the lead manager could restrict the underwriters from reselling the underwritten securities. This was to avoid the practice of some underwriters of subscribing to a larger amount than they could effectively place and then selling the excess at a discount on the grey market. The grey market takes place between the launch date and the closing date. During this period the co-managers and underwriters can buy and sell the issue's securities on a "when-issued" basis. When-issued refers to the fact that since the securities have not actually been issued, trades are subject to their subsequent availability. If an issue is not priced correctly by the management group – the price of the issue is too high or the coupon too low, for example – the issue will trade at a discount on the grey market. Final investors will not want to pay the full issue price if they see that it is already trading at a discount. This is a source of much tension inside the syndicate since the management group is obliged to uphold the price of the issue. In fact, the grey market plays a certain regulatory role insofar as it makes lead managers offer borrowers conditions compatible with the reality of the market.

The role of the selling group is to place the securities with final investors. They have no underwriting responsibilities and take no risk . If they place their securities, they earn a commission of about 1.125% for shorter maturities and 1.5% for longer ones. They lose nothing if they are unable to place the securities they are responsible for. Only their reputation will suffer.

The entire syndication process can be described in six stages:

1. *Preliminary negotiations and preparation.* Potential issuers and lead managers negotiate on their respective needs and capabilities. This stage ends with a written proposition to the prospective borrower on the different financing possibilities concerning the amount of the issue, the coupon rate, the maturity and the issue price.

2. *Preplacement.* Once the mandate has been received the lead manager starts looking for partners. He sends telexes, confirmed by letter, inviting prospective underwriters and sellers to participate in the syndicate. On the launch day a prospectus containing the relevant information on the proposed issue is distributed. In the ensuing period – across about two weeks – the institutions that have been invited to participate sound out potential investors and make their decision on whether or not to participate and for how much.

3. *Fixing the final terms of the issue (pricing day).* Based on the response to his invitation, the lead manager fixes the final terms of the issue, making any modifications that he feels necessary. Once this has been done, the underwriting agreement is completed and signed by the lead manager and the other underwriters.

4. *Apportioning securities (offering day).* On the day following pricing day, the lead manager sends out telexes to the institutions that agreed to participate, stipulating the number of securities that will be allocated to them.

5. *Placing the issue.* During the next two weeks the selling group actively places the issue with final investors and the lead manager supervises the grey market to keep the price in line with the issue price.

6. *Closing the issue (closing day).* The issuer receives the net proceeds of the issue (amount less commissions). The actual securities are issued and distributed to the final investors. The tombstone advertisement is then published in the appropriate financial press.

Bought deal

In this procedure the conditions are fixed by the lead manager and proposed to the issuer. The issuer then has a short time to accept or reject them. This package system is much more rapid than the European procedure and the syndicates much smaller. The goal is to take advantage of market conditions and the deal must be completed before they change. The lead manager often takes all or most of the issue. The bought deal is often employed when the issue will subsequently be swapped.

Listing and trading procedures

In order to gain access to a wide public of final investors, many issuers list the securities on the Luxembourg Stock Exchange or the London Stock Exchange. This is usually done two or three weeks before the effective launch of the issue in order to enable trading to begin as soon as the issue is closed.

Open trading of Eurobonds is handled by market-makers and dealers belonging to ISMA. Prices are quoted bid–ask net of commissions and trades are settled in seven calendar days.

Transaction costs can be high as the bid–ask spread averages about 0.5% on a typical, straight dollar bond transaction. It can reach 1% for bonds denominated in other less common currencies. These rates are usually a little lower for transactions in FRNs and a little higher on equity-linked bonds.

Instruments and trading techniques

The three main types of Eurobonds are:

- fixed rate issues or straight bonds
- floating rate notes (FRNs)
- equity-linked bonds, either convertible or with warrants attached.

The heart of the market consists of the fixed rate issues but, at one time or another depending on market conditions, the other two types have known periods of popularity.

Fixed rate issues

The face value of a typical fixed rate Eurobond varies between USD 1000 and USD 5000 with maturities of three, five, seven and ten years. Some longer maturities are available but are generally limited to the most creditworthy sovereign borrowers. In fact, maturities are linked to the economic uncertainty prevailing at any time with different clientele compartments for the different maturities. Short and medium-term maturities in Eurosterling, for example, are destined for private retail investors and are the object of an active swap market. On the other hand, longer maturities are destined for institutional investors and are issued by the list system. In this system the managers offer portions of the issue at a fixed price directly to a list of investors who have one day to accept or refuse. The contractual guarantees of a fixed rate issue are typically very stringent. They include negative pledge and cross default clauses as well as restrictions on future borrowing by the issuer. They do not, however, usually include collateral requirements whereby the issuer pledges assets to secure payment of the bond in the event of default.

Rates are often fixed as a spread with respect to a benchmark rate in the domestic market of the currency in question, such as US Treasury bonds for the dollar, gilts for sterling, etc. If the issuer is already in the market, the spread is determined in relation to its past issues. If it is new to the market, its reputation and credit rating will determine the spread.

Most issues are straight bullet bonds with annual coupons redeemed *in fine*. Other instruments are also available, however. Zero coupon bonds have been popular in spite of their relatively volatile prices (due to their high duration) and their default risk concentrated at the maturity of the issue. There have also been numerous issues of bonds with call options providing for early redemption.

Other, more exotic issues, include bonds with currency options, bonds with deferred payments, indexed bonds and debt warrant bonds. Bonds with currency options give the investor the right to receive payments in a currency or currencies other than the currency of issue. Dual-currency bonds are denominated in one currency with a coupon and/or repayment of principal at a fixed rate in another currency. Partly paid bonds are paid in installments. Bull and bear bonds are indexed to some benchmark and issued in two tranches. One tranche, the bull tranche, has redemption proceeds that rise as the index rises and the other tranche, the bear tranche, has redemption proceeds that fall as the index falls. Debt warrant bonds have a call warrant attached giving the investor the right to purchase another bond at a given price. The warrant creates leverage for the investor insofar as he gains on the bond and the warrant if interest rates decline. Warrants on zero coupon bonds increase the leverage effect.

Floating rate notes

FRNs are typically issued with higher face values (USD 5000, 10,000, and 100,000) than fixed rate issues because they are directed at institutional investors. The interest rate is variable and determined periodically. It is quoted as a discount or premium to a reference rate, such as six-month Libor + 1%. This spread can be fixed once and for all or can vary over time. For example, it might be 1% for the first three years and 1.5% for the last two. The reference rate is often Libor but other reference rates are also common such as the T-bill for the dollar. The periodicity of the reference rate determines the reference period for the FRN. Thus, the interest rate on an FRN referenced to one-month Libor would be revised monthly and the interest rate on an FRN referenced to three-month Libor would be revised quarterly. Semi-annual is the most common reference period. In some cases, however, coupons are calculated or paid on a schedule different from that of the reference period. For example, the coupon could be calculated as the average six-month Libor observed over the last six months.[2]

In any case, the calculation of the reference rate is the object of numerous clauses in the reference agency agreement. Certain financial institutions are designated as reference institutions: their rates at specified times on given days will be used in the calculation.

The spread determines the discount or premium relative to the reference rate. Because the price of the bond can vary, it does not, however, give an accurate estimate of the spread between the reference rate and the bond's yield. Professional investors have developed several methods to overcome this shortcoming. The simplest method is called the "linear margin" and can be calculated by the following formula:

$$\text{Linear margin} = \frac{s + (1 - B)/n}{B} \qquad (17.1)$$

where s is the spread over the reference rate, B is the market price of the bond and n is the number of years to maturity. For example, the linear margin on an FRN at Libor $+ \frac{1}{4}\%$ with time to maturity of five years quoted at 99.2% is

$$\frac{\dfrac{0{,}25}{100} + \dfrac{1 - 0.992}{5}}{0.992} = 0.413\% \text{ or } 41 \text{ bp.}$$

Another widely used method fixes the reference rate for all future periods and calculates the difference between the yield to maturity (YTM) and the reference rate. It proceeds in two steps. First, the YTM is calculated. If we position ourselves on a coupon payment date, the formula is:

$$B = \sum_{t=1}^{nT} \frac{N(r + s)/T}{(1 + R)^t} + \frac{N_{nT}}{(1 + R)^{nT}} \qquad (17.2)$$

and solving for R, where r is the reference rate, n is the number of years to maturity, T is the number of coupon payments per year, N is the nominal value of the FRN, N_{nT} is the redemption price, and R is the actuarial yield for the fraction of the year $1/T$. Consequently, $[(1+R)^T - 1]$ is equal to the YTM.

The actuarial spread expressed on an annual basis can be found as follows:

$$\text{Actuarial spread} = \left[(1 + R)^T - 1\right] - \left[\left(1 + \frac{r}{T}\right)^T - 1\right] \qquad (17.3)$$

where $(1 + r/T)^T$ is the actuarial yield on the reference rate.

---

[2] This type of operation enables the borrower to take advantage of an upward sloping term structure.

Suppose in the preceding example that the nominal value and redemption value of the bond are the same and equal to USD 10,000. We can use Equation 17.2 to find R:

$$0.992 \times 10,000 = \sum_{t=1}^{5 \times 2} \frac{10,000(0.085 + 0.0025)/2}{(1 + R)^t} + \frac{10,000}{(1 + R)^{nT}}$$

$$R = 0.0447996 \text{ or } 4.47996\%.$$

Substituting this into Equation 17.3 gives

$$\text{Actuarial spread} = 0.48\% \text{ or } 48 \text{ bp.}$$

Perpetual FRNs

Perpetual FRNs were designed as quasi-equity instruments with banks as the most prolific issuers. The FRN bond indenture usually included a subordination clause that subordinated interest payments to all other debts. This and the perpetual nature of the instrument whereby the principal is never reimbursed made the FRN similar to equity capital. Between 1984 and 1986 perpetual FRNs were popular, but they lost their popularity as investors became aware of the risk they were facing and began to require rates of return higher than most issuers could afford.

Minimax and capped FRNs

FRNs have traditionally been issued with a minimum rate embedded in the contract. Some, called minimax FRNs, have been issued with a minimum and a maximum rate. Others, called capped FRNs, have been issued with only a maximum rate. A minimum rate is an advantage for the investor while a maximum rate is an advantage for the issuer.

Convertible and drop lock FRNs

Some issues give the investor the right or the obligation to convert the FRN into a long-term fixed rate bond. Convertible FRNs give the investor the option of converting and are similar to debt warrant FRNs. Drop lock FRNs make conversion automatic if the reference rate falls below some designated floor value. Drop locks have understandably not had much success because they are too constraining for the investor.

Hybrid fixed rate reverse FRNs

Before going too far into financial fantasyland, we can mention one final innovation in the FRN field, the hybrid fixed rate reverse floating rate note. This instrument, developed in 1990 in the Deutschmark sector of the market, pays a high fixed rate coupon (9% or 10%) for the first year or two. Afterwards, investors receive the difference between an even higher fixed rate coupon (15% or 16%) and Libor. This type of instrument can be extremely profitable if short-term rates are expected to fall in the future, which was the case for the Deutschmark in 1990. The reverse is true if short-term rates rise.

Equity-linked bonds

Equity-linked bonds are associated with the right to acquire equity stock in the issuing company. Some have detachable warrants containing the acquisition rights, while others are directly convertible into a specified number of shares.

The market value of a convertible bond can be separated into two parts: the naked value and the conversion value. The naked value is obtained by valuing the bond as if the conversion option did not exist. The conversion value of the bond is added to the naked value to determine the market value of the whole bond.

Consider, for example, a convertible bond with a nominal value of USD 1000 and a conversion ratio of 16.129. The conversion ratio means that each bond can be exchanged for 16.129 equity shares in the issuing company. The conversion price per share is calculated by dividing the bond's nominal value by the conversion factor:

$$\frac{\text{USD } 1000}{16.129} = \text{USD } 62$$

If the market price of the share is less than USD 62, conversion will not happen. The market value of the bond will then be equal to its naked value plus the value of the conversion option (see Chapter 8 for techniques on option valuation). The value of the conversion option depends on the probability that during the period that the bond is convertible the market price of the equity share will go above the conversion price. In Chapter 8 we called this the option's time value. If the equity share price does go above the conversion price, the conversion option will have intrinsic value as well as time value. Figure 17.1 represents these relationships for the convertible bond.

The bond's conversion value can also be expressed as the ratio of the equity share's market price and the conversion price. Suppose that the equity share is quoted at USD 54. The conversion value could be quoted as:

$$\frac{\text{USD } 54}{\text{USD } 62} = 0.87094 \text{ or } 87.094\%$$

If the market price of the convertible bond falls below 87.094%, an arbitrage profit could be made by purchasing the bond, converting it and selling the shares on the market. For example, if the bond price falls to 80%, the investor would purchase it for USD 800, convert it for 16.129 shares, and sell the shares at USD 54 apiece for USD 871.

With this in mind, we can speak of the bond's conversion premium:

$$\text{Conversion premium} = \frac{\text{The bond's market price}}{\text{Conversion value}} - 1$$

Figure 17.1 The value of a convertible bond

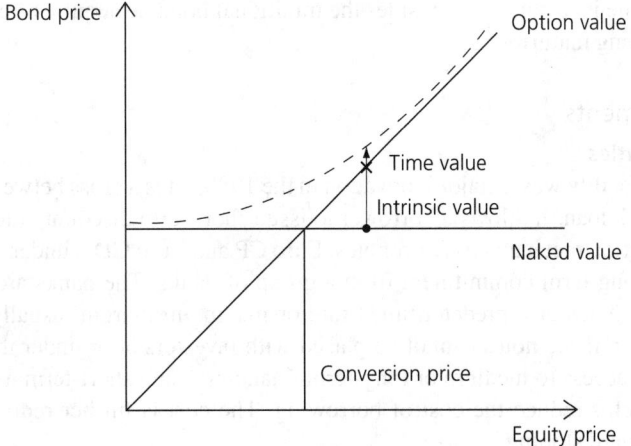

On the issue date, for example, the conversion premium is equal to:

$$\text{Conversion premium} = \frac{100}{87.094} - 1 = 14.82\%.$$

Conversion premiums typically range from 15% to 30% when the bond is issued.

Another way of looking at a convertible bond is to compare the difference between the bond's yield to maturity and the dividend yield with the conversion premium in order to calculate the number of years before the conversion premium will be recovered. This is known as breakeven time. Suppose that the yield on the bond in the preceding example is 7.8% and the dividend yield on the equity share is 2.3%, the difference between the two is 5.5%. We know that the conversion premium is 14.82%. Thus:

$$\text{Breakeven time} = \frac{\text{Conversion premium}}{\text{Bond yield} - \text{Dividend yield}}$$

$$\text{Breakeven time} = \frac{14.82}{7.8 - 2.3} = 2.69 \text{ years.}$$

It would take 2.69 years for the conversion premium to be erased by the convertible bond's yield advantage over the straight equity dividend. The longer the breakeven time the less attractive is the bond for the investor.

It is clear, then, that the performance of convertible bonds depends on the performance of the stock markets. The popularity of convertible bonds grew with the equity markets through the 1980s until the crash of 1987 wiped them out. It should also be noted where convertible bonds are concerned that most of them are subordinated to other classes of debt. Furthermore, besides the conversion option most of them also include an issuer's early redemption option. This option exists in order to force conversion when the market share price is substantially higher than the conversion price. In this context, however, the loss to the investor is limited insofar as the value of the conversion option is composed almost entirely of intrinsic value so that the time value loss is minimal.

Bonds with equity warrants are similar to convertible bonds except that the warrant can be detached from the bond and traded independently. The advantage for the issuer is that it has a double source of financing. The bond remains outstanding even if the warrant is exercised. When a convertible bond is exchanged for equity the debt liability disappears. The advantage for the investor is that besides the traditional bond he acquires a call option with a particularly long maturity.

Other instruments

Euronote facilities

The Euronote facility was a major innovation in the 1980s. It is a cross between a short-term bond and a bank loan. It allows a borrower to issue short-term discount notes via a variety of note distribution mechanisms (Euronotes, Euro CP and Euro CDs) under the umbrella of a medium or long-term commitment from a group of banks. The banks are committed to purchasing the notes at a predetermined rate or maximum margin, usually expressed in relation to Libor, if the notes cannot be placed with investors at or under the margin. The issuer thus has access to medium or long-term financing using short-term negotiable securities, which helps reduce the cost of borrowing. The cost is further reduced if the term structure is upward sloping.

Within the Euronote facility category, a myriad of specific products sporting some creative acronyms has emerged: RUFs (revolving underwriting facilities), NIFs (note issuance facilities), SNIFs (syndicated note issuance facilities), TUFs (transferable underwriting facilities), ENUFs (Euronote underwriting facilities), etc. In fact, the apparent diversity is usually little more than the same basic product packaged differently by the financial institutions doing the marketing.

One issuing procedure entrusts the placement to an arranger. When this formula was created by Merril Lynch under the acronym RUF, the placement was handled by the arranger alone, called the method of the sole placing agent. (This is the same technique used for placing Euro-commercial paper and US commercial paper.) The financing guarantee offered to the issuer was organized as a syndicated backstop credit line. Since then placement has often been syndicated.

Another issuing procedure uses the tender panel. The tender panel is a group, including underwriters, banks and dealers, who are invited to bid on an issuer's paper in an open auction format. If all the paper is not placed or if the required rate is higher than the backstop, the unplaced paper is distributed pro rata among the underwriters.

The set margin procedure resembles a typical syndication where the margin is fixed by the agent and the underwriting banks indicate the amounts they are willing to take at that rate.

Other procedures, similar to those already mentioned, have names like continuous tender panel, split placing agents, authorized placing agents, etc.

Euro-commercial paper

Commercial paper is negotiable, short-term notes or drafts of a governmental agency, bank or corporation. The first Euro-commercial paper dates back to 1971 in response to US regulations on foreign investment. The market really began to develop, though, in the early 1980s and took off in 1986. In fact, Euro CP can be considered a refinement on the Euronote facility because it requires no backup credit. Since 1986 Euro CP facilities have outnumbered Euronote facilities by a large margin.

Euro MTNs

Euro MTNs have maturities of one to five years, fixed coupons and are issued under a program agreement or through one or more dealers. They are small denomination bearer paper listed on the London or Luxembourg stock exchanges.

The secondary market

We have already pointed out that most Eurobonds are registered with a stock exchange during the issuing procedure. Nevertheless, most trading is done over the counter.

On 1 January, 1992 the AIDB changed its name to the International Securities Market Association (ISMA) www.isma.co.uk. ISMA is a Swiss Law Association located in Zürich and regroups all the participants on the Eurobond primary and secondary markets.[3] It aims at facilitating contacts among members, developing their competence and solving any technical difficulties that might crop up in Eurobond trading. It publishes information on prices and transactions in the Eurobond market and has published technical standards (on the calculation of YTM, for example) that are used as a reference by market participants. It was named

---

[3] There is also an association specifically for the primary market called IPMA (International Primary Market Association) (www.ipma.org.uk). IPMA was created on 26 November, 1984 in London. Its role is to keep participants such as lead managers and underwriters informed and to propose standards that will improve the clarity, quality and rapidity of issuing procedures.

by the UK's Securities and Investment Board as a designated investment exchange in 1988 was also approved by the UK Secretary of State for Trade and Industry as an International Securities Self Regulatory Organization under the UK's Financial Services Act.

Like most modern financial markets, the Eurobond OTC market operates on two levels. On the first level are the reporting dealers who have a market-making role quoting bid–ask prices on a specified list of securities. There are about 100 of them registered with ISMA. They are required to supply ISMA with weekly information on the transactions they have effected. Most reporting dealers make markets for bonds denominated in the currency of their country of origin. For example, Japanese banks make markets in Euroyen issues and UK banks make markets in Eurosterling issues.

On the second level are the other traders and the brokers. Non-reporting traders have a role similar to that of the reporting dealers without the market-making obligation. The brokers act as simple intermediaries between buyers and sellers.

In order to increase market liquidity, issuers often use the technique of assimilation whereby different issues have the same characteristics concerning coupons, maturity and redemption. Only the issue price varies in order to conform to market conditions prevailing on the different issue dates. Issues can be in different tranches or on a more regular tap basis.

Prices are quoted bid–ask net of commissions and settlement and delivery are effected seven calendar days after the transaction. The accrued coupon is calculated on the settlement date on a 30/360 basis.

Syndicated Eurocredits

A Eurocurrency is any freely convertible currency, such as a dollar or a yen, deposited in a bank outside its country of origin. In Chapter 5 we looked at the interbank Eurocurrency market and saw that it plays a key role in the international money and banking system. It is a major source of international liquidity and figures prominently in determining exchange rates and financing balance of payments disequilibrium. The retail side of the Eurocurrency market is also important. It is one of the major sources of large-scale financing for a wide range of countries, institutions and firms. Because of the increasing tendency of banks to securitize their riskiest assets,[4] it is also a source of many bonds that are traded on the international bond market. In this section we examine the retail side of the Eurocurrency market, see how it is organized, the different types of instruments available, their advantages, disadvantages and costs, and how they can be used.

Background on the retail Eurocurrency market

Historical background

Syndicated Eurocurrency loans were at the origin of the internationalization of medium-term financing formulas. Although the Eurobond market is older than the Eurocurrency loan market, it offered few possibilities for variable interest rates and went into decline following the sharp interest rate increases at the end of the 1960s. Starting at the end of the 1960s the first syndicated Eurocurrency loan operations began to appear. They thrust the banks back into their fundamental economic role of transforming short-term resources into

---

[4] Brady bonds are the most notorious example of the securitization of bank loans. However, because of the capital requirements in the Cooke ratios and now in the BIS 1998 capital requirements, many other risky loans have been securitized and sold off.

long-term assets. Banks financed medium and long-term loans by borrowing short term. The resulting interest rate risk was transferred to the borrower by making the interest rate on the loans subject to periodic modifications depending on the prevailing conditions.

In 1974 the syndicated Eurocurrency loan market took several bad hits as a result of the first oil shock and the bankruptcies of the Franklin National Bank of New York and Germany's Herstatt Bank. At the time, the bankruptcies of these two important banks were explained away as isolated incidents caused by unauthorized currency speculation. In fact, the financial turbulence of the time was the source of the problem and the bank failures exacerbated the situation, especially on the interbank market.

From the end of 1974 when things began to calm down until 1982, the syndicated Eurocurrency loan market grew almost exponentially due to the necessity of financing balance of payments deficits in the developing countries and some of the major industrialized countries. During this period, more and more banks entered the market, competing for business and squeezing margins to a minimum. Even interest rates above 18 and 19% did nothing to dampen the market's euphoria caused by the developing countries' insatiable appetite for ever-more foreign resources and the banks' willingness to oblige them. The banks were motivated by short-term considerations of large commissions and the prestige and notoriety associated with Eurocurrency loan syndication. The developing countries were motivated by the ease of mobilizing vast sums with few or no strings attached. Together, they managed to end up wiping out massive chunks of bank shareholders' equity and provoking extreme economic hardship in debtor countries.

The trouble began with Poland in 1982 and reached its climax with Mexico's financial default later in the year, followed by Brazil and Argentina and finally by most of the world's indebted developing countries.[5] The resulting slowdown in lending activity was large and lasting, especially if we consider that much of the volume after 1983 was due to refinancing arrangements associated with the rescheduling of outstanding loans. Since 1982 the Eurobond has become a major competitor of the syndicated Eurocurrency loan. Nevertheless, the syndicated Eurocurrency loan has managed to survive and prosper.

Access to international sources of financing

Many firms and institutions are too small, too unknown or too risky to appeal to most segments of the international capital markets. Institutional investors who dominate many of these markets, for example, prefer investment grade securities with low default risk and a large and liquid secondary market. They have neither the means nor the expertise to evaluate the securities of most firms and institutions that do not fulfill these criteria. Banks, on the other hand, because of the nature of their role as intermediary with many agents in a wide range of transactions feel that they have the expertise and means of evaluating and managing risks and maturities that are unattractive to other segments of the international markets. Where other investors see problems and risk, banks see opportunity and profit. Consequently, many borrowers that would otherwise be excluded gain access to international financial resources through the Eurocurrency market.

Diversified sources and large-scale loans

Syndicated Eurocurrency loans can range from USD 50 million to several billion dollars, but sums of USD 200–500 million are most common. The syndication procedure thus

---

[5] Other bankruptcies in 1982 exacerbated the crisis in the Eurocurrency market. The three most notable were the brokerage firm Drysdale Securities in New York, Penn Square Bank in Oklahoma City and the Banco Ambrosiano in Italy with its criminal ramifications.

enables the borrower to obtain large amounts of capital in one single operation, which reduces costs. It also guarantees that the sources of the funding are diversified across a wide range of lenders, thereby avoiding too much reliance on one big lender. Furthermore, once the borrower has signed with the bank or banks that are to organize the syndicate, he is sure to obtain the agreed sum at the negotiated terms.

Speed and flexibility

One of the most attractive qualities of a Eurocurrency credit facility is that it can be mobilized quickly and easily. The documentation is standardized and simple and there is no waiting list to respect as there is in the Eurobond market, for example. The whole procedure takes only four to six weeks.

The actual terms of a Eurocurrency credit facility can be tailored to the borrower's specific needs. This is a big advantage that Euroloans have over other types of financing. Standby credits, for example, make it possible for borrowers to mobilize a large loan just in case they need it. If they need to use it, they pay the interest and commissions just as they would on a normal loan. If they do not use it, they only pay the commissions and perhaps a small fee. This type of facility is especially interesting to borrowers with access to the other segments of the international financial markets who might need temporary alternative financing if they deem conditions in the other markets unfavorable to them. Another advantage is the standard clause that permits the loan to be paid off at any time without penalty.

Most Eurocurrency loans are negotiated for between five and ten years at a small spread over the three-month or six-month interest rate that is revised regularly. History has shown that short-term interest rates are usually lower than medium to long-term interest rates. Consequently, the flexibility of the interest rate on the loan gives the borrower access to medium or long-term capital but only requires him to pay short-term rates.

Characteristics of syndicated Eurocredits

The lead manager

Syndication refers to a number of banks grouping together to make a loan to one borrower. It is usually necessary because of the size of the loans involved. As we said, loans of this type can range from USD 50 million to several billion dollars. What a syndicated loan boils down to is a series of loans by different banks made simultaneously to a common borrower. There is no fundamental legal solidarity among the banks that arises from syndication and many pages of the loan contracts are filled with clauses that take this into account. The number of banks participating in a syndication can go as high as 100 or more but there is a precise hierarchy within the syndicate corresponding to each bank's responsibilities. The lead manager has the most important role in organizing the loan from beginning to end and is always a large, internationally recognized bank. There are currently about 30 banks that can realistically aspire to this rank. The lead manager is responsible for negotiating the overall conditions of the loan concerning rates, maturities, guarantees, etc. with the borrower. It is also responsible for organizing the syndicate by finding the other banks that want to participate.

Sometimes a syndicate will include two or more lead managers. The reasons for having more than one lead manager are usually because of the size of the loan or because financial or commercial strategy dictates it. When more than one lead manager is involved, they usually are of different nationalities in order to cover as many markets as possible. The different lead managers are referred to as co-lead managers, co-managers, or just managers. In practice the "management group" is distinguished from the simple participants by their organizational role and the sums they are pledging. As we will see, this distinction is important for distributing the commissions that are earned on the deal.

Organizing the loan

The lead manager is often chosen directly by the borrower as a result of their ongoing relations or following an announcement by the borrower soliciting propositions. As the head of the syndicate, the lead manager is responsible for drawing up the placing memorandum that is then sent out by telex to certain banks that might be interested in participating in underwriting the loan. The placing memorandum is a confidential document that contains all the relevant information about the borrower and the placement. Generally, banks that are contacted for participation are regular partners of the lead manager. Experience has shown, in fact, that syndicates tend to remain stable over time and there is a strong tradition of reciprocity among members.

A syndicate is rarely formed by one wave of telexes, however. Several invitations are usually necessary. The first wave of telexes is destined for banks that have expressed an interest in the loan so that their demand can be satisfied. The second wave go to banks less known to the lead manager and their number depends on how well the loan is received by the market.

When the lead manager or management group decides that the loan is ready, each participating bank, called an underwriter, is contacted and the amount of their participation is confirmed. Once the syndicate is finally formed and all the details ironed out, the contract is signed and the borrower gets access to its money. Several weeks after the signing ceremony, a "tombstone" is published in the financial press. A tombstone is an advertisement, published as a matter of record to announce completion of the loan, stating the borrower's name, certain terms of the issue, and lists the managers and underwriters.

Most placements are effected in one stage as described above. It will be in one stage if the managers are contractually obligated to cover the entire loan whether or not underwriting participation by other banks is high enough. It can be in several stages if the loan is organized on a "best-effort basis" where the managers only promise to attempt to find purchasers. Sometimes the management group decides to underwrite the operation on its own without the participation of outside banks. This type of syndication is known as a club deal.

Once the loan has been completed, the main role switches from the lead manager to that of the agent bank. The agent bank, which is often the same as the lead manager, is the official intermediary between the borrower and the underwriting syndicate. Its primary responsibilities are to determine the interest rate for each period and to see that the terms of the loan are respected.

Guidelines for choosing the management group

The management group is important for the success of the loan. A badly received loan can make the borrower look bad and hurt its credit standing while a well received one can make it look good and help its credit standing. Consequently, much care should be taken when choosing a management group.

In order to ensure the loan's success, banks in the management group should be large and internationally recognized. They should also be diversified geographically within the management group to ensure that the loan has the widest circulation. Geographical diversification is also good publicity for the borrower. It is often a good idea to include a bank of the same nationality as the borrower. This reinforces the borrower's domestic banking relations and can also be useful for relations with domestic authorities. Other important considerations are the loyalty of the banks, and their capacity for innovation. Innovative financial, organizational or commercial procedures can be helpful in securing the most favorable terms for the borrower.

Different types of credits

There are two basic categories of Eurocurrency credit facilities: term loans and revolving credit facilities. A term loan can be divided into three stages: the drawdown period, the grace period and the **redemption period**. During the drawdown period, which usually lasts about 24 months, the borrower can increase the amount of his loan. The increases can be by simple advance notification or they can be scheduled contractually. The grace period comes after the drawdown period. During this time, the amount of the loan does not change and the only cash flows are those related to interest and commissions. The redemption period refers to the period when the loan is paid off. It can be paid off in one single installment, called a bullet repayment, or in several installments, called a staged repayment. As already mentioned, most Eurocurrency loans give the borrower the right to prepay the loan with no penalty.

A **revolving credit facility** is a loan that permits the borrower to drawdown and repay at its discretion for a specified period of time. This increased flexibility has a cost paid in the form of a commission, called the commitment fee. The commitment fee is paid on the unused portion of a facility. The basis for charging the fee can vary considerably, particularly if it is to remain undrawn for an extended period. As we mentioned, a revolving credit is especially useful for borrowers with access to the other segments of the international financial markets who might need a bridging loan to tide them over between the end of one issue and the beginning of another.

Term loans and revolving credit facilities are only the generic types of syndicated Eurocredits. Since the market is over the counter, loans can be tailored to suit the specific needs of the borrower. This is where innovation can come in handy. Possibilities are unlimited. Evergreen facilities, for example, give the borrower the right to extend the loan indefinitely after its designated maturity. **Multi-currency loans** give the borrower the possibility of drawing the loan in several different currencies. This is especially useful for managing exchange rate risk. Maturities are also flexible. Most Euroloans are medium term, lasting from four to eight years, but it is not surprising to find maturities of up to 20 years.

Borrowing costs: Interest and commissions

Interest

Interest rates on Eurocurrency credit facilities are usually variable, expressed as a percent over a given reference rate: for example, Libor plus $\frac{3}{8}$%. The reference interest rate for most Eurocurrency loans is Libor, which is the rate at which banks are willing to lend to each other on the interbank Eurocurrency market in London.[6] Other reference rates are also used. One of the most popular is the prime rate. In the US domestic market the prime rate is the rate of interest at which a commercial bank offers to lend money to its most credit-worthy customers.

Variable interest rates have advantages for both borrower and lender. They insulate the banks from interest rate risk while they give the borrower access to medium to long-term money at short-term rates. The disadvantage is that variable rates make borrowers more vulnerable to default when interest rates rise. Consequently, by laying the interest rate risk

---

[6] Other financial centers are also used as a reference rate. For example, Pibor in Paris, Luxibor in Luxembourg, Sibor in Singapore and Bibor in Bahrain.

off on the borrower, banks have effectively exchanged interest rate risk for increased default risk.[7] Consider, for example, the situation where a borrower contracts for a variable rate Eurocurrency loan when rates are at 8%. His ability to service his debt might be jeopardized if rates rise to 14% or 15%. This, in fact, is what happened to a number of developing countries that went bankrupt in the 1980s. Dollar Libor went from 6% in 1977 to 16.5% in 1981 and contributed to the well known debt crisis.

Since the reference rate is usually a market rate that varies from one minute to the next, its calculation is the object of numerous clauses in the loan agreement. Certain banks are designated as reference banks whose rates will be used in the calculation. When it comes time to recalculate the reference rate, the agent bank notifies the reference banks specifying the day and the exact time that rates are to be sampled. Most loan agreements apply the rate observed two days before the beginning of the new interest period at a time of day when there is a lot of trading activity. The agent bank then calculates the new reference rate by taking the average of the rates observed by the various reference banks on the day and at the time specified in the loan agreement. It should also be noted that most loan agreements stipulate that any taxes, such as withholding taxes, that lower the lender's return lead to an immediate and automatic readjustment of the reference rate.

The spread over the reference rate is the second element in the determination of the interest rate on a syndicated Eurocurrency credit facility: for example, Libor plus $\frac{3}{8}$%. The spread can be fixed once and for all for the life of the loan or it can vary. It might, for example, be fixed at $\frac{1}{2}$% for the first three years of the loan and then rise to $\frac{3}{4}$% after that. The size of the spread depends on several factors. First of all, it depends on the quality of the borrower and the risk it represents. Where sovereign borrowers are concerned, some authors think that the size of the spread constitutes a pertinent estimation of country risk.[8] It also depends on the prevailing market conditions at the time the loan is negotiated. Finally, the duration of the loan also plays a role in the size of the spread.

Commissions

After interest charges, the second element in the cost of a syndicated Eurocurrency credit facility is the commissions paid to the syndicate. They come in two forms: up-front fees and periodic fees. The up-front fee is called the management fee. It usually does not figure in the loan agreement and is paid to the lead bank when the loan agreement is signed. The lead bank then divides this fee up among the different members of the syndicate according to the role they played in organizing and underwriting the loan.

Praecipium
The praecipium is the lead manager's fee for assuming responsibility for setting up and coordinating the syndication of the loan. Suppose, for example, that the praecipium is $\frac{1}{8}$% and the amount of the loan is USD 250 million. The lead manager will receive

$$0.00125 \times USD\ 250,000,000 = USD\ 312,500.$$

Underwriting fee
This fee is paid to the banks in the management group depending on how much of the loan they underwrote (guaranteed) between the time that their mandate was received and the

---

[7] See O. Grabbe, *International Financial Markets* (Elsevier, 1986).

[8] C. Dufloux and L. Margulici, *Les Euro-crédits: Pourquoi? Comment?* (La Revue Banque, 1984).

time that the loan was placed with the other participating banks. Suppose, for example, that the underwriting fee is $\frac{1}{4}$% and a co-manager underwrote USD 50 million. His commission will be:

$$0.0025 \times USD\ 50,000,000 = USD\ 125,000.$$

Participation fee

This fee is paid to the banks that agree to participate in underwriting the loan. It often increases as the amounts that are underwritten increase. Suppose, for example, that the fee is $\frac{1}{4}$% for amounts between USD 3 and USD 6 million and $\frac{3}{8}$% for amounts higher than USD 6 million. A bank that signs up for USD 4 million will receive:

$$0.0025 \times USD\ 4,000,000 = USD\ 10,000.$$

A bank that signs up for USD 8 million will receive:

$$0.00375 \times USD\ 8,000,000 = USD\ 30,000.$$

If anything is left over after all the fees have been paid, the management group usually divides it up pro rata to their final underwriting share.

Periodic fees can be divided into two groups: the commitment fee and the agency fee. The commitment fee is paid periodically on the unused portion of the loan and rewards the lender for giving the borrower the right but not the obligation to draw on the facility. In this sense it resembles the premium paid for options. The agency fee is a fixed sum paid annually that goes to reward the agent bank for overseeing interest payments and distributing them to participating banks.

Legal aspects

One of the fundamental aspects of the loan agreement is the choice of the legal system and jurisdiction of the court where the case will be tried in case of a conflict. The reason is that the nature of syndicated Eurocurrency loans is such that the nationality of the borrower and the lenders is different. Consequently, the legal system and court jurisdiction must be agreed upon contractually. In practice, English law and the law of the state of New York are the best known and most often chosen. The choice can be influenced, however, by where the borrower holds its assets since it is there that judgements can be most easily executed. For obvious reasons, borrowers like to impose their own domestic legal systems, especially when they are sovereign states. France, for example, usually attempts to impose French law on its Eurocurrency loan agreements. While this is often possible for developed countries with independent, respectable legal systems, it is much more difficult for countries that do not fit into this category.

In general, the legal system of reference should be justified by some objective criteria. For example, an underwriting bank with the same nationality as the legal system of reference would qualify as satisfactory objective criteria. The country whose currency is used in the loan would also qualify. In this case, New York could objectively be chosen as the legal jurisdiction of reference if the loan is denominated in dollars.

Once the legal system of reference has been decided upon, it is necessary to choose the authority competent to render a judgement. It could simply be the court system of the country in question. It could, however, be another non-legal organization such as the international chamber of commerce. Still, to avoid the necessity of falling back into the vagaries of common law, which is often ill-suited to the spirit of Eurocurrency loan transactions, the loan agreement is long and detailed and tries to spell out precise settlement formulas for any and all possible sources of conflict. Certain clauses, for example, aim at outside intervention – usually government intervention – that could have the effect of altering the obligations of one or more parties. The intervention could take the form of fiscal measures, credit limits, foreign exchange controls and the like. In any case, the custom is that the borrower is liable for any extra costs related to difficulties of this type.

Other clauses, called representations and warranties of borrowers, aim at the guarantees supplied by the borrower. The borrower swears to the veracity of the information he has supplied concerning his financial situation and his ability to service the loan. He also commits himself to respect certain norms relating to future debt and subordination. Subordination refers to ranking one type of claim below another for payment in the case of default. These guarantees constitute covenants. A covenant is an agreement by a borrower, which is legally binding on the borrower over the life of an issue or loan, to perform certain acts or to refrain from certain acts. An agreement to refrain from certain acts is called a negative pledge clause. Where subordination is concerned, for example, the borrower agrees to abstain from contracting new loans that would have the effect of subordinating the rights of holders of the current loan. In this way, the borrower is prohibited from weakening the guarantees underlying the loan. The pari passu clause obliges the borrower to treat all members of the syndicate equally. It is designed to prevent the borrower from using divisive tactics within the syndicate in order to gain an advantage. In this way, small banks are on an equal footing with the big banks. The cross default clause stipulates that the borrower will be declared in default on his loan if he is declared in default on any other loan currently outstanding or to be contracted in the future. In other words, if the borrower defaults on one, he defaults on all. The aim of this clause is to protect the lenders in the case where the borrower ceases payment on some debt while continuing payment on other debt. In its absence, creditors receiving regular payments as contracted in the loan agreement could not stop creditors holding defaulted debt from seizing assets to pay themselves off and thereby weakening the ability of the borrower to pay off the undefaulted debt.

Secondary market

One of the consequences of the debt crisis of 1982 was the development of a secondary market for Eurocurrency loans, especially after 1984–85. The market developed as lenders began to realize the necessity for more effective risk management. Diversification was a credible solution. With the secondary market, banks with debt concentrated in one country or area could reduce their risk by trading off part of it for debt in another country or area. For example, a bank with large exposure in Mexico could improve its position by reducing its claims on Mexico in exchange for claims on Bulgaria. This was especially true where sovereign debt was concerned.

The emergence of a secondary market in Eurocurrency loans can also be explained by banks' desire to sell off loans as a means of improving the quality of their balance sheets to enable them to get back into the commission-generating business of loan making. There are three procedures for a bank to sell part or all of its position in a syndicated loan:

- *Novation*: An existing loan is canceled and a new contract is substituted in its place with the agreement of the borrower.

- *Assignment*: This technique is similar to novation and is applied when a drawing has already taken place. It amounts to a contract between the new lender and the old one. The borrower must agree to the new contract. In this case the transfer of rights only applies to interest and principal payments.

- *Sub-participation*: In the case of sub-participation, there is no transfer of rights attached to the original loan and it can be effected without the agreement of the borrower. The purchaser of the sub-participation receives interest that is slightly lower than that prescribed in the loan agreement.

Beyond these simple techniques, the successive reschedulings and renegotiations that affected developing country debt led to active swap markets. The most common types of swaps involved are asset-for-asset swaps and debt–equity swaps. In an asset-for-asset swap creditors exchange the debt of one defaulting borrower for the debt of another. In general, the debt that is exchanged is quoted as a percentage of 100%.

Debt–equity swaps have been used by developing countries to generate direct investment. In the debt–equity swap, debt is purchased at a discount by an investor and traded to the central bank – which takes a percentage in passing – for the domestic currency necessary to make the investment. The investor is thus able to make his investment at a considerable reduction in cost while the country reduces its external debt with no outflows of foreign exchange. Some swap operations are effected on an ad hoc basis by firms wanting to invest in one country or another. This was Nissan's approach in Mexico.[9] Other countries, such as Argentina and Brazil, organized large-scale debt–equity swap programs at the end of the 1980s. They were usually aimed at takeovers or purchases of existing local companies through a system of public auction. Another, more marginal kind of swap, consists of exchanging outstanding debt for other goods, such as raw materials, produced by the borrowing country.

Some indebted countries have taken advantage of the discounts on their debt by buying it back at the lower price. Bolivia, for example, was able to purchase USD 240 million of its outstanding debt for only USD 26.4 million, or 11% of the nominal value. These debt buy-backs are attractive for the borrower but not always accepted by lenders.

Some operations on the secondary market are more elaborate affairs than simple swaps or sales. Take, for example, the Morgan 20-year Aztec bonds at Libor + $1\frac{5}{8}$% issued by Mexico in 1988. These new bonds were auctioned off in exchange for outstanding Mexican debt. Besides the high spread, they had the advantage of being guaranteed by 20-year US Treasury zero coupon bonds. Thus, USD 3.66 billion of outstanding debt was paid for USD 2.56 billion of the new bonds, a discount of 30% that reduced outstanding debt by a net USD 1.1 billion. USD 523 million of zero coupon 20-year US Treasury bonds yielding about 8.265% were purchased by Mexico to guarantee reimbursement of the principal at the end of 20 years. The principal was guaranteed but interest payments were not. Still, lenders had a higher quality claim and Mexico had a lower level of outstanding debt. This Aztec bond was the precursor to the Brady bonds that became the most active market for emerging market debt in the 1990s.

Brady bonds

Brady bonds are bonds that have been restructured from defaulted commercial bank loans. They were introduced in the Brady Plan of 1989, accredited to former US Treasury Secretary, Nicholas Brady, as a means of overcoming the hangover from the debt crisis of the early 1980s. It arose from the failure of conventional restructuring policies that had been tried to restore economic growth and financial stability to the indebted, less developed countries. The Plan was instrumental in restoring access to the capital markets for countries previously considered bad debtors. To date, only one country – Ecuador in

---

[9] See W. Ollard, "The Debt Swappers", *Euromoney* (August 1986).

August 1999 – has ever defaulted on payment, and the Brady bond market has become the largest and most liquid of the emerging markets.

In February 1990, Mexico became the first country to issue Bradys bonds, converting USD 48.1 billion of its eligible foreign debt to commercial banks, it offered banks two options for the exchange of their loans into tradable securities: the discount bonds gave a 35% discount in the face value of the debt, but offered a market-based coupon of Libor plus 0.8125%, while the par bonds were issued at face value, but included a below-market coupon of 6.25%. Banks also had a third option, which allowed them to carry the full principal amount of the loans on their books while providing new lending of at least 25% of their existing exposure over three years. The principal on both types of bonds was fully collateralized in the form of US zero coupon bonds and there was a rolling interest guarantee covering 18 months' worth of interest payments. By May 1994 12 other countries had issued Brady plans for a total of over USD 190 billion.

Although structures have become more complex over time, the basic principles are based on the Mexican deal. One major option added in later issues was the buy-back option, which allows a country to repurchase part of its debt at an agreed discount, thereby enabling it to participate in a debt reduction program. The vast majority of outstanding Brady bonds are US dollar denominated, and although some bonds have been issued in other major currencies, the non-dollar issues tend to be relatively illiquid. The market is largely a longer-dated market and over half of current outstanding Brady bonds have maturities of longer than 20 years, and over 72% have maturities longer than 10 years. Outstandings are evenly divided between fixed and floating rate instruments.

Both investment and commercial banks make active markets in Brady bonds, and the investor base has widened to include mutual funds, money managers, insurance companies and pension funds. Table 17.3 gives an idea of the bid/ask spreads on some of the most popular bonds as of 3 August 2001.

An important point to stress is that although the term "Brady bond" can be used to describe an asset class, because of the wide variation in the characteristics of instruments, performance of a particular country's Brady bonds can vary widely. During 1996, fixed rate par bonds, which are typically longer-dated instruments carrying collateral on both the principal as well as a rolling guarantee on the interest, significantly underperformed uncollateralized floating rate instruments, particularly those at the shorter end of the yield curve. The main reason for this was a decline in the value of the underlying collateral as US Treasury rates rose, and the relative unattractiveness of a fixed rate coupon in a rising interest rate environment.

Besides straight bond trading, the development of this market has led to a number of indices and derivative products that are also actively traded. For example, the CME trades

Table 17.3 Bid–ask prices for selected Brady bonds, 3 August 2001

	Bid	Ask
Argentina Par	58.750	59.750
Brazil Discount	71.250	71.375
Bulgaria IAB	77.750	78.500
Mexico	92.125	92.250
Poland Par	71.500	71.750

Source: Bradynet.com.

futures and options contracts on Brady bonds and JP Morgan publishes a widely used Brady bond index called the Emerging Markets Bond Index (EMBI).

Summary

1. The globalization of the world's capital markets benefits borrowers and lenders. Borrowers benefit from lower rates through competition among the different markets and the possibility of diversifying their financing sources. Investors also benefit from diversification, especially from access to new products with unique characteristics arising from the different legal, fiscal and economic systems of the countries where they are issued.

2. Investing in foreign countries requires a thorough technical knowledge of each domestic market. Products, trading practices and price and yield quotations concerning the various instruments can vary from market to market. Taxes and regulations, such as exchange controls and surtaxes, can also differ.

3. The Eurobond market is a major source of finance for top quality borrowers such as governments and government agencies of developed countries, international organizations, banks from developed countries and large corporations from developed countries.

4. Eurobonds are issued in countries other than the one in whose currency they are denominated. They are not traded on a particular national bond market and, therefore, are not regulated by any domestic authority.

5. The development of the swap market has contributed to the growth of the use of currencies other than the dollar, euro and yen for Eurobond issues.

6. The traditional issuing technique on the Eurobond market, called the European method, is faster than on most domestic markets but still is time-consuming insofar as it involves the constitution of a syndicate and the placing of the issue. In the 1980s, market uncertainty pushed syndicating banks to speed up the issuing procedure in order to enable them and borrowers to take advantage of the ever-changing market conditions. The accelerated issuing procedure, called a bought deal, resembles the banking sector's club deal in the Euroloan market. It involves the offer of a package deal to a potential issuer by a small group of underwriting institutions.

7. Open trading of Eurobonds is handled by market-makers and dealers belonging to the ISMA. Prices are quoted bid–ask net of commissions.

8. The three main types of Eurobonds are fixed rate issues or straight bonds, floating rate notes (FRNs) and equity-linked bonds, either convertible or with warrants attached. The heart of the market consists of fixed rate issues but, at one time or another depending on market conditions, the other two types have known periods of significant popularity.

9. Syndicated Eurocurrency loan facilities are one of the major sources of large-scale financing for a wide range of institutions and firms. They are at the heart of the internationalization of medium-term financing formulas.

10. The Eurocurrency loan market developed for many reasons. (a) It gives access to many firms and institutions that are too small, too unknown, or too risky to appeal to most segments of the international capital markets. (b) The syndication procedure enables the borrower to obtain large amounts of capital in one single operation, which reduces costs. (c) It guarantees that the sources of the funding are diversified across a wide range of lenders, thereby avoiding too much reliance on one big lender. (d) One of the most attractive qualities of a Eurocurrency credit facility is that it can be mobilized quickly

and easily. The whole procedure takes only four to six weeks. (e) The actual terms of a Eurocurrency credit facility can be tailored to the borrower's specific needs.

11. Syndication refers to a number of banks grouping together to make a loan to one borrower. It is usually necessary because of the size of the loans involved. The lead manager is responsible for negotiating the overall conditions of the loan (rates, maturities, guarantees, etc.) with the borrower. It is also responsible for organizing the syndicate by finding the other banks that want to participate. Sometimes a syndicate will include two or more lead managers.

12. The management group is important for the success of the loan. A badly received loan can make the borrower look bad and damage its credit standing, while a well received one can make it look good and help its credit standing. Consequently, much care should be taken when choosing a management group.

13. There are two basic categories of Eurocurrency credit facilities: term loans and revolving credit facilities. A term loan has a fixed maturity and can be divided into three stages: the drawdown period, the grace period and the redemption period. A revolving credit facility is a loan that permits the borrower to draw down and repay at its discretion for a specified period of time. Since the market is over the counter, however, loans can be tailored to suit the specific needs of the borrower. This is where innovation is important and possibilities are unlimited.

14. Borrowing costs are composed of interest and commissions. Interest rates on Eurocurrency credit facilities are usually variable, expressed as a percent over a given reference rate: for example, Libor plus $\frac{3}{8}$%. Variable interest rates have advantages for both borrower and lender. They insulate the banks from interest rate risk while they give the borrower access to medium to long-term money at short-term rates. The disadvantage is that variable rates make borrowers more vulnerable to default when interest rates rise. Consequently, by laying the interest rate risk off on the borrower, banks have effectively exchanged interest rate risk for increased default risk.

15. Commissions come in two forms: up-front fees and periodic fees. The up-front fee is called the management fee. It usually does not figure in the loan agreement and is paid to the lead bank when the loan agreement is signed. The lead bank then divides this fee up among the different members of the syndicate according to the role they played in organizing and underwriting the loan. Periodic fees can be divided into two groups: the commitment fee and the agency fee. The commitment fee is paid periodically on the unused portion of the loan and rewards the lender for giving the borrower the right but not the obligation to draw on the facility. The agency fee is a fixed sum paid annually that goes to reward the agent bank for overseeing interest payments and distributing them to participating banks.

16. One of the fundamental aspects of the loan agreement is the choice of the legal system and jurisdiction of the court where the case will be tried in case of a conflict. The reason is that the nature of syndicated Eurocurrency loans is such that the nationality of the borrower and the lenders is different. Consequently, the legal system and court jurisdiction must be agreed upon contractually. In practice, English law and the law of the state of New York are those most often chosen. Once the legal system of reference has been decided upon, it is necessary to choose the authority competent to render a judgement. It could simply be the court system of the country in question. It could, however, be another non-legal organization such as the international chamber of commerce.

17. One of the consequences of the debt crisis of 1982 was the development of a secondary market for Eurocurrency loans, especially after 1984–85. Debt is actively traded or

swapped in an over-the-counter market and derivative products are actively traded. The largest part of this market is devoted to Brady bonds, which represent repackaged, defaulted debt.

Questions

Solutions to the following questions are set out on the web site, details of which are included in the Preface.

1. What is the most common type of US Treasury debt?

2. On the 5 March, what is the price of a US Treasury bill maturing on 17 July, if the interest rate is 7%?

3. Under US commercial bank regulations, what qualifies a bond as investment grade? What are "junk bonds"?

4. Qualified institutional buyers are:

   a. Primary dealers on the T-bill market.

   b. Dealers on the secondary market for private placements.

   c. Dealers on the secondary market for MTNs.

5. How is the "benchmark" issue decided on in the Japanese market?

6. How would the yield on a JGB with a 6% coupon, a maturity of four years and a price of 96.5% be quoted in Japan?

7. A Samurai bond is:

   a. A yen bond issued in the United States by an institution residing in Japan.

   b. A yen bond issued in Japan by an institution residing outside of Japan.

   c. A non-yen bond issued in Japan by an institution residing outside Japan.

8. What is the name given to UK government bonds?

9. What is a Eurobond and how does it differ from a domestic bond?

10. What is the issuing procedure for a Eurobond?

11. What is the difference between a syndicated Eurocredit and a Eurobond?

12. True or false: Many borrowers that would otherwise be excluded from international sources of financing gain access through the Eurocurrency market. Explain.

13. Why are Euroloans attractive to borrowers?

14. Describe the process for organizing a syndicated loan.

15. What is a "club deal"?

16. What is the difference between a term loan and a revolving credit facility?

17. When speaking of the interest rate on a Eurocurrency loan, what is the reference rate and how is it calculated? What factors go into determining the spread?

18. Define "praecipium", "underwriting fee", "participation fee", and "commitment fee".

19. What are the major legal aspects involved in Eurocurrency loan contracts?

20. How is the secondary market for Eurocurrency bank loans organized?

Managing interest rate risk

To understand the issues involved in managing a portfolio of interest-bearing securities, some background on securities pricing and the term structure of interest rates is necessary.

Bond prices and yields: A review of concepts and techniques

The market price of a bond is found by discounting all future cash flows at the appropriate interest rate. The appropriate rate depends on the term structure of interest rates, which we will take up in the next section. For now, we can assume that the appropriate rate is known. The price of a **zero coupon bond** (pure discount bond) paying USD 100 in one year would be:

$$B_1 = \frac{\text{USD } 100}{1 + {_0}r_{0,1}}$$

where B_1 represents the price of the bond and $_0r_{0,1}$ is the appropriate interest rate. This rate is called a **spot interest rate** or the spot interest rate zero coupon basis. Spot rates are interest rates on bonds with only one cash flow. The subscript before r indicates when the commitment was made, the first subscript after r indicates when the loan is made, and the second subscript indicates when the loan is to be repaid. Thus, $_0r_{0,1}$ means that the commitment for the loan is made at the end of period zero, the loan itself is also made at the end of period zero and the loan is to be repaid at the end of period one. If $_0r_{0,1} = 8\%$, then

$$B_1 = \frac{\text{USD } 100}{1 + 0.08} = \text{USD } 92.59$$

Imagine another zero coupon bond paying USD 1100 at the end of year two with $_0r_{0,2}$, the spot rate on a two-year loan, equal to 12%. Its market price would be:

$$B_2 = \frac{\text{USD } 1100}{(1.12)^2} = \text{USD } 876.91.$$

Consider a third bond with a USD 1000 face value paying a coupon of 10% redeemable "*in fine*" at par and a maturity of two years. *In fine* means at the end of the loan and par means at the bond's face value. The bond's cash flows will then be USD 100 at the end of

475

the first year and USD 1100 at the end of the second year. Since this bond has the same cash flows as bonds one and two together, *ceteris paribus*, it should have the same market price as the sum of their values. Otherwise arbitrage would be possible by buying the cheaper of the two combinations and selling the other. Thus,

$$B_3 = B_1 + B_2 = \frac{\text{USD } 100}{1.08} + \frac{\text{USD } 1100}{(1.12)^2} = \text{USD } 969.50.$$

Correct valuation of a coupon bond involves considering each cash flow as an individual zero coupon bond and discounting it at the appropriate spot rate.

Yield to maturity is the interest figure quoted most frequently by investors and professionals. It is the rate that equates the present value of the future cash flows with the present market value of the bond. In other words, it is the bond's **internal rate of return**. Thus, the yields to maturity on bonds one and two above are their spot rates, 8% and 12% respectively. The yield to maturity on bond three, however, is 11.8% and represents a type of weighted average of the spot rates. Calculating yield to maturity involves setting the bond's market price equal to the present value of its cash flows discounted at the rate r, which is the unknown, and solving. Bond three, for example, has a market price of USD 969.50, a cash flow of USD 100 the first year and a cash flow of USD 1100 the second year. The yield to maturity can be found by solving the following equation for r:

$$\text{USD } 969.50 = \frac{\text{USD } 100}{1 + r} + \frac{\text{USD } 1100}{(1 + r)^2}$$

Trial and error leads to the solution $r = 11.8\%$.

Although yield to maturity is a common tool for bond comparisons it has to be handled carefully. Table 18.1 shows why. Government bonds A and B are the same in all respects except bond A has a high coupon and B has a low coupon. Nevertheless, it seems that B is more advantageous because it has a higher yield to maturity. When we value the bonds at the prevailing structure of spot interest rates, however, it becomes clear that no advantage exists. Both bonds are correctly priced. The illusion of an advantage for bond B is the consequence of using the same rate, yield to maturity, to discount all the cash flows.

The term structure of interest rates

The foregoing result depends on the term structure of interest rates. In the example, the term structure is upward sloping. In other words, shorter maturities have lower rates. Low coupon bonds will have higher yields to maturity with upward sloping term structures because relatively more of their cash flows come later and thus benefit from compounding

Table 18.1 Yield to maturity on a high and low coupon bond

	Face value	Coupon payment	Maturity	Current market value	Yield to maturity
Bond A	USD 1000	USD 152	5 years	USD 1219.80	9.48%
Bond B	USD 1000	USD 87	5 years	USD 963.70	9.65%
Spot rates	1 year = 6%	2 years = 7%	3 years = 8%	4 years = 9%	5 years = 10%

at the higher rates. When the term structure is downward sloping, bonds with higher coupons have the higher yields to maturity because relatively more of their cash flows come at the beginning and benefit from compounding at the higher rate. Figure 18.1 shows an example of an upward sloping term structure, a downward sloping term structure and flat term structure.

Because zero coupon government bonds only exist for a few maturities, most spot rates cannot be directly observed. Methodologies for estimating spot rates have been developed but they are time-consuming and rely on data that is not readily available on a timely basis.[1] Instead of the actual term structure, most analysts use curves that plot yield to maturity for actual bonds against their maturities as a means of approximating the term structure of spot rates.

Term structure theory

Term structure theory deals with the effect that time has on interest rates. It seeks to answer the question of why different maturities should have different yields. We will discuss the three most popular explanations: segmented markets, liquidity preference and pure expectations.

Segmented markets

Segmented market theory is based on the argument that many investors and borrowers have strong preferences for certain maturities and are insensitive to interest rate differentials between their preferred maturities and others. The preferences arise from the desire to balance the maturities of assets and liabilities. The classic example is that of insurance companies with long-term liabilities in the form of life policies. The

Figure 18.1 The term structure of interest rates

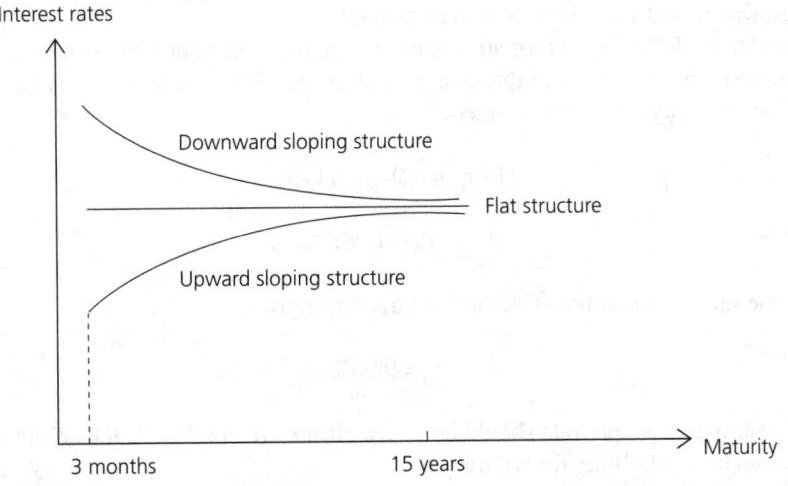

Interest rates

Downward sloping structure

Flat structure

Upward sloping structure

Maturity

3 months   15 years

[1] Several methods for estimating the term structure of interest rates have been discussed in the literature. See, for example: W.T. Carelton and I.A. Cooper, "Estimation and uses of the term structure of interest rates", *Journal of Finance*, Vol. 31 (September 1976), p.p. 1067–1083; J.H. McCulloch, "An estimate of the liquidity premium", *Journal of Political Economy*, Vol. 83 (February 1975), p.p. 95–119; S.M. Schaefer, "Measuring a tax specific term structure of interest rates in the market for British government securities", *Economic Journal*, Vol. 91 (June 1981), p.p. 415–438.

premiums and the payout are determined as a function of the anticipated interest rates and how long the individual is expected to live. To make a profit, the insurance companies have to reinvest the premiums at a rate higher than the payoff on the policy. If they invest in long-term assets, they know the interest that will be earned over the life of the investment and can lock in the return on their principal (not their interest income, which must be reinvested as it is received). In this way they can guarantee a profit for themselves. Similar type arguments are made for borrowers and lenders of medium and short-term maturities.

Market segmentation theory argues that risk aversion is strong enough and widespread enough to keep borrowers and lenders in their preferred maturities. Thus, the supply and demand for long-term maturities determines the rate for long-term maturities, the supply and demand for medium-term maturities determines the rate for medium-term maturities and so on for all maturities. Believers in this theory implicitly accept the absence of arbitrage across different maturity horizons.

Liquidity preference

Liquidity preference theory argues that, other things being equal, investors prefer short-term assets to longer-term assets. The reasons for this are rooted in motives of speculation and precaution in an uncertain world. To induce them to lend for longer periods, a premium must be paid. On the other hand, borrowers prefer longer-term liabilities that enable them to avoid the uncertainties involved in continuously refinancing shorter-term debt in possibly unfavorable conditions. Accordingly, they are willing to pay a premium for longer-term maturities. Consequently, there are pressures from both the supply and demand sides that generate a "liquidity premium" and cause the term structure of interest rates to be upward sloping.

Pure expectations

The pure expectations theory asserts that the long-term interest rate is a geometric average of the current short-term rate and the other short-term rates that are expected in the future. The best way to understand this is with an example.

Consider the following information. The current one-year spot interest rate, $_0r_{0,1}$ is 8%. The one-year spot interest rate that is expected to prevail in one year, $_1r_{1,2}$ is 12%. Then, according to the pure expectations theory:

$$(1+_0r_{0,2})^2 = (1+_0r_{0,1})(1+_1r_{1,2})$$

$$(1+_0r_{0,2})^2 = (1.08)(1.12)$$

Taking the square root of both sides and subtracting 1 gives

$$_0r_{0,2} = 9.98\%.$$

The current two-year spot rate should be 9.98%. If it were not 9.98%, the argument goes, there would be a possibility for arbitrage.

Suppose that the two-year spot rate was 11% rather than 9.98%. An investor could borrow USD 1000, for example, at the current one-year spot rate of 8% and lend it for two years at the two-year spot rate of 11%. At the end of the first year he would owe USD 1080. To pay off this loan he would borrow USD 1080 at 12% for one year, if the spot rate turns out to be what it was expected to be. At the end of the second year he would owe

$$(USD\ 1080)(1.12) = USD\ 1209.60.$$

But he would receive

$$(\text{USD } 1000)(1.11)^2 = \text{USD } 1232.10$$

from his two-year loan. This would leave him with a profit of USD 22.50. In these conditions, all two-year investors would lend for two years. One-period investors have a choice of buying a one-year bond or buying a two-year bond and selling it after one year. If they buy a one-year bond, they will receive USD 1080. If they buy a two-year bond and sell it after a year, the bond they sell will have to offer the same yield as a new one-year bond. Assuming that the one-year spot rate at the beginning of year two turns out to be 12%, they will receive

$$\text{USD } 1000 \times \frac{(1.11)^2}{1.12} = \text{USD } 1100.09.$$

This is more than they would get from the one-year bond. Consequently, they also would buy the two-year bond at the beginning of year one. On the other hand, borrowers would all be trying to borrow at the lower one-year rate. Given this universal preference, prices would have to adjust until the expected return from the two-year bond is the same as the expected return from the two one-year bonds.

We have demonstrated the arguments for the pure expectations theory for two periods. The same reasoning can be applied to obtain the same results for any number of periods. In general

$$(1 + {_0}r_{0,n}) = \left[(1 + {_0}r_{0,1})(1 + {_1}r_{1,2}) \dots (1 + {_{n-1}}r_{n-1,n}) \right]^{1/n}$$

The term structure can be determined from expected future one-period rates. With expectations of rising rates the term structure is upward sloping. With expectations of falling rates, the term structure is downward sloping.

Bond management: Tools and techniques

Terminology

Current yield

The price of a bond is expressed as a percentage of its face or nominal value. Suppose, for example, that a bond with a nominal value of CHF 1000 is quoted at 101.05. This means that it is selling for 101.05% of its nominal value. The price is then CHF 1010.50. A bond's yield can be expressed in many ways. The simplest expression is the ratio of coupon to current price and is called current yield or flat yield. If, for example, the coupon on the foregoing bond was 8.9%, the current yield would be calculated as follows:

$$\frac{8.90\%}{101.50} = 8.81\%.$$

Current yield, however, is only a rough estimation of the bond's true actuarial yield.

Yield to maturity

Yield to maturity gives the bond's true actuarial yield. As we saw above, yield to maturity is the interest figure quoted most frequently by investors and professionals. It is the rate that equates the present value of the bond's cash flows with the present market value of the bond. A bond's cash flows are composed of three elements: interest payments, principal payments and accrued interest payments.

Interest payments correspond to the coupons stipulated in the bond contract. Principal payments correspond to how the loan will be paid back. Some bonds are paid in full on the maturity date. Others have an amortization schedule where the loan is paid off in installments over its life. Accrued interest payments refer to the interest earned but not yet due and payable if the bond has been sold in between coupon dates. Suppose, for example, that an interest payment of CHF 89 is due on 15 April of a leap year and that the bond is sold on 10 January. The seller of the bond is entitled to the interest that corresponds to the fraction of the year that he held the bond. In practice, we have seen that there are several ways to calculate this fraction:

- The actual number of days from the beginning of the calculation period to the end divided by 360, called Actual/360.

- The actual number of days from the beginning of the calculation period to the end divided by 365, called Actual/365.

- The actual number of days from the beginning of the calculation period to the end divided by the actual number of days in the year (366 in a leap year), called Actual/Actual.

- The number of 30-day months from the beginning of the calculation period to the end divided by 360, called 30/360.

Thus, a calculation period that begins on 15 April of one year and ends on 10 January of a leap year will have the following day count fractions according to the different bases:

- Actual/360 = 270/360
- Actual/365 = 270/365
- Actual/Actual = 270/366
- 30/360 = 265/360.

The accrued interest payment is calculated by the formula:

Accrued interest payment = Interest payment due × Day count fraction.

Using this formula and the different day count fractions gives the following accrued interest payments on the CHF 89 interest payment due on 15 April:

$$CHF\ 89 \times {}^{270}/_{360} = CHF\ 66.75$$

$$CHF\ 89 \times {}^{270}/_{365} = CHF\ 65.84$$

$$CHF\ 89 \times {}^{270}/_{366} = CHF\ 65.66$$

$$CHF\ 89 \times {}^{265}/_{360} = CHF\ 65.51$$

Accrued interest payments can differ considerably depending on how the day count fraction is calculated.

With this in mind, we can present a general formula for calculating a bond's yield to maturity. Let

B_0 = the current market value of the bond clean of accrued interest
c = the annual interest payment

f = the fraction of the year until the next interest payment on an Actual/Actual basis

f^+ = day count factor

n = a positive integer representing the number of years to maturity

CF_t = cash flow at time t

r = yield to maturity.

The buyer will pay and the seller will receive the market price of the bond (B) plus the accrued interest (cf^+). In return the buyer receives and the seller gives up the rights to the cash flows for the ongoing year as well as for all the other years until the bond's maturity. This is expressed in Equation 18.1:

$$B_0 + cf^+ = \frac{CF_f}{(1+r)^f} + \frac{CF_1}{(1+r)^{f+1}} + \ldots + \frac{CF_n}{(1+r)^{f+n}} \qquad (18.1)$$

Solving Equation 18.1 for r gives the yield to maturity.

In the case of a bullet bond, the principal is repaid in one installment at the bond's maturity. When P is the principal payment, the cash flows will look like this:

$$B_0 + cf^+ = \frac{c}{(1+r)^f} + \frac{c}{(1+r)^{f+1}} + \ldots + \frac{c+P}{(1+r)^{f+n}}$$

which simplifies to[2]

$$B_0 + cf^+ = c\,\frac{(1+r) - (1+r)^n}{r(1+r)^f} + \frac{P}{(1+r)^{f+n}} \qquad (18.2)$$

Suppose, for example, that a bullet bond selling at 92.75 has a face value of CHF 100, an annual coupon of 9%, a maturity of 8.5 years, and a day count factor of 180/360. Using equation 18.2 we can verify that the yield to maturity is 10.3%.

When interest payments are quarterly or semi-annual instead of annual, yield to maturity has to include the compounding that goes on over the year. In this case, interest payments will have to be discounted at the rate R, where

$$(1+R)^T = (1+r)$$

and T represents the number of coupon payments per year. Thus, if coupon payments are semi-annual and $R = 0.05$

$$(1 + 0.05)^2 = (1 + r)$$

and $r = 0.1025$ or 10.25%.

---

[2] On the right-hand side of the equation we can factor out $c/(1+r)^f$:

$$B_0 + cf^+ = \frac{c}{(1+r)^f}\left[1 + \frac{1}{(1+r)} + \frac{1}{(1+r)^2} + \ldots + \frac{1}{(1+r)^n}\right] + \frac{P}{(1+r)^{f+n}}.$$

In the brackets is a sum equal to

$$\frac{(1+r) - (1+r)^n}{r}.$$

Making this substitution and simplifying gives Equation 18.2 in the text.

Yield to average life

As already mentioned, many bonds are not repaid *in fine*. Instead, they are progressively paid off during their life through a sinking fund provision. When this is the case, many investors and professionals like to speak of the bond's average life. Average life is a weighted average of the bond's principal repayments. If P_j is the principal payment at time j, t_j is the number of periods that separate P_j from the moment of calculation, and n is the number of years to the bond's maturity, average life can be calculated as follows:

$$\text{Average life} = \frac{\sum_{j=1}^{n} t_j P_j}{\sum_{j=1}^{n} P_j}.$$

Take, for example, a bond that will be amortized by a payment of 20 in six months, 30 in 1.5 years and 50 in 2.5 years. Its average life is:

$$\frac{20 \times 0.5 + 30 \times 1.5 + 50 \times 2.5}{20 + 30 + 50} = 1.8 \text{ years}.$$

When there is no amortization, average maturity is equal to the bond's maturity.

In practice, there is some confusion concerning the calculation of yield to maturity (YTM) for bonds with sinking fund provisions. Equation 18.1 is the way it should be calculated. However, some institutions calculate it without taking the amortization schedule into account. In other words, they calculate YTM as if the bond were redeemed *in fine*. Investors should be careful because the difference between the two measures can be large if the bond is selling far above or far below par value. Some institutions also call YTM yield to average life.

Yield to call

Some bonds do not have a sinking fund provision but are issued with a call option where the issuer has the right to "call" back the bond before its maturity date. It will be in his interest to do so if interest rates fall below the bond's coupon rate. In this case, he will be able to call the outstanding bond in, pay it off and issue new debt at the lower rate. Because of this, some investors like to calculate the yield on the bond up to the date that the call option takes effect. They term this yield to call. In this type of calculation, the date that the call takes effect replaces the maturity date in Equation 18.1.

Methods of accounting for options features in bond indentures are well known to experienced investors and their effects should be reflected in the price of the bond. Pricing a bond with a call option, for example, involves breaking the bond down into a bond with no option provision (naked bond) and a call option on the bond. The two are then priced separately. Because the call option is owned by the issuer, the price of the callable bond is found by subtracting the price of the call option from the price of the naked bond. The same procedure can be followed for pricing bonds with other types of option features. These operations in themselves present no serious difficulties because the use of bond valuation and option pricing techniques are commonplace. Options features do complicate the analysis, however. They also cloud the significance of the concept "yield to maturity" because their existence makes the bond's maturity itself uncertain.

Duration

Two of the bond manager's most important analytical tools are **duration** and **convexity**. Duration is the weighted average maturity of a bond where each date is weighted by the present value of the cash flow that the bond pays at that date. On the coupon date it can be written as follows:[3]

$$D = \frac{\sum_{t=1}^{n} tCF_t(1+r)^{-t}}{B} \tag{18.3}$$

where D is the duration index, CF_t is the cash flow for period t, and n is the total number of periods to maturity. Thus, duration depends on the maturity of the bond, the coupon rate, the price of the bond and its yield to maturity. Take, for example, a bond quoted at 96 with a coupon rate of 9%. The next coupon will be paid in six months and the principal payment will take place in 3.5 years. From Equation 18.1 we can calculate the yield to maturity, which is 10.38%. Using Equation 18.3 we can construct Table 18.2.

Remembering that on non-coupon dates the amount paid for a bond includes accrued interest, B in Equation 18.3 must also include accrued interest. Hence, the denominator will be 96, the clean price, plus the accrued coupon of 4.5 (0.5×9). Duration will be equal to:

$$D = \frac{303.51}{(96 + 4.5)} = 3.02 \text{ years.}$$

Duration also expresses the reaction of the bond's price to changes in the interest rate. Remember that there is an inverse relationship between the interest rate and the price of a bond. When the interest rate rises, the bond's price falls and vice versa. Consequently, changes in the interest rate represent a major source of risk for bondholders.[4] Although there

Table 18.2 Calculation of duration

t	CF_t	$CF_t(1+r)^{-t}$	$tCF_t(1+r)^{-t}$
0.5	9	8.57	4.28
1.5	9	7.76	11.64
2.5	9	7.03	17.58
3.5	109	77.14	270.01
		100.50	**303.51**

[3] Duration on dates other than the coupon date or for bonds that pay other than annual coupons can be calculated in the same way by changing the time indices, as we did in the previous paragraph, and discounting at the rate $(1 + R)$ where $(1 + R)^T = (1 + r)$ and T represents the number of discounting periods per year.

[4] There are other sources of risk as well. The risk that the borrower will be unable to honor his financial obligations by making the promised interest and principal payments is called default risk. The risk that inflation will erode the purchasing power of future cash receipts is called monetary risk. Reinvestment risk, which is related to interest rate risk, refers to the possibility that intermediate cash flows of interest and principal will not be able to be reinvested at the bond's current yield to maturity.

are many other ways to express this concept of duration, the most common form assumes proportional changes in a flat (horizontal) yield curve.[5] Taking the first derivative of Equation 18.1 with respect to $(1+r)$, dividing by B, and rearranging gives: [6]

$$\frac{dB/B}{d(1+r)/(1+r)} = -D \tag{18.4}$$

Equation 18.4 expresses the bond's interest rate elasticity. The bond's interest rate sensitivity can be expressed by taking $(1+r)$ to the other side of the equation:

$$\frac{dB}{d(1+r)B} = -\frac{D}{(1+r)} \tag{18.5}$$

$D/(1+r)$ is called modified duration and makes it possible to estimate the percentage change in the bond's price in response to a small change in the interest rate. For example, the price of a bond with a modified duration of 5.4 would be expected to fall by 1.89% if the interest rate rises by 35 bp (0.35%):

$$\frac{dB/B}{0.0035} = -5.4$$

$$\frac{dB}{B} = 0.0035 \times (-5.4) = -0.0189.$$

Higher duration makes for more pronounced percentage changes in the bond's price. Hence, duration can be used in the management of bond portfolios. If a fall in the interest

---

[5] Duration measures can be developed for just about any assumption that one wants to make concerning the term structure of interest rates and the way interest rates change. For a more complete discussion of duration and its applications, see G.O. Bierwag, G. Kaufman and C. Chang, "Duration and bond portfolio analysis: An overview", *Journal of Financial and Quantitative Analysis*, Vol. 13, No. 4 (November 1978), p.p. 671–681; J.E. Ingersoll, J. Skelton and R.L. Weil, "Duration forty years later", *Journal of Financial and Quantitative Analysis*, Vol. 13 (November 1978), p.p. 627–650; H.G. Fong and K.J. Fabozzi, *Fixed Income Portfolio Management*, (Homewood, Illinois: Dow Jones-Irwin, 1985).

[6] On the coupon date Equation 18.1 becomes:

$$B = \frac{CF_1}{(1+r)^1} + \frac{CF_2}{(1+r)^2} + \ldots + \frac{CF_n}{(1+r)^n}$$

The derivative with respect to $(1+r)$ is:

$$\frac{dB}{d(1+r)} = -1\frac{CF_1}{(1+r)^2} - 2\frac{CF_2}{(1+r)^3} - \ldots - n\frac{CF_n}{(1+r)^{n+1}}$$

Factor out $1/(1+r)$, bring it to the left-hand side of the equation, and divide by B

$$\frac{dB/B}{d(1+r)/(1+r)} = \frac{-\sum_{t=1}^{n} tCF_t(1+r)^{-t}}{B}$$

Compare with Equation 18.3 in the text.

rate is anticipated, high duration bonds will benefit most. If a rise in the interest rate is anticipated, low duration bonds will be hurt the least.[7]

Of the many possible duration measures, the modified duration index presented above is the simplest, most widely used and seemingly the most effective. It assumes a flat yield curve and proportional changes in spot rates for all maturities. Empirical evidence shows that these conditions are not met in practice. The yield curve is not flat and long-term interest rates tend to change proportionately less than short-term rates. In these conditions the traditional duration index does not lead to a completely accurate estimate of interest rate risk. In the case of proportional changes in an upward sloping yield curve, interest rate risk will be overestimated; in a downward sloping yield curve it will be underestimated. When longer rates change proportionately less than shorter rates, the traditional duration index will overestimate the actual interest rate risk. The greater the difference in proportional change, the greater the overestimation. This effect acts in the same direction as the effect of an upward sloping yield curve so that when both these conditions are present, the traditional duration index's overestimation will be accentuated. However, it acts in the opposite direction to the effect of a negative sloping yield curve and will tend to reduce or eliminate the traditional index's underestimation arising from the negative curve.[8] It should also be noted, as Figure 18.2 makes clear, that duration is only a relevant risk measure for very small changes in the interest rate. A better estimation of interest rate risk can be obtained by including the concept of convexity.

Convexity

Bond price convexity complements the duration measure of interest rate risk. It can be obtained by taking the second derivative of the bond price function with respect to $(1+r)$ and dividing by the bond's current price: [9]

$$\text{Convexity} = \frac{d^2B}{d(1+r)^2 \, B} \tag{18.6}$$

---

[7] The concept of duration can also be applied to portfolios of bonds. The duration of a portfolio of bonds is equal to the average of the durations of the individual bonds that compose the portfolio weighted by the proportions of the market value of the individual bonds in the market value of the portfolio.

[8] See: E. Clark, "Duration as a risk management tool", *Journal of International Securities Markets*, Vol. 2 (Spring 1988), p.p. 47–53.

[9] Starting from the first derivative:

$$\frac{dB}{d(1+r)} = -1\frac{CF_1}{(1+r)^2} - 2\frac{CF_2}{(1+r)^3} - \dots - n\frac{CF_n}{(1+r)^{n+1}}$$

the second derivative is:

$$\frac{d^2B}{d(1+r)^2} = 2\frac{CF_1}{(1+r)^3} + 6\frac{CF_2}{(1+r)^4} + \dots + n(n+1)\frac{CF_n}{(1+r)^{n+2}}$$

Factoring out $1/(1+r)^2$ gives:

$$\frac{d^2B}{d(1+r)^2} + \frac{\sum (t^2-t)CF_t(1+r)^{-t}}{(1+r)^2}$$

Dividing by B gives Equation 18.6 in the text.

Figure 18.2 Duration

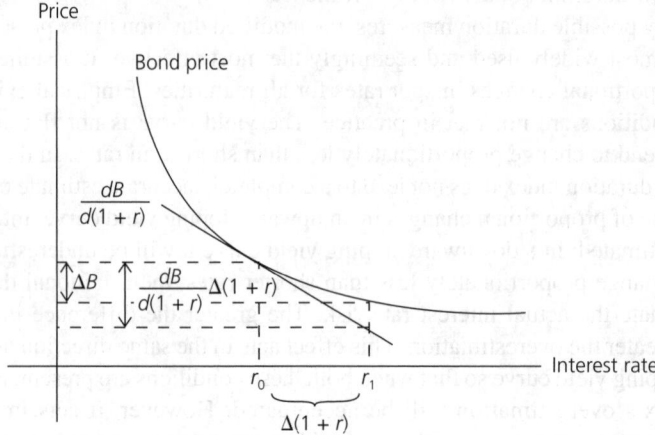

The price changes for a bond can thus be approximated by taking a Taylor series expansion of the bond price function and dividing by B:[10]

$$\frac{dB}{B} = -\frac{D}{(1+r)} d(1+r) + \frac{1}{2} Cd(1+r)^2 \tag{18.7}$$

where C is convexity.

In this expression, convexity can be interpreted as a purchase signal. This is because with higher convexity more is gained when interest rates fall and less is lost when interest rates rise. The reasoning behind this is straightforward. Convexity is a positive number. The change in the interest rate, $d(1+r)$, is squared, which also makes this positive. If interest rates rise, the duration factor causes price depreciation, but the convexity term is positive and, therefore, counteracts the duration effect. If interest rates fall, the duration factor causes price appreciation and the positive convexity term acts as a booster.

Figure 18.3 illustrates these points. At point P, bonds X and Y have equal durations, prices and yields but different convexities. Consequently, as the figure shows, bond Y, the more convex of the two, has greater price appreciation and less price depreciation in response to changes in the interest rate.

Convexity as a measure of risk shares the local properties of duration as well as the shortcomings associated with the assumption of proportional shifts in a flat yield curve.

---

[10] The Taylor expansion for B is:

$$B(r_b) = B(r_a) + B'(r_a)(r_b - r_a) + \frac{1}{2}B''(r_a)(r_b - r_a)^2 + \dots$$

where r_a is the beginning interest rate, r_b is the new interest rate, $B(r)$ is a function, and B' and B'' are the first and second derivatives with respect to $(1+r_a)$. Remember that $(1+r_b) - (1+r_a) = (r_b - r_a)$. Taking $B(r_a)$ to the left-hand side of the equation gives dB. Dividing by $B(r_a)$ gives:

$$\frac{dB}{B(r_a)} = \frac{B'(r_a)}{B(r_a)} (r_b - r_a) + \frac{1}{2} \frac{B''(r_a)}{B(r_a)} (r_b - r_a)^2 + \dots$$

Substituting from 18.5 and 18.6 gives Equation 18.7 in the text.

Figure 18.3 Convexity

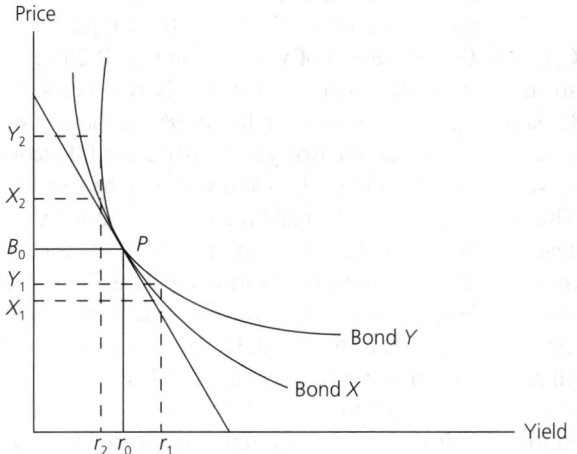

Hence, although Equation 18.7 that combines duration and convexity to explain the reaction of the bond price to changes in the interest rate is more accurate over a longer interval than duration alone, it begins to lose accuracy for larger shocks to the interest rate. Furthermore, where callable bonds are concerned, duration and convexity do not provide a complete analysis of interest rate risk.[11]

Strategies for bond portfolio management

Bond portfolio strategies can be broken down into passive and active strategies. Passive strategies aim at insulating portfolios from shifts in the term structure by using two techniques known as **exact matching** and **immunization**.[12]

Exact matching

Exact matching involves finding the lowest cost portfolio generating cash inflows exactly equal to cash outflows that are being financed by the investment. This strategy is passive because once the bond portfolio is determined, no additional changes are required even if the yield curve changes. In actual practice, changes in the yield curve can produce opportunities for profitable bond swaps, which the manager will be happy to take advantage of. Still, except for defaults, exact matching ensures that liabilities will be met even if the yield curve shifts.

Immunization

Immunization attempts to eliminate sensitivity to shifts in the yield curve by matching the duration of assets to the duration of liabilities. This strategy can succeed only insofar as duration is a true measure of interest rate sensitivity. If this is the case, a change in interest rates will have the same impact on the present value of assets and liabilities so that gains will equal losses.

[11] K. Winkleman, "Uses and abuses of duration and convexity", *Financial Analysts Journal* (September/October 1989), p.p. 72–75.

[12] For some applications of matching and immunization strategies for international bond portfolios, see C. Stoakes and A. Freeman, *Managing Global Portfolios* (London: Euromoney Publications, 1989).

Take, for example, an insurance company that will have to pay GBP 726,000 in two years. Since there is only one cash flow, the duration of the liability is two years (we let the reader verify that this is true). It buys a bond for GBP 600,000 paying GBP 220,000 at the end of year one, GBP 242,000 at the end of year two and GBP 266,200 at the end of year three. The yield to maturity is 10% and the duration is two years, the same as for the liability. Table 18.3 shows that if interest rates fall to 9% at the end of the first year, the company will only be able to reinvest the first year's GBP 220,000 income at 9% instead of 10% for the second year. Instead of GBP 242,000 it will only be worth GBP 239,800 at the end of year two. This loss is offset by the capital gain on the bond which will be sold for GBP 244,220 instead of GBP 242,000. Including the GBP 242,000 cash flow received at the end of year two, GBP 726,020 will be available to meet the liability of GBP 726,000. If interest rates rise to 11%, the gain on investing the first year's cash flow at 11% instead of 10% is offset by the loss on the sale of the bond. Hence, whether interest rates move up or down, the asset will provide enough cash to meet the liability.

The same principle can be applied to a portfolio of assets and liabilities but because the duration of a portfolio of bonds is equal to the weighted average of the durations of the individual bonds, many different combinations could give the same duration for a portfolio. It should also be remembered that immunization strategies are only passive for a particular yield curve. As the yield curve shifts, duration changes, which might cause a differential between the durations of assets and liabilities. Furthermore, if assets and liabilities do not have the same cash flow pattern, their durations will diverge with the passage of time even if the yield curve does not change. These considerations call for some active management, which means that immunization is not a totally passive strategy.

Active strategies

Passive strategies focus on meeting some future liability rather than on period-by-period returns. The main concern of many money managers, particularly investment fund managers, however, is period-by-period returns. This type of problem requires a more active management strategy.

A more active management strategy basically involves the same two steps associated with mean-variance portfolio theory:

- Estimate expected returns, variance and the covariance structure across all bonds.
- Use the correlation structure across all bonds to construct a portfolio with an optimal risk–return tradeoff.

One strategy is similar to stock picking. In this case, the analyst tries to identify bonds that are over or underpriced. The correct price, as we saw above, is the price derived from

Table 18.3 Value of the bond (in GBP) with changing interest rates at the end of period two

Time	Cash Flow	9%	10%	11%
1	220,000	239,800	242,000	244,200
2	242,000	242,000	242,000	242,000
3	266,200	244,220	242,000	239,820
		726,020	726,000	726,020

discounting each cash flow at its risk-adjusted spot rate. If any option clauses are present they should be valued independently. The prices of the individual option features should then be combined with the value of the naked bond to arrive at the price of the whole bond package. Mispricing could occur for many reasons. The risk associated with a given bond may temporarily be incorrectly assessed; the value of an option clause may be mispriced; the spot yield curve may be misestimated, etc. Whatever the reason, underpriced bonds are bought and overpriced bonds are sold. More aggressive managers might even want to buy puts on overvalued bonds or even sell the overvalued bonds short.

Another strategy involves using a single index model based on duration, where the beta is the ratio of the duration of the individual bond or portfolio of bonds to the duration of the index.[13] A model of this type has several advantages as it affords a measure of systematic risk in the duration terms familiar to the money manager. It also affords ease of calculation. Rather than having to estimate the beta in a regression with historical data that will not be available for many bonds, it can be measured directly as the ratio of the durations that can be calculated from the terms of each bond. Furthermore, as a practical matter, consistent bond indexes are becoming available on a wider scale. Salomon Brothers publishes monthly indexes on all major bond markets in *Euromoney* and Lombard Odier et Cie publishes daily indexes in the European edition of the *Wall Street Journal*. Other institutions such as the AIBD publish indexes on the Eurobond market.

This type of model can be especially useful for managers whose performance is judged relative to an index or for managers following many different domestic markets in need of a clear idea of the covariance structure of their portfolios in each currency. It can also be expanded into a multi-index model to include variables that might be another source of covariance, such as liquidity premiums, tax effects, option features and default risk.

We now turn to other active strategies using futures, forwards and options.

Long-term interest rate futures

In October 1975 the Chicago Board of Trade (CBOT) was the first to offer a futures contract directly related to the long-term interest rate. The underlying security, reflecting the American mortgage market, was issued by the Government National Mortgage Association (GNMA), called Ginnie Mae. GNMA is a wholly owned US government corporation whose object is to support the housing market. In August 1977 the CBOT launched the contract on US Treasury bonds, the success of which was beyond all expectations. Contracts on long-term interest rates have spread to other continents and other exchanges, such as the Matif (Marché à Terme International de France) in Paris, Liffe (London International Financial Futures and Options Exchange) in London, Tiffe (Tokyo International Financial Futures Exchange) in Tokyo, and the SFE (Sydney Futures Exchange) in Sydney. Liquid, long-term interest rate futures are now available on many currencies such as the US dollar, the British pound, the Australian dollar, the euro and the Canadian dollar.

In this section, we start by presenting the general principles involved in long-term interest rate coverage. We then outline the basic market procedures and finish by discussing some of the practical difficulties that can be encountered when actively pursuing a strategy on these markets.

---

[13] See E.J. Elton and M.J. Gruber, *Modern Portfolio Theory and Investment Analysis*, second edition (John Wiley and Sons, 1984), p.p. 510–513.

Long-term interest rate hedging

The sources of long-term interest rate risk for a company are numerous. They arise not only from existing assets and liabilities but also from assets and liabilities that will be generated in the future. Table 18.4 lists the situations that can be encountered and how they affect different positions. A fixed long-term asset loses value when interest rates rise whereas a fall in rates raises the value of long-term liabilities. Where planned investments are concerned, a fall in the long-term interest rate will make them less profitable and a rise in rates will make a planned borrowing more costly. The reason for these relationships should be clear. It stems from the way securities are priced. Notice that in the discounting operation the interest rate is in the denominator. A higher interest rate means a higher denominator, which lowers the value of the security. A lower interest rate lowers the denominator and raises the value of the security.

Just as in the case of exchange rate risk, the company's risk exposure depends on the state of its balance sheet as well as on its planned investments and capital requirements. If a company's overall position will be hurt by a fall in the interest rate, we say that it is "long". If its overall position will be hurt by a rise in the interest rate, we say that it is "short".

Hedging the risk of an expected rise

Hedging against an expected rise in the interest rate can be achieved by selling futures contracts. An example will make this clear.

Consider the treasurer of a large French company holding a portfolio of EUR 10 million worth of OATs (*obligations assimilables du trésor*). OATs are long-term bonds issued by the French Treasury. On 1 January the interest rate on the French bond market is 3.5%.[14] The company treasurer fears that between 1 January and the month of June the interest rate will rise to 4%. This fear is based on the conclusions of an in-depth analysis produced by a well known research company that included consideration of the country's macroeconomic outlook, the balance of payments performance, monetary policy and exchange rate forecasts (see Chapters 1–6). He calls his broker and finds that the "notional" contract for June delivery is quoted at 100 on the Matif. Notional refers to the reference bond or theoretical bond with defined characteristics: for example, a ten-year OAT paying a coupon of 3.5%. Contracts are quoted as a percent of the nominal value of the notional contract. On the Matif, the nominal value of the notional contract is EUR 100,000.

Table 18.4 Sources of long-term interest rate risk

	Interest rate rise	*Interest rate fall*
Long-term assets	Yes	No
Long-term liabilities	No	Yes
Planned investment	No	Yes
Planned borrowing	Yes	No

[14] Although we refer to "the long-term interest rate", this is just shorthand for the term structure of interest rates. We have seen above that the market price of a bond is determined by discounting each cash flow at its corresponding zero coupon rate.

Six months later, the treasurer turns out to have been right. The interest rate has climbed to 4%. Given the inverse relationship between interest rates and bond prices, the value of his EUR 10 million worth of OATs has fallen to EUR 9,786,000.[15] This sum includes the market value of the bonds of EUR 9,611,000 plus six months interest worth EUR 175 000. The futures price for June delivery ends at 96.11. How could the treasurer have used the futures market to eliminate the risk associated with his portfolio of government bonds? The answer is straightforward. In January he would sell 100 futures contracts at a price of 100 for a total of EUR 10,000,000. On the last trading day for the June delivery contract, he would buy 100 futures contracts at 96.11 for a net gain of:

$$\text{Price sold} - \text{Price paid} = 100 - 96.11 = 3.89\% \text{ or } 389 \text{ basis points.}$$

Each basis point is worth EUR 10 ($0.01 \times 0.01 \times$ EUR 100,000).[16] His gain on the futures market is thus equal to EUR 389,000 ($389 \times$ EUR 10×100). His total portfolio is:

Value of OAT	9,786,000
Income from 100 futures contracts	389,000
Total	10,175,000

The profit he made on the Matif gives him a return of 1.75% for six months or 3.5% for a year. This result would be the same if the interest rate had fallen instead of rising. Table 18.5 shows the outcome if the interest rate had fallen to 3%. There is a loss on the futures contract of EUR 427,000 but the loss is compensated by the gain in the value of the bond portfolio. By selling the 100 futures contracts, the treasurer locked in his overall profit at EUR 175,000 for the rate of return of 3.5% that prevailed at the time they were sold.

Hedging the risk of an expected fall in the interest rate

Hedging the risk of an expected fall in the interest rate involves buying a forward contract. To see this, let's continue with the preceding example. At the end of June the interest rate has risen to 4%. The treasurer is expecting a payment of EUR 2,000,000 at the end of September that he will want to invest in OATs. He believes that the interest rate is likely to fall between now and then and would like to lock in the 4% interest rate. Unfortunately, he

Table 18.5 Outcome of a bond portfolio hedged with futures when a rise in the interest rate is expected and a fall occurs

Value of the bond portfolio	10,427,000
Futures price sold	100.00
Futures price paid at maturity	104.27
Difference	−4.27
Loss on futures ($427 \times$ EUR 10×100)	427,000
Net	**10,175,000**

[15] Remember that the price of a bond is found by discounting the expected cash flows at the prevailing interest rate structure.

[16] Remember that each basis point is worth 1/100 of 1% (0.01×0.01).

does not yet have the cash and therefore cannot buy the bonds now. No problem! He buys 20 September contracts at 96.11.

Suppose that the interest rate falls to 3.75% by the end of September. The futures contract is settled at 98.14 and he closes out his position by selling his 20 contracts at that price. His gain is:

Sale price in September	98.14
Purchase price in June	96.11
Net gain	2.03

His gain is 203 basis points. Since each basis point is worth EUR 10, his profit is 203 × EUR 10 × 20 = EUR 40,600. This gain will enable him to reduce the price he pays for the bonds that he will buy with his EUR 2,000,000 income. In fact, he buys EUR 2,000,000 worth of government bonds with an interest rate of 3.75% but it only costs him EUR 2,000,000 – EUR 40,600 = EUR 1,959,400. Suppose that the bonds he purchases are ten-year bullet bonds. Bullet means that the bonds are redeemed in full at the end of the ten years. We can verify that the treasurer's effective rate of return, or yield to maturity, on the investment is 4% by solving the following equation for r:

$$1,959,400 = \sum_{T+1}^{10} \frac{75,000}{(1 + r)^t} + \frac{2,000,000}{(1 + r)^{10}}$$

EUR 1,959,400 is the amount effectively paid for the bonds, 75,000 is the annual interest payment every year for ten years on 2,000,000 at 3.75%, and 2,000,000 is the principal repayment. So r equals 4%. The treasurer was able to lock in the 4% rate by purchasing futures contracts. In the case of a rise in the interest rate the result would be the same. The loss on the futures contracts would offset the higher interest on the bonds.

In these two examples everything was made to work out perfectly. The goal was to demonstrate the principle of using the futures market for long-term interest rate hedging. In practice, everything is not likely to work out so well, as we will see further on in this chapter. Nevertheless, the examples serve to underline the major issues involved.

One last comment is in order. It might seem surprising that hedging a rise in the interest rate requires a futures sale while hedging a fall requires a purchase. Foreign currency hedging required a forward purchase when hedging against a rise and a sale when hedging against a fall. The fact is that in interest rate hedging the underlying security is not the interest rate: it is the bond the price of which, as we know, is inversely related to the interest rate. When interest rates rise, the price of the bond goes down and vice versa.

Market characteristics and procedures

Long-term futures markets have the same three characteristics that we saw in Chapter 7: a centralized trading place, standardized contracts and a clearing house. All transactions must pass through an authorized member broker. Only representatives of authorized brokers have access to the trading pits. Trading takes place in a type of permanent auction that ensures transparency, because it is done in public, and competition, because any member is free to participate. In order to facilitate trading, only approved contracts are allowed to be traded. The underlying security is strictly defined and limited to a certain type of bond. Nominal amounts are standardized (such as the contract for EUR 100,000). Maturities are limited in number, usually based on a quarterly schedule of March, June, September and December. Finally, all transactions are recorded with the clearing house. A buy or a sell is simply an accounting entry with the clearing house. Closing out a position amounts to undertaking the reverse transaction. Consequently, opening and closing positions adds to market liquidity and stimulates the market. Finally, the clearing house guarantees all contracts as the ultimate counterparty and manages default risk through mandatory deposits and margin calls. In Appendix 18.1 we give the relevant details for the long term-interest rate contract on the Matif.

When contracts mature, the clearing house ensures settlement for outstanding positions. In practice, few contracts are actually held for settlement. For those that are settled, the clearing house matches buyers and sellers and sees to it that buyers receive the appropriate authorized securities from the designated sellers (see Appendix 18.1 for details of the authorized securities for the Matif contract). It determines the amount to be paid by the buyers as a function of the settlement price and the type of securities that are actually delivered. We will come back to this point later on. For the moment, just let it be said that the securities authorized for delivery do not have to correspond exactly with the "notional" bond in the contract.

With this in mind, the futures price approximates the price of the notional security defined in the contract. In the United States, for example, the notional interest rate is 8% and in France it is 3.5%. Furthermore, futures prices can and do differ from one settlement date to another. This is due to the term structure of interest rates and the anticipations of investors concerning its evolution.

Futures prices and settlement procedures

Open futures positions on the maturity date are settled by physical delivery of Treasury bonds. The contract seller is obliged to deliver the bonds and the buyer is obliged to pay for them. Settlement is effected at the last quoted price, once all margin transactions have been completed. Settlement procedures are strict and precise. Only certain securities are authorized for delivery. They must be government issues and they must have a minimum time to maturity. In the United States and the United Kingdom, for example, the minimum is 15 years, while in France it is 8.5 years. Thus, there are many bonds that qualify for delivery but differ in maturity and coupon. Consequently, their market prices can also differ considerably. In order to account for the different market prices, the exchanges calculate a coefficient, called a conversion factor, for each individual authorized bond issue. The conversion factor corresponds to the theoretical value of the bond in question, calculated by discounting its cash flows at the notional interest rate. The settlement sum that will be paid by the buyer is equal to the conversion factor multiplied by the settlement price. An example will make this clear.

Suppose that the notional interest rate is 8% and that there are two existing bonds fulfilling the delivery requirements. Bond A has a coupon of 10% and a remaining life to maturity of 15 years. Bond B has a coupon of 6% and remaining life of 25 years. The conversion factor of Bond A is 1.1712. For Bond B it is 0.7865.[17] The market price of Bond A is 138.85 and Bond B is quoted at 100. The futures settlement price is quoted at 118.55. The seller has the choice of delivering either Bond A or Bond B. If he delivers A, he receives settlement price × conversion factor = 1.1712 × 118.55 = 138.85,

---

[17] To find the coefficients discount the cash flows on a USD 1 loan at the notional rate of 8%. On Bond A, for example, there would be 14 years of 0.1 (the coupon rate of 10%). On the 15th year there would be the coupon plus the principal repayment for a total of 1.1. Hence:

$$1.1712 = \frac{0.1}{(1.08)^1} + \frac{0.1}{(1.08)^2} + ... + \frac{0.1}{(1.08)^{14}} + \frac{1.1}{(1.08)^{15}}.$$

which is the market value of the bond. If he delivers B he receives

$$0.7865 \times 118.55 = 93.24,$$

which is less than the market value of the bond. It is obvious that he will deliver Bond A because he will lose 6.76 if he delivers B. Bond A is the "cheapest" to deliver.

Bond A will not always be the cheapest to deliver. The cheapest depends on the current term structure of interest rates. Suppose that the term structure is such that Bond A is quoted at 100, Bond B at 63.69, and the futures settlement price is 80.98. In this case, delivery of A will bring in

$$1.1712 \times 80.98 = 94.84$$

and the delivery of B will bring in

$$0.7865 \times 80.98 = 63.69.$$

Bond B is now the cheapest.

Hedging strategies

Obstacles to effective hedging

As we saw in Chapter 7, hedging with futures contracts is complicated by the limited number of maturities that exposes the hedger to basis risk. We can recall that the "basis" is the difference between the futures price and the spot price, determined by the difference in the short-term and long-term interest rates reflected in the equation

$$F_{t,T} = S_t e^{(r-r_B)\pi} \tag{18.8}$$

where r is the short-term rate and r_B is the bond yield, representing the term structure of interest rates. This is the fundamental link between the capital market and the money market. When the term structure is upward sloping, $r < r_B$, the futures price will be below the spot price. When the term structure is downward sloping, $r > r_B$, the futures price will be above the spot price. When the term structure changes, the basis will change.

As an example of how the basis works in interest rate futures, we can go back to the example where the French treasurer is planning to invest EUR 2,000,000 at the end of September. He expects a fall in the long-term rate. Unfortunately, he is not the only one who is expecting a fall and other hedgers have already begun to increase their purchases of futures, thereby bidding up the price. When he contacts his broker for the September futures contract, he finds that it is 96.38 instead of 96.11. He buys 20 contracts at 96.38 and sells them at the settlement price of 98.14 at the end of September. He has a gain of only 176 basis points worth EUR 35,200 on the 20 contracts. The effective cost of the Treasury bonds is EUR 1,964,800. Solving the discounting equation for yield to maturity gives $r \approx 3.968\%$ instead of the yield to maturity of 4% at the time the futures transaction was undertaken. The lower yield is due to the fact that the expected fall in the long-term rate was already reflected in the futures price. Thus, the basis was equal to 27 basis points (96.38 − 96.11).

Hedging with futures is also complicated by the limited number of contracts that are available. The liquidity requirement on futures contracts limits them to a few, high turnover underlying assets. However, since many of the untraded, lower turnover assets are highly correlated with one of the high turnover assets that are traded, a traded asset can be used as a proxy to hedge a cash flow in an untraded asset.

The role of the "cheapest to deliver"

Investors will use the conversion factors and the current term structure of interest rates to determine which bond is likely to be the cheapest on the settlement date. They know full well that the settlement price cannot be far from the ratio of the cheapest bond's market value and its conversion factor. Hence, the price that they are willing to pay for the futures contract is directly linked to the price of the bond cheapest to deliver. Consequently, the futures market reflects market expectations concerning a particular bond.

Hedge ratios

In this section we present some of the most common hedging strategies. Consider the following information:

N = number of contracts
Q = amount of the contract = USD 100,000
C = face value of the bond portfolio = USD 1 million
V = current market value of the bond portfolio with a face value of USD 1 million = USD 900,000
S = spot price of one unit of the portfolio such that $C = V/S = 0.9$
F = futures price = 0.80

In Chapter 7 we defined the hedge ratio as:

$$\beta = \frac{NQ}{C}.$$

Substituting for $C = V/S$, this becomes

$$\beta = \frac{N \times Q \times S}{V}.$$

Consider an investor who holds portfolio V and wants to hedge it. He has several possibilities analyzed in the following four sub-sections.

Equal position

One possibility is to have $N \times Q \times S = V$. In this case $\beta = 1$ and

$$N = \frac{900,000}{100,000 \times 0.9} = 10.$$

Thus he will sell 10 contracts. This will be a good strategy if the spot and futures prices have the same price changes. For example, if there is no maturity or instrument mismatch this would be the strategy to follow.

Match the futures position with the value of the portfolio

In this case, $N \times Q \times F = V$ and

$$N = \frac{900,000}{100,000 \times 0.80} = 11.25$$

and $\beta = 1.125$. Although this type of hedge is convenient and easy to implement, there are no economic or arbitrage arguments to support it.

Minimum variance hedge

In Chapter 7 we dealt extensively with the minimum variance cross hedge, delta hedge and delta cross hedge. The methodology involves running a regression using historical data to capture the covariance between the portfolio and the futures price in the form

$$S = a + \beta F + \varepsilon$$

or

$$\delta S / S = a + \beta \delta F / F + \varepsilon.$$

Suppose we find that $\beta = 0.85$. Then

$$N = 0.85 \frac{900{,}000}{100{,}000 \times 0.9} = 8.5.$$

The problems with this strategy are well known. First of all, since the price of bonds is a complex function of the interest rate, it is probable that the relationship between the two is not linear. Secondly, the estimated coefficients are not stable. Thirdly, a change in the composition of the portfolio will change the slope coefficient. Finally, it is impractical, since it requires large amounts of data and constant re-estimations as the composition of the portfolio changes.

Duration approach

As explained above, duration can be used to obtain the sensitivity of a bond to changes in the interest rate. Let D^* represent modified duration in Equation 18.5. Then,

$$\frac{dB}{B} = -D^* \, d(1 + r).$$

Thus we can write the percentage changes in the portfolio and the position in futures contracts as:

$$\frac{dV}{V} = -D_V^* d(1 + r) \tag{18.9}$$

$$\frac{d(NQF)}{NQF} = -D_F^* d(1 + r) \tag{18.10}$$

where D_F^* refers to the duration of the bond "cheapest to deliver". The hedge is optimal when the change in the value of the bond portfolio is equal to the change in the value of the hedge portfolio: $dV = d(NQF)$. Using 18.9 and 18.10, we get

$$N = \frac{V}{QF} \frac{D_V^*}{D_F^*}$$

and

$$\beta = \frac{NQS}{V} = \frac{S}{F} \frac{D_V^*}{D_F^*} \tag{18.11}$$

Suppose that the modified duration of the bond portfolio is six years and that for the bond "cheapest to deliver" it is nine years, then the optimal hedge ratio is

$$\beta = \frac{0.9 \times 6}{0.8 \times 9} = 0.75$$

and $N = 7.5$.

The duration approach has several advantages. First, it is a forward looking measure and, therefore, requires no historical data. Secondly, it is easy to apply in practice. The duration of a portfolio can be calculated as the weighted average of the durations of the individual bonds and duration figures are routinely available from service vendors and brokerages. Two of the disadvantages are that it is an instantaneous measure that only holds for small changes in the term structure of interest rates and that it changes automatically with the passage of time. Thus, the hedge has to be adjusted each time a change in the term structure causes a change in the durations as well as periodically with the passage of time. Another shortcoming is that the duration approach assumes that the term structure of interest rates is the only source of uncertainty and therefore neglects the other sources of risk such as credit and default risk. Furthermore, the most commonly used measure of duration makes the unrealistic assumption that shifts in the term structure are parallel.

Short-term interest rate futures

On 6 January 1976 the International Monetary Market (IMM) of the Chicago Mercantile Exchange became the first to offer a futures contract on the 90-day US Treasury bill. The success of this contract led them to offer a contract on 90-day Eurodeposits that began trading on 9 December 1981. Since then contracts based on this model have been developed in numerous currencies on many exchanges including the Matif in Paris and Liffe in London, which have several short-term interest rate contracts. The CME itself lists a wide variety of futures and options contracts on short-term US and foreign interest rates. These contracts include: three-month Eurodollars; one-month Libor; 13-week Treasury bills; Euroyen; one-month Federal Funds; the Turn Rate; the Quarterly Bankruptcy Index; Brady bonds; 91-day Mexican Cetes; and 28-day Mexican TIIE. We will begin this section by presenting the general characteristics of futures contracts on short-term interest rates and then we will examine how they can be used.

Basic features of short-term financial futures

The underlying instrument for a short-term financial future can be a negotiable security like a 90-day US T-bill. More often than not, however, a simple index serves the purpose. The indexes used on all the markets are constructed in an identical manner. They are equal to 100 minus the interest rate. For example, the futures contract on the three-month euro quoted on Liffe is 100 minus the interest rate on a three month euro deposit.

The contracts are standardized. The nominal value is fixed. For example, on Liffe it is EUR 1 million for the three-month euro contract, GBP 500,000 for the three-month sterling contract and JPY 100 million on three-month yen. Delivery dates are limited. Liffe, for example, limits its deliveries to the months of March, June, September and December for the contracts on sterling, the Swiss franc and the yen, whereas deliveries take place every month for the euro contract.

Contracts are marked to market at the end of each trading day when all participants are subject to margin calls. Since quotes are made in index points on the underlying instrument, the value of each "tick" is fixed. A "tick" is equal to one basis point. For the Liffe contract on the three-month euro, for example, a change in price from 90.43 to 90.44 implies a change in the interest rate from 9.57% to 9.56%. This variation of 0.01% is worth EUR 25. It corresponds to $0.01 \times 1\%$ multiplied by the contract's nominal value multiplied by $\frac{1}{4}$ of the year (three months):

$$\text{Value of one tick} = 0.01 \times 0.01 \times 1,000,000 \times \tfrac{1}{4} = \text{EUR } 25.$$

Thus, at the end of the day the margin accounts of owners of a futures contract would be credited with EUR 25 per contract and the margin accounts of sellers would be debited by the same amount. The minimum price movement on this contract is half a basis point. In Appendix 18.2 we outline the contract details for Liffe's contracts on three-month sterling, euros, Swiss francs and yen.

At the end of the last trading day, the exchange calculates the interest rate on the underlying instrument in the cash market to use as the settlement price. For example, for its three-month euro contract Liffe uses a representative rate on Libor. This rate is calculated from the closing rates offered by 16 reference banks. The three highest and the three lowest rates are eliminated. The exchange then takes the average of the remaining ten banks which it uses to calculate the settlement price. The settlement price is equal to 100 less the average interest rate. On the day following the settlement date, the remaining margin calls are calculated and compensation is completed. There is no physical delivery with short-term financial futures, only cash settlement.

Principles of hedging with short-term financial futures

Short-term financial futures can be used for hedging, speculation or arbitrage. We will start our presentation with a speculative operation, not because speculation is interesting in itself but because it throws light on the role of the underlying instrument. Afterwards, we will take a look at an arbitrage operation and a hedging operation.

Speculation

A speculator who expects a fall in the interest rate will buy short-term financial futures because the price of the contract will rise as the interest rate falls. On the other hand, a speculator who expects a rise in the interest rate will sell futures. Take the case of a treasurer who, in mid-March, observes the following interest rates on euro deposits: three months = 9% and six months = 9.5%. He believes that these rates can only go up anytime in the near future. At the same time, he notices that Liffe's three-month euro futures contract is quoted at 90.22. He decides to sell ten contracts. Several days later, he is elated at finding out that the euro Libor rates have risen to 9.75% for three months and 9.75% for six months. His elation is short-lived, however, when he finds out that the futures price has risen to 90.48 and that he has lost EUR 6500 [$(90.48 - 90.22) \times 25 \times 10$]. In fact, he cannot understand what is happening. He correctly forecast the rise in the interest rate yet he lost money on his futures speculation. He calls up an eminent professor of Finance at the well known business school where he got his MBA to find out what went wrong.

The professor tells him that he used the wrong instrument for speculating on a rise in the interest rate. The futures contract that he sold was not a bet on a rise in the spot rate. It was a bet on a rise in the expected three-month spot rate for the end of June. When he sold his ten futures contracts, the market was already expecting a rate of 9.78% ($100 - 90.22 = 9.78$) for the end of June. The sharp rise in the spot rate to 9.75% damped down market expectations to the point where the expected spot rate at the end of June is now only 9.52% ($100 - 90.48$). In fact, says the professor, a closer look at the term structure would have made this clear.

According to the pure expectations theory of the term structure of interest rates, a six-month rate higher than the three-month rate implies that the market expects the three month interest rate three months in the future to be higher than the current three-month rate. The expected future rate implied by the term structure is sometimes referred to as the forward/forward. Applying the pure expectations reasoning gives:

$$\left(1 + 0.095 \times \frac{1}{2}\right) = \left(1 + 0.09 \times \frac{1}{4}\right)\left(1 + {}_{\frac{1}{4}}r_{\frac{1}{4},\frac{1}{2}} \times \frac{1}{4}\right)$$

Solving this equation for the interest rate to be made on a three-month loan that will be contracted in three months ($\frac{1}{4}$ of a year) and paid off in six months ($\frac{1}{2}$ of a year) yields:

$$_{\frac{1}{4}}r_{\frac{1}{4},\frac{1}{2}} = 9.78\%$$

It is interesting to note that 9.78% was also the price implied by the futures price.

The same exercise can be applied to the new term structure, which is now flat:

$$\left(1 + 0.0975 \times \frac{1}{2}\right) = \left(1 + 0.0975 \times \frac{1}{4}\right)\left(1 + {}_{\frac{1}{4}}r_{\frac{1}{4},\frac{1}{2}} \times \frac{1}{4}\right)$$

$$_{\frac{1}{4}}r_{\frac{1}{4},\frac{1}{2}} = 9.52\%.$$

This also is the rate implied in the new futures price. A rise in the current spot rate does not imply that the spot rates expected in the future will also rise. "Having forgotten this fact", says the wiley old prof, "is what cost you the EUR 6500".

Arbitrage

As the foregoing example highlighted, the interest rate that is implied by the futures price represents the rate that is expected by the market at maturity. It is also reflected in the term structure of interest rates. If the spot and futures markets are not in phase, opportunities for arbitrage will appear. An example will illustrate the point. Consider the following information: the Eurodollar three-month bid–ask is $9–9\frac{1}{8}$ and the six-month bid–ask is $9\frac{1}{2}–9\frac{5}{8}$. The three-month futures contract is quoted at 89.85. The term structure implies forward/forward bid–ask rates of 9.65%–10.02%.[18] The rate implied by the futures price is 10.15% (100 – 89.85), which is higher than the forward/forward rates. Consequently, there is an opportunity for arbitrage. Borrow for six months, lend for three months, and lock in the gain by buying a three-month futures contract. There is a problem, however, that stems from the fact that the day count on

[18] Calculated as:

$$\left[\frac{1 + 0.09625 \times \left(\frac{183}{360}\right)}{1 + 0.09 \times \left(\frac{91}{360}\right)} - 1\right] \times \frac{360}{92} = 10.02\%$$

when the investor borrows for six months and makes two successive three-month loans. And

$$\left[\frac{1 + 0.095 \times \left(\frac{183}{360}\right)}{1 + 0.09125 \times \left(\frac{91}{360}\right)} - 1\right] \times \frac{360}{92} = 9.65\%$$

when the investor lends for six months and borrows twice for three months.

the Eurocurrency market may be different from the day count in the futures market. All arbitrage calculations should be undertaken using the appropriate day count for each market.

Hedging

Companies are often in a position where a sharp move in the short-term interest rate could hurt them. Short-term financing is the first example that comes to mind such as drawing down lines of credit the interest rate on which is indexed to three-month Libor. Another example is investing temporary cash surpluses in the Euromarket where the interest rate depends on Libid. In the first case, a rise in the interest rate will hurt the company whereas in the second case it is a fall that could do the damage. Hedging against a rise involves selling contracts and hedging against a fall involves buying them.

Suppose that in mid-June a company borrows USD 20 million for one year on the basis of a rollover Libor plus $\frac{1}{4}$. If Libor is 7.05% at the beginning of the operation, the interest cost for the first three months is USD 365,000. Future interest costs on the loan are unknown because Libor can fluctuate between now and the rollover dates. If the company treasurer fears an interest rate rise, he can cover himself with Eurodollar futures on the CME. Since the rollovers are scheduled for September, December and March, he should sell 20 contracts for each of those dates for a total of 60 contracts.

The September contract is quoted at 92.95, which indicates that the term structure is flat for the moment. By September Libor has risen to 7.90% and the contract is settled at 92.10. Since 20 contracts were sold, the company has made a gain of 20 × 85 basis points. Each basis point is worth USD 25 so the profit on the position is USD 42,500. The interest rate on the loan for the next three months is 8.15% or USD 407,500. The interest cost to the company is USD 407,500 minus the USD 42,500 earned on the futures contracts for a total of USD 365,000. The September hedge worked like a charm.

The hedges for December and March would operate in the same fashion. In practice, however, there is a problem with a series of hedges like this. Farther off maturities are usually less liquid than the closer ones. One of the reasons, as we have seen, is that basis risk makes investors choose the closer maturities. Consequently, the treasurer in the foregoing example will probably prefer to hedge with 60 September contracts, rolling over 40 December contracts in September and finishing by rolling over 20 March contracts in December. In this way he will benefit from the liquidity of the shorter maturities and reduce his basis risk. The question of basis risk is important if at some point the treasurer feels that an increase in the interest rate is no longer a threat and wants to close out his position. This system is safer and more dynamic than a series of fixed hedges and is preferred by most practitioners in spite of the cost of regularly rolling over the positions.

Over-the-counter hedging instruments

The banks have developed a wide range of instruments designed to help their clients manage interest rate risk. The range of instruments is so wide, in fact, that it almost seems as if the imagination of the financial engineers is unlimited. It is important to have a good idea of what is available so we will briefly outline the characteristics of some of the main products on the market, such as **forward rate agreements** (FRAs), interest rate swaps, **caps**, **floors**, **collars**, options on FRA's and options on swaps.

Forward rate agreements

In Chapter 9 we saw that FRAs resemble short-term futures contracts. They enable a company or financial institution to protect itself against interest rate risk by fixing the effective rate of interest in advance of the intended borrowing or deposit date. They are a contract whereby two parties agree to exchange the difference between the market rate of interest (usually the interbank offered rate) on the contract's effective date and the fixed rate prescribed in the contract. If a company wishes to guarantee its future borrowing costs, it buys an FRA. If it wishes to guarantee its rate of return on a future deposit, it sells an FRA.

Suppose that a treasurer forecasts a need for USD 2 million in two months that will last for three months. He cannot borrow immediately because he has no use for the funds at the moment but he wants to protect himself against a rise in the interest rate. His banker offers him a rate of 5.50% on USD 2 million. He decides to buy the FRA on the three-month interest rate with a settlement date two months in the future. Remember that if he had used an organized exchange he would have sold a futures contract. The FRA is a private contract between the company and the bank.

On the settlement date two months later, if the interest rate has gone up, the bank pays the company the discounted difference between the current rate and the contract rate of 5.5% multiplied by the contract amount times the fraction of the year. For example, if the current rate is 6.5%, then

$$(0.065 - 0.055)\frac{91}{360} \times USD\ 2,000,000 \times (1 + 0.065\frac{91}{360})^{-1} = USD\ 4973.83.$$

If the interest rate has gone down instead of up, it is the company that pays the bank. It should be clear that the bank does not contract to loan the company any money. Its engagement only concerns paying or receiving the difference in the two interest rates. The company will have to raise the loan separately but the outcome of the FRA guarantees that the cost of the loan will be based on the 5.5% interest rate stipulated in the FRA.

FRA's have some advantages compared to the futures contracts traded on organized exchanges. First of all, they do not require transmitting an order and having it executed on the exchange. Secondly, there are no margin calls to worry about. Thirdly, because there is no standardization, the contract can be tailored to the particular needs of the client in terms of amount, currency and settlement date. However – and this is another plus – standard terms for FRA dealing were published by the British Bankers' Association in August 1985 and these are generally accepted throughout the market. In addition, the revised terms and conditions of the **International Swaps and Derivatives Association** (ISDA) include FRA transactions within their Master Agreement. These advantages have their cost, of course. The banker takes his payment in the form of a spread. At one time this spread could go as high as 20–25 basis points but now it is down to 3–4 basis points and sometimes lower for the more liquid periods up to one year. Furthermore, it is much more difficult to close out a position, even partially, than it is on the organized exchanges so dynamic interest rate management is all but ruled out.

Interest rate swaps

An FRA is basically a short-term instrument for periods up to one year but treasurers often have the need to manage interest rate risk with a much longer-term horizon. **Interest rate swaps** (see Chapter 9) can be a big help in managing risk of this kind.

Remember from Chapter 9 that an interest rate swap is a contractual agreement between two parties to exchange a series of payments for a stated period of time. Only payments resembling or corresponding to the interest payments on a notional amount are exchanged. The principal itself is not exchanged. Usually, one party pays a floating rate and the other party pays a fixed rate. A floating rate refers to the interest rate on a loan that is adjusted periodically according to an index. Although about 75% of swaps are indexed to Libor, other typical floating rate indices are commercial paper, the Fed Funds rate, the prime rate and the T-bill rate.

Swaps can be useful for locking in a fall in the interest rate. Consider a company that has contracted for a floating rate loan in order to benefit from a fall in the interest rate. The interest rate has fallen as expected and now the treasurer wants to protect himself against the possibility of a rise. He could, of course, prepay his loan and negotiate another with a fixed rate. This type of transaction takes time and is costly, especially if there is a penalty for prepayment. He decides instead to enter into a swap agreement negotiated with his bank. The amount he wants to hedge is USD 10 million and the maturity is five years. The swap contract stipulates a notional principal amount of USD 10 million, a term of five years, a fixed rate, called the coupon, of 6.5%, six-month Libor as the floating rate index, and semi-annual payments. Every six months the bank compares Libor with the 6.5% fixed rate. If it is higher, the bank pays the company the difference. If it is lower, the company pays the bank the difference. The company is thus called the fixed rate payer because its interest payments are fixed by the differential payments at 6.5%.

The interest rate swap, then, is like a series of FRAs, one for each payment date. The counterparty to the swap is, of course, the floating rate payer so it is obvious that the swap can be used to transform a fixed rate loan into a floating rate loan in order to benefit from a fall in interest rates. Since swaps generate no increase in liabilities, they can also be used to manage long and medium-term investments. Combined with a foreign exchange swap, they can be used to transform fixed rate debt in one currency into floating rate debt in another. The possibilities are extensive, which explains why swaps have grown into a huge market.

Caps, floors and collars

Having used an FRA or a swap is always a source of intense satisfaction for the company treasurer when his forecast turns out to have been correct. On the other hand, when his forecast turns out wrong he regrets being locked into a position that excludes him from taking advantage of the unforeseen conditions. Ever sensitive to their clients' cares, the banks have come up with some new products, engineered from options theory, that guarantee risk coverage when conditions are bad while making it possible to take advantage of opportunities when conditions turn out to be good. In Chapter 9 we showed how caps, floors and collars can be priced.

Caps

Citicorp introduced the Eurodollar market to "caps" in 1983 but the market really took off in 1985 when a group of 20 large US banks issued USD 2.75 billion of floating rate notes containing an option clause that effectively "capped" the corporate issuer's floating rate exposure at a maximum level. The success of the issue made banks recognize the potential for trading caps for their own account. Since then, the market has developed rapidly, expanding into sterling, euros, yen and Swiss francs. From their origins in corporate finance, caps (and floors) are now traded in a large and liquid over-the-counter (OTC) market where the interbank market plays a major role. The one to five-year maturities are the most actively traded but considerable liquidity can be found for maturities of up to ten years.

A cap, then, enables a company with floating rate debt to limit the risk associated with upward moves in the interest rate while taking full advantage of downward moves. It can be purchased from a bank and amounts to a contract whereby the seller agrees to reimburse the buyer should a chosen reference rate exceed the cap's interest rate level. To compensate the seller for taking on the interest rate risk, the buyer makes a premium payment. The cap contract stipulates the maturity, the interest rate level, the reference floating rate (usually Libor), the reset period (tenor) and the notional principal amount.

Suppose, for example, that a company has USD 20 million worth of five-year floating rate debt at Libor plus $\frac{1}{4}$%. To limit the risk of an excessive rise in the interest rate, the company buys a cap – not necessarily from the bank that issued the loan – with a maturity of five years, a strike price of 7.5%, a reference rate of Libor, a notional principal amount of USD 20 million and a reset period of six months. For this contract the company pays a premium, which, as we showed in Chapter 9, is calculated as the value of the series of ten options involved in the deal. Every six months Libor is compared to the strike price of 7.5%. If Libor is below 7.5%, nothing happens and the company pays the lower rate on its loan. If Libor is above 7.5% – at 9.5%, for example – the company pays 9.75% on its loan (Libor plus 0.25%) but it receives the difference between 9.5% and 7.5% multiplied by $\frac{1}{2}$ (the reset period is six months) multiplied by the notional principal amount from the bank that sold the cap. The cost to the borrower as a result of the cap payment is effectively limited to 7.75%, the strike price of 7.5% plus the 0.25% over Libor.

Floors

Floors are similar to caps except that where caps protect against upward moves in the interest rate floors protect against downward moves. Like caps, they can be purchased from a bank and amount to a contract whereby the seller agrees to reimburse the buyer should a chosen reference rate fall below the floor's interest rate level. To compensate the seller for taking on the interest rate risk, the buyer makes a premium payment. The floor contract stipulates the maturity, the interest rate level, the reference floating rate (usually Libor), the reset period and the notional principal amount.

The mechanics of a floor are symmetrical to those of a cap. Suppose that a company has excess funds of USD 10 million that it wants to invest in three-month Eurodeposits at a rate of Libor minus $\frac{1}{2}$%. To guard against a fall in the interest rate, the company buys a floor with a maturity of three years, a strike price of 5%, a Libor reference rate, a three-month reset period and a notional principal amount of USD 10 million. For this contract the company pays a premium calculated, as shown in Chapter 9, as the value of the series of ten options involved in the deal. If Libor stays above 5%, the company pays the premium but benefits from the higher interest rates. If Libor falls below 5% – to 4%, for example – the company receives the lower interest rate from its investment but it also receives the difference between 5% and 4% for $\frac{1}{4}$ of one year multiplied by the notional principal amount (USD 25,000). As a result of the payoff on the floor, the lowest return that the company can receive is 4.5% (5% less 0.5%) and its upside return possibilities are unlimited.

Collars

By combining a cap with a floor, the banks invented the collar. As would be expected, the collar is a contract that fixes a maximum and a minimum interest rate. When used to manage a liability, the company buys the cap and sells the floor. Thus, it limits risk due to upward moves in the interest rate but it also limits the opportunities for benefiting from falls. When used to manage an investment, the cap is sold and the floor is purchased, thereby limiting the risk due to downward moves in the interest rate as well as the gains to be made from upward moves. The advantage of the collar is that the strike prices of the cap and the floor are usually calculated in such a way that the premiums offset one another and the company has no initial cash outlay. Although there is no initial cash outlay, the collar is not free. The cost comes in the form of the potential gains that have been surrendered in the option that was sold.

Let's go back to the company that has USD 20 million of five-year debt at six-month Libor plus 0.25%. The purchase of a cap with a strike price of 8% and the sale of a floor with a strike price of 5% enables the company to partially cover its risk. If six-month Libor stays between 5% and 8%, no payments are made on the collar and the company's cost of the loan is six-month Libor plus 0.25%. If six-month Libor goes above 8%, the bank pays the difference and the cost of the loan to the company is 8.25%. If it goes below 5%, the company pays the bank the difference and the cost of its loan is 5.25%.

The premiums on the two options do not have to offset each other exactly. The strike prices can be chosen so that either the company or the bank makes a cash outlay. In any case, the outlay will be considerably lower than if only one side of the transaction had been undertaken.

Options on FRAs and on swaps

Options on FRAs can be used for short-term debt while options on swaps can be used for medium to long-term debt.

Options on FRAs

Forward rate agreements have the advantage of locking in the interest rate on a future loan. When borrowing, it is a good deal if the interest rate goes up but a bad deal if it goes down. When lending, it is a good deal if the interest rate goes down but a bad deal if it goes up. A treasurer who is not sure of what will happen in the future might prefer to leave himself some room for maneuver. As a borrower, he will buy a call on an FRA. If the interest rate goes up, he exercises his call and locks himself into the lower rate. If the interest rate goes down, he will let the call expire worthless and borrow at the lower rate. In both cases, the cost of the loan is increased by the premium that was paid for the call. In Chapter 8 we showed how to price options on futures contracts. As a lender, he will buy a put on an FRA. If the interest rate goes down, he exercises his put and locks himself into the higher rate. If interest rates go up, he lets the put expire worthless and lends at the higher rate. In both cases, his return is reduced by the amount of the premium.

Options on swaps

The growth in the swap market generated a demand for options on swaps, sometimes called swaptions. Corporate treasurers, faced with the choice of remaining unhedged or fixing their funding costs for a given period of time, began to search for more flexible alternatives. Flexibility is especially useful when the yield curve is upward sloping and long-term rates are considerably higher than short-term rates. Swaptions offer this flexibility.

A swaption, as we saw in Chapter 9, is the right to enter an interest rate swap as either the payer or the receiver of the fixed side of the swap. A payer swaption is the right to pay the fixed rate in the swap. If rates rise above the swaption strike price, the purchaser exercises the option and locks in the lower rate. The seller is obliged to receive the fixed rate at the strike price and pay the floating rate. If rates do not rise above the strike price, the swaption expires worthless.

A receiver swaption is the right to receive the fixed rate in the swap. If rates fall below the swaption strike price, the purchaser exercises the option and locks in the higher rate. The writer of the swaption is obliged to pay the higher rate in return for the floating rate. If rates do not fall, the swaption expires worthless.

Since swaptions are over-the-counter products, they can be tailored to suit particular needs. A typical swaption has an option period of less than a year, a swap maturity of between three and ten years, and a notional principal amount of between USD 50 million and USD 100 million.

Consider a company that plans to borrow USD 50 million for five years in three months time. Its treasurer thinks that interest rates are likely to fall but in order to cover himself he buys a payer swaption with an option maturity of three months, a strike price of 8%, a swap maturity of five years and a notional principal amount of USD 50 million. For this he pays 70 basis points (USD 350,000). If interest rates fall as he expects, the option will expire worthless and he will borrow at the market rate, either fixed or floating, depending on his expectations on interest rates. If, however, the prevailing five-year swap market rate is above 8%, the treasurer borrows USD 50 million for five years at a floating rate of interest and exercises his option. His cost will be the fixed rate of 8% per year plus the premium. In Chapter 9 we showed how to calculate the premium of a swaption.

Summary

1. Interest rates determine the prices of assets and liabilities. Interest rate risk is associated with the fact that interest rates can change, thereby changing the value of existing assets and liabilities as well as the value of those that are anticipated in the future. Interest rate risk is not limited to whether rates will go up or down. It also concerns variations in the term structure of interest rates. Term structure theory deals with the effect that time has on interest rates. It seeks to answer the question of why different maturities should have different yields.

2. Yield to maturity is the interest figure quoted most frequently by investors and professionals. It is the rate that equates the present value of the future cash flows with the present market value of the bond. In other words, it is the bond's internal rate of return. Care must be taken when using yield to maturity as an investment guideline because it represents only a weighted average of the underlying term structure.

3. Expected future rates, or forward rates, can be deduced from the yield curve (term structure).

4. The organized exchanges worldwide have developed a range of contracts in numerous currencies designed for managing long-term interest rate risk. Long-term futures markets have the same three characteristics that we saw in the organized exchanges trading foreign currencies: a centralized, public trading place, standardized contracts and a clearing house. All transactions must pass through an authorized member broker. Only representatives of authorized brokers have access to the trading pits. Trading takes place in a type of permanent auction that ensures transparency, because it is done in public, and competition, because any member is free to participate. In order to facilitate trading, only approved contracts are allowed to be traded. The underlying security is strictly defined and limited to a certain type of bond. Nominal amounts are standardized. Maturities are limited in number, usually based on a quarterly schedule of March, June, September and December. Finally, all transactions are recorded with the clearing house.

5. The basis is the difference between the futures price and the spot price and is determined by the difference between long and short-term interest rates. Although spot and futures prices converge at maturity, the basis can change if there is a change in the term structure. Term structure induced changes in the basis is called basis risk and must be managed carefully if the maturities of the futures contract and the hedged assets are not perfectly matched.

6. Because of settlement procedures that permit delivery of bonds with different characteristics, one bond will turn out to be the "cheapest to deliver". Since this is the bond that is likely to be delivered, the futures price will tend to approximate the price of the cheapest to deliver divided by the conversion factor.

7. When the prices of futures contracts are not perfectly correlated with the asset to be hedged, a cross hedge has to be constructed. A cross hedge means that the futures

contract is different from the asset being hedged. The success of the cross hedge depends on the hedge ratio, which can be defined as the ratio of the nominal value of the futures contracts that are bought or sold to the nominal value of the assets to be hedged. Successful cross hedging requires finding the ratio that minimizes the variability of the returns of the hedged portfolio.

8. Short-term financial futures can be used to hedge short-term interest rate risk. The underlying instrument for a short-term financial future can be a negotiable security like a 90-day US T-bill but, more often than not, a simple index serves the purpose. The indexes used on all the markets are constructed in an identical manner. They are equal to 100 minus the short-term interest rate. The contracts are standardized. The nominal value is fixed and delivery dates are limited. Contracts are marked to market at the end of each trading day when all participants are subject to margin calls. At the end of the last trading day, the exchange calculates the interest rate on the underlying instrument in the cash market to use as the settlement price. There is no physical delivery with short-term financial futures, only cash settlement.

9. Arbitrage ensures that the interest rate that is implied by the futures price represents the rate that is expected by the market at maturity as well as the rate reflected in the yield curve (term structure).

10. The banks have developed a wide range of instruments designed to help their clients manage interest rate risk. Some of the best known and most popular instruments include interest rate swaps, forward rate agreements (FRAs), caps, floors, collars, options on FRAs and options on swaps.

Questions

Solutions to the following questions are set out on the web site, details of which are included in the Preface.

1. If a bond is quoted at 107.5% and the coupon is 10.3%, what is its current yield?

2. A zero coupon bond maturing in one year is selling for 92.59%. A two-year bond paying an annual coupon of 8% is selling at 99.15%. What is the price of a zero coupon bond maturing in two years?

3. A bond pays a 10% coupon on a face value of EUR 1000. The coupon date is 16 February. On 12 May the bond is sold. What is the accrued interest payment calculated on a 30/360 basis?

4. What is the average life of a bond that has amortization payments of GBP 2000 in three months, GBP 1800 one year later and GBP 1600 one year after that?

5. The modified duration of a bond is equal to four years. By how much will its price vary if the interest rate increases by 25 basis points? (a) 1%; (b) –1%; or (c) –2%.

6. What is the difference between "immunization" and "exact matching" as strategies for bond portfolio management?

7. Choose the correct response (responses). The sale of notional futures contracts makes it possible

   a. to speculate on a fall in the interest rate

   b. to hedge a bond portfolio

   c. to generate temporary funds

   d. to hide recent losses on a bond portfolio.

8. On the maturity date of a futures contract, three bonds are available for delivery:

	Clean price	Accrued interest	Conversion factor
Bond A	128.70	7.056	118.6748
Bond B	126.30	3.279	115.5783
Bond C	107.90	1.477	98.6970

If the futures settlement price is 108.60, which of the three bonds is the cheapest to deliver?

9. The "cheapest to deliver" has the following characteristics: clean price = 100.56; conversion factor = 92.0947; sensitivity = 5.57. How many futures contracts (notional value USD 100,000) must be sold to hedge a portfolio of USD 6,000,000 composed of $\frac{1}{3}$ of Bond A and $\frac{2}{3}$ of Bond B. The characteristics of Bonds A and B are as follows:

	Clean price	Sensitivity
Bond A	107.38	5.68
Bond B	98.03	6.52

10. The interest rates on the euro and the dollar are quoted in London as follows:

	Three-month	Six-month
Euro	$12\frac{1}{4}$	11
US dollar	$3\frac{1}{4}$	$3\frac{1}{2}$

What is the forward/forward rate for the two currencies?

11. Choose the correct response. A cap can be used

 a. to protect the value of future investments

 b. to limit the fall in the value of a bond portfolio

 c. to limit the cost of future borrowing at a variable rate.

12. In what ways are FRAs and short-term futures contracts similar?

13. Show that an interest rate swap (fixed/variable) can be broken down into a succession of FRAs.

14. A company benefiting from a government guarantee can take out a seven-year loan at a fixed rate of 10% or at a variable rate of Pibor + $\frac{1}{10}$%. At the same time, a company not benefiting from the government guarantee can borrow for seven years at a fixed rate of 11% or a variable rate of Pibor + $\frac{4}{10}$%. The company with the guarantee wants to borrow at a variable rate while the company without the guarantee wants to borrow at a fixed rate. As a banker, propose a deal using swaps that will improve both companies' conditions and pay you a commission of $\frac{2}{10}$%.

15. What is the difference between a swaption and a series of options on an FRA?

16. The borrowing opportunities for Company X and Company Y have the following profile

	Fixed rate	Floating rate
Company X	9.0%	Libor + 0.4%
Company Y	10.9%	Libor + 0.7%

Could a swap be arranged so that X could borrow floating rate funds and Y fixed rate funds more cheaply than the rates indicated in the table? If the bank commission is 40 basis points and the two companies agree to split everything evenly, what would be the all-in cost for each company?

17. Annual coupons on loans in Swiss francs and US dollars have the following profile:

Maturity	Annual coupon rate in CHF	Annual coupon rate in USD
One year	8.5%	3.6%
Two years	8.3%	3.9%
Three years	8.1%	4.2%
Four years	7.9%	4.5%
Five years	7.8%	4.9%

The spot exchange rate in Zürich is CHF 1.6 = USD 1.

a. What are the zero coupon interest rates (spot rates) implied by the annual coupon rates given above?

b. A Swiss company has an outstanding loan of USD 6 million paying a 4.8% annual coupon and an *in fine* principal payment due in four years. The prevailing market rate on an equivalent loan is now 4.5%. Using the zero coupon rates calculated in question a, calculate the present value of the yearly savings generated by the lower market rate of interest.

c. Express the answer to question b in basis points.

18. Discuss the different kinds of risks involved in swap transactions.

19. If one of the parties to an interest rate swap defaults, what is at risk for the non-defaulting party?

Appendix 18.1 The Matif long-term interest rate futures contract

Matif euro notional future

- **Symbol:** ELT
- **Underlying instrument:** 8½ to 10½ year notional government bond, redeemable at maturity, 3.5% coupon. At each first trading day, Euronext Paris SA establishes the list of sovereign issuers of EMU whose bonds can be part of the bond pool
- **Trading unit:** EUR 100,000
- **Price quotation:** Percent of the nominal value, quoted to the second decimal point
- **Minimum price fluctuation (tick):** 0.01% of the nominal value, equivalent to EUR 10
- **Contract cycles:** Three successive quarterly contract cycles out of: March (H), June (M), September (U), December (Z)
- **Regular initial margin:** EUR 1,500
- **Last trading day:** The second trading day preceding the third Wednesday of the contract month at 11.00 a.m.
- **First trading day:** First trading day following the closing of a contract month
- **Settlement:** Based on settlement price. Bonds are selected by the seller from an official list of 8½ to 10½-year deliverable government bonds, possibly of other sovereign issuers of EMU, redeemable at maturity, minimum outstanding amount of EUR 6 bn paid one month before the settlement date of the contract month
- **Daily price limit:** + / – 135 bp

- **NSC trading hours:** Pre-opening 7.45 a.m–8.00 a.m. Trading session 8.00 a.m–10.00 p.m. Settlement day changeover 5.30 p.m. (all Paris time).

Delivery procedures and deliverable securities for open maturities

Delivery month = June 2001
Last trading day = 18 June 2001
Repartition day = 19 June 2001
Settlement/delivery day = 22 June 2001
Conversion factor calculated on 19 June 2001
Accrued interest calculated on 22 June 2001.

Deliverable securities	Redeeming date	ISIN code	Conversion factor (CF)	accrued interest in % (AI)
Bund 5.375%	4 January 2010	DE0001135135	113.6217	2.488700
OAT 5.50%	25 April 2010	FR0000186603	114.9854	0.874000
Bund 5.25%	4 July 2010	DE0001135150	113.3605	5.938050
OAT 5.50%	25 October 2010	FR0000187023	115.6966	3.616000
Bund 5.25%	4 January 2011	DE0001135168	113.9525	3.520990
OAT 6.50%	25 April 2011	FR0000570731	124.6198	1.033000

Invoice amount (in EUR) due by the buyer to the seller for one futures contract: $IA = 1{,}000 \times (SP \times (CF/100) + AI)$ where SP is the settlement price.

Appendix 18.2 The Liffe long-term interest rate futures contract

Contract	Three-month sterling	Three-month euro (Libor)	Three-month Euro-Swiss franc	Three-month Euroyen (Libor)
Exchange contract number	16	30	33	47
Currency specified by the Board	Sterling	Euro	Swiss franc	Yen
Unit of trading	GBP 500,000	EUR 1 million	CHF 1 million	JPY 100 million
Delivery months	Mar, Jun, Sep, Dec	All calendar months	Mar, Jun, Sep, Dec	Mar, Jun, Sep, Dec
No. of delivery months available for trading	20 Quarterly 2 serial	16 Quarterly 2 Serial	8 Quarterly	12 Quarterly
Basis point value	GBP 12.50	EUR 25.00	CHF 25	JPY 2,500
Minimum price movement	1 basis point	Half basis point	1 basis point	Half basis point
Quotation	100.00 minus rate of interest	100.00 minus rate of interest	100.00 minus rate of interest	100.00 minus rate of interest
Last trading day	Third Wednesday of the delivery month	Two business days prior to the third Wednesday of the delivery month	Two business days prior to the third Wednesday of the delivery month	Two business days prior to the third Wednesday of the delivery month
Interest rate basis	Actual/365	Actual/360	Actual/360	Actual/360

OTHER INTERNATIONAL MARKETS

International commodity markets: Inventory and supply management

Manufacturing firms usually carry three types of inventories: finished goods, work in progress and raw materials. Levels of inventories of finished goods depend on anticipated sales and the skill of the financial manager in coordinating production and sales. Work in progress also depends on anticipated sales but it is strongly influenced by how long it takes to produce the finished good. A longer production period automatically generates higher levels of inventories of work in progress.

Inventories of raw materials are somewhat different. They do, of course, depend to a large extent on expected sales. However, their levels are also affected by whether or not their production is seasonal, by the reliability of sources of supply, and by how effectively the financial manager can coordinate raw material purchases with the firm's production plans. Management of inventories of raw materials is particularly relevant to international finance because production of raw materials is generally international in scope. In the case of raw materials like oil and metals, it depends on the geographic location of the resources themselves. In the case of agricultural raw materials like coffee and bananas, it depends on climate. Consequently, the financial manager's supplies of raw materials will often come from foreign countries where they are subject to political interference, natural catastrophes, and the vagaries of climate and the weather.

Even when raw materials are produced domestically, their price is dependent on international supply and demand. In fact, commodities as diverse as wheat, corn, cotton, pork bellies, coffee, copper, iron, lead, silver, tin, petroleum, aluminum, zinc, gold and orange juice, to mention only a few, are traded worldwide. They serve as basic inputs for the production of breakfast cereals, TV dinners, cars, televisions, jeans, whiskey, aspirin and all the other familiar products integral to our everyday lives. As such, their availability, quality and cost play an important role in corporate decision making concerning what is produced, how it is produced, and the quantities and timing of output. Besides being traded on the spot market, most of these products are also traded on futures markets. The futures markets are an invaluable tool in managing the problems associated with raw material prices and supplies. In the first place, they reflect how prices are expected to evolve in the future. Secondly, they make it possible to manage the risk associated with commodity price fluctuations, thereby reducing production costs for innumerable products. Finally, they are a valuable aid in managing stock levels and ensuring timely supplies.

In this chapter we begin by describing the international commodity markets, both spot and derivative, and analyzing where and how the vast majority of commodities are traded. To this end we detail the roles of the major players in the physical markets: the producers, the consumers and the trading companies that ensure worldwide distribution and supply.[1] We then outline the issues involved in inventory management in general and review the principles of hedging the risk associated with raw material supplies by using commodity futures. Next, we present the principles involved in determining a hedging strategy for the management of raw material inventory supply risk. Finally, we see how futures contracts combined with supply timing can play an important role in solving the overall problem of more efficient inventory management.

International spot and derivative commodity markets: An overview

The world commodity markets can be broken down into markets for energy, metals and minerals, agricultural commodities, and other miscellaneous commodities. Many of these markets are organized exchanges. The others are over-the-counter (OTC) markets that use **reference prices**. A reference price is a price that is recognized as a fair price by both parties negotiating the contract. Reference prices are often prices posted by a major producer. In the diamond market, for example, until recently the reference prices were those posted by the De Beers Central Selling Organization. Other reference prices can come from specialized organizations such as Bloomberg, Reuters and Platt's. Platt's, for example, is often the reference for spot oil prices.

Data sources on commodities

There are many vendors that supply short-term data suitable for commodity trading. These data vendors usually offer online and real-time data on commodity markets and indexes with suitable charts giving the evolution of prices over various periods of time from anywhere between a day to several years. Most of these data vendors also supply data on financial and foreign exchange markets as well as real-time market news and analyses.

Three of the most important data vendors are:

- Reuters (www.reuters.com) is a UK company specialized in the supply of real-time financial data. It supplies online and real-time data and charts on both physical and derivative markets for a large number of commodities, including energy, metal and agricultural commodities. It also publishes news concerning all these markets.

- Bloomberg (www.bloomberg.com) is a US company that supplies services similar to those of Reuters.

- The Bridge Commodity Research Bureau (Bridge-CRB) is more specialized in commodities and in forecasting. It also publishes one of the most important commodity indexes, the Bridge-CRB Commodity Index (www.crbindex.com).

These commercial data sources are supplemented by many newspapers, such as the *Wall Street Journal*, the *Financial Times* and the *International Herald Tribune*, that supply both physical and derivative commodity market prices along with financial market prices in their daily issues. There are also a number of professional journals, publications and databases concentrating on specific commodities and groups of commodities. Table 19.1 gives some examples.

---

[1] For a comprehensive presentation and analysis of the international commodity markets see Clark, Lesourd and Thiéblemont (2001).

Table 19.1 Examples of sources of information concerning various classes of commodities

Commodity	Data sources
Non-ferrous metals	*Metal Bulletin*, *Mineral Commodity Summaries*, US Geological Survey, Raw Materials Group, LME, NYMEX/COMEX, Reuters, Bloomberg
Iron and steel products	International Iron and Steel Institute (IISI), US Geological Survey
Precious metals (Gold, silver, PGM metals)	Gold Institute, Johnson Matthey, Minemet, Raw Materials Group, CBOT, NYMEX/COMEX, TOCOM, Reuters, Bloomberg
Oil and gas	*Oil and Gas Journal*, *Petroleum Economist*, Platt's, Raw Materials Group, US Department of Energy, IPE, NYMEX/COMEX, Reuters, Bloomberg
Petrochemicals	*Oil and Gas Journal*, *Petroleum Economist*, Chemical Data, Chemical Industries Services, Morgan Stanley, Goldman Sachs
Coal	*Coal Week*, Raw Materials Group, US Department of Energy, NYMEX/COMEX
Cereals	International Wheat Council, Topfer, USDA, CBOT, Liffe, MATIF, Reuters, Bloomberg
Oilseeds and edible oils	*Oil World*, CBOT, Reuters, Bloomberg
Coffee	Reuters, Bloomberg, International Coffee Organization, Liffe, NYBOT
Cocoa	E.D. & F. Man, Liffe, NYBOT, Reuters, Bloomberg
Natural rubber	IRSG, Safic Alcan, FAO, Reuters, Bloomberg
Sugar	E.D. & F. Man, International Sugar Organization, Liffe, NYBOT, Reuters, Bloomberg

All major commodity exchanges have web sites, which supply a wide range of usually free information and pertinent data, including general information on the exchange, contracts, prices and charts, educational information and other topics. Some of the most important exchanges are the

- Chicago Board of Trade (www.cbot.com)
- Chicago Mercantile Exchange (www.cme.com)
- NYMEX/COMEX (www.nymex.com)
- London International Financial Futures Exchange (Liffe) (www.liffe.com)
- London Metal Exchange (www.lme.co.uk)
- International Petroleum Exchange (www.ipe.com).

Other sites worth mentioning that supply free information on physical and derivative markets are:

- USDA (www.usda.gov). This site gives detailed information on agricultural commodity markets, such as crop reports, weather, agricultural statistics, supply and demand, foreign trade information, satellite imagery and periodic reports on specific commodity markets.

- US Geological Survey (USGS) (minerals.er.usgs.gov). This site provides forecasting data for the metals markets.

Markets for energy commodities

The major energy commodities are crude and refined oil, kerosene and naphtha, liquefied petroleum gas, natural gas and coal. Pure electricity has also become a traded commodity.

The major spot markets for oil products are in Amsterdam-Antwerp-Rotterdam, New York and Singapore. Derivatives are traded on the London International Petroleum Exchange (IPE) and the New York Mercantile Exchange (NYMEX/COMEX). For example, the IPE trades futures and options contracts on North Sea "Brent" oil (1000 barrels of 158.987 liter, USD/barrel), and on gasoil (heating oil No.2 or light fuel oil, 1000 metric tonnes, USD/metric tonne). The New York Mercantile Exchange (NYMEX/COMEX) trades futures and options on a number of products including:

- "Light Sweet" crude oil (1000 barrels, USD/barrel)
- Heating oil No.2 (42 000 US gallons: USD/gallon)
- Unleaded gasoline (42 000 US gallons: USD/gallon)
- Natural gas (1 000 000 MBTU: USD/MBTU).

The spot markets for natural gas are mainly OTC while the spot markets for coal are found in the major producing countries such as Australia, the United States, South Africa and Canada. Futures and options are traded on the NYMEX/COMEX in both natural gas and coal.

Due to the deregulation of electricity utilities in various regions of the world, including North America and Europe, efficient spot markets in electricity appeared at the beginning of the 1990s in the United Kingdom and the Nordic countries (Denmark, Finland, Norway and Sweden) in Europe and in California in the United States. Futures and options contracts corresponding to US-produced electricity are traded on the NYMEX/COMEX in New York. Futures and option contracts corresponding to electricity produced in the Nordic countries are traded on the Nord Pool in Oslo. The commoditization of electricity is, however, expanding very fast and other spot and futures markets are soon expected to develop in other countries and regions of the world, such as Australia.

Markets for metals and minerals

Metals and minerals can be grouped into ferrous and non-ferrous metals, precious metals and other mineral commodities.

The most common non-ferrous metals are aluminum, copper, lead, nickel, tin and zinc. The major spot market that serves as a benchmark for these commodities is the London Metal Exchange (LME), which is a centralized exchange rather than an OTC market. Futures and options prices are also quoted on the LME with possible delivery in LME warehouses throughout the world. Futures and options contracts on aluminum and copper are also traded on the NYMEX/COMEX. Other non-ferrous metals that can be used as alloys in the steel industry such as cobalt, magnesium, vanadium and zirconium generally use producers' prices as reference prices and there are no organized derivative markets for these commodities. The same is true for iron and steel. Other metals, such as antimony, bismuth, cadmium, chromium, cobalt, titanium sponge, ferro-manganese, ferro-molybdenum, mercury, selenium and tungsten are quoted on an active spot market in London.

Gold and silver are traded on spot, forward and futures markets in many places throughout the world. Spot markets exist in London (London Bullion Exchange), New York, Paris, Zürich, Singapore and many other financial centers. Gold futures and options are traded on both NYMEX/COMEX in New York and CBOT in Chicago (100 oz. contracts, USD/oz.), while silver futures and options are traded on both NYMEX/COMEX and CBOT (5000 oz. contracts, USD/oz.). The CBOT also offers a 1000 oz. futures contract on silver and a 1 kg gold futures contract. Other precious platinum group metals (PGM) such as platinum and palladium are traded on NYMEX/COMEX (50 and 100 oz. contracts, respectively, USD/oz.) and on the Tokyo Commodity Exchange (TOCOM) for platinum. Rhodium, another platinum group metal, is a rare and very speculative metal with an active spot market.

Another important market for a mineral commodity other than a metal is the international diamond market. Until very recently, reference prices for diamonds were those fixed by the De Beers Central Selling Organization, a cartel that was dismantled in 2000 by De Beers. A more competitive market is now expected to develop.

Markets for agricultural commodities

Agricultural commodities can be grouped as grains, edible oils and sugars, fibers, tropical commodities and other agricultural commodities. The first group includes wheat, corn, soybeans, canola, olive oil and sugar, among others. Fibers include cotton, wool and silk. Tropical commodities include coffee, cocoa, tea and natural rubber. Other agricultural commodities include cattle, hogs and meats, milk and dairy products, lumber, pulp and paper. The spot markets for these commodities are generally located in the areas where they are produced.

The Chicago Board of Trade (CBOT) is the largest futures and options market for many US-produced agricultural commodities. It trades futures and options contracts on:

- wheat (Hard Red Winter, 5000 bushels, USD/Bu)
- corn (No.2 Yellow, 5000 bushels, USD/Bu)
- soybeans (No.2 Yellow, 5000 bushels, USD/Bu)
- soybean meal (100 short tons, USD/ton)
- soybean oil (60 000 lb., USD/lb.).[2]

The Chicago Mercantile Exchange (CME), also located in Chicago, is another traditional market for agricultural commodities and its derivative products are complementary to those offered by the CBOT. It trades futures and options contracts on:

- live cattle (40 000 lb., USD/lb.)
- boneless beef meat (20 000 lb., USD/lb.)
- milk (200 000 lb., USD/lb.).

It also runs a butter and cheese spot market and trades contracts on forestry products, including lumber (in particular, Western, North Central, South Western and South Eastern lumber, 100000 board square feet, USD/1000 board square feet of standardized board panels of lumber four feet wide, eight feet long, and $\frac{7}{16}$ inch thick).

---

[2] 1 bushel (Bu) = 35.239 liter (27.216 kg of wheat, 25.4 kg of corn, 27.216 kg of soybeans); 1 lb=0.453 kg; 1 short ton = 2000 lb = 906 kg.

The New York Board of Trade (NYBOT) is the result of the merger in 1998 of the New York Coffee, Sugar and Cocoa Exchange (CSCE) and the New York Cotton Exchange. Its futures and options contracts include:

- coffee (Arabica, 37 500 lb., USD/lb.)
- cocoa (any origin, 10 tons, USD/ton)
- raw cane sugar (any origin, 112 000 lb or 50 long tons, USD/long ton)
- cotton (50 000 lb., US cents/lb.)
- orange juice (15 000 lb., US cents/lb.)
- milk index futures (15 000 lb., USD/lb.).

The London International Financial Futures Exchange (Liffe) has recently developed its futures and options products on agricultural commodities:

- futures on tropical products: coffee (robusta, 5 tonnes, USD/tonne); cocoa (10 tonnes, USD/tonne)
- futures and option contract in white sugar (any origin, cane or beet sugar, grade No.5, 50 tonnes, USD/tonne)
- wheat (100 tonnes, GBP/tonne)
- European Union barley (100 tonnes, GBP/tonne)
- British potatoes (20 tonnes, GBP/tonne).

The Paris Marché A Terme International de France (Matif) trades futures in milling wheat, corn, rapeseed, rapeseed meal and rapeseed oil (all are contracts of 50 tonnes, priced in EUR/tonne). It is also launching a futures contract on fine wines of the Bordeaux area.

Other organized markets for agricultural commodities are the Kansas City market, which competes with CBOT for several futures contracts on wheat, the Winnipeg Commodity Exchange, which offers contracts on cereals such as rye, and the Sydney auction market for wool, which gives a reference quotation on wool.

Markets for miscellaneous commodities and services

Among the commodities that can neither be classified as energy nor mineral commodities nor as agricultural commodities, are seafood and fish. These products include various seawater species of fish in the form of fresh, canned, smoked or frozen fish and salmon, shrimps and crabmeat. The spot markets for these products are located in the various areas of production.

There are also a few services that may be considered as commodities. These include shipping freight, for which there is a large international market, especially in the large seaports, such as London, Rotterdam, New York and Yokohama. Shipping services include in particular tanker rates, for which there are OTC markets in the Gulf of Mexico and in Rotterdam, and dry cargo rates. There is also a new futures market for one of the representative indexes, which is quoted on the Liffe in London. This market trades a shipping freight index, the BIFFEX Baltic Panamax Index, a representative index for dry cargo freight.

Futures and options contracts on weather indexes were launched in 2000 by the CME in Chicago. They comprise daily Heating Degree-Day indexes (daily HDD indexes) in cities scattered around the United States. These cities are Atlanta, Chicago, Cincinnati, Dallas, Des Moines, Las Vegas, New York, Philadelphia, Portland and Tucson, and they represent most of the climatic conditions that prevail in the United States.

There are also two futures and options contracts traded on commodity indexes. Both are in the United States. One is a futures contract on the Goldman Sachs Commodity Index (GSCI)

Table 19.2 Composition and weighting of the GSCI (dollar weights for individual commodities and groups of commodities, 22 September 2000)

Sector	Components
Energy commodities: 67.97%	American crude oils: 27.47% Brent crude oil: 12.53% Unleaded gasoline: 5.13% Heating oil: 8.21% Gasoil: 3.52% Natural gas: 11.11%
Base metals: 6.91%	Aluminum: 3.38% Copper: 1.89% Lead: 0.22% Nickel: 0.61% Tin: 0.10% Zinc: 0.70%
Precious metals: 2.02%	Gold: 1.62% Platinum: 0.21% Silver: 0.19%
Agricultural commodities and livestock: 23.10%	Wheat: 3.09% Red wheat: 1.19% Corn: 3.33% Soybeans: 1.85% Cotton: 2.14% Sugar: 1.96% Coffee: 0.82% Cocoa: 0.18% Orange juice: 0.52% Live cattle: 5.63% Lean hogs: 2.39%

Note: GSCI® is a registered trademark of Goldman, Sachs and Co.

Table 19.3 Current composition of the Bridge/CRB Futures Index (2000)

Sector	Components
Energy commodities (3)	Crude oil (NYMEX/COMEX) Heating oil (NYMEX/COMEX) Natural gas (NYMEX/COMEX)
Base metals (1)	Copper (NYMEX/COMEX)
Precious metals (3)	Gold (NYMEX/COMEX) Platinum (NYMEX/COMEX) Silver (NYMEX/COMEX)
Agricultural commodities and livestock (10)	Wheat (CBOT) Cocoa (NYBOT) Coffee (NYBOT) Corn (CBOT) Cotton (NYBOT) Lean hogs (CBOT) Live cattle (CBOT) Orange juice (NYBOT) Soybeans (CBOT) Sugar No. 11 (NYBOT)

Note: Bridge/CRB® is a registered trademark of Commodity Research Bureau.

quoted on the CME in Chicago, and the other is a futures contract on the Bridge-Commodity Research Bureau (Bridge-CRB) Index, which is quoted on the NYBOT. Tables 19.2 and 19.3 describe these indexes, which can be useful for managing risk.

International commodity trading

Major market participants

The principal actors in commodity trading are the producers, the industrial end-consumers and the trading companies linking the two that ensure worldwide distribution and supply.

These players are complemented by the insurers, banks, brokers and certifying companies on the financial side and by transport services such as shipping, air cargo, railways, road transport and pipeline companies on the distribution side.

The fundamental activity of international commodity trading companies is to ensure physical transfers for basic commodities between one place and another worldwide. This includes:

- transporting the product from its production site to the port of embarkation
- storage before, during and after shipment and trans-shipment
- conditioning and/or other industrial transformations of the product
- international transportation of the product
- other post-shipping operations.

From this it is clear that the activity of an international trading company can go far beyond the scope of its core activity of trading to include tasks that require industrial facilities adapted to the nature of the commodities being processed. However, although the foregoing activities can be carried out directly by the trading company, they can also be done through specialized sub-contractors. Thus, a trading company will often be present in the industry of basic commodities itself and, conversely, producers and industrial end-users of commodities can also maintain trading subsidiaries and trading divisions. The three largest trading companies in terms of turnover are Cargill, Glencore and Louis Dreyfus.

Besides actually ensuring the movement of commodities from producer to end-user, commodity trading also requires the input of financial operators to offset the risk inherent in commodity trading that could, if unchecked, inhibit transactions. To manage the risk, operators can either use insurance or, more generally, transfer the risk to other parties. This means using the services of the financial community such as banks and insurance companies.

Trading overview

The complete process of an operation in the international trade of basic commodities is complex and the role of the various actors can vary according to the commodities being traded. The tasks to be completed are many and varied. They can require the participation of shipowners, shipbrokers, forwarding agents, companies specialized in control, physical management and transportation of raw materials, as well as banks and insurance companies. All these agents are specialized in functions that can be required for the execution of a commercial commodity contract. The actual number of agents and intermediaries varies according to the commodity in question:

- In the case of energy, secondary energies, such as refined petroleum products and coal, there are a small number of intermediaries (trading companies and wholesalers only, and no transformation industry for these products) because these commodities are end-user products that may be used directly by end-consumers and distributed by retailers.
- In the case of agricultural commodities where storage and conditioning are the most important steps of the commercial sequence of operations, the number of intermediaries is small.
- Metals require a larger number of intermediaries because the steps to transform the commodity into a final consumption good are more complex. Thus the intermediaries on these markets include large trading companies, secondary merchants, wholesalers and brokers.

Besides the trading companies, the brokerage companies and their clients, other participants on physical markets that are neither commodity suppliers nor commodity purchasers, such as financial institutions and transport service providers, are also important. Table 19.4 summarizes the main operators.

Physical commodity contracts

A commercial commodity contract is an agreement concluded between a purchaser and a seller, either of which can be a physical producer, a consumer, an end-user or an intermediary such as a trading company.

Preparation of a sale proposal

In a commercial operation on commodities markets, the sale proposal is extremely important and must be carefully prepared by the seller. It must take into account the potential client's needs and it must also be adapted to his culture. A well prepared proposal will make the negotiation and the conclusion of a draft agreement for a final offer much easier.

In basic commodity contracts, the selection of suppliers is seldom submitted to formal tenders. Formal tenders for commodities are usually reserved for large markets and official contractors such as governments and other public bodies.

Table 19.4 The main operators on international commodity markets

Commodity class	Types of operators
Energy products	Oil and gas companies, coal mining, oil refiners, electricity generators and distributors, gas distributors, large traders and merchants in oil products, natural gas, LPG and coal, secondary traders or merchants, stockists/distributors, banks, other financial intermediaries, including brokerage companies, investment funds and pension funds, speculators (hedge funds and public speculators), transport services
Metals	Mining companies, smelters and refiners, rolling and extrusion companies, secondary smelters and refiners, metal industries, large traders and merchants in steel products, common non-ferrous metals, other non-ferrous metals, and precious metals, secondary traders or merchants, stockists/distributors, banks, other financial intermediaries, including brokerage companies, investment funds and pension funds, speculators (hedge funds and public speculators), transport services
Agricultural products	Large farmers and farming companies, elevator companies and other stockists, basic food industries, textile industries, and other related industries, secondary food industries textile industries, and other related industries, other transformation industries, secondary food industries, textile industries, and other related industries, secondary traders or merchants, stockists/distributors, banks, other financial intermediaries, including brokerage companies, investment funds and pension funds, speculators (hedge funds and public speculators), transport services

The commercial proposal usually takes the form of a letter of intent (LOI) expressing a firm proposal from the producer-seller that is sent to the potential purchaser. The LOI is more than an informal statement or a document issued for the sake of information. It expresses the irrevocable commitment of the selling party who legally binds itself to the terms of its offer, if accepted. Any such offer must stipulate the period over which it is valid. In the case of acceptance, the LOI may also require presentation of a performance bond, which will be explained below.

The LOI often takes the form of a pro forma, which enables the potential buyer to know the amount and the various conditions of the order and can be useful in order to apply for authorizations, such as import licenses and/or to apply for documentary credit. Completion of this first step will enable the two parties to continue their negotiations towards the final commercial contract.

Producers, industrial end-users and trading companies

Because of the quantities, quality, pricing arrangements and delivery terms required by most industrial end-users, the latter are usually not involved in direct negotiations with a producer. On the other hand, commodity producers typically arrange to sell their output before it is available in order to manage the risks associated with production, inventory management, pricing and turnover. Therefore, both industrial end-users and producers tend to deal through a commercial intermediary such as a trading company. The function of intermediaries on these markets, then, consists of reconciling the producers' needs with the requirements and objectives of final purchasers.

In its role as intermediary the trading company fulfills four major tasks. It negotiates the terms of the commercial contract with the producer on the one hand and the industrial end-user on the other. It also manages the physical goods that are the object of the transaction. In many cases, it also manages stocks of the commodity and/or effects an industrial transformation of the commodities. Finally, it matches the operational timing of both the producer and the purchaser inasmuch as there is a time lag between them.

Carrying out these various tasks opens the trading company to a number of risks arising from the risk of price mismatch between selling and buying, the physical risks related to the conditions of delivery of the goods with respect to the date of delivery, freight risks, and financial risks such as credit risks and exchange rate risks. These features and risks that are specific to commodity markets are reflected in the attributes of commodity contracts and in the financial instruments corresponding to the legal terms of these commodity contracts.

The commodity contract

For every physical transaction, the parties sign a purchasing/selling contract giving the precise details of the agreement. Individual contracts are often the adaptation of a standard contract issued by one of the professional trading associations. For example, in the case of grains, standard contracts are issued by the British Grain and Feed Trade Association (GAFTA). Thus, although individual contracts follow standard contracts, the terms of the contract are freely negotiated and adjusted to the particular context of each transaction.

Each contract must specify the legal and regulatory environment for settling disputes. For this, most commercial contracts refer to RUU 500, which are uniform rules and specifications issued by the International Chamber of Commerce (ICC). This reference is internationally recognized and makes it easier to handle clauses related to letters of credit, for instance, or clauses related to risk transfers in the case of incoterms (international commercial terms). Since international regulations and national legislation are generally inadequate for solving all the problems of interpretation that may arise during the execution of a contract, most commercial contracts provide for an arbitration procedure, which may be more costly than using national legislation, but is more generally accepted. Disputes may then be submitted to reference arbitration courts, such as the ICC in Paris, GAFTA in London or the Geneva Arbitration Court.

Financial terms of contracts enable both parties to address problems such as method of payment and the various risks that can occur in the execution of any commercial operation, in addition to the price and exchange rate risks, which are normally covered through derivative instruments. Thus, the contract must specify what happens in the case of seller or purchaser default, how to ensure that the seller delivers at the right time, in the right place in the right quantity and adequate quality of the good, and how to handle the other miscellaneous risks such as freight risks and transportation risks.

Finally, in any contract there are further exceptional clauses that determine the rules applicable to problems that may arise due to events beyond the control of the parties, usually termed force majeure or an act of God?[3]

Economic specifications of a commercial commodity contract

The economic specifications of the contract are market-related variables such as quantities, quality, prices, delivery dates and other conditions of delivery.

Quantities are expressed in some unit of measurement (weight, volume, energy), which may be a metric unit (metric tonne, cubic meter, kWh), an Anglo-Saxon unit (ounces, pounds, bushels and tons) or in some traditional measurement unit (such as a barrel of oil). Quality is linked to quantity in the sense that the physical unit used may be ambiguous if the quality is not specified precisely. Quality is often specified in terms of tolerances with respect to exactness. Typical tolerances may range between ± 1% and ± 5 %. Up to these tolerances, the seller guarantees the quantity and quality. Contracts shipped by a third party will usually provide for verification of quantity and quality on which both the seller and the buyer agree. Independent and reputable companies that supply specialized verification services, such as Société Générale de Surveillance (SGS, headquartered in Geneva), are often mentioned in commercial contracts.

For medium or long-term contracts, "take-or-pay" provisions can be included in the contract to guarantee the buyer against the risk of supply disruption while ensuring the seller a minimum revenue.

Incoterms are defined as clauses of a commercial contract that refer to how certain costs, including transportation costs, freight-related costs and other logistical costs, conditions and responsibilities are shared between the two parties. In the case of maritime transportation, liner terms must also be covered in commercial contracts. FOB (free on board) and CIF (cost, insurance and freight) are some of the most usual incoterms.

Prices in most commodity contracts are specified as fixed within the framework of a forward transaction or for the duration of the contract if it involves several deliveries over a short period of time. If there is an efficient futures market for the commodity, the futures price can be used as the reference price which is used for calculation of the forward price. Commodity prices can also be specified as spot prices or producers' prices at the date of delivery or at some related date close to delivery. More precisely, they may be calculated at

---

[3] Due to innovations in financial instruments, risks that were previously considered as beyond the control of economic agents, such as weather-related risks, tend to lend themselves to the development of new marketable hedging instruments: weather derivatives, for example. These instruments may become important in the future and they have significant implications for the markets in a number of commodities – agricultural commodities because crops are submitted to climatic hazards, but also commodities such as heating oil, the demand for which varies according to the temperature.

a given date of delivery on the basis of a reference price that is accepted as such by both parties. For forward operations and for ongoing longer-term contracts as well, commodity contracts may also specify that the price applicable to the operation in question will be the average of some reference price, usually the average of a spot price recognized as a reference price by both parties, over a specified period of time. Under such terms, price risks will usually be significantly reduced because upward and downward fluctuations in price with respect to a trend will cancel out.

Premiums or discounts with respect to the reference price may also be provided for in the contract. Premiums and discounts can provide the incentive to avoid defaults by suppliers and clients. If, for example, prices rise above the fixed contract price, there is a risk that the supplier will default and sell the commodity on the spot market. Providing for a premium, which will give the supplier an incentive not to default, might mitigate this risk. If, on the contrary, spot prices are lower than the fixed price, the supplier might accept a discount on the reference price in order to secure a client. Premiums and discounts with respect to the reference price can also be used to compensate for product quality that might be either better or worse than the reference quality. Finally, premiums and discounts can be used to compensate for differences in transport costs when the contract delivery site differs from the reference price delivery site.

Miscellaneous conditions are also important, including notice and penalties in case of cancelation, extent of the responsibility of the supplier and penalties in the case of partial or non-delivery, and settlement procedures for conflicts and disputes.

Treating risks in commercial contracts

The major risks involved with commodities transactions are price risk, currency risk, purchaser and supplier default risk, quality risk and supply disruption. We have seen that financial instruments such as futures and options are available for hedging price and currency risk. Financial instruments have also been developed to handle the other types of risk.

Bid bonds and **performance bonds** are bank guarantees of the seller's ability to fulfill his obligations. They play a fundamental role in the negotiations that take place before the conclusion of any commercial commodity contract as well as in the execution of the contract. A bid bond, or a tender bond in cases where a formal tender has been organized, is a financial instrument aimed at eliminating the risk that a commodity supplier will withdraw from the negotiations after it has been selected or that it will be unable to supply the commodity that is the object of a commercial contract under negotiation. It may be requested by the buyer at the preliminary phase of the negotiation, in order to ensure that the seller, once chosen, will effectively sign the contract and not withdraw before signature and, moreover, that it has the ability to fulfill its obligations. Once the seller has been selected and has signed the contract, a performance bond will usually be requested by the buyer. A performance bond is a bank guarantee aimed at eliminating the risk that a commodity supplier will be unable to supply the commodity in question over the life of the contract.

Both bid bonds and performance bonds are issued by the seller's bank. They irrevocably guarantee that the bank will pay the client the value of the bond should the seller not fulfill its obligations either before signing the contract (i.e. withdrawing before signing in spite of an otherwise firm commitment) or after the contract is signed (i.e. being unable to deliver the commodity on time or in accordance with the quality provided for). The value of a bid bond usually ranges between 2% and 5% of the amount of the commercial contract. For a performance bond this value is between 2% and 25%.

While bid bonds and performance bonds are financial instruments aimed at handling the counterparty risk from the point of view of the purchaser, letters of credit, discussed in Chapter 13, address the counterparty risk from the point of view of the seller.

Quality risk – the risk that the supplier does not supply the quality of the commodity specified in the contract – is covered by the performance bond. Quality verification is guaranteed by **third party certification**. Third party certification means that a third party (recognised by both the seller and its client) will, at some stage of shipping of the commodity, verify that the quality supplied meets the technical quality specifications set out in the contract. Where documentary credit is concerned, the letter of credit will only be issued once the buyer is in possession of the quality certificate and the performance bond. The certifying party is usually a specialized company, such as Société Générale de Surveillance (SGS).

Finally, other physical risks and in particular risks that occur during the transportation and the delivery of the commodity, are a matter of conventional insurance, which may be either the seller's or the buyer's responsibility, depending on the terms of the contract and the incoterms that have been agreed. Freight risk itself can be hedged with derivatives on the BIFFEX Index traded on Liffe (see above).

Principles of inventory management

There are three basic elements in inventory management. First of all, the stock must be large enough to fulfill normal production requirements. Secondly, a little extra should always be on hand to avoid the costs of not having enough in case of an unexpected increase in demand or delay in delivering new supplies. Thirdly, additional amounts might be necessary to take advantage of increased demand or new sales opportunities. Anyone familiar with monetary theory will recognize these three reasons for holding inventories as similar to the transaction, precautionary and speculative motives for holding cash balances. In fact, inventory management is similar to cash management or, indeed, the management of any type of asset. As such, effective inventory management requires that the costs of holding incremental inventory be compared to the benefits derived from it.

Identifying costs

Some costs rise with larger inventories; other costs fall. Some of the costs that rise are interest payments on the funds used to finance the inventory, storage costs and insurance premiums, and the increased risk of damage or obsolescence. Some of the costs that fall are associated with a reduction in lost sales because of delivery delays, fewer production interruptions due to stock outs and increased discounts for buying in quantity. The problem in inventory management is to identify the costs and benefits of holding inventories and apply them in a rigorous analysis as a means of determining when and how much to order.

Carrying costs

Carrying costs associated with holding inventory include:

- interest
- storage
- insurance
- handling
- depreciation
- obsolescence
- taxes.

These carrying costs usually rise as the level of inventories increases. Frequent orders mean lower inventories, whereas infrequent orders mean higher inventories. Since inventories are usually run down on a more or less continuous basis while orders are placed on a punctual basis, carrying costs can be determined as a function of the average inventory level between orders. The average inventory level can be calculated as the sum of the beginning inventory and ending inventory divided by two. Suppose, for example, that a firm has 2000 units of inventory at the beginning of the year. It receives no deliveries during the year and at the end of the year it has no units left. Its average inventory for the year is $(2000 + 0)/2 = 1000$ units.

Ordering, shipping and receiving costs

There is a fixed and variable component to ordering, shipping and receiving costs. The personnel, office space and equipment assigned to the purchasing and receiving department can be considered as relatively fixed. Costs arising from things such as computer time, fax messages, telephone calls, setting up for a new production run, etc., are variable and depend on how many orders are placed. The more orders that are placed, the higher costs will be. Some of the major fixed costs associated with ordering, shipping and receiving are:

- personnel
- office space
- equipment.

Some of the major variable costs are:

- telephone, fax, etc.
- shipping and handling
- production set-up costs
- hedging costs (foreign exchange, supplies)
- foregone quantity discounts.

A simple decision model

Once the costs and benefits related to inventory management have been identified, they should be employed in a decision-making model to determine the timing and quantities of supplies. Some of the models for inventory control techniques can get quite complicated and a full treatment of the problem is beyond the scope of this book. Nevertheless, one simple model underlies most of the more complicated systems. In spite of its simplicity, it is probably the most widely used inventory decision model around. A look at this model will make it possible to illustrate most of the important issues involved in efficient inventory management.

The crux of the inventory management problem is to find the optimal amount to be ordered at any one time. To solve the problem, we can compare the costs and benefits associated with higher inventories. Remember that some costs rise with higher inventories, some costs fall and others are constant. The notation we will use is independent of the notation we have used elsewhere in this book and is as follows:

U = number of units
q = the number of units per order
A = $q/2$ = the average inventory
n = U/q = the number of orders per year
v = variable cost per order

c = carrying cost expressed as a percent of the unit price
P = price per unit
F = fixed cost per year
C_c = carrying cost
C_o = cost per order
C_T = total cost.

Assume that sales and production are equally distributed over the year so that inventories decline smoothly. Total carrying costs can be expressed as the cost per unit multiplied by the average inventory level:

$$C_c = cP\frac{q}{2} \tag{19.1}$$

They increase as the average inventory increases.

Ordering, shipping and handling costs are equal to the fixed costs plus the variable costs:

$$C_o = F + nv \tag{19.2}$$

They increase as the number of orders increases. Remember that $n = U/q$. As q gets larger, n falls, which makes C_o fall also. On the other hand, from Equation 19.1 we can see that as q gets larger C_c gets larger. Carrying costs rise with a higher quantity per order while ordering, shipping and receiving costs fall. The total cost of the inventory is

$$C_c + C_o = C_T = cP\frac{q}{2} + F + \frac{U}{q}v \tag{19.3}$$

To find the optimal ordering quantity, we can differentiate Equation 19.3 with respect to q, set the result equal to zero and solve for q:

$$\frac{\partial C_T}{\partial q} = \frac{cP}{2} - \frac{vU}{q^2} = 0$$

$$q = \sqrt{\frac{2vU}{cP}} \tag{19.4}$$

Equation 19.4 determines the number of units that should be ordered each time that inventory is replenished in order to minimize inventory costs.

To take an example, suppose that variable costs are USD 217 per order, 5000 units are sold each year, and carrying costs are 25% of the cost price, which is USD 50 per unit.

v = USD 217
U = 5000
c = 0.25
P = USD 50

Substituting into 19.4 gives:

$$q = \sqrt{\frac{2 \times USD\ 217 \times 5000}{0.25 \times USD\ 50}} = 416.67.$$

Because only whole units can be ordered, the optimal ordering quantity is 417 units. The average stock level is 417/2 = 208.5 units worth USD 10,425 at USD 50 per unit. The number of orders per year is 5000/417 = 11.99 or about once a month.

The cost of buffer stocks

Up to now we have been assuming that there is no uncertainty concerning the number of units to be used over the year or the reliability of our suppliers. In reality, neither of these assumptions is likely to be justified. Sales can vary as demand fluctuates or new markets open up. Suppliers may also be unable to meet delivery schedules. Uncertainty of this type makes the firm vulnerable to a stock out. A stock out occurs when the company is unable to supply customers or continue production because of a lack of inventory. Costs associated with this situation come in the form of lost sales and customer goodwill, disruption of production schedules, employee stress and irritation, and other expenditures necessary to correct the situation. The decision model should be modified to allow for costs generated by uncertainty. The usual procedure is to include a safety stock.

The optimal safety stock should be at the point where the increased carrying cost is just equal to the costs associated with a stock out. Unfortunately, stock out costs are difficult to quantify with any precision. Nevertheless, there is no doubt that they exist and, in fact, they may be the largest single component of inventory management costs. The question of safety stocks is particularly pertinent for supplies of raw materials that may be produced in far away lands, subject to political interference, climatic hazards, natural catastrophes and the like.

Inventory management and the principles of hedging with commodities futures

Inventory control presents a number of problems for the financial manager. Outside of raw materials, however, once the foreign exchange risk has been accounted for, they are more or less the same whether at the domestic or international level. Raw materials are different because their source depends on geography and climate. Most countries outside of the United States have only a few of the many raw materials necessary for the diversified output of a modern industrial economy. Consequently, the market for most raw materials is intrinsically international. Furthermore, even without the political risk associated with many countries producing basic commodities, prices and supplies are often vulnerable to discoveries of new resources, the weather or the instability of the production process itself. All this makes managing raw material inventory and supply a very complicated and risky proposition. As we saw in Chapter 7, futures markets are one of the financial manager's most valuable tools for managing the inventory risk associated with supplies of raw materials.

Hedging with futures

The principles of commodities hedging with futures contracts are the same as those for financial assets. Long positions in the commodity (the producer, for example) take short positions in futures while short positions in the commodity (the trader, for example) take long positions in futures contracts. At maturity the position can be closed out by making an offsetting buy or sell. It is interesting to notice that in neither case was the futures market used as a source of supply. The desired goal was a price differential that would offset unfavorable moves in the spot price. Furthermore, it is clear that both buyers and sellers have an interest in the market and are likely to be present on a continuous basis. This is important for liquidity where the presence of both is indispensable.

Inventories of raw materials: The case of an expected price rise

Consider the case of a manufacturer at the beginning of September who is expecting a large jump in the price of copper for the end of the year. The current price of copper is USD 1.025 per pound. He feels that this relatively low price is due to a momentary excess supply that will disappear in short order. He realizes that if he is wrong, however, the price is likely to drop lower than it is now. A December futures contract is selling at USD 1.0825 per pound and it is a contango market with a positive basis of 5.75 cents per pound.

He could buy a December futures contract to protect himself against the expected price rise, but if he does and the price falls he will be a big loser. In order to take advantage of his analysis of the current and expected market situation, the manufacturer decides to increase his inventory at the current spot price of USD 1.025 beyond what his normal needs would be. But, just in case he is wrong and the price falls rather than rising, he decides to hedge the excess stock he is going to carry by selling a December futures contract at USD 1.0825 per pound.

At the end of December the price of copper has risen to USD 1.22 per pound and his futures contract is settled at this price. Thus, the manufacturer has lost 13.75 cents per pound (USD 1.0825 – USD 1.22) on his futures contract. However, the cost of his excess stock is only USD 1.1625, the USD 1.025 spot price he paid plus the 13.75 cent loss on the futures contract. This is 5.75 cents lower than the spot price of USD 1.22. On the other hand, it is 8 cents higher than he would have paid if he had made a straightforward purchase of a futures contract at USD 1.0825 per pound. The disadvantage of the straightforward futures purchase is that if the spot price had fallen – to USD 1.00, for example – he would still have paid USD 1.0825 for his copper supply. With the solution that he actually chose, a fall in the spot price to USD 1.00 would give him a gain of 8.25 cents on the futures and his net cost would be USD 0.9425 per pound, 5.75 cents lower than the spot price of USD 1.00. Thus, by adjusting his inventory and using the futures market, he was able to secure his supply of raw materials at a price more favorable than the going market price. Of course, he would have to compare his 5.75 cent gain with his carrying costs and convenience returns to determine his net benefit on the operation.

The case of an expected price decline

Suppose that at the beginning of March the spot price of copper is USD 1.1725 per pound. The market is expecting the price to fall and the June futures contract is selling for USD 0.9925 per pound. The market is in a situation of backwardation and the basis is negative by 18 cents.

The manufacturer decides to avoid paying the high spot price by running down his inventory. Nevertheless, he wants to cover himself in case prices do not fall and proceeds to buy a June contract at USD 0.9925 per pound. By the end of April the bottom has fallen out of the market and the spot quote is USD 0.885 while the June futures contract is selling at USD 0.95. It is now a contango market and the basis is positive by 6.5 cents.

Having run down his inventory, the manufacturer must now make a purchase at USD 0.885 per pound. He closes out his futures position and loses 4.25 cents per pound (USD 0.95 – USD 0.9925). His total cost is USD 0.9275 per pound (USD 0.885 + USD 0.0425). This is 24.5 cents better than the USD 1.1725 he would have paid in March. Of course, he would have to compare this gain with his convenience losses due to lower inventory levels and the savings on foregone carrying costs to determine his net benefit on the operation.

In any case, these two examples give an idea of how futures markets can be combined with the timing of inventory supplies to contribute to more cost-efficient inventory management.

Hedging with options

Hedging against a price rise by purchasing calls

Consider a manufacturer on 5 July with a need for 50 000 pounds of copper in September. The current spot price for copper is USD 0.75 per pound. He feels that the price could go as high as USD 0.95 per pound by September and does not want to be left holding the bag if it does. He also feels that the price could fall as low as USD 0.55 per pound. The current price for a September copper futures contract is USD 0.80 per pound. If he purchases one September contract he can lock in his price at USD 0.80 per pound but if the price falls, he will reap none of the benefits of a lower price. He decides to purchase one September futures call option with a strike price of USD 0.76 currently selling for USD 0.0375 per pound for a cost of

$$50\,000 \times USD\ 0.0375 = USD\ 1875.$$

Outcome if the price rises to USD 0.90 on the expiry date

The manufacturer exercises his option and closes out his futures contract. Since the futures price converges to the spot price on expiry, he receives:

$$50\,000 \times (USD\ 0.90 - USD\ 0.76) = USD\ 7000$$

His total gain is USD 5125, the difference between the cash payment and the cost of the option. When he purchases the 50 000 pounds of copper at the spot price of USD 0.90 his all-in cost is:

$$50\,000 \times USD\ 0.90 - USD\ 2562.50 = USD\ 39,875.$$

This works out to a cost of USD 0.7975 per pound.

Outcome if the price falls to USD 0.60 on the expiry date

The manufacturer lets the option expire worthless and buys his copper at USD 0.60 per pound. When he adds in the cost of the option, his total cost is

$$50\,000 \times USD\ 0.60 + USD\ 1875 = USD\ 31,875.$$

This works out to USD 0.6375 per pound. The price is higher than the spot price but is much lower than if he had locked himself into the futures contract at USD 0.80 per pound.

Outcome if the price remains unchanged

The benefits of an option strategy can only be realized if there is a sizeable move in the price. If, for example, the price in September was USD 0.75, the option would expire worthless but the cost per pound would be USD 0.7875 because of the cost of the option.

Hedging against a price fall by purchasing puts

Consider a copper broker on the same day, 5 July, with an excess 50 000 pounds of copper on his hands in September. The situation is the same as above. The current spot price for copper is USD 0.75 per pound. The copper broker has made the same analysis as the manufacturer. He feels that the price could go as high as USD 0.95 per pound by September and would like to take advantage of the situation if it does. He also feels that the price could fall as low as USD 0.55 per pound and does not want to get hurt. The current price for a September copper futures contract is USD 0.80 per pound. If he sells one September contract he can lock in his price at USD 0.80 per pound but if the price rises, he will reap none of the benefits of a higher price. He decides to purchase one September futures put option with a strike price of USD 0.76 currently selling for USD 0.0475 per pound for a cost of

$$50\ 000 \times USD\ 0.0475 = USD\ 2375.$$

Outcome if the price rises to USD 0.90 on the expiry date:
The option contract expires worthless and he sells his copper for

$$50\ 000 \times USD\ 0.90 = USD\ 45,000.$$

His total income is USD 22,500 less the cost of the option

$$USD\ 45,000 - USD\ 2375 = USD\ 42,625$$

for an all-in price of USD 0.8525 per pound.

Outcome if the price falls to USD 0.60 on the expiry date
The broker exercises his option and takes delivery. Since the futures price converges to the spot price on expiry, he receives a cash amount for the option equal to:

$$50\ 000 \times (USD\ 0.76 - USD\ 0.60) = USD\ 8000.$$

He also receives 50 000 × USD 0.60 = USD 30,000. His total gain is USD 30,000 + USD 8000 less the cost of the option. This works out to USD 0.7125 per pound.

Outcome with a small price change
Again, the benefits of an option strategy can only be realized if there is a sizeable move in the price. If, for example, the price in September rose to USD 0.82, the option would expire worthless but the price per pound would be only USD 0.7725 because of the cost of the option.

Hedging with swaps

In a commodity swap, one party agrees to pay the other a fixed price for a given quantity of a commodity at certain specified dates in the future while the other party agrees to pay the first party a variable price, for example, the ongoing spot price or the futures price, for the same quantity of the commodity on the same specified dates.

Hedging against a price rise

Consider an airline company that consumes 40 000 tons of kerosene per month hedging against a price rise by making a deal with the bank whereby it agrees to pay the bank USD 200 per ton on the first day of every month for the next 12 months. In return the bank agrees to pay the company the price recorded on the Rotterdam spot market on the last working day of the preceding month. Thus, on the first of every month, the company owes USD 200 × 40 000 tons = USD 8,000,000. The bank's liability will depend on the spot price. Suppose that on the last working day of the first month the spot price on the Rotterdam market is USD 225. The bank will owe USD 225 × 40 000 tons = USD 9,000,000. The bank will pay the company the difference between the two liabilities: USD 9,000,000 − USD 8,000,000 = USD 1,000,000. If on the last working day of the second month, the Rotterdam spot price is USD 185, the company must pay the bank (USD 200 − USD 185) × 40 000 tons = USD 600,000. No kerosene changes hands. The company obtains its kerosene on the Rotterdam market where its effective price is always USD 200 no matter what the spot price of the moment happens to be.

Hedging against a price fall

A swap can also be used to hedge against a price fall. Consider a small oil producer with 10 000 barrels of oil per month that hedges by making a deal with the bank whereby it agrees to pay the bank on the first working day of every month for the next 24 months the spot price on the last working day of the preceding month reported by Platt's for Brent crude. In return the bank agrees to pay the company USD 22 per barrel for 10 000 barrels on the first working day of every month. Thus on the first working day of the month the company would receive (USD 23 − S) × 10 000. If the spot price were USD 20, it would receive (USD 23 − USD 20) × 10 000 = USD 30,000. Its total income from the oil plus the contract would be USD 20 × 10 000 + USD 30,000 = USD 230,000. If the spot price rises to USD 30 per barrel in the next month, its total income would still be USD 230,000. It would receive USD 150,000 from the sale of the oil on the spot market but would have to pay the bank (USD 30 − USD 23) × 10 000 = USD 70,000 on the difference between the fixed price and the flexible price.

Other hedging techniques

As we have seen, there are many other hedging instruments adapted to the commodity markets. Average rate options are popular for firms with regular sales or purchases over time. Caps, floors and collars can be used to guarantee maximum and minimum prices for a series of sales or purchases. Basket options are useful for those with needs in several commodities at the same time. Swaptions guarantee swap terms if a swap is needed. The possibilities are virtually limitless as new products are created and hedging strategies evolve.

Summary

1. The world commodity markets can be broken down into markets for energy, metals and minerals, agricultural commodities and other miscellaneous commodities. Many of these commodities are traded on organized exchanges for both spot and derivatives. Commodities not traded on organized exchanges are traded OTC and use reference prices provided by producers or specialized organizations.

2. The principal actors in commodity trading are the producers, the industrial end-consumers and the trading companies linking the two that ensure worldwide distribution and supply. These actors are complemented by the insurers, banks, brokers and certifying companies on the financial side and by transport services such as shipping, air cargo, railways, road transport and pipeline companies on the distribution side.

3. A commercial commodity contract is an agreement concluded between a purchaser and a seller, either of which can be a physical producer, a consumer, an end-user or an intermediary such as a trading company. It stipulates quantities, quality, pricing arrangements and delivery

terms. It must also specify financial terms and the regulatory authority for settling disputes. Individual contracts are often the adaptation of a standard contract issued by one of the professional trading associations.

4. The major risks involved with commodities transactions are price risk, currency risk, purchaser and supplier default risk, quality risk and supply disruption. Financial instruments such as futures and options are available for hedging price, currency and freight risk. Bid/performance bonds cover supplier default risk and documentary credit deals with purchaser default risk. Insurance is available for the other types of risk.

5. The problem in inventory management is to identify the costs and benefits of holding inventories and apply them in a rigorous analysis as a means of determining when and how much to order.

6. Inventory control presents a number of problems for the financial manager. Outside of raw materials, however, once the foreign exchange risk has been accounted for, they are largely the same whether at the domestic or international level. Raw materials are different because their source depends on geography and climate. Most countries outside of the United States have only a few of the many raw materials necessary for the diversified output of a modern industrial economy. Consequently, the market for most raw materials is intrinsically international. Furthermore, even without the political risk associated with many countries producing basic commodities, prices and supplies are often vulnerable to discoveries of new resources, the weather, or the instability of the production process itself. All this makes managing raw material inventory and supply a very complicated and risky proposition.

7. There is a wide range of instruments available for managing supplies of raw materials and inventory levels, including the basic futures, options and swaps as well as the more exotic derivatives such as Asian options, basket options, swaptions, caps, collars and floors.

World equity markets

In Chapter 11 we saw that the wide diversity of stock market organizations across countries is a major source of risk when making international portfolio investments. These differences include market size and turnover, the key market participants, transaction, settlement and delivery procedures, the types of instruments available to investors, fees and commissions, taxation, and other regulations such as foreign exchange controls that could affect the foreign investor's cash flows. We also saw that information and management costs are higher for international portfolio management than they are for a purely domestic portfolio. In Chapters 17 and 18 we studied these factors in the context of the bond market. In this chapter, we want to look at them in the context of financing and investing in the international equity markets. We begin with presentation of the general issues involved in equity investment and how equities are evaluated and priced. We then look at some of the major aspects associated with international equities. We conclude with an examination of the world's three largest equity markets – the United States, Japan, and the United Kingdom – and a discussion of the developments in what have come to be called the "emerging markets".

Valuing equities

Discounted dividends

In Chapter 18 we saw that bond valuation involves lining up the expected cash flows for each period and then discounting each cash flow at the appropriate rate back to the present. The same method can be applied for equity valuation. For equities, the relevant cash flow is the dividend paid to the shareholder. However, whereas most bonds have a maturity date, equity shares typically do not. Theoretically, they can provide dividends forever. With this in mind we can write the basic formula for the valuation of a common stock as:

$$P_0 = \frac{Div_1}{(1 + r_1)} + \frac{Div_2}{(1 + r_2)^2} + \frac{Div_3}{(1 + r_3)^3} + \dots \qquad (20.1)$$

where the dots indicate that dividend discounting continues on forever and:

Div_t = the expected dividends per share to be received at the end of period t
r_t = the appropriate risk-adjusted discount rate for a dividend to be received at the end of period t
P_t = the price of the share at the end of period t.

Just as in bond valuation, Equation 20.1 takes account of the term structure of interest rates. However, cash flows from bonds are considerably easier to estimate than dividends. The relative accuracy of forecasting bond cash flows warrants attention to this detail whereas the relative difficulty of forecasting future dividends makes most analysts feel that it is inappropriate for equity valuation. Consequently, a single discount rate for all dividends is typically used for equities (in Chapter 21 we take up the question of how this rate should be determined) and no attempt is made to identify a term structure. When r represents the appropriate discount rate for all dividends, Equation 20.1 becomes:

$$P_0 = \frac{Div_1}{(1+r)} + \frac{Div_2}{(1+r)^2} + \frac{Div_3}{(1+r)^3} + \dots \tag{20.2}$$

Equations 20.1 and 20.2 apply to investors with an infinite horizon. Most investors, however, plan on holding a stock for something less than forever. Suppose, for example that an investor plans on holding the stock for one year. His cash flows will be composed of the dividend he will receive at the end of the year plus the price he will receive for the sale of the share. Lining these two cash flows up and discounting at the appropriate rate gives:

$$P_0 = \frac{Div_1}{(1+r)} + \frac{E(P_1)}{(1+r)} \tag{20.3}$$

where E indicates the expectations operator.

This equation seems different from Equations 20.1 and 20.2. In fact, it is based on the same principle. In order to estimate the price that will prevail at the end of the first period, expected dividends must be lined up and discounted at the appropriate rate. At the end of the first period, this gives:

$$E(P_1) = \frac{Div_2}{(1+r)} + \frac{Div_3}{(1+r)^2} + \frac{Div_4}{(1+r)^3} + \dots \tag{20.4}$$

If we substitute 20.4 into 20.3 we get:

$$P_0 = \frac{Div_1}{(1+r)} + \frac{1}{(1+r)}\left[\frac{Div_2}{(1+r)} + \frac{Div_3}{(1+r)^2} + \frac{Div_4}{(1+r)^3} \dots\right] \tag{20.5}$$

which is the same as Equation 20.2. There is no difference in the valuation procedure because of a change in the investment horizon.

Earnings per share, value and growth

Because of the difficulty of forecasting future dividends, analysts often make assumptions about how dividends are likely to evolve. The procedure is usually accomplished in three steps. First, the company's financial statements are studied to estimate the company's earnings per share (EPS) and its dividend policy. The dividend policy refers to how much of the EPS will be distributed as dividends and how much will be retained to finance investment opportunities. Secondly, the company's investment opportunities based on its individual competitive position and the overall evolution of its market are analyzed. Thirdly, the results of steps one and two are combined to arrive at an assumption about the growth of the dividend.

One assumption is that the dividend will remain constant. This does not mean that the dividend will not deviate from year to year. It just means that on average it will not grow.

It also implies that there is no net investment and that total EPS is distributed as a dividend.[1] In this case, the price of the share will be given by:[2]

$$P_0 = \frac{Div_1}{r}$$ (20.6)

Take, for example, a firm with an EPS of GBP 5, a dividend of GBP 5 per share and an appropriate discount rate of 10%. Its price will be

$$P_0 = \frac{GBP\ 5}{0.1} = GBP\ 50.$$

Another possible assumption is that the dividend will grow at a constant rate for ever. This does not mean that there will be no year-to-year deviations from the trend. It only means that the expected dividend will grow at a constant rate. It also implies that a part of EPS will be retained by the company to finance investment opportunities. In this case, the price of the share will be given by:[3]

---

[1] An investment that generates no incremental cash flows has a negative net present value and should not be undertaken. See Chapter 21.

[2] This formula is derived by starting with Equation 20.2 where the dividend is the same for all periods:

$$P_0 = \frac{Div_1}{(1+r)} + \frac{Div_1}{(1+r)^2} + \frac{Div_1}{(1+r)^3} + \ldots.$$

Factor out the dividend and assume that the dividend will last for n periods: $P_0 = Div_1[(1+r)^{-1} + (1+r)^{-2} + (1+r)^{-3} + \ldots + (1+r)^{-n}]$. The term in brackets is the sum of a geometric progression: $Sum = (1+r)^{-1} + (1+r)^{-2} + (1+r)^{-3} + \ldots + (1+r)^{-n}$. Multiply this sum by $1+r$, which gives $(1+r)\ Sum = 1 + (1+r)^{-1} + (1+r)^{-2} + \ldots + (1+r)^{-(n-1)}$. Subtract the first sum from the second and rearrange:

$$Sum = \frac{1-(1+r)^{-n}}{r}.$$

As $n \to \infty$, $(1+r)^{-n} \to 0$, which gives $Sum = 1/r$.

[3] This formula is known as the Gordon-Shapiro model. See M.J. Gordon and E. Shapiro, "Capital equipment analysis: The required rate of profit", *Management Science*, Vol. 3 (October 1956), p.p. 102–110. It is derived as follows. If the dividend grows at a constant rate the price of a share can be written as:

$$P_0 = \frac{Div_0(1+g)}{(1+r)} + \frac{Div_0(1+g)^2}{(1+r)^2} + \frac{Div_0(1+g)^3}{(1+r)^3} + \ldots$$

Factoring out Div_0 gives:

$$P_0 = Div_0 \left[\frac{1+g}{1+r} + \frac{(1+g)^2}{(1++r)^2} + \ldots \right]$$

Using the same technique as in the previous footnote, it can be shown that if $r > g$, the term in brackets is an infinite series that converges to: $(1+g)/(r-g)$ so that

$$P_0 = Div_0 \left[\frac{1+g}{r-g} \right].$$

Remembering that $Div_1 = Div_0(1+g)$ gives Equation 20.7 in the text.

$$P_0 = \frac{Div_1}{r - g} \tag{20.7}$$

where g represents the growth rate.

Suppose, for example, that a firm has the same earnings per share of GBP 5 and the same discount rate as the no-growth firm above, that it distributes 50% of its earnings as dividends, and that it reinvests the rest at an after-tax rate of 12%. Reinvesting at an after-tax rate of 12% means that every pound invested will increase after-tax earnings by 12 pence. Thus, if 50% of every pound earned is reinvested at 12%, the growth rate of the dividend will be equal to:

$$g = 0.5 \times 0.12 = 0.06 \text{ or } 6\%.$$

Since the firm distributes 50% of its earnings per share as dividends, the dividend will be $0.5 \times$ GBP 5 = GBP 2.50.

Substituting this information into Equation 20.7 gives the price of the share as:

$$P_0 = \frac{\text{GBP } 2.5}{0.1 - 0.06} = \text{GBP } 62.5$$

It is important to note that the expected growth of the dividend adds GBP 12.5 to the share price of the growth firm compared to the no-growth firm. We will come back to this point in the following section.

So far we have assumed situations of no growth and constant growth. Many other hypotheses could also be made. For example, we could assume a period of exceptionally high growth followed by constant normal growth. Or, we could assume a period of very high growth followed by a period of slower growth followed by no growth.[4] Whatever the assumptions, the valuation procedure is the same. Higher growth prospects lead to higher share prices.

The price/earnings ratio

The price/earnings (P/E) ratio is a common term in stock market jargon. Analysts speak of high P/E stocks and low P/E stocks. Newspapers print P/E ratios alongside stock market prices. In order to use P/E ratios effectively, however, it should be clear exactly what information is represented in a P/E ratio.

We pointed out above that the price of a share depends on the expected rate of growth of the dividend. The implications for P/E can be shown if we remember that the dividend is equal to earnings per share minus retained earnings.

Let s represent the percent of EPS that is retained by the firm. Then EPS$(1-s)$ is equal to the dividend, and we can rewrite Equation 20.7:

$$P_0 = \frac{\text{EPS}(1 - s)}{r - g} \tag{20.8}$$

Taking EPS to the left-hand side of the equation gives:

$$\frac{P_0}{\text{EPS}} = \frac{(1 - s)}{r - g} \tag{20.9}$$

---

[4] For more on valuation and growth see any standard textbook on corporate finance such as Brealey and Myers (latest edition) or Copeland and Weston (1988).

The P/E ratio is on the left-hand side of Equation 20.9. It depends on the rate at which earnings are retained by the firm, the appropriate discount rate, and the growth rate. This is a lot of information for one simple ratio and it is clear that indiscriminate comparisons across firms is a risky business. P/Es can vary across firms because of different rates of retaining earnings, different risk levels reflected in r, and different investment opportunities reflected in g. Therefore, the P/E ratio does not indicate anything precise about the discount rate or the growth rate. The P/E could be high in the face of a high discount rate if the growth rate is also high. It could also be high in the face of a low growth rate if the discount rate is also low. Furthermore, EPS is hard to interpret because it is an accounting concept that can be modified arbitrarily by applying different accounting conventions. Inventory valuation and depreciation methods are the two that come most quickly to mind.

With all these qualifications clearly in focus, the P/E ratio can be used as a crude barometer of a company's growth prospects. Retention ratios are usually quite stable and the CAPM can be used to estimate the required discount rate. A good analyst can iron out accounting anamolies. Thus, other things being equal, a higher P/E ratio suggests good investment opportunities and growth.

Different market structures

By now most countries have created a national stock exchange. Although the individual exchanges tend to have unique trading characteristics and legal structures, most relate back to one of three types of market organization: the public exchange, the private exchange and the bankers' exchange.

- Public exchanges are designed as public institutions where brokers are appointed by the government and enjoy a monopoly over all transactions. France originated the public exchange under Napoleon I. Consequently, stock exchanges organized under the authority of the state are found in the countries in Napoleon's historical sphere of influence: France, Belgium, Italy, Spain, Greece and many Latin American countries.

- Private exchanges are founded by groups of individuals and private institutions for the purpose of trading securities. They are typically found in countries with a strong Anglo-Saxon influence such as the United States, Canada, Australia and South Africa as well as in Japan and the Far East, countries that have adopted the Anglo-Saxon model. Private exchanges tend to be ruled by a mix of self-regulation and government supervision where self-regulation is the dominant feature. Unlike in countries with the public exchange tradition, countries in this category are likely to have several exchanges that compete with each other for business.

- Bankers' exchanges are those where membership is generally limited to the banking community. They tend to be found in countries within Germany's historical sphere of influence such as Austria, Switzerland and Scandinavia. In fact, Germany's Banking Act granted a brokerage monopoly to banks. Bankers' exchanges tend to be ruled by government regulation on the exchange as well as directly on the banks.

Price quotation

The methods for quoting prices can generally be divided into two categories: auction markets and dealer markets.

- In auction markets, also known as order-driven markets, supply and demand are both a function of the price and, consequently, there is a transaction price that equates supply and demand. Typically, because of market liquidity, auctions (or "fixings") can only take place a few times a day. Orders are either market orders or limit orders. A market order implies acceptance of whatever price is established through the auction. A limit order states the maximum price to be paid for a share or a minimum price to be received for the sale of a share. As the price rises (falls) some limit purchase orders are eliminated (added) from the demand side and other limit sell orders are added (eliminated) to the supply side, thereby leading to a price that clears the market.

- In contrast to the auction markets with a limited number of fixings per day, dealer markets, also known as price-driven markets, are continuous in the sense that transactions take place throughout the day. They are characterized by **market-makers**, who guarantee liquidity at virtually any point in time. Market-makers quote a bid–ask spread, representing a firm commitment to purchase or sell a minimum number of shares at those prices. Market-makers adjust their prices continuously as supply and demand ebbs and flows.

Price quotation and computerized trading

The trend in recent years has been from the physical trading floor to the virtual world of computerized trading. Computerization makes it possible to handle orders more efficiently through automated price quotation, order routing and order matching. Individual computerized trading systems have generally been designed to reflect the characteristics of the individual exchanges by simply reproducing an automated version of the trading rules adopted by each exchange. For example, although auction markets have moved to computerized continuous trading, the system still confronts supply and demand with the transaction price determined by electronic auction. Thus, although all exchanges are resorting to computer technology to automate the trading process, the actual process itself can differ fundamentally from one market to another.

Two basic types of automated trading systems have evolved. The first is the price-driven system developed for exchanges that have traditionally been dealer markets. The US Nasdaq and the London SEAQ are examples of these. This type of system posts firm quotes by the market-makers. There is no centralized limit order book or automated trading mechanism. The market-maker's firm quotes represent nothing more than limit orders to buy and sell and he does not know what trades it will generate. The second is the order-driven system developed for exchanges that have traditionally been auction markets, such as Paris. In this system the computer stores all the orders and makes them public. As with the traditional fixing, the limit order book is the heart of the system. With knowledge of all standing orders, a trader knows exactly which trades will be executed if he enters a new order.

Some drawbacks to computerized trading

Automation has many advantages in speed and costs of trading. The disadvantage is that it forces one side of the trade to expose its position. A limit order is like a trading option offered free of charge by the one who posts it. If it is advantageous to the other side of the trade, it will be exercised. Otherwise, it will not be. This opens the one who posts the limit order to getting "picked off" if there is a big move in the market. Suppose, for example, that the price of ATT is USD 100 and an investor enters a limit order to sell at USD 110. If new information arrives that causes the price of ATT to jump to USD 130, the investor that posted the USD 110 limit order will get picked off at USD 110, the exercise price of the de facto option, and lose USD 20. In an order-driven market it is the trader that posts the limit order who is at risk. In a price-driven market it is the market-maker who is at risk.

Thus, the first drawback of an automated system is that liquidity will be reduced if investors (in an order-driven system) or market-makers (in a price-driven system) are reluctant to place limit orders. Another drawback relates to market orders in an order-driven market. In the absence of market-makers, the arrival of a large market order could cause a huge price swing, thereby generating large losses for the one who places it. For this reason, most large transactions are handled off the automated system.

International equities

Valuing international equities

Generally speaking, there is nothing especially unique about valuing foreign companies. The discounting techniques and fundamentals of financial analysis are basically the same from one country to another. In fact, many analysts are even likely to be familiar with international variables because they must be considered when analyzing most reasonably sized domestic firms that have foreign suppliers and clients. This is even more obvious when the domestic firm owns a network of foreign subsidiaries. As we saw in Chapter 11, the main problems of international equity analysis stem from the element of foreign exchange risk, the complexity of applying an international asset pricing model and the general shortcomings of available information where international equities are concerned.

Foreign exchange risk and international asset pricing can be handled in the traditional risk–return framework. Data problems, however, are different. They stem from many sources. Corporate reporting requirements regarding content and timeliness differ from country to country. Accounting standards are also often different, which, for a given level of economic reality, can change the magnitude of the relevant financial ratios from one country to another. The P/E ratio, mentioned above, is especially sensitive to different accounting procedures. Furthermore, cultural and institutional differences can affect financial relationships and analytical concepts.

Many of these problems can be overcome with specialized financial services and outside consultants. The same goes for problems arising from different market structures, instruments, trading procedures, taxes and fees. These services are costly, however. Consequently, although there is no real difference in the fundamental procedures for valuing domestic and foreign equities, the costs of realizing the analysis can differ significantly. Looked at another way, we might say that the risk of a loss due to ignorance is increased by the international dimension. Whether we look at the issue as a cost or a risk, if its effects are considered to be significant, they should be included in the valuation analysis.

The international equities market

The development of the international equities market is a relatively new phenomenon, only having begun in 1983 with an issue by Alcan and Bell Canada. It offers another dimension to firms seeking fresh sources of equity financing.

Three approaches to international equity issues are possible. In the first approach, a firm's shares are listed on one exchange and sold by an international syndicate in several countries. In the second approach, a firm has its shares listed simultaneously on an exchange in the country of incorporation as well as on one or more exchanges in other countries. London, New York and Luxembourg are the most popular foreign exchanges. The third approach corresponds to a real Euroequity issue. In this approach, the firm's shares are listed simultaneously on the home exchange as well as on one or more foreign exchanges and they are issued by an international syndicate in a Eurocurrency.

Advantages of international equities

An international equity issue has a number of advantages for both the issuing firm and the investor. For the issuing firm, the main advantages are:

- Issuing internationally makes it possible to issue in larger amounts. Therefore, it is often used in **privatizations** and reverse **leveraged buyouts** (LBOs). A privatization is when a government-owned firm is sold back to the public and a reverse LBO is when a privately held firm is sold to the public.

- Issuing internationally increases and diversifies the shareholder base, which makes takeover operations more difficult (see Chapter 23 concerning international mergers and acquisitions). However, this argument must be handled with care because the international equity market tends to be dominated by institutional investors. In this case, an international issue would tend to concentrate share ownership in their hands.

- Listing internationally improves the firm's image and increases public awareness.

- Listing procedures for international issues are often less constraining than those for domestic issues. For example, listing procedures for the London International Stock Exchange are much simpler than those for the New York Stock Exchange (NYSE). This explains why London is the world's leading exchange for trading international equities. In 1991, 647 international equities were listed on the London International Stock Exchange while only 105 foreign companies were listed on the NYSE.

- The secondary market for international issues is active and liquid, especially on the major intenational exchanges such as London and New York.

For investors, international equities basically offer two advantages:

- As we saw in Chapter 11, portfolio diversification is the major advantage of international equities for investors.

- A second advantage stems from the possibility of favorable tax treatment.

Making a public equity issue

Public equity issues can be primary or secondary. In a primary issue new shares are sold and new funds are raised for the company, whereas in a secondary issue existing shares simply change hands and the company, receives no new funds. Some of the biggest secondary issues of the 1980s and 1990s occurred through privatizations (that is, government sell-offs of their shareholdings). Many public equity issues are a combination of the two.

Most equity issues are straight cash offers to the public at large where shares are traded for cash. Some, however, are restricted to existing shareholders and are called rights issues. In a rights issue, existing shareholders are issued a number of warrants, called rights, based on the number of shares they own. These warrants confer the right to purchase a certain number of new shares at the official subscription price. The warrants can then be sold, exercised or discarded, depending on the shareholder's inclination and the market price of the stock.

Public issues are handled by a syndicate of underwriters. The syndicate, led by the lead manager, provides the company with procedural and financial advice, buys the issue and then resells it to the public. For this it is paid a fee.

One of the most sensitive responsibilities of the syndicate is to help determine the price of the issue. The company does not want to sell the shares for less than they are worth. The underwriters, on the other hand, do not want the price too high because they guarantee the issue and will be left with any unsold shares. The pricing procedure involves in-depth financial analysis where the company's ratios, including the P/E ratio, are estimated and compared with those of competing firms. Numerous discounted cash flow scenarios like those described above are also worked through and compared. Based on the results of all this activity, a price is agreed upon between the company and the syndicate.

The procedures for bringing an issue to the public are often complicated and costly. For example, the United States requires a prospectus for public distribution as well as a registration statement for submission to the Securities and Exchange Commission (SEC) that includes detailed information about the firm's history and existing business, its plans for the future and the proposed financing. Each state also has laws that must be respected by the issuer. Finally, a registrar to record the stock issues and a transfer agent to oversee the transfer of newly issued stock must be appointed.

The costs of a public issue can be considerable. The underwriters must be paid as well as the lawyers, accountants and advisers that prepared the prospectus and registration statement. Furthermore, there are registration fees and printing and distribution costs.

Issuing procedure

The issuing procedure for international equities is similar to that for Eurobonds. A lead manager obtains a mandate from the issuer. He is responsible for negotiating the overall conditions of the issue as well as for organizing a syndicate to market it. The syndicate is composed of a management group, an underwriting group and a selling group. The co-managers in the management group are always internationally recognized financial institutions and are chosen according to geographical diversification, the ability to effectively place securities and past relations with the issuer.

The underwriting group is much larger than the management group. Its role is to guarantee the placement of the securities. The role of the selling group is to place the securities with final investors.

Fees and commissions are paid according to the role of each institution. The lead manager receives a praecipium, members of the management group receive a management fee, underwriters receive a fee based on how much of the issue they guarantee and members of the selling group receive a commission based on how much they sell.

Up to the early 1990s, most issues were divided into tranches assigned to a specific country or geographic zone. The new trend is towards the "pot method", whereby all orders by institutional investors are centralized by the lead manager in a common "pot". It gives the lead manager more control because, in this way, he can see exactly where demand is coming from. This makes it difficult for individual underwriters to exaggerate the level of demand they can guarantee or to get a monopolistic lock on a certain geographic area.

International stock market indexes

Stock market indexes make it possible to measure the performance of a national market. They can also be used in the asset pricing models such as the CAPM and APT for portfolio management. Most national markets have one or several indexes. For example, the United States has the Dow Jones Industrials, the Standard and Poor's 500, the NYSE Composite, the Nasdaq and the AMEX, among others. Canada has the TSE, Japan has the Nikkei Average, Hong Kong has the Hang Seng, France the CAC 40, and the United Kingdom has the FT-SE 100 and the FT All Share indexes.

There are also some international indexes. For example, Morgan Stanley Capital International (www.msci.com) publishes a World Index, a Europe Index and a Europe, Australia, and the Far East Index (EAFE). The *Financial Times* publishes the FT-Actuaries World Indexes and the *International Herald Tribune* has launched some indexes of its own.

There are also a number of indexes devoted to the emerging markets. The International Finance Corporation (IFC, at www.ifc.org), an organization of the World Bank, produces emerging market stock indexes such as the IFC Global that includes most of the emerging markets and the IFC Investable that trys to include all stocks in the emerging markets that are available to foreign investors. It also publishes a regional index for Latin America, Asia and Europe and the Middle East. MSCI publishes several indexes on emerging markets including the Emerging Markets Global and several regional indexes. Baring has also published an emerging market index. Table 20.1 lists the addresses for some of the most important stock market indexes.

The three major equity markets

The three major equity markets in the world are the United States, Japan, and the United Kingdom. The three markets differ in many ways. They are organized differently, they trade and settle differently, their listing requirements are different, and they have different regulatory systems and tax treatment. In this section we will try to give a comprehensive overview of the major characteristics of these three markets.

The United States

The main US stock exchanges are the New York Stock Exchange (NYSE at www.nyse.com), the American Stock Exchange (AMEX at www.amex.com) and the Nasdaq market (at www.nasdaq.com).[5] The NYSE is the largest in the world, dating back to 1792. In 1863 the exchange moved to the premises that it still occupies today and adopted the name "New York Stock Exchange".

Nasdaq is the second largest stock market in the United States and the fastest growing. It is an OTC market using a blend of screen-based trading technology and market-maker competition. In January 1992 it installed computer facilities in the United Kingdom to become the world's first inter-continental stock market.

AMEX has a reputation for introducing new ideas and new products. Its listing requirements are less stringent than those of the NYSE and it encourages the registration of young companies as well as foreign ones. In September 1985, AMEX and the Toronto Stock Exchange introduced the first two-way electronic link between equity markets in different countries.

Shareholding is widespread in the United States. On the NYSE individuals account for 30% of turnover; they account for about 49% on AMEX and 57% on Nasdaq. Institutions account for 46% of turnover on the NYSE, 33% on AMEX and 43% on Nasdaq. The rest is accounted for by member firms dealing on their own behalf.

[5] The Philadelphia Stock Exchange, founded in 1790, is the oldest in the United States. In 1953 it merged with the exchanges in Washington D.C. and Baltimore. The Boston Stock Exchange, founded in 1834, was the first US exchange to open its membership to foreigners (in 1968). The Midwest Stock Exchange was established in 1882 as the Chicago Stock Exchange. In 1949 it merged with the exchanges in St. Louis, Cleveland, and Minneapolis-St. Paul to form the MSE. The New Orleans Exchange became a part of the MSE in 1959. The Pacific Stock Exchange, specializing in listing new technology companies, was formed in 1957 by the merger of the San Francisco and Los Angeles exchanges. The Cincinnati Stock Exchange dates back to 1885. It began operating the National Securities Trading System in 1976.

Table 20.1 International market indexes

Market	Index	Address
New York Stock Exchange	NYSE Composite	www2.nyse.com/marketinfo/marketinfo.html
Nasdaq	Nasdaq Composite	www.nasdaq.com
American Stock Exchange	AMEX	www.amex.com
Amsterdam	AEX Index	www.aex.nl
Athens	Composite Index	www.ase.gr
Bangkok	SET Index	www.set.or.th
Bombay/NSE	CNX Nifty	www.nseindia.com
Brussels	BET-20 Index	www.stockexchange.be
Copenhagen	KFX Index	www.xcse.dk
Frankfurt	DAX	www.exchange.de
Helsinki	HEX General Index	www.hex.fi
Hong Kong	Hang Seng	www.sehk.hk
Istanbul	National 100 Index	www.ise.org
Jakarta	Composite Index	www.jsx.co.id
Johannesburg	All Market	www.jse.co.za
Kuala Lumpur	Composite	www.klse.com.my
London	FT-SE 100	www.stockex.co.uk
Madrid	Bolsa Index	www.bolsamadrid.es
Manila	PSE Index	www.pse.org.ph
Mexico	Bolsa Index	www.bmv.com.mx
Milan	MIB Telematico	www.borsaitalia.it
Oslo	OBX Index	www.ose.np
Paris	CAC-40	www.bourse-de-paris.fr
Sao Paulo	Bovespa Index	www.bovespa.com.br
Seoul	Composite Index	www.kse.or.kr
Shenzen	B Shares Index	n.a.
Singapore	Straits Times	www.ses.com.sg
Stockholm	OMX Index	www.stockholmsborsen.se
Swiss Exchange	SPI	www.bourse.ch
Sydney	All Ordinaries	www.asx.com.au
Taipei	Stock Market Index	www.tse.com.tw
Tel Aviv	Tel Aviv 25 Index	www.tase.co.il
Toronto	TSE Industrials	www.tse.com
Vienna	ATX Index	www.wbag.at
Wellington	NZSE-40 Index	www.nzse.co.nz

Types of instruments

The principal types of equity instruments traded on the US exchanges are common stock, preferred shares, American depository receipts and trust receipts of beneficial interest. **American depository receipts** (ADRs) are negotiable certificates in registered form, issued in the United States by a US bank, certifying that a specific number of foreign shares have been deposited with an overseas branch of the bank or another financial institution, which acts as custodian in the country of origin. Usually, only shares traded on a recognized foreign exchange are represented by ADRs. A holder of ADRs can request the underlying shares at any time. ADRs can be either sponsored or unsponsored. Unsponsored ADRs are issued without an agreement from the issuer of the shares while sponsored ADRs are issued with an agreement.

A trust certificate of beneficial interest represents an equity share in the underlying assets of a trust owning financial securities. Holders of the certificates have the right to receive dividends.

Trading

Trading on the NYSE takes place on a dealer-to-dealer basis. It is a mixture of an auction and a dealer market. The largest membership category is the commission broker. Commission brokers work for one of about 500 stockbroking firms. They execute orders for their firm on behalf of their firm's clients or for their firm's own account. Each stock is assigned to a single specialist. Specialists act as market-makers in the stocks for which they are registered as specialists. In this role they can act as brokers, executing orders, or as a dealer, buying and selling for their own account. Registered traders are individual members who buy and sell for their own account.

Orders are communicated to the trading floor through Superdot 250, an electronic order-routing system. Superdot 250 routes market and limit orders directly to the post where each stock is traded or to the member firm's booth on the trading floor. The brokers then execute the order.

Nasdaq uses a screen-based system. Unlike the NYSE's single specialist system, trading is carried out by competing market-makers, representing some of the largest and best capitalized securities firms in the world. A typical stock will have about ten competing market-makers while the most actively traded stocks like MCI and Apple will have 40 or more.

Market-makers enter their bid–ask prices into their workstation terminals. Trades are negotiated, executed and reported through the workstation terminals as well. Nasdaq in turn sends the trade details to the clearing corporation for clearance and settlement.

Since May 1975 when fixed commissions were abolished, commissions in the United States have been negotiable. The maximum commission for a single round lot or odd lot is USD 80.73. Commissions can range from as high as 10% of the transaction value to as low as several tenths of one percent for very large orders. Commissions in OTC trades are included in the bid–ask spread.

Settlement and transfer

From the time a trade is executed on any major US exchange, a computerized system handles recording, settlement, delivery and safekeeping. Unless otherwise specified, all transactions must be settled on the Five Day Delivery Plan. Under this plan, "regular way" transactions, which constitute the lion's share of all transactions, are due for settlement by delivery of the securities against payment on the fifth business day after the transaction date. Late fees can go as high as USD 100 per day.

Taxes and regulations affecting foreign investors

In the absence of a tax treaty, withholding tax is 30% on dividends. Tax treaties usually reduce this to 15% for portfolio investments. The United States does not impose exchange controls. Consequently, dividends, interest and capital can be freely repatriated. There are no registration requirements on foreign capital or loans, although restrictions on direct investments do exist in certain sensitive fields such as communications, coastal shipping and defense.

Reporting and required information

Reporting requirements for listed companies are the most stringent of all the major industrialized countries. Public issues must be accompanied by a detailed prospectus.

The Securities Exchange Act of 1934 imposes annual and quarterly reporting require-ments on corporate issuers registered under the Act. Companies listed on the NYSE are required to give prompt notice of any fact that could have a material impact on a company or its financial position such as a suspension of a business, a change of char-acter or nature of the business, increases or reductions of capital, mergers, dividends and stock splits.

An alternative set of listing standards exists on the NYSE for companies organized outside the United States. For example, the NYSE accepts shares and shareholders on a worldwide basis. Also, since many countries make widespread use of bearer shares (as opposed to the registered shares in the United States), the NYSE waives the 5000 round lot shareholder requirement and allows foreign firms to make a simple attestation concerning the liquidity and market depth for their shares. The NYSE, however, could not obtain SEC approval for admitting companies on the basis of home country disclosure that did not conform to SEC standards. Other requirements are:

- pre-tax cumulative income of USD 100 million in the most recent three years with a minimum of USD 25 million in any one of them
- net tangible assets of USD 100 million worldwide
- aggregate market value of publicly held shares of USD 100 million worldwide
- 2.5 million shares publicly held worldwide.

On the AMEX foreign issuers face the same requirements as domestic firms: USD 4 million in shareholders' equity, pre-tax income of USD 750,000 in the last fiscal year or in two of the three last fiscal years, USD 3 million in capitalization, 800 shareholders worldwide, and one million shares publicly held worldwide. Nasdaq listing requirements are essentially the same for US and foreign companies.

Investors are protected by the Securities Investor Protection Act of 1970 that established the Securities Investor Protection Corporation (SIPC). All brokers and dealers registered with the SEC must be a member of the SIPC. The SIP Act provides for a fund paid by assessments of members to the SIPC that guarantees protection to investors against financial loss resulting from brokers/dealers who fail.

Insider trading and market manipulation are illegal in the United States, backed up by heavy penalties and strict enforcement.

Japan

The Tokyo Stock Exchange (TSE) was established in 1878. There are now eight stock exchanges in Japan located in Tokyo, Osaka, Nagoya, Kyoto, Hiroshima, Fukuoka, Niigata, and Sapporo.

Before World War II, stocks were concentrated in the hands of a few large holding companies and were generally speculative investments. Long-term financing was handled by the banking sector. The exchanges were closed for a time during and after World War II. When they were reopened in 1949, based on the US Securities and Exchange Law of 1948 shareholdings were redistributed and democratized. Since then, shares have once again become concentrated, this time in institutional hands.

The OTC market is currently the fastest growing equity market in Japan. It expanded from 161 registered companies in 1986 to over 450 at the end of 1991. Its primary role is to facilitate the raising of funds from the investing public by unlisted, small and medium-sized companies. The Japan Over-The-Counter Trading Company acts as the intermediary for OTC issues between securities companies.

Types of instruments

Ordinary shares, preferred shares, deferred shares, shares to be retired with profits, shares without voting rights and convertible shares are all traded on the exchanges. Preferred and deferred shares refer to how they are treated in the distribution of profits or surplus assets on liquidation. Shares to be issued with profits are issued by a company that is scheduled to be dissolved at a given future date. Preferred shares, deferred shares, shares to be retired with profits and shares without voting rights are rare. Most equity issues take the form of ordinary voting shares.

Trading

In Japan, all securities must be traded through an authorized securities dealer who is a member of the Japan Securities Dealers' Association. On the TSE, which is traditionally an auction or order-driven market, there are two types of members, regular members and Saitori members. Regular members are securities companies engaged in trading on the exchange as a principal or an agent. There are about 100 regular members. Saitori members are securities companies acting as intermediaries between regular members on the exchange. They manage the limit order book and execute transactions according to the rules of the exchange. Priority is determined first by price: the highest bid and lowest ask have priority over all other orders. The second priority is determined by time: orders at the same price are executed on a "first come-first served" basis. Market orders have priority over limit orders. There are four Saitori members and they are prohibited from trading on their own account.

Trading is based on the auction method. Prices are opened at the beginning of the trading session with a special auction based on orders that have reached the the Saitori book before opening. All these orders are executed at a single price. Other investors then enter the market. Their orders are transmitted to the floor by computer or by telephone and executed as they arrive in a continuous auction. Floor clerks of the regular members carry the order slips to the traders where buys and sells are matched by an open auction. Commissions range from 1.15% on the smallest trades to 0.075% for the largest.

Settlement and transfer

Japan uses a book-entry system for all clearing transactions. Regular settlement covers about 99% of transactions effected on the exchange. It is due on the third business day following the day of the trade. Cash delivery is due on the day of the trade or the following business day. Trades can also be settled on a date agreed to by both parties, which cannot be later than 14 calendar days following the trade.

Taxes and regulations affecting foreign investors

Non-resident shareholders are subject to Japan's 20% withholding tax on dividends. Reduced rates, ranging from zero to 15% depending on the country, might apply if the investor is a resident of a country that has a tax treaty with Japan. To benefit from the tax treaty status, the investor has to submit an advance application to the tax authorities. Unless specifically excluded by a tax treaty, capital gains are subject to a 20% income tax as well as to a 6% local tax. There are no real exchange controls concerning the repatriation of income and capital, which can be repatriated freely.

Reporting and required information

The Security and Exchange Law spells out the basic requirements for a stock exchange listing. The individual exchanges deal with the listing criteria and reporting procedures.

The range of information that must be supplied to the Ministry of Finance and to the stock exchange includes annual, semi-annual and extraordinary reports. The stock exchange also requires that prompt notice must be given of any fact that could have a material impact on a company such as a suspension of a business or an unhonored bill or check. Notice must also be given on corporate decisions or resolutions relating to increases or reductions of capital, mergers, dividends and stock splits. The disclosure requirements for foreign companies have been simplified in order to facilitate cross-border capital flows. The TSE publishes a booklet entitled *A Listing Guide for Foreign Companies* that details the rules and regulations for foreign companies seeking a listing in Japan.

Insider dealing and market manipulation are illegal in Japan. Japan does not, however, have any compensation fund designed to protect shareholders against loss caused by fraud.

The United Kingdom

The United Kingdom is Europe's biggest equity market. It is also the world's most international exchange. Over 60% of cross-border trading in the world and 93% of European cross-border trading passes through London.

Dealing began among merchants around London's coffee houses in the 17th century. In 1773, New Jonathan's Coffee House became the stock exchange, which was formally constituted in 1802. Other exchanges also developed around the country. They began to amalgamate around 1890 with the constitution of the Council of Associated Stock Exchanges. By 1967, the provincial exchanges had grouped into six regional exchanges and in 1973 all seven exchanges in the British Isles merged to form the Stock Exchange of Great Britain and Ireland, with trading floors in London, Birmingham, Manchester, Liverpool, Glasgow, and Dublin. Exhibit 20.1 provides a brief history of the London Stock Exchange (LSE, at www.londonstockexchange.com), the largest and most important of these markets.

The basic system of the stock exchange remained unchanged from 1911 until 1985 when the government obliged the exchange to abolish the practice of fixed commissions. Since the rigid division of member firms between brokers and jobbers (market-makers) was considered incompatible with negotiated commissions, it was abolished in the general market deregulation of October 1986, called the "Big Bang". Now member firms are broker-dealers and trading is based on a system of market-makers who are free to conduct brokerage business.

Although there are over 11 million private shareholders in the United Kingdom, the proportion of shares owned by private individuals has fallen. In 1975 about 37.5% of UK quoted equities were owned by private individuals. Today this figure has fallen to about 20%, with 68% owned by institutions and foreigners owning the rest.

Types of instruments

The share capital of a company may be divided into many types of classes subject to the general rule that all shares rank equally as to dividends and capital. The different rights associated with each class of share are left to the specific terms of the memorandum and articles of association of each company. Most companies issue both ordinary and preference shares.

Trading

Trading on the exchange is computerized under the Stock Exchange Automated Quotations (SEAQ) system. Member firms are allowed to act as brokers or as dealers on their own account. They can also become committed market-makers that are required to make markets at all times in their registered stocks during the mandatory quote period between 8.30 a.m. and 4.30 p.m.

Exhibit 20.1 Short history of the London Stock Exchange

1760:	150 brokers kicked out of the Royal Exchange for rowdiness form a club at Jonathan's Coffee House to buy and sell shares.
1773:	Members vote to change name to Stock Exchange.
1914:	The Great War meant the exchange market closed at the end of July until the new year. The Stock Exchange Battalion of Royal Fusiliers was formed – 1600 volunteered, 400 never returned.
1972:	Her Majesty the Queen opened the exchange's new 26-storey office block with its 23 000 sq ft trading floor.
1973:	First female members admitted to the market.
1986:	Big bang:
	Ownership of member firms by an outside corporation is allowed.
	All firms become broker/dealers able to operate in a dual capacity.
	Minimum scales of commission are abolished.
	Individual members cease to have voting rights.
	Trading moves from being conducted face-to-face on a market floor to being performed via computer and telephone from separate dealing rooms. This is enabled by SEAQ and SEAQ International–2 computer systems displaying share price information in brokers' offices around the UK. The exchange becomes a private limited company under the Companies Act 1985.
1991:	The governing Council of the Exchange is replaced with a board of directors drawn from the exchange's executive, customer and user base.
1995:	AIM – a market for growing companies – is launched.
1997:	SETS (Stock Exchange Electronic Trading Service) is launched to bring greater speed and efficiency to the market.
	The settlement service – transferring stock from seller to buyer and arranging the movement of money – is no longer provided by the exchange, moving to CRESTCo.
2000:	The role as UK Listing Authority with HM Treasury is transferred to the Financial Services Authority (FSA).
	Shareholders vote to become a public limited company, called London Stock Exchange plc. Dealing in shares is conducted via an off-market trading facility operated by Cazenove and Co.
2001:	Exchange listed in July.

Source: www.londonstockexchange.com.

Since 14 January 1991, stocks have been quoted in normal market size (NMS). There are 12 bands ranging from 500 to 200 000 shares based on each stock's average market turnover.

As discussed, commissions are fully negotiable and there is a stamp duty of 0.5% on all share transfers.

Taxes and regulations affecting foreign investors

UK corporations are required to pay advance corporation tax (ACT) on dividends distributed to shareholders. Residents of countries having a tax treaty with the United Kingdom can claim a tax credit equal to the amount of ACT paid less a withholding tax, usually about 15%.

There are no exchange controls on inward or outward movements of capital and investment income, nor are there any specific regulations applying solely to foreign equity investors except in certain sensitive industries as provided in the Industry Act of 1975, Part II.

Reporting and required information

Reporting requirements in the United Kingdom are the strictest in Europe. Applications for new listings must be submitted to the stock exchange for approval along with details of the company and its business. The details must then be published in at least one national daily newspaper. The procedures necessary to obtain a full listing are set out in the manual entitled *Admission of Securities to Listing*.

Once a listing has been obtained, disclosure obligations include the immediate release of any information that could reasonably be expected to affect the market in that company's shares. Dates of board meetings, dividend payments, profits and losses and changes in capital structure are some of the most obvious examples. Semi-annual reports must be prepared and published and preliminary profit statements must comply with them. The annual report and accounts must be issued by the company within six months of the end of the financial period to which they relate.

Foreign companies are subject to a simplified set of continuing obligations if they are already listed on their domestic stock exchanges.

The Financial Services Act of 1986 lays down the rules and regulations for all activities relating to the securities markets. Overall responsibility lies with the Securities and Investments Board (SIB), which supervises the various autonomous self-regulating organizations. Insider trading and price manipulation are illegal.

Emerging markets

The growth of emerging stock markets has been nothing short of spectacular. From the mid-1980s to the late 1990s, their trading volume multiplied by a factor of 30 and market capitalization by a factor of 20. This performance has been accompanied by progressive deregulation and liberalization in the context of financial globalization and competition for foreign investment funds. Nevertheless, wide disparities across countries still exist. Some countries, such as Argentina, have virtually no restrictions on foreign stock market participation and repatriation of income and capital. Others, like China, restrict foreign shareholding to certain classes of stock but impose no restrictions on repatriation of income and capital, while others restrict shareholding to certain approved investors, in certain classes of shares with repatriation restrictions on income and capital. It should also not be forgotten, however, that even when there are no restrictions, they can easily be imposed at the stroke of a pen. Witness the Malaysian restrictions imposed in the wake of the Asian meltdown of 1997.

The case for investing in emerging markets is based on the principle of diversification developed in Chapter 11. Although the emerging markets stand out as highly volatile, they generally seem to have low correlation with the stock markets of the developed countries. They also seem to offer higher average returns than those of the developed countries. Too much should not be made of this, however, as correlations are unstable over time and often rise in times of crisis. This was the case in the worldwide stock market crash of 1987 that was repeated in the Mexican peso crisis of 1994, the Asian meltdown of 1997 and the Russian default of 1998. The higher returns must also be measured against the political risk associated with the emerging markets (see

Chapters 10, 11 and 12), the costs associated with corruption and insider trading that is endemic to many emerging markets as well as the increased costs of information gathering in an underdeveloped economy.[6]

Where information gathering on emerging stock markets is concerned, the IFC (www.ifc.org) is a major source of data. Other official sources of information include the International Chamber of Commerce (www.icc.org), the Emerging Markets Trade Association (EMTA at www.emta.org), the World Bank (www.worldbank.org) and the International Monetary Fund (IMF at www.imf.org). There are also many private suppliers of information on emerging markets.

Summary

1. Valuing equities is similar to valuing bonds. Cash flows must be determined and discounted back to the present at the appropriate discount rate. Cash flows to equities are usually in the form of dividends.

2. Determining equity cash flows is more difficult than determining bond cash flows. The procedure is usually accomplished in three steps. First, the company's financial statements are studied to estimate the company's earnings per share and its dividend policy. Secondly, the company's investment opportunities based on its individual competitive position and the overall evolution of its market are analyzed. Thirdly, the results of steps one and two are combined to arrive at an assumption about the growth of the dividend.

3. The ubiquitous P/E ratio is more complicated than it looks and should be handled carefully. It depends on the rate at which earnings are retained by the firm, the appropriate discount rate and the growth rate. P/Es can vary across firms because of different rates of retaining earnings, different risk levels reflected in r and different investment opportunities reflected in g. Therefore, the P/E ratio does not indicate anything precise about the discount rate or the growth rate. Furthermore, EPS is hard to interpret because it is an accounting concept that can be modified arbitrarily by applying different accounting conventions. Only after all these qualifications have been allowed for can the P/E ratio be used as a crude barometer of a company's growth prospects.

4. Although the individual exchanges tend to have unique trading characteristics and legal structures, most relate back to one of three types of market organization: the public exchange, the private exchange and the bankers' exchange.

5. The methods for quoting prices can generally be divided into two categories: auction markets and dealer markets.

6. The trend in recent years has been from the physical trading floor to the virtual world of computerized trading. Computerization makes it possible to handle orders more efficiently through automated price quotation, order routing and order matching. The drawbacks to computerized trading stem from potential loss of liquidity due to risks associated with publicly posting prices.

7. Most equity issues are straight cash offers to the public at large where shares are traded for cash. Some, however, are restricted to existing shareholders and are called rights issues.

---

[6] For information on political risk and economic freedom, see www.freetheworld.com. For corruption, see www.transparency.org.

8. Public issues are handled by a syndicate of underwriters, led by a lead manager, that provides the company with procedural and financial advice, buys the issue, and then resells it to the public. It is a relatively complicated and costly process.

9. There is nothing especially unique about the fundamental techniques involved in valuing foreign companies. It should be remembered, however, that certain informational shortcomings must be taken into consideration as well as the differences in market characteristics that might exist from one country to another.

10. There are several advantages to international equity issues. Issuing internationally makes it possible to issue in larger amounts; it increases and diversifies the shareholder base; it improves the firm's image; it often offers less constraining listing procedures; and the secondary market on international issues is active and liquid, especially on the major intenational exchanges such as London and New York.

11. For investors, international equities offer the benefits of portfolio diversification and the possibility of favorable tax treatment.

12. The issuing procedure for international equities is similar to that for Eurobonds. A lead manager obtains a mandate from the issuer. He is responsible for negotiating the overall conditions of the issue as well as for organizing a syndicate to market it. The syndicate is composed of a management group, an underwriting group and a selling group. The co-managers in the management group are always internationally recognized financial institutions and are chosen according to geographical diversification, the ability to effectively place securities and past relations with the issuer.

13. The three major equity markets in the world are the United States, Japan and the United Kingdom. The three markets differ in many ways. They are organized differently, they trade and settle differently, their listing requirements are different, and they have different regulatory systems and tax treatment.

14. Stock markets in emerging countries have become popular with international investors for the apparent diversification benefits they offer. These apparent benefits might be lower than expected insofar as correlations across markets seem to rise in times of crisis. These apparent benefits must also be compared with the increased information costs as well as increased risks associated with politics and corruption.

Questions

Solutions to the following questions are set out on the web site, details of which are included in the Preface.

1. A share of Henway Inc. is quoted at GBP 25 on the stock exchange. The next dividend to be paid in 12 months time is expected to be GBP 1 and it is expected to grow at a constant annual rate of 10%. What is the appropriate risk-adjusted discount rate that should be applied when valuing Henway's stock?

2. What is the difference between an order-driven market and a price-driven market?

3. What is the role of computerized trading in today's stock markets?

4. What are the drawbacks to computerized trading?

5. What is a rights issue?

6. Explain what is meant by a Euroequity issue.

7. In an international equity issue, what measures can be taken to keep any one underwriter from establishing a monopoly in a specific country or geographic zone?

8. What use are stock market indexes?

9. What is an ADR and where is it traded?

10. What is the role of the Saitori members of the Tokyo Stock Exchange?

11. Where is the world's most international stock exchange located?

CAPITAL BUDGETING AND FOREIGN DIRECT INVESTMENT

Foreign direct investment: Capital budgeting and political, economic and financial risk management

The large multinational corporations (MCNs) – many with internationally recognized household names, such as Coca-Cola, McDonald's, Sony, Nestlé and Fiat – have followed development strategies based on direct investment in foreign countries. Remember from Chapter 1 that direct investment involves the investor taking an active role in the management of the assets he is acquiring. In this chapter we concentrate on capital budgeting and the management of exposure to country-specific economic and financial risk in the context of foreign direct investment.

Reasons for cross-border investing

Cost of labor

The economic reasons for cross-border investing are many and varied. The cost of labor is a prime example. Lower labor costs are an important incentive for foreign investment in labor-intensive industries. In more capital-intensive industries labor costs are liable to play a less important role. On the other hand, the quality and skills of the labor force might even make investing in high-wage countries attractive when productivity depends on technology and know-how.

Transport costs

Transport costs are also an important consideration. For products with high transaction costs, the establishment of factories around the world might be justified as a means of reducing costs. For example, processing plants might be set up close to raw material sources. Where scale economies in manufacturing are limited, costs may be lowered by using smaller factories and locating them close to their markets, thereby reducing costs on transporting goods to market. Some countries are even attractive to foreign investors because of their central geographic location or efficient transportation systems.

Diversification

Diversification of cash flows is another important economic motive for cross-border investment. It is based on the same principle as financial diversification. Insofar as company cash flows are correlated with the performance of individual national economies, and the performances of these economies are not perfectly correlated among themselves, by spreading investments across countries cash flows can be stabilized and the risk–return trade-off can be improved.

Operational constraints

Operational constraints may also induce direct investment. Government policies or fear of government policies that favor local production over imported goods can induce foreign companies to invest in the domestic market. For example, many developing countries link the availability of certain rare resources to the establishment of local processing plants.

Investing abroad can also make it possible for companies to avoid regulations at home. The banking industry is a prime example. Banks often move offshore in order to avoid reserve requirements, deposit insurance, and credit and interest rate controls as well as taxes. Witness the growth of offshore banking operations in the so-called "tax haven" countries such as Luxembourg, Panama, the Bahamas, Jersey, Guernsey and the Isle of Man. Manufacturing firms can be motivated to move offshore by a desire to escape from stifling regulations such as environmental controls and safety standards. In fact, one of the main arguments against the North American Free Trade Area (Nafta) was that US manufacturing jobs would be lost to companies moving to Mexico to take advantage of relatively lax environmental standards and labor laws.[1]

Special incentives

Incentive measures are also often cited as important for attracting foreign investment. Incentive measures can be grouped as follows:

- Tax concessions, such as investment write-offs, tax concessions on sales, exports, licence fees, etc.
- Tariff concessions such as the exemption or reduction of tariffs on imported inputs or the provision of protective tariffs.
- Financial incentives such as investment grants, local loans at preferential interest rates, and subsidies.
- Other incentives such as exchange control concessions, curbing labor unions, or lowering environmental or safety standards.

As attractive as these incentives sound, however, there is some doubt as to how effective they are in influencing cross-border investment. Many case studies have shown that the main incentive for private investment is a sound economic policy that allows prices of products and resources to reflect real scarcities.[2]

Market considerations

Market considerations influence foreign investment decisions. As a matter of fact, several major analyses of US firms have found that the main consideration in their decision to invest abroad was a concern for markets.[3] Market dominance, for example, is

[1] For information on Nafta see www.ffas.usda.gov/info/factsheets/nafta.html.

[2] See, for example, Aharoni (1966).

[3] See Polk, Judd, et al. (1966) and Spitaller (1971).

a primary criterion, which, it has been shown, has a positive relationship with long-term profitability.[4] Declining margins in the home market may also induce the firm to invest abroad. This argument, known as the product life cycle hypothesis, maintains that a new product will be produced in the country that developed the innovation, regardless of cost, because of its price insensitive demand.[5] Foreign demand will be satisfied by exports at the beginning but, as the product catches on, the market matures and competitors appear both at home and abroad. At this point, the firm is obliged to invest abroad as a means of fighting competition and avoiding tariffs.

Some firms are obliged to invest abroad rather than rely on licensing agreements in order to protect their reputations. McDonald's, for example, had a bad experience with a licensing arrangement in France in the 1970s. Cleanliness and quality standards were not respected to the point that the company felt obliged to abrogate the agreement and undertake management of the operation itself.

Exploiting a reputation can also be an argument for investing abroad. Fields such as accounting and finance, where reputation and image are the essential product ingredient, are an example.

Factor advantages

A monopolistic advantage in technology is an obvious incentive to invest abroad. Other types of advantages include capital market access and management know-how. Access to capital markets lowers the firm's cost of capital and allows it to operate more cheaply than the smaller local firms that do not have the same financing opportunities. Management know-how might be one of the single most important factors in motivating a firm to invest abroad, since it is probably one of the most important factors in the success or failure of a business venture. Eastern Europe's transition to a market economy, for example, has been hampered by an acute shortage of management expertise. The organization theory of direct investment is on shaky theoretical ground (and even shakier legal ground), however, when it emphasizes broad management objectives such as market presence, size and sales growth as opposed to the traditional management role of profit maximization and creation of shareholder wealth.

The orthodox theory of investment

Net present value

In Chapter 10 we pointed out that the orthodox theory of investment under uncertainty taught in most business schools and economics departments revolves around the net present value (NPV) rule. According to this rule, expected flows of income and expenditure are estimated for each period. These flows are then discounted at the appropriate discount rate. The NPV is found by subtracting the present value of the expenditure stream from the present value of the income stream. If the NPV is positive, the project is accepted. If it is negative, the project is rejected. If it is zero, we are indifferent.

Consider, for example, a project that involves an initial outlay of USD 2250. The income for year zero is USD 250. There is a 50% probability that in one year's time annual income will rise to USD 350 and remain there for ever. There is also a 50% probability that in one

---

[4] See Gale (1972).

[5] See Vernon and Wells (1976).

year's time annual income will fall to USD 150 and remain there for ever. The expected annual income in one year's time is equal to:

$$(0.5 \times USD\ 350) + (0.5 \times USD\ 150) = USD\ 250.$$

If we suppose that the appropriate discount rate is 10%, the NPV is equal to the present value of the expected cash flows minus the expected outlay:

$$NPV = -USD\ 2250 + \sum_{t=0}^{\infty} USD\ 250(1.1)^{-t} = USD\ 500.$$

Where foreign direct investment is concerned, the two main questions for the NPV rule revolve around just how the expected cash flows should be estimated and what discount rate should be used for calculating present values.

Identifying the cash flows

In the international context, determining the cash flows to be incorporated in the capital budgeting process and estimating their expected values is more complicated than in the traditional domestic capital budgeting problem. First of all, a distinction must be made between the cash flows accruing to the project and the cash flows accruing to the parent company. The nature of cross-border investing is such that a substantial difference can exist between the two. Exchange controls, for example, can reduce the flows to the parent relative to the project whereas fees and royalties can increase them. Judicious project evaluation requires that the analysis include all the pertinent incremental cash flows to the parent arising from the project.

Joint projects

The proposed project might have a direct effect on the company's already existing operations. A company contemplating an investment in a country where it is already exporting must consider whether or not export sales will be lost as a result of the investment. On the other hand, incremental sales from other units of the company might be generated if those units are suppliers of inputs to the project's production process. When determining the cash flows, lost exports should be deducted and incremental sales should be added.

The subject of incremental sales brings up the sensitive problem of transfer pricing. Market prices do not always exist for some of the intermediate products moving through a vertically integrated firm. The question then is how much to charge for them. Theoretically, the price should be equal to the firm's marginal cost of production. In practice, however, many intermediate goods moving between different divisions of the same firm are sold at monopolisitc prices, thereby distorting the relative price system and the true incremental cash flows that should be generated by the project. Furthermore, transfer pricing is often used as a means of skirting foreign exchange controls and other types of government interference. For example, the parent company might charge excessively high prices for project inputs in order to get around limits on profit and principal repatriation. It can achieve the same effect by paying excessively low prices for the project's outputs.

Fees and royalties

Supervisory fees and royalties are a source of flows to the parent company. They should be included in the assessment of the project. As with intermediate inputs, fees and royalties are often used as a means of remitting funds to the parent.

Scale economies

Certain production processes feature important economies of scale. Thus, individual small projects should be charged for the incremental costs or diseconomies associated with decentralization.

Taxes and subsidies

Non-economic considerations such as taxes and subsidies can have important consequences for parent cash flows. Although tax laws and treaties vary from country to country and change over time, most countries acknowledge that dual taxation is unjust and give full credit for taxes paid in another country. However, for individual investments, even where tax treaties and special incentive programs exist, tax consequences on cash flows should be carefully analyzed. For example, withholding taxes on dividends remitted to the parent should be charged to the project.

Tax laws are notoriously complex and subject to the vagaries of individual interpretation. In fact, the complexity of calculating after-tax cash flows often makes it necessary to make simplifying assumptions. For example, assuming the most unfavorable tax scenario in the first stage of a project evaluation might be justified under the argument that if the project is acceptable under the most unfavorable conditions it will certainly be acceptable under more favorable ones. While this is a good way to avoid bad investments, many good investments will also be eliminated. In the next chapter we will present an approach to investment decision making under uncertainty that makes it possible to overcome this drawback.

Currency fluctuations

The preceding chapters have emphasized the importance of the exchange rate on base currency cash flows. Where direct investments are concerned, however, it is important to remember the relationships developed in Chapter 2. Currency fluctuations can affect the demand for a product as well as its price. However, because of varying time lags and demand elasticities, the prices of different products will react in different ways to currency fluctuations. If, for example, the project is producing for a client-base that gains as a result of the devaluation, cash flows to the project in host country currency might increase enough to more than offset the effects of the depreciation in the exchange rate and thereby increase parent company cash flows. On the other hand, the cost of inputs will also vary and could offset the gains. Parent cash flows could also be affected if project output varies as a result of the devaluation and changes the quantities of transferred inputs or the amount of royalties and fees that are due. Hence, besides the direct effect of a lower exchange ratio, devaluation scenarios should also include estimates of the consequences on the cash flows of the project itself.

Techniques for project evaluation

The first step in the traditional capital budgeting process involves determining the relevant cash flows. When estimating cash flows, it is important to use the correct concept of expected returns. Table 21.1 is an example of an income statement. As we shall see below in the discussion of the cost of capital, investment decisions and financing problems should be studied separately. Therefore, income from operations should include financing costs, and the relevant concept of expected returns is net operating income or earnings before the deduction of interest and taxes (EBIT). The cash flow is thus equal to EBIT less taxes that would have to be paid on this amount in the absence of interest charges plus depreciation less the change in net working capital. Depreciation must be added back because, although it is a cost, it is not an expenditure. The change in net working capital (change in stocks plus change in accounts receivable less change in accruals) must be subtracted because, although it is a component of profits, it has not yet been converted into cash.

Thus, from Table 21.1 EBIT is USD 100,000 and at the marginal tax rate of 40%, taxes would be USD 40,000. Depreciation is USD 50,000 and if there is no change in net working capital, the relevant cash flow would be

$$\text{Cash flow} = \text{EBIT} - \text{Tax} + \text{Depreciation}$$

$$\text{Cash flow} = \text{USD } 100,000 - \text{USD } 40,000 + \text{USD } 50,000 = \text{USD } 110,000.$$

It is important to note that all costs of financing are already included in the expected cash flow. This is because it is generally admitted that the returns to the project should be independent of the way the project is financed. This position is upheld by strong theoretical arguments.[6] However there are cases when these arguments are inappropriate, and, in these cases, it will be necessary to make modifications in the techniques for estimating the cash flows. We will deal with these topics later in the chapter.

Cash flow estimation is not a mechanical operation. Increased output and sales revenue resulting from the investment must be calculated as well as the cost implications coming from the quantity and quality of direct labor, fuel costs, maintenance expenses, down time, etc. Many variables are involved and their effects on cash flows require input by the engineers, accountants, economists, cost analysts and others competent to make such evaluations.

The most common techniques for project evaluation are net present value (NPV) and internal rate of return (IRR). The only difference between the two is the rate at which the cash flows are discounted. The NPV method discounts at the project's cost of capital while the IRR method discounts at the rate that will make the the NPV just equal to zero. The two methods will give the same accept-reject signals for specific projects. If the IRR is greater than than or equal to the cost of capital (r), the project is acceptable. Consequently, with $r <$ IRR, the NPV will be greater than zero and the project will also be acceptable under this criterion.

Table 21.1 Pro forma income statement (in US dollars)

Sales	400,000
Operating costs	−250,000
Earnings before depreciation, interest and taxes	150,000
Depreciation	−50,000
Net operating income	100,000
Interest charges	−20,000
Earnings before taxes	80,000
Taxes at 40%	−32,000
Net income	48,000

[6] See Modigliani and Miller (1959 and 1963).

However, where several projects are concerned, the two methods can rank projects differently. Rankings can differ if the cost of the projects differ, if the temporal profiles of the cash flows differ or if the expected lives of the projects differ. When the two methods yield conflicting rankings, the conflict can be resolved by assuming that management should seek to maximize the value of the firm. Under this assumption the correct decision is to choose the project with the highest NPV, since NPV measures the project's contribution to the firm.

An export project versus a direct investment

Expert project

The main issues involved in cross-border project evaluation can be illustrated with some simple examples. Suppose that firm XYZ in a country called Nafta, whose currency is the dollar, is planning on marketing its projects in Argenuay. Two projects have been proposed. The first project is the simple export project with a five-year time horizon presented in Table 21.2. It involves an investment of USD 200,000 in equipment for the increased output of 55 000 units that the company expects to sell in Argenuay at USD 2.00 per unit. Argenuay will be billed in dollars. The sales price includes the insurance and freight charges necessary to get the product to market. Operating costs are USD 40,000 and depreciation is straight line. Because of the nature of the investment, it is assumed that it will have no salvage value at the end of the five years. The company feels that even if Argenuay has economic or financial problems over the next five years and its exports are lower than expected, there will be no difficulty in making up the lost sales in the home market. All sales will be guaranteed with a confirmed letter of credit. Consequently, XYZ feels that the export project is no riskier than its ongoing activity in the home market and decides to evaluate the project at the firm's current cost of capital of 10%.

The initial outlay at the beginning of year one will be equal to the investment in equipment of USD 200,000 plus the investment in working capital for a total of USD 210,000. The cash flows from operations to be received at the end of years one to five are equal to after-tax income of USD 18,000 plus depreciation of USD 40,000 for a total of USD 58,000. At the end of year five the investment in working capital will be recuperated

Table 21.2 Cash flows (in US dollars) generated by the export project to Argenuay

Investment in equipment	200,000
Increase in working capital	10,000
Tax rate = 40%	
Cost of capital = 10%	
Sales	110,000
Operating costs	–40,000
Depreciation	–40,000
EBIT	30,000
Taxes at 40%	–12,000
Net income	18,000

as stocks, accounts receivable and payable, and accruals are wound down. In these conditions, the NPV of the project will be:

$$NPV = -\ USD\ 210,000 + USD\ 58,000 \sum_{t=1}^{5} (1.10)^{-t} + USD\ 10,000 \times (1.10)^{-5}$$

$$= -USD\ 210,000 + USD\ 219,866 + USD\ 6210$$

$$= USD\ 16,076.$$

Since the NPV is positive and, at about 13%, the IRR is above the cost of capital, the project is acceptable. However, the export project and the direct investment are mutually exclusive. Therefore, the project for the direct investment must be evaluated and compared to the export project in order to determine which project should be chosen.

The direct investment

Table 21.3 shows the relevant information in dollars for the direct investment as estimated by company XYZ based on their experience in countries similar to Argenuay and on the assumption that the exchange rate will not change over the life of the investment. Since producing directly in Argenuay will make it possible to sell considerably more, the project is much more costly than the export project and its horizon of ten years is considerably longer. The investment in equipment at the beginning of year one is USD 1,000,000 and the investment in working capital is USD 30,000. As in the export project, depreciation is straight line and it has been agreed that at the end of ten years the government will inherit what is left of the production facility free of charge. At 30%, the tax rate in Argenuay is lower than the 40% rate in Nafta and, according to the tax treaty negotiated between the two countries, taxes owed in one country can be offset by taxes paid in the other.

Because the project would not be internationally competitive, import tariffs have been negotiated to protect the project from external competition. Consequently, the output could only be sold in Argenuay, which makes the investment vulnerable to the economic and financial dilemmas that might befall the economy over the ten-year life of the investment. The managers of XYZ feel that this makes the project riskier than the company's ongoing operations and therefore, after careful analysis, the cost of capital is set at 12%.

Net income is estimated at USD 70,000. After-tax earnings of sales of materials by the parent company to the subsidiary are estimated at USD 24,000. Taxes owed in Nafta on profits earned in Argenuay are USD 40,000 but, since taxes paid in Argenuay can be credited against taxes owed in Nafta, the net tax liability is only USD 10,000 (USD 40,000 – USD 30,000 paid in Argenuay). With the annual straight line depreciation of USD 100,000, the estimated annual cash flows to the parent from years one to ten are USD 184,000.

The total investment is the outlay for equipment of USD 1,000,000 plus the investment in working capital of USD 30,000 for a total of USD 1,030,000. The USD 30,000 of working capital will be recuperated at the end of the tenth year. Discounting these cash flows at the project's cost of capital of 12%, the NPV of the project will be

$$NPV = -1,030,000 + USD\ 184,000 \sum_{t=1}^{10} (1.12)^{-t} + USD\ 30,000 \times (1.12)^{-10}$$

$$= USD\ 19,260.$$

The direct investment project has an NPV of USD 19,260 while the export project only has an NPV of USD 16,076. However, because the lives of the projects are different, the

Table 21.3 Cash flows (in US dollars) generated by direct investment in Argenuay

Cash flows generated by operations in Argenuay	
Investment in equipment	1,000,000
Increase in working capital	30,000
Tax rate in Argenuay = 30%	
Cost of capital = 12%	
Cost per unit = USD 1.00	
Price per unit = USD 2.00	
Number of units sold = 200 000	
Sales (200 000 x USD 2.00)	400,000
Operating costs (200 000 x USD 1.00)	–200,000
Depreciation	–100,000
EBIT	100,000
Taxes at 30%	–30,000
Net income	70,000
Earnings on sales of materials by parent company	
Sales (200 000 x USD 0.50)	100,000
Cost (200 000 x USD 0.30)	–60,000
Profit before taxes	40,000
Taxes at 40%	–16,000
Profits after taxes	24,000
Tax Adjustment	
Taxes owed in Nafta (0.4 x USD 100,000)	40,000
Tax credit from Argenuay	–30,000
Tax liability in Nafta	10,000
Cash Flows	
Net income from operations	70,000
Depreciation	100,000
Profits from sales of materials	24,000
Tax liability in Nafta	–10,000
Cash flow	184,000

NPVs cannot be compared directly. Two theoretically sound methods for handling this problem are available. The first method is to assume that each project is continuously replaced as it wears out and then to find the NPV of each infinitely replaced alternative. The other method is to equate the lives by assuming a reinvestment rate for the shorter project for the additional years required to equate the lives.

NPV assuming infinite replacement

There are three steps involved in estimating the NPV of an infinitely replaced investment project, which we will note as NPV$^\infty$.

1. Estimate the NPV of each project for the original life and applicable cost of capital, as we have already done.
2. Find the equivalent annuity (x) for the life and cost of capital of each project that will yield the corresponding NPV.
3. Find the net present value of this annuity (NPV$^\infty$) if it is received to infinity.

Thus, for the export project, the NPV is equal to USD 16,076 and the annuity is equal to the NPV divided by the present value interest factor of a five-year annuity at an interest rate of 10% ($PVIFA_{5\,years,10\%}$):[7]

$$x_{Export} = NPV / PVIFA_{5\,years,10\%}$$

$$= USD\ 16,076/3.7908$$

$$= USD\ 4,240.80.$$

The net present value of this annuity received to infinity is thus:[8]

$$NPV_{Export}^\infty = \frac{x_{Export}}{r_{Export}} = \frac{USD\ 4,240.80}{0.10}$$

$$= USD\ 42,408.$$

The same procedure can be applied to the direct investment project:

$$x_I = NPV_I / PVIFA_{10\,years,12\%}$$

$$= USD\ 19,260/5.6502$$

$$= USD\ 3,408.72$$

$$NPV_I^\infty = \frac{x_I}{r_I} = \frac{USD\ 3,408.72}{0.12}$$

$$= USD\ 28,406.$$

[7] The PVIFA is the sum of a geometric progression:

$$Sum = (1+r)^{-1} + (1+r)^{-2} + (1+r)^{-3} + \ldots + (1+r)^{-n} \tag{1}$$

Multiply this sum by $1 + r$, which gives:

$$(1+r)Sum = 1 + (1+r)^{-1} + (1+r)^{-2} + \ldots + (1+r)^{-(n-1)} \tag{2}$$

Subtract the first sum from the second and rearrange:

$$Sum = \frac{1 - (1+r)^{-n}}{r} \tag{3}$$

[8] From Equation 3 in the preceding footnote, as $n \to \infty$, $(1+r)^{-n} \to 0$, which gives $Sum = 1/r$.

Since NPV* is higher for the export project than for the investment project, the export project is preferable. It is interesting to note that this outcome is the direct result of the higher cost of capital associated with the direct investment. If the direct investment had been evaluated at the 10% cost of capital of the export project, then the direct investment project would have been preferred. This illustrates the importance of accurate estimations of the cost of capital for cross-border capital budgeting.

Reinvestment rate assumptions and terminal value

The NPV and IRR methods for project evaluation assume that cash flows are reinvested at the corresponding discount rates (the cost of capital for the NPV method and the internal rate of return for the IRR method). The rate at which these cash flows can actually be invested, however, might be quite different from the project's cost of capital or its internal rate of return. Consider, for example, a one-shot project with an exceptionally high rate of return. This could be the case if the government of Argenuay was offering generous investment incentives and a high level of protection. Since it is a one-off affair, the cash flows it generates could not be reinvested at the exceptionally high rate. In order to estimate the investment's contribution to the firm's value, the real rate of reinvestment must be taken into consideration. Otherwise, the project's value will be overestimated. On the other hand, a firm whose investment opportunities have a higher rate of return that its cost of capital would underestimate the contribution of a project to the firm's value if the reinvestment rate were not considered.

The terminal value concept involves three steps.

1. The reinvestment rate must be determined.

2. The reinvestment rate is applied to each cash flow for the number of periods remaining until the end of the project. The sum of these compounded values represents the terminal value of the cash flows.

3. The terminal value is discounted at the cost of capital and the original outlay is subtracted to yield the NPV adjusted for the reinvestment rate, noted as NPV*.

The terminal value concept provides another method for comparing projects with unequal lives. It involves estimating the terminal value of the shorter project and then applying the reinvestment rate to the terminal value for the number of periods necessary to equate the lives of the two projects.

Assume, for example, that it is decided that the reinvestment rate for the cash flows from the export project is 12%. The terminal value of the cash flow received at the end of the first year would be the cash flow of USD 58,000 compounded for the four periods until the end of period five:

$$USD\ 58,000 \times (1.12)^4 = USD\ 91,264.$$

The cash flow received at the end of year two would be compounded over the three remaining periods and so on until the last year. The cash flow for the fifth year (the USD 58,000 from operations plus the USD 10,000 of working capital) is not compounded because it is received on the terminal date:

$$USD\ 58,000 \times (1.12)^3 = USD\ 81,486$$

$$USD\ 58,000 \times (1.12)^2 = USD\ 72,756$$

$$USD\ 58,000 \times (1.12)^1 = USD\ 64,960$$

$$USD\ 68,000 \times (1.12)^0 = USD\ 68,000.$$

The terminal value of the export project at the end of year five is:

$$TV_5 = 91,246 + 81,486 + 72,756 + 64,960 + 68,000$$

$$= USD\ 378,466.$$

The terminal value at the end of year ten is the terminal value at the end of year five compounded for five periods at 12%, the reinvestment rate:

$$TV_{10} = USD\ 378,466 \times (1.12)^5$$

$$= USD\ 666,986.$$

The net present value adjusted for the reinvestment rate is equal to the terminal value at the end of year ten discounted over ten years at the project cost of capital of 10% less the outlay for the investment:

$$NPV^* = \frac{USD\ 666,986}{(1.10)^{10}} - USD\ 210,000$$

$$= USD\ 47,152.$$

At the reinvestment rate of 12% the NPV* of the direct investment project is the same as its NPV because all discounting was already done at 12%. Since the export project has a higher NPV*, this is the one that should be accepted.

Foreign exchange exposure from direct investments

In the foregoing examples we assumed that all cash flows could be repatriated with no difficulty at a constant exchange rate. From Chapters 2 and 3 we know that this assumption

Exhibit 21.1 Adjusted net present value

Adjusted net present value (APV) is an interesting offshoot of the orthodox NPV rule. Instead of one average discount rate applied to the overall net cash flows, APV breaks the cash flows down into their component parts and discounts each one at the appropriate risk-adjusted discount rate. This makes it possible to analyze the interactions between investment and financing decisions. For cross-border projects, the APV approach is particularly useful since these projects often include complicated financial arrangements that would be difficult, if not impossible, to account for in a single discount rate. Three steps are involved:

- discount the project's operating cash flows at the all equity required rate of return
- analyze the financing side effects of the project and discount them at the the appropriate rate adjusted for the systematic risk they represent
- add the net present values of the operating cash flows and the financial side effects to obtain APV.

Consider, for example, a USD 10 million investment in Thailand lasting for five years financed with 50% equity and 50% debt. Normally, the cost of debt would be 12% for a project of this type in Thailand.[9] The World Bank, however, is willing to lend the USD 5 million at a subsidized rate of 10%. The project is expected to generate USD 3 million in operating cash flows before interest expenses every year for five years and the marginal tax rate is 40%. Thus, there are three cash flow streams to consider: the operating cash flows, the tax saving on interest payments, and the interest rate subsidy on the loan.

Suppose that the all equity discount rate for the project is 14.6% as calculated in Equation 21.4. The present value of the operating cash flows is then equal to:

$$\text{USD } 3 \sum_{t=1}^{5} (1.146)^{-t} = \text{USD } 10.152 \text{ million.}$$

Annual interest payments are equal to 10% × USD 5 million = USD 0.5 million and the tax saving is 40% × USD 0.5 million = USD 0.2 million. The tax saving is only as risky as the debt that generates it. In the absence of the interest rate subsidy, the debt would cost 12%, so 12% is the appropriate discount rate for calculating the present value of tax savings on interest interest payments:

$$(40\% \times \text{USD } 0.5) \sum_{t=1}^{5} (1.12)^{-t} = \text{USD } 0.721 \text{ million.}$$

Without the interest rate subsidy from the World Bank, interest on the USD 5 million debt would be 12% × USD 5 million = USD 0.6 million. Thus, the subsidy is worth USD 0.6 million – USD 0.5 million = USD 0.1 million. As with the tax saving, the interest rate subsidy is only as risky as the debt that generates it, i.e. 12%. The present value is:

$$\text{USD } 0.1 \sum_{t=1}^{5} (1.12)^{-t} = \text{USD } 0.360 \text{ million.}$$

Thus:

$$APV = -\text{USD } 10.000 + \text{USD } 10.152 + \text{USD } 0.721 + \text{USD } 0.360 = \text{USD } 1.233 \text{ million.}$$

[9] The CAPM can be used to estimate this rate. It will be equal to the cost of debt reflecting the country's systematic financial risk plus a premium for the project debt's systematic risk. As explained above, the cost of debt reflecting the country's systematic risk can be estimated through option pricing techniques. The risk premium for the project debt's systematic risk can be estimated using the same methodology as for the project's systematic operating and economic risk. First, the required rate of return on debt is presented in terms of its systematic risk relative to the performance of the overall economy:

$$\overline{R}_{ib} = r_f + \beta_{ib} (\overline{R}_c - r_f)$$

where

$\overline{R}_{ib}$ represents the required rate of return on the project's debt and β_{ib} represents the measure of the debt's systematic risk of relative to the economy's performance.

Second, systematic risk on the project's debt is combined with systematic country risk:

$$\overline{R}_{ib} = r_f + \beta_{ib} \beta_c (\overline{R}_w - r_f)$$

Thus, $\beta_{ib} \beta_c (\overline{R}_w - r_f)$ represents the risk premium for the debt's systematic risk.

implies constant relative prices and the same rate of inflation in both countries, a clearly unrealistic assumption. Relative prices can and do vary, rates of inflation differ widely across countries and exchange rates move constantly. These realities can cause a disequilibrium in the supply and demand for foreign currency and have consequences for cash flows to both the project and the parent. These unanticipated variations in cash flows due to disequilibrium in the supply and demand of foreign currency can be called foreign exchange exposure.

Foreign exchange controls: blocked funds

When a country's exchange rate is under attack, one of the most popular measures for blunting the attack is the imposition of controls that limit or forbid movements of funds into and out of the country. These exchange controls can have an important impact on the project's value to the parent, even when the exchange rate and other relevant variables remain unchanged.

Consider, for example, the foregoing direct investment project in a country whose exchange rate is under pressure for a devaluation. In order to relieve pressure on the exchange rate, the government installs a number of foreign exchange controls. One of the controls concerns cash flows from direct foreign investments and forbids the repatriation of profits and depreciation until an investment is either sold or terminated. Consequently, the project's funds are effectively blocked and must be reinvested in the host country until the termination of the project in ten years' time. After careful analysis, it is decided that the funds can be reinvested in the host country's money market at the rate of 10% per year. Furthermore, it is also decided that the exchange controls will be effective and that the exchange rate will remain at one peso for one dollar. In light of the new conditions, we can re-evaluate the project's value for the parent company.

The investment is still USD 1,030,000 or PES 1,030,000. Since the exchange rate is expected to remain constant, the annual cash flows to the project are USD 160,000 or PES 160,000 (USD 70,000 net income plus USD 100,000 depreciation less USD 10,000 tax liability in Nafta) but they will not be received by the parent until the end of the tenth year. Reinvested at 10% their terminal value is:

$$\text{USD } 160,000 \sum_{t=1}^{10} (1.10)^{t-1} = \text{USD } 2,549,988.$$

Adding the USD 30,000 from the investment in working capital, gives a total terminal value of USD 2,579,988. Discounting the total terminal value at the 12% cost of capital for the project gives

$$\text{USD } 2,579,988 \times (1.12)^{-10} = \text{USD } 830,687.$$

The NPV of the investment for the parent is the cash flows to the project plus the present value of the USD 24,000 annual profit from sales of materials less the investment outlay:

$$\text{NPV} = -\text{USD } 1,030,000 + \text{USD } 830,687 + \text{USD } 136,605 = -\text{USD } 62,708.$$

The NPV of the investment is a negative USD 62,708, which means that blocking the funds has made the project unacceptable to the parent. If the investment had already been made before the fund blockage occurred, the project would be exposed to measures of this type. In the present case, the exposure amounts to USD 62,708 but would change from year to year as the project neared its maturity date. As a practical matter, measuring exposure to foreign exchange controls such as blocked funds is difficult because there is such a wide range of measures and combinations of measures that could be applied by the authorities. Nevertheless, its existence is a reality, even in the most advanced industrial countries, and some account should be taken of it.

Economic exposure

In Chapter 13 we saw that the economic exposure to exchange risk is associated with how the company's cash flows in domestic currency will be influenced by variations in the exchange rate. In fact, the relationship is subtle and often very complicated. The simplest case is the *ceteris paribus* case when only the exchange rate changes and everything else remains the same.

Scenario 1: Only the exchange rate changes

Suppose, for example, that just after the investment of USD 1,030,000 is made in Argenuay, the exchange rate falls from PES 1 for USD 1 to PES 1.05 for USD 1. After careful analysis, the company concludes that this will have no effect on the sales price, the number of units sold or the cost of domestic inputs. Table 21.4 shows the results of this scenario on the cash flows to the parent company. They can be compared to the cash flows before the devaluation in Table 21.3. (Remember that in Table 21.3 we assumed that the exchange rate remained stable such that the flows in dollars and pesos were the same.)

Profits fall from PES 100 000 before the devaluation to PES 95 000 because the cost of imported inputs in pesos rises from PES 0.5 to PES 0.525 (P1.05 / USD 1×USD 0.5), which makes the cost per unit equal to PES 0.5 + PES 0.525 = PES 1.025.

The consequences on the cash flows to the parent are even more striking. Only profits on the after-tax earnings on sales of materials by the parent company are unaffected by the devaluation. At the exchange rate of 1.05, the net income of PES 66,500 falls to USD 63,334, depreciation falls to USD 95,238 and the tax liability in Nafta falls to USD 9,048. The total annual cash flow falls from USD 184,000 to USD 173,524. The dollar value of the investment in working capital falls to USD 28,571 (PES 30 000/1.05). Putting all this together gives a NPV of

$$NPV = -USD\ 1,030,000 + USD\ 173,524 \sum_{t=1}^{10} (1.12)^{-t} + USD\ 28,571 \times (1.12)^{-10}$$

$$= -USD\ 1,030,000 + USD\ 980,449 + USD\ 9199$$

$$= -USD\ 40,352.$$

The NPV falls from a positive USD 19,260 before the devaluation to a negative USD 40,352 after the devaluation. In this case, we could say that the project's exposure to a 5% devaluation is USD 59,612. We could also express the exposure as an elasticity and say that the 5% devaluation caused a variation in the present value of the cash flows of

$$\frac{-USD\ 59,612}{USD\ 1,049,260} = -5.68\%$$

where USD 1,049,260 is the present value of the cash flows to the parent in the case of constant prices and constant exchange rates. Even in the simplest case where only the exchange rate changes and all the other variables remain the same, the consequences on the cash flows to the parent ae substantial.

Table 21.4 Cash flows generated by direct investment in Argenuay (1)

Cash flows generated by operations in Argenuay

Investment in equipment	USD 1,000,000
Increase in working capital	USD 30,000
Tax rate in Argenuay = 30%	
Cost of capital = 12%	
Cost per unit = PES 1.025	
Price per unit = PES 2.00	
Number of units sold = 200 000	
Sales (200 000 x PES 2.00)	PES 400,000
Operating costs (200 000 x PES 1.025)	–PES 205,000
Depreciation	–PES 100,000
EBIT	PES 95,000
Taxes at 30%	–PES 28,500
Net income	PES 66,500

Earnings on sales of materials by parent company

Sales (200 000 x USD 0.50)	USD 100,000
Cost (200 000 x USD 0.30)	–USD 60,000
Profit before taxes	USD 40,000
Taxes at 40%	–USD 16,000
Profits after taxes	USD 24,000

Tax Adjustment

Taxes owed in Nafta (0.4 x USD 90,476)	USD 36,190
Tax credit from Argenuay	–USD 27,142
Tax liability in Nafta	USD 9,048

Cash Flows

Net income from operations (PES 66,500/1.05)	USD 63,334
Depreciation (PES 100,000/1.05)	USD 95,238
Profits from sales of materials	USD 24,000
Tax liability in Nafta	–USD 9,048
Cash flow	USD 173,524

Scenario 2: The devaluation causes a change in host country prices

From Chapter 2 we know that a change in the exchange rate causes changes in relative prices. A relative price change could affect the cost of a company's inputs as well as the price of its outputs. Take the case of a company producing a good whose only demand comes from local consumption but using a large proportion of imported inputs. A devaluation would cause a rise of the local currency cost of its imported inputs. The reaction of the price of its output depends on who its clients are and whether or not they lose in the devaluation. A company producing an import substitute that is consumed by those who gain from a devaluation is likely to see its prices rise considerably. On the other hand, a company producing a non-exchanged good consumed by losers in the devaluation is likely to see a fall in demand and its prices: relative prices for sure and possibly absolute prices. Changes such as these cause changes in the cash flows to the subsidiary and alter its market value. They also cause changes in parent company cash flows and, consequently, its economic exposure to foreign exchange risk.

Suppose that the project is producing import substitutes and that, after the devaluation, demand increases. Since the project is already operating at full capacity, output cannot be increased and prices rise by 5% to PES 2.10 per unit. Suppose further that since Argenuay is a price-taker and the supply elasticities for its imports are very high, the foreign currency cost of imports stays constant so that their domestic price rises by the full amount of the devaluation to PES 0.525 per unit. Finally, suppose that the domestic input has a low supply elasticity and that the devaluation raises demand so that its price rises by 7.5% to PES 0.5375. Total cost per unit will be PES 1.0625, an increase of 6.25%. Table 21.5 shows the effects of this scenario on parent company cash flows.

It is interesting to note that, in spite of a larger percentage increase in costs than in the sales price, net income to the project is higher in pesos and dollars than it is when the exchange rate is not expected to change (USD 71,667 versus USD 70,000). The reason is that the sales price is twice as large as the cost per unit. This gain is offset by by higher taxes in Nafta and a loss on the dollar value of depreciation. Total annual cash flows are equal to USD 180,667 compared to USD 184,000 in the constant exchange rate scenario. NPV falls to

$$NPV = -USD\ 1,030,000 + USD\ 180,667 \sum_{t=1}^{10} (1.12)^{-t} + USD\ 28,571 \times (1.12)^{-10}$$

$$= -USD\ 1,030,000 + USD\ 1,020,809 + USD\ 9199$$

$$= USD\ 8.$$

The NPV is positive but close to zero. In this case the foreign exchange exposure was USD 19,252 or -1.83%.

Scenario 3: A constant exchange rate and domestic inflation

It is clear from the two foregoing examples that a project's economic exposure to exchange risk depends on many factors such as the type of product, its competitors, its client-base, taxes, the composition of its costs and the situation of its suppliers. The exchange rate does not have to change, however, for a project to be exposed to exchange risk. Another kind of exchange risk can arise from a constant exchange rate in the face of local inflation. Remember from Chapter 2 that the central bank can intervene in the market to make up the difference between the supply and demand for foreign currency in order to keep the exchange rate constant. Central bank intervention is usually effected in such a way that the decrease in the money supply that would normally result from the intervention is neutralized. In this case, intervention is accompanied by money expansion and a rise in prices. When the exchange rate is constant and prices rise, the economic exposure to exchange rate risk comes about through a change in the real exchange rate. The real exchange rate refers to an economy's overall terms of trade and measures an economy's competitiveness. It is equal to the nominal exchange rate deflated by the ratio of the price levels in the two countries.[10] It can be written

$$\text{Real exchange rate} = S(D\ /\ F) \times \frac{P_F}{P_D}$$

---

[10] Sometimes the real exchange rate is expressed in a multilateral context as an index of the real exchange rate of a representative basket of foreign currencies, each weighted by its importance in trade with the country in question. In this case it is called "the real trade-weighted exchange rate".

Table 21.5 Cash flows generated by direct investment in Argenuay (2)

Cash flows generated by operations in Argenuay	
Investment in equipment	USD 1,000,000
Increase in working capital	USD 30,000
Tax rate in Argenuay = 30%	
Cost of capital = 12%	
Cost per unit = PES 1.0625	
Price per unit = PES 2.10	
Number of units sold = 200 000	
Sales (200 000 × PES 2.10)	PES 420,000
Operating costs (200 000 × PES 1.0625)	–PES 212,500
Depreciation	–PES 100,000
EBIT	PES 107,500
Taxes at 30%	–PES 32,250
Net income	PES 75,250
Earnings on sales of materials by parent company	
Sales (200 000 × USD 0.50)	USD 100,000
Cost (200 000 × USD 0.30)	–USD 60,000
Profit before taxes	USD 40,000
Taxes at 40%	–USD 16,000
Profits after taxes	USD 24,000
Tax Adjustment	
Taxes owed in Nafta (0.4 × USD 102,381)	USD 40,952
Tax credit from Argenuay	–USD 30,714
Tax liability in Nafta	USD 10,238
Cash Flows	
Net income from operations (PES 75,250/1.05)	USD 71,667
Depreciation (PES 100,000/1.05)	USD 95,238
Profits from sales of materials	USD 24,000
Tax liability in Nafta	–USD 10,238
Cash flow	USD 180,667

where P refers to the price level and D and F refer to domestic and foreign. Thus, if the nominal exchange rate is constant and the foreign price level rises relative to the domestic price level, the real exchange rate depreciates. In other words, domestic currency has less purchasing power. It implies a gain in competitiveness insofar as domestic goods are relatively cheaper compared to foreign goods. On the other hand, if the nominal exchange rate is constant and the domestic price level rises relative to the foreign price level, the real exchange rate appreciates and the domestic currency has more purchasing power. It implies a loss of competitiveness insofar as domestic goods are relatively more expensive than foreign goods.

A change in the real exchange rate suggests that purchasing power parity is violated. Remember from Chapter 3 that purchasing power parity holds that the exchange rate should reflect the ratio of price levels in the two countries. The foreign exchange exposure comes from the effects of maintaining a constant exchange rate, despite inflation differentials, on the company's cash flows.

Suppose that the domestic price level rises by 5% as a result of the government's intervention in the foreign exchange market. The unit cost of production rises only by 2.5% to PES 1.025 because 50% of inputs are foreign sourced and their price does not change. On the other hand, the prices of imports that compete with the project's output do not rise either. Consequently, if project output prices rise in line with its costs, sales will be lost. Suppose that the decision is made to maintain market share by holding prices constant. Table 21.6 shows the effects on the parent company's cash flows. Annual parent cash flows

Table 21.6 Cash flows generated by direct investment in Argenuay (3)

Cash flows generated by operations in Argenuay	
Investment in equipment	USD 1,000,000
Increase in working capital	USD 30,000
Tax rate in Argenuay = 30%	
Cost of capital = 12%	
Cost per unit = PES 1.025	
Price per unit = PES 2.00	
Number of units sold = 200 000	
Sales (200 000 × PES 2.00)	PES 400,000
Operating costs (200 000 × PES 1.025)	−PES 205,000
Depreciation	−PES 100,000
EBIT	PES 95,000
Taxes at 30%	−PES 28,500
Net income	PES 66,500
Earnings on sales of materials by parent company	
Sales (200 000 × USD 0.50)	USD 100,000
Cost (200 000 × USD 0.30)	−USD 60,000
Profit before taxes	USD 40,000
Taxes at 40%	−USD 16,000
Profits after taxes	USD 24,000
Tax Adjustment	
Taxes owed in Nafta (0.4 × USD 95,000)	USD 38,000
Tax credit from Argenuay	−USD 28,500
Tax liability in Nafta	USD 9,500
Cash Flows	
Net income from operations (PES 66,500/1.00)	USD 66,500
Depreciation (PES 100,000/1.00)	USD 100,000
Profits from sales of materials	USD 24,000
Tax liability in Nafta	−USD 9,500
Cash flow	USD 181,000

fall from USD 184,000 when prices and the exchange rate are constant to USD 181,000 when prices are allowed to change. NPV falls to

$$NPV = -USD\ 1,030,000 + USD\ 1,022,691 + USD\ 9659 = USD\ 2350,$$

which is a loss of USD 16,910 or –1.61%.

Accounting exposure

The question of accounting exposure arises because the balance sheet accounts of foreign subsidiaries must be translated from foreign currency into home currency before consolidation with the parent company's accounts. The value of the various assets and liabilities can vary depending on whether they are translated at the exchange rate that prevailed when they were acquired (historical rate) or at the current exchange rate. The question boils down to which assets and liabilities should be translated at which rate. The question is important because, although it has little economic meaning, it can have substantial tax consequences. Four general translation methods are available:

- current/non-current
- monetary/non-monetary
- temporal
- current rate.

Current/non-current method

In the current/non-current method all the foreign subsidiary's current assets and liabilities are translated into home currency at the current exchange rate. Non-current assets and liabilities are translated at the historical rate, which is the rate that prevailed when they were acquired. The income statement is translated at the average exchange rate over the period, except for items like depreciation that are associated with non-current assets or liabilities.

Monetary/non-monetary method

The monetary/non-monetary method discriminates on the basis of monetary and non-monetary assets and liabilities. It translates monetary assets and liabilities that designate a payment of a fixed amount of foreign currency units (cash, accounts receivable, accounts payable and debt) at the current exchange rate. Non-monetary items, such as inventory and fixed assets, are translated at their historical rates. The income statement is translated at the average exchange rate over the period, except for non-monetary items like depreciation and cost of goods sold, which are translated at the same exchange rate as their corresponding balance sheet items.

Temporal method

The temporal method and the monetary/non-monetary method differ in their theoretical underpinnings. The monetary/non-monetary method discriminates on the basis of the types of assets in question, whereas the temporal method discriminates on the basis of cost evaluation – historical versus market. The only practical difference between the two concerns inventories. In the temporal method, if inventory is shown on the balance sheet at market value, it is translated at the current rate. The income statement is translated at the average rate over the period except for the cost of goods sold and depreciation.

Current rate method

The current rate method makes no discrimination between different items and translates all of them at the current exchange rate.

The option approach to investment under uncertainty

As useful as it is, the NPV rule has a weakness in that it is based on the unrealistic implicit assumptions that the investment is either a now-or-never proposition that will be unavailable in the future or that it is reversible and that the expenditures can somehow be recovered in case things do not turn out as expected. Most investments do not meet these conditions. In fact, in practice, irreversibility and the possibility of delay are important characteristics of most investments. The option approach to investment under uncertainty complements the NPV rule by directly incorporating these characteristics into the decision-making process. An example will make this clear.[11]

Going back to the example at the beginning of the chapter, we had a project that involved an initial outlay of USD 2250. The income for year zero was USD 250 and there was a 50% probability that in one year's time annual income would rise to USD 350 and remain there for ever. There was also a 50% probability that in one year's time annual income would fall to USD 150 and remain there for ever. The expected annual income in one year's time was equal to:

$$(0.5 \times USD\ 350) + (0.5 \times USD\ 150) = USD\ 250,$$

and, supposing that the appropriate discount rate was 10%, the NPV was:

$$NPV = -USD\ 2250 + \sum_{t=0}^{\infty} USD\ 250(1.1)^{-t} = USD\ 500.$$

Since the NPV is positive, according to the NPV rule, the investment should be undertaken. Suppose, however, that we decide to wait and see what happens. If income falls to USD 150, the NPV will be equal to the project's net value at the beginning of period one discounted back one period (remember that there is no income or expenditure in year zero):

$$NPV = \left[-USD\ 2250 + \sum_{t=0}^{\infty} USD\ 150(1.1)^{-t} \right] \frac{1}{1.1} = [-USD\ 600]\frac{1}{1.1} = -USD\ 545.45.$$

Since the NPV is negative, the project will not be undertaken. If income rises to USD 350, the NPV will be:

$$NPV = \left[-USD\ 2250 + \sum_{t=0}^{\infty} USD\ 350(1.1)^{-t} \right] \frac{1}{1.1} = [USD\ 1600]\frac{1}{1.1} = USD\ 1454.54.$$

and the project will be undertaken. Thus, since no income or expenditure occurs if the project is not undertaken, the NPV of the project is equal to the NPV of the project if it is undertaken times the probability (50%) that it will effectively be undertaken:

$$NPV = 0.5[USD\ 0.00] + 0.5[USD\ 1454.54] = USD\ 727.27.$$

---

[11] See Dixit and Pindyck (1994), Trigeorgis (1996) and Amram and Kulatilaka (1999).

By waiting a year, the value of the project is USD 727.27 whereas it is only worth USD 500 if we invest today. It is clearly preferable to wait and the value of the option to wait is the difference between the two NPV's:

$$USD\ 727.27 - USD\ 500 = USD\ 227.27.$$

In Exhibit 21.2 we show how to value the investment using option pricing methods.

Simple applications: A Sportswear factory in Russia

Ekan Inc., a US sportswear company, is negotiating to build a factory in Russia near Leningrad. The initial investment will amount to USD 25 million and will generate expected net cash flows of USD 11 million per year for ten years at which point the personnel and local investors will inherit the plant. Given the ongoing economic, social and political turmoil in the country, Ekan has estimated its required rate of return at a relatively high 15% but, even with this, the project still looks worthwhile with an NPV of USD 30.2 million:

$$NPV = -USD\ 25 + \sum_{t=1}^{10} USD\ 11(1.15)^{-t} = USD\ 30.2.$$

Exhibit 21.2 Valuing the investment as an option

The investment can also be valued using the binomial methodology developed in Chapter 8:

Step 1: Sell one call and buy Δ units of output for a cash flow of $C_0 - \Delta \times USD\ 250$.

Step 2: Choose Δ so that the outcome of the portfolio will be the same in an up-move or a down-move. In an up-move the call will be worth USD 1600. The Δ units of output will be worth $\Delta \times USD \times 350$ plus the interest of 10% on the investment for a cash flow of $\Delta \times USD\ 350 + 0.10 \times \Delta \times USD\ 250$.[12] In a down-move the the call is worth USD 0 so the cash flow will be $USD\ 0 + \Delta \times USD\ 150 + 0.10 \times \Delta \times USD\ 250$. Equating the two cash flows gives:

$$USD\ 1600 + \Delta \times USD\ 350 + 0.10 \times \Delta \times USD\ 250 = USD\ 0 + \Delta \times USD\ 150 + 0.10 \times \Delta \times USD\ 250$$

$$\Delta = 8$$

Step 3: Borrow $(\Delta \times USD\ 150 + 0.10 \times \Delta \times USD\ 250)/(1.10)$. Since the portfolio is riskless with a zero outcome in all cases, its value is zero:

$$C_0 - 8 \times USD\ 250 + \frac{8 \times USD\ 150 + 0.10 \times 8 \times USD\ 250}{1.10} = 0$$

$$C_0 = USD\ 727.27.$$

[12] The interest arises from the fact that the expected price is USD 250, the same as the current price. There is no expected gain. The opportunity cost of holding this investment is 10%. Thus, no one would make this investment unless he was guaranteed the opportunity cost of holding it. Thus, in order to make the sale the short seller has to pay the opportunity cost. See Dixit and Pindyck (1994).

Ekan still has some doubts however. Although cash flow repatriation has been negotiated with the government and guaranteed, Ekan's directors are worried that the national elections due in two years time will bring in a new government that will throw out the agreement and make the project unprofitable. The company's political analyst is asked to assess the situation. His conclusion is that there is a 40% possibility that such a government will come to power in two years time. In this case, cash flows will fall to zero. He also estimates that in the political turmoil leading up to the election there is a 40% probability that cash flows will fall to zero. Thus, he estimates that expected cash flows over the ten years will be:

$$(0.6 \times USD\ 11) + (0.4 \times USD\ 0) = USD\ 6.6$$

and that NPV falls to

$$NPV = USD\ 25 + \sum_{t=1}^{10} USD\ 6.6(1.15)^{-t} = USD\ 8.12.$$

The NPV is still positive and it seems that it should be undertaken. By waiting two years, however, the analyst points out that the NPV can be calculated as the probability of the favorable outcome multiplied by the net value of the investment if the favorable outcome occurs, discounted two periods to the present (the discounting occurs because we are looking at the net value of the investment two years in the future if the favorable outcome occurs):

$$NPV = 0.6 \left[-USD\ 25 + \sum_{t=1}^{10} USD\ 11(1.15)^{-t} \right] \frac{1}{(1.15)^2} = USD\ 13.7.$$

This is USD 5.58 million higher than if the investment were undertaken immediately. Thus it is clear that it would be better to wait.

With this in mind, the Marketing Department feels that waiting two years is feasible but, in the meantime at least, some presence is absolutely necessary as a means of maintaining contacts and keeping a finger in the market. The Economics Department brings up the objection that the cost of the project could vary considerably in the course of two years. To this the analyst points out that USD 5.58 million, the value of the option to wait, could be spent to get the project under way and keep involved in the country. He also calculates how high the cost of the project would have to go to make waiting undesirable. This he does by equating the NPV of investing now and the NPV of waiting and leaving cost as the unknown:

$$USD\ 8.12 = 0.6 \left[-Cost + \sum_{t=1}^{10} USD\ 11(1.15)^{-t} \right] \frac{1}{(1.15)^2}$$

$$Cost = USD\ 37.3.$$

The cost of the project would have to rise by almost 50% to USD 37.3 million to make immediate investment preferable to waiting for the outcome of the elections in two years time. The Economics Department figures that cost could rise by a maximum of 15% and could even fall by that much. Thus, it is decided that the investment will be put off for two years but that in the meantime USD 2.5 million will be invested in office space and recruitment and training of management personnel.

More complex applications: Investments in natural resources

Assumptions and methodology

Projects involving exploitation of natural resources with an active spot market lend themselves particularly well to the options approach to investment evaluation. Natural resources on the whole are homogeneous and with an active spot market furnish a perfect "spanning" asset – that is, an asset whose risk tracks the risk of the investment. Brennan and Schwartz showed that the purchase and exploitation of a gold mine is equivalent to a series of options on the gold contained in the mine.[13] Paddock, Siegel and Smith used the same approach to evaluate investments in oilfields.[14] Many other applications have followed.[15]

In its simplest form, the procedure involves associating the income from the investment with the market price of the natural resource that is being produced. The life of the investment is divided into periods (years, quarters, months, etc.) and the decision to produce or not to produce at the beginning of each period is considered as an option that can be valued using traditional option pricing techniques. The information required to value the options is either directly observable or can be calculated from observable data. Using the notation from Chapters 8 and 12, it includes:

- V_0 = the market price of the spanning asset at time 0, which can be directly observed;
- t_i = the length of time ($i = 0, 1, 2, \dots n$) between time 0 and the beginning of each future period ($t_1, t_2, \dots t_n$);
- X_0 = the after-tax production costs at time 0 which make it possible to estimate after tax production costs ($X_1, X_2 \dots X_n$) for the following periods. It is assumed that production costs evolve slowly and predictably;
- σ = the standard deviation of the spanning asset's continuously compounded annual rate of return, calculated from historical data on the market price;
- r_i = the continuously compounded riskless rate of interest corresponding to each period ($i = 0, 1, 2, \dots n$), which can be observed directly or calculated from current data.

Thus, C_0^i, the value of the call option for period i, is given by the traditional Black-Scholes formula:

$$C_0^i = V_0 N(d_1) - X_i e^{-r_i} N(d_2) \tag{21.1}$$

where $N(d)$ is the value of the standardized normal cumulative distribution evaluated at d.

The project's NPV is equal to the sum of the option values less the amount of the investment:

$$NPV = -Cost + \sum_{i=0}^{n} C_0^i \tag{21.2}$$

---

[13] See Brennan and Schwartz (1985).

[14] See Paddock, Siegel and Smith (1988).

[15] See, for example, R. Morck, R. E. Schwartz and D. Strangeland, "The valuation of forestry resources under stochastic prices and inventories", *Journal of Financial and Quantitative Analysis*, Vol. 24, (December 1989), p.p. 473–487; R. Gibson, and E. Schwartz, "Stochastic convenience yield and the pricing of oil contingent claims", *Journal of Finance*, Vol. 45 (July 1990), p.p. 959–976.

This procedure has several advantages over the traditional NPV approach. First of all, the well known, tried and tested Black-Scholes option pricing formula can be used. Secondly, it overcomes the difficulty of forecasting long-term commodity prices, well known for their unpredictability. Thirdly, since all discounting is done at the riskless rate, it eliminates the necessity of estimating the risk-adjusted discount factor. It does, however, make some unrealistic assumptions above and beyond those that we pointed out in Chapter 12. The central assumption is that the exploitation activity can be stopped or started at will with little or no cost. (In many countries, where exploitation of natural resources is concerned, this assumption may not be far from the truth, however.) It is also assumed that overhead and maintenance costs during shutdowns are negligible and that there is no middle ground between full production and full stop. Stocking is impossible as well and all output is sold at the going market price. In fact, all income and expenditure is realized at the beginning of the period, with deliveries taking place during the period.

In many situations, these assumptions will not be too far from the truth and, consequently, will not distort the analysis. When this is not the case, the analysis must be adapted to the specific situation.

Exploiting an oilfield: Petroleum Capital L.C. in South America[16]

Consider the classic case of a South American government that has decided to concede the exploitation of a fully equipped oilfield and invites bids on an international tender for an initial period of ten years. The installed capacity of the oilfield is 1,000,000 barrels per year.

Petroleum Capital L.C., a small oil company operating out of Dallas, Texas, was considering bidding on the project. To arrive at an estimate of how much they could bid, they used the options approach and decided to reason on a yearly basis. They realized that more frequent evaluations based on a shorter time unit (the month or the quarter, for example) would give a more precise estimate but they knew that the difference is relatively small. They also knew that more frequent evaluations would give the project a higher value. Since they wanted to avoid overbidding at all cost, the undervaluation resulting from the lower frequency of evaluation guaranteed them a safety margin.

They continued their estimate by making several assumptions:

1. The wells would either function at full capacity or not at all, and the cost of turning them on and off as well as maintenance costs during shut-downs were null. In fact, the wells could operate at less than full capacity and the start-up/shut-down and maintenance costs were not zero but they were very low. After analysis, Petroleum Capital L.C. concluded that the gain from flexible output just about offset the costs and justified the assumption.

2. Production costs, including royalties and taxes, were equal to USD 12 per barrel and would remain constant over the life of the contract. They represent the exercise price, X, in the options pricing model.

3. The decision on whether or not to produce would be made at the beginning of each year. If the spot price of oil was higher than the after-tax cost of production, the decision to produce would be made. On that day, expenditure for the total year's production costs would be made and the total year's output would be sold at that day's spot price. If the spot price of oil was less than the cost of production, the field would be shut down for the year. Thus, income would either be equal to the difference between the spot price and and the cost of production or zero, whichever was larger.

---

[16] See Clark and Marois (1996) for a similar example.

4. The standard deviation of the percentage change in the spot price of oil would be constant and equal to the historical standard deviation, which was estimated as 0.25.

5. The riskless rate of interest for each option would be constant over the life of the option and equal to the current riskless rate. The current term structure, estimated by a well known investment bank, was given as follows. Zero coupon riskless rates:

1 year: 8.00%
2 years: 8.20%
3 years: 8.35%
4 years: 8.45%
5, 6, 7, 8, 9, 10 years: 8.50%.

At the time of the analysis, the current spot price of a barrel of crude oil was USD 15 and, thus, all the information necessary for the estimation exercise can be summarized as follows:

$V_0 = \text{USD } 15$
$\sigma = 0.25$
$X_0 = X_1 = \ldots = X_{10} = \text{USD } 12$
$t_i, (i = 0, 1, 2, \ldots, 10) = 1, 2, 3, 4, 5, 6, 7, 8, 9, 10$
$r_{f1} = 8.00\%$
$r_{f2} = 8.20\%$
$r_{f3} = 8.35\%$
$r_{f4} = 8.45\%$
$r_{f5\ldots10} = 8.50\%$

Using Equation 21.1, Petroleum Capital L.C. estimated the maximum price that they could bid for the oil concession by calculating the value of each option to produce one barrel of oil and multiplying by the number of barrels of output. This information is summarized in Table 21.7. It shows that the maximum they could bid was USD 75,464,190.

On the merits of the project itself, the Managing Director of Petroleum Capital L.C. had no problem with a bid in the USD 70 million range. He did, however, fear that once the contract was signed and the payment had been made, politics in the host country might disrupt his operations. The danger was not so much for the immediate future but a populist, nationalistic, anti-American movement was starting to spread from some of the less populous regions of the country to the cities. He feared that if it gained too much force, operations such as his would be jeopardized. Consequently, he hired a consulting firm to estimate the probabilities for each year of the contract that some unforeseen political event would not upset his oilfield operations. The results of the analysis are summarized in Table 21.8.

Using the probabilities supplied by the consulting firm, the MD then recalculated the price he was willing to pay for the oilfield concession by multiplying each year's expected cash flow by the corresponding probability as shown in Table 21.9. He thus concluded that he could make a top bid of $64 million.[17]

---

[17] The project's systematic operating risk was effectively prived in the Black-Scholes formula. The country-specific risk, however, was not. Given the nature of an oilfield exploitation concession where costs are generally determined by international prices or fixed by contract and output is sold abroad for dollars, there is little in the way of country-specific economic, financial or currency risk. Country-specific political risk is another question, however, and the MD, acting as he did, was treating the political risk as totally non-diversifiable.

Table 21.7 Values of the option to produce and present values of expected cash flows for oilfield exploitation

1 Option value for year i (USD)	2 No. of barrels per year	3 PV (in USD) of expected cash flow (column 1 × column 2)
$C_0^1 = 4.09785$	1 000 000	4,097,850
$C_0^2 = 5.11485$	1 000 000	5,114,850
$C_0^3 = 6.00967$	1 000 000	6,009,670
$C_0^4 = 6.80599$	1 000 000	6,805,990
$C_0^5 = 7.51478$	1 000 000	7,514,780
$C_0^6 = 8.14213$	1 000 000	8,142,130
$C_0^7 = 8.71136$	1 000 000	8,711,360
$C_0^8 = 9.22965$	1 000 000	9,229,650
$C_0^9 = 9.70271$	1 000 000	7,702,710
$C_0^{10} = 10.13520$	1 000 000	10,135,200
Total = 75.46419		Total = 75,464,190

Source: E. Clark and B. Marois, *Managing Risk in International Business* (London: Thomson Learning, 1996).

Table 21.8 Probability of no disruptions due to unforeseen political events

Year	1	2	3	4	5	6	7	8	9	10
Probability	0.95	0.95	0.93	0.90	0.90	0.85	0.85	0.80	0.75	0.75

Table 21.9 Expected cash flows adjusted for political risk

1 PV (in USD) of expected cash flow	2 Probability	3 PV (in USD) of expected cash flow adjusted for political risk
4,097,850	0.95	3,892,957.50
5,114,850	0.95	4,859,107.50
6,009,670	0.93	5,588,993.10
6,805,990	0.90	6,125,391.00
7,514,780	0.90	6,763,302.00
8,142,130	0.85	6,920,810.50
8,711,360	0.85	7,404,656.00
9,229,650	0.80	7,383,720.00
9,702,710	0.75	7,277,032.50
10,135,200	0.75	7,601,400.00
Total = 75,464,190		Total = 63,817,370.00

Source: E. Clark and B. Marois, *Managing Risk in International Business* (London: Thomson Learning, 1996).

Conclusions on the option approach to investment

In this section we have outlined the principles behind the option approach to investment under uncertainty and shown some of its simplest applications to problems associated with foreign direct investment. In fact, insofar as the option approach itself is concerned, we have done little more than scratch the surface. There is a rich and growing literature on the subject, employing relatively complicated techniques, that has opened the science of investment decision making to significant new horizons. The techniques involved are generally beyond the scope of this book, although we did use some of them in the appendices at the end of several chapters. It is important to remember, however, that these new techniques are not substitutes for judicious, country-specific risk assessment in the decision-making process. If anything, they increase its importance insofar as they make it possible to exploit country-specific risk analyses more effectively and creatively. This having been said, they do require more focus and precision than traditional country-specific risk analysis has been able to supply. It is no longer sufficient, for example, to signal the existence of a general political risk or the probability of an unfavorable outcome. The analyst must be able to distinguish between political risk that is diversifiable and that which is not. He must also be clear as to how unfavorable outcomes will affect the investment in question. Consequently, it is important for the analyst to understand the requirements of the option approach as well as its strengths and weaknesses. It is also important to understand how the country-specific element can be integrated into the analysis. The background to this exercise was developed in Chapters 10 and 12. We will take up these questions again in Chapter 22.

Beyond mean-variance

Political risk and the shortcomings of mean-variance analysis

The thrust of our analysis up to now has relied on the mean-variance criterion and the Markowitz paradigm. As useful and powerful as it is, however, this analytical framework does have some shortcomings. The main shortcoming is that it is not always consistent with expected utility maximization. In fact, it is certain to be consistent with expected utility maximization only in the cases of a quadratic utility function or normally distributed outcomes. Although the central limit theorem considerably expands the number of density distributions that can be incorporated under the normal distribution label, there is a growing body of empirical evidence that casts considerable doubt on the validity of routinely assuming normally distributed outcomes. To see how the mean-variance criterion can differ from the criterion of expected utility maximization consider, for example, two investments with the characteristics set out in Table 21.10.

In mean-variance space any rational individual would prefer investment 1 to investment 2 because investment 1 has the higher mean and the lower variance. Now consider an individual with a logarithmic utility function $u(R) = \ln(R)$. He will choose the investment that will give him the highest expected utility:

$$E\left[u(\widetilde{R}_1)\right] = 0.8u(1) + 0.2u(100) = 0.8 \ln 1 + 0.2 \ln 100 = 0.4$$

$$E\left[u(\widetilde{R}_2)\right] = 0.99u(10) + 0.1u(1000) = 0.99 \ln(10) + 0.01 \ln(1000) = 1.02$$

Investment 2 gives the higher expected utility and is preferred to investment 1 even though its variance is higher and its mean lower. In this case, mean-variance is not a good decision-making criterion.

Table 21.10 A comparison of two investments

Outcome	Probability	Mean	Variance
Investment 1			
1	0.8	20.8	1468
100	0.2		
Investment 2			
10	0.99	19.9	9703
1000	0.01		

The foregoing is important for political risk analysis because political risk often manifests itself in ways that make the assumption of normally distributed outcomes and the validity of the mean-variance criterion inappropriate. In fact, the precise nature of political risk often depends on the performance of a firm or the state of the economy. For example, some governments have a tendency to act mainly in bad times when the firm or the economy is in trouble. Others may act mainly in good times. Their actions can take many forms. They may reduce employers social charges or increase them, grant investment tax credits or impose price controls, expand credit or cut red tape, raise or lower the minimum wage, etc. The options are virtually limitless. The point is that the action they take is generated by the outcome or the state of nature. In this sense, the risk associated with their actions is said to be dependent. When this is the case, the criterion of expected utility maximization rather than the mean-variance criterion should be used in the analysis.

Clark and Jokung have shown that where the dependent risk occurs is important when discriminating among investments.[18] In fact, as we show in Appendix 21.1, *ceteris paribus,* projects where the political risk is associated with good outcomes are preferred to projects where the political risk is associated with less favorable outcomes. They call this theorem the "good times" rule. Thus, besides estimating what the risks are, it is also important to establish in what conditions the different risks are likely to occur. With this in mind, the criterion of expected utility maximization can be combined with the mean-variance criterion to discriminate between mutually exclusive investments. The procedure involves five steps.

1. Pinpoint the dependent political risk and then estimate the magnitude of its effects and the probabilities of its occurrence.

2. Assume that the dependent political risk is completely diversifiable and then estimate expected cash flows and the required rate of return according to the methods presented in the foregoing chapters.

3. Choose a well behaved utility function, meaning one that is strictly concave so that

$$u'(w) > 0, u''(w) < 0, u'''(w) > 0$$

where w represents wealth and the primes indicate the first, second and third derivatives. Any function with these characteristics will do since we are not interested in precisely

---

[18] See Clark and Jokung (1998).

how much expected utility is involved in each investment but rather in the ranking by which investment has more expected utility. We find that the logarithmic function is the easiest to work with.

4. Apply the information generated in step one in the chosen utility function to calculate the estimated utilities of the individual investments.

5. Compare the expected utilities and choose the one with the highest.

Pinpointing the political risk: An investment in the United States

In 1992, Little Snay, a British producer of wood furniture, had been considering building a factory in the southern United States for over three years. All the preliminary studies had been completed and, because of capacity constraints in its other factories, the decision could no longer be put off. It was decided to locate in the area of the lowlands of South Carolina at a cost of USD 100 million. The decision was based on three equi-probable scenarios drawn up by the Economics Department. Using traditional techniques, the required rate of return on the project had been estimated at 10%. Figure 21.1 shows the NPV for the three scenarios as well as the expected NPV, estimated at USD 600 million.

The only decision left to be made was the actual site of the factory. The choice had been narrowed down to two cities, Charleston, South Carolina and Savannah, Georgia, located about 100 miles to the south of Charleston. There was little to differentiate the two cities. Both had good port facilities, road and rail links to potential markets as well as a well developed economic infrastructure and a supply of relatively cheap, well qualified labor. The only significant difference was in city government. Joe Riley, Charleston's long-standing mayor, had a well earned reputation for high quality management and long-term planning. His strategy was to act in economic good times using tax breaks and subsidies to attract companies and property taxes and targeted assessments to fund developemnt projects and improve city services. This smoothed the ride through the bad times and made it possible to avoid costly or unpopular emergency measures. Savannah, on the other hand, had a history of not acting until the last minute and under duress. When the decisions were finally undertaken, they were generally sound, however, which is why Little Snay was seriously considering Savannah as the home for its factory. In fact, the Little Snay personnel who had visited both cities were indifferent between Savannah and Charleston as a place to live.

When Little Snay's Economics Department was asked to assess the effects of local government on the investment project, it came to the conclusion that the effects would basically be the same for both cities. For Charleston there was a 50–50 probability of plus or minus USD 100 million on the rosy scenario while for Savannah there was a 50–50 probability of plus or minus USD 100 million on the rainy scenario. Thus, there was still nothing

Figure 21.1 The project's NPV under different scenarios and the expected NPV

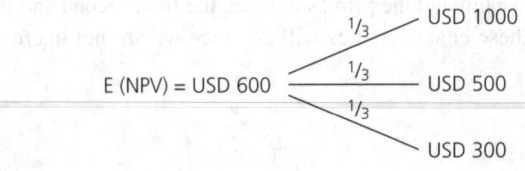

to separate the two cities. The project's expected NPV and standard deviation was the same for both. This information is summarized in Figure 21.2.

Finally, following the advice of an external consultant, the Economics Department decided to class the investments on the basis of expected utility using the logarithmic function with the following result:

Charleston

$$Eu(NPV_c) = \frac{1}{6}\ln(\text{USD }1100) + \frac{1}{6}\ln(\text{USD }900) + \frac{1}{3}\ln(\text{USD }500) + \frac{1}{3}\ln(\text{USD }300)$$

$$= 6.273$$

Savannah

$$Eu(NPV_s) = \frac{1}{3}\ln(\text{USD }1000) + \frac{1}{3}\ln(\text{USD }500) + \frac{1}{6}\ln(\text{USD }400) + \frac{1}{6}\ln(\text{USD }200)$$

$$= 6.256$$

On the criteria of expected utility, Charleston was clearly superior to Savannah and, consequently, the decision was made to build the factory in Charleston.

Figure 21.2 The project's expected NPV and standard deviation – Charleston and Savannah

Charleston

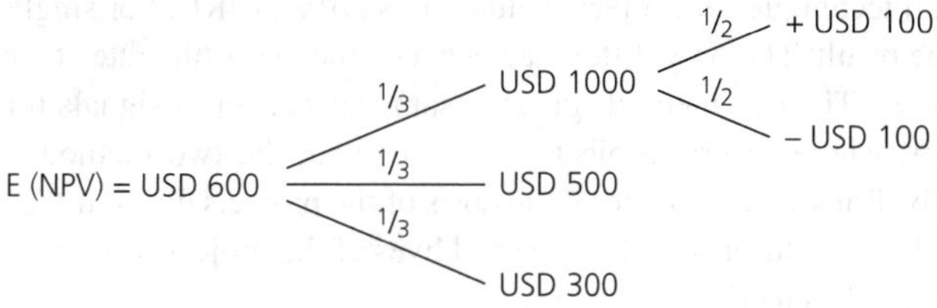

$\sigma^2 = \frac{1}{6}(1100 - 600)^2 + \frac{1}{6}(900 - 600)^2 + \frac{1}{3}(500 - 600)^2 + \frac{1}{3}(300 - 600)^2 = 90{,}000$

$\sigma^2 = \sqrt{90{,}000} = 300$

Savannah

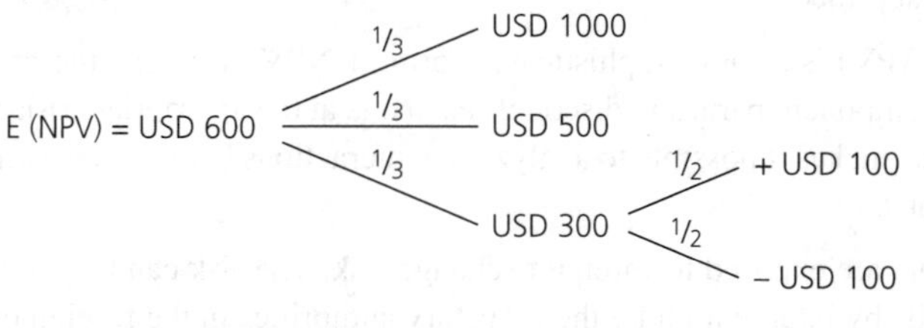

$\sigma^2 = \frac{1}{3}(1000 - 600)^2 + \frac{1}{3}(500 - 600)^2 + \frac{1}{6}(400 - 600)^2 + \frac{1}{6}(200 - 600)^2 = 90{,}000$

$\sigma^2 = \sqrt{90{,}000} = 300$

Source: E. Clark and B. Marois, *Managing Risk in International Business* (London: Thomson Learning, 1996).

Summary

1. The reasons for investing abroad are many and varied. They include the cost of labor, transport costs, diversification, operational constraints, special incentives, market considerations and factor advantages.

2. Whatever the reasons for investing abroad, the ultimate success of the investment and its effects on the firm's profitability depend on the cash flows that the investment generates. Hence capital budgeting and techniques for cash flow evaluation are crucial elements in the decision to invest. In the international context, determining and evaluating cash flows is more complicated than in the traditional capital budgeting problem.

3. The orthodox theory of investment is based on the rule of net present value. According to this rule, expected flows of income and expenditure are estimated for each period. These flows are then discounted at the appropriate discount rate. The NPV is found by subtracting the present value of the expenditure stream from the present value of the income stream. If the NPV is positive, the project is accepted. If it is negative, the project is rejected. If it is zero, we are indifferent. Where foreign direct investment is concerned, the two main questions for the NPV rule revolve around just how the expected cash flows should be estimated and what discount rate should be used for calculating present values.

4. The first step in the capital budgeting process involves determining the relevant cash flows. First of all, a distinction must be made between the cash flows accruing to the project and the cash flows accruing to the parent company. For cash flows to the parent, all incremental cash flows and costs – including lost export sales, supervisory fees, royalties and linked sales – should be charged to the project. Finally, taxes, subsidies and currency fluctuations should be included.

5. The most common technique for project evaluation is NPV or IRR. For single projects they give the same result. The only difference between the two is the rate at which cash flows are discounted. The two methods give the same accept-reject signals for specific projects. However, where several projects are concerned, the two methods can rank projects differently. Rankings can differ if the costs of the projects differ, if the temporal profiles of the cash flows differ or if the expected lives of the projects differ. In this case the NPV is theoretically superior.

6. When the lives of the projects are different, the NPVs cannot be compared directly. Two theoretically sound methods for handling this problem are available. The first method is to assume that each project is continuously replaced and then to find the NPV of each infinitely replaced alternative. The other method is to equate lives by assuming a reinvestment rate for the shorter projects for the additional years required to equate their lives to the longest project.

7. Adjusted NPV (APV) is a more sophisticated form of NPV. It breaks the cash flows down into their component parts and discounts each one at the appropriate risk-adjusted discount rate. This makes it possible to analyze the interactions between investment and financing decisions.

8. Direct investments are exposed to foreign exchange risk. The risk can be generated by exchange controls, by intervention by the monetary authorities in the foreign exchange markets or by a change in the exchange rate.

9. Because balance sheet accounts of foreign subsidiaries must be translated from foreign currency into home currency before consolidation with the parent company's accounts, direct investment projects are also vulnerable to accounting exposure. The value of assets

and liabilities can vary depending on whether they are translated at historical or current exchange rates. The question is simply, "Which assets and liabilities should be translated at which rate?" The question is important because, although it has little economic meaning, it can have substantial tax consequences. Four general translation methods are available; current/non-current, monetary/non-monetary, temporal and current rate.

10. The weakness of the conventional NPV rule is that it is based on the unrealistic implicit assumptions that the investment is either a now-or-never proposition that will be unavailable in the future or that it is reversible and that the expenditures can somehow be recovered in case things do not turn out as expected. Most investments do not meet these conditions. In fact, in practice, irreversibility and the possibility of delay are important characteristics of most investments. The option approach to investment under uncertainty complements the NPV rule by directly incorporating these characteristics into the decision-making process.

11. If we go beyond mean-variance analysis, it can be shown that for a well behaved utility function $- u'(w) > 0, u''(w) < 0, u'''(w) > 0 -$ incremental risk that is associated with good investment outcomes is preferred to risk associated with less good outcomes. This "good times" rule makes it possible to distinguish between otherwise equivalent investments.

Questions

Solutions to the following question are set out on the web site, details of which are included in the Preface.

1. What motivates corporations to invest abroad?

2. In capital budgeting for an international project, how can cash flows to the parent company differ from cash flows to the project itself?

3. What is the difference between the NPV and the IRR methods for project evaluation?

4. Consider two investment projects A and B with the following characteristics:

	Project A	*Project B*
Investment outlay	USD 1,000,000	USD 2,000,000
Investment in working capital	USD 50,000	USD 30,000
Annual EBIT	USD 133,333	USD 280,000
Project life	5 years	10 years
Cost of capital	10%	12%
Depreciation	USD 200,000 per year	USD 200,000 per year
Tax rate	40%	40%

Which one would you choose assuming:

a. infinite replacement

b. a reinvestment rate of 14% for both projects.

5. Suppose the funds of project A are blocked at the central bank at no interest until the end of the project when they can be repatriated in full. Is project A still acceptable?

6. Consider a five-year project with an outlay of GBP 1,000,000, annual cash flows of GBP 300,000, an initial exchange rate of 1 peso = GBP 1, and a cost of capital of 11%. The exchange rate is expected to go to PES 1.5 = GBP 1 at the beginning of year three. Other things being equal, would you accept the project?

7. Is it likely that other things would remain the same after a devaluation as we assumed in the preceding question? What could happen and how could it affect the project?

8. Is it possible to have foreign exchange exposure even if the nominal exchange rate remains unchanged? Explain.

9. What is accounting exposure and how is it measured?

10. Given the following information, calculate the project's APV.

$R_m^* = 12\%$

$r_f = 6\%$

$\beta_s = 1.8$

$\beta_b = 1.0$

$B = £10$ million

$S = £10$ million

$T = 40\%$

EBIT$(1-T)$ + depreciation = GBP 5.95 million

Cash outlay = GBP 20 million

Project life = 5 years.

11. How does the options approach to investment differ from the traditional NPV rule?

Appendix 21.1: Investment choice with dependent political risk

Consider a company with initial wealth, w_0, considering two investments, both with outcomes x_1, x_2, x_3 where $x_1 > x_2 > x_3$ and $Pr(x_1) = Pr(x_2) = Pr(x_3) = \frac{1}{3}$. Investment one has an equi-probable additive political risk, ε, associated with outcome one while investment two has the same equi-probable additive political risk associated with outcome two. Figure 21.3 shows the firm's position depending on which investment it makes.

Figure 21.3 Investment choice

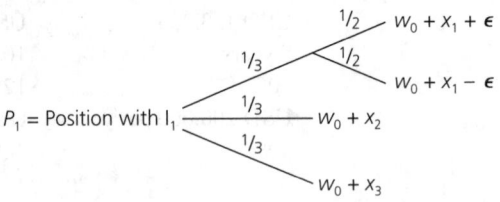

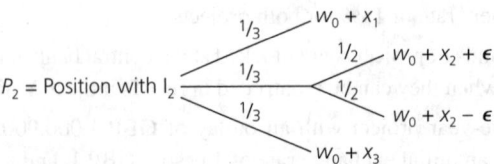

Source: E. Clark and B. Marois, *Managing Risk in International Business* (London: Thomson Learning, 1996).

Assume a strictly concave utility function, $u(w)$, where $u'(w) > 0, u''(w) < 0, u'''(w) > 0$ and the primes denote first, second, and third derivatives. $u'(w) > 0$ implies that investors prefer more to less. $u''(w) > 0$ implies that investors are risk averse and $u'''(w) > 0$ implies that the risk aversion decreases as wealth increases. Then in mean-variance space, the two investments are equivalent:

$$E(P_1) = E(P_2) = w_0 + E(x) \tag{A21.1.1}$$

$$\sigma_{P_1} = \sigma_{P_2} = \sigma_x + \frac{1}{3}\varepsilon^2 \tag{A21.1.2}$$

Taking the expected utility, however, shows that the expected utility of P_1 is greater than the expected utility of P_2:

$Eu(P_1) - Eu(P_2) =$

$$\left[\frac{1}{6}u(w_0 + x_1 + \varepsilon) + \frac{1}{6}u(w_0 + x_1 - \varepsilon) + \frac{1}{3}u(w_0 + x_2) + \frac{1}{3}u(w_0 + x_3)\right]$$

$$- \left[\frac{1}{3}u(w_0 + x_1) + \frac{1}{6}u(w_0 + x_2 + \varepsilon) + \frac{1}{6}u(w_0 + x_2 - \varepsilon) + \frac{1}{3}u(w_0 + x_3)\right]$$

$$= \frac{1}{6}[\{[u(w_0 + x_1 + \varepsilon) - u(w_0 + x_1)] - [u(w_0 + x_1) - u(w_0 + x_1 - \varepsilon)]\}$$

$$- \{[u(w_0 + x_2 + \varepsilon) - u(w_0 + x_2)] - [u(w_0 + x_2) - u(w_0 + x_2 - \varepsilon)]\}] \tag{A21.1.3}$$

The four terms in parentheses represent marginal utility and are positive because the utility function is well behaved and $u' > 0$. The two terms in braces are negative because the differences between the two parentheses in each brace represent the differences between the successive slopes of the utility function. The slopes are decreasing because $u'' < 0$. The difference between the two terms in braces is positive because marginal utility is convex and $u''' > 0$. Thus, Equation A21.1.3 is positive, which signifies that the expected utility of P_1 is greater than the expected utility of P_2:

$$Eu(P_1) > Eu(P_2).$$

Foreign direct investment: Measuring and managing risk

The previous chapter outlined the basic issues and techniques involved in generating the acceptance criteria for cross-border investment projects. One of the key variables was the cost of capital that should be applied to the project. The question is important . First of all, the cost of capital is a major input in the accept-reject analysis of project evaluation. Secondly, the cost of capital and the firm's financial structure can affect both the size and riskiness of the firm's cash flows and, hence, the value of the firm.

Estimating the risk

Once the various cash flows arising from the project have been identified, present values for these cash flows must be estimated. This is a well known problem in capital budgeting and there are no easy solutions. Where foreign direct investment (FDI) is concerned, the process is complicated by the existence of political risk and the possibility of currency fluctuations. In Chapter 10 we showed how political risk could be integrated into the analysis by either including a probability of loss factor when estimating the cash flows or adding a risk premium to the discount factor when calculating the NPV. As we pointed out, however, there is some serious doubt about the theoretical justification for incorporating political risk in this way. First of all, a probability of loss factor applied to the overall expected cash flow implicitly assumes that the consequences of political risk affect all components of the overall cash flow in exactly the same way. This is a highly dubious proposition. Different types of flows are likely to be affected in different ways depending on how the political risk manifests itself. Furthermore, if the cash flow analysis is thoroughly done, the consequences of political risk will be directly accounted for. Adding a probability of loss factor to account for political risk amounts to double counting. Secondly, as we mentioned in Chapter 10, accounting for political risk in a premium added to the discount factor treats all political risk as non-diversifiable and, thus, does not distinguish between systematic risk, which, according to portfolio theory, should be priced, and unsystematic risk which should not. This section proposes several methods for determining the cost of capital for FDI.

The capital asset pricing model: Levered and unlevered betas

Before going into the various methods for estimating the cost of capital for FDI, we should make the distinction between levered and unlevered betas. A levered beta refers to the systematic risk on the stock of a company or project that has debt. The unlevered beta refers to the systematic risk on a stock of a company or project with no debt. To see the relationship between the two we start with the Modigliani-Miller proposition 2 with taxes: [1]

$$r_s = r_u + (r_u - r_b)\frac{B(1-T)}{S} \tag{22.1}$$

where:

r = weighted cost of capital
r_u = required rate of return on the stock of a company with no debt
r_s = required rate of return on the stock of a company with outstanding debt
r_b = component cost of debt
S = market value of the company's stock
B = market value of the company's outstanding debt
$V = S + B$ = total market value of the company
T = the company's marginal tax rate.

Using the CAPM, we can write the required rate of return on the unlevered company, the levered company and the component cost of debt as:

$$r_u = r_f + \beta_u (\overline{R}_M - r_f) \tag{22.2}$$

$$r_s = r_f + \beta_s (\overline{R}_M - r_f) \tag{22.3}$$

$$r_b = r_f + \beta_b (\overline{R}_M - r_f) \tag{22.4}$$

where r_f is the riskless rate and $\overline{R}_M$ is the expected return on the market. Substituting Equations 22.2, 22.3 and 22.4 into Equation 22.1 gives the relationship between the betas:

$$\beta_s = \beta_u + (\beta_u - \beta_b)\frac{B(1-T)}{S} \tag{22.5}$$

Rearranging gives:

$$\beta_u = \frac{\beta_s + \beta_b[B(1-T)/S]}{1+[B(1-T)/S} \tag{22.6}$$

Estimating systematic economic risk

Without getting into the theoretical complications concerning optimal capital structure and the cost of capital, we can say that it is generally accepted that a project be discounted at the rate that reflects its systematic riskiness. In cross-border projects, systematic riskiness should include economic, financial, currency and political risk. One possibility is to use APT or a multi-index model to account for the systematic risk of each risk source taken individually. The drawback to this method is that it is practically impossible to estimate the individual betas. New projects, by definition, have no historical data to regress on. Given the intricate relationships among the different risk sources, subjective estimation of the

[1] See Modigliani and Miller (1963).

individual betas also looks like a dead-end street. Another method involves a straight-forward application of the CAPM or the ICAPM, where systematic risk is estimated in the absence of country-specific economic, financial and political risk. A risk premium is then either added to the required rate of return or deducted from the expected cash flows. The shortcomings of these methods were discussed in Chapter 10. A third method involves using the required rate of return estimated in the CAPM or ICAPM to estimate the NPV of the project in the absence of country-specific economic, financial and political risk. The losses accruing to country-specific economic, financial and political risk are then computed as the value of a hypothetical insurance policy against these losses. The value of the insurance policy is then deducted from the NPV to give the NPV adjusted for country-specific risk (see Chapter 10).

Another promising method involves a three-step procedure using the CAPM and the international index developed in Appendix 12.2 (Chapter 12). The method proceeds as follows. In step one the project's required rate of return is presented in terms of its systematic risk relative to the performance of the overall economy. This is information that the investor either already knows from experience or can estimate with little difficulty. In step two systematic country risk is estimated according to the procedures outlined in Chapter 12. In step three systematic project risk is combined with systematic country risk to determine the project's required rate of return.

Step one

Start with the following definitions:

r_f = riskless rate of interest on the dollar

$\overline{R}_i$ = expected return on an unlevered project in dollars

$\overline{R}_c$ = country's expected return in dollars (see Chapter 12 for estimation procedure)

$\overline{R}_w$ = expected return on the world index

β_i = a measure of the systematic variation of the unlevered project's returns with respect to the performance of a national economy

β_c = a measure of the systematic variation of the performance of the national economy with respect to the performance of the world economy.

The required rate of return on an unlevered project can be expressed in the CAPM as follows:

$$\overline{R}_i = r_f + \beta_i (\overline{R}_c - r_f) \tag{22.7}$$

where β_i measures the systematic variation of the unlevered project's returns with respect to the performance of a national economy. We use the unlevered rate of return in order to establish a common standard of comparison among the different projects that will be used in the estimation of beta. The assumption here is that similar projects will have similar reactions to macroeconomic performance in all countries. A company in the tool and dye industry, for example, should have a good idea of how cash flows from tool and dye projects react to macroeconomic performance just as a car manufacturer or textile producer should for its products. Thus, past data from similar projects in other countries can be used to get an estimate of the project's systematic correlation with macroeconomic performance. From a practical standpoint, this assumption will be all the more robust if the project being considered is similar to others that have already been undertaken elsewhere in similar conditions. Least squares regressions and other more sophisticated statistical techniques can be used to arrive at a precise estimate of the beta.

Step two

Step one captures the systematic relationship between the project and the performance of a national economy. We know, however, that because of their dotation in human and natural resources, their institutional and social organization, their economic management, etc., individual national economies have their own particular risk characteristics that must be taken into consideration. Again, only systematic risk should be considered. We can capture the systematic relationship between an individual national economy and the overall world economy in the expression:

$$\overline{R}_c = r_f + \beta_c(\overline{R}_w - r_f) \tag{22.8}$$

In Chapter 12 we showed how to estimate individual country betas using $\overline{R}_c$, the country's ROI, and $\overline{R}_w$, the return on the international market index. It is important to remember that the resulting β_c captures the systematic, country-specific, economic, currency and political risk. It does not, however, include the country's financial risk. This is because we use ROI, the return on total investment, rather than the return on investment financed by local residents. In this sense the resulting β_c is an "unlevered" beta. The country's financial risk must be considered separately. We will show how this can be done later on.

Step three

Total systematic economic and operating risk associated with the project is a combination of the systematic risk of the project relative to the country's economy and the systematic risk of the country's economy relative to the world economy. This can be found by substituting Equation 22.7 into 22.8 and simplifying:

$$\overline{R}_i = r_f + \beta_i \beta_c(\overline{R}_w - r_f) \tag{22.9}$$

Thus, $\beta_i \beta_c$ measures the project's total systematic economic and operating risk.

An example: A retail investment project in Pakistan

In 2000, PHI Consultants was asked to estimate the economic and operating risk premium in US dollars for an investment project in Pakistan. After explaining the methodology outlined above to its client, a well known retail manufacturer, PHI worked with them to determine the beta that would capture the systematic relationship between the proposed project and the performance of the Pakistani economy. This was done by looking at the performance of other similar investment projects that the company had undertaken in the past. It was found that 1.25 was an accurate estimate. Using the international market index and 20 years of historical data on the Pakistani economy, PHI then estimated that the Pakistani economy's beta was 1.4. The average return on the market index over the same period was 10% and the riskless rate at the time of the analysis was given as 5%. PHI thus had the following information:

$r_f = 5\%$
$\overline{R}_w = 10\%$
$\beta_i = 1.25$
$\beta_c = 1.4.$

This information was applied to Equation 22.9:

$$\overline{R}_i = 5\% + (1.25)(1.4)[10\% - 5\%] = 13.75\%$$

and the project's required rate of return necessary to compensate for systematic, country-specific economic, currency and political risk as well as project-specific operating risk was calculated as equal to 13.75%. PHI was careful to point out to its client that this analysis reflected only unlevered systematic risk because it was carried out using unlevered betas. Besides the project-specific operating risk and the country-specific economic, currency and political risk, the proper discount rate for the project should also include the risk arising from the Pakistani economy's foreign debt.

Estimating systematic country financial risk

The relationship in Equation 22.9 gives the project's required rate of return in terms of systematic economic risk relative to the world economy. Country financial risk is not included. Most countries, however, have outstanding foreign debt. Servicing this debt can jeopardize project flows to the parent company to the extent that debt payments eat up available foreign exchange. Consequently, country financial risk should be included in the project's required rate of return.

As with economic and operating risk, only systematic financial risk should be considered. The most obvious way to estimate systematic financial risk is with the CAPM. Extending the CAPM to debt instruments poses no serious theoretical problems. Furthermore, as we show in Appendix 22.1 at the end of the chapter, the relationship between the CAPM and the Black-Scholes options pricing model is such that the Black-Scholes formula can be used to estimate the risk premium associated with systematic financial risk. You will remember that this is exactly what we did in Chapter 12. Thus, the country financial risk premium estimated in Chapter 12 measures systematic risk and is appropriate for investment decision making.

Estimating the appropriate discount rate

Without bankruptcy costs

The orthodox theory of project evaluation says that the appropriate discount rate must account for systematic financial risk as well as economic and operating risk. Remember that for purposes of comparison, we are considering an unlevered project. If, however, the country has outstanding foreign debt that can affect cash flows to the parent, this leverage must be considered in the project's cost of capital. Equation 22.9 measures systematic economic and operating risk. It gives the required rate of return on a project in a country with no outstanding foreign debt. We can get from Equation 22.9 to r_s, the required rate of return when systematic financial risk is included, by using Modigliani-Miller (MM) proposition 2 without taxes. MM proposition 2 expresses the required rate of return on levered equity as the required rate of return on unlevered equity plus a risk premium weighted by the debt/equity ratio:[2]

$$r_s = r_u + (r_u - r_b) \frac{B}{S} \tag{22.10}$$

---

[2] The debt/equity ratio is just another way of expressing the debt/total assets ratio used in the options pricing formula:

$$\frac{B}{S} = \frac{{}^B/_V}{1 - {}^B/_V}; \frac{B}{V} = \frac{{}^B/_S}{1 + {}^B/_S}.$$

where:

r = weighted cost of capital
r_u = required rate of return on the project in a country with no foreign debt
r_s = required rate of return on the project in a country with outstanding foreign debt
r_b = component cost of foreign debt
S = market value of the portion of the country's economy owned by residents
B = market value of the country's outstanding foreign debt
V = $S + B$ = market value of the country's economy.

Thus, r_u corresponds to $\overline{R}_i$ in Equation 22.9 and r_b corresponds to the riskless rate plus the financial risk premium as calculated in Chapter 12. We recognize S as the value of the call option in Chapter 12 and B as the difference between V and S. We showed how to estimate V in Chapter 12. Thus, we have all the necessary information to estimate the appropriate required rate of return.

Example: The investment project in Pakistan with country financial risk

Remember that the discount rate adjusted for systematic country-specific economic, currency and political risk as well as project-specific operating risk was 13.75%. Suppose that at the same time Pakistan's cost of foreign borrowing was 8% and that the procedures outlined in Chapter 12 gave the total value of the economy as USD 1800 with a resident equity value of USD 1500. We would the have the following information:

r_u = $\overline{R}_i$ = 13.75%
r_b = 8%
V = 1800
B = 300
S = 1500.

To find r_s we use Equation 22.10:

$$r_s = 13.75\% + (13.75\% - 8\%)\frac{300}{1500}$$

$$r_s = 14.9\%.$$

Thus, r_s would be the appropriate discount rate for the investment project in Pakistan completely financed with equity. This rate includes, however, a 1.4% financial risk premium caused by the country's foreign indebtedness.

With bankruptcy costs

It is conceivable that the debt/equity ratio becomes so large that it threatens the viability of the firm or, in the case that interests us, of the country. This situation engenders incremental costs associated with bankruptcy and reorganization. Where a country is concerned, bankruptcy costs include the loss of access to credit plus the money, time and effort spent negotiating with creditors and the international organizations such as the IMF and the World Bank. Reorganization can be even more costly because it implies political changes and social upheaval. Long before these difficulties come to pass, however, other costs, such as capital flight, reduced import credits, emigration, etc., will manifest themselves. At this point, MM proposition 2 (Equations 22.1 and 22.10) no longer holds and the costs of bankruptcy and reorganization begin to raise the average cost of capital and reduce the value of the firm or the country. The appropriate discount rate will then be equal to the riskless rate plus a premium for systematic economic and operating risk plus a premium for systematic financial risk:

$$r_s = r_f + \lambda_u + \lambda_b \tag{22.11}$$

where:

λ_u = the premium for systematic economic and operating risk
λ_b = the premium for systematic financial risk.

From Equation 22.9, λ_u is equal to $\beta_i \beta_c (\overline{R}_w - r_f)$ and λ_b can be estimated in the Black-Scholes formula using the procedures outlined in Chapter 12.

Example: The investment in Pakistan with bankruptcy costs and financial risk
Remember the following information:

r_f = 5%
$\overline{R}_w$ = 10%
β_i = 1.25
β_c = 1.4.

From Equation 22.9 we derive the economic and operating risk premium:

$$\lambda_u = (1.25)(1.4)[10\% - 5\%] = 8.75\%.$$

To calculate the financial risk premium we have the following information:

V = the foreign exchange value of the economy = 1800
σ = the volatility of the return on V = 0.45
X = the nominal amount of foreign debt outstanding including interest and principal (see Chapter 12, Equation 12.26) = 650
t = the duration of the foreign debt (see Chapter 12, Equation 12.26) = 4 years
r' = the continuous time interest rate = 4.88% (the discrete rate is 5% so the continuous time rate is ln(1.05)).

Substituting this information into Black-Scholes (Chapter 12, Equation 12.23) we find that the market value of the foreign debt is 500.8. We calculate the continuous rate as

$$\ln\left[\frac{650}{500.8}\right]/4 \approx 6.5\%.$$

The discrete rate is given as $e^{0.065} \approx 0.067$. Thus, r_b, the required rate of return on foreign debt, is 6.7% and the financial risk premium is 6.7% − 5% = 1.7%.

Thus, from Equation 22.11, the appropriate required rate of return (discount rate) is

$$r_s = 5\% + 8.75\% + 1.7\% = 15.45\%.$$

The option approach to investment under uncertainty

In the option approach to investment developed in Chapter 21, the methodology is such that discounting is always done at the riskless rate of the base currency. This is because the pricing technique (developed in Chapter 8) is based on the rule of no arbitrage and the construction of a riskless portfolio, which makes it possible to discount at the riskless rate. Thus, if the base currency is the US dollar, the riskless rate will be the rate on the US Treasury security whose duration is closest to that of the investment. In the case of infinitely lived investments, the longest duration, that of the 30-year STRIP, would be the closest.[3]

With political risk

Determining the discount rate

In Chapter 10 we presented four ways to include political risk in the capital budgeting process for FDI:

1. Include all the effects of political events directly in the estimation of the cash flows. Monte Carlo simulations are often used in this context. In this case discounting should be done at the rate that reflects the systematic risk reflected in the cash flows. For example, for a country not facing bankruptcy costs, Equation 22.10 could be used to estimate the discount rate. For a country so highly indebted that it is facing bankruptcy costs, Equation 22.11 would be appropriate.

2. Estimate the cash flows without political risk and then adjust the cash flows to reflect the country-specific political risk. This methodology assumes implicitly that the political risk is fully diversifiable and has no effect on the project's cost of capital. In this case, a straight application of the CAPM reflected in Equation 11.6 (or 22.7 in this chapter) can be used to determine the discount rate.

3. Estimate the cash flows without political risk and then adjust the discount rate on a typical project of this type to reflect the incremental political risk. It should be remembered that this method is strictly ad hoc.

4. Estimate the NPV of the project without political risk. Estimate the value of a hypothetical insurance policy that would pay all losses accruing to political events. Subtract the value of the policy from the NPV of the project without political risk. In this methodology, the cash flows of the project are discounted at the appropriate rate for a typical project without political risk. Equations 11.6 and 22.7 can be used to this effect. Given the option pricing techniques used to value the hypothetical insurance policy, discounting on the policy is done at the riskless rate of the base currency (US dollars in our examples).

Ranking equivalent investments

In practice, it will often be the case that alternative investments are more or less equivalent based on mean-variance analysis. If we go beyond mean-variance analysis, the "good times" rule developed by Clark and Jokung (1998) (see Chapter 21 and Appendix 21.1) can be applied to political risk. According to this rule, if the political risk is associated with a particular investment outcome, for well behaved utility functions – $u'(w) > 0, u''(w) < 0, u'''(w) > 0$ – it is preferable for the political risk to be associated with good investment outcomes rather than with less good outcomes. This "good times" rule makes it possible to distinguish between otherwise equivalent investments. Thus, an investment that is likely to

---

[3] See Chapter 17 for information on STRIPS.

incur political penalties when it is successful is preferred to an otherwise equivalent investment that is likely to incur political penalties when it is unsuccessful.

Managing exposure of foreign direct investment to political risk

Hedging exposure of FDI to political risk has two basic techniques. The firm can resort to some kind of "internal" coverage that it sets up itself or it can take out an insurance policy against political risk.

Internal hedging techniques

Limiting investment to countries offering a good legal environment

The most obvious way to hedge the exposure of FDI to political risk is to limit investments to countries with a respectable legal environment. Most industrial countries have signed various bilateral "agreements on protection of foreign investment". These agreements, normally covering a span of 10 to 15 years with a rollover option, stipulate that no expropriation is valid except if compensation is fair. "Fair" is defined as the market value of the expropriated assets. An international organization, called the International Center for Settlement of Investment Disputes (ICSID, at www.worldbank.org/icsid), can be called in as arbitrator if any dispute occurs.

Founded in 1966, ICSID belongs to the World Bank group. So far 149 countries have signed the Convention on the Settlement of Investment Disputes, which ICSID is responsible for enforcing. ICSID can provide binding arbitration for foreign investors if a dispute arises between them and the host country. In this case, a conciliation commission or an arbitration tribunal is set up to judge the issue. Besides this, ICSID adopted five directives in September 1992:

1. defining the scope of intervention by ICSID
2. giving guidelines for host countries in their dealings with foreign investors
3. defining investment "norms" with regard to investment remittances
4. identifying cases of expropriation considered as "legitimate"
5. explaining the conciliation process.

As a result, ICSID is becoming recognized as an arbitration tribunal. Twenty-seven countries recognize it in their national legislation and 286 bilateral treaties as well as Nafta identify it as the appropriate body for arbitration purposes.

Limiting the transfer of funds to the subsidiary

Limiting the transfer of funds to the subsidiary is another obvious way to minimize the potential loss on a direct investment due to political risk. Various schemes can be devised to achieve this aim. First of all, the investor can rely more heavily on leasing than on purchased assets. This involves paying rents in local currency for company premises, manufacturing equipment, computers and vehicles. The scope for leasing may well be constrained by the availability of local leasing opportunities. Secondly, when it is feasible, the investor can employ amortized or second-hand equipment rather than risk the full cost of new equipment. This avenue can have surprising tax consequences and should be studied carefully. Thirdly, the investor can reduce his equity stake by financing the local subsidiary with debt from third parties. To limit transfer risk, preference can also be given to loans in local currency. Higher debt, of course, means higher financial risk. Local authorities also often resent financing structures that are too obviously designed to reduce exposure since reduced exposure means that their control is reduced as well.

Introducing "sleeping partners"

Several international or regional organizations, such as the International Finance Corporation (part of the World Bank group), the Inter-American Development Bank (IADB, at www.iadb.org) or the Asian Development Bank (ADB, at www.adb.org), stand ready to take minority stakes in the equity of foreign subsidiaries. These institutions are supposed to help developing countries on the way to industrialization by bringing in new investors. They typically take 10% to 15% of the equity but without exercising their voting rights. In this way the investor's exposure is reduced and he can take some comfort in the knowlegde that his association with an important international institution may shield his investment from the worst abuses of the local authorities.

Setting up joint ventures is another way to reduce exposure since it diminishes the funds to be transferred from the parent company. There is a risk, however, that the "sleeping partner" will wake up and demand a say in the management of the subsidiary. Thus, it is wise for parent company management to keep as much control as possible over intellectual property, such as patents, licenses, and marketing and manufacturing know-how.

Organizing an "international division of production"

Remember that the international division of production is a system in which each subsidiary is linked to other subsidiaries of the same multinational in various countries, buying from them and selling to them components and parts of the final products. A similar method would consist of making foreign subsidiaries dependent on the parent company's technology. As we said earlier, a more complex, interdependent system reduces exposure. Any measures taken by the local authorities against the subsidiary would result in its destruction. In fact, firms that integrate their production at a world or region-wide level make any form of nationalization useless. It is important to remember, however, that effective exposure reduction depends on the host country understanding to what extent the local investment is dependent on parent technology or integrated production. Otherwise, blinded by ignorance, the host country might undertake measures that are revealed as self-damaging only after it is too late. The automotive industry, computers, electronics and the aircraft industry are some of the sectors particularly adapted to an international division of production.

Adopting a "good citizen" policy

Table 22.1 outlines the advantages and disadvantages of FDI for the host country. In a "good citizen" policy, the foreign investor will try to accentuate the positive side of the investment by creating new jobs, favoring transfers of technology and bringing in hard currency. He will also try to reduce the negative side by favoring locally produced inputs over imports and limiting remittances. The foreign investor should also keep an eye on the image that its subsidiary is conveying locally by informing public authorities on its development projects and making sure that its record as a "good citizen" is well known. Again, establishing a joint venture with a local investor can be a plus by increasing the local aspect and bringing in new supporters ready to lobby in favor of the foreign investor.

Practical applications

In practice, most firms will use a combination of the techniques outlined above to control their political risk exposure. The eventual combinations depend on the host country in

Table 22.1 Advantages and disadvantages of FDI

Advantages	*Disadvantages*
Hard currencies brought in through investment and exports	Hard currencies taken out through remittances and imports of components and raw materials
Employment (new jobs)	Cultural contamination[1]
Transfers of technology	Environmental damage and pollution
Local development through sub-contracting	Competition to local producers for markets and resources[1]

[1] Although these features are actually positive rather than negative (competition, for example, benefits consumers by lowering prices, while foreign cultural influence can help to eliminate some undesirable practices), they are often perceived as a threat to local business and local cultural traditions.

question and the particular situation of the firm itself. For example, when Remy Cointreau made its initial investment in China in the late 1970s, it concentrated on minimizing its political risk. It limited its exposure by signing a cooperative agreement with a local partner for an initial period of 11 years and restricting its contribution to equipment imported from the parent. It also took advantage of the new Foreign Investment Code established in June 1979 by the Chinese authorities. During the negotiations, Remy Cointreau was aided by the China International Trust and Investment Corporation (CITIC). Finally, in order to guarantee the remittance of profits made by the subsidiary, a formal agreement was signed with the Chinese Foreign Investment Commission.

In its investment in Poland in the early 1990s, ABC, a major manufacturer for power generation, transmission and distribution, issued a number of guidelines to manage its exposure to political risk. The guidelines emphasized a "good neighbor" policy and included such items as

- get close to the unions
- encourage minority employee ownership
- start training before signing the contract to show good faith and to get a flying start
- be honest, even on uncomfortable facts such as overstaffing
- do not over promise on such things as expected investment and exports.

They also urged prudence with such admonitions as

- be prepared for high inflation and unrealistic exchange rates
- be highly selective, look for synergies, and give priority to companies you know
- adopt a "survival strategy" including such things as a crash plan for exports, emergency raw material supply, alternative transport and telecommunications networks.

Finally, in order to help guarantee fund transfers they mandated that costs for technology transfer and training be multiplied by three.

External hedging techniques

The first and most effective type of external hedging technique involves reducing the probability of a dispute occurring. This can be done by signing a special agreement with the host country government or the appropriate authority such as the Foreign Investment Committee. When the country is a member of ICSID and a signatory of the Convention on the Settlement of Investment Disputes, the agreement can make explicit reference to the Convention and detail how it will be interpreted. If the country is not a member and signatory, the special agreement can be used as a substitute and ICSID can be designated as the arbitration body.

The second type of technique is a straightforward insurance policy that protects the foreign subsidiary against political risk. Insurers for this type of risk belong to one of the following categories:

- multilateral institutions such as the Multilateral Investment Guarantee Agency (MIGA, at www.miga.org), a branch of the World Bank
- national institutions such as Overseas Private Investment Company (OPIC, at www.opic.gov) in the United States, ECGD (www.ecgd.gov.uk/graphic/homepages/normal.asp) in the United Kingdom, Coface (www.coface.fr) in France, Treuarbeit in Germany and MITI in Japan
- private institutions such as Lloyd's of London, American Insurers Guarantee (AIG) and UNISTRAAT in France.

The Multilateral Investment Guarantee Agency

MIGA was established in 1988 by 42 World Bank members. It currently includes 118 members and 26 others are scheduled for membership in the near future. Its objective is to complement national programs such as ECGD and Coface, but not to compete with them. MIGA offers the following types of coverage:

- *Currency transfers:* MIGA policies protect against losses arising from the investor's inability to convert local currency returns from the guaranteed investment into foreign exchange and to transfer it abroad.
- *Expropriation:* MIGA policies protect against losses due to actions depriving an investor of ownership or control of a local subsidiary. The actions include direct nationalization as well as creeping expropriation.
- *War and civil disturbance:* MIGA offers protection against losses from damage to tangible assets caused by politically motivated acts of war or civil disturbance in the host country.

In addition, MIGA can insure any new investment originating in a member country and destined for a member developing country. A wide range of investment vehicles such as equity, shareholder loans and management agreements are likely to be covered. However, the maximum amount of coverage is set at USD 50 million and the standard term is 15 years. MIGA cannot unilaterally cancel the contract whereas the investor has the right to cancel after three years.

Government insurance

Government insurance typically covers three specific risks:

- the risk of nationalization, either direct or indirect, resulting in the foreign investor being pushed out of his subsidiary
- the risk of non-payment of an indemnity
- the risk of non-transfer of the indemnity.

To obtain a guarantee, government insurance usually requires the submission of a substantial dossier with detailed information on the investor (name, location, financial statements, foreign subsidiaries, etc.), reasons for investing (market potential, choice of local partners and prospects with regard to profits), main features of the investment (type of investment, financing sources, local incentives, if any, and attitude of local authorities) and the scope of the guarantee applied for (initial investment, dividend remittances, retained earnings).

The guarantee can include the amount invested as well as profits but often coverage is limited to less than 100% of the sums involved. The duration of the guarantee is also limited. The cost of the insurance is usually low.

Private insurance

Private insurers usually cover items such as investments consisting of net asset value, loans from the parent company, bank loans guaranteed by the parent, dividends, equipment and inventories. Premiums, of course, depend on country ratings and project specifics. Both multi-country and "first loss" policies are available.

The private insurance schemes have several advantages over government-sponsored ones. First of all, there is greater flexibility in terms of the adequacy and scope of the risks covered. Leased assets, for example, can be included in the coverage. Secondly, the guarantee can reach 100% of the amount invested and, in the case of nationalization, the market value of the assets expropriated can be reimbursed. Thirdly, already existing projects can be covered. Finally, confidentiality is preserved.

The drawbacks are that the duration of the coverage is limited and usually does not exceed three years. Coverage for war-related damage is usually limited to 12 months. The amount of the premium can also be increased if the country's risk increases.

The cost of private insurance is not necessarily higher than that of government-backed schemes. Usually, industrial firms looking for political risk guarantees get in touch with specialized brokers like Marsh McLennan, Gras & Savoy, or CAURI. These intermediaries help their clients with writing the insurance contracts and negotiating with insurers. Sometimes the private insurers pass on part of their risk to reinsurers such as Skandia, Lloyd's or SCOR.

Summary

1. In cross-border projects, systematic riskiness should include economic, financial, currency and political risk. One possibility is to use APT or a multi-index model to account for the systematic risk of each risk source taken individually. Another method involves a straightforward application of the CAPM or the ICAPM, where systematic risk is estimated in the absence of country-specific economic, financial and political risk. A risk premium is then either added to the required rate of return or deducted from the expected cash flows. A third method involves using the required rate of return estimated in the CAPM or ICAPM to estimate the NPV of the project in the absence of country-specific economic, financial and political risk. The losses accruing to country-specific economic, financial and political risk are then computed as the value of a hypothetical insurance policy against these losses. The value of the insurance policy is then deducted from the NPV to give the NPV adjusted for country-specific risk.

2. Another method involves a three-step procedure using the CAPM and the international index developed in Appendix 2 of Chapter 12. In step one the project's required rate of return is presented in terms of its systematic risk relative to the performance of the overall economy. In step two systematic country risk is estimated according to the procedures outlined in Chapter 12 that use the concept of macroeconomic market value. In step three systematic project risk is combined with systematic country risk to determine the project's required rate of return.

3. The Black-Scholes option pricing formula can be used to estimate the systematic country-specific financial risk.

4. Hedging exposure of foreign direct investment to political risk involves two basic techniques. The firm can resort to some kind of "internal" coverage that it sets up itself or it can take out an insurance policy against political risk.

5. Internal hedging techniques include limiting investment to countries offering a good legal environment, limiting the transfer of funds to the subsidiary, introducing "sleeping partners", organizing an "international division of production" and adopting a "good citizen" policy.

6. The first and most effective type of external hedging technique involves reducing the probability of a dispute occurring. This can be done by signing a special agreement with the host country government or the appropriate authority such as the Foreign Investment Committee. When the country is a member of ICSID and a signatory of the Convention on the Settlement of Investment Disputes, the agreement can make explicit reference to the Convention and detail how it will be interpreted. If the country is not a member and signatory, the special agreement can be used as a substitute and ICSID can be designated as the arbitration body.

7. The second type of external technique is a straightforward insurance policy that protects the foreign subsidiary against political risk. Insurers for this type of risk belong to one of the following categories: multilateral institutions such as MIGA; national institutions such as OPIC, ECGD and Coface; and private institutions such as Lloyd's of London and American Insurers Guarantee (AIG).

Questions

Solutions to the following questions are set out on the web site, details of which are included in the Preface.

1. Why is it difficult to incorporate political risk into the capital budgeting decision?

2. What is one of the major obstacles to integrating country risk into the cost of capital estimate?

3. How can a country's systematic risk be estimated?

4. Does a country's indebtedness affect the cost of capital that applies to direct investment projects?

5. Calculate the project's required rate of return, given:

   β_u of the country Argenuay = 1.2

   β_u of the project in Argenuay = 1.375

   Expected return on the world economy, $R_w^* = 10\%$

   Riskless rate = 6%

   Cost of Argenuay's foreign debt, $r_b = 8\%$

   Argenuay's debt/equity ratio, $B/S = 0.5$.

6. How can systematic country financial risk be estimated?

7. What are the four ways of incorporating political risk into the capital budgeting decision?

8. What are the internal techniques for hedging exposure to political risk?

9. What are the external techniques for hedging exposure to political risk?

Appendix 22.1: The relation between the CAPM and the Black-Scholes option pricing formula

In Chapter 12 we showed how the equity in a levered company can be valued as a call option on the firm's assets. If, at the debt's due date, the value of the firm's assets is higher than the the amount of the debt to be paid, the debt is paid and shareholders keep the difference. In the opposite case, the shareholders walk away and leave the firm's assets to the debtholders. In this scenario, where the firm issues only one class of zero coupon debt, the Black-Scholes formula gives the firm's equity value as:

$$C_0 = V_0 N(d_1) - Xe^{-r_f t} N(d_2) \qquad \text{(A22.1.1)}$$

where:

C_0 = the present value of the firm's equity
V_0 = the present value of the firm's assets
X = the debt's face value
$N(d)$ = the value of the standardized normal cumulative distribution evaluated at d
rf = the continuously compounded riskless rate of interest
t = the debt's time to maturity
σ = the standard deviation of the continuously compounded annual rate of return on the firm's assets.

d_1 and d_2 are given by

$$d_1 = \frac{\ln(V_0 / X) + (r_f + \sigma^2 / 2)t}{\sigma \sqrt{t}} \qquad \text{(A22.1.2)}$$

$$d_2 = \frac{\ln(V_0 / X) + (r_f - \sigma^2 / 2)t}{\sigma \sqrt{t}} \qquad \text{(A22.1.3)}$$

In footnote 15 of Chapter 12 we showed that the market value of the bond could be calculated directly by remembering that B, the market value of the bonds, is equal to $V_0 - C_0$. Substituting this into Equation A22.1.1 gives the value of the bond:

$$B_0 = V_0 N(-d_1) + Xe^{-r_f t} N(d_2) \qquad \text{(A22.1.4)}$$

Finally, so that the assumptions of the Black-Scholes formula and the CAPM are consistent, we can express the required rate of return on risky bonds in the continuous time version of the CAPM derived by Merton (1973):

$$\overline{R}_b = r_f + \beta_b (\overline{R}_m - r_f) \qquad \text{(A22.1.5)}$$

where:

$\overline{R}_b$ = required rate of return on a risky bond
$\overline{R}_m$ = expected return on the market portfolio
β_b = $Cov(R_b, R_m) \div Var(R_m)$
$\overline{R}_b - r_f$ = the financial risk premium expressed in the CAPM.

In order to link the Black-Scholes formula, Equation A22.1.4, to the CAPM in Equation A22.1.5, we can use Ito's lemma to write:[4]

$$dB = \frac{\partial B}{\partial V} dV + \frac{\partial B}{\partial t} dt + \frac{1}{2} \frac{\partial^2 B}{\partial V^2} \sigma^2 V^2 dt \qquad (A22.1.6)$$

Taking the limit of Equation A22.1.6 as dt goes to zero and dividing by B, gives

$$\lim_{dt \to 0} \frac{dB}{B} = \frac{\partial B}{\partial V} \frac{dV}{B} = \frac{\partial B}{\partial V} \frac{dV}{V} \frac{V}{B} \qquad (A22.1.7)$$

dB/B is the bond's rate of return, R_b, and dV/V is the rate of return on the frim's assets, R_V. Therefore:

$$R_b = \frac{\partial B}{\partial V} \frac{V}{B} R_v \qquad (A22.1.8)$$

Using Equation A22.1.8 and the definition of beta, we can write the instantaneous covariance as:

$$\beta_b = \frac{\partial B}{\partial V} \frac{V}{B} \beta_v \qquad (A22.1.9)$$

Taking the first partial derivative of Equation A22.1.4 with respect to V gives:

$$\frac{\partial B}{\partial V} = N(-d_1) \qquad (A22.1.10)$$

so that Equation A22.1.9 becomes:

$$\beta_b = N(-d_1) \frac{V}{B} \beta_v \qquad (A22.1.11)$$

Substituting Equation A22.1.11 into A22.1.4 gives:

$$\overline{R}_b = r_f + \beta_v N(-d_1) \frac{V}{B} (\overline{R}_m - r_f) \qquad (A22.1.12)$$

From the CAPM, we know that $\overline{R}_v - r_f = \beta_v (\overline{R}_m - r_f)$. Substituting this into Equation A22.1.12 and rearranging gives the risk premium in terms of the option pricing formula:

$$\overline{R}_b - r_f = N(-d_1) \frac{V}{B} (\overline{R}_v - r_f) \qquad (A22.1.13)$$

[4] See Hsia (1981).

International mergers and acquisitions

23

In Chapters 21 and 22 the emphasis was on direct foreign investment starting from scratch. Direct foreign investment, however, can also be undertaken by acquiring an already existing company. In fact, the 1980s were noted for their cross-border mergers and acquisitions (M&A) activity as companies jockeyed for position in the world's major consumer markets. This is not surprising since M&A as a foreign investment vehicle often seems to have many advantages over the "start from scratch" approach. One of the main arguments is that it gives the acquiring firm instant local expertise, clients and business contacts that would otherwise take years to develop. Unfortunately, there are many disadvantages associated with M&A in general and cross-border M&A in particular. The object of this chapter is to look at M&A as a cross-border investment strategy. We start with a presentation of the nuts and bolts of M&A operations and then look at the complications arising from the cross-border aspects. We conclude with an analysis of the current state of international M&A activity.

Advantages and disadvantages of M&A as an investment strategy[1]

Estimating the value of a merger

Valuing the acquisition of a going concern is somewhat different from valuing a ground-up investment project. The reason is that the owners of a going concern are not likely to sell it for less than its economic value. In fact, they are likely to want a premium as an incentive to sell. If this is the case, the NPV of the acquisition valued as an individual investment project will be negative. At best, it will be zero. The value of the acquisition comes from the economic gains to be derived from the two firms operating as a single unit. The sources of potential economic gains, which we will come back to later in this section, are many and varied, ranging from scale economies and the elimination of inefficiencies and redundancies to tax shields, diversification of cash flows and lower financing costs.

---

[1] The definitions and interpretations in this section follow those set out in R.A. Brealey and S.C. Myers, *Principles of Corporate Finance* (Singapore: McGraw-Hill Book Co., 1988), p.p. 793–826.

Suppose that firm A is thinking of acquiring firm B. The gain from merging the two firms into a single unit can be represented as the difference between the value of the two firms as a single unit minus the value of the two firms operating individually:

$$\text{Gain} = V_{AB} - (V_A + V_B)$$

where V refers to the market value of equity plus debt as in Chapters 12 and 22.

The cost of the acquisition for firm A is equal to the price paid for acquiring B, including the fees and commissions of investment bankers, lawyers and accountants, less B's market value:

$$\text{Cost} = \text{Price} - V_B$$

It is interesting to notice that if the acquisition had been valued as an individual project, its NPV would have been (V_B – Price). In other words, the cost is represented by the negative NPV of the acquisition valued as an individual investment project.

Thus, the acquisition of a going concern is worthwhile if the gains are larger than the cost:

$$\text{Gain} - \text{Cost} = V_{AB} - (V_A + V_B) - (\text{Price} - V_B)$$

An example will illustrate the point. Consider the following information:

V_A = USD 5,000,000
V_B = USD 2,000,000
Change in net cash flow resulting from merged operations = USD 50,000 per year for ever
Sales price of firm B = USD 2,260,000
Fees and commissions = USD 40,000
Project cost of capital = 10%.

The total amount paid for the acquisition of firm B is the sales price of USD 2,260,000 plus USD 40,000 for the fees of the bankers, lawyers and accountants:

$$\text{Price} = 2,260,000 + 40,000 = \text{USD } 2,300,000.$$

The cost of the acquisition is

$$\text{Cost} = \text{Price} - V_B$$
$$= 2,300,000 - 2,000,000 = 300,000$$

The value of the merged firm is equal to the value of each firm taken separately plus the NPV of the incremental net cash flows resulting from the merged operations:

$$V_{AB} = V_A + V_B + \text{NPV}_{AB}.$$

The NPV of the incremental cash flow of USD 50,000 per year received for ever is:[2]

$$\text{NPV}_{AB} = 50,000/0.1 = \text{USD } 500,000.$$

---

[2] For the derivation of the formula for the present value of a constant annuity received for ever see Chapter 20, footnote 2.

Therefore,

$$V_{AB} = 5{,}000{,}000 + 2{,}000{,}000 + 500{,}000 = \text{USD } 7{,}500{,}000$$

and

$$\text{Gain} = V_{AB} - (V_A + V_B)$$

$$= 7{,}500{,}000 - (5{,}000{,}000 + 2{,}000{,}000) = \text{USD } 500{,}000.$$

The value of the acquisition for firm A is:

$$\text{Gain} - \text{Cost} = 500{,}000 - 300{,}000 = \text{USD } 200{,}000.$$

Hence, the acquisition is worthwhile. When it is announced, the value of B's stock will rise by 13% from USD 2,000,000 to USD 2,260,000 and, if investors share management's assessment of the gains from the acquisition, the value of A's stock will rise by 4% to USD 5,200,000.

Motives for M&As

M&As are often categorized as horizontal, vertical, or conglomerate. Horizontal M&As take place between two firms in the same line of business. Vertical M&As expand the firm upstream towards the production of raw materials or downstream towards the production of consumer products. Conglomerate M&As combine companies in different lines of business.

As we mentioned, the motives for M&As are many and varied. Some, as we will see, are sensible and some are dubious. Even when the motives are sensible, however, the purported gains may not be as great as promised or they may not exist at all. When they do exist, the share price of the two firms is likely to rise. When they do not exist, the share price of the acquiring firm is likely to fall.

Sensible motives

Economies of scale

Economies of scale exist when costs increase less than proportionately with output. One way to achieve this is to spread fixed costs over a larger volume of output. An example would be writing a book. Clearly, the effort is the same whether subsequently 1000 or 100 000 copies are sold, and the cost per unit declines with each incremental copy. In M&A, economies are supposed to come from sharing central services such as management, accounting, control, research and development. The problem is that it is often very difficult to get the personnel of the two companies to work together as a single unit.

Economies of vertical integration

Vertical integration refers to undertaking successive stages in the production process of a particular consumer good. The petroleum industry is a good example of vertical integration. The major firms undertake exploration, drilling and extraction, transport to distribution outlets and ownership of those outlets. There may be technical economies to be gained from vertical integration. An example is the physical proximity of successive processes such as iron ore smelting and the production of steel. Important savings may also arise from improvements in coordination between stages of production, which comes about if control is centralized.

Combining complementary resources

Complementary goods are those whose usefulness increases when they are used together. Peanut butter and jelly, cigarettes and matches, and cars and gas are some obvious examples. In M&A, gains from combining complementary resources come about if each acquires something that the other has more cheaply than if they acted on their own. An example is the large computer software company that acquires a software firm with a unique program but where the latter is too small to produce and market it on a large scale. The large firm gets the unique program that would cost much more if it tried to produce it on its own and the small firm gets the production and marketing expertise that it lacks.

Unused tax shields

Some companies have potential tax deductions but lack the profits to take advantage of them. An example of a tax shield is interest payments on outstanding debt. Merging with a profitable company would avoid the tax shields going to waste.

Improved management

Badly managed companies are often M&A targets because it is often the only way that incompetent managers can be ousted. Gains should then be realized through the activities of the competent managers that replace them. Arguments such as this should be handled with extreme skepticism. Brealey and Myers make the point by quoting Warren Buffet, the chairman of Berkshire Hathaway:[3]

> Many managers were apparently overexposed in impressionable childhood years to the story in which the imprisoned, handsome prince is released from the toad's body by a kiss from the beautiful princess. Consequently, they are certain that the managerial kiss will do wonders for the profitability of the target company. Such optimism is essential. Absent that rosy view, why else would the shareholders of company A want to own an interest in B at a takeover cost that is two times the market price they would pay if they made direct purchases on their own? In other words, investors can always buy toads at the going price for toads. If investors instead bankroll princesses who wish to pay double for the right to kiss the toad, those kisses better pack some real dynamite. We've observed many kisses, but very few miracles. Nevertheless, many managerial princesses remain serenely confident about the future potency of their kisses, even after their corporate backyards are knee-deep in unresponsive toads.

Dubious Motives

Diversification

In past chapters we have shown that diversification can reduce risk for a given level of return or increase return for a given level of risk. When diversification is used as an argument for a corporate merger or acquisition, however, the question is whether the firm can achieve diversification more cheaply than the individual investors can on their own. Although in some particular cases corporate diversification might be realized more cheaply than individual diversification, on the whole this is not true. It is especially not true when capital markets are perfect.[4] In fact, diversified firms that become the targets of hostile

---

[3] Berkshire Hathaway *1981 Annual Report*, cited in R.A. Brealey and S.C. Myers, *Principles of Corporate Finance* (Singapore: McGraw-Hill Book Co., 1988) p. 799.

[4] See R.A. Brealey and S.C. Myers, *Principles of Corporate Finance* (Singapore: McGraw-Hill Book Co., 1988), p.p. 824–826.

takeovers often use the tactic of "un-diversification" to concentrate on core activities as a major element of their defense strategy. This was Goodyear's strategy when it came under attack by J. Goldsmith in 1986. Other companies like Knight-Ridder, Toys-R-Us, and Pillsbury began divesting in 1988 as a means of avoiding a hostile takeover bid.

Lower financing costs

Economies of scale can be achieved at the level of issuing new debt. However, it is often argued that a larger firm can also obtain lower interest rates and that this justifies a merger. In fact, merged firms often can obtain lower rates than could be obtained if each firm borrowed individually. Unfortunately, this does not mean that there is a net gain to the merger. The lower interest rate is achieved at the cost of each firm guaranteeing the other's debt. The mutual guarantee raises the market value of the bonds but it reduces the value of the shareholders' stock. There is no net gain.

This can be more easily grasped if we remember from Chapter 12 that the value of shareholders' equity can be considered as a call option on the firm's assets. Remember also from Chapter 8 that the value of a call option is positively related to the volatility of the underlying security (vega). In the case of shareholders, the underlying security is the value of the firm's assets. The volatility of the value of the merged firm's assets will be lower insofar as the cash flows of the individual firms are not perfectly correlated. The lower volatility lowers the value of the call option (the equity value of the firm). In other words, the lower cost of debt is offset by an increase in the cost of equity.

Increased earnings per share

An acquisition or a merger can generate increased earnings per share without producing any evident economic gains. If this is the case, any apparent benefits are mere illusion and there is no justification for the operation.

Consider the information in Table 23.1. The situation of firms A and B before the acquisition is set out in the first two columns. The higher price/earnings ratio (P/E) for firm A indicates that firm A has better growth prospects than firm B. Since there are no economic gains from the acquisition, the value of the firms together should be the sum of their values when they are apart. Their individual market values are equal to the price per share (line two) multiplied by the number of shares (line four), that is, USD 12 million and USD 3 million respectively. Together, then, they are worth USD 15 million (line six). Total earnings (line five) are equal to the sum of the earnings of A and B when they are separate.

If A acquires B by issuing its shares to the shareholders of B, it will have to issue 50 000 shares:

$$\frac{\text{Market value of B}}{\text{Price per share of A}} = \frac{\text{USD 3,000,000}}{\text{USD 60}} = 50\,000 \text{ shares.}$$

Earnings per share rise from USD 5 to USD 6. However, there is no gain for either group of shareholders. In line seven we can see that the shareholders of firm A end up with higher earnings per dollar invested. This is offset by lower growth prospects (the P/E falls from 12 to 10). The shareholders of firm B end up with lower earnings per dollar invested but this is offset by higher growth prospects (the P/E ratio rises from 6 to 10). The only way that the operation could produce any gains is if investors are fooled by the increase in earnings per share and mistake it for real growth. They might momentarily bid up the stock price of the merged company. Gains of this type would be shortlived, however, and investors would sell the stock when they recognized the increased earnings per share for the technical illusion that it is. In fact, if B had acquired A, the earnings per share would have fallen from USD 5 to USD 3. We leave the exercise of making the relevant calculations for this result to the reader.

Table 23.1 Impact of acquisition on market value and earnings per share of firm A

	Firm A	Firm B	Firm A after acquiring B
1. Earnings per share	USD 5	USD 5	USD 6
2. Price per share	USD 60	USD 30	USD 60
3. Price/earnings ratio	12	6	10
4. Number of shares	200 000	100 000	250 000
5. Total earnings	1,000,000	500,000	1,500,000
6. Total market value	12,000,000	3,000,000	15,000,000
7. Current earnings per dollar invested in stock	USD 0.0833	USD 0.167	USD 0.10

Mechanics of international M&A

M&A transactions can be extremely complex affairs that require the expertise of a battery of expensive specialists to iron out the details and bring the operation to a successful conclusion. International M&A is even more complicated due to the different political, economic, judicial and social systems involved. The object of this section is to point out some of the most important issues associated with cross-border M&A.

Form of acquisition

The form of acquisition refers to the level of control, the corporate fit and the form of payment. Inevitably, local laws and takeover regulations will influence a company's final decision in these matters so that an appropriate form for the takeover will be in keeping with both the local laws and traditions of the country of origin and of the target.

Level of control

The level of control refers to the percent of the target company to be owned by the acquiring company. It depends on what the acquiring company intends to do with the target. Simple management control over a company remaining free standing and independent might be achieved with a relatively small minority shareholding. On the other hand, if the acquirer wishes to absorb the target's business, incorporate its management and dispose of certain assets, a high level of equity control will be necessary, maybe even 100%.

Many countries have laws that limit the level of control by foreign entities. Where these laws exist the acquirer will have to co-exist with minority shareholders. The cost of acquisition is considerably reduced if less than 100% of the target company is purchased. However, the expense of running a company with minority shareholders is higher than that of a wholly owned subsidiary, since there are costs associated with the management time involved in dealing with minorities as well as the direct expense of holding public meetings and printing and distributing the required reports and accounts. Furthermore, most countries have laws designed to protect minority shareholders from abuse by majority shareholder control. Consequently, important elements in determining the parent company's cash flows, such as transfer pricing and fees and royalties, might be difficult to implement in the presence of minority shareholders. In most OECD countries 75% equity control allows the buyer to pass special resolutions commiting the target company to whatever is so approved. Thus, in many M&A transactions 75% control is the key figure to be achieved.

As we mentioned, tax shields can represent important gains from an acquisition. The possibility of grouping tax shields and liabilities between parent and subsidiary often depends on control threshold levels. For example, US grouping occurs at 80% while UK grouping occurs at 75%. The relevant tax treaties and legislation should be carefully examined to determine appropriate control levels.

While simple majority control (51%) is usually enough to exercise effective control over any acquired company, effective control over publicly held companies can often be achieved at far lower levels. In the United Kingdom, for example, the *City Code on Takeovers and Mergers* defines this level as 30%. When this threshold is reached it triggers the requirement for a full offer.

Internationally, there are two instances when a company may choose effective management control without equity control. The first is when restrictions on foreign ownership prohibit a foreign entity from owning more than 50% of a locally resident company. The second is when share purchase restrictions lead to loss of the target company's exchange listing if any buyer gains majority control.

Corporate fit

Corporate fit refers to the target company's role in the acquiring company's operations. Will it be a stand-alone subsidiary, an operating division or a fully integrated operation. Corporate fit is important because regulators have shown increasing interest in this aspect and its relationship to public welfare. It is also important because the successful outcome of the acquisition often depends on whether the target company's existing shareholders, management and personnel agree with the acquiring company's plans for the target company's role in the acquiring company's organizational structure.

The stand-alone subsidiary holds out the promise of operational independence to the target's management. In effect, the stand-alone subsidiary operates as an independent company that reports to its shareholders, which includes the acquiring company. Consequently, it is the fit likely to cause the least disruption to the target company and its management and the least friction between the target company and the acquiring company. It is considered appropriate for control levels between 51% and 90% where there are minority shareholders.

At the 75% control level or whatever control level allows for special resolutions to be passed, the appropriate corporate fit might be the operating division. This format includes the target's management within the operating framework of the acquirer. The target may be required to work to a common set of objectives with other divisions or to a budget imposed by the acquirer. It may also be required to enter into trading arrangements with its sister divisions, which would not apply if it were a free-standing subsidiary, although these arrangements cannot operate against the interests of the minority shareholders.

Full integration is appropriate once the target is owned 100% by the acquirer. Full integration means that management may be transferred within the acquirer's other operations, assets may be disposed of or switched to other companies in the group, and trademarks reallocated within the acquiring group. In short, the acquirer can do just about anything it wants and, for all practical purposes, the target company could eventually lose its corporate identity. It is easy to see that full integration causes maximum disruption to the target company and its management. Consequently, resistance on the part of target company management and personnel can be a source of problems for the acquirer. The resistance is often strong enough to make the outcome of the acquisition a failure.

Form of payment

Form of payment refers to how the acquisition will be paid for. Will it be cash, will it be shares, will it be debt or will it be some combination of these?

Shares for shares is a true merger. The acquiring company effectively issues new shares, gets some new shareholders and increases its equity base. Existing shareholders see their holdings diluted. If the target company has a higher P/E ratio than the acquiring company, they will also see a dilution in their earnings per share. If it has a lower P/E ratio, they will see it increase. We have shown, however, that this of itself has no effect on the shareholders' wealth. Whether or not to issue shares depends on many considerations, such as the current share price, the dividend yield, currency restrictions on dividend payments, foreign share ownership restrictions and requirements for local stock exchange listings.

Cash or deferred cash payments for the shares of the target company is an acquisition. This means of payment can have heavy tax consequences for the shareholders of the target firm insofar as it generates tax liabilities if there is a capital gain and tax shields if there is a capital loss. For the acquiring firm it can have consequences on short, medium and long-term liquidity, as we will see in the next section when we look at some of the new financing instruments. It can also have consequences on foreign exchange exposure if payment is deferred and target company cash flows are insufficient to meet the payments.

Regulatory approvals

Most countries have legislation governing corporate takeovers and mergers. In some countries like the United Kingdom and Hong Kong monitoring is carried out by informal bodies. Other countries like the United States have a rigid system of laws enforced by the courts and government agencies. Furthermore, many countries have legislation directed at foreign entities seeking to acquire local companies.

Regulatory approvals are of two distinct types. The first type is composed of the formal consents and clearances that must be obtained before the completion of a takeover. The second type consists of the informal clearances from the quasi-regulatory bodies like trade unions, trade federations, government agencies and supranational industrial watchdogs. Knowledge of local trade practices and political attitudes is as important as the official regulatory processes.

Formal consents

The central bank is often the main supervisor of all capital flows into and out of the country. Thus, any purchase, sale, or merger of a company that involves a foreign counterparty is subject to central bank clearance. If a country has a foreign investment review board whose task is to ensure that overseas investment into the local economy is restricted to transactions that will be in the national interest, a cross-border M&A operation will also require its accord. The Ministry of Finance or the Ministry of Commerce often fulfill this role. Besides monitoring capital flows into and out of the country, the central bank also monitors currency controls when they exist. If they do, clearance for the payment of interest, dividends, fees, royalties and other cash flows is often required.

Another important regulatory body for M&A transactions is the national anti-trust agency. Its role is to see that the public interest is protected by ensuring free competition. If the anti-trust agency has good reason to believe that a merger or acquisition is against the public interest, it usually has the legal authority to prevent the transaction from taking place. For a company planning a cross-border acquisition, definitive clearance from the anti-trust agency is a necessity.

Informal consents

Informal consents refer to clearances by those organizations whose approvals are not legally binding but can be instrumental to the success or failure of the operation. Union opposition to a takeover, for example, might create enough uncertainty to make it unattractive. Furthermore, some countries such as Germany require worker participation on the boards of directors of domestic companies. In this case, opposition, or clearance, for that matter, would operate on two important levels. Some trade associations, like the Accepting Houses Committee in Britain, restrict membership to domestically controlled interests. Lack of membership could damage the business of the intended target. Pertinent informal consents depend ultimately on the particularities of each transaction concerning the industry, the company and the country. The important thing is to realize that such consents may be needed and to find out what they are for each situation.

Techniques

The techniques for undertaking an M&A transaction differ depending on whether the takeover is friendly or hostile. In hostile takeovers of publicly quoted companies, there is typically little time for negotiation. On the other hand, friendly takeovers, where both counterparties can see the benefits of the transaction, are characterized by detailed negotiations.

Negotiated acquisitions

In a negotiated acquisition, sellers are in the most delicate position. They often have to part with sensitive information in order to complete the sale. If news of the expected deal leaks out, they may have problems with customers and suppliers who are uncomfortable with the uncertainty surrounding the company's future. Employees worried about their jobs will begin to look around for other openings. Unfortunately, it is usually the best that leave first. Furthermore, if the deal falls through in its final stages there may be suggestions that a hidden problem was discovered that made the buyer withdraw. Therefore, sellers need to have some assurance that the buyer is serious and not merely shopping around or, even worse, that he is not seeking to extract some vital industrial intelligence that would not otherwise be legally available.

One common practice is the use of a confidentiality letter. The confidentiality letter is signed by the buyer whereby he promises:

- that no information will be divulged to third parties, including advisers, without the sellers written permission
- that access to the information within the buyer's company will be severely restricted on a need-to-know basis
- that all information will be returned uncopied when discussions are terminated
- that the information will not be used for competitive purposes.

If leaks occur and it can be shown that the buyer was negligent, he is liable to legal action and damages. Consequently, by signing the letter, the buyer proves his serious intention because he would not assume the potential legal liability if he were not.

As negotiations proceed to a fairly advanced stage a letter of intent or heads of agreement will be drafted and signed by both parties. The letter of intent goes beyond the confidentiality letter by covering the major issues that have been discussed and agreed to. The substance can vary considerably but it usually includes a statement of the structure of the deal, who the buyer is, who the seller is, what is being sold (shares or assets) and what is the intended payment (amount and form, such as cash, shares, notes). Exactly what is included in the letter of intent depends on how far the negotiations have gone. Typically, a letter of intent is non-binding unless payment is made to make it binding. For example, sometimes payment will be made for a binding element such as the exclusive right to negotiate for a set period.

Finally, when the deal is close to consummation, a more formal announcement will be made in the form of a press release. The last stage involves signing the final contract.

Contested bids

Contested bids or hostile takeovers have little in common with the foregoing negotiated bids. In fact, their jargon of dawn raids, pre-emptive strikes and black and white knights suggests that they have more in common with war than with corporate finance.

Most hostile takeovers begin with discreet purchases of the target company's shares. This enables the predator company to strengthen its negotiating position with the target's board and to establish a significant holding to deter new bidders as well as to provide a consolation prize in capital gains should a new bidder materialize and win the company. The allowable size of the share purchases before disclosure is required varies from country to country. In the United States and the United Kingdom it is as low as 5%.

Several strategies are possible at this initial stage. One is to engage in a quiet, protracted build up, and another, called a dawn raid, is to launch a sudden large-scale purchase of the target's shares. An alternative to buying an outright stake is to secure an irrevocable call option over someone else's shares.

Once the initial stake has been established, the next step is to make a bid. One possibility is to make a bid, called a pre-emptive strike, at a price high enough to deter third parties from making their own bids. Another possiblity is to make a low bid, called a "low ball offer", in the hopes of acquiring the target for less than its true worth. A wrinkle on the low ball offer is the "planned revision" whereby the bidder starts low but is prepared to go higher.

In some countries it is common to take control of a company by capturing a majority of seats on the board of directors rather than by acquiring a majority of its shares. This type of operation is called a "proxy fight" because votes for board seats are typically cast *in absentia* through postal voting cards called proxy forms. In practice, proxy fights are rare in cross-border takeovers since nationalistic solidarity is likely to unite domestic shareholders against the foreign predator.

Once the takeover war has begun, the predator will press his case on all fronts. He will use a press campaign, political lobbying, performance comparisons and promises of many good things to come. The target company managers, galvanized by the possible loss of their lucrative jobs, will fight back tooth and nail. They will use a press campaign, political lobbying, performance comparisons and promises of many good things to come. In fact some have become so desperate that they endanger their company's very existence through tactics like "shark repellents", "poison pills", "golden parachutes" and "crown jewels lock-up". Shark repellents and poison pills are designed to make their company so unpleasant that it is attack proof. One tactic is a loan covenant that makes debt instantly repayable and the company insolvent in the event of a takeover. Another is an onerous commercial agreement if the predator passes a certain level of shareholding. Golden parachutes are unacceptably high compensation packages that must be paid to managers if they are forced to leave the company. The crown jewels lock-up is a contract to sell the company's most valuable assets at below market prices if the hostile bid succeeds. All of these ploys look suspiciously designed to protect the interests of entrenched management at the expense of the shareholders, whose interests the managers are supposedly defending, and their legality is often successfully challenged.

Financial techniques in M&A

Junk bonds

Junk bonds, created by Michael Milken, became the most popular form of takeover financing in the 1980s.[5] Before Milken, high risk bonds, called fallen angels, were those that had been issued by a high quality firm that subsequently fell upon hard times. Milken's idea was to issue bonds that were risky right from the outset. As we mentioned in Chapter 17, bonds are rated according to the risk they represent. A bond's rating is important because it helps issuers determine the coupon rate and potential investors. Ratings above BBB- for Standard and Poor's and Baa3 for Moody's are considered investment grade. Any ranking below investment grade qualifies the bond as junk. Junk bonds are often called high yield bonds.

The success of the junk bond was based on the idea that the price of risk on high yield bonds was too high. Numerous studies had aimed at determining the rate of default on high yield bonds compared to investment grade. Many of them concluded that the rates were not all that different, at least not different enough to merit the price differentials observed in the market. Milken's achievement was to convince investors of this. Later studies showed, however, that after the creation of the junk bond market, default rates were higher than supposed.[6] Nevertheless, as we can see in Table 23.2, between the first junk bond issue in 1977 and 1989, the market for high yield bonds grew at a breathtaking rate.

The growth of the junk bond market was aided by deregulation of US financial markets, notably in legislation concerning savings and loan associations (S&Ls). An S&L is an institution whose primary business is to take local deposits and lend then for financing mortgages. They are also called thrifts and are known as building societies in the United Kingdom. US deregulation allowed the S&Ls to fix the rates they paid for deposits and lifted controls on what they could invest in. Table 23.3 shows that by 1988 S&Ls accounted for 7% of the total junk bond market. As fate would have it, this ultimately proved their undoing.[7]

Continued M&A activity in the face of rising P/E ratios increased the need for more sophisticated financing methods. Remember that company cash flows can be approximately described as after-tax profit plus depreciation. Unless investment has been extremely high, a high P/E ratio suggests that cash flows generated by the target company might be insufficient to cover interest payments. One way of lowering interest charges, as

Table 23.2 Growth of the US high yield bond market (in US dollars bn), 1977–89

	1977	1978	1979	1980	1981	1982	1983	1984	1985	1986	1987	1988	1989
Amount	24	26	28	30	32	35	43	59	82	123	138	183	205

Source: Drexel Burnham Lambert.

[5] Milken began his career with Drexel Firestone of Philadelphia. In 1973 Drexel Firestone became Drexel Burnham and eventually Drexel Burnham Lambert.

[6] See P. Asquith, D.W. Mullins and E.D. Wolff, "Original issue high yield bonds: Aging analyses of defaults, exchanges and calls", *Journal of Finance*, Vol. XLIV, No. 4 (September 1989), p.p. 923–952.

[7] When the junk bond market crashed in 1989, S&Ls had an overall deficit of USD 250 billion that the US taxpayer had to make good because S&L deposits were insured by the government.

Table 23.3 High yield bond ownership, end-1988

Type of investor	%
Insurance companies	30
Mutual funds, money managers	30
Pension funds	15
Foreign investors	9
Savings and loans	7
Individuals	5
Corporations	3
Security dealers	1

Source: Drexel Burnham Lambert.

we saw in Chapter 17, is to issue bonds with warrants or with a conditional conversion clause. There is a double advantage for the borrower. First of all, he pays a lower coupon rate. Secondly, the lender will be less likely to throw the borrower into liquidation since, by doing so, he will lose the time value of the option embedded in the warrant or the conversion clause. "Pay in kind" notes (PIK) are another invention devised by junk bond issuers to avoid liquidity problems caused by insufficient cash flows. PIKs are bonds whose coupons are paid in the form of another bond, thereby pushing back the date when cash must actually be disbursed.[8]

Financial strategy

There are three basic financial strategies in takeover transactions: the "raider", the "builder" and the "tax saver".

The raider is looking for a quick profit. His most favorable outcome is associated with "greenmail" payments. Greenmail is the purchase by the target company at a substantial premium of the shares acquired by the raider. In the absence of greenmail payments, the raider's profit comes from "asset stripping" that is, selling off the target company's assets piece by piece, hopefully at a considerable profit. The raider strategy requires sources of financing that can be quickly mobilized, that can withstand high levels of risk and that can be paid back at any time.

The builder is looking for a long-term improvement in the company's management and profitability. In this case, cash flows will be weak in the first years following the takeover, improving as improved management increases efficiency and profits. This strategy requires financing with deferred repayment, progressive interest rates, or option kickers that allow the borrower to pay lower coupons.

The tax saver is looking for the tax advantages available through financial leverage. In order for this strategy to be effective, target company cash flows generated by current or exceptional before-tax profits must be higher than financial charges. Financing costs can be high as long as cash flows are adequate and the rate of return on capital is higher than the after-tax cost of the debt. A key variable is the ratio of debt to equity (B/S), which is associated with the concept of the leveraged buyout (LBO). The LBO is designed to take the

---

[8] In the raid on RJR-Nabisco, KKK issued USD 1 billion worth of PIK subordinated debentures and USD 4.1 billion worth of zero coupons at 48% of face value.

target company private for a number of years, increase its profitability and sell it back to the public at a substantial gain.

Before we get into the specifics of the financial antics involved in LBOs, we ought to take a look at some of the arguments behind their existence. Jensen argues that publicly quoted companies are unable to show their real capabilities because of the latent conflict of interest between shareholders and managers.[9] Managers have many personal advantages associated with their positions that they do not want to give up. In declining sectors of the economy where growth is weak and cash flows are high, excess liquidity should be returned to shareholders. If managers do this, however, they lose benefits associated with their positions (power, money and perks). Instead they waste the money on loose management and doubtful investments. They can get away with it because traditional shareholders do not have effective means of controlling the managers. On the other hand, when the capital of a firm is held by a small group of active shareholders, they can control the managers directly or even participate in management themselves. Furthermore, the existence of a high level of debt substituted for the previous passive shareholders acts like a watchdog and obliges the managers to regularly extract large sums from their cash flows in order to service their debt.

There are two currents of thought on the future of the publicly quoted corporation. The first, championed by Jensen, figures that the role of this type of institution is destined to decline even though it does have the advantage of risk diversification for a large number of investors. The decline will vary from sector to sector, depending on the possibilities it offers for growth.

The second trend, championed by A. Rappaport, figures that the role of the public corporation will remain dominant.[10] He argues that the LBO can only be a transitory phenomenon because it creates no value in itself except for the shock therapy of reorganization. It could, however, be the best instrument for limiting managerial autonomy, and the principles applied in LBOs should be applied to the publicly held corporation.

S.N. Kaplan finds that LBOs are transitory in nature.[11] Other studies have sought to determine if LBOs really achieve improved company performance. C.J. Muscarella and M.R. Vetsuypens studied 72 reverse LBOs (privately held firms going public) and found that "reverse LBOs have experienced significant improvements in profitability when compared with random samples of publicly traded firms over similar time periods".[12] A. Smith studied the consequences of the structural reorganization that follows a leveraged management buyout.[13] He underlines the marked improvement in profitability resulting from the operation. Other studies confirm these conclusions.

It seems then that the financial strategies associated with LBOs, whether by raiders or by builders, have made it possible for the original shareholders to obtain some of the gains resulting from the reorganization. It is estimated by the SEC that the premiums paid for LBOs in the United States between 1980 and 1987 amounted to USD 20 billion and that the value-weighted average premium paid to shareholders was 32%.[14]

---

[9] M.C. Jensen, "Eclipse of the public corporation", *Harvard Business Review* (September–October, 1989), p.p. 61–74.

[10] A. Rappaport, "The staying power of the public corporation", *Harvard Business Review* (January–February, 1990), p.p. 96–104.

[11] S.N. Kaplan, "The staying power of leveraged buyouts", *Journal of Financial Economics*, Vol. 29 (1991), p.p. 287–313.

[12] C.J. Muscarella and M.R. Vetsuypens, "Efficiency and organizational structure: A study of reverse LBOs", *Journal of Finance*, Vol. XLV, No. 5 (December 1990), p.p. 1389–1413.

[13] A. Smith, "Corporate ownership, structure and performance: The case of management buyout", *Journal of Financial Economics*, Vol. 27 (1990), p.p. 143–164.

[14] S.M. Rubin, *Junk Bonds after the Crisis* (Euromoney Publications, London: 1991).

LBO financing

In the preceding section we looked at the strategies underlying LBOs. In this section we are going to consider some of the financial operations that make them possible.

LBO financing usually takes place in two stages. The first stage covers the tender period when the takeover is being organized, while the second stage finances the actual takeover. In the first stage, which is transitory, the relay credit plays a crucial role. The financing of the actual takeover itself requires more permanant arrangement and includes equity, senior debt and subordinated or mezzanine debt.

During a takeover bid, a group of investors is organized by the raider. The capital that they bring to the operation should be substantial enough to ensure the availability of the supplementary financial resources necessary for the operation to succeed. The supplementary resources are obtained in the form of a relay credit from a major financial institution that pledges the funds in a letter of confirmation. The funds are guaranteed by the assets of the target company and by the the the suspension clause that makes the credit conditional on the success of the takeover.

The success of the first stage depends on the ability to mobilize large sums and to mobilize them rapidly. This ability was the source of Milken's and Drexel Burnham Lambert's success. The sums themselves can go as high as several billion dollars[15] and the operations, often put together over a weekend, are supposed to remain absolutely secret.[16]

Financing the takeover itself takes more time. The technique is to create a holding company financed with equity, senior debt, and subordinated or mezzanine debt.

Equity

Equity usually represents between 10% and 30% of total financing. The proportion has to remain low so that investors can take maximum advantage of the leverage effect. Lenders, however, often prefer higher equity levels because high financial leverage translates into high risk. Equity participation cannot go too high in any case because the nature of the LBO is to concentrate ownership as a means of rationalizing the company and taking it public after a few years.

Equity is usually comprised of ordinary shares and preferred shares with no voting rights. Sometimes there is a "sweet equity" deal that assigns different financial conditions for different shareholders. In the 1989 takeover of Comet, a subsidiary of Air Liquide, for example, the arranging English venture capital company, 3i, got a lower price than the other shareholders as a reward for putting the deal together.[17] Sellers credits can also be included in the holding firm's equity. For example, in the LBO on Swedish Match, the target's mother company, the Swedish group Stora, granted the acquiring company an interest-free sellers' credit for 8% of the total. This credit can be included as equity because it ranks last along with equtiy in the order of payouts.

---

[15] The first operation of this type was organized for USD 1.7 billion in December 1984 by Milken when he was assisting T. Boone Pickens in his raid on Gulf Petroleum.

[16] In spite of this, Milken was indicted in 1988 for insider trading with several arbitragers, notably Ivan Boesky. He was convicted and condemned to ten years in prison and USD 600 million in fines. Of course, in 1988 alone he earned USD 550 million from Drexel. Drexel itself declared bankruptcy on 14 February 1990.

[17] In practice, the operation must take place in two steps. In the first step, the holding company is created with the sweet equity beneficiaries as shareholders. In the second step, capital is increased to include the other shareholders.

Senior debt

Senior debt usually accounts for between 50% and 80% of total financing and is obtained from a group of banks in a syndicated loan with a maturity of less than seven years. In fact, deals of this type sparked the comeback of the Eurocurrency loan market that was in decline because of the debt crisis.

The loan indenture is tailored to the needs of the LBO operation and is backed up with strong guarantees. The guarantees often refer to the target or the acquiring company's assets as collateral. They also refer to covenants regarding required financial ratios and the relationship between senior and subordinated debt. The interest rate is almost always variable. For example, the takeover of Swedish Match in 1990 by a group of investors led by Gillette and J.P. Morgan gave rise to syndicated senior debt of USD 409 million with a six-year maturity at Libor plus 2%. It represented 65% of the total transaction. The LBO of Secap, organized by Alspi et Lazard in the same year, led to syndicated senior debt of FRF 450 million with a maturity of 8.5 years at Pibor plus 1.75% and represented 65% of the total financing.

Mezzanine debt

Mezzanine, or junior, debt typically has a longer maturity than senior debt. The longer maturity and the fact that it is subordinated make it considerably riskier than the senior debt. In fact, the term mezzanine comes from the Italian *mezzanina* and refers to its position as somewhere between senior debt and equity. Mezzanine debt is usually issued in the form of junk bonds. Average interest rates are between 18% and 22% but can go up to 25% or 30% for private issues that cannot be traded on the secondary market. It is interesting to note that the junk bond market is strictly a US phenomenon and has never invaded Europe.

In recent years a new wave of junk bonds has appeared. They have features like progressive interest rates or interest rates that vary with the market price of the bond. If the price of the bond falls, the company is required to raise the interest rate it pays. Thus, the company has an incentive to purchase its bonds on the secondary market to avoid a fall in the price. These new features have the effect of reducing market risk but they do nothing for default risk, which is still a major risk for junk bond holders.

Actually, it seems that market risk is lower for junk bonds than many analysts predicted. In the stock market crash of October 1987 the Standard and Poor's 500 Index fell by 12.2% while Drexel Burnham Lambert's High Yield Bond Index fell by only 2.4%. Generally, because of their lower duration, junk bonds are less sensitive to interest rate risk than investment grade bonds, long-term Treasuries or equities. On the other hand, industry and firm-specific risk is much higher. Recognizing this has made it necessary to adapt financial leverage to the cash flow capabilities of the target company. Consequently, leverage ratios have become lower.

Mezzanine financing has made its appearance in Europe over the past few years through equity-linked issues. The United Kingdom was the testing ground and France followed suit. Several investment funds specializing in mezzanine investments have been created. For example, the company Euromezzanine was created in 1990 by Banexi, a subsidiary of the BNP, and Financière Saint-Dominique, a subsidiary of Crédit National. It invests in units of FRF 10 million or more. Nevertheless, the mezzanine market in Europe is quite modest compared to the US market.

Some mezzanine transactions are straightforward, like the Libor plus 4% bonds issued by Gillette in its acquisition of Swedish Match. Others are more complex. In the LBO on Techpach International, the mezzanine took the form of subordinated participating shares, where the rate varies between a minimum of 5% and a maximum of 20% depending on

Techpach's results. The LBO on Secap gave rise to a two-part issue of FRF 90 million. The first part, for FRF 67 million, had a maturity of 9.5 years and an interest rate of 13.1% for the first three years and 15.8% from there on. The second part, for FRF 23 million, had an interest rate of 1% and was repayable in equity shares.

In fact, the mezzanine should be adapted to the LBO operation itself. In the Secap operation, for example, the issuer wanted to limit cash payouts, especially in the first few years. This explains the progressive interest rate on the FRF 67 million issue and the 1% rate on the FRF 23 million issue. Furthermore, the part of the issue repayable in equity shares was smaller than the other part of the issue in order to avoid too much equity dilution. Finally, obligatory repayment in equity shares was chosen over a warrant or convertible issue as a means of guaranteeing the character of the bonds as quasi-equity.

Summary

1. The value of an acquisition comes from the economic gains to be derived from the two firms operating as a single unit. In order for a takeover to be justified, the gains must be larger than the cost.

2. M&As are often categorized as horizontal, vertical, or conglomerate. Horizontal M&As take place between two firms in the same line of business. Vertical M&As expand the firm upstream towards the production of raw materials or downstream towards the production of consumer products. Conglomerate M&As combine companies in different lines of business.

3. The motives for M&As are many and varied. Some are sensible and some are dubious. Even when the motives are sensible, however, the purported gains may not be as high as promised or they may not exist at all.

4. M&A transactions can be extremely complex affairs that require the expertise of a battery of expensive specialists to iron out the details and bring the operation to a successful conclusion. International M&A is even more complicated due to the different political, economic, judicial and social systems involved.

5. In international M&A, attention must be paid to the form of acquisition, regulatory approvals and allowable techniques. The form of acquisition refers to the level of control, the corporate fit and the form of payment. Regulatory approvals are of two distinct types. The first type is composed of the formal consents and clearances that must be obtained before the completion of a takeover. The second type consists of the informal clearances from the quasi-regulatory bodies like trade unions, trade federations, government agencies and supranational industrial watchdogs.

6. The techniques for achieving an M&A transaction differ depending on whether the takeover is friendly or hostile. In hostile takeovers of publicly quoted companies, there is typically little time for negotiation and predator and prey often act as if they were at war, using dawn raids, pre-emptive strikes, poison pills and shark repellents to achieve their ends. On the other hand, friendly takeovers, where both counterparties can see the benefits from the transaction, are characterized by detailed negotiations.

7. M&A transactions are sensitive to economic and political conditions and can vary considerably from year to year.

8. The junk bond became one of the most popular forms of financing for takeovers in the 1980s. They are often associated with LBOs. The LBO is designed to take the target company private for a number of years, increase its profitability, and sell it back to the public at a substantial gain.

Questions

Solutions to the following question are set out on the web site, details of which are included in the Preface.

1. What are the three major categories of M&A?

2. Discuss the pros and cons of the principal motives underlying M&A operations.

3. Consider the following information for Akron and Tardus:

	Akron	Tardus
EPS	GBP 8	GBP 4
Price per share	GBP 64	GBP 56
Number of shares	300 000	200 000

a. Based on the foregoing information, how many shares must Akron issue to acquire Tardus?

b. What will the EPS of the merged company be?

c. Because of synergies arising from the merger, the EPS of the merged company is expected to remain at GBP 8 per share with a P/E ratio equal to 10. Is this situation likely to satisfy both groups of shareholders? What will be the gain for both groups of shareholders?

4. What are shark repellents and poison pills and what purpose do they serve?

5. Explain why junk bonds are less sensitive to changes in the interest rate than investment grade bonds.

Appendix 23.1: M&A regulations in some major countries

The United States

M&A regulations in the United States come from three sources: the Securities and Exchange Commission (SEC), federal legislation and state legislation. The SEC is the authority that controls US stock exchange activity. It has considerable power compared to equivalent bodies in other countries. It is financed by the federal budget and has ten times more employees than the Consob in Italy, which is Europe's largest. It is 15 times larger than the Commission des Operations de Bourse (COB) in France or the Securities and Investment Board (SIB) in the United Kingdom.

Rule 13d of the Securities Exchange Act of 1934 requires anyone owning 5% or more of a company's shares to file a document with the SEC within 10 days of acquiring this amount. In addition, the various states have specific legislation governing takeovers. Some states, in an effort to attract corporate residents, have adopted legislation aimed at eliminating takeovers. Delaware is the leader in the field, followed by Pennsylvania and Indiana. For example, in 1987 in Indiana the state supreme court validated legislation stipulating that takeovers would be accepted only if the purchaser obtained the consent of a majority of shareholders owning 10% or less of outstanding stock. This makes hostile takeovers virtually impossible.

Besides the legal aspects associated directly with takeovers, there is also anti-trust legislation (the Scott-Rodino Anti-Trust Improvement Act of 1976) as well as laws designating certain protected sectors in the economy.

The United Kingdom

The United Kingdom was the first European country to be touched by the wave of takeovers in the 1980s. UK capital markets function in a similar way to the US capital markets; shareholding is widespread but institutional investors play a major role.

The UK system is based on the principle of self-regulation by professional organizations. The *City Code on Takeovers and Mergers* was created in 1968 and is administered by the Takeover Panel that defines the rules of good conduct in matters of M&A. Since 1983, the rules apply to all public companies, whether or not they are quoted on an exchange. One of the main provisions of the Code is that all shareholders be treated in an equal manner by the acquirer. Although the Code does not have the force of law, the Takeover Panel can pronounce sanctions that range from a simple reprimand to the interdiction of voting shares at shareholder meetings.

The government takes a pragmatic position that allows professionals to adapt law to practice. It did, however, introduce the Companies Act in 1985 and the Financial Services Act in 1986. The Companies Act stipulates that when a predator company owns 90% or more of the target company's shares, it can force the minority shareholders to sell their shares. On the other hand, minority shareholders can oblige the 90% majority shareholder to purchase their shares. The Financial Services Act provides the framework for all regulations relating to financial markets and instruments.

The Monopolies and Mergers Commission has the power to oppose any public takeover bid. Before being referred to the Commission, all large acquisitions must be reported to the Office of Fair Trading. The OFT then makes a report on the effects of the proposed acquisition and market competition. If its report is unfavorable, the matter is referred to the Commission. Few cases go that far.

The main thrust of UK M&A law and practice can be summarized as follows:

- An obligatory statement of intention to the target company and to the authorities is required at 10% ownership (at 5% if the target asks for it) as well as a one-week ban on public purchases. (The rule applies to totals if more than one acquiring firm is involved.)
- Shares continue to be quoted and traded during the takeover.
- A 30% stake in a company requires a public bid for all outstanding stock.
- With respect to the principle of equal treatment, any investor can initiate a takeover bid without the authorization of any Ministry or regulatory body.

France

Over the past few years, French financial markets have been the object of government efforts to increase efficiency and transparency. These efforts were codified in the Law of 2 August 1989. This law, most recently modified in April 1992, contains the legislation relating to mergers and acquisitions.

In practice, French regulation occurs at three levels. The COB monitors operations on the exchanges and seeks to maintain truthfulness of public information. The Conseil des Bourses de Valeurs (CBV) is the authority that has the power to authorize or refuse public takeover bids. Finally, the Société des Bourses Françaises (SBF), a professional organization, is responsible for communicating the measures taken by the CBV to the public.

The general principles behind French regulations are based on the Civil Code and the XIIIth European Directive (see below). As in the UK legislation, one of the main provisions is that all shareholders be treated in an equal manner by the acquirer:

- A public bid for 100% of outstanding shares is required by any investor acquiring ownership of one-third or more of a company's stock.

- At 95% ownership, an investor can require minority shareholders to sell their shares, or vice versa.

- Investors acting together are treated as one single investor.

- On acquiring shares representing ownership of 5%, 10%, 20%, 33.33%, 50% and 66.67% the authotities must be notified within five days.

- When a public bid is made, trading is suspended for a time to give the CBV time to make a ruling on the bid.

- No obstacles, such as shareholder agreements, to the free exchange of shares are tolerated.

- During a bid, managers are required to limit their activities to day-to-day operations. Thus, once a bid is launched, managers have less latitude to initiate poison pills and the like in order to discourage predators. Nevertheless, pre-bid defense measures are numerous.

Germany

German takeover legislation is limited to anti-trust law monitored by the Bundeskartellamt. Nevertheless, the organization of German business is such that hostile takeovers are very difficult.

First of all, German equity capital is concentrated in a few hands. Stock market capitalization is a very small percentage of GNP. The reason is that a large number of German businesses are family affairs. Furthermore, German owners seem to be concerned by the social role of their commercial activities.

Secondly, banks are important players in German business life. They lend money, participate in management decisions, and often hold blocking minority shareholding positions. In 1985 banks were represented on the boards of 318 of the 400 largest German corporations. Furthermore, German law allows banks to vote the shares that they manage for their clients.

Thirdly, cross and reciprocal shareholdings are permitted. Also, because no explicit legislation exists, managers can protect themselves by statutory clauses that limit the voting rights of certain categories of shares or that confer multiple voting rights on other classes.

Spain

Spanish law on takeovers dates back to 1984 and was completed in 1988. Nevertheless, it remains somewhat unclear. For example, where obligatory public bids are concerned, it is not certain at exactly what level of shareholding this is required because the law of 1988 mentions only "substantial stakes". Partial bids are also permitted if the acquirer does not intend to change the target's status. In practice, however, it is difficult if not impossible to know the true intentions of the predator. The sanctions and penalties for those who fail to respect these fuzzy laws are explicit and severe.

European legislation

The XIIIth Directive of 22 December 1988 aimed at harmonizing EU takeover legislation. Some governments, like France, for example, did adapt their legislation. Most did not, however, and legislation is still too diverse to allow the XIIIth Directive to be applied. Of course, the Directive is only a recommendation and not a law. EU anti-trust legislation does have "teeth" and is the principal EU-wide means of monitoring and controlling takeover activity.

Selected web sites

- Asian Development Bank (ADB): www.adb.org
- Bloomberg: www.bloomberg.com
- Brady Bonds: www.bradynet.com
- Bridge-CRB commodity index: www.crbindex.com
- Chicago Board of Trade: www.cbot.com
- Chicago Mercantile Exchange: www.cme.com
- Coface: www.coface.fr
- Corruption: www.transparency.org
- ECGD: www.ecgd.gov.uk/graphic/homepages/normal.asp
- Emerging Markets Trade Association (EMTA): www.emta.org
- IFC: www.ifc.org
- Inter-American Development Bank (IADB): www.iadb.org
- International Center for Settlement of Investment Disputes (ICSID): www.worldbank.org/icsid
- International Chamber of Commerce: www.icc.org
- International Monetary Fund (IMF): www.imf.org
- International Petroleum Exchange: www.ipe.com
- International Primary Market Association: www.ipma.org.uk
- International Securities Market Association: www.isma.co.uk
- J.P. Morgan Emerging Market Bond Index: www.jpmorgan.com/Home/Research/Research.html
- Liffe: www.liffe.com
- London Metal Exchange: www.lme.co.uk
- London Stock Exchange (LSE): www.londonstockexchange.com
- Matif: www.matif.fr
- Morgan Stanley Capital International (MSCI): www.msci.com
- Nafta: www.ffas.usda.gov/info/factsheets/nafta.html.
- NYMEX/COMEX: www.nymex.com
- Overseas Private Investment Company (OPIC): www.opic.gov
- Political risk and economic freedom: www.freetheworld.com/
- Reuters: www.reuters.com
- Sydney Futures Exchange: www.sfe.com.au
- The Multilateral Investment Guarantee Agency (MIGA): www.miga.org

- Tiffe: www.tiffe.or.jp
- US Geological Survey (USGS): www.minerals.er.usgs.gov
- USDA: www.usda.gov
- VaR: www.jpmorgan.com
- World Bank: www.worldbank.org

International market indexes and their internet addresses

Market	Index	Address
New York Stock Exchange	NYSE Composite	www2.nyse.com/marketinfo/marketinfo.html
Nasdaq	Nasdaq Composite	www.nasdaq.com
American Stock Exchange	AMEX	www.amex.com
Amsterdam	AEX Index	www.aex.nl
Athens	Composite Index	www.ase.gr
Bangkok	SET Index	www.set.or.th
Bombay/NSE	CNX Nifty	www.nseindia.com
Brussels	BET-20 Index	www.stockexchange.be
Copenhagen	KFX Index	www.xcse.dk
Frankfurt	DAX	www.exchange.de
Helsinki	HEX General Index	www.hex.fi
Hong Kong	Hang Seng	www.sehk.hk
Istanbul	National 100 Index	www.ise.org
Jakarta	Composite Index	www.jsx.co.id
Johannesburg	All Market	www.jse.co.za
Kuala Lumpur	Composite	www.klse.com.my
London	FT-SE 100	www.stockex.co.uk
Madrid	Bolsa Index	www.bolsamadrid.es
Manila	PSE Index	www.pse.org.ph
Mexico	Bolsa Index	www.bmv.com.mx
Milan	MIB Telematico	www.borsaitalia.it
Oslo	OBX Index	www.ose.np
Paris	CAC-40	www.bourse-de-paris.fr
Sao Paulo	Bovespa Index	www.bovespa.com.br
Seoul	Composite Index	www.kse.or.kr
Shenzhen	B Shares Index	NA
Singapore	Straits Times	www.ses.com.sg
Stockholm	OMX Index	www.stockholmsborsen.se
Swiss Exchange	SPI	www.bourse.ch
Sydney	All Ordinaries	www.asx.com.au
Taipei	Stock Market Index	www.tse.com.tw
Tel Aviv	Tel Aviv 25 Index	www.tase.co.il
Toronto	TSE Industrials	www.tse.com
Vienna	ATX Index	www.wbag.at
Wellington	NZSE-40 Index	www.nzse.co.nz

Glossary

Accounting exposure. The change in the value of a firm's accounts denominated in foreign currency due to a change in the exchange rate.

Accrued interest. Interest that has been earned but is not yet due to be paid.

Adjusted present value. The net present value of an asset if financed solely by equity plus the present value of side effects associated with financing.

ADR. See **American depository receipts**.

AIBD. Association of International Bond Dealers. See ISMA.

American depository receipts. Negotiable certificates in registered form, issued in the United States by a US bank, certifying that a specific number of foreign shares have been deposited with an overseas branch of the bank or another financial institution that acts as custodian in the country of origin.

American style option. An option that can be exercised at any time over the option's life.

APV. See **Adjusted present value**

Arbitrage. The purchase of goods or securities in one market for immediate resale in another market in order to exploit price discrepancies between the two markets.

Arbitrage pricing theory (APT). A pricing theory based on a mechanism that derives asset prices from arbitrage arguments, once a pre-specified return generating process has been given.

Asian options. Also called average price or average rate options, these are path-dependent options whose payoff depends on the average price of an asset, an index or rate calculated over a predetermined part of the option's life.

Ask price. The price quoted by a market-maker at which he is willing to sell.

Asset for asset swap. Creditors exchange the debt of one defaulting borrower for the debt of another.

At-the-money option. An option where the strike (exercise) price is equal to the market price of the underlying asset.

Backwardation. When the basis is negative.

Balance of payments. The record of the economic and financial flows that take place over a specified time period between residents and non-residents of a given country.

Bank for International Settlements was originally set up in 1930 to enable the various national central banks to coordinate their receipts and payments arising from German war reparations. Since then, it has acted as a bank for central banks by accepting deposits and making short-term loans.

Barrier options. Options where the payoff depends on whether the price of the underlying asset reaches a pre-specified level over a given time period.

Basis. The difference between the futures price and the spot price.

Basis point. One one-hundredth of 1% (i.e. 0.01%).

Basket options. Options written on portfolios or "baskets" of risky assets.

Beta. The measure of systematic risk in the CAPM. Beta is calculated as the covariance between returns on the asset and returns on the market portfolio divided by the variance of returns on the market portfolio.

Bid bond (tender bond in cases where a formal tender has been organized). A financial instrument aimed at eliminating the risk that a commodity supplier will withdraw from the negotiations after it has been selected or that it will be unable to supply the commodity that is the object of a commercial contract under negotiation.

Bid price. The price quoted by a market-maker at which he is willing to buy.

Bid–ask spread. The difference between the quoted bid and ask prices.

Bill of exchange. See **draft**.

Bill of lading. A contract between the shipper (exporter) and a transportation company in which the latter agrees to transport the goods under specified conditions that limit its liability. It is the shipper's receipt for the goods as well as proof that the goods have been or will be shipped.

Binary options (also known as digital options). Options with discontinuous payoffs such as cash or nothing or asset or nothing.

Black option formula. Option pricing formula universally used by the market to price options on futures contracts.

Black-Scholes options pricing formula. The original options pricing formula universally used by the market to price options.

Bond. A long-term debt security with precise contractual obligations regarding interest and principal payments.

Brady bonds. Bank debt of emerging countries repackaged in the form of bonds under a plan named after a former US Secretary of the Treasury.

Bretton Woods system. The system negotiated by the Allied powers in 1944 that included the gold exchange standard along with the International Monetary Fund and the World Bank to administer it.

Call option. The right but not the obligation to buy at a given price.

Cap. A contract involving a series of call options with the same strike price and different expiration dates.

Capital account. In the balance of payments this is the net result of private and public borrowing, lending and investing between residents and non-residents.

Capital asset pricing model (CAPM). The first well known and widely used model of market equilibrium. It assumes that the investor must be compensated for the time value of money plus systematic risk – that is, risk that cannot be eliminated through diversification. Systematic risk is measured by beta.

Caplet. One component of a cap.

CAPM. See **Capital asset pricing model**.

Certificates of deposit (CDs). Certificates of deposit are negotiable instruments that can be traded on the secondary market.

Change in reserves. The account in the balance of payments that records changes in the monetary authorities' holdings of international liquidity. This account differs from the other accounts in the balance of payments insofar as it is the only account that records transactions with residents as well as non-residents.

CHAPS (Clearing House Automated Payments System). A computerized clearing system for sterling funds that began operations on 9 February, 1984. It includes 14 member banks and nearly 450 participating banks, and is one of the clearing companies within the Association for Payment Clearing Services (APACS) structure.

Cheapest to deliver. The bond that is cheapest to deliver as settlement in a futures contract.

CHIPS (Clearing House Interbank Payments System). A computerized network for international transfers of dollar funds that links depository institutions with offices in New York City. The system is owned and operated by the New York Clearing House Association whose members comprise 12 New York money center banks.

Circus swap. A fixed rate currency swap against floating US dollar Libor payments.

Clean price. The price of a bond quoted net of the accrued interest.

Clearing House. An organization that guarantees and settles trades on the organized derivative markets.

Clearing House Interbank Payments System. See **CHIPS**.

Collar. A combination of a cap and a floor.

Collateralization. The percent of the economy's total value that is realistically vulnerable to actions undertaken by foreign creditors in the case of default.

Common market. An agreement between two or more countries that permits the free movement of capital and labor as well as all goods and services.

Compound option. An option on an option.

Contango. When the basis is positive.

Convenience returns or yields. The advantages of actually owning an asset that come in the form of the planning benefits of having a secure supply and the elimination of costs associated with stock-outs or avoiding stock-outs.

Convexity. A measure of the change in duration with respect to changes in the interest rate.

Correspondent bank. A bank located in another city, state or country that provides a service for another bank.

Counterpart items. In the balance of payments there are analogous to unrequited transfers in the current account. They arise because of the double-entry system in balance of payments accounting and refer to adjustments in reserves owing to monetization or demonetization of gold, allocation or cancelation of SDRs and revaluation of the various components of total reserves.

Country beta. Covariance of a national economy's rate of return and the rate of return of the world economy divided by the variance of the world economy.

Country economic risk. Developments in the national economy that can affect the outcome of an international financial transaction.

Country financial risk. The ability of the national economy to generate enough foreign exchange to meet payments of interest and principal on its foreign debt.

Country risk. See **Cross-border risk**.

Covered interest arbitrage. This exploits interest rate differentials by borrowing in one currency, selling the borrowed currency on the spot market, investing the proceeds of the sale, and simultaneously buying back the borrowed currency on the forward market.

Crawling peg. This is an automatic system for revising the exchange rate. It involves establishing a par value around which the rate can vary up to a given percentage. The par value is revised regularly according to a formula determined by the authorities.

Credit risk. Reflects the counterparty's credit standing and its ability to meet its obligations in a swap agreement.

Cross hedge. A hedge using a futures contract on an asset that is different from the asset being hedged.

Cross rate. The exchange rate between two currencies that do not involve the US dollar calculated from the dollar rate for each currency.

Cross-border risk. The volatility of returns on international investments caused by events associated with a particular country as opposed to events associated solely with a particular economic or financial agent.

Currency option. A contract that gives its owner the right for a given period of time to buy or sell a given amount of one currency for another currency at a fixed price, called the exercise price or the strike price.

Currency swap. The exchange of a loan in one currency for a loan in another currency where both the principal and interest payments are exchanged.

Current account. In the balance of payments this is the net flow of goods, services and unrequited transfers between residents and non-residents.

Customs union. An agreement by two or more countries to erect a common external tariff and to abolish restrictions on trade among members.

Debt–equity swap. Debt is purchased at a discount by an investor and traded to the central bank (which takes a percentage) for the domestic currency necessary to make an investment.

Default risk. The risk that a counterparty will not be able to make his interest and principal payments.

Delta. The derivative of the price of an option with respect to the underlying asset price.

Delta hedge. An imperfect hedge using futures contracts where the maturities do not match.

Derivatives. Securities such as options, forwards, futures and swaps, whose value is derived from the value of another asset.

Devaluation. A decrease in the spot value of a currency.

Dirty price. The total price of a bond that includes accrued interest.

Domestic bonds are issued by a domestic borrower in the domestic market, usually in domestic currency.

Draft or **bill of exchange**. An unconditional order in writing, initiated and signed by the exporter, ordering the importer to pay on demand or at a given future date a given sum of money.

Duration. The present value weighted average of a bond's maturity. It is also a measure of the bond's sensitivity to changes in the interest rate.

Economic exposure to currency risk. The degree of variation of cash flows in home currency from foreign operations due to changes in the exchange rate or relative price levels.

Economic union. An agreement between two or more countries that allows the free movement of capital, labor all goods and services, and involves the harmonization and unification of social, fiscal and monetary policies.

Economies of scale exist when costs increase less than proportionately with output.

Efficient markets theory. This holds that a all relevant information is fully and immediately reflected in a security's market price.

Efficient portfolio. A portfolio that gives the highest expected return for a given level of risk.

Euro. The common currency of the countries belonging to the European Monetary System.

Eurobonds are issued in countries other than the one in whose currency they are denominated. They are not traded on a particular national bond market and, therefore, are not regulated by any domestic authority.

Eurocurrency (sometimes referred to as offshore currency). Any freely convertible currency, such as a US dollar or a Swiss franc, deposited in a bank outside its country of origin.

European Currency Unit (ECU). The accounting unit of the European Monetary System. It is a weighted average of each of the EMS currencies plus the Greek drachma.

European Economic Community (EC). Now called the European Union, the EEC was founded by the Treaty of Rome on 25 March 1957 by Belgium, France, Italy, Luxembourg, The Netherlands and West Germany.

European Monetary System (EMS). Created in 1979 by the major countries in the EC, the EMS is a fixed exchange rate system with an accounting unit called the European Currency Unit (ECU), which is a weighted cocktail of the participating countries' currencies.

European style option. An option that can only be exercised on the option's expiration date.

Exact matching. A bond portfolio management strategy that involves finding the lowest cost portfolio generating cash inflows exactly equal to cash outflows that are being financed by the investment.

Exchange rate. The price of foreign currency in units of local currency or, conversely, the price of local currency in units of foreign currency.

Exchange risk. The variability of the value of financial stocks and flows due to uncertainty about changes in the exchange rate.

Exercise price. See strike price.

Expected return. The average return.

Factoring. The sale of company receivables to a specialized buyer at a discount.

Fedwire. The Federal Reserve system for domestic money transfers between institutions that have accounts at the Federal Reserve banks.

Financial leverage. A measurement of the extent to which the assets of a firm are financed with debt.

Fisher relation or **Fisher open condition**. This gives the ratio of nominal investment values in terms of relative real rates of interest and expected rates of inflation. It should not be forgotten that this relation is not a market arbitrage condition like PPP and interest rate parity. It is a general equilibrium condition derived from first-order optimality conditions from individuals' utility optimization.

Fixed exchange rate. The price of the home currency in terms of another currency or commodity is fixed by the government. The gold standard and the gold exchange standard are two of the fixed rate systems that have been adopted in the recent past.

Flexible or floating exchange rate. The exchange rate is allowed to adjust freely to the supply and demand of one currency for another.

Floating rate loan. A loan where the interest rate is adjusted periodically according to an index.

Floating rate notes (FRNs). Generally medium-term CDs where the interest rate is fixed at a percentage above Libor (usually 15 to 30 basis points). Adjustments are made at regular intervals (every three or six months) according to the prevailing Libor.

Floor. A contract involving a series of put options with the same strike price and different expiration dates.

Floorlet. One component of a floor.

Foreign bonds are issued on the domestic market by a foreign borrower, usually in domestic currency. The rules and regulations governing issuing and trading procedures are under the control of the domestic authorities.

Foreign branch. An operation in a foreign country incorporated in the home country.

Foreign exchange. In the balance of payments this includes monetary authorities' claims on non-residents in the form of bank deposits, Treasury bills, short-term and long-term government securities, and other claims usable in the event of balance of payments need, including non-marketable claims arising from inter-central bank and inter-governmental arrangements, without regard to whether the claim is denominated in the currency of the debtors or the creditors.

Foreign subsidiary. An operation in a foreign country that is incorporated under the law of the foreign country.

Forward exchange rate. The current price of one currency for another for delivery at a specified date in the future.

Forward market. The market where goods, securities and currencies are traded for future delivery.

Forward rate agreement (FRA). An agreement between two parties concerning a future notional loan.

Forward rate parity hypothesis. This states that the forward exchange rate quoted at time 0 for delivery at time t is equal to what the spot rate is expected to be at time t.

Forward start options. Options that become effective some time after they are bought or sold.

Free on board (fob). This implies that distributive services like transport and handling performed on goods up to the customs frontier of the economy from which the goods are exported are classed as merchandise.

Fundamental analysis. This involves examining the macroeconomic variables and policies that are likely to influence a currency's performance.

Futures contract. A contract for future delivery of goods, securities or currencies. A futures contract is similar to a forward contract except that futures contracts are standardized, traded on an organized exchange and marked to market each day.

Gamma. The second partial derivative of the option price with respect to the price of the underlying asset.

Gold exchange standard. A system of fixing exchange rates adopted in the Bretton Woods agreement. It involved the United States pegging the dollar to gold and other countries pegging their currencies to the dollar.

Gold standard. This is a system whereby governments of participating countries fix the prices of their home currencies in terms of a specified amount of gold.

Gross domestic product (GDP). A measure of an economy's output defined as the total flow of goods and services produced by an economy over a specified time period. It is obtained by valuing the outputs of both final and investment goods and services at the market prices of the country in question and then aggregating.

Gross national product (GNP). A measure of an economy's total income. It is equal to GDP plus the income from abroad accruing to domestic residents minus income generated in the domestic market accruing to non-residents.

Hedge ratio. The percentage of the position in an underlying asset that is hedged with derivatives.

Hedging refers to the technique of making offsetting commitments in order to minimize the impact of unfavorable potential outcomes.

Immunization. A strategy for bond portfolio management that attempts to eliminate sensitivity to shifts in the yield curve by matching the duration of assets to the duration of liabilities.

Implied volatility. The volatility given by using the option's observed market price in the option pricing formula with volatility as the unknown.

Incoterms. Clauses of a commercial contract that refer to how certain costs, including transportation costs, freight-related costs and other logistical costs, conditions and responsibilities are shared between the two parties.

Interest rate parity relation. This states that on perfect money markets the forward discount or premium on the foreign exchange market is equal to the relative difference between the two interest rates.

Interest rate swap. The exchange of fixed rate interest payments for floating rate payments on a notional amount.

Internal rate of return. The discount rate that equates the present values of a stream of income and expenditure.

International Bank for Reconstruction and Development (IBRD). Also known as the World Bank, the IBRD was established at Bretton Woods along with the International Monetary Fund. Its purpose is to encourage capital investment for the reconstruction and development of its member countries either by channeling the necessary funds or by making loans from its own resources.

International Monetary Fund. The IMF is an international organization created at Bretton Woods in 1944 to administer a code of fair exchange practices and provide compensatory financial assistance to member countries with balance of payments difficulties.

International Securities Market Association. See **ISMA.**

International Swaps and Derivatives Association (ISDA). An association of swap dealers formed in 1985 to promote standard practices with respect to trading swaps and other derivative products.

In-the-money option. An option where the price of the underlying asset is above the strike price.

Intrinsic value. The non-negative difference between the price of the underlying security and the option's strike price.

Investment income. Income derived from the ownership of foreign financial assets. It includes interest and dividends for portfolio investment but excludes the earnings of incorporated enterprises that are not formally distributed.

ISDA. International Swaps Dealers Association.

ISMA. International Securities Market Association. ISMA, formerly called AIBD, is a Swiss Law Association located in Zürich that regroups all the participants on the Eurobond primary and secondary markets.

Junk bonds (high yield bonds). Any bond with a ranking below investment grade.

Law of one price. This states that identical commodities or goods must have the same price in all markets.

Lead manager. The bank in charge of organizing a syndicated bank credit or bond issue.

Letter of credit. A document addressed to the exporter that is written and signed by a bank on behalf of the importer. In the document, the bank undertakes to guarantee for a certain time span the payment for the specified merchandise, either by paying directly or by accepting drafts, if the exporter conforms to the conditions of the letter of credit by presenting the required documents.

Leveraged buyout (LBO). A corporate takeover designed to take the target company private for a number of years, increase its profitability and sell it back to the public at a substantial gain.

Libor (London interbank offered rate). The deposit rate on interbank transactions in the Eurocurrency market quoted in London.

Limit order. An order to buy or sell a security at a specific price.

Liquidity ratio. The measure of a firm's ability to meet its maturing short-term obligations.

Lookback option. An option the payoff on which depends on the maximum or minimum price of the underlying asset within the life of the option.

M1. This measure of money supply is equal to demand deposits plus the currency and coins outside the banking system.

M2. This measure of money supply is equal to M1 plus quasi-money.

Macroeconomic accounting discipline. This means that an economy's consumption and investment of resources cannot be greater than the resources that it produces plus the resources that it borrows.

Macroeconomic profits. The dollar value of exports minus imports plus the net gain in the the economy's market value.

Maintenance margin. The minimum margin that must be kept on deposit.

Managed float. Sometimes called a "dirty float", this is a system of flexible exchange rates whereby the authorities occasionally intervene by buying or selling domestic currency to smooth the transition from one rate to another.

Margin. The amount that must be deposited by an investor as collateral to cover positions taken on the financial markets.

Market order. An order to buy or sell immediately at the best available price.

Market prices. The amount of money that a willing buyer pays to acquire something from a willing seller, when buyer and seller are independent and when such an exchange is motivated only by commercial considerations.

Market risk. Reflects the difficulty in reversing positions due to market illiquidity.

Market-maker. Traders who stand ready to buy and sell on a more or less continuous basis.

Marking to market. The procedure whereby the profits and losses on a futures contract are paid on a daily basis.

Merchandise. All movable goods such as cars, textiles and appliances.

Modified duration. The duration of a bond divided by one plus the yield to maturity, which measures sensitivity of the bond price to changes in the interest rate.

Monetary gold is gold held by the authorities as a financial asset.

Money base (Mo). This is composed of currency and coins outside the banking system plus liabilities to the deposit money banks.

Multi-currency loans give the borrower the possibility of drawing a loan in several different currencies.

Multi-option financing facility (MOFF). A syndicated confirmed credit line with attached options.

Nationalization. A government takeover of a private company.

Net errors and omissions. In balance of payments accounting these record the statistical discrepancies that arise in gathering balance of payments data.

Netting. Reducing transfers of funds between subsidiaries to a net amount.

Nominal interest rates (or exchange rates). Actual market rates that do not compensate for inflation.

Non-financial services. Such things as freight, insurance, passenger services and travel.

Non-tradables. Goods and services produced and consumed domestically that are not close substitutes of exportables and importables.

Official unrequited transfers. These include voluntary subsidies, military aid, voluntary cancelation of debt, contributions to international organizations, indemnities imposed under peace treaties, technical assistance, taxes and fines.

Open interest. The total number of futures or option contracts that have not been closed out by an offsetting purchase or sale.

Option. A contract that gives its owner the right for a given period of time to buy or sell a given amount of an underlying asset at a fixed price, called the exercise price or the strike price.

Option premium. The price of the option.

Organization of Petroleum Exporting Countries. OPEC is a cartel of oil producing countries.

Other capital. In the balance of payments this is a residual category that groups all capital transactions that have not been included in direct investment, portfolio investment and reserves. It is divided into long-term capital and short-term capital and, because of its residual status, can differ from country to country. Generally speaking, other long-term capital includes most non-negotiable instruments of a year or more like bank loans and mortgages. Other short-term capital includes financial assets of less than a year such as currency, deposits and bills.

Out-of-the money option. An option where the price of the underlying is below the strike price.

Over-the counter (OTC). A securities market composed of dealers outside an organized exchange, where trading takes place electronically or by telephone.

Performance bond. A bank guarantee aimed at eliminating the risk that a commodity supplier will be unable to supply the commodity in question over the life of the contract.

Pibor (Paris interbank offered rate). The deposit rate on interbank transactions in the Eurocurrency market quoted in Paris.

Poisson process. A jump process describing events that happen at random with a probability per time period, called an intensity parameter.

Political risk. A term used by industrial firms to describe adverse events outside their particular market sector. The events can be traced to macroeconomic, social, political or strategic factors.

Political subordination. The de facto right of countries to subordinate claims of non-residents to those of residents.

Praecipium. The lead manager's fee for assuming responsibility for setting up and coordinating the syndication of the loan.

Price earnings ratio. The ratio of the share price divided by the earnings per share.

Price elasticities. Defined as the percentage change in the quantity divided by the percentage change in price.

Price specie flow. This means that balance of payments disequilibrium will be adjusted through adjustments in the country's money supply.

Private unrequited transfers. Mainly resident immigrant workers' remittances to their country of origin as well as gifts, dowries, inheritances, prizes and charitable contributions.

Privatization. A government-owned firm is sold to the public.

Promissory note. A written promise by the importer to pay a given sum on a given date in the future.

Purchasing power parity (PPP). The theory linking inflation and exchange rate movements.

Put option. The right but not the obligation to sell at a given price.

Put–call parity. The relationship between the value of a put option and the value of a call option with the same strike price and the same expiration date.

Rating. Classification of the credit quality of a company or a country by a rating agency such as Moody's or Standard & Poor's.

Real interest rate (or exchange rate). The rate after compensating for inflation.

Real options. The option approach to investment under uncertainty calls real options the possibilities that management has to delay investment, abandon investment, increase and decrease the size of an investment, and switch inputs and outputs of an investment.

Reference price. A price in the commodity markets that is recognized as a fair price by both parties negotiating the contract.

Reinvoicing center. A centralized operation that handles all foreign exchange transactions between group subsidiaries and third party clients. It takes title to all goods sold, pays the seller and collects from the buyer.

Reserve position in the Fund. Basically the difference between the member's IMF quota plus other claims on the Fund less the Fund's holdings of that member's currency.

Reserves. In the balance of payments this includes monetary gold, special drawing rights (SDRs), the reserve position in the Fund and foreign exchange.

Revolving credit facility. A loan that permits the borrower to drawdown and

repay at its discretion for a specified period of time.

Rho. The first partial derivative of the price of an option with respect to the interest rate.

Risk. See **Standard deviation**.

Risk premium. The difference between the expected return on a security and the risk-free rate.

Separation theorem. The ability to determine the optimum portfolio without having to know anything about the investor except that he is risk averse .

Short sale. The sale of a borrowed security.

Single European Act (SEA). A European Community Act in 1987 that affirmed the EC's intention to make the transition from a common market to a full economic union by 1992.

Sovereign risk. The possibility that a government will not be able to meet its external obligations because of a lack of foreign exchange.

Special drawing rights (SDRs). Reserves created by the International Monetary Fund (IMF) as bookkeeping entries and credited to the accounts of IMF member countries according to their established IMF quotas. A decision to create SDRs requires the approval of a majority of the member countries holding 85% of the weighted voting power of the IMF. Once created they may be used in the settlement of balance of payments imbalances among countries participating in the Special Drawing Account administered by the IMF.

Spot exchange rate. The exchange rate for the closest delivery date (usually two working days).

Spot interest rates are interest rates on bonds with only one cash flow.

Spot price. Current market price of an asset.

Spread option. Options written on the difference between two indices, prices or rates. Where interest rates are concerned, for example, one popular spread is a long-term Treasury rate minus a shorter-term Treasury rate.

Spreads. Combinations of options of different series but of the same class, where some are bought and others are written.

Spreads. The difference between bid and ask prices when quoting securities prices.

Standard deviation is the simplest statistical measure of how much a variable is likely to diverge from its expected value. It is sometimes referred to as "volatility" and in finance it is often used to indicate the riskiness of an asset, a portfolio of assets or a market. The standard deviation is the square root of the variance.

Straddle. Long position in a call and a put with the same strike price.

Strangle. A long position in a call and a put with different strike prices.

Strike price. The price at which an option can be exercised.

Subordination refers to ranking one type of claim below another for payment in the case of default.

Swap. An exchange of streams of payments between two counterparties, either directly or through an intermediary.

Swap rate. This presents the forward rate as a discount or premium on the spot rate.

Swaption. An option to enter into a given swap at a later date.

SWIFT (Society for Worldwide Interbank Financial Telecommunications). A special satellite communications network based in Belgium that connects over 1800 banks, brokerage firms and non-banking financial institutions worldwide.

Syndication refers to a number of banks grouping together to make a loan to one borrower.

Systematic risk. Risk that cannot be eliminated through diversification.

Tap. The procedure by which a borrower can keep issuing additional amounts of an old bond at its current market value.

Technical analysis. This makes no use of the economic and financial fundamentals deemed relevant to exchange rate determination. It focuses on prices and seeks to detect repetitions of past price patterns.

Term deposit. Conventional term deposits are non-negotiable bank deposits with a fixed term where the interest rate is fixed for the duration of the deposit.

Terms of trade. The number of units of imports that one unit of exports will buy (or vice versa), which can be calculated by dividing the price of exports by the price of imports.

The zero rate solvency test. The methodology whereby the country financial risk premium calculated using the Black-Scholes formula is compared with the country's rate of return to determine if the country is financially solvent.

Theta. The first partial derivative of the option price with respect to time.

Third party certification. A third party (recognized by both the seller and its client) who at some stage of shipping of the commodity verifies that the quality supplied meets the technical quality specifications set out in the contract.

Trade balance. Merchandise exports and imports fob.

Transfer price. The price at which one unit of a firm sells goods or services to an affiliated unit.

Transfer risk. The risk that a government might impose restrictions on debt service payments abroad.

Underlying. The asset on which a derivative is written.

Value at risk (VaR). A loss that will not be exceeded at some specified confidence level.

Variance. See **Standard deviation**.

Vega. The first partial derivative of an option with respect to volatility.

Velocity of money. The rate at which the stock of money circulates through the economy in order to finance transactions.

Volatility. See **Standard deviation**.

Wiener process. A stochastic process where the change in the variable for each short time period has a normal distribution with a mean equal to zero and a variance equal to dt.

World Bank. See **International Bank for Reconstruction and Development**.

Yankee bond. A foreign bond issued in the US market, payable in dollars, and registered with the SEC.

Yield curve. A curve showing the relationship between interest rates and maturity.

Yield to maturity is a bond's internal rate of return.

Zero coupon bond. A bond that pays no interest premiums but which is issued at a discount to its face value.

Zero coupon swap. Allows a zero coupon debt issuer to convert a zero coupon liability into a conventional floating or fixed rate liability.

References

Abuaf, N. and Jorion, P., "Purchasing power parity in the long run", *Journal of Finance* (March 1990), p.p. 157–174.

Adler, M., "Global fixed income portfolio management", *Financial Analysts Journal* (September–October 1983).

Adler, M. and Dumas, B., "International portfolio choice and corporation finance: A synthesis", *Journal of Finance* (June 1983), p.p. 925–984.

Adler, M. and Jorion, P., "Universal currency hedges for global portfolios", *Journal of Portfolio Management* (Summer 1992).

Adler, M. and Prasad, B., "On universal currency hedges", *Journal of Financial and Quantitative Analysis*, *27(1)* (March 1992).

Agmon, T. and Lessard, D.R., "Investor recognition of corporate international diversification", *Journal of Finance* (September 1977), p.p. 1049–1056.

Alesina, A. and Tabellini, G., "External debt, capital flight and political risk", *Journal of International Economics*, *27* (1989), p.p. 199–220.

Alexander, G.J., Eun, C.S. and Janakiramanan, S., "International listings and stock returns: Some empirical evidence", *Journal of Financial and Quantitative Analysis* (June 1988), p.p. 135–151.

Alexander, S.S., "Effects of a devaluation on a trade balance", *Staff Papers*, Vol. II, No. 2 (IMF, April 1952), p.p. 263–278.

Aliber, R., "The interest rate parity theorem: a reinterpretation", *Journal of Political Economy* (1973), p.p. 1451–1459.

Aliber, R. and Stickney, C.P., "Accounting measures of foreign exchange exposure: The long and the short of it", *The Accounting Review* (January 1975), p.p. 44–57.

Aliber, R., *Exchange Risk and International Corporate Finance* (London: Macmillan, 1978).

Amram, M. and Kulatilaka, N., *Real Options: Managing Strategic Investment in an Uncertain World* (Boston MA: Harvard Business School Press, 1999).

Anderson, R. "Some determinants of the volatility of futures prices", *Journal of Futures Markets* (Fall 1985), p.p. 331–348.

Ang, J. and Pohlman, R.A., "A note on the price behavior of Far Eastern stocks", *Journal of International Business Studies* (Spring 1978).

Antl, B. (Ed.), *Swap Finance* (London: Euromoney Publications, 1986).

Asquith, P., Mullins, D.W. and Wolff, E.D., "Original issue high yield bonds: Aging analyses of defaults, exchanges and calls", *Journal of Finance*, Vol. XLIV, No. 4 (September 1989), p.p. 923–952.

Bahamani Oskooee, M. and Das, S.P., "Transactions costs and the interest parity theorem", *Journal of Political Economy* (August 1985), 793–799.

Bailey, W. and Stultz, R.M., "Benefits of international diversification: the case of Pacific Basin stock markets", *Journal of Portfolio Management* (Summer 1990), p.p. 57–61.

Baldwin, R. and Krugman, P., "The persistence of the US trade deficit", *Brookings Papers on Economic Activity*, No.1 (1987), p.p. 1–43

Bank for International Settlements, *Evolution de l'Activité Bancaire et Financière Internationale* (November 1991).

Barnett, W.A. "New indices of money supply and the flexible Laurent demand system", *Journal of Business and Economic Statistics, 1* (January 1983), p.p. 7–23.

Bates, P.S. and Saini, K.G., "A survey of the quantitative approaches to country risk analysis", *Journal of Banking and Finance* (1984), p.p. 341–356.

Belongia, M.T. and Chalfant, J.A., "The changing empirical definition of money: Some estimates from a model for money substitutes", *Journal of Political Economy, 97(2)* (1989), p.p. 387–397.

Bennett, P. "Applying portfolio theory to global bank lending", *Journal of Banking and Finance* (1984), p.p. 153–169.

Bierwag, G.O., Kaufman, G. and Chang, C., "Duration and bond portfolio analysis: An overview", *Journal of Financial and Quantitative Analysis, 13(4)* (November 1978), p.p. 671–681.

Black, F., "The pricing of commodity contracts", *Journal of Financial Economics, 3* (1976), p.p. 167–179.

Black, F. "Universal hedging: Optimizing currency risk and reward in international equity portfolios", – *Financial Analysts Journal* (July-August 1989).

Black, F., "Equilibrium exchange rate hedging", *Journal of Finance*, Vol. XLV, No. 3 (July 1990).

Black, F., "Fact and fantasy in the use of options", *Financial Analysts Journal, 31* (1975), p.p. 36–72.

Black, F. and Litterman R., "Global portfolio optimization", *Financial Analysts Journal, 48(5)* (1992), p.p. 28–43.

Black, F. and Scholes, M., "The pricing of options and corporate liabilities", *Journal of Political Economy* (June 1973), p.p. 637–659.

Bouchet, M., Clark, E. and Groslambert, B., "Revisiting the Asian financial crisis: Were capital markets caught by surprise?", *International Journal of Finance* (in press).

Brealey, R.A. and Myers, S.C., *Principles of Corporate Finance* (Singapore: McGraw-Hill Book Co., 1988).

Brennan, M. and Schwartz, E., "Evaluating natural resource investments", *Journal of Business, 58* (January 1985), p.p. 135–157.

Brewer, T., *Political Risk in International Business: New Directions for Research, Management, and Public Policy* (New York: Praeger, 1985).

Brewer, T. and Rivoli, P., "Politics and perceived country creditworthiness in international banking", *Journal of Money, Credit and Banking, 22(3)* (1990), p.p. 357–369.

Brigham, E.F. and Weston, J.F., *Managerial Finance* (Hinsdale, IL: The Dryden Press, 1981).

Broadie, M., Glasserman, P. and Kou, S.G., "Connecting discrete and continuous path-dependent options", *Finance and Stochastics, 2* (1998), p.p. 1–28.

Callier, P. "One-way arbitrage, foreign exchange, and securities markets: A note", *Journal of Finance* (December 1981), p.p. 1177–1186.

Carelton, W.T. and Cooper, I.A., "Estimation and uses of the term structure of interest rates", *Journal of Finance, 31* (September 1976), p.p. 1067–1083.

Carli, G., "Eurodollars: A paper pyramid", *Banca Nazionale Quarterly Review* (June 1971).

Carter, E.E., "The behavioral theory of the firm and top level corporation decisions", *Administrative Science Quarterly* (December 1971).

Cassel, G., "The present situation in the foreign exchanges", *Economic Journal* (1916), p.p. 62–65.

Cataquet, H., *Bank lending to developing countries and the capital asset pricing model: how diversifiable are the risks?*, paper presented at the annual meeting of the Applied Econometrics Association in Lille, France, 9–11 December 1987.

Cavaglia, S., Verschoor, W.F.C. and Wolff, C.P., "Further evidence on exchange rate expectations", *Journal of International Money and Finance, 12* (February 1993).

Chang, C.W. and Chang, J.S.K., "Forward and futures prices: Evidence from the foreign exchange markets", *Journal of Finance, 45* (1990).

Chollerton, K. Pieraerts, P. and Solnik, B. "Why invest in foreign currency bonds?", *Journal of Portfolio Management* (Summer 1986).

Clark, E., "Le système monétaire international: Liquidités privées et reserves officielles", *Eurépargne* (Septembre 1978).

Clark, E., "Country risk analysis in globalized financial markets", *The Business Economist, 19(1)* (Winter 1987).

Clark, E. "L'analyse du risque-pays des années 70 à la période actuelle", *Revue Banque, 477* (November 1987).

Clark, E., "Duration as a risk management tool", *Journal of International Securities Markets, 2* (Spring 1988), p.p. 47–53.

Clark, E., *Cross-Border Investment Risk* (London: Euromoney Publications, 1991).

Clark, E., "A general international market index", *International Journal of Finance, 7(3)* (1995), p.p. 1288–1312.

Clark, E., "Valuing political risk as an insurance policy", *Journal of International Money and Finance, 16* (1997), p.p. 477–490.

Clark, E., "Political risk in Hong Kong and Taiwan: Pricing the China factor", *Journal of Economic Integration, 13(2)* (1998), p.p. 278–293.

Clark, E. "L'effet de réunification sur le risque politique à Hong Kong", *Banque et Marches* (July–August 1999), p.p. 50–55.

Clark, E., "Agency conflict and the signaling snafu in the Mexican peso conflict of 1994", *International Journal of Public Administration*, Vol. 23, No. 5–8 (2000), p.p. 837–876.

Clark, E. and Jokung, O., "Capital budgeting, political risk and prudence", *International Journal of Finance, 10(1)* (1998), p.p. 933–943.

Clark, E., Lesourd, J.B. and Thiéblemont, R., *International Commodity Trading: Physical and Derivative Markets* (London: John Wiley and Sons, 2001).

Clark, E. and Marois, B., *Managing Risk in International Business* (London: Thomson Learning, 1996).

Clark, E. and Tunaru, R., "Valuing and managing multiple political risks", *Middlesex University Business School Discussion Paper,* Series 4 (May 2000).

Clark, E. and Zenaidi, A., "Sovereign debt discounts and the unwillingness to pay", *Finance, 20(2)* (1999), p.p. 185–199.

Clendenning, E.W., "Eurodollar and credit creation", *International Currency Review* (March–April 1971).

Clinton, K. "Transactions costs and covered interest arbitrage: Theory and evidence", *Journal of Political Economy* (April 1988), p.p. 358–370.

Cobbaut, R. *Theorie Financière* (Paris: Economica, 1987).

Cochran, S.J. and Mansur, I., "The interrelationships between US and foreign equity market yields: Tests of Granger causality", *Journal of International Business Studies* (Fourth Quarter, 1991), p.p. 723–736.

Cohen, D., "A valuation formula for LDC debt", *Journal of International Economics, 34* (1993).

Copeland, T.E. and Weston, J.F., *Financial Theory and Corporate Policy* (Reading, MA: Addison Wesley Publishing Company, 1988), p.p. 17–76.

Cornell, B. and Reinganum, M., "Forward and futures prices: Evidence from the foreign exchange markets", *Journal of Finance*, 36 (1981), p.p. 1035–1045.

Cosset, J.C. and Roy, J., "The determinants of country risk rankings", *Journal of International Business Studies, 22(1)* (1991), p.p. 135–142.

Cox, J., Ingersoll, Jr., J. and Ross, S., "The relation between forward prices and futures prices", *Journal of Financial Economics, 9* (1981), p.p. 321–346.

Cox, J., Ross S. and Rubenstein, M., "Option pricing: A simplified approach", *Journal of Financial Economics, 7* (1979), p.p. 229–264.

Cox, J. and Rubenstein, M., *Options Markets* (Englewood Cliffs NJ: Prentice Hall, Inc., 1985).

Crockett, A.D., "The Eurocurrency market: An attempt to clarify some basic issues", *Staff Papers* (IMF, July 1976).

Cumby, R. and Obstfeld, M., "A note on exchange rate expectations and nominal interest differentials: A test of the Fisher hypothesis", *Journal of Finance* (1981), p.p. 697–703.

Deardorff, A.V., "One-way arbitrage and its implications for the foreign exchange markets", *Journal of Political Economy* (April 1979), p.p. 351–364.

Deppler, M.C. and Ripley, D., "The world trade model: Merchandise trade flows", *Staff Papers* (IMF, March 1978), p.p. 147–206.

Dixit, A.K. and Pindyck R.S., *Investment Under Uncertainty* (Princeton: Princeton University Press, 1994).

Dornbusch, R., "Expectations and exchange rate dynamics", *Journal of Political Economy* (December 1976), p.p. 1161–1176.

Dornbusch, R. and Krugman, P., "Flexible exchange rates in the short term", *Brookings Papers on Economic Activity, (3)* (1976), p.p. 537–575.

Dufloux, C. and L. Margulici, *Finance Internationale et Marchés de Gré à Gré* (Paris: Economica, 1991).

Dufloux, C. and Margulici, L., "Les Euro-crédits: Pourquoi? Comment?", *La Revue Banque* (1984).

Earl, P. and F.G. Fisher, III, *International Mergers and Acquisitions* (London: Euromoney Publications, 1986).

Eaton, J., Gersovitz, M. and Stiglitz, J., "The pure theory of country risk", *European Economic Review, 30* (1986), p.p. 481–513.

Edison, H.J. "Purchasing power parity in the long run: A test of the dollar/pound exchange rate (1890–1978)", *Journal of Money, Credit and Banking* (August 1987), p.p. 376–387.

Elton, E.J and Gruber, M.J., *Modern Portfolio Theory and Investment Analysis*, 5th edition (New York: John Wiley & Sons, 1995).

Elton, E.J., Gruber, M.J. and Rentzler, J., "The performance of publicly offered commodity funds", *Financial Analysts Journal* (July–August 1990), p.p. 23–30.

Enders, W., "ARIMA and cointegration tests of PPP under fixed and flexible exchange rate regimes", *Review of Economics and Statistics, 70* (August 1988).

Engel, C., "On the foreign exchange risk premium in a general equilibrium model", *Journal of International Economics, 32* (1992).

Ergueta, A.J. and Shrieve, R., "Assessing the debt servicing capacity of Peru", in G. Feiger and B. Jacquillat (Eds.), *International Finance: Text and Cases* (Boston, MA: Allyn and Bacon, 1982).

Eun, C.S. and Resnick, B., "Exchange rate uncertainty, forward contracts, and international portfolio selection", *Journal of Finance* (March 1988), p.p. 197–215.

Fama, E., "Efficient capital markets: A review of theory and empirical work", *Journal of Finance* (May 1970).

Fama, E. and French, K.R., "The cross-section of expected stock returns", *Journal of Finance*, Vol. XLVII, No. 2 (June 1992), p.p. 427–465.

Feder, G. and Just, R.E., "A study of debt servicing capacity applying logit analysis", *Journal of Development Economics* (1977), p.p. 25–39.

Feiger, G. and Jacquillat, B., *International Finance: Text and Cases* (Boston, MA: Allyn and Bacon, 1982).

Fisher, I., *The Theory of Interest* (New York: Macmillan, 1930).

Fisher, III, F.G., *Eurobonds* (London: Euromoney Publications, 1988).

Folks, Jr. W.R. and Stansell, S.R. "The use of discriminant analysis in forecasting exchange rate movements", *Journal of International Business Studies* (Spring 1975), p.p. 71–81.

Fong, H.G. and Fabozzi, K.J., *Fixed Income Portfolio Management* (Homewood, IL: Dow Jones-Irwin, 1985).

Fox, S. and Reuschoff, N., *Principles of International Accounting* (Austin TX: Austin Press, 1986).

Frank, C.R. and Cline, W.R. "Measurement of debt servicing capacity: An application of discriminant analysis", *Journal of International Economics* (1971), p.p. 327–344.

Frenkel, J. and Levich, R., "Transaction costs and interest arbitrage: Tranquil versus turbulent periods", *Journal of Political Economy* (1977), p.p. 1209–1226.

Frenkel, J.A., "Test of rational expectations in the forward exchange market", *Southern Journal of Economics* (1980), p.p. 1083–1101.

Frenkel, J.A. and Froot, K. "Using survey data to test standard propositions regarding exchange rate expectations", *American Economic Review, 77* (March 1987).

Friedman, M. (Ed.), *Studies in the Quantity Theory of Money* (Chicago: The University of Chicago Press, 1956).

Friedman, M., "The Eurodollar market: Some first principles", *Morgan Guaranty Survey* (October 1969).

Froot, K.A. and Obstfeld, M., "Exchange rate dynamics under stochastic regime shifts", *Journal of International Economics, 31* (1991).

Gale, B.T., "Market share and rate of return", *Review of Economics and Statistics* (December 1972).

Galliot, H.J. "Purchasing power parity as an explanation of long term changes in exchange rates", *Journal of Money, Credit and Banking* (August 1971), p.p. 348–357.

Garman, M., "Recollection in tranquility", *Risk, 2(3)* (1989), p.p. 16–19.

Garman, M. and Kohlhagen, S., "Foreign currency options values", *Journal of International Money and Finance* (December 1983), p.p. 231–237.

Gelach, S., "Intertemporal speculation, devaluation and the J-curve", *Journal of International Economics, 27* (1989), p.p. 335–345.

Gerakis, A.S., "Recession in the initial phase of a stabilization program: the experience of Finland", *Staff Papers*, Vol. XI, No. 1 (IMF, November 1964), p.p. 434–445.

Geske, R., "A note on an analytic valuation formula for unprotected American call options on stocks with known dividends", *Journal of Financial Economics, 7* (1979) p.p. 375–380.

Geske, R., "The valuation of compound options", *Journal of Financial Economics, 7* (1979), p.p. 63–81.

Geske, R., "Comments on Whaley's note", *Journal of Financial Economics, 9* (1981), p.p. 213–215.

Geweke, J. and Feige, E. "Some joint tests of the efficiency of markets for forward exchange", *Review of Economics and Statistics* (1979), p.p. 334–341.

Gibson, R. and Schwartz, E., "Stochastic convenience yield and the pricing of oil contingent claims", *Journal of Finance, 45* (July 1990), p.p. 959–976.

Giddy, I.H. and G. Dufey, "The random behaviour of flexible exchange rates", *Journal of International Business Studies* (Spring 1975), p.p. 1–32.

Girardin, E. (Ed.), *Finance Internationale: L'Etat Actuel de la Théorie* (Paris: Economica, 1992).

Glen, J.D., "Real exchange rates in the short, medium and long run", *Journal of International Economics, 33* (1992).

Goldberg, L. and Spiegel, M.M., "Debt writedowns and debt equity swaps in a two sector model", *Journal of International Economics, 33* (1992).

Goldman, B., Sosin H. and Gatto M.A., "Path dependent options: Buy at the low, sell at the high", *Journal of Finance, 34* (1979), p.p. 1111–1127.

Goodman, L. "Bank lending to non-OPEC LDCs: Are risks diversifiable?", *Federal Reserve Bank of New York Quarterly Review* (Summer 1981).

Gordon, M.J. and Shapiro, E., "Capital equipment analysis: the required rate of profit", *Management Science, 3* (October 1956), p.p. 102–110.

Grabbe, O., *International Financial Markets* (Amsterdam: Elsevier, 1986).

Grangeas, G. and Saucier, P., *Comptabilité Nationale* (Paris: Editions Cujas, 1992).

Gujarati, D.N., *Basic Econometrics*, third edition (New York: McGraw-Hill, Inc., 1995).

Hagger, E., "Grand Met snubs the syndicators", *Euromoney* (December 1991).

Hana, H., "Why Americans should have diversified", *Euromoney* (March 1980).

Haner, F.T., *Business Environment Risk Index*, BERI Ltd.: A system for selected countries (August 1981).

Hansen, L.P. and R.J Hodrick, "Risk-averse speculation in the forward exchange market: An econometric analysis of linear models", in J.A. Frenkel (Ed.), *Exchange Rates and International Macroeconomics* (Chicago: University of Chicago Press, 1983).

Hayek, F., *Monetary Theory and the Trade Cycle*, trans. N. Kaldor and H.M. Croome (London: Jonathan Cape, 1933).

Hayek, F., *The Pure Theory of Capital* (London: Routledge and Kegan Paul, Ltd., 1941).

Hayek, F., *Prix et Production*, trans. Tradecom (Vienne: Calmann-Levy, 1975).

Heller, L. (Ed.), *Eurocommercial Paper* (London: Euromoney Publications, 1988).

Hertz, D.B., "Uncertainty and investment selection" in J.F. Weston and M.B. Goudzwaard (Eds.) *The Treasurer's Handbook* (Homewood, IL: Dow Jones-Irwin, 1976), p.p. 376–420.

Hewson, J. and Sakakibara, E., "The Eurodollar multiplier: A portfolio approach", *Staff Papers* (IMF, July 1974).

Hicks, J., *A Contribution to the Theory of the Trade Cycle* (Oxford: Clarendon Press, 1950).

Hicks, J. *Capital and Time: A Neo-Austrian Theory* (Oxford: Clarendon Press, 1987).

Hodgson, J. and P. Phelps, "The distributed impact of price level variation on floating exchange rates", *Review of Economics and Statistics* (February 1975), p.p. 58–64.

Hoss, S. and Working, H., "Wheat futures prices and trading at Liverpool since 1886", *Wheat Studies of the Food Research Institute* (November 1938).

Hsia, C.C., "Coherence of the modern theories of finance", *Financial Review* (Winter 1981), p.p. 27–42.

Hull, J. C. *Options, Futures and Other Derivatives* (London: Prentice Hall International, 2000).

Hunter, J.E. and Coggin, T.D., "an analysis of the diversification benefit from international equity investment", *Journal of Portfolio Management* (Fall 1990), p.p. 33–36.

Ingersoll, J.E., Skelton, J. and Weil, R.L., "Duration forty years later", *Journal of Financial and Quantitative Analysis*, *13* (November 1978), p.p. 627–650.

Inter-Bank Research Organization, "CHAPS: A new approach to payments systems" (April 1982), reprinted with additions by APACS (August 1991).

International Monetary Fund, *Balance of Payments Manual,* 4th edition (IMF, 1977)

International Monetary Fund, *The Monetary Approach to the Balance of Payments* (IMF, 1977).

International Monetary Fund, *International Financial Statistics*, published monthly,

International Monetary Fund, *Report on the World Current Account Discrepancy* (IMF, September 1987).

Isard, P., "How far can we push the Law of One Price?", *American Economic Review* (December 1977), p.p. 942–948.

Ishikawa, J., "Learning by doing: Changes in industrial structure and trade patterns, and economic growth in a small open economy", *Journal of International Economics*, *33* (1992).

Jacquillat, B. and Solnik, B., "Multinationals are poor tools for diversification", *Journal of Portfolio Management* (Winter 1978), p.p. 8–12.

Jaffee, J. and Westerfield, R., "Patterns in Japanese common stock returns: Day of the week and turn of the year effects", *Journal of Financial and Quantitative Analysis* (June 1985).

Jensen, M.C., "Eclipse of the public corporation", *Harvard Business Review* (September–October 1989), p.p. 61–74.

Johnson, R. A., Srinivasan, V. and Bolster, P.J., "Sovereign debt ratings: A judgemental model based on the analytic hierarchy process", *Journal of International Business Studies* (1990), p.p. 95–117.

Jorion, P., "International portfolio diversification with estimation risk", *Journal of Business*, *58(3)* (1985), p.p. 259–278.

Jorion, P. and Schwartz, E., "Integration versus segmentation in the Canadian stock market", *Journal of Finance* (July 1986), p.p. 603–616.

Kaminsky, G. and Peruga, R., "Can a time varying risk premium explain excess returns in the forward market for foreign exchange?", *Journal of International Economics* (1990).

Kane, E. and Rosenthal, L., "International interest rates and inflationary expectations", *Journal of International Money and Finance* (April 1982).

Kaplan, S.N., "The staying power of leveraged buyouts", *Journal of Financial Economics, 29* (1991), p.p. 287–313.

Kapoor, G. and Grub, A., *Multinational Enterprise in Transition* (Princeton: Darwin Press, 1973).

Kasanen, E. and Trigeorgis, L., "A market utility approach to investment valuation", *European Journal of Operational Research* (Special Issue on Financial Modeling) *74(2)* (1994), p.p. 294–309.

Kato, K. and Schallheim, J. "Seasonal and size anomalies in the Japanese stock market", *Journal of Financial and Quantitative Analysis* (June 1985).

Kemma, A. and A. Vorst, "A pricing method for options based on average asset values", *Journal of Banking and Finance, 14* (1990), p.p. 113–129.

Kennedy, Jr., C.R., "Multinational corporations and political risk in the Persian Gulf", *International Journal of Middle East Studies* (August 1984), p.p. 391–403.

Keynes, J.M., *A Treatise on Money* (London: Macmillan, 1930).

Klein, J. and Marois, B., *Gestion et Stratégie Financière Internationale*, second edition (Paris: Dunod, 1993).

Klopstock, F. "Money creation in the Eurodollar market: A note on Professor Friedman's views", *Monthly Review*, Federal Reserve Bank of New York (January 1970).

Kobrin, S., "Expropriations as an attempt to control foreign affiliates, 1960–1979", *International Studies Quarterly, 3* (September 1984), p.p. 329–348.

Kouri, P.J.K. and Porter, M.G., "International capital flows and portfolio equilibrium", *Journal of Political Economy* (May—June 1974), p.p. 443–467.

Kravis, I.B. and Lipsey, R.E., "Price behaviour in the light of balance of payments theory", *Journal of International Economics* (May 1978), p.p. 193–246.

Kritzman, M., "A simple solution for optimal currency hedging", *Financial Analysts Journal* (November–December 1989).

Krugman, P., "Internal debt strategies in an uncertain world", in G. Smith and J. Cuddington (Eds.), *International Debt and the Developing World* (Washington DC: World Bank, 1985).

Lee, J.P. and Schwartz, R., *Global Custody: A Guide for the Nineties* (London: ICB Publications, 1991).

Lee, P., "Enterprise fires up the 144A Yankee bond", *Euromoney* (December 1991).

Leroux, F., *Marchés Internationaux des Capitaux* (Sillery, Quebec: Presses Universitaires du Quebec, 1988).

Levasseur, M. and Quintart, A., *Finance*, second edition (Paris: Economica, 1992).

Levi, M.D., *International Finance* (New York: McGraw-Hill, Inc., 1990).

Little, I. and Mirrlees, J., *Manuel d'Analyse des Projets Industriels dans les Pays en Voie de Développement*, Vol. II of *L'Analyse Co-ts-Avantages du Point de Vue de la Collectivité* (Paris: OECD, 1969).

Liu, P. C., and Maddala, G.S., "Rationality of survey data and tests of market efficiency in the foreign exchange market", *Journal of International Money and Finance, 11* (August 1992).

Longin, F. and Solnik, B., "Is the international correlation of equity returns constant: 1960–1990?", *Journal of International Money and Finance* (February 1995).

Machlup, F., "Eurodollar creation: A mystery story", *Banca Nazionale del Lavoro Quarterly Review* (September 1970).

Marchal, J. and Lecaillon, J., *Les Flux Monétaires* (Paris: Editions Cujas, 1967).

Mark, N., "Real and nominal exchange rates in the long run: An empirical investigation", *Journal of International Economics, 28* (February 1990).

Markowitz, H., *Portfolio Selection: Efficient Diversification of Investments* (New York: John Wiley & Sons, 1959).

Marois, B. *Le Risque Pays* (Paris: Presses Universitaires de France, Collection "Que Sais-Je", 1990).

Marois, B., "Foreign Investment Risk and the Multinational Corporation", *Les Cahiers de Recherche* (HEC, 1992).

Marston, R.C., "Interest arbitrage in the Eurocurrency markets", *European Economic Review* (1976).

Mason, S.P. and Merton, R.C., "The role of contingent claims analysis in corporate finance", in E. Altman and M. Subrahmanyam (Eds.), *Recent Advances in Corporate Finance* (Homewood, IL: Richard D. Irwin, 1985), 7–54.

McCulloch, J.H., "An estimate of the liquidity premium", *Journal of Political Economy, 83* (February 1975), p.p. 95–119.

McKnown, R. and Wallace, M., "National price levels, purchasing power parity and cointegration: A test of four high inflation countries", *Journal of International Money and Finance, 8* (December 1989).

Merton, R.C., "An intertemporal capital asset pricing model", *Econometrica* (September 1973), p.p. 867–887.

Merton, R.C., *Continuous Time Finance* (New York: Basil Blackwell, Inc., 1990).

Merton, R.C., "On the mathematics and economic assumptions of continuous time models", in R.C. Merton (Ed.) *Continuous Time Finance* (New York: Basil Blackwell, Inc., 1990), p.p. 57–93.

Meyer, H., "Multiplier effects and credit creation in the Eurodollar market", *Banca Nazionale del Lavoro Quarterly Review* (September 1971).

Milonas, N., "Price variability and the maturity effect in futures markets", *Journal of Futures Markets,* Spring (1986).

Minor, M., "The demise of expropriation as an instrument of LDC policy, 1980–1992", *Journal of International Business Studies, 25(1)* (1994), p.p. 177–188.

Miron, S. and Swannell, M., *Hedging and Pricing Swaps* (London: Euromoney Publications, 1990).

Mishkin, F.S., "Are real interest rates equal across countries? An empirical investigation of international parity relations", *Journal of Finance* (December 1984).

Morck, R., Schwartz, E. and Strangeland, D., "The valuation of forestry resources under stochastic prices and inventories", *Journal of Financial and Quantitative Analysis, 24* (December 1989), p.p. 473–487.

Muscarella, C.J. and Vetsuypens, M.R., "Efficiency and organizational structure: A study of reverse LBOs", *Journal of Finance*, Vol. XLV, No. 5 (December 1990), p.p. 1389–1413.

Nagy, P., *Country Risk* (London: Euromoney Publications, 1984).

Neftci, S.N., *An Introduction to the Mathematics of Financial Derivatives* (San Diego, CA: Academic Press 1996).

Noetzlin, B. and Solnik, B., "Optimal international asset allocation", *Journal of Portfolio Management* (Fall 1982).

Officer, R.R., "Seasonality in Australian capital markets", *Journal of Financial Economics* (March 1975).

Ollard, W., "The debt swappers", *Euromoney* (August 1986).

Otani I., and Tiwari, S., "Capital controls and interest rate parity: The Japanese experience 1978–1981", *Staff Papers* (IMF, 1981), 793–815.

Paddock, J., Siegel, D. and Smith, J., "Option valuation of claims on real assets: The case of offshore petroleum leases", *Quarterly Journal of Economics, 103* (August 1988), p.p. 479–508.

Park, H.Y. and Chen, A.H., "Difference between futures and forward prices: A further investigation of marking to market effects", *Journal of Futures Markets, 5* (1985), p.p. 77–88.

Paveau, J. et al., *Exporter* (Paris: Editions Foucher, 1992).

Pearce, I.F., "The problem of the balance of payments", *International Economic Review*, Vol. II, No. 1 (January 1961), p.p. 1–28.

Phylaktis, K., "Purchasing power parity and cointegration: The Greek evidence from the 1920s", *Journal of International Money and Finance, 11* (October 1992).

Pippenger, M.K., "Cointegration tests of purchasing power parity: The Swiss case", Journal of International Money and Finance, *12* (February 1993).

Polak, J.J. and Argy, V., "Credit policy and the balance of payments", in International Monetary Fund, *The Monetary Approach to the Balance of Payments* (Washington DC: IMF, 1977), p.p. 205–225.

Polk, J. et al., *US Production Abroad and the Balance of Payments* (New York: National Industrial Conference Board, 1966).

Popper, H., "Long-term covered interest parity: Evidence from currency swaps", *Journal of International Money and Finance, 12* (August 1993).

Poynter, J., "Government intervention in less developed countries: The experience of multinational companies", *Working Paper No. 238*, University of Ontario (March 1980).

Raff, H., "A model of expropriation with asymmetric information", *Journal of International Economics, 33* (1992), p.p. 245–265.

Rappaport, A., "The staying power of the public corporation", *Harvard Business Review* (January–February 1990), p.p. 96–104.

Ricardo, D., *On the Principles of Political Economy and Taxation* (New York: Dutton, 1948).

Richardson, J.D., "Some empirical evidence on commodity arbitrage and the Law of One Price", *Journal of International Economics* (May 1978), p.p. 342–351.

Robock, S. and Simmons, K., *International Business and Multinational Enterprise* (Homewood, IL: R. Irwin, 1973).

Roddock, D., *Assessing Corporate Political Risk* (Totowa, NY: Rowman and Littlefield Publishers, 1986).

Rogalski, R.J. and Vinso, J.D., "Price variations as predictors of exchange rates", *Journal of International Business Studies (*Spring-Summer 1977), p.p. 71–83.

Rogriguez, R.M. and Carter, E.E., *International Financial Management*, third edition (Englewood Cliffs, NJ: Prentice-Hall, Inc., 1984).

Roll, R., "An analytic valuation formula for unprotected American call options on stocks with known dividends", *Journal of Financial Economics, 5* (1977), p.p. 251–258.

Roll, R. "A critique of the asset pricing theory's test: On past and potential testability of the theory", *Journal of Financial Economics, 4* (March 1977), 349–357.

Roll, R., "Violations of purchasing power parity and their implications for efficient commodity markets", in M. Sarnat and G.Szego (Eds.) *International Finance and Trade (*Cambridge, MA: Ballinger 1979).

Roll, R. and Ross, S.A., *On the Cross-Sectional Relation between Expected Returns and Betas*, paper presented at the French Finance Association's International Conference in Finance (29 June 1992).

Roll, R. and Solnik, B., "A pure foreign exchange asset pricing model", *Journal of International Economics* (May 1977).

Root, F., "Analyzing political risks in international business", in Kapoor and Grub (Eds.), *Multinational Enterprise in Transition* (Princeton: Darwin Press, 1973).

Root, F.R., *International Trade and Investments*, sixth edition (Cincinnati, OH: South-Western Publishing Co., 1990).

Ross, S. A., "The arbitrage theory of capital asset pricing", *Journal of Economic Theory, 13* (December 1976), p.p. 341–360.

Rousseau, P., *Théorie Financière et Décision d'Investissement* (Paris: Economica, 1990).

Rubin, S.M., *Junk Bonds after the Crisis* (London: Euromoney Publications, 1991).

Rutledge, D., "A note on the variability of futures prices", *Review of Economics and Statistics, 58* (1976), 118–120.

Samuelson, P.A., "Proof that properly anticipated prices fluctuate randomly", *Industrial Management Review, 6* (1965), 41–49.

Sarnat, M. and Szego G. (Eds.), *International Finance and Trade* (Cambridge, MA: Ballinger 1979).

Schaefer, S.M., "Measuring a tax specific term structure of interest rates in the market for British government securities", *Economic Journal, 91* (June 1981), p.p. 415–438.

Schwartz, E.S. and Zurita, S., "Sovereign debt: Optimal contract, underinvestment, and forgiveness", *Journal of Finance*, Vol. XLVII, No. 3 (July 1992).

Shapiro A.C., *Multinational Financial Management*, third edition (Needham Heights, MA: Allyn and Bacon, 1989).

Shapiro, A.C., "What does purchasing power parity mean?", *Journal of International Money and Finance* (1983), p.p. 295–318.

Sharpe, W.F., *Investments* (Englewood Cliffs, NJ: Prentice-Hall, Inc., 1985).

Smith, A., "Corporate ownership, structure and performance: The case of management buyout", *Journal of Financial Economics, 27* (1990), p.p. 143–164.

Smith, A., *An Inquiry into the Nature and Causes of the Wealth of Nations* (New York: Random House, 1937).

Smith, G. and Cuddington, J., *International Debt and the Developing World* (Washington DC: World Bank, 1985).

Solnik, B. "Why not diversify internationally rather than domestically", *Financial Analysts Journal* (July–August 1974), p.p. 48–54.

Solnik, B., "An equilibrium model of the international capital market", *Journal of Economic Theory* (August 1974).

Solnik, B., "Why not diversify internationally rather than domestically", *Financial Analysts Journal* (July 1974).

Solnik, B., *International Investments* (Reading MA: Addison Wesley Publishing Co., Inc., 1996).

Solnik, B. and Noetzlin, B., "Optimal international asset allocation", *Journal of Portfolio Management* (Fall 1982).

Spithaller, E., "A survey of recent quantitative studies of long-term capital movements", *Staff Papers* (IMF, March 1971).

Stoakes, C. and Freeman, A., *Managing Global Portfolios* (London: Euromoney Publications, 1989).

Stockman, A.C., "Risk, information and forward exchange rates", in J.A. Frenkel and H.G. Johnson (Eds.), *The Economics of Exchange Rates* (Reading, MA: Addison Wesley, 1978).

Svensson, L.E.O., "The foreign exchange risk premium in a target zone with devaluation risk", *Journal of International Economics, 33* (1992).

Swoboda, A.K., "The Eurodollar market: An interpretation", *Essays in International Finance*, No. 64, Princeton University Press, 1968.

Tagaki, S., "Exchange rate expectations: A survey of surveys studies", *Staff Papers* (IMF, June 1991).

Tapley, M., (Ed.), *International Portfolio Management* (London: Euromoney Publications, 1986).

Thomas, L.R., "The performance of currency hedged foreign bonds", *Financial Analysts Journal* (May–June 1989).

Topsacalian, P., *Principes de Finance Internationale* (Paris: Economica, 1992).

Triffin, R., *Gold and the Dollar Crisis* (Yale University Press, 1960).

Triffin, R., "The myth and realities of the so-called gold standard", in *The Evolution of the International Monetary System: Historical Reappraisal and Future Perspective* (Princeton University Press, 1964).

Trigeorgis, L., *Real Options* (Cambridge, MA: The MIT Press, 1996).

Tucker, H., *A Graduate Course in Probability* (New York: Academic Press, Inc, 1967).

Turnbull, S.M. and Wakeman, L.M. "A quick algorithm for pricing European average options", *Journal of Financial and Quantitative Analysis, 26* (September 1991), p.p. 377–389.

UNIDO, *Directives pour l'Evaluation des Projets* (New York: United Nations, 1973).

United Nations, *A System of National Accounts, Studies in Methods*, Series No. 2, Rev. 3 (New York, 1968).

Vernon, R. and Wells, L.T., *Manager in the International Economy*, fourth edition (Englewood Cliffs, NJ: Prentice-Hall, 1976).

Weston, J.F. and Goudzwaard, M.B., *The Treasurer's Handbook* (Homewood, IL: Dow Jones-Irwin, 1976).

Whaley, R., "On the valuation of American call options on stocks with known dividends", *Journal of Financial Economics*, *9* (1981), p.p. 207–211.

Wheeler, D. and Mody, A., "International investment location decisions", *Journal of International Economics*, *33* (1992).

Williams, M., "The extent and significance of the nationalization of foreign owned assets in developing countries", *Oxford Economic Papers*, *27* (1975), p. 260.

Wilmott, P., *Derivatives* (New York: J. Wiley, 1998).

Wilmott, P., Howison S. and Dewynne, J., *The Mathematics of Financial Derivatives* (Cambridge: Cambridge University Press, 1998).

Winkleman, K., "Uses and abuses of duration and convexity", *Financial Analysts Journal* (September–October 1989), p.p. 72–75.

Working, H., "Price of cash wheat and futures at Chicago since 1883", *Wheat Studies of the Food Research Institute* (November 1934).

World Bank, *World Debt Tables* (Washington DC: World Bank) published annually.

Zhang, P.J., *Exotic Options* (Singapore: World Scientific Publishing Co., 1998).

Zinc, D.W., *The Political Risks for Multinational Enterprise in Developing Countries* (New York: Praeger, 1973).

Name index

Subject index